PERSPECTIVES
ON
WORLD EDUCATION

PERSPECTIVES
ON
WORLD EDUCATION

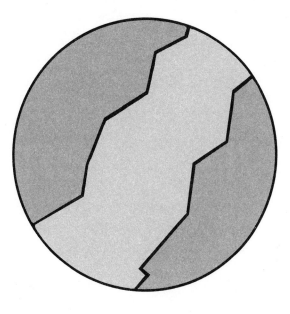

Edited by
Carlton E. Beck
University of Wisconsin—Milwaukee

Area Chairmen

Donald Bewley, Asia
Douglas Ward, Latin America
John Carpenter, Middle East

WM. C. BROWN COMPANY PUBLISHERS

To the memory of the late Professor Robert Frogge
Scholar, Colleague, and Dear Friend—
A man who knew no boundaries of color or nations

Preface

This book contains original essays on education written especially for *Perspectives on World Education* by scholars from many nations. It is not the usual "book of readings" consisting of reprinted journal articles. Although the writing styles and approaches vary greatly (Will some future critic call it "uneven"?), each individual has tried to do his best to present in brief form a response to the editor's originally posed question, which was almost the only guideline for their work. The question: "What would you say to an intelligent layman from another nation if he asked you to tell him about the main points in the history of education in your country, a description of education now, and what influences seem likely to shape it in the foreseeable future?" Of course, many books and articles have been written on most of the nations—but that was not the intent of the question. As the Romans stated, "Art is long and time is short." At the risk of the charge of "superficiality" (the easiest of all charges to level against any sort of summary or synthesis), each person has done his best, within the space allotments assigned by an unbending editor-organizer, to present the picture as simply as possible. No knowledge of educational jargon on the part of readers is presupposed; no knowledge of history of a specific nation is presupposed beyond the "general" knowledge of an intelligent layman. Naturally, *some* authors have succeeded for *certain* readers better than others have.

Spellings and other technical matters, such as bibliographies, presented a great editorial problem. Does one retain the English *-our* or shorten it to the American *-or* spelling? Is it pro*gram* or pro*gramme*? Should the style of dropping the publication place, common in some parts of the world when the place appears in a footnote, be retained? In general, the editor has tried to retain the maximum amount of the individual author's own words consistent with readability. While such a practice does not always contribute to editorial niceties, and may indeed lead to criticism for "loose" editing and inconsistency, the editor believes that these matters are of small consequence to most of the intended audience and will upset primarily purists who make a career of being upset anyway.

Every attempt has been made to be true to the meaning of each contributor. The editorial prerogative of shortening, omitting, rephrasing, and toning down blatantly biased and unnecessarily unkind statements has been exercised. Some of the printed "asides" which have been cut are in themselves most interesting, but they added little to the assigned task and might have detracted unnecessarily from the main points of the essays.

The book was produced over a period of four years. It suffered all the pains of any international writing venture of such scope—deaths, sudden changes of responsibilities which led to withdrawal by some, too many commitments to meet deadlines, physical illnesses of long duration, wars and international incidents, changes of geographic names and boundaries, and other hindrances. Thus, some of the statistics are unavoidably more current than others. This is also true because of the practice of some nations of relying on decennial census and of others using five-year figures.

The "area essays" included at the beginning of each major section of the book are intended to add meaning to the individual national essays by presenting an overall glimpse of the area in which the nations are located and also to avoid repetition of regional-type statements in each individual national essay. Some are historical, some are philosophical, others are primarily economic; all are intended to add some dimension of understanding to the area as a whole. Interested readers who wish more depth either in the area history and problems or in the educational system of a nation are referred to the carefully selected bibliographies at the conclusion of the individual essays on education. Often these bibliographies contain reference to nations *not included* in this book but whose problems are similar to or closely related with those of a specific nation herein represented.

Explanation is in order concerning the inclusion or omission of nations. Certainly omission does not imply diminished importance on the world education scene, nor does inclusion always imply the opposite. An attempt has been made to select nations in each section of the world which present some special set of circumstances, some colonial tradition, some unique approach, or perhaps just a rather typical (if such exists), representative nation in that part of the world. To include all nations would be desirable, but for the present editor such a task of organization and timing would seem impossible, and the repetition of circumstances and description of system would be great, with diminishing benefit. At the rate at which new nations are today being created, some new nation might be unavoidably slighted by the simple fact of time required to proofread and print the book.

Most of the usual statistical tables have been eliminated, since they become dated rather soon anyhow and because they are typically tangential to the intent of the book. UNESCO and individual embassies will do a far better job of providing updated figures upon request than can any book. Other excellent sources are *International Yearbook of Education* and *The Statesman's Yearbook*.

The ideal of the "educated man" varies from nation to nation. As these ideals pass in review, the editor suggests that the reader approach it not from the standpoint of "Am I *for* a given ideal or against it?" but rather, "What can I learn from it?" No nation has a direct pipeline to truth. It is the intent of this book to examine the oil in each pipeline which converges to aid in lighting the universal torch of knowledge.

Special thanks are in order to all the men and women who contributed to this endeavor, especially to the "area chairmen" who aided in assembling the writing team; they are Donald Bewley for Asia, Douglas Ward for Latin America, and John Carpenter for the Middle East. Agencies, churches, ministries of education, professors, and others have aided in the selection of writers in Europe and Africa.

C. E. B.

Contents

PART ONE: EDUCATION IN EUROPE

PART TWO: EDUCATION IN ASIA

PART THREE: EDUCATION IN THE MIDDLE EAST

Part One

Education in Europe

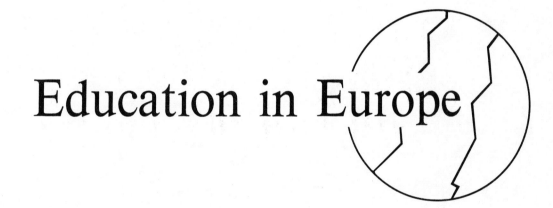

AREA ESSAY: EUROPE

Martin Kilcoyne

Long before the dawn of history, in the first half of the Pleistocene Age, men lived on the continent of Europe. But civilization was a stranger to it, brought in from outside during the second millennium B.C. It is because of this fact that historians usually begin the story of Europe by describing the parent civilizations of the Near East.

EARLY CIVILIZATION

These cultures existed in the so-called Fertile Crescent that curved northward from the Nile, through present Israel, and on to the mouths of the Tigris and Euphrates Rivers. The people of this region had already lived through two thousand years of history when the products of their cultures began to be exported to Europe through the maritime empire of Crete, a Mediterranean island lying between Egypt and Greece. The activity of the Cretans created a host of trading towns on the islands of the Aegean Sea and on the Greek mainland where, in spite of invasions, a flourishing culture began to emerge. Before 1000 B.C. the Greeks had developed the characteristic features of their society, later portrayed by Homer (*ca.* 850 B.C.) in the *Illiad* and *Odyssey*. But increasing population, a scarcity of arable land, and other factors caused the people to take to the seas in an effort of trade and colonization that eventually established Greek towns from southern Italy to the northern shores of the Black Sea. Although this world was not uniform, it shared the same language and religious ideas.

The highest achievement of Greek political life was the close-knit city-state (*polis*), ideally made up of a few thousand families. In the city-state the member found himself part of a polity for which he could freely work and to which he could creatively devote his talents. He had a duty to hold himself ready to serve and had a right to participate in all public affairs and offices. The *polis* stressed its localistic spirit, remaining by choice apart from others. Thus the city-states differed widely, and in social and political forms their experiments extended from the military, totalitarian regime of Sparta to the relatively open society of Athens, the most famous of the cities.

Classical Greece swiftly mounted to its apogee. In war the Greeks at Salamis and Marathon (479 B.C.) turned back the threat of invasion by the vast Persian Empire, a theocratic despotism. The stimulation of these surprising victories, together with the natural intellectual bent of the people, led to an outburst of creativity that probably never has been equalled anywhere in the world. Although there was a dark side to Greek thought, full of fatalism and gloom, this is not what was passed on in western culture. The Greeks sought beauty, not just the sensuous beauty of visible things, but that which lived in the mind— the perfectly constituted idea or concept. But they never became completely abstract. To them man was always the measure of all things. They delighted in life and believed that it was worth living, even with its trials and pains. To them the natural world in which men existed was not inevitably hostile. It was governed by rational laws that man's mind could know.

Despite their successes, the Greeks were all too human, and their civilization had weaknesses; it was these that led to its decline. They placed small value on any attempt to search for a rational orthodoxy, even one that provided hope of accommodation to evolutionary change. They had a love of dialectical argument, sometimes for its own sake. There was never a people more interested in the possibilities of unfettered speculation, more willing to demolish established ideas and institutions, and more intoxicated by the search for beauty. But many of them failed to realize that these great goals could best be achieved only when a stable social order afforded men the chance to think and act in freedom. In the realm of practical action they sometimes were back-

3

ward; in adversity their leaders showed a hackneyed sense of political opportunism and factionalism. The Athenians for all their brilliance had a poorly developed sense of obligation to the other cities. The provincialness of the Greeks prevented their genius from inventing anything larger than the *polis* for organizing the life of man.

Thus the Greeks spent the last quarter of the fifth century B.C. in destructive civil strife (the Peloponnesian War) that by 404 B.C. temporarily exhausted most of the cities. The anarchic and nihilistic tendencies inherent in a collection of competing city-states prohibited unity and left the way open for foreign powers to play a role in Greek affairs: first Persia, then Macedonia, and finally Rome. The Macedonians lived to the north; they were in the orbit of Greek civilization but were regarded by the Greeks as uncouth and barbarian. In 338 B.C. at the Battle of Chaeronea, the Macedonians defeated the Greeks and soon made them part of their empire under their king Alexander the Great.

Alexander was the pupil of the philosopher Aristotle and in many ways was thoroughly imbued with the ideals of Greek culture. In 334 B.C. he began his wars of conquest. He fought all over the Near East, crushed the Persians, and reached the edges of India. Before his meteoric career suddenly ended in 323 B.C., he created a state embracing much of the civilized lands of the old Egyptian, Assyrian, and Persian empires.

But his realm did not last long; the successor states were unable to remain together, for Alexander never learned how to fuse his disparate lands into one. He thought that Greek ideas would provide much of the needed bonding agent, although he later tried to strengthen unity by adding the oriental concept of the divine king.

In the arts this Hellenistic era has generally been regarded as a silver age. There was much activity, but it explored old themes in well-worn styles and invented no new forms. In philosophy, for instance, its characteristic schools were Stoicism, Epicureanism, and Cynicism, which stressed withdrawal and concern with the isolated individual as opposed to the Hellenic thought which stressed that the individual was part of a harmonious nature and community and could best discover himself in active involvement in the world. Lacking in optimism, somewhat sterile in creation, the Hellenistic Age was addicted to the monumental in art and stressed realism and naturalism rather than beauty. But progress was made. In fact, the era provided many technological discoveries and added distinguished names to the roster of scientists. Hipparchus stated that the earth moved around the sun; Eratosthenes figured the circumference of the earth; Hero explained the nature of the vacuum; Hippocrates proposed a scientific medicine; and Euclid and Archimedes made important contributions to mathematics. At the great library and museum of Alexandria many scientific thinkers worked among the precious resources that included much of the written work of the ancient world.

It is not right to compare Hellenistic times with the Golden Age of classical Greece. First of all, it is unhistorical to insist that all eras must measure up to the standards of what is at present considered the highest stage. Periods of rest and gestation may be as necessary for human progress as are the dynamic, creative eras. Ideas must be sifted and tested after they are born. The soon-to-come great age of Rome and the rise of Christianity may have required the seed time that preceded them. Finally, Greek learning in this age was able to permeate thoroughly the entire eastern Mediterranean world; culture in general was unified, digested, and spread to many peoples from India to the Balkans; and economic prosperity extended to a large part of the civilized East. The scene was set for the next act in the drama of European history: the rise of Rome.

ROMAN CIVILIZATION

Rome began as a town on the Tiber River in central Italy, probably about 1000 B.C. For a long time it was a client state of neighboring peoples such as the Etruscans, but the Romans eventually threw off the domination of others and established a republic about 509 B.C. Although the government of the city had some democratic features, it was always dominated by an aristocracy, and the internal history of Rome was characterized by dissension between upper and lower classes, with the latter gradually gaining important rights. Political institutions evolved in the direction of a rule of law and a constitutional republic, with more popular participation in affairs than one usually finds in the ancient world outside classical Greece.

While these things were happening, Rome developed a reasonably cohesive society with each citizen expected to dedicate himself to the idea that he should always put the interests of the republic above his own. The Romans were a disciplined people and they were somewhat dour, destined, it can almost be said, to hold sway over a huge empire. But although they were disciplined, they were not ruled by tyrants. Their sense of order came from the belief that the citizen was obliged to carry within him a feeling of duty toward Rome. The city in turn recognized that the citizen possessed rights, and these were protected by law and were honored by all the institutions of Rome.

The empire was built slowly and methodically— in a way expressing the deliberate and cautious spirit of the people. They gradually extended their sway over all the principalities and towns of the Italian peninsula, improvising as they went and designing new institutions and ideas to suit their needs. For instance, to join the other communities to Rome and to avoid the excesses of crude imperialism, they developed a system of treaties and pacts, the first time any state had ever used such a concept to allow for diversity and unity in a political league. Once the peninsula was brought under their sway, the Romans began to extend their power to nearby lands in the central Mediterranean. This drive brought them finally into collision with the Carthaginian Empire of North Africa. A difficult series of wars followed in which, for a while, it seemed that the Carthaginians under Hannibal might win. Hannibal, one of the world's great generals, led a host through Spain and down the Alps Mountains. He fought in Italy and came up to Rome, but as the Romans said, he could not ride his cavalry through their walls. By 200 B.C. the stolid and persevering Romans won out, and in the next two centuries they conquered most of the Mediterranean world.

But too many of their institutions were best suited to rule the city-state and were not suited for a large empire. The result was inevitable: the republic got into trouble. Social strife grew severe. The upper classes dreamed of seizing the state and the commoners feared that they would be left with only the power to revolt. Fierce battles raged over questions ranging from land reform to political patronage. After a period of decline and destructive civil war, the republic was irretrievably lost in 23 B.C. when Augustus Caesar inaugurated an era of one-man rule by emperors.

This new arrangement brought political stability. Augustus tried to create a synthesis of politics that solved the worst problems afflicting the empire: corruption of offices, inefficient provincial administration, lack of harmony among social classes, and most of all the need to give the people a new faith in Roman greatness. But in politics Rome was no longer creative, so Augustus had to look back and draw upon the past for ideas. He was partly successful in his quest, but most of the old problems continued in one form or another to plague the empire, and to these another dangerous one was added: the problem of succession to the imperial title.

While Romans were going through their time of troubles, they constructed a solid heritage to pass on to other peoples. It was in the development of law that they made their greatest contributions to civilization. They differentiated between internal and international law, developed a system of legal codification and interpretation, and created magistrates and lawyers to administer the law. In art and philosophy they were content to copy Greek and Hellenistic forms, sometimes, as in the case of the poet Virgil, mastering them with much technical virtuosity. But their art was decorative and, at times, reached in the direction of sheer size and reportorial naturalism. In sculpture they were highly competent but flatly pictorial, preferring to depict character rather than to search for truth. However, they were great engineers and builders, putting large bridges over rivers, constructing massive aqueducts, to bring potable water to metropolises, and building military roads that are still in use.

The rather unintellectualized Romans were not too concerned with what others thought of them; they cherished respect rather than love. They freely wore their vices on their sleeves for envious detractors to see and relish. Nevertheless, their achievements were impressive. They organized the world of their time into a viable whole, for a while joining peoples in a unity they had never before known. Although they finally failed, they made the first attempt to create the universal state based on law and statecraft rather than on the sheer power of theocratic despotism.

HEBRAIC-CHRISTIAN CONTRIBUTIONS

The almost universal sway of Rome over the classical world and the use of the Latin and Greek tongues offered the chance to a new faith to spread along the well-developed channels.

Some observers have said that the stream of western culture has two sources: Hellenism and Hebraism. The rise of Hellenism has been charted. At this moment in history, at the height of Roman power, Hebraism in the form of Christianity made its appearance in the West. For several generations after the death of Jesus Christ, Christianity grew among its Jewish adherents. Then in the face of sporadic persecutions it expanded in the prosperous eastern parts of the empire. The new faith had a powerful ability to win converts, especially among the lowly elements of society. By the early fourth century its membership formed a significant minority of the eastern empire. In 313 A.D. the emperor Constantine recognized it as the state religion and gave it favored status. As Christianity grew it developed an organized system of administration based on Roman models and its learned men created a body of official doctrines and literature.

Christianity arose as Rome slowly declined. Spasmodic attempts to save Rome proved to be mere short-term remedies. Efforts were made to force men to serve the decaying local regimes and to pay increased taxes, but such measures only increased the alienation of the people. Violent internal dissension, the decline of population and trade in the western empire, the loss of a sense of civic pride among the citizens, a succession of bad emperors, the growth of large estates using landless workers, insecurity of personal life, the invasions of barbarians—these were the signs of Rome's decline. But the most dramatic evidence of the end appeared in the growing separation of the eastern and western parts of the empire, a process recognized by Constantine when he transferred his capital to the new city of Constantinople in 330 A.D.

In such a weakened condition Rome could not hold back barbarian invaders who sacked the city in 410 and 455. In the West, barbarian successor states appeared, while in the East, the empire was reconstituted and began to grow into a flourishing trading realm that endured for one thousand years. In fact, however, the Greco-Roman world was not shattered beyond repair until the Arabic invasion swept over North Africa and parts of the Near East in the seventh century A.D.

THE DARK AGES

Now began the Dark Ages, a time when many of the arts of civilized society declined sharply. The barbarians had been incorporated in the empire, but cultural forces were overwhelmed and could not teach the ways of civilization to these people. The Christian church became the most important agency in debarbarizing the tribal invaders and converting them into the human material from which nations could be developed. Although the empire and many of its institutions had perished, the church preserved the Latin tongue, and stressed Roman organization, law, and discipline in rebuilding a rational social order.

The Byzantine or East Roman Empire was Greek in culture and staunchly Christian in religion. Its principal role in history was to preserve the heritage of the classical world and to pass it on in a missionizing effort directed toward the peoples of Eastern Europe, especially the Slavs. It was a conserver, not an innovator. It also stood as a European bastion, along with Russia from the ninth to thirteenth centuries, holding Asia at bay. For instance, in 683 and 718 A.D. Constantinople turned back massive Arabic assaults from its walls, forcing an Islamic flanking movement to make a great sweep across Africa and up through Spain and into France where it was finally turned back by the Frankish king, Charles Martel, at the decisive Battle of Tours in 732 A.D. Thus two powers at opposite ends of Europe saved the continent from being made part of the Arabic East.

Although Islam was extra-European and was often hostile, it influenced Europe by passing on some elements of Hellenistic culture. The Arabs had their own religion and literature and therefore were uninterested in Greek literature, but as practical empire builders they were fascinated by Greek science. To this they added many of their own discoveries in mathematics, chemistry, astronomy, and medicine. In late Medieval times much of this learning found its way into Europe.

MEDIEVAL CONTRIBUTIONS

For a modern European, the Medieval centuries are the most difficult part of his heritage to understand because the Medieval world view and its values are so different from his. The pulse of life was slower, and there was a deep concern with spiritual rather than with worldly affairs. In addition, the continent was politically split into a host of small principalities, although the idea of a united Christian world remained alive for a long time, preserved in the concept of a Holy Roman Empire. But the civil rulers were usually weak. On the other hand, the church played an important role in the life of every man, and it successfully struggled to assert its independent power, even to the point of claiming its primacy over the secular prince. The social, economic, and political organization of Medieval Europe is also strange to the modern mind. It was marked by a subsistence economy with little trade, a manorial system of agricultural production, and a hierarchical system of social organization in which every man was supposed to have his assigned place.

It was not an era of spectacular achievements. It has generally been regarded as colorful or even quaint, with a dash of barbarism that made it interesting. But one should remember that it produced modest but solid advances in many forms of human endeavor, from farming technology to philosophy.

However, the growth of trade, the revival of towns and cities, and the impact of the crusades all signified the end of Medieval times. Vital forces were appearing in Europe, turning the attention of men to new problems and creating new interests. The mind of Europe was launched on a voyage of discovery in the age of the Renaissance which began about 1400.

RENAISSANCE

Among the energies feeding the Renaissance were the growth of internal and foreign trade and the perfection of economic institutions to finance and control the elaborate operation of the growing economies of the continent: banking, insurance, and credit operations. Most of the forces behind the Renaissance came from inside Europe, but there had been early cross-fertilization of ideas by Arabic knowledge and Byzantine art. From the trading cities of northern Italy the Renaissance spread beyond the Alps and eventually to the rest of the continent. Wherever it went it produced remarkable outbursts of activity.

In the Renaissance, stability, order, and otherworldliness became less important than they had been in Medieval times. The typical man of the new age was vigorous and active, had confidence in his own powers of mind and will, and wanted to test himself in the world and to explore the meaning of his humanness and to discover what was unique about himself as an individual. He was venturesome and experimental in his approach to life and determined to be a master of many affairs. Thus with dramatic suddenness, over a few generations, the values of European life swiftly changed and pushed in an entirely new direction.

Princes and popes competed with each other to collect manuscripts of the great writers and thinkers of the Greco-Roman world. The entire heritage of that distant era was reclaimed when men in the early Renaissance went back to the past for guidance and inspiration. At the same time men of action set out on voyages to cruise all the seas of the world and to bring all the continents under their sway.

The Renaissance was a complex era and was not always uniform in its trends; it was a time of violently clashing ideas and of contradictions of purpose, but it centered its interest on man and nature. Many artists and scholars sought to study these in various fields of learning. Much of this passion for knowing was found in the visual arts—painting, architecture, sculpture. In these pursuits and in literature, a score of great names appeared such as da Vinci, Raphael, Titian, Michelangelo, Dürer, Machiavelli, Erasmus, More, Rabelais. In typical Renaissance fashion the artists concerned themselves with psychology, perspective, and anatomy.

REFORMATION

Some of the leading thinkers were critical of existing institutions, feeling that they did not conform to the demands of the new humanistic spirit. Inevitably some turned their attention to the most powerful institution of all—the church. Because it had grown so strong and entrenched, the church had changed relatively little and in this condition it failed to meet many of the requirements the critics set for it. A monk, Martin Luther, in 1517 attacked the most serious abuses and in a few years found himself the leader of a full revolt in Germany. In the remainder of the century, the revolt, called the Reformation, spread across Europe as Protestant churches, independent of Rome, were set up in many countries. Although the papacy finally answered the challenge with its own reformation and succeeded in regaining some of the people who had gone over to Protestantism, the unity of western-Christendom was broken.

Protestantism did not grow as a united faith but quickly divided into a number of varieties. Politically the key role of these churches was in giving support and legitimacy to the most important new political institution of early modern Europe: the nation-state.

NATION-STATES

During the next two centuries nation-states grew in power, consolidating the hold on lands within the realm, gathering in pieces of neighboring territories, and developing the resources of the kingdom. By creating a system of diplomacy and a recognized set of rules of behavior they learned, more or less, to live together in a system of states. Large and small wars often broke out, but they were usually contained and did not threaten the essential progress of Europe.

Although the political and social order of these states differed somewhat from place to place, with England and Russia being the major deviants, it generally was marked by a pyramidal structure: at the top, strong monarchs asserted the absolute and God-given nature of their power and sought to centralize the operations of the government; beneath them were the privileged orders of the nobility who staffed the offices and managed the main enterprise of the economy: agriculture; beneath them were the majority of the people, peasants or serfs who paid the taxes and tilled the land.

The kings maintained efficient bureaucracies, judiciaries, and administrations, all tightly controlled and supported by the crown. They concentrated on increasing the wealth of the nation by paternalistically looking after trade in accordance with the prevailing economic theory called mercantilism.

MERCANTILISM

Growth of commercial life and improvement of agriculture begot a numerous and active middle class, mostly concentrated in cities, in whose hands the new wealth accumulated. These aggressive and practical men of affairs liberated themselves from the fetters of feudal institutions and turned to help the new monarchs with advice and money and with all their talents and energies. In this way they were able to make the monarch independent of the nobles on whom he had once depended and who had acted as competitors in the struggle for power.

When such a state behaved as it was expected to, it could produce a bounteous supply of revenue; in theory it could become a wealth-producing engine for the king, who had first call on all its resources and who could use the tax system to extract money from it. The accumulation of riches that he could tap made it possible for him to accomplish things undreamed of by the impecunious Medieval ruler. For instance, the combination of wealth and power permitted him to send out conquerors, merchants, and missionaries to the ends of the earth. Through this process the Europeanization of the entire world was well under way by 1700.

SCIENCE

It was during this time that modern science arose. Of all the contributions Europeans have made to the world, this may be the most important. It is certainly unique; no other people were able, despite advances in technology and isolated instances of speculation about the natural world, to develop science and its methodology, vocabulary, and viewpoint. It is hard to say why science appeared in Europe and not in some older civilization. No doubt the answer will be found in the past, in the heritage of classical thought and the scholastic training of Medieval times. Whatever the cause, the effect was impressive. Copernicus, Galileo, Kepler, and Newton described the universe and the forces and laws that controlled it. Harvey helped turn the scientific revolution toward man when he described the circulation of the blood in the body. Others such as Descartes and Bacon provided important philosophical underpinnings for the new science.

All these discoveries and the consequent thinking about them had important ramifications in many fields of thought. Even art, in the so-called Baroque Era, reflected the energy, confidence, and concern with form that the interest in science evoked. Religious thinkers were forced to check their beliefs against the concrete knowledge of the new learning and to begin painful efforts to accommodate faith and science. Science reaffirmed in a spectacular way the essential Faustian nature of western man, his relentless vitality, and the searching nature of his voyage through history. While this attitude produced valuable knowledge, it also caused misgivings. The new discoveries sometimes shattered man's vision of himself and left him with a feeling of apprehension—dread, as some modern existential thinkers have called it—and a sense of loss. Individual warnings such as those coming from the seventeenth century French thinker Pascal, himself a scientist who stood on the threshhold of the new era, were ignored. The full implication of this untrammeled quest for scientific knowledge is even yet unknown.

POLITICAL PROBLEMS

In early modern times Europeans were not concerned with such things. The development of overriding importance seemed to be the growth of the new monarchies. In central and eastern Europe these states, with their powerful sovereigns, their system of military despotism and submissive estates, were usually unchallenged from within. But in western Europe they were built on the partly demolished foundations of feudalism. These remnants fitted poorly into the new states and contributed to social and economic instability. In addition the very success of the nation-states created forces whose full development was frustrated by barriers of old laws and customs. In directing public and private affairs they emphasized the guiding role of tradition and custom, principles that contradicted the very dynamism they had created. Their most dangerous weakness, however, was found in the absence of legitimate procedures for permitting reform and change to take place. They had not solved the age-old problem of how to harmonize an expanding social-economic structure with a slower changing political structure. Even the so-called Enlightened Despots of the eighteenth century, who were honestly dedicated to progress and who were earnestly willing to sponsor change, failed to overcome the inertia of resistance offered by some parts of their societies. (Not until the founding of the American constitutional system in 1787 was any nation given a recognized and written set of laws providing for such change.) In western Europe as time passed, many people felt that such things as guilds, established churches, and chaotic systems of laws and special privileges were hindering progress and were anachronistic.

In England and Holland, where many political and civil rights had been accorded to the most restive groups, the pressure for reform did not threaten orderly government. But France was different. It had a large educated leisure class, was in many ways the most advanced country in Europe, and had the largest population and greatest wealth. The future seemed to beckon appealingly to France, with all its potential for progress. But the juxtaposition of antique laws and hopes for the future highlighted the contradictions of the situation, and together with certain other causes of tension sparked the outbreak of revolution in 1789.

REVOLUTION

The French Revolution was probably the most important event in modern history. It set in motion many dramatic incidents that completely changed France and, ultimately, the rest of Europe. In a few years the king and queen were deposed and beheaded, a republic was proclaimed, a variety of experiments were tried such as the fixing of prices and the prohibition of religion, foreign armies invaded the country, there was internal rebellion, and several new varieties of government appeared. The revolution deepened and became more radical as time went on. No one seemed able to control its fury: thousands perished in massacres, proscription, and rebellions. It beheaded many nobles and then turned to "devour its own children." Eventually, after teetering on the brink of anarchy, it was brought under control by a young officer, Napoleon Bonaparte. With his arrival the revolution entered its heroic age. He launched a series of wars of conquest that gave France domination over much of the continent and the opportunity to indoctrinate it with revolutionary ideas such as "Liberty, Equality, Fraternity."

After a generation of war and turmoil, the revolution was finally beaten on the battlefield of Waterloo, and peace was restored at the Congress of Vienna in 1815. But the threat of revolution hung over Europe for most of the nineteenth century. The generation of 1815 tried to turn back this threat by firmly uniting the forces of throne and altar which were to cooperate in ferreting out conspiracies and joining to fight uprisings.

But the revolution transformed Europe. The old order survived but it was changed, and within the next two or three generations vestiges of it disappeared, either cut down in a series of short revolutionary outbursts or transformed through periodic changes as in England. Never again did aristocracies feel that they were natural rulers, nor did kings believe they could reign without thinking of the new power—public opinion. These currents began in western Europe and by the end of the century had marched over all the kingdoms, reaching Russia and Turkey.

The French Revolution also hastened the transformation of thought. In the Enlightenment or Age of Reason of the eighteenth century men had confidence in the faculties of the logical mind, believing that human reason could solve all problems. At the same time, feeling and emotion were mistrusted. But in the nineteenth and early twentieth centuries, the Age of Romanticism, men turned to the heart and emotions as sources of truth.

PEACE AND PROGRESS

The nineteenth century really began in 1815 and lasted until the outbreak of World War I in 1914. Although it was a time of fast-paced change, it was not disturbed by many wars, and those that occurred were usually short. It was a time of relative peace.

At the start of this era, Europe had few roads, wooden sailing ships, horse-drawn wagons, and seasonal transportation. Men and beasts supplied the power to do work, large areas were thinly inhabited, most of the population was illiterate, and the fruits of civilization were enjoyed by a small minority. At the end of the era, on the other hand, there was mass transportation over thousands of miles of track in high-speed trains, steamships connected all ports of the world and tied European markets together. Telephone and telegraph lines brought news around the earth in minutes. In western Europe the majority of people could read and write, and the amenities of civilization were available to a large and growing minority.

Science, which had been speculative and concerned with general laws of nature, now began to turn to man and his world and to apply the laws in solving practical problems. The geologists searched for the earth's beginnings and Darwin looked at human origins. There was an explosion of new inventions that profoundly changed the lives of most people. The knowledge of electricity provided telegraphs, radio, and x-rays. Discoveries in medicine cured or prevented diseases and made surgery possible. In cities, public health laws controlled communicable diseases, streets were lighted and cleaned, pure drinking water brought in, and police protection provided. Such things added a dimension of comfort, leisure, and security to life that men had never known before.

Meanwhile, the Industrial Revolution, which had started in England about the middle of the eighteenth century, spread across Europe to Poland and southern Russia, and indeed, had leaped the boundaries of the continent to Japan and North America. The essence of it was the application of technology and capital to problems of production. For its full development there had to be a modern, reliable system of transportation

(at first canals and later railroads) to bring markets and materials together. Until well into the twentieth century, men struggled to increase production. This, in fact, seemed to be the central problem.

Europe had begun the solving of this problem, but it also discovered that the solution created other problems. Eventually, in the name of the all-important goal of efficiency a new industrial society was created. But some of the values and ideals of society often remained rooted in an earlier era and their bad adjustment to the new reality created social pressures. For some people the promise of the new era appeared to be a long way off. The Industrial Revolution in its early stages was oppressive and exploitative; only a very small minority seemed destined to benefit from it. Critics arose either to denounce the economic system, called capitalism, or to accept it but to demand reform. One of the most radical critics was Karl Marx who called for a total revolution. He may not have been the wisest critic, but in the twentieth century his ideas became the basis for several schools of socialist thought and is the official ideology of all Communist states.

In the open societies those who found fault with the industrial system could express their fears and resentments in political action. Parliamentary institutions expanded; reform of voting laws enfranchised almost all adult males in Great Britain by 1867. In many countries legislatures met and expressed the desires of most of the population. In other words, for those attracted to the hope of non-violent change there was a belief that men could progress to the building of a just and stable society either through increasing freedom in the existing institutions or through creating new institutions such as labor unions. But the growth of wealth could not keep pace with the soaring hopes and the demands of the people for a larger share of the products of the industrial system. Increased communication of news via the mushrooming press spread restiveness and dissatisfaction faster than hope could be requited. So despite the solid achievements of the century, there was an underground current of frustration and rebellion that sometimes took violent forms as in the bombs, daggers, or guns of the anarchists and other radicals.

WAR

The political history of the era was not remarkable aside from the absence of large wars. The early mood of defensive conservatism was gradually corroded and it died away in the year of 1848, a time of upheaval in many countries. Although the last one-third of the century was a time of enlargement of European empires, the focus of events remained on the continent. Italy was united and became a nation by 1860. The Germans followed suit, and after several wars created the German Empire in 1871. This empire burgeoned economically and tended to dominate the continent.

Toward the end of the nineteenth century growing tension between the powers led to the failure of the diplomatic system. The principal states, as they gathered in two camps, were frozen into hard alliances: the Entente (France, Russia, and after 1907, Great Britain) and the Central Powers (Austria-Hungary, Germany, and Italy). The early years of the new century were punctuated by severe international crises in which the two groups of powers faced each other. The Austrian and Russian empires were becoming increasingly embittered in their clashes in the Balkan Peninsula, where they moved into the vacuum left by the retreat of the Turks. In 1914 these two empires collided and set off a chain reaction of events that dragged the other powers into the conflagration of World War I. Eventually, France, Russia, England, Italy, and several allies faced Germany, Austria, Turkey, and their allies in a drawn-out war of attrition that lasted until 1918.

The German, Austrian, Turkish, and Russian empires were destroyed in this holocaust along with millions of men who died in battle. Germany lost the war but the Entente powers cannot be said to have won it. The fighting exhausted both sides. Economically, they recovered, but in the realm of the spirit Europe, in the estimation of some, seemed permanently hurt. Although there were few objective reasons for the malaise, it became fashionable among the intellectuals to take a pessimistic view of Europe's future. Even if this was an overly dark picture of the situation, it was true that the continent's position in the world had slipped. The U.S.A., for instance, had become an important power. So had Japan.

The most important event of the war was the collapse of tsarist Russia early in 1917. The tsars were replaced by the Provisional Government, a democratic regime dedicated to the creation of a constitutional system. Late in 1917 it was overthrown when a radical Marxist group calling itself the Bolsheviks (Communists), led by Lenin, grabbed power. Despite their measures to control the election that followed, the Communists were roundly beaten. In the next few years a civil war raged as an inept coalition, including opponents of the Communists ranging from liberals to radical socialists assisted at times by an equally inept intervention of the Entente Allies, tried to pry loose Lenin's grasp of power. They failed, however, and Lenin was free to set about creating the first Communist state. In 1917 the Communists had proclaimed their determination to destroy the governments of all other nations and to build a regime of total power at home. The second goal was reached in about a decade; it was not until the later stages of World War II that the march toward the first goal began.

The general trend of politics in the post-war world tended to reinforce the feelings of pessimistic observers. The peace signed at Versailles in 1919 was obviously only an uneasy truce. The system of treaties created by the Allies was not firm from the start because the U.S.A. withdrew from European diplomacy and began to turn its eyes toward the Pacific. England and France could not cooperate to protect the peace.

The depression of the 1930s created more problems. Unemployment and declining markets brought a major crisis to the continent. In Germany widespread fear and confusion caused the rise of totalitarian political forces, Communism and Nazism. Eventually, the country early in 1933 fell victim to the Nazis under Hitler. Using his National Socialist dogma as a basis, he began to create a police state similar in many ways to the U.S.S.R., a country he both hated and admired.

Germany had been humiliated and unjustly accused of causing World War I. Hitler never failed to remind Germans of the shame, using this tactic to arouse mass support for his program. He rearmed the nation after tearing up treaties, and then he brilliantly outmaneuvred the divided and vacillating democracies in every contest in which he engaged. In the process he seized Austria and Czechoslovakia. The U.S.A. was absent, and the democracies did not trust the U.S.S.R. Therefore, there was no hope of outside help in the attempts to stop Nazi Germany. Appeasement was tried on the dictator; it only whetted his appetite and convinced him that his foes were weak. Finally with their backs to the wall, the western states stood up to him and his ally, the Soviet Union. War began in 1939 and continued until Germany was defeated in 1945. It was the most destructive experience the continent had gone through in many centuries.

POST-WAR PERIOD

After the war Europeans required help and the passing of two decades to assist them in recovery. Through all this time the U.S.S.R. loomed large on the horizon. In the war it had made important territorial gains with the aid of its ally, Nazi Germany, and then it had made other important gains when Hitler's attack drove it unwillingly into the camp of the democracies. As a result of being an ally with both sides the U.S.S.R. by 1945 held much of eastern Europe. It hoped, in addition, that the dislocations of the post-war world might bring in more prizes such as the great industrial area of the Ruhr and the Dardenelles. When it became apparent that the continent did not have the strength or resources to revive itself and that the U.S.S.R. intended to sovietize it, the U.S.A. offered large sums of capital to vitalize industry again and prepare European nations to protect themselves. The aid program was highly successful.

The two decades after the war were a time of a search for unity. The unrelenting pressure of the

U.S.S.R. gave birth to the North Atlantic Treaty Organization, a defensive diplomatic alignment sponsored by the U.S.A. This military pact created a broad political mood favoring some form of unification. In addition, as their empires melted away, Europeans turned more to their own affairs. The flourishing economies surprised many observers who had assumed that the wealth of Europe was derived from exploitation of colonies. In fact, prosperity was never greater than in the post-imperial age that was dawning. In every category of economic activity, statistics showed sharp rises despite the existence of some problem areas such as southern Italy where unemployment and the need for land division continued to blight the general picture. But Germany bounded back to new industrial heights. France, in spite of the decline of its democratic political structure after De Gaulle's take-over of power in 1958, and despite being stripped of its colonies, experienced a burst of economic growth that gave it a feeling of confidence it had not had since the years before World War I. This very assurance, however, when expressed by De Gaulle, revived national sentiment and became a block to the movement for continental unity, temporarily or permanently the world cannot yet know.

In the second half of the 1960s, Europe felt renewed faith in its ability to look after itself. Although in scientific research it lagged behind the two largest powers, it was still the intellectual leader of the world, the incubator of important new ideas.

There was a widespread feeling among intellectuals that fundamental changes had taken place in the Communist world and it was therefore no longer such a danger to western Europe, which consequently could afford to be more independent of its protector, the U.S.A. This feeling was communicated to political leaders who presumed it to be a fact and who, as a result, began to act in domestic and international politics in accordance with it. After the crisis over jurisdiction in the divided city of Berlin ended in 1962 in a Communist victory, the major diplomatic events began to occur outside the continent.

Since the end of the Second World War several dozen new countries appeared in the world, all of them eager to adopt basic European institutions. Although this was a form of flattery, it led to a relative decline in Europe's position and a watering-down of its influence in the United Nations. Then a new concern arose. Since the end of the war, Arabic nationalism, frustrated for more than a generation and stimulated by the creation of the state of Israel, was growing restless. The Egyptian dictator, Nasser, stirred up the fires of rebellion and led the attempts of these countries to oust western control or influence. The vital Suez Canal was closed and Europe's oil supplies were jeopardized. Next came the spectre of Soviet power in the Mediterranean, creeping in with diplomatic success and with naval forces until in the late 1960s it was well established, outflanking Europe to the South. Despite this threat, many Europeans accepted De Gaulle's estimate of the future: Europe was meant to be a collection of nation-states and it was with the nation-state that each people would reach its destiny. Such thinkers had hope that the U.S.S.R. would succumb to this putative law and permit the remainder of the continent to go its own way.

ALBANIA

Jani I. Dilo

ECONOMIC BACKGROUND OF EDUCATION IN ALBANIA

Albania is on the Adriatic sea, in the western part of the Balkan peninsula, bordered by Greece and Yugoslavia. The area of the country is 11,099 square miles and the population, according to a 1968 estimate, is about 2,000,000.

The country, called Illyria in ancient times, has been known in modern times as Albania. To the inhabitants themselves, the country goes by the name of Shqipëria. It is hemmed in on three sides by almost impenetrable mountain ranges that have kept it in a state of isolation which, while detrimental to the development of trade and social intercourse, made it easier for the Albanians to keep their language, their customs, and their individuality. However, Albania has a wide coastal belt on the Adriatic and the ports of Durrës and Vlorë are convenient heads of communication for penetration into the Balkans. While the average altitude is over 2500 feet above sea level, more than two-thirds of the country's area is largely unproductive. The rivers rise at a high altitude in the interior and descend swiftly to the coastal plains through steep gorges, and none of the rivers is navigable. However, there is an abundance of water and Albania has a great potential capacity for the production of cheap hydroelectric power from the torrential streams and waterfalls. There is a mean annual rainfall of forty inches; the climate along the coast is typically Mediterranean and in the uplands is decidedly continental.

Although Albania was once heavily forested, this natural resource has been largely dissipated; what remains is little exploited because of poor communications. The chief crops are corn, wheat, rice, oats, barley, rye, potatoes, tobacco, sugar beets, cotton, grapes, citrus fruit, pomegranates, and figs.

While Albania was under Turkish yoke, little mining was done. After it became independent, serious consideration was given to the development of na-tional mineral resources that had been exploited in ancient times by the various conquerors of the land. In recent years the government has given considerable attention to the discovery of ores and the development of mines, and Albania now produces about 2 percent of the world's chromium ore and a good quantity of copper ore, lignite, asphalt, rock salt, bauxite, and pyrite. Petroleum is the chief mineral wealth of the country and limestone, quarried throughout the land, is one of the principal raw materials for the building industry.

Commerce plays a less important role in Albania than in the other Eastern European countries. Transportation and communication are poorly developed. While Albania has as many miles of national highways per square mile as other Balkan countries, it has very few local roads and about half of the total mileage is in very bad repair.

A relatively sparsely settled country, with a density of about 175 inhabitants per square mile, Albania is a nation of small landowners. Almost every family head owns his own home and almost 80 percent of the Albanian population is engaged in agriculture. After the Second World War the Communist regime introduced collectivization and today there are over 2000 agricultural cooperatives with 83 percent of all the arable land. However, the means and methods of farming are still quite primitive and most of the farming is done without labor-saving machinery. Pastoral industries (which form a large part of the Albanian economy) have been included into cooperatives, as has the whole handicraft sector of manufacturing. The collectivization of agriculture together with the nationalization of manufacturing industries has changed entirely the historic way of life in Albania. Until this change Albania had been a nation of self-sufficient small landholders, who for the most part gained their living by tilling the field and watching their flocks, much after the fashion of their remote ancestors.

DEVELOPMENT OF EDUCATION
IN ALBANIA

Certain peculiar combinations of events in the history of the Albanian people have had a profound effect upon the development of education in the nation.

The Albanian people are descendants of the old Illyrians, the original Indo-European settlers of the eastern coast of the Adriatic Sea. Their name is that of the Illyrian clan of Albani, mentioned by Ptolemy in the second century A.D. They inhabited what is today Central Albania. Alexander the Great characterized them as the stoutest and most warlike of all Europeans, and the Albani may well have been the toughest of the race since they succeeded in surviving Roman, Slavic, and Byzantine invasions.

In the fifteenth century the Albanians performed miracles under Scanderbeg in fighting one of the most heroic wars in history at a time when all around them fell before the triumphant Turk. This was the golden age of Albania; it distinguished itself as a nation and assumed a rank among the powers of Europe. When the Byzantine Empire disappeared and the rest of the world trembled before the Turks, Albania made its great contribution. But this glory was short-lived and Albania finally succumbed to the Turks. Then for over four centuries, until 1912, Albania was a subject-nation.

During this period the Albanian language was forgotten by many people because even the memory of it was proscribed by the Turkish conquerors. Nevertheless, it survived to form the basis of the rejuvenation of Albania in the latter half of the nineteenth century, a rejuvenation that was largely educational.

Even before the invasion of Albania by the Turks, there existed documents in the Albanian language. During the first three centuries of Turkish domination, there was some Albanian literature but it was purely ecclesiastical in character. It was not until the latter half of the nineteenth century that an Albanian literature of a nationalistic character appeared. It appeared first in Italy, written by Albanians whose ancestors had emigrated in order to escape the yoke of the Turks. The Albanians of Italy were also able to found schools for the education of their children; by 1794 they possessed an excellent institution, the Collegio di San Demetrio Corone in Calabria, where the Albanian language was taught.

The movements for the unification of Italy served as a stimulus to the Italo-Albanians. It was in the liberated Naples of 1848 that de Rada published his patriotic political and literary newspaper *L'Albanese d'Italia*. In the rhapsodies of an Albanian poem entitled "Milosao," de Rada lauded the pre-Turkish state of freedom of the Albanians, their wars against the Ottoman invaders and told of their surrender and exile.

De Rada's guiding motive, his sun by day and star by night, was a belief in the 'mission' of the Pelasgian race now scattered about the shores of the Indian Sea —in Italy, Sicily, Greece, Dalmatia, Roumania, Asia Minor, Egypt—a belief as ardent and irresponsible as that which animates the *Lost Tribe* enthusiasts of England. He considered that the world hardly realized how much it owed to his country-folk; according to his views, Achilles, Philip of Macedon, Alexander the Great, Aristotle, Pyrrhus, Diocletion, Julian the Apostate . . . were all Albanians. (All his writings) . . . throb with a resonant note of patriotism; they are "fragments of a heart", and indeed, he utilized even the grave science of grammar as a battlefield whereon to defy the enemies of Albania. His "Fiamuzi Arbërit" (the Banner of Albania) became the rallying cry of his countrymen in every corner of the earth.

This was the spark that set off the flame that grew into the conflagration that won Albanian independence. Other books followed from the pens of other authors; congresses and committees met to establish schools; Albanian emigrants contributed from their meager earnings to start institutions in several places. In the meantime, the Albanian League for the Defense of the Rights of the Albanian Nation was created at Prizren, Kossovo, in 1878.

The League placed great stress upon the importance of language and schools. During this period Albania continued to have Turkish schools for the Moslems and Greek schools for Orthodox Christians, none of which were at all Albanian in spirit. However, there were two Albanian Catholic institutions in Shkodër: a Franciscan seminary, opened in 1861, and a Jesuit school (Collegio Saveriano), opened in 1877, under the auspices of Austria, which had taken Albanian Catholics under protection.

From the time of the formation of the League of Prizren, the problems of the schools never ceased to be of concern to Albanian leaders. In 1884 a secondary school for boys was opened in Korça by the Albanian society of Bucharest. A year later, a private Albanian school was established in the same town, followed by others in surrounding villages. In 1891 a school for girls began to function in Korça. However, in 1902 all the schools of the province of Korça were closed by the Turkish government and their teachers were persecuted. Moreover, the clergy of the Greek Church excommunicated the teachers in the Albanian schools and the Albanian language was prohibited and anathematized.

After the Young Turk Constitution of 1908, a surge of educational activity rose in Albania. A congress was held in Monastir (Bitolj) in November, 1908, and this group decided upon a unified alphabet. The resolution of the alphabet question was a significant step toward the unification of the Albanian people and it also contributed toward making Moslems and Christians more conscious of their common patrimony. Many Albanian schools were opened, even in villages. The progress of the Albanians alarmed the

Young Turks and the new Albanian schools were closed again by the end of 1910. As the prospects for liberation from the Turkish yoke became increasingly bright, conferences and meetings were held in various places to determine the plans and characteristics of the proposed national system of schools. But, because World War I broke out shortly after Albania declared her independence (November, 1912), there was little time for progress in national education until 1920, when a Ministry of Education was created by the newly-formed government. This Ministry faced enormous problems. There were few good teachers in the country. Illiteracy was very high. (As late as 1938, approximately 75 percent of the population was illiterate.)

The Ministry of Education also faced the problem of creating an educational system for the entire country. From time to time, various changes were made. The most significant reform came in 1933-34 when, following the nationalization of education, a law was passed re-organizing the entire educational system. It was the most important and complete educational law ever made in Albania. Prepared by Ivanaj, the Minister of Education, it aimed at creating an integrated national education program. The program covered both elementary and secondary education in detail.

Elementary

Free elementary education was made obligatory for the children of all Albanian citizens from age four to thirteen. In villages where there were no kindergartens, education began in the elementary schools at the age of seven. Five grades of instruction were given in elementary schools. Upon completing elementary school, the pupil could enter a gymnasium or other secondary school.

Secondary

There were five types of secondary school:

1. The *gymnasium* consisted of eight years of instruction, divided into two levels. The lower, comprising the first four grades, was the basis for all secondary education. (There was also a state secondary institution, the National Lycée of Korça, whose program consisted of nine years of instruction, the first two of which were non-specialized.)
2. The *Normal School* consisted of four years. Students could enter this school after four years at a gymnasium.
3. The *Town School* consisted of four years; it was a separate unit constituting the lower division of the professional schools and it corresponded to the lower level of the gymnasium.
4. The *Commercial Institute* consisted of four years; students could be admitted after they finished town school.

5. The *Technical School* consisted of three to five years; students could be admitted after they finished town school.

Secondary schools had the following fields. The gymnasia had classical and scientific divisions, beginning with the third year. The National Lycée of Korça, following the French system, had a liberal arts division and a science division. The normal schools trained teachers for elementary and kindergarten instruction; they had a two-year curriculum for kindergarten training and a four-year curriculum for elementary training. In their last two years normal school, students specializing in elementary education attended training schools to obtain practice teaching. In the town schools students were taught business, wood-carving, dairy production, agriculture, or home-economics. Technical schools provided theoretical teaching and practical training in agriculture and various crafts.

There were no universities in pre-war Albania and advanced study had to be pursued outside the country. In 1930, the National Organization of Albanian Youth was founded to direct the activities of all Albanian youth societies and to improve "the patriotic, moral, and physical education of the youth of the country," both in and out of school. This new departure in Albanian education reflected the control and regimentation of public activities by the state.

When Fascist Italy occupied Albania, a few months before the beginning of the Second World War, Albanian education came completely under Italian control. In 1941, after the collapse of Yugoslavia, Kossovo-Metohia, a province whose population was preponderantly Albanian, was annexed to Albania. This provided an incentive for the spread of education and the founding of Albanian schools in that province.

After the capitulation of Italy in 1943, the Germans recognized Albanian neutrality and left them free to run their own schools along nationalistic lines. However, because of the unsettled conditions in the country, little education was actually accomplished.

Private and Minority Schools

There were private schools in Albania prior to the suppression of private education in 1934 when education was nationalized. They included schools owned by private individuals, schools founded by the Franciscan and Jesuit orders, *medreses* (the religious schools of the Moslem community) and the seminaries of the Orthodox Church. There were also a few private schools established by American organizations. The only schools for ethnic minorities were the Greek schools in the prefecture of Gjinokaster, where some 30,000 Greeks lived. In 1936 a bill was passed that divided schools into state schools and "authorized" schools, the latter being a euphemism for private schools. As a result, the Franciscan gymnasium and the Greek minority schools were re-opened under government control.

This is a very brief sketch of the important movements in Albanian education prior to the Second World War. If the reader is interested in learning more about the history of education in Albania, he is referred to two excellent works by Stavro Skendi:

"The Beginnings of Albanian Nationalist Trends in Culture and Education (1878-1912)." *The Journal of Central European Affairs.* Vol. 12, No. 4, January 1953.

Albania, Frederick A. Praeger, Inc., New York, 1956.

EDUCATION UNDER THE COMMUNIST REGIME

Communists have been in power in Albania since November, 1944, before the end of the Second World War; since then education has been built on Marxist-Leninist foundations. The Educational Reform Act of 1946 provides that textbooks be prepared on the principle of Communist ideological content. Education is slanted to make the pupil identify with the world Communist movement and to show him that communism represents the inevitable development of Albania's national heritage and culture.

At the beginning, the main goal of the Communist program for education was elimination of illiteracy, and great progress has been made in this field. Today, according to the Albanian government, illiteracy has disappeared from the country. General education schools (according to the Soviet model, elementary, seven-year and secondary) were made uniform throughout Albania. The gymnasia were preserved. The elementary schools consist of four grades and the seven-year schools of seven grades, the first four corresponding to the elementary school. The secondary schools have four grades beyond the seven-year school. The seven-year schools of the Greek minority in the district of Gjinokaster were preserved but the Albanian language is also taught and these schools are under strict governmental control. Professional education was introduced for the preparation of cadres "in various fields of the economic, social and cultural life of the country." Night schools were opened to give adults an opportunity to begin or to continue their education without leaving work. Toward the end of 1946, the first Pedagogical Institute was founded in Tirana to provide two-year training for teachers. As time passed, greater emphasis was placed on professional and technical training. The objectives are

1. to increase the number of students in order to have qualified workers.
2. to build a broad network of schools with professional courses in order to help in the creation of technical *cadres,* skilled and semi-skilled workers, who will bring about the realization of plans;
3. to take all steps to increase the theoretical and professional knowledge of qualified workers.

A government decree established secondary professional schools called *teknikums* based on Soviet lines. By 1950, Albania had professional schools for medicine, finance, commerce, agriculture, and the petroleum industry. In 1951, three "High Institutes" —the High Pedagogical Institute, the High Polytechnical Institute, and the High Agricultural Institute— were founded to give "science, culture, and technology in our country broader perspectives and to create conditions for their further development, according to the example of the Soviet Union . . . and in order to form the intelligentsia of our fatherland." In 1952, the foundation of High Institutes of Economics and Medicine followed. In 1957, the government made its most important step with the foundation of the University at Tirana

to train highly qualified specialists, educated on the basis of Marxist-Leninist theory; to carry out research in order to disseminate scientific and political knowledge among the workers; to raise the qualifications of specialists working in the national economy, culture and education.

In 1963 a law was passed reforming the Albanian school system on the basis of "unity between thoughts and action, study and work, theory and practice." The new system of education calls for eight years of compulsory education. There are no fees for higher education in Albania and the majority of students receive monthly grants.

Current Organization

There is no entrance examination in any Albanian school. Education is now nominally compulsory for eight years (from age seven to sixteen) in what is called the "incomplete secondary school." Pupils may stay on for an additional three or four years and obtain a complete secondary education. The first four grades are called the elementary school.

In the eight-year school the curriculum is divided so that 42 percent of the time is given to the humanities, 34 percent to science, 17 percent to handicrafts and labor training, and the rest to physical education. In grades nine to eleven, the curriculum is 30 percent humanities, 32 percent science, 34 percent vocational training plus theoretical, practical, and productive labor, and the rest physical education. (See Table 1, page 16, Curriculum for the Eleven-Year School.)

The Albanian educational system is centralized, and all schools work in accordance with a common curriculum. Schools are non-religious; that is, there is no religious instruction and no religious assemblies are held. They are co-educational except for the military schools.

TABLE 1

Curriculum for the Eleven-Year School

	CLASS										
	1	2	3	4	5	6	7	8	9	10	11
Subjects	Hours Per Week										
1. Albanian Language	12	12	12	10	6	5	3	2	-	-	-
2. Literature	-	-	-	-	2	3	2	3	3	3	3
3. Mathematics	6	6	6	6	6	6	6	5	5	4	4
4. Civics	-	-	-	-	-	-	1	-	-	-	-
5. History	-	-	-	2	2	2	2	2	3	3	3
6. Constitution	-	-	-	-	-	-	-	-	-	-	2
7. Nature Study	-	-	-	3	-	-	-	-	-	-	-
8. Geography	-	-	-	-	2	2	2	2	-	2	2
9. Biology	-	-	-	-	2	2	2	2	3	-	-
10. Physics	-	-	-	-	-	2	2	3	5	4	2
11. Astronomy	-	-	-	-	-	-	-	-	-	-	1
12. Chemistry	-	-	-	-	-	-	2	2	2	3	2
13. Technical Drawing	-	-	-	-	-	-	1	1	2	-	-
14. Russian Language	-	-	-	-	4	3	3	3	3	3	3
Totals:	18	18	18	21	24	25	25	26	26	22	22
15. Drawing	1	1	1	1	1	1	1	-	-	-	-
16. Singing & Music	1	1	1	1	1	1	1	1	-	-	-
17. Physical Education	2	2	2	2	2	2	2	2	2	2	2
18. Training in Labor & Socially Useful Work	2	2	4	4	5	5	5	5	-	-	-
19. General Technical Subjects, Theoretical & Practical Work and Training	-	-	-	-	-	-	-	-	8	12	12
Totals:	24	24	26	29	33	34	34	34	36	36	36
20. Voluntary Subjects	-	-	-	-	-	-	-	-	3	2	2

NOTE: The Albanian school year consists of thirty-three weeks.

To cope with the large numbers of students entering the inadequate schools, the two-shift system was introduced just after World War II, and it has been in existence ever since, especially in the towns. Although a large number of new schools have been built, building has never caught up with the needs of Albanian education because of the increased population and the raising of the age for leaving school.

Every Albanian school has a patron. In towns the patrons may be factories, enterprises, theaters, or other organizations. A patron factory supplies the school with equipment for technical work (such as machines and tools) and provides the facilities for pupils to do practical work in its shops. In villages, the schools are linked to state or collective farms.

As in all countries, progress depends on good teaching and there are good, bad, and indifferent teachers in Albania, as there are everywhere. However, in Albania the Party exercises strict control and teachers are given help so that they can improve themselves.

A great deal of research is being devoted to teaching methods and many teachers are doing research work. The textbooks, which are standard for all schools, follow the programs. The content of the subjects taught in Albanian schools is similar to that of Soviet schools. Chemistry students make field trips to factories to see the processes; arithmetic problems deal with everyday life and plans for the development of industry and agriculture; biology includes work with plants and crops. All subjects are supplemented by practical work.

Education for the Party

In 1949 a Central Party school was opened in Tirana to prepare leaders for the Party, for government organizations, and for professional unions. Other Party schools have the usual ideological courses and set an example for all other schools.

The *Pioneer Organization*, under the direction of the Albanian Communist Party, is for children between nine and fourteen. It is based on the school, where its function is closely linked with that of the pupils' committees of the school, or it is run by factory workers or other agents of the Union of Working Youth of Albania. The Youth Organization of Albania has branches in schools where there are pupils over fourteen. Every secondary school has a Pioneer organizer on the staff. Young people may join the Youth Organization from the age of fourteen; in schools they are mainly responsible for running the Pioneers. The aims of the Pioneer organization are to help its members to study well, to enjoy their leisure hours in a positive way, and to develop into party-minded citizens. The Pioneers have regular meetings and activities and have their own room in almost every school in which they keep banners, musical instruments, and equipment for producing wall newspapers.

"*Circles*" are organized by the Pioneers or by the Youth Organization for the general and political education of youth. They are assisted by "*Red Workers*" whose function is to bring "socialist culture" to people in cooperatives, offices, plants, and schools.

In villages the collective farm clubs often organize activities for the children; these consist of social evenings, dances, and singing groups. They are arranged in conjunction with the school. Most "out-of-school" activities actually take place in the school building which is in fact the only cultural center of the village.

Albanian Communists believe that out-of-school activities are as important as lessons learned during school time. Socialist culture as well as music, foreign languages, technical subjects, art, and literature can be followed by adults in their clubs. Young people who have a taste for sports, of whom there are many, can transfer to adult clubs when they leave school.

School summer camps and school excursions are becoming a feature in Albanian schools. These are often arranged by the leaders of the Pioneers, after-school "circles," or factory unions.

Regulation

All schools in Albania are subject to the central government through the Ministry of Education and Culture, but the principles of Albanian education are laid down in the program of the Workers' (Communist) Party; directives on education are given by the Party's Central Committee. Laws and decrees on education in general are made by the People's Assembly and its Council of Minister. They determine such matters as the type of school that may be opened, when to open higher institutes, what ages students may enter and leave schools, when to confer degrees and professorships, and the amount of the budget. The university and higher educational institutions are entirely under the Council of Ministers. Others are under both the Ministry of Education and the Ministry with which they are mostly concerned. The Committee of Arts and Culture, the Radio Broadcast Committee, and the Direction of Publications are under the control of the Ministry of Education, which now bears the title of Ministry of Education and Culture. Regional and local educational authorities are not only under the Ministry of Education and

Culture but are also linked with the district and local People's Councils. Each local authority has an Education Committee to help carry out the education plan. The inspectors have charge of the work in the elementary and secondary schools and act as agents of the Ministry of Education in dealing with local governmental authorities and school committees.

Union Membership

There is one Union of Workers in Education and Trade which includes teachers in schools, all workers in higher institutes and in the university, and also scientific workers. It is affiliated with the General Syndical Union of Albania. Membership in a school union is open to all who work in it; that is, to cleaners and administrative staff as well as the teachers. The district committees of the Union as well as the Central Committee are elected at conferences of delegates from local branches. The Teachers' Union helps to provide facilities for further study and organizes courses, exhibitions, and conferences. Because committee members, are themselves teachers, working among their colleagues, they are able to see and understand the difficulties that arise and take action to overcome them. In schools the Union arranges social evenings, runs a wall newspaper, sees that sick members get hospital treatment, and helps resolve any difficulties that may arise between the administration of the school and the staff. The Teachers' Union provides clubs and builds rest homes for its members and runs summer camps for their children.

Teachers in Albania are paid on the scale of other state workers and highly-skilled workers in factories. It is obvious that the lot of labor in Albania, in terms of living standards, is far inferior to that of Western workers and is even considerably below Soviet and other Eastern European standards. However, the status of teachers in Albania is high. They may be elected Members of the People's Councils as well as Deputies to the People's Assembly. Teachers with long service and good records are honored with such titles as "distinguished educator," "distinguished teacher," "meritorious teacher," or "teacher of the people."

The latest figures show that 10 percent of the total Albanian budget is spent on education. The expenditure for 1960 was 2,466 million leks (at the official Albanian rate of 50 leks to one dollar), of which 64.7 percent was spent on general education (schools, children's homes, kindergartens, boarding-schools, out-of-school activities), 23 percent was spent on training teachers and other personnel, and 12.3 percent on political and cultural education and the press, research institutions and art. However, the financial conditions are so disturbed and the lek so depreciated that any references to salaries, school expenditures, and the like would be more misleading than informative.

A picture of the growth of Albanian schools can be seen in Table 2.

Although one might contest the figures given by the post-war regime in the Table 2, there is no doubt that Albania has made the school a center of attraction for young people and their elders. Today one out of 4.5 Albanians attends school and 48 out of 10,000 Albanians participate in higher education.

Albania in the past had a system of schools that was largely continental, modified by national historical development, political organization, and social customs, and reorganized after World War II by a government "of the Communists, by the Communists, and for the Communists." Therefore, as described by Thomas Molnar, "today the whole community is a potential participant in a 'popular' culture lacking in taste, tradition and meaning"—an exact reflection of the new Albanian educational situation.

Prior to the break with Moscow, some 1,213 Albanian students were enrolled in Soviet schools and almost as many were attending higher institutes in other East European countries. Since 1961, Soviet and East European universities have closed their doors to

Albanian students and have withdrawn their teaching personnel from Albanian higher schools. Tirana State University could not cope with all the technical and intellectual problems which suddenly faced it. It is evident that Peking, Albania's only friend, can by no means fill the gap created in this sector. On the other hand, the Albanian regime is extremely cautious about having any cultural relations with the West, about allowing its students to travel to Western Europe as they did in the past, or of engaging western teachers for its higher schools. So higher education in Albania is suffering, and the consequences of these disturbances may be felt even more in the future.

FUTURE PROSPECTS

It is difficult to be up-to-date on the development program in Albanian schools because, in this period of completing the establishment of the eight-year compulsory school for all, the Communist leaders and the educationalists are already discussing and organizing the next stage. The development of polytechnical training is taking varied forms. In many

TABLE 2

Growth of Albanian Schools

A. GROWTH OF POPULATION AND SCHOOLS IN ALBANIA				
	1923	1938	1961	1964
Population	803,659	1,040,353	1,660,300	1,820,000
Schools	574	677	3,524	4,000
Pupils	25,250	58,717	334,621	405,000
Teachers	865	1,551	10,948	15,000

B. SUMMARY OF SCHOOL STATISTICS OF ALBANIA						
	1938-1939			1961-1962		
Type of School	Schools	Teachers	Pupils	Schools	Teachers	Pupils
Kindergarten	23	40	2,434	421	1,068	23,087
General Education	649	1,477	55,404	3,065	10,069	310,605
Secondary Pedagogical Education	3	18	675	12	246	7,501
Higher Education	-	-	-	7	414	9,287
Totals:	677	1,551	58,717	3,524	12,138	359,978

C. NUMBER OF PUPILS GRADUATING FROM SCHOOL		
	Years	
	1938	1961
Elementary School (Four years)	2,745	35,189
Seven-Year School	514	17,490
Secondary School	224	3,453
University & High Institutions in Albania	-	814
Abroad	91	132

cases the work is of a useful nature and serves as a means of helping the community. At the present time no matriculating certificate is complete without evaluating the practical work done by the pupil; poor grades on practical subjects may be a reason for keeping a pupil back to repeat a year.

In the next four or five years the number of pupils in Albanian schools will rise from 405,000 to 525,000 and the number of teachers to over 20,000. It is estimated that schools will eventually last twelve years and give pupils an opportunity to continue their general education or to choose a particular group of subjects for special study during the last two or three years. However, the details of this plan have not been worked out; one proposal is that after an eight-year general education, pupils transfer to specialized schools. The first graduates of re-organized schools are expected to come in 1970 or 1971, depending on whether the secondary school lasts eleven or twelve years. Boarding-schools are being expanded to include some 20,000 pupils within the next few years.

School syllabuses are being revised and improved. Great effort is being made to have textbooks prepared for all subjects covered in the secondary schools and in higher education. Most of the textbooks are literal translations of Soviet textbooks into Albanian, but there is some good work being done by the Institute of Sciences in the fields of Albanian literature, language, and folklore.

The emphasis at the present time is on the relationship between schools and daily life in Albania; "the school, the Party and the government should, in the first place, concentrate their efforts to transform the Albanian family in accordance with Communist doctrine." By this transformation Albanian leaders and educationalists intend to produce "productive labor and cultural activity and active participation in the development of our fatherland."

It is of course easy to make generalizations and one can always prophesy. Time will give a proper setting to the work of the Workers' (Communist) Party in Albania[1] and history will record all of its acts in their proper relationship. But no matter what injustice and unfairness exist there, in the long run, as far as education is concerned, the good will outweigh the bad.

BIBLIOGRAPHY

Anuari statistikor I RPSH, Drejtoria e Statistikes. (The Annual Statistical Yearbook of the People's Republic of Albania.) Directorate of Statistics. Tirana, 1961.

BURGESS, ALINE. "Home Economics in an Albanian School." *The Journal of Home Economics*, XXIII, 1931.

DOUGLAS, NORMAN. *Old Calabria.* Harcourt, Brace and Co. New York, 1956.

Il Collegio Saveriano di Scutari d'Albania nei Primi Cinquant 'Anni (1877/8-1927/8) Chieri. G. Atesano, 1928.

KONITZA, FAIK. *Albania: The Rock Garden of Southeastern Europe.* Vatra, Boston, Mass., 1957.

KREMNEV, P. "Podëm prosveshcheniia i kul'turi v narodnoi respublike Albanii," (The Rise of Education and Culture in the People's Republic of Albania) *Sovet-Skaia Pedagogika.* (Soviet Pedagogy) Moscow. VII, 1952.

NOLI, BISHOP FAN S. *George Castrioti Scanderbeg*, International Universities Press, New York, 1947.

PETROTTA, GAETANO. *Svolgimento Storica della Cultura e della Litteratura Albanese*, Palermo, 1950.

PIPA, FEHIME. *Nji shekull Shkolle Shqipe (1861-1961)* (One Century of Albanian Schools (1861-1961) Arti Grafiche Editorali A. Urbinati, 1961.

SKENDI, STAVRO. *Albania. Published for the Mid-European Studies Center of the Free Europe Committee, Inc.* Frederick A. Praeger. New York, 1956.

———. "The Beginnings of Albanian Nationalist Trends in Culture and Education (1878-1912)." *The Journal of Central European Affairs.* Vol. 12, 1953, pp. 356-67.

———. "The History of the Albanian Alphabet. A Case of Complex Cultural and Political Development." Südost-Forscfiungen. XIX. R. Oldenbourg. München, 1960.

Periodicals

The Albanian Resistance. (News bulletin of the National Democratic Committee for a Free Albania. Paris, France, 1954 ———.

Aresimi Popullor (Popular Education). Monthly organ of the Ministry of Education and Culture of the Communist regime, 1945 ———.

Bashkimi (The Union). Tirana. Daily organ of the Democratic front of the Communist regime, 1944 ———.

SHELJZAT—*Le Pleiadi* (The Pleiades). Rome, Italy, 1957 ———. (This magazine contains a variety of studies by Albanian and Italian scholars.)

Shqiptari i Lirë (The Free Albanian). New York, 1959 ———. (Organ of the "Free Albania" Committee.)

Zeri i Popullit (The Voice of the People). Tirana. Organ of the Workers' (Communist) Party of Albania. 1944 ———.

1. Jani I. Dilo. *The Communist Party Leadership in Albania.* Institute of Ethnic Studies. Georgetown University, Washington, D. C. 1961.

ENGLAND

W. D. Halls

To a foreign observer, the outstanding characteristic of English education has been its slowness of growth. Not until 1833 did Parliament first vote public money to promote the education of the common people. By this time England's powerful Continental neighbors, France and Prussia, had already established the foundations of a complete primary and secondary education system. English tardiness may be ascribed to nineteenth-century liberalism, with its belief in individual liberty. The French Revolution had provided a grim warning of the excesses which an unbridled central power might commit. Empirical, pragmatic, putting his trust in common sense rather than "reason," the English liberal was content to leave education to private or religious initiative.

Religious belief has almost everywhere provided the initial motivation for education. In England the Anglican Church, by law the established church, naturally took the lead, but its motives for so doing were religious and moral rather than social and pedagogical. Events in France had stimulated the educational zeal of many within the Anglican Church, not with the aim of enlightening the masses but in order to control their thinking.[1] Victorian England, devout in Church attendance, saw no wrong in singing hymns that extolled "the rich man in his castle, the poor man at his gate" or reciting prayers which exhorted: "God bless the squire and his relations and keep us all within our proper stations."

The second largest religious group, the Dissenters, sprang from a more robust religious tradition such as had inspired the Puritan Pilgrim Fathers. It must not be forgotten that it was the Puritan regime of Cromwell which first attempted to establish a national educational system in England. The Dissenters believed in education for its own sake, Yet, whereas in the New World the Puritans flourished, gaining the religious tolerance denied them in the land of their birth, in England they had been deprived of their liberties and their schools had been closed. The Dissenting Academies were held to be anti-monarchical, anti-episcopal, and consequently dangerous to the established order.

The "old faith," Catholicism, had been banished from England after the Reformation, but with the relaxation of the penal laws many Catholics returned and started schools patronised by the many Irish immigrants to England and by others. But their motives for so doing were also not disinterested: education was regarded as a means of proselytising.

Economically the Industrial Revolution had created a need for schooling. A literate working force equipped with at least the bare minimum of knowledge, enough to read instructions on how to work a machine or to add up figures in simple bookkeeping, was required. But whereas other countries soon realised that industrial advance would create further educational needs, the English head-start on the rest of the world blinded it to this necessity, an oversight for which it paid dearly later. On the other hand, some Englishmen saw in education a mitigating factor in the use of child labour. Trevelyan speaks of the Factory Act of 1833 as "the children's charter," principally because it forbade the employment of children under the age of nine. Coupled with this humanitarian overtone is apparent the early influence of socialism, typified in Robert Owen, who regarded education not only as a means of enlightenment but also of banishing or at least alleviating the lot of the new industrial poor. He believed also that an effective educational system was only possible under direct state control.

One other influence, that of humanism, may be mentioned. Humanism represented a reaction against superstition and allegedly erroneous beliefs and practices. Its *cause célèbre* in the nineteenth century was the debate on evolution between Bishop Wilberforce and the anti-Darwinists and men such as Herbert

1. *Cf.* Asa Briggs, *The Age of Improvement, 1783-1867*, London, 1959, p. 224.

Spencer and Thomas Huxley. Both scientists and secularists allied in this struggle which they saw as one directed against the ecclesiastical dominance of education. The new scientists wished to establish a scientific curriculum in the schools, and thus make them more relevant to life.

Thus, looking back over the past century and a half, one can detect a shift in English education from religious to secular control; from an elitist to a meritocratic principle; from a nationalist and imperialist concept to a less insular and blinkered attitude; from the ideal of the "gentleman" to the ideal of the "professional"; from the belief in a non-intellectual approach to education to one with a more intellectual orientation. This essay shows how these diverse changes were fulfilled and indicates possible future trends.

The eighteenth century was largely hostile to the interference of the state in educational matters. It was argued that politicians could not establish a good educational system and in fact it was no part of the business of society. A society that did so would in fact produce a harmful uniformity. Even a shrewd observer such as Adam Smith regarded a national educational system as a marginal institution for those who were unable to find education for themselves. Much later, John Stuart Mill[2] summed up general feeling by deprecating any state interference at all. All this is in accordance with the principle of laissez faire:

In all the more advanced communities the great majority of things are worse done by the intervention of the government than the individuals most interested in the matter would do if left to themselves.

The lack of central control in English education might be ascribed to various factors. The tradition of empiricism, for example, dies hard. The religious lobby and local interests in educational matters have always been strong. This has been coupled with indifference on the national level, perhaps because the ruling classes did not see the use of any state system of education, particularly when their own children were educated in the so-called "public schools." The result was that until 1944 a policy of Malthusianism in education was practiced, with an insistence upon the "educational minimum." Perhaps the typical posture of the ruling classes at the beginning of the nineteenth century is exemplified in the words of Lord Eldon, who gloomily predicted that universal education would one day cause to march "a hundred thousand tall fellows with clubs and pikes against Whitehall."

Despite this overt hostility, however, the nineteenth century started with the elements of an educational system. In elementary education four types of school existed: the "dame school," mainly merely a child-minding establishment; the "hedge" school,

usually run by a man in his shop, where pupils might pick up a little learning; the workhouse apprentice school designed for the children of the destitute; and the charity school, with a religious rather than an educational aim. Secondary education had really made very little progress since the Reformation. Three main types of school existed: there were first and foremost the "public schools," particularly the nine largest—Eton, Charterhouse, Harrow, Merchant Taylor's, Rugby, St. Paul's, Shrewsbury, Westminster, and Winchester. These schools were then decadent institutions characterised by the harshness of their regime. At Rugby School the soldiers had to be summoned in 1797 to suppress a revolt by the students after a magistrate had been called to read the Riot Act. Despite this, Hans has estimated that half the nation's leaders went through the public school mill.[3] (But it must not be forgotten that another third were also educated at home.) The other group of secondary schools were the old grammar schools, some dating back to the Tudor period or even earlier. These had also been allowed to fall into decay, so much so that some positions of headmaster, or "usher," were merely sinecures. Both public and grammar schools remained strongholds of the classical curriculum. Trust deeds prevented this classical curriculum being supplemented by modern subjects. Lord Eldon (of the "pikes against Whitehall" fame) had delivered a legal judgement in 1805 which ruled that anything other than the classics could not legally be taught in such institutions. A third category of schools was the dissenting and private academies. The dissenting academies, run by the Nonconformists, were more progressive and even introduced a little science into their curriculum. The academies were in effect private grammar schools which might be vocational, technical, or classical. If vocational, the schools prepared mainly for a seafaring career or for the army. On the whole, however, secondary education was in an even more parlous state than elementary education.

The universities also stagnated. In England only two existed: Oxford and Cambridge. The students who entered them at the age of fifteen were either of aristocratic families or destined for the Church. Examinations were a farce. Lord Eldon declared that for his bachelor's degree he was asked two questions only: what the Hebrew word was for "the place of the skull," whereupon he answered "Golgotha"; and and second, who was the founder of University College, Oxford. Paying due lip service to the legend, he answered "King Alfred," and was thereupon awarded his degree! The universities were still very much under Church influence and the state had little power over them.

2. J. S. Mill, *Essay on Liberty*, London, 1859, p. 126, quoted in W. O. Lester Smith, *Education: An Introductory Survey*, 1966.
3. N. Hans, *New Trends in Education in the Eighteenth Century*, London, 1951, p. 19.

Although the current of influential opinion in the country was against state interference in education, a precedent was set by the passing in 1802 of the Health and Morals of Apprentices Act. This prescribed, *inter alia*, a twelve-hour day for factory apprentices, and provided for instruction in the three R's to be given. It was followed in 1833 by another Factory Act which provided that after work was finished, children aged nine to thirteen should attend school for two hours a week. Inspectors were appointed to see that this regulation was enforced. A further step forward was the introduction of the Bell and Lancaster monitorial system, which provided a model for elsewhere in Europe.[4] This monitorial system gave rise to a form of teacher apprenticeship. Other national events combined to favour the extension of education. The Reform Act of 1832 enfranchised many more of the enlightened classes. It was followed by Chartist riots arising partly from a demand for further extension of the franchise. Such national unrest provoked concessions, particularly in educational matters. Meanwhile, Parliament had made its first grant of £20,000 to the two religious societies, the National Society and the British and Foreign Society, "for the education of the children of the poorer classes in Great Britain." This was the beginning of a series of annual grants. In 1839 a Committee of Council on Education inaugurated under the secretaryship of Shuttleworth to see that the parliamentary grants were wisely spent, and also to start a normal school. It also established an inspectorate.

The predominantly moral purpose of such educational provision is, however, apparent in the Instructions that the Committee issued to inspectors in 1840:

The inspectors will inquire, with special care, how far the doctrines and principles of the church are instilled into the minds of the children. The inspectors will ascertain whether church accommodation of sufficient extent and in a proper situation, is provided for them; whether their attendance is regular, and proper means are taken to ensure their suitable behaviour during the service; whether enquiry is made afterwards by their teachers how far they have profited by the public audiences of religion which they had been attending. The inspectors will report also upon the daily practice of the school with reference to divine worship: whether the duties of the day are begun and ended with prayer and psalmody; whether daily instruction is given in the Bible; whether the catechism and the liturgy are explained, with the terms most commonly in use throughout the authorised version of the scriptures.

In these instructions can also be seen the beginnings of religious instruction for all children and of the daily "act of worship" which even today, by law, must begin the school session. One may discern also the beginnings of what for a time was an oppressive inspection system.

The Committee of Council was faced with a problem of teacher supply, particularly as the Bell and Lancaster system was falling into disrepute. Thus in 1846 the apprentice-teacher system was officially adopted.[5] In 1848 Shuttleworth, the first secretary of the Committee, was forced to resign because of ill-health. To him, more than to anyone else, can be ascribed the creation of a public system of elementary education in England, in which a working partnership had been inaugurated between the religious and secular authorities. In 1852 the Committee of Council came under fire because it was not subject to direct parliamentary control. Thus in 1856 its status was changed from that of a subordinate organ of the Privy Council to that of an Education Department, presided over by the Lord President of the (Privy) Council, but with a Vice-President in the House of Commons who was answerable to Parliament.

Once Parliament had more direct control over educational expenditure an outcry was raised against its growing cost. In the decade from 1847 to 1857 the expenditure quintupled. The result was the establishment of a Royal Commission presided over by the Duke of Newcastle "to inquire" into the present state of education in England and to consider and report what measures, if any, are required for the extension of sound and cheap elementary instruction to all classes of the people." The insistence upon "sound and cheap elementary instruction" set the tone for the Report of the Newcastle Commission. Yet undoubtedly the criticisms the Commission made of the existing system, that it was neither cheap nor sound, were justified by the facts. It recommended that there should be no further centralisation of education; that the denominational system that had hitherto appertained should continue to exist with any secular schools that were in existence; that grants made by the central authority should be supplemented by local taxation. Furthermore, the system of raising funds by charitable means should also continue. It came out against making education either free or compulsory and, in fact, wrote trenchantly:

Any attempt to replace an independent system of education by a compulsory system managed by the government will be met by objections, both religious and political, of far graver character in this country than any with which it has had to contend in Prussia.

Thus was evolved the first of the many compromises that have characterised English education since that date. The Vice-President of the new Education Department, Sir Robert Lowe, accepted also the principle of payment by results—the Commission had suggested that a capitation grant of up to six shilling per head yearly should be made for every pupil who, after examination by the inspectors, had made satis-

---

4. For an account of how the system worked *cf.* G. D. H. Cole & Raymond Postgate, *The Common People, 1746-1946*, London, 4th Edition, 1949, p. 308.

5. *Cf. Minutes of the Committee of Council of Education, 1839-40*, London (official government publication).

factory progress. This was embodied in a Revised Code of regulations, which became the ultimate authority for the giving of grants. Speaking in the House of Commons, Lowe confessed with brutal frankness:

I cannot promise the House that this system will be an economical one and I cannot promise that it will be an effective one, but I can promise that it will be one or the other. If it is not cheap it shall be efficient; if it is not efficient it will be cheap.

Not only did Lowe favour the principle of payment by results, as it became known, but also of payment by attendance. His instruments in this matter were the inspectors. On the other hand, he rejected the principle of education aided by local taxation.

How did the new code introduced by Lowe work? In its favour it must be said that it improved the general efficiency of the school and achieved higher standards and better attendance figures. On the other hand, the minimum standards necessary to qualify for a grant became the maximum ones and as Matthew Arnold, himself an Inspector, declared, the general quality of education declined, particularly the quality of the teachers; other side effects were also injurious to the schools.

Meanwhile the revival of the "public schools" had begun under the impetus that had been given to it by Thomas Arnold, father of Matthew Arnold, when he had been headmaster of Rugby in the 1840s. The original public schools such as Winchester, Eton, and Westminster were royal or ecclesiastical foundations. In the eighteenth and nineteenth centuries other schools, such as Harrow, Rugby, Charterhouse and Shrewsbury, gradually grew in importance. They were independent of state control and even semi-independent of church control, despite the ecclesiastical origins of many of them. Possessing strong links with the universities, they had gradually become national rather than local institutions, serving a clientele composed of the aristocracy and of the newly rich middle classes. According to Lytton Strachey, Arnold wanted for Rugby School: "first, religious and moral principle; second, gentlemanly conduct; thirdly intellectual ability." Moral education, as can be seen, loomed larger than intellectual education which, in any case, consisted mainly of Latin and Greek. The public schools retained the classics as the basis of their curriculum, stressed the virtues of duty and discipline, reinforced by corporal punishment, compulsory attendance in chapel, a sometimes ruthless self-government by the boys themselves, and the establishment of an authoritarian prefect system.[6]

In 1861 it was felt by many that the time was ripe to overhaul the public schools. As a result the Clarendon Commission was appointed. Its Report recommended that the managements of the schools should be controlled so as to prevent financial and other abuses. It also desired a broadening of the curriculum so that mathematics, science, modern languages, some social studies, and aesthetic subjects should be included. The Act of Parliament that followed the Report omitted curriculum matters. But it did end the managerial abuses undoubtedly prevalent, although finally permitting the continuing autonomy of the schools. Meanwhile, the public schools themselves had heeded the danger signals and in 1869 established an organisation known as the Headmasters' Conference, which still exists and exercises an informal regulating function over its members.

Another body, the Schools Enquiry Commission (the Taunton Commission) sat from 1864-1868 in order to inquire into the position of schools not covered by the Newcastle and Clarendon Commissions respectively. It found that secondary education was inadequately provided for, both as regards curriculum and buildings. It cast an admiring glance at American secondary schools which, although of more recent origin, were as good as English ones; as for Prussia, it was considered to have the best system of education of all. Following the Prussian example it was proposed that three grades of secondary school should be established based upon the length of secondary schooling desired, the beginnings of the so-called tripartite system. The curriculum given should include as a minimum languages, mathematics, and science. It advocated a central Ministry of Education which would control the endowments on which the present secondary schools existed, which in return would receive support from local taxation. It not only proposed that more girls' schools should be established but also wanted some kind of central examination board and a system of teacher certification. However, few of the recommendations were followed. One practical outcome was the passing of the Endowed Schools Act in 1869, which placed the schools under the control

---

6. The importance of the "public schools," self-cast in the role of providing national leaders, can be seen from the following facts: the last three Conservative Prime Ministers of Great Britain, Sir Alec Douglas Home, Mr. Macmillan, and Lord Avon (Anthony Eden) were all old-Etonians. In the period 1931-1936 old-Etonians provided 27 percent of recruits to the Foreign Office. In 1934 over one-sixth of the Members of Parliament, 89 in all, were old-Etonians. Even in the first post-war Labour Government 30 percent of the M.P.'s were educated in public schools, as were 11 out of 34 ministers. Although the number of children, mainly boys, in the public schools has never exceeded 6 percent of the total school population, the above statistics give some measure of their influence. From figures given by Guttsman it would also appear that from 1918-1955 51 percent of all Conservative M.P.'s were educated in public schools as were 71 percent of all Cabinet Ministers. What is more, 36 percent of all Conservative M.P.'s and 45 percent of all Conservative Cabinet Ministers were educated at either Eton or Harrow. For the Socialists, over the same period, 13 percent of all M.P.'s and no less than 25 percent of all Cabinet Ministers were educated in public schools. Guttsman concludes (writing in 1963): "There exists today in Britain a ruling class, if we mean by it a group which provides the majority of those to occupy positions of power and who, in their turn, can materially assist their sons to reach similar positions." Such is the power of the public schools even today. The above statistics are taken from T. W. Bamford, *The Rise of the Public Schools*, London, 1967, Ch. 9.

of the Charity Commissioners. The proposal for a central authority was not taken up, for reasons that Matthew Arnold described as being due to class interests.

From the beginning of the nineteenth century many economists had considered education from a utilitarian viewpoint, believing that schools could act as agents for the reduction of crime. In a parliamentary debate in 1807 Whitbread had declared:

Search Newgate (prison) calendar. The great majority of the executed in London every year were the Irish; the next, in order, were English, and the last Scots. This was in exact proportion with their respective systems of education among the lower orders.[7]

It was these practical arguments for education rather than moral or idealistic ones which finally led to the Education Act of 1870; by then it was also agreed that English industrial prosperity would depend upon adequate provision of public education. The victories of the North over the South in the American Civil War and the Prussian defeat of Austria were ascribed to the respectively better educational systems. Moreover, pressure now arose from the working classes themselves for an education that would be non-denominational, free, compulsory, and universal. The 1867 Reform Act had enfranchised a larger number of the urban population, so much so that Lowe is reported to have said, "Now we must educate our masters." The growth of secularism had been furthered by the setting up of a National Secular Society. There was a feeling of unrest expressing itself in a republicanism which aimed at deposing Queen Victoria, by then "the Widow of Windsor" grieving for her lost husband.[8] It fell to Forster, a wealthy Quaker and a radical, who was also the brother-in-law of Matthew Arnold, to introduce into Parliament the appropriate measures.

On the eve of the 1870 Education Act the total education grant was £415,000, distributed among 13,000 schools. This meant that about 1.5 million children were being educated with the help of the state. But the number was very unevenly distributed. In Liverpool, for example, it was estimated that one in four children did not go to school at all. Among the working classes only two-thirds of children aged six to ten attended school and only one-third aged ten to twelve. Education was in effect still part-time. The leaving of the establishment of schools to voluntary local initiative in the hands of religious denominations meant that where no schools had been started no state help had been sought. Forster saw the problem as nothing less than how to establish a national public system without destroying what had already been built up largely through local support.

As regards administration, Forster's bill proposed that the country be divided into districts. Where adequate provision for education already existed, no further administrative measures need be taken. In other areas school boards should be elected to set up schools. These schools would provide compulsory education from age five to thirteen if the local school board deemed it desirable. Schools would not be free but would be sustained by three sources of contribution: a central fund; the local taxation system ("rates"); and fees charged to parents. The thorniest issue was the religious question. Forster said:

We have no doubt whatever that an enormous majority of the parents of this country prefer that there should be a Christian training for their children—that they should be taught to read the Bible.

This principle was finally accepted in an amended form (known after its author as the Cowper-Temple Amendment) which ran:

No religious catechism or religious formulary which is distinctive of any particular denomination shall be taught in the school.

Denominational schools already existing were, however, allowed to give religious instruction either at the opening or the close of the school session, but with provision for a "conscience clause." Non-denominational religious instruction might be given in non-denominational schools set up by school boards, but this would be at local discretion. The denominational schools would not receive local aid but in its stead would receive an additional grant from the central Treasury.

The 1870 Act can only be regarded as a compromise. The denominational or voluntary schools and the school board schools henceforth existed side by side in a so-called "dual" system. Looking back with the benefit of hindsight, writers on the Left have condemned the Act. In 1924 R. H. Tawney declared:

The elementary schools of 1870 were intended in the main to produce an orderly, civil, obedient population, with sufficient education to understand a command.

Similarly H. G. Wells later wrote:

The Education Act of 1870 was not an act for a common universal education; it was an act to educate the lower classes for employment on class lines.[9]

One important detrimental result was indeed that elementary education became further isolated from secondary education. In other respects the Act was disappointing. Education, even elementary, was not made free; fees of up to ninepence per week could be charged. Nor was it made compulsory unless the local school board decided it should be so. Little wonder that families of the poorest classes existing on

7. Quoted in E. G. West, "The Role of Education in Nineteenth Century Doctrines of Political Economy," *British Journal of Educational Studies,* May 1964.

8. For a description and analysis of the Socialist movement in education *cf.* B. Simon, *Education and the Labour Movement, 1870-1950,* London, 1965.

9. Quoted in B. Simon, *op. cit.*

a total income of only eighteen shillings a week regarded the Act as an intolerable hardship. Moreover, the system worked to the disadvantage of the voluntary denominational schools. It is true that they now received a 50 percent grant from the Education Department, but this was intended only as a yearly subsidy for running expenses, and all new building grants were henceforth cut off. The school boards were empowered to levy a local tax (rate) far less than what was really required to produce a complete elementary education system. On the other hand, the school boards represented the beginning of what today is termed the "partnership" between the central authority and local education authorities. But the necessary teachers were not trained in sufficient numbers. The iniquitous Revised Code, with its "payment by results," continued right up to 1897 with the result that lessons were formalized, rote memory was encouraged, knowledge was drilled into the children, discipline was harsh, and little beyond the three R's was taught. The board schools, as the local secular schools came to be known, did not flourish. In 1902 there were only 5,700 of them against 14,000 voluntary schools, but even the latter were in a parlous financial state.[10]

As regards religious instruction, the London School Board—the largest—laid down that in its schools Bible reading "with explanations," together with instruction in the principles of morality and religion should be given, but this should be non-denominational. This example was followed by most of the other new school boards.

On the other hand, many school boards did not enforce the provision regarding compulsory attendance. Thus in 1876 an Act was passed placing a duty on parents to see that the child was instructed in the three R's. This did not necessarily imply compulsory school attendance and, in fact, if a sufficient schooling is given, even today a child need not attend school. Even in those areas where by-laws regarding compulsory attendance were passed, many exemptions were possible. A particular scandal was caused by children still working in factories, although their employment under the age of ten had been stopped by the 1870 Act. The so-called "half-time" system, in which a child was allowed to spend half his time in gainful employment and the other half in school, persisted right up to 1918.

The working of the 1870 Act proved so inefficient that a new Commission, the Cross Commission, was appointed to inquire into how the new elementary education system was operating. It reported in 1888. One of its main criticisms concerned the iniquitous "payment by results" system; this led eventually to a new Code in 1890, which considerably modified the previous grant regulations. The Commission also gave its approval to what were becoming known as "higher grade schools," where education was being continued beyond the elementary stage. It also urged the necessity for more and better teachers.

The "higher grade" schools were perceived in some quarters as giving advanced technical and commercial education. The move to provide a more scientific and technological education had started as far back as 1851, when the Great Exhibition had awakened many to the fact that Britain's industrial lead was being narrowed. Grants had been given after this for teachers to obtain scientific qualifications. In 1884 a Royal Commission on Technical Instruction had been set up to investigate technical and science teaching, because at this time much alarm was growing at competition from the U.S.A. and the newly created German Empire. The Technical Instruction Act of 1889 allowed local school boards to levy a special local tax for technical instruction. At the same time the government used money obtained from an extra duty on wines and spirits to subsidise technical education, a source of funds which became appropriately known as the "whiskey money."

If the Education Act of 1870 at long last established a skeleton public system of elementary education, secondary education was still very deficient. It was the aim of the Bryce Commission (1895) also to set secondary education on a firm basis. The commission defined secondary education as

The education of the boy or girl not simply as a human being who needs to be instructed in the mere rudiments of knowledge but a process of intellectual training and personal discipline conducted with special regard to profession and trade to be followed.

It recommended the setting up of a central authority for all education which would work in partnership with local authorities—County Councils, County Boroughs and boroughs with a population of over 50,000 —for it was by local initiative, they considered, that adequate secondary education should be provided. They also recommended that certain "higher grade" schools should henceforth be treated as true secondary schools.

The Board of Education Act of 1899 provided the central authority hitherto lacking in English education. The Board was given the superintendance of all educational matters in England and Wales and was composed of a President, a Secretary of State, the First Commissioner of the Treasury and the Chancellor of the Exchequer, all political appointments. It lasted for forty-five years (until 1944) but, and perhaps this is symptomatic of the neglect from which

---

10. The tests that the inspectors were obliged to make in order to allocate the grant a school could "earn" are ridiculous, as can be seen from the following examples. 1. Children had to write correctly from dictation: "If you twist that stick so long you will make your wrist ache." 2. They had to solve the following arithmetical problem: "5 1/2 yards make one pole. Draw a diagram to show that 30 1/2 square yards make one perch." If the luckless children inquired what a diagram was, they were given the reply: "Never mind what a diagram is—work the sum!"

English education has suffered, never once met as a full body because its most important member, the Chancellor of the Exchequer, who controlled the purse strings, failed to attend a single meeting.

The work of the Bryce Commission came to full fruition in 1902. By then there was need for a new general dispensation for education. In the elementary non-denominational schools there were now slightly more pupils than in the Anglican schools, yet the Anglican schools had at their disposal only about half the amount of money. For international reasons the need for reform became even more apparent. As Halévy put it:

Victoria's England began to doubt itself. A people of amateurs was obliged to recognize that it was ill equipped to face up to a people of professionals (the Germans).[11]

The Act of 1902 that emerged was therefore not a result of educational, but rather of political, economic, and religious forces. It established a much stronger network of local administration, identifying the local education authorities (L.E.A.'s) with the local councils and giving them power to levy a local tax for education. The school boards were abolished. The religious schools were also henceforth subsidised by local taxation rather than from the central exchequer, and the so-called "dual" system of official and voluntary schools continued side by side. It is usually said that this Act created an educational 'ladder' for the poorest to climb to university education. Yet, save for the few selected, secondary education was still not placed "end-on" to elementary education but was considered to be different in kind, fee-paying, and intended for a different clientele. However, it may fairly be said that by 1902, almost a century later than France and Prussia, England had at last achieved a national system of education.

From 1902 to 1944 there was steady but slow progress in both elementary and secondary education. The Education Act of 1918 (perhaps it is significant that most educational reform in Britain takes place immediately after a war) raised the leaving age to fourteen, regulated child employment, promoted the transfer of a few children from the elementary to the academic secondary school (until then, children not selected for secondary education remained at the elementary school before leaving at fourteen), and put pressure on the L.E.A.'s to extend their educational provision. The advent of the Labour Party to power for a short while in 1924 popularised the slogan "secondary education for all." This new view of secondary education gained ground, and a Committee under the chairmanship of Hadow reported in 1926 on *The Education of the Adolescent*. The report favoured a break in the educational process between the ages of eleven and twelve. At this age all children should be moved to secondary schools or senior schools of a post-primary kind, termed "modern" schools. The recommendations had to wait for full implementation until the 1944 Education Act, but the

report did have the effect of promoting an eleven-plus examination which selected a slightly larger elite for the secondary grammar schools.

Although the economic crisis slowed down educational development, by 1938 over 60 percent of school children were being educated in schools reorganized in accordance with the Hadow recommendations. As before, the stimulus of war brought about a new deal for education. The 1944 Education Act ranks with the Acts of 1870 and 1902 as one of the milestones in English education and is still the basis of the present system. Pamphlet No. 1 of the newly-formed Ministry of Education expressed the educational hopes of the nation in optimistic terms:

We are not, of course, planning a new educational edifice on a cleared site: the educational system exists. But the task before us is certainly not one just of repair and patching: it is rather one of extension and modernising to secure a new structure. . . .

Elsewhere, it declared: "We must now write the vision and make it plain upon tables."[12]

The Board of Education was replaced by a Ministry whose duty it was not merely to "advise and supervise," but to "control and direct"—a significant change of wording. The local education authorities were reconstituted and it was envisaged that the relationship between the central and local authorities would be that of a partnership, with finance coming approximately half from the central and half from local sources. These arrangements affected the position of the voluntary schools. The majority of such schools became officially recognised as "aided" schools, if they were able to match capital funds provided by the central authority with a voluntary contribution of the same amount. New capital grants for building were provided on the same basis. In all schools, whether voluntary or otherwise, the Education Act made religious instruction compulsory unless parents withdrew their children from it, and each school day had to begin with an act of worship for all children. The ideology behind this arrangement, which in many cases merely confirmed what was already local practice, is interesting. Those instrumental in producing the Act (whose main architect was Mr. [now Lord] Butler) sought for some philosophy to match the Nazi Ideology. They found it in the Christian religion which was (and still is) the "established" religion of England.

It was hoped also under the Act to raise the leaving age to fifteen immediately. This measure had eventually to be postponed until 1947 when a Labour government minister, Miss Ellen Wilkinson, did so in what has been described "an act of faith rather than an act of wisdom."

---

11. Halévy, *Histoire du Peuple Anglais, 1895-1906*, Paris, p. 152.
12. Ministry of Education Pamphlet No. 1: *The Nation's Schools: Their Plan and Purpose*, London, H.M.S.O., 1945.

The chief feature of the Act, however, was the establishment of the principle of "secondary education for all." Without explicitly specifying types of secondary schools, the new Ministry envisaged that a tripartite system of secondary education would emerge. A grammar-school type of education, academic in nature and leading on to the university, would be most suitable for the gifted, estimated at about 20 percent of the school population. For a further 5 percent, secondary technical education would be developed, building upon the existing junior technical schools. In point of fact, secondary technical education failed to develop, and the number of pupils in such schools in relative terms consistently fell. Most children would, however, move at age eleven to a new type of school known as the secondary modern school, the senior schools envisaged and partly realised after the Hadow Report. This type of school suffered under the disadvantage that its purposes were never made sufficiently clear. Ministry of Education Pamphlet No. 1 postulates "that in these schools will be a considerable number of children whose future employment will not demand any measure of technical skill or knowledge." This prediction of the future trends of industry and the economy proved completely out of touch with reality. The three types of school mentioned were not necessarily envisaged as separate institutions but might, it was held, be housed under one roof as a multilateral school. This was in germ the beginnings of the comprehensive system of education which is now official government policy. However, the immediate effect of this tripartite structure was an insistence by parents that their children should enter a grammar school now made entirely non-fee-paying, which they rightly saw as remaining the royal road to success in life. From this followed the institutionalisation of the 11+ examination, which had such iniquitous effects upon the secondary system.

Since the re-organisation of 1944 a number of significant reports concerning English education have appeared. The Crowther Report of 1958 dealt with the education of the adolescent, as its title "Fifteen to Eighteen" implies. Its main recommendations concerned the raising of the leaving age to sixteen with the eventual establishment of part-time education for all young people up to the age of eighteen in institutions known as County Colleges. In view of the present economic situation it does not now look as if even the first recommendation, the raising of the leaving age, will take effect until about 1972. On the other hand, the massive increase in numbers staying on at school beyond the statutory leaving age is sufficient cause for a complete rethinking of the latter stages of secondary education. A second report, known as the Newsom Report, and entitled "Half our Future," deals with the education of children of average intelligence or below between the ages of thirteen and sixteen. It had no mandate to consider the structures of secondary education, but did highlight the educational black spots of the present system. It

demonstrated that the present tripartite structure was itself a function of social class; five out of six children attending the secondary modern school, for example, came from the homes of manual workers. It pleaded for a better deal for the average child and postulated a curriculum for him that was "realistic, practical, vocational and offering a choice." Yet another report, the Robbins Report (1963) dealt with higher education. It attempted to forecast future economic needs and predicted that by 1980 about 17 percent of the relative age group would be in higher education, a conservative estimate compared with North America or some other Western European countries. However, as a result of such forecasts the number of universities in Britain has now been doubled, technological institutions have been granted full university status and other institutions, now known as "polytechnics," have been similarly upgraded. The most recent report, the Plowden Report, which deals with primary (elementary) education, again highlighted the defects of the present system.

There is no doubt that these reports of advisory bodies have spurred successive governments on to some action, although tardy. In two areas, that of curriculum change[13] and secondary structures, the discussion has been particularly fruitful. In 1964 the Ministry of Education (now expanded and rechristened the Department of Education and Science) set up an independent body known as the Schools Council for the Curricula and Examinations. This body began to review the whole of the secondary curriculum in the light of educational objectives has stirred up discussion and produced concrete proposals for reform. One example of this may suffice. It concerns the structure of what is known as the sixth form—in American terms, the college-bound students of the eleventh and twelfth grade upwards. The sixth form has been the normal mode of entry to the university and has been oriented towards a series of university examinations known as the General Certificate of Education. This G.C.E. examination functions on two levels: Ordinary and Advanced. For entry to a university the sixth former must have achieved a combination of O (Ordinary) and A (Advanced) level subjects, including English, a foreign language, mathematics, a science and one other subject. In practice, O level is taken before the sixth form in the equivalent of the tenth grade. The sixth form curricula have therefore been oriented towards the passing of two or at the most three subjects at the Advanced level, practically either in the field of the humanities or in the field of sciences. The ensuing curriculum specialisation for England's most gifted students is now almost universally condemned. The Schools Council has come forward with proposals for

---

13. For an account of curriculum change in England see: W. D. Halls, "England: Sources and Strategies of Change" in Thomas, Sands & Brubaker (eds.), *Strategies for Curriculum Change: Cases from Thirteen Nations, Scranton,* Pa.: International Textbook Co., 1968.

reform that are still a subject for debate. A broadening of the curricula on the lines appertaining in most countries of Western Europe is desired by many, but the vested interests involved are such that the constraining collar of the G.C.E. examinations will not easily be broken. At this and other levels of curriculum reform the Schools Council has performed a useful task in shaping an informed opinion and stimulating action (such as the introduction of modern languages into the elementary school).

The reform of educational structures, in practice the institution of a system of comprehensive education roughly on American high school lines, has now become a political question. The Labour Party desires the comprehensive school on largely social grounds (because the old system had demonstrated clearly that the grammar school was a middle-class preserve); some (but not all) Conservatives fear that the abolition of the grammar school or its absorption into a comprehensive structure will eliminate much that was good in the old elitist concept of education. The decisive step was taken by the Labour government when Circular No. 10 of 1965 ordered all L.E.A.'s to prepare plans for secondary re-organization on comprehensive lines. Freedom of choice was given these bodies as to the form these structures might take. In fact, no less than six patterns have been favoured. Unfortunately the one seemingly preferred by the Department of Education and Science, possibly on grounds of cheapness, is a comprehensive unitary school for all between the ages of eleven and eighteen. If this is to become the general pattern, it would again place England as being out of step with secondary reform elsewhere in the world. Three other schemes propose variants of the American junior and senior high schools. Another postulates a division of education into three (not two) stages: primary education from age five to nine, a middle school from age nine to thirteen, and a senior school from age thirteen to eighteen. The last proposal, which is finding increasing favour in some quarters, is for a sixth form college, which in effect means a senior high school from age fifteen to eighteen. But the final decision as to which pattern should be adopted lies in local hands. This carries with it so many disadvantages that one can hardly understand why it is acceptable to the central government. Nevertheless English education, proceeding as always empirically, is undoubtedly evolving towards a fairer concept of equality of opportunity than hitherto.

In higher education also it is now apparent that by the end of the century there will be a gradated order of institutions, some of which will be universities in the traditionally European sense of the term, and others of which will operate at a lower level. In fact, this means that the former restricted meaning of "higher education" is being expanded to include a variety of forms of post-secondary education, just as has already occurred in the U.S.A.

Reviewing the course of English education, one notes the increasing intervention of the state in the schools. The laissez-faire policy of the nineteenth century was followed by a period of benevolent state interest and is now being superseded by active state direction of education. Since this is now an enterprise that swallows up some 5 percent of the gross national product each year, it clearly cannot be left entirely to local amateurs. Like most modern nations, England has now accepted the theory that investment in education is a necessary condition of economic growth. Such intervention must mean, however, to some extent the "manipulation" of education for national ends. There are signs, of which student unrest is one, that such an approach is resented. The problem of the right balance between education for the individual and education for society is still not solved. Nor has the question of how considerable freedom in education can be reconciled with a democratic concept of equality. But England has now come to realise that the concept of a static educational system is gone forever. Structures and curricula, like everything else, will need to be constantly updated. England is plunged into a period of rapid educational development to which there can now be no end.

SELECT BIBLIOGRAPHY

ADAMSON, J. W. *English Education, 1789-1902*. London: Cambridge University Press, 1930.

BANFORD, T. W. *The Rise of the Public Schools*. London: Nelson, 1967.

BANKS, O. *Parity & Prestige in English Secondary Education*. London: Routledge & Kegan Paul, 1955.

BARNARD, H. C. *A Short History of English Education, 1760-1944*. London: University of London Press, 1947.

BERNBAUM, G. *Social Change & the Schools, 1918-1944*. London: Routledge & Kegan Paul, 1967.

BRIGGS, ASA. *The Age of Improvement, 1783-1867*. London: Longmans, 1959.

COLE, G. D. H., and POSTGATE, RAYMOND. *The Common People 1746-1946*. 4th ed. London: Methuen, 1949.

CRUIKSHAUNK, M. *Church & State in English Education*. London: Macmillan, 1965.

CURTIS, S. J. *History of Education in Great Britain*. The best succinct history of British education. 4th ed. London: University Tutorial Press, 1957.

EDMONDS, E. L. *The School Inspector*. London: Routledge & Kegan Paul, 1962.

HUGHES, T. *Tom Brown's Schooldays*. 1st ed. London: Blackie, 1857.

McCLURE, S. *Educational Documents 1816-1963*. An invaluable reference work. London: Chapman & Hall, 1965.

SIMON, B. *Education and the Labour Movement, 1870-1920*. London: Lawrence & Wishart, 1965.

SMITH, W. O. LESTER. *Education in Great Britain*. 4th ed. London: Oxford University Press, 1964 (and Penguin Books).

WILKINSON, R. *The Prefects*. London: Oxford University Press, 1964.

FINLAND

O. K. Kyöstiö

THE COUNTRY AND ITS PEOPLE

Finland is the most eastern of the Scandinavian countries, lying as a whole in the very North. Though its most southern tip is only at the same latitude as Greenland, the climate is rather warm in the summer and the annual average temperature is about six degrees centigrade higher than at the same latitude in North America and Asia. Therefore, it is possible to carry on some farming up to the Arctic Circle. Even above this line, there are many forests.

The whole area of Finland is 337,000 square kilometers, 9 percent of which is water (55,000 lakes) and of the land area, about 72 percent is covered by forests, so that only about 9 percent is cultivated. The abundance of lakes, rivers, and swamps is the cause of many difficulties for school districts. Most elementary schools in the countryside are therefore small and have only one to three teachers. Because of the long distances between school and home, many elementary schools in northern and eastern Finland are equipped with dormitories.

Finland is also thinly settled; there are 4.6 million people or a ratio of only fifteen people per square kilometer. Of the entire population 93 percent speak Finnish and about 7 percent Swedish as their mother tongue. Most of the people or 92 percent belong to the Lutheran Church. All these factors influence Finland's system of education.

From the economic point of view, Finland is among the top fifteen countries in regard to its standard of living (national production per capita). Agricultural production (20 percent) and industry (41 percent) absorb a bigger proportion of the net national production than in the more highly-developed countries; the services, a smaller proportion (39 percent). In terms of the numbers of workers involved, agriculture and forestry take up a large percentage of the manpower (28 percent). These factors must be considered, especially in vocational education.

Finland is a republic.

DEVELOPMENT OF FINNISH EDUCATION

Until 1809 or for about 500 years, Finland was a part of Sweden. During this time and even a little later, the Church controlled all public education. Since the Middle Ages, the most important subjects in the schools were Latin and religion since the schools tried primarily to train clergymen. After the Reformation, Latin gradually disappeared as the language of teaching, and instead, Swedish, unfortunately for the nation, replaced Latin. Finland was not nearly as well provided with schools as was Sweden. One university, however, was established in 1640, but the number of grammar schools was proportionately much smaller in Finland than in Sweden. The education of the common people was cared for by the clergymen, especially through their so-called confirmation schools. The parents had to teach their children to read. If they could not do this, the Church sometimes arranged village schools to teach the children.

When Sweden lost Finland during the Napoleonic War, Finland was established autonomously under the Russian Empire. Since this change, Finland was able to develop its own school organization to meet its own needs and purposes. During the first half century after separation from Sweden, the supremacy of the Church and the Swedish upper classes prevailed in the field of education. But since that time a rapid change began. In 1858 the first Finnish language grammar school was founded; in 1863 the first normal school for training elementary school teachers was established; in 1866 the elementary school system was organized; in 1870 the Church and school were separated; and in 1872 a secondary school ordinance was passed which is still the foundation for the parallel secondary school system. Elementary schools became general after this time, and more Finnish-speaking people began to send their children to secondary schools.

But it was not until the real independence of the country in 1917 that full opportunity to develop the nation's education in all fields came to Finland. In the 1920s and 1930s the six-year obligatory day school was made common in the whole country and illiteracy practically disappeared. However, at that time the percentage of children who continued their studies in secondary schools was rather small (about 10 percent of each age class), and in the universities, only about 1 percent. The most important accomplishment during this time was certainly the comprehensive coverage of the six-year obligatory day school and its two-year continuation classes. In the countryside, however, such classes were just part-time.

After World War II, the general interest in grammar schools increased. The number of secondary schools and the number of enrollees has tripled in the last twenty years. Then, too, poorer parents wanted to send their children to these schools, but there were not enough secondary schools to meet the demand, for the system which provided them was old. Secondary school was a selective grammar school and the upper grades (five to eight) of the elementary school were parallel with the lower levels of the secondary school. Only those who passed an entrance examination at the age of eleven years were allowed to enter a secondary school, and if they passed an examination at the end of this school, they could enter a university. The number of university students also increased during this period so that about 5 percent of each age group continued their studies in a university.

This period also brought a rapid development of education. Earlier there were rather few vocational schools and institutes. The number of students tripled at least. Besides day schools shorter vocational courses became numerous. More general adult education also became common, although it had been in existence much earlier.

The next period of Finnish education will probably be characterized by the expansion of higher and adult education. Secondary education in varying forms as in England also will become more common than it is now. A comprehensive school system will probably be realized in the distant future.

GOALS OF EDUCATION

The 1957 law of obligatory elementary school education defines the goals of public education. Each citizen is assured a basic elementary school education. The elementary school is obliged to educate its pupils morally so as to form good habits and to train them to acquire the practical knowledge and skills needed for life. In addition, the elementary school has to help the students in broadening their cultural understanding. Then, too, the school must work closely with the pupils' homes.

Laws formulated for the other types of schools stress the acquisition of still greater knowledge and skills, which are important in pursuing further studies or in practicing a vocation. Many people think that an emphasis on the humanities is not as necessary in a rapidly-changing society.

In discussing the goals of education, it is worthwhile to mention the goals selected by a committee which prepared the curricula for the elementary schools. According to the committee's 1952 report, the goals are

1. Individual aim: awakening of cultural interests
2. Social aim: educating citizenship and to humanity
3. Economic aim: developing economic thinking and behavior
4. Personal aim: building a harmonious and sound personality.

These goals, then, define at least in theory what is an educated man. It is often said that manners make the man, but in Finland in actual practice the formal training and passing of examinations are often given primary importance. In the past when only about 2 percent of the entire population earned a grammar school education, this attainment really defined the educated man.

There are, of course, very few goals that people in a country are unanimously willing to accept, especially goals which are emotionally linked to value systems involving religion, political ideas, traditions, and the like. Therefore, knowledge and skills are stressed as short-range goals that can be objectively realized. How far teachers try to reach the so-called long-range goals depends very much on the cultural milieu in which the teacher was reared and on the professional training he has received.

OBSTACLES TO ATTAINMENT OF GOALS AND EFFORTS TO OVERCOME THEM

Certain skills and knowledge are always important goals of all schools. To attain these goals, schools need money for equipment, buildings, school services, and teaching aids. Because Finland has a cold climate, the building assumes more importance, perhaps, than in a warm country. Buildings cost a great deal, so the cost of education generally is proportionately higher than in other countries with similar education. This fact explains why the obligatory education for all children in Finland is only an eight-year period. However, plans to lengthen this period have been made.

About half of all the children now have some opportunity to continue their studies in general or vocational schools, but these schools are not free of fees.

Another obstacle to the free and democratic education in Finland is the old-fashioned parallel school system. This system does not allow all children equal opportunities for education, for the social-economic status of the family too often determines whether a child's full capabilities are used. The attitudes among the higher social classes are still rather conservative and against the proposed school reform. In theory they recognize that Finnish school organization is out of date, but they still favor a system that is selective beginning even from the young age classes. In such a system children from poor and rural homes do not have the same educational opportunities as the children whose home backgrounds are more advantageous to attaining a good education.

Finland is a bilingual country. This fact could be an asset for education as it is in Switzerland. But the situation in Finland is unfavorable because both languages of the country are minority ones in international usage. For traditional reasons all Finnish children in secondary schools must learn Swedish. Usually they have to study at least two other foreign languages besides. The result is that languages absorb a great proportion of the time, leaving little time for the sciences; nor can the student concentrate on one widely-used living language. In general, the pupils should have more opportunity to choose between different subjects. But such a system is strange in Finland where the curriculum is restricted.

Teacher education has, of course, much influence on the short- as well as the long-range goals of education. Teachers for different types of schools are trained separately in their own normal schools. Therefore, one cannot generally speak about academic training for the teaching profession. This is without doubt one of the worst obstacles to the attainment of educational goals. Universities are not very keen to involve themselves in this matter and school authorities do not have the ability to improve the situation. A proposition to reorganize teacher training was made, but until now it has not had any practical consequences.

FINNISH SCHOOL SYSTEM

Compared with countries where there is a comprehensive school system, Finnish school organization is much more complicated. Finnish children enter rather late, at seven years of age. Very few of them have been in a kindergarten because there are such institutions only in cities. In Finland, kindergarten is not considered as a part of education but of social welfare. Therefore, kindergarten children are generally from poor homes where there is an absence of either mother or father or where both parents are working. A discussion, however, has arisen concerning whether the kindergarten should be made a part of the public school system and thus be made available to all children.

Only the lowest four grades of the elementary school are common to all children. After this period at least half of children in grade four try to enter a grammar school on the basis of selection. These 11-plus entrance examinations in reading, writing, and arithmetic are arranged at the same time in grammar

schools, not in the elementary schools. For this reason and some related ones, many capable children do not take part in the examinations at all.

Schooling of Finnish pupils at the age of eleven years is definitely divided into two tracks. Some elementary school children try later, from the fifth or sixth grade, to move to a grammar school. If they pass the entrance examinations, they must begin from the first class of the grammar school as the figure shows. Pupils also lose the extra years they may have spent in the elementary school beginning with the fifth grade. Thus the grammar school is the only type of "secondary" school in Finland. The upper grades of elementary school (five to nine) run parallel with the lower classes (one to five) of the grammar school. But the graduation of the former does not give the same rights as the certificate of the latter. Therefore, the upper grades of elementary school are not considered as secondary school. The same was true also with so-called prevocational schools, which the pupils could formerly enter from the sixth or seventh grade of elementary school. Almost all these schools now require the full obligatory school.

The only officially obligatory school in Finland is the eight-year elementary school. Everywhere it is at least a seven-year day school with additional day courses for a year after. In all cities and population centers in the countryside, too, the elementary school has two parts, a common six-year school and a two-year centralized citizenship school with some prevocational training. The following statistics show the duration of citizenship schools: two-year schools, 48 percent; one-year schools, 28 percent; less than one year, 24 percent. The latter type follow the seventh grade of elementary school. Some two-year schools (27 percent of them) have a voluntary ninth grade. Because elementary school is obligatory, it is also free and provides as well books and other materials, meals, health services, and transportation without payment. This is true, too, if a communal middle school has been established in a district. The lower grades of elementary school give a thorough foundation in reading so that there is no illiteracy in Finland, if formal reading skills are in question. This favorable situation is partly explained by the fact that Finnish is a phonetic language, which is spelled regularly.

It has been mentioned earlier that small elementary schools are characteristic of Finland. The following 1964 percentages indicate this: One-teacher schools employ 8.5 percent of teachers; two-teacher schools, 55.6 percent; three-teachers, 20.2 percent; four or more teachers, 15.7 percent.

The grammar school had its roots in the old Latin school but assumed its present pattern from the German Gymnasium. In general, German influence has been very important on the whole cultural life of Finland. However, the grammar school is not focused as much on the humanities as it still is in Germany. Greek is taught in a few schools and Latin is rather seldom obligatory. But foreign languages play a very great role in grammar-school curriculum. This is easy to understand because Finnish is spoken by few people and knowledge of foreign languages is important in Europe.

Grammar schools have different names in Finland; they might be called "lyseo," "tyttökoulu," "yhteiskoulu," depending on whether the school is for boys or for girls or for both sexes. Coeducation is very common in Finland. The lower classes of the grammar school are called middle school (keskikoulu). Middle school has the same curriculum whether it is part of a grammar school or a separate institution. Thus the middle school does not form a different school category; that is, it is not a separate school between elementary and grammar school as it is in Germany. Finnish middle school is not, however, a normal continuation school for all children as the American junior high school nor one type of secondary school among others as the English grammar school. In Finland the grammar school is the only way to higher education and the only type of school which is considered as a form of secondary education. Therefore, Finnish statistics on secondary schools do not give a realistic picture because they usually include only grammar schools. There are also other types of schools for the youth of this adolescent age, but these schools do not grant the privilege of further studies as the successful completion of grammar school does.

A usual grammar school course requires eight years for graduation. But in most girls' schools the course takes nine years because the girls in these schools have a longer course in home economics than girls in coeducation schools. This additional year comes during middle school, which school is therefore six years in a girls' school. Sometimes middle school is only three or four years; that is, if all the pupils come from the upper grades of the elementary school. However, this type is rare. Usually the children who enter a grammar school later than the fourth grade lose the years they have spent in elementary school after the fourth grade.

At the end of grammar school written matriculation examinations are organized at the same time in all schools. Those who pass the examination in four obligatory subjects have the right to study in a university if they can find a free place in one. These examinations are esteemed rather highly, even more so in the past than now. The numbers who pass the examination is now about ten times as great as fifty years ago; in 1964 there were 11,500 who successfully took the examination. This fact has, thus, diminished the actual value of the grammar school examinations. Another reason for the diminished value of the examinations is the fact that graduation from vocational institutes has become more common.

After the end of the obligatory school age, Finnish youth must choose from among many kinds of schools. But none of these schools has a direct working relationship with the elementary school (citizenship school). And they do not belong to the same organizational scheme. They have other school authorities, building entrance requirements, teachers and teachers' training programs. The pupils of middle school are in a little better position for they can continue their studies in the upper classes of grammar school, if such classes exist in the school.

About three-fourths of the elementary school graduates go directly into industry, agriculture, forestry, or business. The rest immediately or later find places in a trade or other vocational school or assume an apprenticeship.

Many middle school graduates also have to take the same path as elementary school graduates because there are not enough places in vocational institutes, even though they were originally established for middle school graduates. The scarcity of places in colleges is sending more and more grammar school graduates to the vocational institutes, thus taking the places from middle school graduates. Of course, ultimately, the elementary school graduates suffer most from this trend.

Only grammar school graduates have the right to continue their studies in universities. Some professional colleges give this right also to the best graduates of vocational institutes. But a scarcity of available places creates a situation annually so that only about half of the grammar school graduates are able to enter a university, which will now also give an additional entrance examination. Those who do not find a place in the university go to *alempi koulu* or translated literally "down to a lower school," to vocational institutes, or directly to earning a living. About half of the grammar school graduates are girls. In vocational schools and institutes the ratio of girls is smaller.

Folk high schools and other institutes of adult education form an essential part of training after the obligatory school is completed. Folk high schools are day schools, usually with dormitories, which offer particularly to the youth of the countryside a chance to study different subjects during a winter term. Originally folk high schools were quite oriented toward the humanities, but now they also offer vocational courses. Working men's institutes and citizenship institutes represent another type of free adult education. They are open to everyone who wants to study either an academic or a non-academic subject outside of working hours. Private correspondence institutes are also used mainly by adults.

FINANCING OF SCHOOLS

There are both private and public schools in Finland. All elementary schools are public, owned by cities or counties (communes). But the state substantially supports them, contributing 25 percent of all the costs in city schools and in the countryside 90 percent of teachers' salaries and two-thirds of all costs, as well as giving outright grants or loans for building, from 60 percent to 95 percent of the cost; the size of the grant or loan is dependent on the prosperity of the commune.

Grammar and vocational schools are either public, that is owned by the state or communes, or private. But the state also pays about 80 percent of the operating costs of private grammar schools. The remainder of the expenditures are mainly covered by student fees. The amount of state support for vocational schools and adult institutes is about 70 percent of the total costs. Universities are either state-owned or are heavily-financed by the state as other schools are.

SCHOOL ADMINISTRATION

The highest authority in school administration is the Parliament, which passes the laws affecting schools. On the basis of such laws, the government issues ordinances. All important matters are fixed by law. For example, the subjects which are taught in the elementary schools are listed in the Elementary School Act of 1957. The state supports the schools financially and also controls them by regulations and inspection.

Finnish school organization is administratively centralized. But it is a centralization which is also divided according to the various kinds of schools involved. There are eight departments in all, all of which have different schools under their control. There is very little cooperation in school matters between the departments. Each department makes its own regulations, maintains its own teacher education program, and has its separate salary system. The three main controlling departments in the field of education are Ministry of Education, Ministry of Commerce and Industry, and Ministry of Agriculture. The Ministry of Education controls all elementary and grammar schools as well as free adult education. The Ministry of Commerce and Industry controls vocational schools concerned with commercial and industrial training. The Ministry of Agriculture controls its special vocational schools.

Most of the departments directly control their own schools in the entire country. The Ministry of Education, however, has a central board to which immediate control belongs. There are superintendents for elementary, secondary, and adult education. The country is divided into forty-eight districts for inspection of the elementary schools; cities with over 10,000 inhabitants have their own inspector. But for the inspection of the other type of schools, the whole country is viewed as a district and the inspection staff originates from the capital, Helsinki. There are no local school authorities in Finland who can take care of school matters concerning different types of schools in the same district, so in a city each type of school has its own board, which does not work with the board of another type of school.

Each school, additionally, has its own board except city elementary schools; this is true whether the school is a public or private institution. State school boards have very limited power because everything is set either by law or by ordinance or by the central board. Private and communal school boards have in theory more freedom to develop their schools, but they very seldom use this freedom. Of course, there are some exceptional cases. Each school, also, has its own principal, who is one of the teachers usually proposed by the other teachers to this position, but who continues to work as a teacher.

TEACHERS' TRAINING, SELECTION, UNIONS, AND SALARIES

Teacher training is organized or strongly supported by the state. A typical characteristic of Finnish teacher training is separation; each type of school has its own training institutions. The aim has been that each teaching level forms a closed profession and movement from one group to the other, as from elementary to secondary school teaching, is not possible. Another typical feature of teacher training is the presence of the normal schools established in the last century.

Kindergarten teachers are trained in private normal schools or seminaries, usually with middle school education as a prerequisite for entrance. Normal schools for elementary education have traditions that go back a hundred years. There are three types of these normal schools. The highest type requires grammar school graduation for its applicants and the course is two years. The second group accepts middle school graduates for a four-year course. And the third group enrolls elementary school graduates in a six-year course of study. Two training colleges are connected with universities, but the training is nevertheless typical of normal schools.

Teachers of certain school subjects, for example, handicrafts, arts, home economics, and physical education, are trained in their own normal schools and usually require a matriculation examination from their applicants. Vocational schools have their own normal schools which usually set a vocational certificate as a requirement of entrance.

The training of grammar school teachers is organized in another way. The applicants must have first earned an academic degree from a university (B.A. or M.A.) before they come to a normal school. This school is really a grammar school where these graduate students do their two terms of student teaching. Because only a few grammar schools are authorized to take student teachers, there may be 100-200 student teachers in the same school. In addition to practice teaching, the student teachers have to pass a written examination in education given by a university professor and one also in school administration given by a superintendent.

In-service training is not organized in Finland. After the training described above, the teachers are certified for life. Job openings are announced in newspapers and all the applicants send their papers to the board concerned. This board either nominates one of the applicants or sends its recommendation to a higher board. The certificate the applicant has earned at the normal school usually is of great importance in job selection.

Teachers have their own unions. These have also been organized along school-type lines. Elementary school teachers have the largest union, which is also the most coherent one. Grammar school teachers have a common organization, but they are also divided into small groups according to subjects taught. Vocational school teachers do not have any general union because they are organized by school type only, such as agricultural, technical, or commercial school. In addition to this differentiation, teachers who work in the same field but on different levels have joined to form still other organizations. Cooperation between the groups is rare. The reason for this may be explained partially by their different teacher-training backgrounds.

Teachers' salaries depend on the school level in which they work. Kindergarten teachers have the lowest salaries, but their working time is also the shortest, only four hours a day. With the exception of big cities having their own salary schedules, elementary teachers, who teach thirty hours per week, have the same salary throughout the country. There are two salary groups in grammar schools: junior and senior lecturers. To the former group belong teachers of the non-academic subjects (arts, music, physical education, home economics) or also those teachers of other subjects if they teach only on the lower levels. Senior lecturers are those who teach the upper levels of academic subjects (mathematics, science, languages, social studes). They have higher salaries than junior lecturers and instead of twenty-six hours a week, they teach only twenty-four hours. Usually teachers have more than the minimum number of hours, but they are then paid extra for each hour including homework. Teaching duties for a lecturer in a normal school are limited to eighteen hours a week. The salary schedule of secondary school teachers is the same in the whole country.

Compared with other professions, teachers' salaries in secondary schools are a little lower than those of officials in state offices where the same academic degree is required. But one must remember that the daily and yearly working time in teaching is much shorter. In elementary schools there are 200 and in secondary school only about 185 working days a year. Summer vacations are three months long and there are many other holidays in each month. Very few

skilled laborers have as good wages as elementary school teachers and when the wages are comparable, the skilled workers' working time is longer, working conditions worse, vacations shorter, and the security not as good. In general, the calibre of teachers in state schools is higher than that of teachers in private schools.

The teaching profession, especially in secondary schools, but as well in elementary ones in the countryside, is rather highly esteemed. The jobs are secure, salaries fair, vacations long, and pupils disciplined. No wonder that trained teachers in Finland seldom move from teaching to another occupation (only about 2 percent). It would probably be advantageous to good teaching if the movement were greater. If most teachers have only experienced the academic world, either as students or teachers, they may know very little about life around them.

REFORM PLANS

Many committees have discussed the problems of Finnish school organization and have given their proposals. It is generally accepted that the system is in many ways out of date for today. The organization, such as it is, does not offer equal opportunities to all. The communication between schools is poor. The curricula are outmoded, the administration and teacher training unsuitable. How to solve these problems seems to be a very difficult task. The majority political parties have found a solution, in principle, so that a committee concerning new school organization proposed in 1963 a general school law. The main points of this proposal are the following:

1. A new system will be organized according to the principles of comprehensive schools. The old parallel system will be abolished in 20 years and in its place a new school of nine grades will be organized everywhere.
2. The pupils are to be taught in different groups in the upper grades for certain subjects (languages and mathematics). This will take into account variation in ability of students.
3. A kindergarten will be a part of the public school and then education may begin earlier than now.
4. The whole obligatory system will be communal,
5. The schools after the obligatory school age will be more directly related with the lower levels. In this way all students will have an opportunity to continue their studies to the senior high school level if they want to do so. These schools may be called grammar, technical, or vocational schools. They may be owned by the State, communes, or private corporations. An essential matter is that they all work together to offer students suitable opportunities according to the needs of society.

So the old system tried to select and eliminate students, but the new one will try to encourage students to continue their studies.

Reforms suggested for school organization will not by themselves be sufficient. Reforms in other fields are needed, too. Especially in the area of teacher training, improvement is urgently needed. There must also be more cooperation on the administrative level. Then it will be possible to do cooperative planning on reforming curricula and methods of teaching to meet today's needs.

REFERENCES

The Historical Developments

These can be studied in W. Sjöstrand's work *Pedagogikens historia* I-III:1 (Lund 1954-61). There is a detailed bibliography in each volume. Another important work is *Svenska folkskolans historia* 1-5 (Stockholm 1940-50).

As regards modern developments, reference can be made in the first place to the reports of the various educational commissions. Since 1922 these have been included in the series entitled *Statens offentliga utredningar* (SOU). Here will be found all the reports of, for example, the 1940 committee of inquiry, the 1946 commission and the 1957 preparatory committee. These reports contain actual historical expositions of different problems. A detailed account of the endeavours for reform in the present century will be found in E. Arrhén's book *Enhetsskolan, vardagen och atomtidsåldern* (Uppsala 1956).

Another important source is the series entitled *Aktuellt från Skolöverstyrelsen* (1948-63), which includes, for example, reports on the experimental work in the 1950s on the comprehensive school. The National Board of Education's series of publications should also be mentioned, especially Nos. 42, 46, 59, 60, 61 and 68 (*cf.* under "Literature in foreign languages"), which are reports and documents connected with the educational reforms.

Statistical Information

Sweden has an excellent series of population statistics from 1749. A summary of it can be studied in *Historisk statistik för Sverige*, 1-3 (1955-60). A detailed account of the statistics for the last century year by year is given in two publications: *Bidrag till Sveriges officiella statistik* (1880-1911) and *Sveriges officiella statistik* (1911-63).

BIBLIOGRAPHY

1. *Care and education of the exceptional children in Finland.* Central Union of Child Welfare in Finland, Helsinki, 1956, p. 36.
2. *Education in Finland,* UNESCO education abstracts 1960:2, Paris, 1960, p. 17.
3. *Finland and its students.* Ed. board: P. Burman, P. Opas, and P. Sjöblom. Publ. by National Union of Students of Finland. Helsinki, 1957, p. 51. Rev. ed. Helsinki, 1962.
4. "A general survey of University level education in Finland comprising a summary of the requirements for the different degrees together with an evaluation on those degrees in American terms." Publ. by The Finnish Committee on Study and Training in the United States. Helsinki, 1952, p. 20.
5. HALILA, A. *Suomen kansakoululaitoksen historia* I-IV (History of Finnish Elementary School), Porvoo, 1950.
6. HANHO, JUHO T. *Suomen oppikoululaitoksen historia* I-II (History of Finnish Grammar School), Porvoo, 1947, 1955.
7. KALLIO, N. *The school system of Finland.* Helsinki, 1956, p. 86. (also in French, German and Swedish).
8. ———. *Finland's Schools.* Helsinki, 1957, p. 20 (43), ill.
9. KYÖSTIÖ, O. K. Die Schule und Schulerziehung in Finnland. Jyväskylä, 1961, p. 95.
10. LUND, R. *Scandinavian adult education.* Denmark, Finland, Norway, Sweden, Finland: Viljo Kosonen, pp. 85-159. Copenhagen, 1952.
11. NIINI, A. (ed.) *Vocational education in Finland.* Subordinated to the Ministry of Commerce and Industry. Helsinki, 1963.
12. PAUTOLA, L. (ed.) *Youth services and organizations in Finland.* Helsinki, 1954, p. 74, ill.
13. *Popular and adult education in Finland,* Publ. by the Society for Popular Culture. Helsinki, 1957, p. 12.
14. RUGE, H. *Educational Systems in Scandinavia.* Oslo, 1962.
15. *Workers' adult education in Finland.* Summary of the original work by S. Kiuru. English transl. by A. Tuomikoski. Compiled by The Finnish Workers' Educational Association. Helsinki, 1954, p. 29.
16. *World Survey of Education*: I. Handbook of Educational Organization and Statistics. Paris, 1955. Finland, pp. 229-236.
17. ———. II. Primary education. Paris, 1958. Finland, pp. 364-376.
18. ———. III. Secondary education. Paris, 1961. Finland, pp. 463-476.

Periodicals

1. *Kasvatus ja koulu* (*Education and School*, with English summary), published by the University of Jyväskylä, 6 numbers a year.
2. *Kasvatusopillinen Aikakauskirja* (*Educational Review* —Acta Paedagogica Fennica—with English summary), published by the Finnish Educational Association, Helsinki, 4 numbers a year.

FRANCE

Shirley N. Kersey

Two major distinguishing characteristics of the French educational system are (1) a high degree of centralization, and (2) an emphasis upon an intellectual education. Critics of the system have suggested that centralization has been responsible for limiting reforms in education and for molding teachers to a prescribed image. While the lack of emergence of effective local educational leaders is sometimes attributed to the powerful control in Paris, the motivation for such a system is evident in the overall governmental administration in France, a consistently strong centralized operation dating from the time of Napoleon Bonaparte.

Although Frenchmen reserve their foremost respect for an intellectual education, traditional emphasis upon human values is slowly making room for an education that will contribute to the means to meet the practical, daily demands of life. The average Frenchman now sees the need for an extended period of time in school as well as for the education of more than a limited number of intellectual elite. It is an inescapable fact, however, that a rigid, classical, traditional education for a select group remains the educational goal of many French educators and students.

In addition to centralization and a humanistic education, the third major factor in the French educational system is the influence of the Roman Catholic Church. Frequent laws of the past 150 years have lessened the influence of the church upon education, although these laws have been countered, occasionally, by pro-religious laws. The emotions of the French citizenry were a strong factor in maintaining religious control of a large portion of education. However, one may reflect upon the almost total control of education by the church a few centuries ago in contrast to the fact that over 80 percent of French school children today attend neither a church-affiliated school nor a private secular school but rather the public school,[1] which has gained strength from compulsory education laws.

Compulsory education begins at age six; many youngsters drop out of school at age fourteen or fifteen. The average adult Frenchman has completed elementary school and has completed, as well, a certain amount of vocational training. However, figures demonstrate the continuance of an intellectual elite in showing that in 1960 less than 12 percent of the eligible age group completed secondary school. Concurrently, only 3.3 percent received the first university degree or an equivalent diploma,[2] but an encouraging statistic indicates that school enrollment increased 50 percent during the decade 1950-1960.[3]

France, along with the rest of the modern industrial and technical world, notes a decrease in the number of agricultural workers and an increase in the need for technical workers and intellectually trained personnel.

In order to better comprehend French education today, and to contemplate French education in the future, this essay will present a brief resumé of the history of French education. Twentieth-century French education will be categorized into primary, secondary, and higher education, teacher education, and the role of the Roman Catholic Church in education.

This account of French educational history will begin with the Middle Ages, roughly, the sixth to the thirteenth centuries.

MIDDLE AGES

Throughout the Middle Ages, church influence and interest in education increased: in fact, it was thought until recent years that the flame of intellec-

---

1. *Education in France*, No. 11, September, 1960. p. 42. (Published by the Cultural Services of the French Embassy, New York.)

2. *L'Education Nationale*, 15 février 1962, p. 12.

3. Raymond Poignant. *The Planning of Educational Expansion in Relation to Economic Growth*. Paris: Organisation for European Economic Co-operation, 1961, p. 33.

tualism was kept alive only within the confines of medieval monasteries. Scholars of today maintain that there were no dark ages in education but that a steady, although weak, flame was sustained. Almost certainly, education was restricted to boys and to those boys of means or of desire and ability to enter the clerical life. The Roman Catholic Church was keenly interested in perpetuating an educated clergy.

Recovery of many of Aristotle's writings in the eleventh and twelfth centuries led to the use of Aristotelian rational inquiry and deduction, a welcome replacement for the strict memorization method formerly used. Another eleventh-century development in higher education was the growing prominence of the cathedral school and the declining influence of the monastic school.

The dominating educational philosophy of the later Middle Ages was Scholasticism, which was characterized by argumentation, disputation, and dialectical analysis. The corresponding educational goal was that each pupil learn to read Latin.

The Middle Ages contributed the apprenticeship system, wherein a boy begins as an apprentice to a skilled tradesman, advances to journeyman under his watchful eye, and finally becomes a master. Perhaps it is not an exaggeration to consider the apprenticeship system of the Middle Ages the forerunner of vocational education.

Development of the university is of particular interest to the student of French education, since the University of Paris was the first university in the modern sense. The University of Paris was founded in the eleventh century by clergymen from the Cathedral School of Notre Dame and the collegiate church of St. Genevieve. These clergymen organized themselves into guilds in an attempt to achieve autonomy. The awesome attraction of the inspired teacher, Abelard, drew throngs of students to the embryonic university. The major prominence and excellence of the institution rested in its faculty of theology. By the close of the thirteenth century the University of Paris was acclaimed the greatest contemporary university, and it paved the way for the familiar years of "re-birth."

RENAISSANCE

The fourteenth-, fifteenth-, and sixteenth-century Renaissance brought impressive changes in educational thought. Emphasis turned from the rigidity of Scholasticism to classical humanism, which glorified the worth of the individual and stressed the belief that improvement results from a study of the great minds and characters represented in the ancient classics.

Philosophers of education favored humanism over religion and science and were reasonably successful in producing fifteenth-century reform. Educators formed new schools in which to exercise their ideas since church schools opposed the change. This humanistic reform of five centuries ago formed the backbone of French education. As was suggested in this essay's introductory paragraphs, even today the classical tradition dominates.

France is an outstanding example of the absolutism common to the sixteenth centry; here one finds the accomplishment of strong, centralized royal power. The rigid class system prevailed, but youngsters whose parents were members of the rural gentry and the city merchant class began to attend schools and, subsequently, these classes contributed financial aid to the schools. Religious and philanthropic agencies attempted to provide some education for the poor, but the subject matter coverage was minimal.

In the seventeenth century the French government commanded the church to establish schools in all towns and to institute compulsory education. This move perpetuated the dominant educational role played by the church, specifically by the ubiquitous, powerful Jesuits. Huguenots, members of the Calvinist faith in France, attempted to counteract the influence of Catholicism and rendered a brief and relatively ineffective influence upon French education. In other words, the Protestant reformation was of little consequence in French education.

In all facets of human endeavor, absolutism was about to give way to what historians have termed the Enlightenment.

ENLIGHTENMENT

Frenchman who outwardly opposed the absolute monarchy, rigid social class system and religious authoritarianism embodied the spirit of the eighteenth-century Enlightenment. This revolutionary Frenchman made demands upon education, which was totally controlled by the Catholic church. He regarded secular, modern, and practical studies preferable to a religious, classical education. Members of the revolutionary group sensed that education would help them to achieve their goal of a new society. Condorcet drew detailed plans for a state system of secular schools and, although these plans were not instituted, they provided ideas for future French educators.

However, enlightened ideas did not produce instant reform; contrary to activity in Germany, the French universities remained under the control of the church. Similarly, desired freedom of thought was stifled. For example, censorship prevented widespread reading of Rousseau's innovative book dealing with the education of a boy, *Emile*.

The eighteenth century firmly established the highly intellectual character of French education. It also produced a centralized administrative control of education, a natural outgrowth of the absolute monarchy which had prevailed in France for several centuries. Actually, the people of France considered monarchs an improvement over the prior leaders, the local over-lords, and the people trusted in the strong, centralized rulers to bring order and justice.

The eighteenth century demonstrated a growing commitment to humanism. The great philosophers, notably Descartes, Rousseau, and Montaigne, influenced acceptance of humanism rather than a continued allegiance to theology. However, change was slow to come and the influence of the Jesuits remained predominant. Bourbon monarchs considered education a matter for the church, not for the state.

Education continued to be elitist, a concept accepted by the Bourbons, who regarded education a privilege deserved by the wealthier, aristocratic youth. The result was widespread illiteracy, since only a few common people were educated by Christian Brothers and several other charitable teaching orders.

Against this background, philosophers continued to speak boldly in favor of humanistic education with governmental support rather than church influence.

In the France of 1789 over 75 percent of the women and over 50 percent of the men were illiterate.[4] Education was not free. In an attempt to meet the urgent need for educational reform, France was organized into departments. Each department was a geographic region in which its chief city could be reached in one day from any location within its boundaries. In 1789 the French government also established a system of public schools under civil control and abolished church control of education.

In 1791 legislators established the centralized system of education that exists in France today.

The Law of Daunou in 1795 showed greater concern for secondary and higher education than for lower education; however, it did call for a primary school in each large population center. It required one secondary school in each department. An important facet of the law was its emphasis upon a progressive curriculum to replace the classical. Schools were encouraged to develop the rational powers of each student in addition to his scientific background. Modern languages were to dominate although Latin and Greek still were to be taught. Thus the curriculum included mathematics, science, grammar, literature, drawing, and the laws of the First Republic.

The Daunou Law also provided for a polytechnical school, a Conservatory of Arts and Trades, and a sorely needed National Normal School to provide competent teachers, a rare commodity at the time.

Educational proposals of the 1790s prepared the way for the post-revolutionary years of Napoleon Bonaparte.

NAPOLEON BONAPARTE

Predictably, Napoleon Bonaparte regarded education as the means to mold the minds of French youth to his ideology and to perpetuate *his* government through education. Unfortunately, he overlooked the long-term value of the primary schools and sadly neglected them, leaving them unfinanced and unsupported by the national government. Religious orders and private agencies carried the responsibility for the education of the very young. Since Napoleon saw a need for scientists, technicians, and an intellectual elite, he directed educational funds to be used by seminaries of military science.

The Law of 1802 clearly reflected Napoleon's goals for French education. The law returned elementary education to the control of the church while it presented the framework for a state system of secondary education. Legal provision permitted priests to be principals and teachers in the public schools and designated bishops to license teachers.

Specifically, the Law of 1802 made a major impact upon French education by creating the Lycée, a public secondary school supported and controlled by the national government. The lycée of the twentieth century is virtually unchanged; it is a boarding school operating on a fee system, under state control and offering a classical curriculum. Located in the larger towns, it became the path to the universities. The clientele was primarily aristocratic because the fees were prohibitive to the common people and the humanistic education offered no vocational education. An interesting feature of the curriculum of the original lycée was that it did not include philosophy and history since either might encourage independent thought. The general character of the earliest lycée was Napoleonic in essence: the schools maintained military discipline and replaced the traditional school bell with a stirring drum roll.

The Collège developed as a modified version of the lycée. It was established by local communities and was less well endowed, financially and physically, than was the aristocratic lycée. The collège of today retains its tradition as a boarding school, state controlled and financed by student fees.

Briefly turning his attention away from secondary education, Napoleon formed special faculties or schools of law, medicine, and letters, and science. In 1804 he reinstated the faculty of theology and installed technical higher schools.

On March 17, 1808, Napoleon founded the Universite Imperiale. There was not a university in the usual sense but rather was an agency to administer and regulate all public education. Its primary aim was to emphasize the desire for fidelity to Catholicism. The highest executive official was the Grand Master, who wielded immense power.

In order to facilitate this new organization France was divided into twenty-seven administrative districts, known as academies. This division is not to be confused with departments which dealt with internal government and not education; these departments

---

4. *Education in France.* Paris: Editions France Actuelle, 1956, p. V.

later became the units for the administration of primary education.

After he placed the secondary schools, *i.e.* the lycées and collèges, under the control of the Universite Imperiale, Napoleon closed the universities. He directed that at least one lycèe be established in each academie. It has been pointed out that Napoleon stressed the importance of secondary education but one should note that he did *plan* institutions of higher education; perhaps he failed to implement these plans because of inadequate time.

Napoleon, aware of the need for teacher education, established Normal Schools in 1810 for the express purpose of preparing teachers for the lycèe. This school was named the Higher Normal School and exists today.

Bourbon monarchs accepted the reins of state from the determined hands of Napoleon and placed their own stamp upon French educational history.

BOURBON RESTORATION

In direct opposition to the philosophy of Napoleon, throughout the Bourbon Restoration from 1815 to 1830 monarchs put forth effort to strengthen their hold on the country by means of church control of education. The emphasis shifted to elementary education, and by 1830 state grants were given to the long-neglected elementary schools. Rulers permitted the Jesuits to conduct influential pre-seminaries in spite of their being illegal. Additional support was given to the Roman Catholic Church by allowing many priests to hold positions of authority in the educational system, which was officially controlled by the government.

Bourbon monarchs renamed the Universite Imperiale the University of France and renamed the Grand Master of the Minister of Public Instruction. Approximately one century later, during the time of the regime of Adolf Hitler, the name of this high executive officer of French education was changed to the Minister of National Education. Withstanding the name changes, the original organization remains virtually unaltered in the mid-twentieth century; it is this body that gives France the reputation of having the most centralized major system of national education the world ever has seen.

Further strides toward modern education were made under the July Monarchy of Louis Philippe.

JULY MONARCHY

The effective Guizot Law of 1833 bears the name of the man who was the first Minister of Public Instruction under the July Monarchy. Many authorities consider this law to mark the true beginning of the public school system in France. At this time, Louis Philippe established a national system of elementary schools to be kept separate from secondary and higher education. The law provided for the establishment of a primary school in each department capital and in each commune, a division similar to a township. The local citizenry was responsible for the building and maintenance of these schools. Taxes partially financed the schools and, with the exception of the poor, students paid fees. To ensure national uniformity, a Manual of Primary Instruction was given to each teacher. The curriculum consisted of reading, writing, mathematics, the French language, morality, and the Roman Catholic religion. Guizot's law did widen educational opportunity for the masses but would have reached a higher degree of effectiveness had it made lower education compulsory. To the credit of their citizens, local communes were painstaking in executing the law.

The Guizot law required each department to establish a Normal School to train primary teachers: this was in addition to the existing normal schools which prepared teachers at the secondary education level. To help in meeting the practical needs of the early nineteenth century, the law required the establishment of higher elementary schools to offer vocational preparation for commerce, agriculture, or industry.

Civil authorities were authorized to license and appoint public school teachers. A Bishop and the Mayor of the commune certified private school teachers.

The July Monarchy made contributions to various other areas of education. For example, 1836 marked the authorization of French adult classes, although this phase of education was not well developed for fifty years.

Turning their attention from adults to the very young, legislators established Infant Schools in the following year. In 1840 national funds were given to the Infant Schools. During this same period educational opportunities for girls were expanded.

Secondary education was not neglected and national funds were granted to lycées and collèges in 1845.

Fading into history, the July Monarchy gave way to the Second Republic and an increasing homage to democracy.

SECOND REPUBLIC

The Second Republic (1848-1870) of Louis Napoleon carried with it strong sentiments favoring education for the masses and promoted free, public, compulsory elementary education.

The Falloux Law of 1850 appeased Roman Catholics by permitting bishops to be members of the committee which appointed the head of each academie; it followed, naturally, that it became easier for the clergy to teach in public schools. In addition, the law required only limited government inspection of Catholic schools and served to intensify the church-state educational conflict.

The 1850 law aided private secular schools also, since the law stated that any French citizen of twenty-five years of age or older with five years of teaching experience and a baccalaureat certificate, or an equivalent diploma, was permitted to open a private school.

The Falloux Law made a significant change in secondary education by issuing direct aid to secondary schools, but following the pattern observed frequently in French educational history, this particular law had no significant effect upon elementary education.

In 1867 the Duruy Law provided free education for the needy and thereby increased school attendance. It also required communes with a population of five-hundred or more to establish elementary schools for girls.

Having enjoyed the leniency of the Second Republic, the Catholic Church was forced to adjust to the more secularly oriented reforms of the Third Republic.

THIRD REPUBLIC

The Prussian military victory over France in 1870 was influential in altering the French attitude toward education; Frenchmen tended to attribute this victory to Prussian education. This assumption led to ever-increasing attention to educational reforms and advancements. However, conservatives and the Catholic party continued to oppose mass education by the state.

To support its views that the state would benefit from widespread education, the government in 1878 made public money available for new schoolhouses and normal schools.

Generally, laws passed in the 1880s tended to move toward a gradual secularization of schools. Specifically, the laws of the 1880s abolished fees in public elementary schools. Education became compulsory for youngsters from six to thirteen years of age. With the repeal of an 1850 law, the clergy no longer had the right either to supervise in public schools or to nominate teachers. Only secular personnel were allowed to teach in public schools, while private schools were more closely supervised than before in order to uphold Republican ideology. The government built a number of higher primary schools to provide education at a post-elementary level for those students who were not necessarily university-bound.

Introduction of lycées and collèges for girls extended feminine educational opportunity but did limit their secondary education to five years, while lycées and collèges for boys were seven-year institutions. The curriculum for girls included elementary mathematics and science but no classical languages. Prior to the Law of 1880 only a few French girls received a secondary education, and then only in convent or private schools.

The 1880s provided firm support for national control of education and gave the Minister of Public Instruction complete control over details concerning examination and appointment of teachers, actual payment of teachers' salaries, textbook selection, and curriculum.

French universities remained virtually inactive throughout earlier years of political turmoil. In 1885 the Republic gave the universities the right to own property as corporate bodies and to conduct their own affairs under a board of governors. The mid-1890s showed a marked improvement in university management, as well as the advent of fifteen universities.

Statistics reveal the accomplishments of the laws of the 1880s. The number of students increased 70,000 between 1882 and 1900.[5] The 20 percent illiteracy rate of 1872 declined to 4.2 percent in 1910.[6] Thus the twentieth century in France was born amidst educational expansion and reform.

TWENTIETH CENTURY

Primary Education

Modern French primary schools have inclined toward progressive methods; for example, there is demonstrable concern for the individual differences of each student. William Heard Kilpatrick, the eminent American pragmatist, influenced French education through its acceptance of his activity method, interest centers, and group work. Pupil participation increased, notably in dramatics and journalism; simultaneously, teachers reduced the amount of homework.

The majority of French primary schools are not coeducational, the separate sexes being placed at opposite ends of a building. An occasional primary school is attached to a secondary school and in this case might be coeducational.

Private church-sponsored primary schools are especially popular for girls and it is fairly common for a family to send its sons to a state school and its daughters to a Roman Catholic school. Since the number of state schools is inadequate to meet the needs of the population, the national government does offer some support to these church schools.

Prior to 1925, it was necessary for girls who desired to continue their education through the university level to attend a private primary school because the public primary school simply did not provide a path to the university. A welcome change in feminine education occurred in 1925 when the government permitted schools for girls to offer the same curriculum as was offered in schools for boys.

Pre-school instruction is available in state-sponsored infant schools for children two to five years old. A number of these schools have independent physical facilities, while others are attached to primary schools. Pre-schools are of special value since

5. Jean Debriesse. *Compulsory Education in France.* Paris: UNESCO, 1951, p. 23.
6. Editions France Actuelle, *op. cit.*

they provide care for the children of working mothers. These schools for the very young utilize the Montessori method and stress development of the senses. In addition, there are private, coeducational pre-schools known as mother-schools.

Elementary education is compulsory for youngsters from six to eleven years of age, with certain classes of the classical and modern lycée an alternative to attendance at the primary school.

The French primary curriculum includes civic and moral instruction along with the traditional reading, writing and arithmetic.

Special schools, or, in some instances, special classes are available for the physically and mentally handicapped.

The observation stage (*cycle d'observation*) resembles the junior high school in the United States. An orientation period for youngsters from eleven to thirteen years old, its most important function is to delay for two years the decision determining the child's future educational track. At the conclusion of this stage, a committee consisting of the teacher, a psychologist, and a medical doctor examines the two-year record of the student and recommends the secondary course which, hopefully, will best suit the interests and aptitudes of the individual. Frenchmen have great faith in their educational administrators and seldom argue with the recommendation, but a parent does have the right to request a review, in which case a psychologist re-tests the pupil and makes a judgment. It is interesting to note that the second decision almost always supports the original decision. The observation school has provided a bridge between the primary school and the secondary school.

Secondary Education

Since secondary education had been reserved for the upper classes in this class-conscious society, a change of vital importance took place when steps were initiated in 1933 to abolish fees for the lycée. By 1937 the French lycée was totally free of tuition for everyone.

Thoughtful educators and parents have disagreed with a system which has prevented reversal of an educational choice made for an adolescent. Gradually, the two-track system has been de-emphasized and students now are able to cross tracks.

Compulsory education laws have provided a major contribution to the growth of the French secondary school. The law of 1882 stated that youngsters from six to thirteen years old must attend school. Subsequent laws retained the school entering age of six years but extended the years in attendance to (1) age fourteen in 1936, (2) age fifteen in 1947, and (3) age sixteen in 1959.

Contrary to the progressive education adopted by the French primary school, the secondary school, until recently, remained tradition-bound. The public secondary school emphasized modern languages and science along with the classics, but these schools were not recognized as equal to the lycée. Basically, the highly respected lycée remained unchanged throughout its first 150 years, offering a classical education and providing the preferred path to a university. Lower in status, the collège has continued to offer an alternative path to the university although it is still located in smaller cities, supported by local communities and less well endowed with facilities than the lycée.

Lecture continued to be the major method in secondary education. There have been few libraries, and there has been inadequate concern for social studies and technical education. A few schools, known as *classes nouvelles*, represented one early attempt to experiment with progressive education at the secondary level.

In 1902 the secondary curriculum was divided into four options: (1) Latin and Greek, (2) Latin and modern foreign languages, (3) Latin and natural science, and (4) modern languages and sciences. The student chose either philosophy or mathematics in the seventh (final) year. A six-year course of general subjects for everyone was adopted in 1925.

A widely influential 1930 law permitted girls to enter lycées and collèges formerly limited to boys.

Broad major changes in secondary education were not achieved until the 1940s. An important motivational factor was the apparent need for a greater percentage of the population to be educated. Further, it no longer seemed fitting that education be limited to the aristocratic class. The apparent need for modernized education was recognized.

Currently, French youth between the ages of thirteen and eighteen are divided into five types of schools: (1) a five-year "general long" course offered by lycées, divided into classical, modern and technical streams, and concluded with the awarding of a baccalaureaté, (2) a four- or five-year "professional long" course offered at lycées and other technical schools; (3) a three-year "professional short course available at colleges; (4) a three-year "general short" course, which provides preparation for the non-technical professions and teacher training institutions; and (5) a three-year terminal course offering a general education and vocational training. The contemporary French secondary education system demonstrates a proud, traditional school system bending to meet the needs of modern society.

The influence of Rousseau's *Emile* is not lost in present-day France, where a youngster may be educated at home provided a state school inspector makes an annual investigation. Simultaneously, the youngster may be undergoing an apprenticeship outside the home in order to become prepared to earn a living.

Typically, when a student is seventeen or eighteen years old he takes a local probationary examination to determine whether he shall continue his education. If the result is satisfactory the student faces a difficult two-day written examination followed by an oral examination, both administered by university professors. Close communication is characteristic between French secondary schools and the universities.

Higher Education

In spite of the fact that a primary purpose of the lycée is to prepare secondary students for the university, only one-third of its graduates accept the opportunity to seek a higher education. Students are admitted upon acquisition of the baccalaureate. Specifically, admittance rests upon successful completion of seven years of secondary school, a physical examination and both a written and an oral national examination.

French universities are state institutions and charge only a modest fee. Reminiscent of medieval universities, the student retains a large amount of responsibility and academic freedom. Each student determines his own choice of studies, whether to attend lectures and where to live. Also, students are influential in such matters as curriculum changes.

Americans are wont to compare the French university to the American graduate school. An unspecified number of years is needed to complete a university education, with a range of from one to seven years. It is possible to generalize, however, that the first degree, the *Licence-es-Lettres*, is attained at the end of two years. The second degree, the *Diplome d'Etudes Superieures,* is granted only in the humanities and its American equivalent would fall between a master's degree and a Ph.D. A thesis leads to the highest degree, the *Doctorat-des-Lettres.*

French universities are divided into faculties of law, medicine, pharmacy, science, and letters. Higher education is provided, too, by observatories, free faculties (some of which are Catholic), and various schools offering professional and technical instruction.

Beyond the universities are the Grandes Ecoles, specialized institutions which provide for the truly intellectual elite of France. Roughly one dozen of these schools exist and together they provide the majority of French leaders in science, government, education, and the military.

Teacher Education

As stated earlier, Napoleon Bonaparte established a normal school to prepare teachers for the secondary level, and a law in 1833 established a normal school to prepare teachers of the elementary level. Consistently, the emphasis in normal schools serving to prepare elementary teachers has been on method and Pestalozzian ideals, while the emphasis in normal schools serving to prepare secondary teachers has been upon subject matter.

A fault of nineteenth century normal schools was the leaning toward academic inbreeding. Eighteen-year-old elementary school teachers had been educated in elementary schools and in normal schools specifically dedicated to the preparation of elementary teachers. A similar situation prevailed in secondary schools, since the twenty-one-year-old teacher at the lycée or collège was a graduate of a secondary school and had attended a normal school which was connected with a university and was geared to preparation of secondary teachers. These teachers had known only a humanistic, classical education.

Among post-World War II efforts to improve the professional background of teachers was an attempt to alter the tradition of in-breeding and to broaden preparation of teachers. Normal schools for elementary teachers introduced some amount of general education at the secondary level. By providing at least a token amount of secondary education to all elementary teachers, this was a step toward answering the demand that in the future all teachers shall have two years of higher education. The French normal school today offers elementary teachers four years of secondary level education and includes a general education as well as one year of professional training, often with student teaching.

Concurrently, normal schools to prepare secondary teachers added several professional courses to the curriculum and thereby offered an improved balance in preparation.

Cautiously, a one-year probationary period of teaching precedes the attainment of permanent professional status.

A normal school for elementary teachers is located in each department (county). More accurately, there are two schools, since there is one for boys and one for girls. These schools provide room and board facilities and are under the direct control of the Minister of Education. The government is willing to pay all expenses with the understanding that the student eventually teach for ten years in a state school or repay the government for his normal school education.

Students aspiring to become secondary teachers attend either a two-year non-coeducational normal school, or occasionally, a university. Rigid standards of professional attainment and ability are held for secondary teachers.

An inadequate supply of teachers creates a major problem in French teacher education today. A second important problem relates to the firm national control of education which contributes to the fact that teachers have too small a voice in educational affairs.

Since the Roman Catholic Church is an element in society that has offered a consistent, clamorous voice in French educational affairs, its twentieth-century participation will be examined separately.

Role of the Church

Catholic teaching orders dominated pre-revolutionary education. The influence of the Roman Catholic Church upon French education has been a prominent twentieth-century issue. Perhaps a brief chronological, political summary of modern France will be helpful in interpreting this influence.

The role of the Roman Catholic church in French education follows:

1815-1830 (Restoration)	Increased
1830-1848 (July Monarchy)	Decreased
1852-1870 (Second Empire)	Increased
1870-1940 (Third Republic)	Decreased [7]
1940-1944 (Vichy Government)	Increased
1945-1969	Decreased

A bill in 1901 forced thousands of monks and nuns out of teaching positions and placed rigid state control over those religious orders still authorized to teach in public schools. Three years later a bill ordered teaching by *authorized* religious orders to end within the following ten-year period. Further opposition to the church came with the Separation Law of 1905, which relieved the state of its obligation to pay the salaries of the clergy involved in public education. At this time the church remained in control of private schools, but in order to relieve the oppressive financial burden, bishops instructed Catholic children to attend public schools on condition that they receive religious instruction outside the school.

World War I prompted the government to suspend enforcement of a law that had closed private schools controlled by religious orders. Out of deference to a need for national unity, members of the clergy were allowed to teach in private schools during the period between the two world wars.

The Vichy government of the early 1940s gave public money to church schools and made religion a compulsory subject in public schools. However, public teachers objected and were instrumental in the government decision to rescind the decree in the latter part of 1941. A decree of 1942 rescinded the Association Law of 1901, which had been anti-religious in character; now, religious orders had a legal right to organize. The German occupation forces located in France encouraged dissension in order to further the division of France within itself.

Between 1910 and 1950 80 percent of the elementary schools were public and 20 percent were private.[8] Enrollment in Catholic secondary schools increased steadily. The struggle lessened between public and Catholic schools when a growing security in the Republic became evident. In 1951 scholarships were offered at public expense to Catholic students and allotments were made to Catholic parents' associations. Governmental officials hoped that this money would be spent for salary increases to improve the teaching in private schools, where the teaching was judged to be inferior.

Events of the past twenty years have indicated that Catholic parents are tradition-bound to parochial schools and count heavily upon church-operated schools to strengthen the religious faith of their young-

sters. National scholarships were given to students of private schools which met national standards for buildings, teacher qualifications, and instructional hours. Private schools were given a five-year period in which to raise the qualifications of their teachers; at the end of the five-year period, 609 of the 891 Catholic schools were disqualified because they were judged to be sub-standard.[9]

Private secondary school enrollment decreased substantially in the 1950s. In 1951, 35.2 percent of secondary pupils attended private schools, but in 1959 this figure stood at only 28.4 percent.[10]

The French political situation wielded powerful influence and inflicted frequent change upon private education throughout modern history. In 1958, for example, Parliament was composed predominantly of supporters of Catholic schools; consequently, there was an increase in government aid to private schools. Perhaps an additional reason for state assistance to private schools is the hard fact that there is an insufficient number of state schools to meet the needs of all French school children. Economic aid does not permit independence, however, and public school inspectors continue to supervise private schools.

The 1960s showed a decrease in private school influence. In 1955 the percentage of children entering elementary and secondary non-public schools was 19.9 percent but by 1961 this figure had decreased to 16.2 percent.[11] Further evidence of a secular trend is the fact that throughout the 1960s the proportion of lay teachers in Catholic schools has been increasing. Figures for 1965 and 1966 show that approximately 14 percent of infant and elementary students attended private schools while the remainder enrolled in French public schools.[12]

SUMMARY

The history of French education is also a partial history of the contributions and influence of the Roman Catholic Church. Contemporary French education is a highly centralized system emphasizing intellectual values. Recent trends suggest that French education in the future will undergo continued reforms that will increase the administrative influence of teachers, provide a greater number of years in school for a greater number of students, and enhance

7. R. Freeman Butts. *A Cultural History of Western Education: Its Social and Intellectual Foundations.* New York: McGraw-Hill Book Company, 1955, p. 353.

8. Debiesse, *op. cit.,* p. 90-91.

9. Olive Wykes. "The Fifth Republic and the Catholic Schools." *Melbourne Studies in Education,* 1959-1960. Melbourne, Australia: Melbourne University Press, 1961, p. 77.

10. *Informations Statistiques,* No. 34-35, décembre 1961, p. 311.

11. "News from the Field." *Catholic Educational Review,* March 1962, p. 201.

12. *The Statesman's Year Book.* 1968-69. New York: St. Martin's Press, p. 992.

public and professional opinion of a practical, general education. It is too early to tell what influence the 1969 resignation of De Gaulle will have on education.

SELECTED BIBLIOGRAPHY

BELDING, ROBERT E. *European Classrooms*: *Schools of Four Nations*. Iowa City, Iowa: Sernoll, Inc., 1966.

BUTTS, R. FREEMAN. *A Cultural History of Western Education*. New York: McGraw-Hill Book Company, Inc., 1955.

GOOD, H. G. *A History of Western Education*. 2nd ed. New York: The Macmillan Co., 1960.

MAYER, FREDERICK. *A History of Educational Thought*. Columbus, Ohio: Charles E. Merrill Books, Inc., 1960.

MEYER, ADOLPHE E. *An Educational History of the Western World*. New York: McGraw-Hill Book Company, 1965.

STEINBERG, S. H. ed., *The Statesman's Year Book*. 1968-69. New York: St. Martin's Press, 1968. Macmillan: London, Melbourne, Toronto, pp. 989-992.

THUT, I. N., and ADAMS, DON. *Educational Patterns in Contemporary Society*. New York: McGraw-Hill Book Company, 1964.

U. S. Department of Health, Education and Welfare. *Education in France*. Office of Education. U. S. Government Printing Office, Washington, D. C. 20402.

GERMANY

Susanne M. Shafer

German education today writhes between time-honored principles and the apparent demands of the future, between long-time traditions and those innovations which have been sought to adjust the school system to a technologically-oriented democracy eager to capture an expanding share of world trade. Germans want to maintain or even better their present relatively high standard of living. They are depressed by the diminished size of the Federal Republic and by the obvious stumbling blocs which obstruct the path to reunification with their brethren in East Germany. That the split between the generations constitutes a greater chasm than elsewhere or than in times past is probably true. Pervading all these relationships is a widespread sense of mistrust of those who hold positions of genuine power in the national government. Over some of these personages there hangs yet the pall of certain associations with National Socialism.[1] Others are disdained as second-raters and opportunists who have succeeded in gaining political power in place of the economic power which had eluded them via the more traditional career-building through one's chosen vocation. Democracy as a political process is not yet esteemed to the extent it is in Anglo-Saxon nations where democratic institutions have passed the test of time, comparison, and trial by fire. Nor has democracy produced such national heroes as Disraeli, Winston Churchill, Abraham Lincoln, Theodore Roosevelt, or John F. Kennedy.

In view of these prevailing currents in German thinking, schools find themselves caught in a variety of cross-winds. Certainly there is a total awareness of educational advances being made in other Western nations, be it in the percentage of youth secondary schools or the role of early childhood education, or even the use of television in classrooms. Knowledge of what Germany's neighbors and economic competitors are achieving creates pressures to do as well at home. If the Federal Republic is to continue to advance in its technology, the general level of education must be raised further. Pupils must also be channeled into vocational fields which will continue to require their labors (even if new skills must be taught to them from time to time). Universities must expand to absorb more of those seeking higher education and then entrance into a profession.

Germans are also eager to maintain those elements in the society which they feel have given it stability and fundamental values. Schools should strive to make all pupils literate, diligent, respectful of authority, knowledgeable, practicing Christians,[2] and sensitive to the German cultural heritage. It is in the course of any analysis of the last, the study of German history and the work of German artists, that the split between the young and their parents develops. As yet the former cannot fully grasp that their elders lacked the courage or the ability to withstand Hitler, to overthrow him, and, surely, to prevent the murder of six million Jews. These same young Germans grow impatient with the study of the works of Walter von der Vogel Weide, Wolfram von Eschenbach, and even Goethe and Schiller, men who failed to inspire their elders sufficiently to keep them from participating in National Socialism. The young turn to the postwar generation of writers, to Boll, Brecht, and Gunter Grass, in order to search for the meaning of life. And when they consider what governments should do, they look at both democratic and communist countries. They are reluctant to accept unquestioningly what teachers explain in civics class about the merits of a democracy. Often teachers skirt the controversial issues which surround their national government. Thereby they also mask the dynamics

1. Chancelor Kurt Kiesinger not long ago testified in a war crimes trial in Bonn that ". . . he had joined the Nazi Party in 1933, 'but not out of conviction or opportunism.'" *Arizona Republic,* July 5, 1968, p. 8.

2. The Jewish population in West Germany remains small. Jewish pupils as well as others whose parents request it are excused from attending either Protestant or Catholic "Religion" classes.

of that government, knowledge essential for a person who wishes to participate in the process by which his democracy operates.

What then have been the educational practices in times past which Germans now wish to alter? As in other European nations, the Medieval Church once constituted virtually the sole educational institution. In order to perpetuate itself, it was forced to recruit and to train boys who would ultimately serve as monks, priests, bishops, and diverse church functionaries. The first included not only the men who copied manuscripts but also those who studied their content and constituted the learned part of the church's officialdom. Monasteries prepared priests who went out to teach the fundamentals of Christianity in each parish. In order to ensure an adequate supply of churchmen, the bishops eventually opened schools for boys in conjunction with the great cathedrals in their domain. Here youth were given a classical education which placed heavy emphasis on the study of Latin and Greek, the languages required for later ecclesiastical study. Germany had its share of such schools, institutions which tended to serve the well-to-do and nobility rather than the peasantry. Universities similar to that of Paris and of Bologna were begun in German areas with the University of Heidelberg opening in 1385. Others followed throughout the fifteenth century.

Along came Martin Luther with his 95 Theses that he posted on the doors of the church in Wittenberg in 1517. The convulsions which that act set off had several major effects on education in the various German states. Luther's translation of the Bible into the vernacular resulted in a stabilization and eventual standardization of German in its written form. His insistence that every person should have access to the Bible and to God as well implied that all would have to learn to read that basic guide to Christianity. He proposed, and himself organized, vernacular schools which taught reading and writing, the fundamentals of Protestantism through the catechism, church hymns, and prayer, together with obedience to authority. Luther considered the last one important because the peasants were to be obedient to their temporal as well as to their ecclesiastical superiors. Intended for the masses, the German schools, or *Volksschule*, developed in villages and towns. They became sanctioned by the state starting with Wüerttemberg in 1559.

Secondary education was affected by Martin Luther through his followers, particularly Johannes Sturm. At Strasbourg, Sturm organized a humanistic *Gymnasium* which soon became a model for other such secondary schools throughout Germany. Here he fashioned a curriculum which placed Latin the center. Greek, the study of classical antiquity, religion, and science, formed the remainder of the pupils' studies. Religion was included, for obedience to God had to be fostered. The impact of the Renaissance and of humanism explains the presence of science. The *Gymnasium* served the boys from the upper social classes, a pattern which persisted well into the nineteenth, if not really also the twentieth, century.

One further impact of Martin Luther affected the universities. Originally these had consisted of the faculties of theology, law, medicine, and the arts (or philosophy). With the conversion of certain German states to Protestantism, universities in these states—and they were always supported by the rulers of each state—had to change the orientation of their faculty of theology; if there was no university, a new one had to be organized in order to assure an adequate supply of clergy. Hence Protestant universities were founded at Marburg, Jena, Strasbourg, and Koenigsberg, each in distinctly Protestant states.

The Enlightenment brought German thinkers in close contact with Paris, the recognized cultural center of Europe during the seventeenth and much of the eighteenth centuries. Secularization of higher education in Germany could be noted through the interest in rationalism, the increased skepticism directed against religion, and the growing concern with science. The faculty of philosophy led in this movement. At the secondary level a kind of negative reaction to the Enlightenment caused philological studies to further dominate the *Gymnasium*. In contrast, the *Realschule* was founded to bring secular subjects to pupils who would enter business or government service in German towns and cities.[3]

Elementary schooling for the masses in the *Volksschule* became more institutionalized as states took full responsibility for these schools and made attendance compulsory. Prussia led the way by insuring four years of schooling for everyone, and in the nineteenth century even eight years. Prussia organized training institutions where successful *Volksschule* graduates were prepared to become teachers. For that purpose they extended their general knowledge during a three-year period of studies followed by an additional year devoted to the study of pedagogy, including methodology, philosophy of education, and religion. Prospective teachers would also observe pupils and do some practice teaching at the elementary school which formed a part of the teacher training institution. That pattern of teacher education came to be widely copied, particularly in the United States through the efforts of Horace Mann who instituted a similar plan in his Lexington, Massachusetts, Training School for Teachers.

In Prussia and elsewhere in Germany certain individuals made an indelible mark on the educational system. Luther had been one of the earliest whose influence could be identified. There followed Johann Amos Comenius, the Moravian bishop who drew up picture books with German and also Latin captions

3. Roger D. O'Connor, *Education for Real Life, A Study of the Curriculum of the German Mittelschule*, Detroit, Michigan: Wayne State University, unpublished dissertation, *passim*.

to teach the child language, religion, and information about his environment at one and the same time. Rathke urged direct experience and an emphasis on understanding for genuine learning. Wilhelm von Humboldt led much of the effort to strengthen the *Volksschule* in Prussia after Napoleon's successful attack in 1806. He also urged that the *Gymnasium* broaden the education it offered to include more history, geography, science, and mathematics. At the University of Berlin, von Humboldt succeeded in having established a faculty of science where genuine scientific research began to be conducted. He also contributed to having that research orientation extended throughout the university, giving professors the freedom to explore all knowledge without interference from either church or state and allowing students to pursue learning in the same critical manner.

Friedrich Froebel brought Johann Heinrich Pestalozzi's teaching to Germany when he organized his kindergarten. Here appeared Pestalozzi's high regard for interest in the pupil and affection for him just as it did when teacher education was institutionalized in Prussia. Johann Friedrich Herbart brought clarity to the questions of methodology by his delineation of the five steps in learning, namely preparation, presentation, association, generalization, and application. He brought additional satisfaction to German educators when he showed how history and literature could be used to teach morality.

By World War I German education rested on the *Volksschule*, an eight-year, compulsory elementary school attended by the workers' children in urban centers and by nearly everyone in the many villages. Besides literacy, religion, and arithmetic, children were taught local geography, nature study, some music, some hand work or crafts, drawing, and physical education. Thereafter pupils either went to work in the fields or as apprentices in factories and businesses. One day a week, the latter might return to a classroom for some theoretical instruction in their skill or craft. Pupils whose parents had aspirations of rooting their offspring firmly in the middle class would send them to the *Realschule* or *Mittelschule* to age sixteen at which time they would be eligible for middle-level positions in industry, commerce, or the civil service.

An entirely separate set of schools were attended by children of the upper classes. These started their education in a preparatory school, often privately organized, from which after three years they moved to the *Gymnasium*, a nine-year school. The less able or diligent pupils left it at age sixteen preferably having passed the *Miltlere Reife,* or middle maturity examination, the same one taken by the graduates of the *Realschule.* Those who wished to prepare for the university continued in the *Gymnasium* for another three years and then had to pass *Abitur,* a test of general knowledge. Success on the *Abitur* assured

entrance into any of the German universities. Except in the villages, these pupils never attended school with children of the middle and lower classes. By World War I girls had achieved educational opportunities nearly equal to those existing for boys.

The educational practices delineated above remained largely unchanged after World War I. Although German liberals sought reforms such as strengthening the education of teachers of the *Volksschule,* offering free tuition in the *Gymnasium* to able children of the poor, and a decrease in church influence on the *Volksschule,* few changes were adopted in all sections of Germany because of the economic difficulties as well as the political weakness of the Weimar Republic.

The period of National Socialism and World War I constituted a further setback to the extension of education. Schools soon were utilized for propaganda purposes by Hitler and his followers. Indoctrination rather than the search for knowledge and understanding began to come into classrooms from the *Volksschule* to the *Gymnasium* and even to the university. Physical training often became more important than academic subjects. Jewish children were excluded altogether as Hitler's campaign against their parents accelerated. With the increasing pressures brought on by the war, secondary education was curtailed. Teachers as well as the older boys were drafted. The schools in heavily bombed cities closed while their pupils were sent to rural areas for temporary shelter. By the end of the war in 1945 the disruption of the educational system was fairly complete.

Perhaps surprisingly, when the rebuilding process was begun under the close supervision of the occupation powers, Great Britain, France, the Soviet Union, and the United States, the Germans resurrected their educational edifice to resemble that of the pre-Hitler days. In the three Western zones, liberalizing modifications were added at the urging of both the occupation powers and those German educators who were asked to give leadership once again. Most had been removed from positions of influence during the Third Reich; many had been the youthful standard bearers of liberalism during those years of the Weimar Republic when it was thought democracy might succeed in bringing Germany through the difficult economic crises of the 1920s.

Reforms which each occupation power sought in its zone reflected that power's perception of a satisfactory educational system. In East Germany, the Russians substituted the symbols of communism for those of national socialism. The schools which emerged resembled those in the Soviet Union although even today underlying vestiges of German educational practices remain in evidence.

In the French and in the British zones the policy was to allow the Germans to retain the basic structural characteristics of their educational system. Selectivity in secondary education, early separation of lower middle class and workers' children from those planning to enter the professions or, at least, the more remunerative and prestigious positions in commerce and government was an accepted practice in both France and England. It did not seem to run counter to genuine democracy. The British did insist that those German fairy tales in which brutality and ruthlessness inspired fear in the children be eliminated from texts used in schools. They, too, opened information centers to give Germans access to a wide range of books and periodicals. They organized workshops to reorient teachers from authoritarianism in classrooms toward a sense of respect for pupils as persons of dignity and worth. In the French zone a key policy was an exchange of students and teachers in order to break down the long-standing animosity between the French and the Germans.

Of the three Western powers the United States attempted by far the most ambitious program of reform. The occupation authorities took seriously the slogan "de-Nazification, demilitarization, and democratization." They screened out teachers known to have been very active Nazis. Having removed the textbooks whose content had been tainted by National Socialist ideology, they organized writing teams to produce new textbooks. To make the German schools more in accord with democratic ideals, they sought to establish a single-ladder educational system to replace the three-track system (Volksschule, Realschule, and Gymnasium which overlapped for pupils age ten to fourteen). When the proposal failed, in part because it had become associated with Soviet school reform in East Germany, the United States Military Government did insist that education in the Volksschule be upgraded, that the teachers of Volksschule be graduates of the Gymnasium before beginning their studies at a teachers college, that tuition charges be removed for the Gymnasium, that transfer from one track to another be permitted after the fifth grade or even later, that P.T.A.'s and student governments be inaugurated, and that civic education be instituted to prepare youth for participation in the democratic state expected to be organized in Germany before long. In addition, the United States held many teachers' workshops to introduce teachers to educational practices generally being followed in American schools, such as guidance and counseling. A research institute was also established in order to study various aspects of education in conjunction with the evolvement of educational policies.[4] A look at German education today will indicate the extent to which American proposals for reform have been put into effect.

PEDAGOGY TODAY

To acquaint oneself with the present interrelationship of education and West German society, one needs to study the organizational as well as the instructional patterns of schools. These must be seen against the cultural context out of which they have emerged. The one-time three-track system which once tended to reinforce the social class system of Germany has been greatly modified since World War II partly through the persistent American influence and partly through the general European trend toward egalitarianism. All children spend the first four years[5] together in an elementary school. Although it is a neighborhood school, classes are organized heterogeneously. Private schools are few and far between, and the separate pre-Gymnasium schools (Vorsschulen) have remained closed down since the days of the Weimar Republic.

At age ten (at the conclusion of fourth grade) a pupil's parents can ask to have him placed either in a Realschule or a Gymnasium. Most West German states give no formal entrance examination to either school nor do school authorities rigidly screen the applicants. Rather, a half-year trial period is beginning to serve the purpose of identifying any pupil who has been placed in too difficult a program. Counseling by the elementary school teacher who often has had the same group of pupils for the entire four years, grades one to four, tends to decrease the number of such mistaken placements.[6]

Those who remain in the elementary school, now called the Hauptschule, continue their study of fundamental skills in language and arithmetic along with geography and later also history, civics, science, music, art, physical education, industrial arts for boys and home arts for girls. Foreign language, usually English, is offered as an elective. The Hauptschule has been lengthened from four to five years by now in nearly all places. Except in rural communities, it is beginning to contain the weakest learners, a characteristic deplored by the teachers of the Hauptschule. In most German towns its more promising pupils have annual opportunities to transfer to the Realschule. Once a pupil concludes the Hauptschule, today usually at age fifteen after nine years of schooling, he becomes a paid apprentice in industry or in a commercial establishment, large or small. In either case he receives some on-the-job training. Once a week he is given broader theoretical instruction at a vocational school. The larger the city the greater is the variety of vocational classes available for training in a specialized skill. At the end of three or three and a half years he concludes the apprenticeship by presenting a record of his work experiences and his exercises at the vocational school. By this time he is well launched on a career in one occupation or another in the employ of a particular individual or

4. Henry P. Pilgect. *The West German Educational System*, (U. S. Office of the U. S. High Commissioner for Germany, Historical Division, 1953), pp. 13-17.
5. Six Years in West Berlin.
6. *Die Welt*, Hamburg, August 15, 1967, p. 5.

company. Few deliberately make a change in later years.

While about 60 percent[7] of German teen-agers are actively participating in the world of work, 15 to 20 percent are in the *Gymnasium*, the academic secondary school. Here they have little direct contact with the economic life of their nation nor are they likely to be in touch with those of their peers who are apprentices. In the *Gymnasium* from fifth grade to thirteenth grade they participate in a rigid regimen of learning subject matter in German language and literature, in mathematics and the sciences, in foreign languages, mainly English and Latin and sometimes French or Greek, in history and geography, and today also in government; music and art are also taught, as is physical education. Germany's cultural heritage is stressed, with pride; her political inheritance is scrutinized often with great candor. In the academic subjects much memorization is required. Homework assignments often are lengthy and difficult. Especially in the case of the younger pupils, a parent must help his son or daughter, for many times the classes are large and teachers fail to give adequate assistance to their young learners. Those who fail because they lack either the maturity or the ability to learn may have to transfer to the *Hauptschule* or they may drop out at age sixteen at the conclusion of tenth grade. At that time they may take the middle maturity examination and enter a full-time vocational school for one or two years. Girls more interested in marriage than in an academic career often choose this path.

The more successful learners remain in the *Gymnasium* until age nineteen with the intent of seeking higher education thereafter. During the last three years they continue their general education as they prepare for the *Abitur*, an examination which if passed permits the individual to enter any of the West German universities.

For most students the *Abitur* consists of written examinations in German language and literature, mathematics, physics, and English. Substitutions of subject matter are made for pupils who in eighth grade had entered an alternate stream which gave more emphasis to the study of Latin in place of English or which stressed the sciences more than the study of foreign languages. The earlier concentration on classical languages and antiquity in most instances has been modified in favor of more modern languages and even science. Regardless of the pupil's choice of stream, he will submit to an oral examination in some or all of the other subjects he has studied in the Gymnasium. Often 10 percent of the examinees fail the *Abitur*. Most repeat it a year later after repeating the thirteenth year.

A third alternative for West German youth is to move from the elementary school to the *Realschule*. Here they continue to receive a general education taught by teachers who teach those subjects in which they have a major, in contrast to the elementary and *Hauptschule* teachers who must teach all basic subjects to their classes. In the *Realschule* English is a required subject[8] and some prevocational courses are available. At age sixteen the pupils take the middle maturity examination and either enter the labor market as apprentices or a full-time vocational school as a means of qualifying for middle-level positions in commerce, industry, and the civil service. Some transfer to the *Gymnasium* because they wish to enter institutions of higher learning. The rising percentage of youth in the *Realschule* is a testament both to parental desire to have their children attain more education and hopefully a higher occupational status than they have as well as to the general recognition that in a modern technological society, a strong general education base is desirable for all who wish to have more than a non-skilled job. In Germany's cities the *Realschule* draws an ever larger portion of the lower middle class just as the middle and upper middle classes send their children to the *Gymnasium* in increasing numbers.

No matter which school a child attends, he will have from two to four periods per week of religious instruction. Very few parents ask to have their children excused from these classes. They may be taught either by teachers who are willing to do so or by clerics, depending on the particular state. Hamburg does not permit a cleric in the schools while other states find that the state's neutrality in religion is more readily maintained by replacing teachers with clerics during the classes in religion. The curriculum for these classes consists of church hymns, prayers, the catechism, and Bible stories in the earlier years, and comparative religion and even ethics in the most advanced grades of the *Gymnasium*.

Schools further religion in still another way in those German states which have a tradition of being largely Catholic. In North Rhine Westphalia, in Bavaria, in Rhineland-Palatinate, and even in parts of Baden-Württemberg elementary schools, *Volksschulen*, are organized on a denominational basis. Catholic, Protestant, and common schools are maintained, often side by side and even in the same building, each with its own principal and teachers. Although the latter were trained in a teachers' college of their own religious preference, instruction rarely reveals denominational tendencies. In contrast to past practices in American parochial schools, textbooks are not used as vehicles for religious training (except, of course, those used in the subject "Religion"). In the many villages in rural areas served by a single school, the predominant religion is used to determine the school's denomination. In most instances this procedure means (1) that the village school operates as a

---

7. The figure ranges considerably higher in rural villages and lower in metropolitan areas.

8. With the exception of areas very close to France where French is the first foreign language taught.

Catholic school, (2) that Protestant children have no choice but to attend that school, and (3) that somewhat unofficially the village priest represents the Catholic Church to assure that its youthful flock receives a suitable education, one which is in accord with Papal encyclicals. Fearful of losing its influence on the schools and thus a part of its political power, the Church in those German states with Catholic majorities has opposed the consolidation of one- or two-room schools located in villages often less than two miles apart.

To obtain a view of West Germany's educational system from another vantage point, one needs to explore the German perception of the "educated man." Such an individual has attended the *Gymnasium* and in all likelihood a university. He is believed to have been introduced to the major disciplines and to have learned to think clearly, to analyze events and phenomena in a rational manner. Intellectual competence is generally attributed to those who are "educated," or in the Germans' terminology, "gebildet." President John F. Kennedy appealed to the Germans in part because they thought he was "gebildet." He displayed intelligence, rational thought, and learnedness. He was familiar with the liberal arts. Today one senses in many a German's conversation that he believes a person is either "gebildet" or he is not. The differentiation is a reflection of the socially and intellectually divisive multiple-track educational system.

That distinction may be reinforced by the language used to deal with the concept of education. Whereas the English word "education" can be applied to what a young child receives at home or at school, to what an adolescent receives in either place or even on the street, and to what a student receives at a university, the Germans have two words which are certainly not interchangeable. One, *Bildung*, refers to education of the intellect, and it is provided in the *Gymnasium* and at universities. To some extent it is equivalent to the American concept of general education. A person acquires *Bildung* by an absorption of a broad spectrum of subject matter as well as by an analysis of the meaning of that subject matter. Without intellectual ability, *Bildung* is not obtainable.

All youth regardless of intelligence require *Erziehung*, or training, the second concept of education. *Erziehung* includes the upbringing that parents provide. It is the social learning which a child achieves at the hands of his elementary school teacher. It refers to the basic discipline that is imposed on an individual by the society to whose mores he is to conform. Probably the acquisition of the fundamental skills of reading, writing, and arithmetic are also included. This type of training, *i.e.* *Erziehung*, is the particular responsibility of the *Volksschule*. The resulting dichotomy can easily be identified: The graduate of the *Gymnasium* has an abundance of *Bildung*, while the *Volksschule* graduate is adequately trained. He has *Erziehung* but no *Bildung* despite the recent efforts to upgrade the curriculum of the *Hauptschule*.

The dichotomy between the graduates of the *Volksschule* and those of the *Gymnasium* may be decreasing now that the teachers in the former schools themselves have successfully completed the latter. To teach in a *Volksschule* one needs the *Abitur* as well as six semesters at a teachers' college. The latter, frequently a part of a university, offers the students some general education, training in pedagogy, and course work in a major field of their choice. Student teaching occurs during the rather long period between semesters when the college is closed but the schools are open. If a person wishes to qualify for teaching at *Realschule*, he must select a second major field to study more intensively. Examinations follow, as does a three-year probationary period with supervision, additional training, and examinations. Those who seek to teach in the *Gymnasium* attend a university after completion of the *Gymnasium* and the *Abitur*. They major in two fields and often minor in a third. After four to five years they submit to the *Staatsexamen*, an oral examination, which if passed allows them to begin a two-year internship in a *Gymnasium*. During these years they teach part time, they receive their pedagogical training, and they observe master teachers usually in two different *Gymnasia*. After additional examinations they are appointed to a full-time position. By then they are in their later twenties and thoroughly "gebildet." They often perceive themselves to be scholars in their field and yet their pupils may be only ten, eleven, or twelve years of age.

Much tension has surrounded German universities in recent years. That students have several reasons to be dissatisfied has been made clear by their various demonstrations. Like the French students at the Sorbonne, German students have found themselves in overcrowded lecture halls and seminars because universities have not expanded during the postwar period along with the increase in size of their student bodies. The full professors (*Ordinarius*) who serve as department chairmen and directors of their own research institutes are largely to blame. They have failed to appoint additional faculty despite legislative authorization of new positions. Their intransigence may be in part due to a fear that standards are lowered when too many places are made for students at the universities. They may be reluctant to share the direction over their students with additional professors. They still receive lecture fees in proportion to the number of students in their lecture. Whatever the reasons, universities have become badly overcrowded, a condition for which some relief is in sight as the new universities at Constance, Bochum, Bremen, and Regensburg become fully operational.

A second student complaint also involves the faculty, for students object to the kind of control wielded by the full professors over who is to receive assistantships. These frequently lead to an appointment as a *Dozent*, or instructor, a position which gives its holder permanent civil service status as a university faculty member.

As in other countries, universities have become the center of political demonstrations. At the Free University of Berlin, in particular, students have taken inspiration from the Berkeley revolt in their objections both to the university administration and to certain political postures of their government. In the last few years they organized demonstrations against the American war in Vietnam, against Vice-President Humphrey as a representative of the administration that has conducted that war, against the Shah of Iran, and against the national emergency legislation to be included in the Federal Republic's Basic Law. Though Maoists and those who subscribe to Herbert Marcuse's principle of "repressive tolerance" led the demonstrations, a sizeable group of followers inside and outside the S.D.S. (Sozialdemokratischen Studenten) are willing to listen, to consider the leftists' position, and to take part in their demonstrations.

Other facets of university life remain relatively unaffected by student unrest. The various science faculties and research institutes are more immune than the social sciences and philosophy in which a direct confrontation of the issues in question often becomes necessary. Most students continue to attend lectures, to participate in occasional seminars, and to take their examinations at the end of a four- or five-year period of study. During that time they very likely spend at least a semester at a second university in order to broaden their grasp of their specialization. On the *Staatsexamen* (state examination) they will be expected to be familiar with the full breadth of their subject and with the theories and findings of its various scholars.

German students continue to live free of university supervision. There are only a few student residences and these are maintained by student unions and lie virtually outside university jurisdiction. Students often live in rooming houses unless, of course, they continue to live at home. Intercollegiate athletics and intra-university sports are non-existent. Social life is still fostered by the fraternity-like "corporations," the *Burschenschaften*. Here young men gather to drink beer and sing songs. Sometimes they also still duel, a sport which is supposed to prove the participants' manliness.[9] If one doesn't flinch in spite of the oncoming sword and the chance of being cut in the face, one will be known for one's valor. Those who bear the scars of these duels on their faces do so proudly. The diagonal scar across their cheek marks each as a university graduate, obviously well educated, *i.e. gebildet*. If, on the other hand, one meets a *Bundeswehr* (army) officer with a scar, one may be seeing a university dropout. Ordinarily, university graduates do not choose an army career. The *Burschenschaften* may foster certain political view-

points among their youthful members. They have also been found to provide channels by which a university student can obtain respectable employment in commerce and industry. Former corporation members assist present members to locate career positions that match the social status of a university graduate.

REVISIONS OF EDUCATIONAL PRACTICES

What then are the issues whose debate reveal the Germans' dissatisfaction with the existing educational system? Looming large on the horizon are the proposals for the reform of higher education. These include the push in Catholic states to begin to educate Protestant and Catholic teachers in the same institution, to have prospective *Gymnasium* teachers of history and social studies take more university courses in the social sciences and modern history than in ancient and medieval history, and to create a greater awareness among students of areas of the shortages and surpluses in the labor market. Not long ago, for example, the Technical University of Munich held an open house for the advanced students in a local *Gymnasium*.[10]

Several individuals have enunciated their views of the needed reforms at universities. The *Wissenschaftsrat*, an officially-constituted national group of scholars, issued a plan. The prominent German sociologist Ralf Dahrendort with others produced a plan for Baden-Württemberg. In it the recommendation was made that some students remain at the university only three years to complete what an American might describe as an undergraduate specialization in his major and professional field. The five-year program was to be reserved for those wishing to do research and advanced study in a special field.

Bavaria's Minister of Education and Culture, Ludwig Huber, mentioned six practices which needed to be changed. He urged that more of the administration of the university be taken centralized to lighten the responsibilities of the *Rektor* of each faculty. The *Rektor*, or president, is a faculty member, elected to that post by this fellow professors. He serves in the post for one or two years. Minister Huber also concurred with the idea of developing departments for each specialization to reduce the power as well as responsibility presently centered in the full professor who heads up the research institute for his area of specialization. Like others, he saw no satisfactory way yet to allow students to have a voice in university affairs, an issue which demands resolution. He liked the notion of publicly announcing vacancies to be filled at universities. Eligible university graduates would be able to compete with their peers, and again reliance on the largesse of the full professor would

---

9. The University at Frankfurt recently tried to disenfranchise its dueling societies but was told by the courts that such organizations have a right to exist alongside the other "corporations." *New York Times*, Nov. 13, 1964, p. 15.

10. Munich, *Suddeutsche Zeitung*, July 13, 1967, p. 14.

be diminished, if not eliminated. The present practice to conduct another major research study following the awarding of the Ph.D. (the *Habilitation*) if one wishes a professorial appointment at a German university might be limited to those with exceptional promise in research. Others would be utilized more to teach, a step that would improve the instruction for the bulk of the students. Huber finally proposed academic counseling for new students, improved oral final examinations (*Staatsexamen*), the use of television and other mass media for instructional purposes, and the year-around utilization of university facilities.[11]

Although many voices are concurring with the irate German university students that reforms like those discussed by Minister Huber must be made, the full professors at universities appear reluctant to make any changes. Whatever reforms might be instituted are almost certain to diminish their power over the distribution of assistantships, over conduct of research, and over instruction in their field.

Other issues are periodically discussed. Georg Picht elaborated on a number of these in his book, *Die deutsche Bildungskatastrophe* (Munich: Deutscher Taschenbach Verlag, 1965), a study of Germany's educational deficiencies. He points to the persistent teacher shortage that has come about not only through the extension of schooling for most youth but also through the requirement (1) of a *Gymnasium* education for all applicants to the teachers' colleges and (2) of competency in two or even three disciplines for certification as a *Gymnasium* teacher. In the case of the former, graduates of the *Gymnasium* find themselves equally eligible to enter a university, a more prestigious institution than the teachers' college. As to the latter, prospective *Gymnasium* teachers find that on the *Staatsexamen*, they must compete with students who have majored in a single discipline in contrast to their two or three fields. The existence of the teacher shortage was corroborated by an August, 1967, report of the impending unfilled vacancies in the secondary schools of Lower Saxony.[12]

Picht also described the malfunction of the present assignation of fiscal and administrative responsibility for education. States administer the schools and provide most of the funds, but they show little concern with any national planning to overcome educational deficiencies. Equalization of tax resources or of teacher supply has been virtually impossible so far, as has been the undertaking of cooperative measures to anticipate the kinds of skills demanded by the West Germany economy.

Another topic which draws attention to itself is the relationship between church and school. Many individuals oppose the denominational elementary school as breeding narrowness, as being divisive in a religiously mixed nation like Germany and in these days of ecumenism, and as constituting an infringe-

ment of religious freedom. State school laws often conflict here with the Basic Law of the Federal Republic.[13] Other people wonder whether the present system of religious instruction in the schools really insures adherence to Christian principles as a person reaches adulthood.

Of the educational innovations being adopted in West Germany the evening *Gymnasium* is one of the first. Here working youth complete their academic secondary education on a part-time basis, generally prior to seeking higher education in the line with the vocational training they obtained originally. An alternative such youth have is to attend a *Kolleg*, a full-time *Gymnasium* for older youth who already have worked at their vocation and have completed the equivalent of the *Realschule*. Voluntary effort by pupils is at the base of another experiment. A *Gymnasium* in Buxtehude utilizes independent study, small group seminars, elective courses, and extensive student self-government.[14]

Meanwhile other experiments deal with educational television for teacher in-service education; they concern the organization of field trips for pupils to the courts, to war-crimes trials, and to Bonn and Berlin. Pupils should learn about their country's past and its hopes for a genuine democracy in the future. A type of science fair has been tried in order to stimulate interest in the exploration of the natural sciences. Adult education centers are popular and are growing everywhere as West Germans seek to extend their knowledge and upgrade themselves professionally. These steps give an indication of the present ferment that pervades education in the Federal Republic of Germany today.

SELECTED BIBLIOGRAPHY

ABENDROTH, WOLFGANG. *Wirtschaft, Gesellschaft und Demokratie in der Bundesrepublik*, Frankfurt/M.: Stimme-Verlag, 1965.

ALMOND, GABRIEL, and VERBA, SIDNEY. *The Civic Culture: Political Attitudes and Democracy in Five Nations*, Princeton (N. J.): Princeton University Press, 1963.

ARENDT, HANNAH. *The Origins of Totalitarianism*, New York: Harcourt Brace & World, Inc., 1961.

BINDER, GERHART. *Lebendige Zeitgoschichte, 1890-1945*, Handbuch und Methodik. Munich: Chr. Kaiser Verlag, 1961.

BLATTNER, FRITZ. *Das Gymnasium*, Heidelberg: Quelle & Meyer, 1960.

BOSSENBROOK, WILLIAM T. *The German Mind*, Detroit: Wayne State University, 1961.

BRANDT, WILLY. *The Ordeal of Coexistence*, Cambridge, Massachusetts: Harvard University Press, 1963.

---

11. Ludwig Huber, "Die 6 Neuralgischen Punkte," *Die Zeit*, Hamburg, May 21, 1968, p. 10.
12. *Hannoversche Allgemeine Zeitung*, Hannover, August 24, 1967, p. 9.
13. Hamburg, *Die Zeit*, April 2, 1968, p. 7.
14. Hamburg, *Die Zeit*, October 31, 1967, p. 10.

BUCHHEIM, HANS. *Das Dritte Reich*, Munich: Koesel Verlag, 1959.

DAHRENDORF, RALF. *Gesellschaft und Demokratie in Deutschland*, Munich: R. Piper & Co., 1966.

Deutscher Ausschuss für das Erziehungs-und Bildungswesen. *Empfehlen und Gutachten*. 1st ed., Stuttgart: Ernst Klett Verlag, 1955.

Deutscher Ausschuss für das Erziehungs-und Bildungswesen. *Rahmenplan zur Eingestaltung und Vereinheitlichung des allgemeinbildenden öffentlichen Schulwesens*, Stuttgart: Ernst Klett Verlag, 1959.

DILL, MARSHALL, JR. *Germany, A Modern History*, Ann Arbor: The University of Michigan Press, 1961.

ELLWEIN, THOMAS. *Was Geschieht in der Volksschule?* Berlin: Cornelsen Verlag, 1960.

ELLWEIN, THOMAS, and FINGERLE, ANTON. *Vernunft und Glaube, Ein Gespräch über die politische Erziehung in der Schule*, Berlin: Cornelson Verlag, 1958.

FLITNER, WILHELM. *Hochschulreife und Gymnasium*, Heidelburg: Quelle & Meyer, 1959.

FLITNER, WILHELM, and KUDRITZKE, GERHARD. *Die Deutsche Reform—Pädagogik*, Munich: Verlag Helmut Kupper, 1961.

FREUND, GERALD. *Germany Between Two Worlds*. New York: Harcourt, Brace & World, Inc., 1961.

GABLINGS, ILSE, and MÖRING, ELLE. *Die Volksschullehrerin*, Heidelberg: Quelle & Meyer, 1961.

GRABERT, HERBERT. *Sieger Und Besiegte: der deutsche Nationalismus nach 1945*, Tübingen: Verlag der Deutschen Hoch schullehier-zeitung, 1966.

GRABING, HELGA. *Geschichte der deutschen Arbeiterbewegung*, Munich: Nymphenburger Verlag, 1966.

GRACE, ALONZO G. "Education," *Governing Postwar Germany*, ed. Edward H. Litchfield and Associates, Ithaca, New York: Cornell University Press, 1953.

HEITGER, MARIAN. *Buildung und Moderne Gesellschaft*, Munich: Kösel Verlag, 1963.

HELMREICH, ERNST CHRISTIAN. *Religious Education in German Schools*, Cambridge, Massachusetts: Harvard University Press, 1959.

HOFER, WALTER. *Der Nationalsozialismus, Dokumente 1933-1945*, Frankfurt/M.: Fischer Bücherei, 1957.

HUEBNER, THEODORE. *The Schools of West Germany*, New York: New York University Press, 1962.

HYLLA, ERICH J., and KEGEL, FRIEDRICH O. *Education in Germany*, Frankfurt/M.: Hochschule für Internationale Pädagogische Forschung, 1953.

IRVING, DAVID. *The Destruction of Dresden*, New York: Holt, Rinehart & Winston, 1963.

JASPERS, KARL. *Wohin Treibt die Bundesrepublik*, Munich: R. Piper, 1966.

KANDEL, I. L. *The Making of Nazis*, New York: Bureau of Publications, Teachers College, Columbia University, 1935.

KERSCHENSTEINER, GEORG. *Education for Citizenship*, London: George G. Harrap & Company, Ltd., 1915.

KNAPPEN, MARSHALL. *And Call It Peace*, Chicago: University of Chicago Press, 1947.

KNELLER, GEORGE F. *The Educational Philosophy of National Socialism*, New Haven: Yale University Press, 1941.

KOHN, HANS. *The Mind of Modern Germany*, New York: Charles Scribner's Sons, 1960.

KOPP, OTTO. *Widerstand und Erneuerung*, Stuttgart: Serwald, 1966.

KUHN, HELMUT. *Die deutsche Universität im dritten Reich*, Munich: R. Piper, 1966.

LAWSON, ROBERT F. *Reform of the West German School System, 1945-1962*, Ann Arbor, Michigan: School of Education, University of Michigan, 1965.

LEONHARDT, RUDOLF WALTER. *This Germany*, Greenwich, Conn.: New York Graphic Society, 1964.

LEVY, GUENTER. *The Catholic Church and Nazi Germany*, New York: McGraw-Hill Book Company, 1964.

LILGE, FREDERIC. *The Abuse of Learning; The Failure of the German University*, New York: The Macmillan Co,. 1948.

MOSSE, GEORGE L. *Nazi Culture*, New York: Grosset & Dunlap, Inc., Publishers, 1966.

PAULSEN, FRIEDRICH. *German Education* (translated by T. Lorenz), New York: Charles Scribner's Sons, 1912.

PICHT, GEORG. *Die deutsche Bildungskatstrophe*, Munich: Deutscher Taschenbuch Verlag, 1965.

PINSON, KOPPEL. *Modern Germany*, New York: The Macmillan Co., 1954.

SAMUEL, R. H., and THOMAS, R. HINTON. *Education and Society in Modern Germany*, London: Houtledge & Kegan Paul, Ltd., 1949.

SCHELSKY, HELMUT. *Anpassung oder Widerstand?*, Heidelberg: Quelle & Meyer, 1961.

SCHULTZE, WALTER, and FÜHR, CHRISTOPHER. *Schools in the Federal Republic of Germany*, Weinheim: Julius Beltz Verlag, 1967.

SHAFER, SUSANNE MUELLER. *Postwar American Influence on the West German Volksschule*, Ann Arbor, Michigan: School of Education, University of Michigan, 1964.

SHIRER, WILLIAM L. *The Rise and Fall of the Third Reich*, New York: Simon and Schuster, Inc., 1960.

STAHL, WALTER, ed. *Education for Democracy in West Germany*, New York: Frederick A. Praeger, Inc., 1961.

STAHL, WALTER. *The Politics of Postwar Germany*, New York: Frederick A. Praeger, Inc., 1963.

STERN, FRITZ. *The Politics of Cultural Despair: A Study in the Rise of the Germanic Ideology*, Berkeley: University of California, 1961.

TAUBER, KURT P. *Beyond Eagle and Swastika: German Nationalism since 1945*, Middletown, Conn.: Wesleyan University Press, 1967.

ULICH, ROBERT. *The Education of Nations*, Cambridge: Harvard University Press, 1961.

WACHENHEIM, HEDWIG. *Die deutsche Arbeiterbewegung 1844 bis 1914*, Cologne: Westdeutscher Verlag, 1967.

WALDMAN, ERIC. *The Goose Step is Verboten*, The German Army Today, New York: The Free Press of Glencoe (Macmillan), 1964.

WENKE, HANS. *Education in Western Germany*, Washington, D. C.; Library of Congress, Reference Department, European Affairs Division, 1953.

ITALY

Aldo Caselli[*]

Italy was unified in 1870. The occupation of Rome by the Italian troops completed the dream of a United Italy, a dream known as the *Risorgimento*; at the same time, it compelled the Pope to become a prisoner in his own palaces. So he remained until 1929, when the Lateran Pacts of February 11 sounded the end of his seclusion but also paved the road for today's position of compulsory religious education in Italian schools.

Italian education, according to Medieval and Renaissance tradition, was basically church-oriented. The Catholic Church had a monopoly. Social developments elsewhere in Europe during the eighteenth century began to shake the position of the Jesuits in the running of secondary schools. The Napoleonic Wars, and the breeze of freedom which they carried with them, gave the Italian Liberals an infusion of new ideas in the field of education. This did not last long. Napoleon was defeated and the Church took over again. But the seed had been imported from France and would germinate. The first manifestation was in the little state of Piedmont, where the unification movement began. They conceived and passed the Boncompagni Law (1848) which eliminated clerical interference in State schools by the simple device of abolishing a great number of the privileges of the clergy. But it was a subsequent law of the state of Piedmont, the Casati Law (November 13, 1859), later carried into all of Italy, which was the basic charter of Italian education at that time. From a practical point of view, it continued as a basic document until philosophical and structural reforms were brought about by Gentile in 1923.

The Casati Law, 374 Articles long, covers the full spectrum of education from elementary grades to the university. The Napoleonic code of education is the framework within which this law was written. Its concept of centralizing authority in the hands of the national government was to continue into the future, and even today it is accepted and enforced.

The Law is divided into five sections: administration of the system of public education, universities, classical education at the secondary level, vocational education, primary education, and teacher training. Academic freedom is a fundamental idea inherent in the Law and guaranteed by the government. This concept is very important, following, as it does, centuries of church-controlled education in which dogma was of primary importance and prevented the recognition of individual points of view. Individual freedom is the basic motivation of the changing Italian society, and, as such, it must be recognized and cherished in the schools of the nation. Building on this concept of freedom, private groups were permitted to open schools in competition with those of the government, provided they met governmental requirements. Elementary education was made the responsibility of the local community. Local municipal governments had the task of managing and staffing the elementary schools. Education was required between the ages of six and twelve. Parents were held responsible for children's attendance, and procedures were established for their carrying out this responsibility. Education was free, and so the idea developed that education was not a service offered by the local government to the citizens but was one of the basic rights of citizenship.

After the Casati Law, there was no major change until 1877. In that year the Coppino Law intensified enforcement of school attendance between the ages of six and nine. During these years of compulsory education, fines were instituted for parents who evaded the law. Elementary education was still in the hands of the local government and could be implemented as the local authorities saw fit, thus creating disparate sets of standards throughout the peninsula, resulting in some excellent real facilities and others which existed in theory only.

[*]Acknowledgment is here given to the aid received from the Haverford College Research Fund.

Another change took place in 1904 with the Orlando Law. Elementary education was extended to six years, with those students going on to upper schools, being permitted to enter the *scuola media* after the fourth grade, while those for whom elementary education was terminal had to continue in the school, which had two final years of vocational training. Compulsory education was now established between the ages of six and twelve. Not only were parents held responsible for their failure to send children to school, but employers were held liable if they gave jobs to youngsters who had not fulfilled their scholastic obligations. Adult education and an organized fight against analphabetism began to form, at this time, in Italian education.

A final step in the development of this first phase of education in Italy came with the Credaro Law of 1911, a difficult law which required the enactment of numerous rulings before it could operate smoothly. Elementary education, with its compulsory nature, had been the main concern of legislators since the early Casati Law. A final step now was made to reorganize the very structure of elementary education. It was no longer the responsibility of the local governments (which had often used it to suit their political aims) but became the responsibility of the central government. This was a significant turn in education. The nation witnessed the shifting from an era of freedom in which the municipalities could operate as they saw (or did not see) fit to an era of guidance and control by the central government which was to continue to increase. Peripheral administrative offices were created to bring directives from Rome to the local level.

The next station on this road is the Gentile reform of 1923. Giovanni Gentile was Fascism's intellectual showpiece, Italy's outstanding philosopher after Benedetto Croce. As Minister of Education, Gentile conceived the most notable reforms in the structure of Italian education since the Casati Law. Gentile, as a philosopher, was well known prior to the days of Fascism and, on his assumption of the role of Minister of Public Instruction, he changed its title to the Minister of National Education as a way to introduce the values of his philosophical system.

Benedetto Croce was the originator, in Italy, of that school of idealistic philosophy which Giovanni Gentile applied to pedagogy and which Giuseppe Lombardi-Radice, by carrying out the working details of Gentile's "actual idealism," successfully formulated as a complete philosophical movement in education: School is not preparation for life, but life itself. Life, for Lombardi-Radice, means the solution of any problem in all its individuality as it has been put before the student, hence a spiritual communion between the student and teacher. The teacher then does not repeat himself like a phonograph from class to class nor from year to year, but he is new and fresh each time he approaches the subject because he is develop-

ing it with the student, and, while he leaves them to find their solutions, he educates them in the largest sense as he makes them citizens of their time.

The most appealing example of practical results of this philosophy of teaching was achieved in language, either foreign languages, or the national languages, when seen from an area where a local dialect is spoken. The old system consisted of teaching the rules of an abstract grammar without any feeling of entering into the foreign culture. The new concept is that "we can speak in someone else's language only insofar as we are capable of creating a spiritual unity between ourselves and them." Grammar then becomes "neither a *quid prius* nor a *quid posterius*" in our relation to the language. It coincides with the ability the student may develop in grasping the language itself. The cold abstract grammatical rule is left out of the system, and the warm comparative grammar is presented as the student develops his linguistic experience. In the writings of Gentile, as in those of Lombardi-Radice, one finds many pages, inspired by Hegel perhaps, which formed the basis of the educational system of Italy between 1923 and World War II.

Education is a blending of individuals in a common conscience. The real teacher leaves his own problems on the doorstep of the classroom as he detaches himself from his Ego and plunges into the topic of his lecture and develops that transcendental Ego which identifies itself with the object at hand. Pupils and teachers do not exist per se, but together they form one unity which witnesses all the happiness of a single identity and none of its handicaps. It is only an empiric statement when we say that one man teaches another because the real teacher of man is *tutto*, the invisible spirit.[1]

Identification of teaching with the development of personality was put to good use by the Fascist regime, but it is inappropriate to say that the various Fascist youth organizations were part of the educational process. They were rather the second half of the formula by which youth was made to fit the need of the State: "Libro e Moschetto: Fascista Perfetto" ("Books and Muskets: a Perfect Fascist"), and after years of well-engineered propaganda, the identity "Italian ergo Fascist" became accepted by the majority.

Before terminating this review of the trends in Italian education prior to the end of World War II, one must mention the significant happenings of February 11, 1929, which, as a crescendo had been influential in shaping national life, particularly in recent years when democratic form of government had been reestablished and the Christian democrats had an opportunity to express themselves. This was the pact between the Holy See and Italy for the recognition of the Vatican State and its prerogative in Italian

1. G. Hessen. *Idealism. Pedagocico in Italia,* Roma, 1960. p. 16.

life. This agreement bearing the signatures of Cardinal Gasparri and Benito Mussolini is known as the Lateran Treaty. It regulates the position of the clergy, the Church and its various instrumentalities, and all transactions pertaining to Church operation. Five Articles are concerned with education, specifically Articles 35 and 38 on Catholic schools, Article 36 on Religious education in the Italian educational system, and Articles 39 and 40 on seminaries and Catholic universities (schools of theology, philosophy, Church history, missionary work, and canonic law). The institution of the seminary for those wishing to dedicate themselves to the priesthood had its roots in the Council of Trent; but now again they have their own legal physiognomy, are directly dependent on the Vatican, and are spared taxation. Similarly, the Catholic universities, such as the Gregoriana in Rome, are fully recognized, but like all foreign schools, their degrees have value only as recognition of academic achievements.

Catholic schools, as mentioned in the Treaty, are organized for the education of those who prefer church-sponsored education to the laic school system of Italy. There are many of these schools, topped by that masterpiece of higher education known as the Sacred Heart Catholic University (Università Cattolica del Sacro Cuore) with its various schools in Milano, Piacenza, Rome, Passo della Mendola, and Bergamo. The Church bases its right to educate on four concepts: (1) Jesus Christ's mandate to make disciples (Mathew 28:19), (2) the Motherly function of the Church toward those who became its children by virtue of baptism, (3) an historical tradition based on medieval educational patterns and the scholastic life in the monasteries, and (4) the right that man has to educate himself according to his own desire, outside the State monopoly, if he so wishes.

The article which is most far-reaching is Article 36, concerning religious teaching in governmental schools. Religious education returns to the educational system of the State, and its administration is subject to Church control, using books carrying the Church imprimatur. Pius XI had a pithy sentence in this connection. He said, "We have caused God to return to Italy and Italy to God." Religious teaching is compulsory for one hour a week and is part of the overall curriculum (Law, June 5, 1930, No. 824). Dispensations for reason of family belief can be obtained by the student's parents only if they apply in writing at the beginning of the school year.

As the reader will notice, this far-reaching decision and one which will shape education in Italy for the years to come, because the language of the Lateran Treaty is such that the concept is not changeable unless Italy wants to return to the *status quo ante,* which is highly improbable, especially in the democratic climate of today's Italy.

EDUCATION SINCE WORLD WAR II

Presentation of current practices and trends in Italian Education must start with an analysis of the Italian Constitution, the one enacted on December 22, 1947, and which established the rights and the duties of the central government in the matter of public education.

The articles which are of particular significance are the following:

Article 9: The Republic promotes the development of culture as well as scientific and technical research. It safeguards the landscape and historical artistic landmarks.

Article 33: Arts and sciences are free and so is their teaching. The Republic lays down general rules for education and establishes State schools of all kinds and grades. Organizations and private citizens are allowed to create schools and educational institutions, provided this does not involve charges on the State.

Article 34: Schools are open to all. Elementary education, imparted for at least eight years, is compulsory and free. Capable and deserving pupils, even if without financial resources, are entitled to pursue the highest courses of study. The Republic enacts this privilege by means of scholarships, of contributions to the families of the pupils, and other provisions, to be secured by competitive examinations.

These articles embody essential principles, all of which seek to assert the obligation of the government to standardize education and the responsibility for making it available to those who are capable of acquiring it, even if they do not have the financial ability. They also grant freedom in teaching and the right of private groups to establish their own schools provided they do not draw on the national budget.

These broad powers have certain limitations imposed by the Institute of Regioni, another concept which has come into existence under the New Constitution. It provides that in those parts of Italy where a regional government exists, the central government may delegate some of its powers in matters of education to the regional authorities.

CENTRAL LEVEL: THE MINISTRY OF PUBLIC EDUCATION (Ministero della Publica Istruzione)

This is the central governmental unit which has control of all educational activities. The Minister is the supreme authority. He establishes the goals and paves the road for their enactment (Law, July 16, 1923, No. 1753, Article 4). A big, and in a certain sense, evolving area is the one relating to the curricula which are standardized all over the Republic. It is with the Minister that all steps toward these changes, necessitated by changing times, originate. As examples, civics became a field of study only in 1958-59 and the history curriculum was considerably changed in 1960. These changes were achieved by laws sponsored by the Ministry. Social work is not yet a recognized field of study in Italy. Teaching at the university level, and for that matter, research, do not escape Ministry control, as without spelling out all details, it establishes the directive to be followed. The Minister is responsible for the budget for Italian education, which at the university level means determining the contribution the central government will pay to various universities toward their local expenses (Law, December 18, 1951, No. 1551, Article 1), and this is obviously an important means of control.

The Ministry exercises control over the rulings issued by the dependent peripheral units. Its control is exercised after a ruling has been issued, by revision and prevention of its enforcement, if it violates other laws, or if it is otherwise illegal. In various instances, outlined in various laws, authorization of the Ministry is requested before certain steps are taken. For example, university administration needs Ministry approval in order to dispose of equipment valued at more than half a million lira (Law, June 30, 1955, No. 766, Article 4).

The Ministry is organized according to a pattern established by law (Article 97 of the Constitution; Law, December 7, 1961, No. 1264, Article 2). It includes thirteen general directorates (direzioni generali), four inspectorates (ispettorati), and one central office (servizio). Each of these eighteen sections is concerned with one particular phase of the broad area within which the Ministry has jurisdiction.

The task of the Ministry is aided by the presence of eleven additional collegiate bodies which act as consultants in various cases and which have different degrees of authority according to the case presented to them. One of these is the top advisory board for education (Consiglio Superiore della Publica Istruzione) which has a wide range of responsibilities in the shaping of national educational policies. Others have to do with such fields as discipline of teachers, supervision of local administration, the budget, and auxiliary matters.

LOCAL LEVEL

Provincial School Boards (Provveditorati agli Studi) enact ministry policy and regulations at the provincial levels. Under them, principals (Presidi or Direttori) of secondary schools or principals (Ispettori Scolastici or Direttori Didattici) of elementary schools carry the provisions on all levels: the school building, the classroom, and the teacher.

These school boards are headed by a superintendent (Provveditore). (See above: Credaro Law of 1911) His functions are various. He represents central government at the local level and supervises the enactment of rules and regulations in the field of secondary education. In the area of elementary education, the Provveditore has a higher degree of authority as he appoints the teachers, makes local decisions, and administers the complex pattern of schools according to his judgment in an overall frame of reference established by ministerial policy.

The Provveditore has no authority over universities or institutions of higher education which may be located within his province. Some sidelines of his activities concern athletics, buildings and grounds, scholarship administration. The principals are responsible to him for the operation of the various secondary schools to which they have been appointed after proper examination. The Provveditore, like the Minister of Public Education, may rely on the help of collegiate bodies especially organized to assist him in solving problems of elementary or secondary instruction.

THE EDUCATIONAL PATTERN

The School System

Schools are public institutions since they serve the public and may be considered as a peripheral branch of the government. Schools may be classified by levels (primary, secondary, university) and by type (secondary cultural: ginnasio, liceo; and secondary vocational: istituti professionali). Schooling is free and compulsory from the age of six to the age of fourteen (Constitution, Article 35). There are private schools in Italy, mostly parochial, but they must teach state-established curricula, any additional discipline being considered facultative. Students have to pass state-controlled examinations in order to receive official certificates or degrees, which, in all cases, are issued in the name of the Minister of Public Education.

Pre-elementary Years

Kindergartens or nursery schools are generally privately owned and subject to the overall control of the local Provveditore. Teachers must hold the proper Italian teacher's certificates for this level. Enrollment in 1967 was about 1,300,000 (total of both private and public pre-school programs).

Elementary Schooling

This is the first step where children begin to face organized forms of schooling. It is divided into sections, a first cycle (first and second grades) and a second cycle (third, fourth, and fifth grades). There are written examinations at the end of a cycle, within a cycle promotions are made without examination at the discretion of the teacher. A child is eligible to enroll in the first grade if he is six years old, or if he will be six years old by December 31 of the calendar year when he enrolls (Law, February 5, 1928,

No. 577 Article 171). Teachers are selected by the Provveditore from among those who have the appropriate school diploma and have passed special competitive examinations, thereby earning the right to a teaching position. Competitive examination is the standard form of selecting teaching personnel throughout the entire educational system and this principle applies to any level of the educational system. Elementary schools, like all other schools below university level, are financed by the Ministry budget, three-quarters of which is for teachers' salaries throughout the national territory.

The school year lasts ten months, with not less than one hundred and eighty school days. The school day is four hours and ten minutes, with a total of twenty-five hours a week. The basic teaching includes Religion, Italian, Arithmetic, Physical Science, Civics, Penmanship, Design, and Choral Singing. Note that Religion is the first discipline on the curriculum as it is "Foundation and goal of any education based on the teaching of the Catholic Doctrine."

Middle Schools (Scuola Media)

This is the most controversial step recently carried out by the government of Italy (Law, December 31, 1962, No. 1859), in order to fulfill the requirements of Article 34 of the Constitution. It is compulsory, it is free; in subsequent schools students must pay a school tax. Such a tax had formerly been payable for the first three years of post-elementary education, but it has now been abolished. These three years are those which, in the past, were used to begin the training which led to the final degree toward which the student was working. Now the years have been diverted to complement the student's elementary education rather than being the first step toward a personal goal. It is a controversial issue; more on this subject later. It is a result of social concepts which have been taking Italy by storm since the end of World War II and because of which, in the expectation of enlarging the numbers of those receiving the benefits of additional education, the qualitative element of the curriculum had to be compromised. The curriculum is basically Religion, Italian, Social Science, one foreign language, Mathematics, Physical Science, and Physical Education. During the first year, as a continuation of the elementary school, a course in music appreciation is given as is a course in craft. During the second year, Italian is not taught per se, but is presented in connection with elements of Latin, and the relationship between the two languages is investigated. Latin is available as a discipline during the third year but on an elective basis. The diploma (*esame di licenza*) is the appropriate final document and a prerequisite for seeking admission to any one of the other schools at a higher level.

Secondary School, Cultural Type

In this category one finds (1) the ginnasio and liceo classico, remnants of the old school which had been the preparation for a classical education. The original eight-year curriculum is now cramped into five. While the liceo was and still is three years, the ginnasio was five and now is two; it is preparatory for the liceo and the emphasis on Greek and Latin in the preparation for a classical education is condensed, in such a way that, even by changing pedagogic methods, final results are not comparable with the old school; (2) The Lyceum for scientists (Liceo Scientifico) is a five-year school, created in 1923, with emphasis on science and is the preparation for a scientific career. The place of Greek is taken by Mathematics, though the Latin programs are comparable to those of the Liceo Classico. A prerequisite for admission is one year of ginnasio. Again, the results are not comparable to those achieved in the old school; (3) The Art School (Liceo Artistico) lasts four years, specializes in the arts, and leads to the School of Architecture. All these schools, as well as the Magistero, mentioned below, grant at the end of the course a diploma of accomplishment (Diploma di Maturità) if the student passes a state-controlled examination.

Secondary School, Vocational Type

The first school to be mentioned is the Istituto Magistrale which is the teachers' training school. Its course lasts four years, and it is a crucial school. After four years, at age eighteen, young men and women are ready to teach children at the elementary level. Children in those years are extremely eager to discover the meaning of personal experiences. It is essential that their teachers, boys and girls in their teens be properly trained, and one may wonder if they are not too young for the task. In 1967 about 170,000 students were enrolled in these schools.

Philosophy, Psychology, and Pedagogy are basic disciplines in the Istituto Magistrale. It follows a complete representation of the cultural spectrum: Italian, Latin, History, Science (Geography, Physics, Chemistry, Mathematics, Natural Science), one foreign language, arts (History, Music, Singing, Crafts), Civics, Religion, and Physical Education. Recent changes in the curriculum call for practical teaching experience during the last two years. Generally attached to this kind of school there is a Nursery School (Giardino d'Infanzia). The Scuola Magistrale also grants a diploma for teachers at nursery school level. It is given to those students who apply for it at the end of the third year, and who can pass the required examination.

Another school in this group is the five-year vocational course (Istituto Tecnico) leading to a Certificate of Expertness in a specific field (Diploma di Perito). These schools specialize in various fields, such as Agriculture (Istituto Tecnico Agrario), Commerce and Surveying (Istituto Tecnico Commerciale e per Geometri), Industries (Textile, for example) (Istituto Tecnico Industriale), and, for students going to sea, Navigation (Istituto Tecnico Nautico).

Special Schools

Before concluding this speedy survey of Italian primary and secondary education one should consider special schools that are either made necessary by special conditions or qualifications of individual students. In the first category are the following: open-air schools for children have a predisposition toward various diseases, schools for children with physical defects, schools for the blind or deaf and dumb, schools for inmates in correctional institutions for juvenile delinquents. To the second category belong some Terminal Schools, the most important of which are the *Conservatori* & *Istituti of Musica* dedicated to the teaching of music.

Higher Education

Roots of institutions of higher learning in Italy are deep and widely spread. Bologna opened its doors in the eleventh century followed by Padua and Naples in 1222 and 1224, while Pisa goes back to the fourteenth century. Pavia, probably the oldest, although not formally organized until 1361, was famous as a Law School even before the scholastic reputation of Bologna was established. These early Italian centers of higher learning attracted students from all over the world. They were originally established in an independent way with their own statutes and their own sources of income. With the passing of time and with the demand for education increasing, the universities turned to the local governments for aid and were connected more and more closely with government, until today, when, although they have administrative autonomy, they are consistently regulated from the central government of Italy.

The central government also exercises control over the universities and comparable institutions by means of the State examination. This is required of all graduates who expect to enter the professions. This examination is comparable to the examination given in the United States to doctors entering the medical profession, to lawyers becoming members of the bar, to accountants qualifying for CPA, and the like. Through these examinations the State exercises control over the quality of the teaching provided by individual institutions and also make sure that applicants have the necessary preparation for entering the field of their choice.

There are also private universities and other institutes of higher learning which, although fully financed by local sources, have a status comparable to the State universities; their diploma carries the same rights and privileges; and the central government exercises control over their curricula and over the quality of their teaching. As a matter of fact, a university cannot be established by any private group unless the plans are submitted in complete detail to the central government and approved.

Direct or indirect contributions which the central government makes for the operation of each individual university (here and elsewhere the word "university" must be understood to include all institutes of higher learning which have university status) are established by law.

When Italians talk of *Università* they mean the administrative organization, while by the name of *facoltà* they indicate the teaching organization which through a pre-established curriculum, generally from four to six years, brings the student to the conclusion of his journey through learning and grants him academic recognition. The government determines which facoltà can be instituted in various universities and also what secondary education is prerequisite for admission. The basic curriculum is also established by the government, which decides what should be taught and for how long.

By-laws of each university have to adhere to the general national educational goal. In addition to the compulsory courses, there are certain elective subjects. The by-laws of each institution will determine which of these elective subjects will be taught at the university and this document will also establish what courses of specialization the university will run; and finally, it is the responsibility of the university to establish the sequence of presentation to the student of the required material and to enact all those administrative regulations which must be fulfilled before a final certificate can be granted.

Italian universities issue two degrees, one called Laurea and the other Diploma. While both documents have the same legal value, the name is determined by the legal character of the school which issues the document. A Diploma is a degree which usually entails less work than a Laurea, either in years of study or in number of courses required.

Not all universities grant all diplomas, and while there are a number of schools granting a law degree, there is only one school granting a Laurea in Statistical Science. An analysis of degrees issued is further complicated by the fact while there may be a school specializing intensively in a specific field and granting a degree, the same degree may also be granted elsewhere in Italy as part of the program of a school which includes this field among other specializations. A good example is the Laurea in foreign literatures and languages granted by the special Institute in Venice. But a student need not go to Venice to seek such a degree, since seventeen additional *facoltà* offer the degree as part of their program in the school of education and eleven more schools of Italian Literature offer a degree in modern foreign languages.

In addition, Universities offer a considerable number of post-graduate courses in specialized fields which last one to three years and which allow further specialized instruction for scientific or professional ends.

To evaluate an Italian University degree, one would need to study the official transcript or the libretto which a student carries with him on which his grades are entered after an examination. This is necessary since, in addition to certain basic courses, there are many electives which vary from one university to another. A graduate is called Dottore, which is not on a par with Ph.D. since it lacks the high degree of concentrated specialization, but it covers, in theory at least, much broader and deeper work, such as that required in our educational system for an M.A. The difficulty in making comparisons is further complicated by the fact that pedagogic methods are so different in Italy and in America that the ultimate results are not what one might expect they would be, considering America's system of reading assignments and tests, for example, both unknown to the European student. The Italian student may or may not go to the big lectures, mostly overcrowded, and he works largely on his own, generally at the zero hour, for a final examination.

Administration of Universities

From the administrative standpoint, universities are free to organize as they see fit (Constitution, Article 35). Universities having their special autonomous organization, have special organs with which the power is rendered. The top authority is called Rettore (Direttore, in the case of Institutes of Higher Learning), a counterpart of the president in similar U. S. organizations. The difference is that he is appointed by the *Corpo Accademico,* or the faculty of the university on permanent appointment. This body also generally rules on issues of broad general interest for all the schools which make up the university. The *Senato Accademico* consists of the heads of the various schools and is close to the Academic Council of American institutions. This group is concerned with educational policy and rules on those issues which the Rettore presents to them. Each school has its own *Preside* (roughly equivalent to Dean of the Faculty) elected by the faculty of the school from among its own professors. The faculty meeting rules on educational policy pertaining to the specific school. In conclusion:

1. Each university has its own charter which establishes the schools and the departments which will make up the university and the rules pertaining to mid-year examinations and finals.

2. Discipline is the responsibility of the university through its regularly constituted bodies (such as the Rettore and the Senato Accademico).
3. Budgets and fiscal reports are not subject to the approval of the Ministry.
4. The head of the administrative offices is in a position subordinate to the Rettore.
5. The appointment of professors to fill a vacant chair is a faculty responsibility.

A professor cannot be removed or transferred to another university except with the approval of all parties concerned, the appointee and the faculty. The procedures for the selection of a new faculty member are interesting. The faculty of a school makes known to the Ministry that a chair is vacant. The Ministry establishes and makes known the terms of a national competition. These usually require consideration of published works, and occasionally a sample lecture is given. A Commission, charged with the task of examining the applicant's credentials, is elected by the faculty of the school where the vacancy occurs. When all credentials have been examined, the Commission makes known the names of three candidates they think suitable for the chair, listing them in order of merit. The faculty then makes the selection and asks the Ministry to make the appointment.

Academic freedom is an accepted prerequisite of the profession and even in unsettled times professors jealously defend this right.

These broad freedoms allowed to a university mean that their degrees have value only in the academic world. As previously seen, certification to practice a profession for which one has been trained requires that one pass a state examination which is very competitive indeed. (Law, August 31, 1933, No. 1592, Article 172)

COMMENTS AND TRENDS

Italy's population in 1968 was estimated to be about 56,000,000. In spite of all provisions written in the laws, illiteracy is always high, especially in the south. The total national illiteracy rate is about 7 percent. The goverment is determined to expand educational facilities to the less fortunate social classes in all possible ways. The law of December 1961, No. 1264, was enacted to direct more attention to this important need. The ratio of adult students to teachers was 1:178.

The Italian TV network started a few years ago what turned out to be a very successful series of educational programs entitled, *It's Never Too Late.* A report by André Lestage (UNESCO Education Branch) on this experiment indicates that

to date, three experiments have been made with television in order to reduce illiteracy—two in the United States and one in Italy. . . . The educational method used in Italy to teach listeners how to read and write, the employment of those technical aids that television provides and the imagination shown are, in my opinion, exemplary. . . . This was the opinion of all who watched the screening and they offered warm applause. . . .

A number of elementary school teachers have followed these lessons for adults in order to learn the new technique used and thus improve their own methods.

Regular televised lessons in the first year of this program totalled 2,044, while a further 1,298 were given during the summer. They were taken by 48,113 adults; of these, 34,326 won certificates attesting to successful completion of the series and admission to the second year cycle.

Related to the problem of illiteracy is the problem of drop-outs or students dragging their feet, a widespread problem in Italy.

As indicated in Table 1, male and female university graduates make up less than 2 percent of the total (1.3 percent), with men far in the lead (75.8 percent) over women (24.2 percent), since only a small, select group of women succeeds in completing university training.

TABLE 1

Italian Population over Six Years of Age
Classification According to Educational Level

Grade of Education	Male	Female	Total	% Male of Total
University Graduate	2.0	0.6	1.3	75.8
Secondary School Diploma	4.8	3.8	4.2	64.9
Lower Secondary School Diploma	11.2	8.0	9.6	57.1
Elementary School Diploma	60.0	61.5	60.8	48.1
Total Possessors of Degrees, Diplomas, etc.	78.0	73.9	75.9	50.1
Total with no Educational Diplomas	22.0	26.1	24.1	44.5
of which:				
Able to read and write	15.4	16.0	15.7	47.8
Unable to read and write	6.6	10.1	8.4	38.4
Total	100.0	100.0	100.0	48.7

Students successfully obtaining diplomas at the various senior secondary schools (lycée, classical, scientific, art, teachers' college, commercial, industrial, agricultural, and the like) amount to little more than 4 percent (4.296 percent), but the number of males is not far different from that of females (54.9 percent and 45.1 percent respectively), since this category includes a large number of elementary school teachers.

Holders of lower secondary school diplomas are estimated at almost 10 percent (9.6 percent), with 57.1 percent boys and 42.9 percent girls. The introduction of a standard secondary school curriculum will enable a far larger number of boys and girls to obtain this educational level in the future. Those in possession of a lower secondary school diploma total more than 60 percent (60.896 percent), and in this category girls exceed boys (51.9 percent and 48.1 percent respectively). In all, persons holding some form of degree or diploma comprise three quarters (75.9 percent) of the population of over six years of age (half male, half female).

From a social viewpoint, it is the illiterates who are a serious and important problem. This group consists of 3,831,926 persons, of whom 1,471,241 are men and 2,360,685 are women. Educational illiteracy is also frequently accompanied by an incapacity to qualify in any trade or profession.

Foreign students are attracted by special courses in Italian language and culture given at some of the oldest universities of Italy. These are, generally speaking, incidental to one's visit to Italy, rather than the reason for the visit. Italy has not yet reached the level of France where there is a segment of the educational system geared to the needs of the foreigner and the foreign student profits from these special arrangements in a unique way which may lead him to official degrees which have official value in the French educational system. Italy still has a long way to go before it can match what France offers. Although the attraction may be on a smaller scale, the cultural facilities of Italy could well be used by students of the classical world or of the Renaissance in order to acquire a knowledge and an awareness which they may cherish for life.

Foreign undergraduate attendance in Italian universities is not very large. About 2,000 foreign students attend Italian universities each year. Greece sends the largest contingent, followed by the United States of America. During the academic year 1959-60, 281 foreign students obtained degrees from Italian Institutes of Higher Learning. Most were in Medicine, with 128; Engineering was second, with 37.

Italian teachers are not well paid by American standards of living nor by Italian standards. They are civil servants. Their status is divided into categories, and they can be paid only what their particular category allows them to have. This explains, especially in periods of inflation and growing costs, their eagerness to give private lessons or to seek subsidiary work. Teachers, holders of an appointment, do not leave the profession since it was difficult to obtain the appointment, and the mere fact of having an appointment gives them status in the community. So they struggle along and tolerate all the difficulties of making ends meet. Italy will have to soon face a rearrangement of its bureaucratic setup and approach the matter of salaries in a more realistic way. In the meantime salaries are a major problem waiting for solution. It results from tremendous changes in the social condition of the country, coupled with political unrest in which no single party has had the stable majority needed for a productive form of government.

A stable middle class, which emphasized savings and morality, which existed in Italy prior to World War II has been replaced by the newly uplifted lower class, which brought with it free spending and, as a result, inflation. In such a society which has not yet found its point of stabilization, schools attempt to keep pace with the changes in order to provide the services which are required. Yet, socially Italy is in a turmoil. Agriculture is in decline and ex-farmers want to become factory workers. Internal migration is displacing many people very rapidly; while certain social classes have much more money to spend than they ever had, others, mostly the former middle class, find that at the new levels of cost their incomes are not sufficient for maintaining the old standards. Such turmoil creates a need for better understanding between peoples. To overcome the traditional apathy of some groups; to overcome the dogmas of others and to understand the motivation of the new society, these are the tasks of the educational system of Italy which, in the long run by presenting a progressive approach to civic affairs, must be able to use the experience of the classroom as a preparation for the experience of life. Seen from this point of view, a point of view familiar in other countries, it is clear that the entire structure of the educational system needs a revision. The programs of certain disciplines need to be changed and the students must focus on everyday happenings in the family, in the nation, and in the world to understand the role of the citizens in an expanding society. Italy seems to have adopted this aim in long-range planning, and a first step has been to revise the *scuola media*, the methods of teaching Latin. The basic concept on which it is possible to curtail Latin studies is Article 34 of the Constitution which establishes eight years of compulsory and free education, but the critics point out that this does not specify which curriculum students should follow. On the other hand to impose on all students a standard curriculum, a curriculum without Latin, regardless of the students' final educational aims, denies the fundamental idea on which the humanistic teaching has taken place for centuries. By osmosis, from classical culture the student was learning the essential culture of the land. In addition, classical studies were imposing on the student a regimen of application which remained with him late in life and which he could apply to other fields. Furthermore, the long study of the classical language has for too long conditioned the formation of a citizen's personality so that it is hard to envision or welcome the idea of a ruling class which would draw less heavily from direct and extensive reading of the Latin Classics. From such reading and translation the student was gaining

an ability to reason, argue, and write in Italian, to say nothing, for instance, of the joy of discovering in the verses of Horace a forerunner of Carducci, and of finding ways to become a nonconformist in a conformist world.

Returning to the basic point, probably there was no need to level the curriculum, since Article 34 of the constitution also provides that "capable and deserving pupils even without financial resources" are entitled to follow the highest grade of studies. This is an old concept in the Italian educational system. Benedetto Croce, Minister of Public Instruction in 1920, sent a directive to the various *Provveditori* requesting the institution in each Italian school of a scholarship fund. Private enterprise was called into an otherwise public system, to provide contributions to enable the *Preside* to make grants to deserving students who, for financial reasons, might be inclined to drop out. Increases in school taxes, increases in the cost of books, small salaries in the lower strata of the middle class, all were among the problems which suggested this directive over forty years ago. Soon thereafter a move was started to organize such scholarship funds as the main business of independent non-profit corporations with their approved by-laws, rather than leaving these funds free to be spent at the discretion of the *Preside*. In a post-World War II development, private foundations have come to be created in Italy, and these are often aimed at helping deserving students. They have a legal status comparable to the non-profit corporations which manage scholarship funds. The original purpose of Student Aid has recently been expanded in addition to include prizes, grants for studying abroad, and funds for research. The by-laws of these non-profit corporations establish the way in which application must be filed. Unfortunately the current available income is not sufficient for all grants which need to be made in accordance with the constitutional commitment, and since 1954 the government has often subsidized these *casse scolastiche* so that stipend may be standardized from the minimum of thirty thousand lira to a maximum of ninety thousand. But scholarships are not enough. The social background from which some students come remains as a frequent deterrent to his scholastic work. It takes more than free tuition, free books, free luncheons to help a child who, however great his potentialities, comes from a family where education is an empty concept. Some steps should be taken to offset the subjective influence of the surroundings. It is part of the task of making education available to all who are capable, it is a form of social work, it is something essential in the present social revolution of Italy.

The population explosion of other parts of the world is also felt in Italy. During the next six years the high school will see a growth in population of 64.8 percent; universities, a growth of 54.8 percent. The first figure will call for 14,500 new teachers in the fields of mathematics and physics alone, and these are the least popular fields of all. The problem of teachers, competent teachers, is one of the hardest to solve, and the first step toward the solution must be taken by the universities. The forecast of the Ministry for the next six years indicates that new universities are to be created to achieve better geographic distribution. Italy may not go to the extreme of France which has divided its territory into educational districts with the head of the university assuming responsibility for each district. But certainly Italy needs a better geographical distribution of its Institutes of Higher Learning, to say nothing of a reorganization of schools already existing, if it is to fulfill adequately the aims of the various curricula. (Something patterned on the United States' system of higher education is in the making with various levels of higher education granting different degrees.) Research demands a straight-forward approach, since some professions in the social sciences need recognition and status. Italy, by virtue of being a Catholic country, has not yet accepted social service as a profession for which training may be obtained through established schools at university level; yet in the *Mezzogiorno* there is need, a very great need, for trained social workers to help solve problems at the human level, and none are available. These idiosyncrasies and others need quick revision. The forecast of the Ministry also looks forward to the creation of a national universities' council to coordinate the efforts of the Institutes of Higher Learning.

Another problem the government must settle soon is the matter of government aid to parochial schools. On this very issue the cabinet of Aldo Moro fell on June 26, 1964. It is true that the constitution establishes that private schools can be organized if they do not call on public funds. This article means that private schools have no right to expect aid, but it does not necessarily mean that the government cannot extend aid if it so chooses. The State has been helping the private school in the past because it sought to offset some of the financial stress experienced by private schools as a result of the government's request that they pay private school teachers the same salaries as those in the public school system. Until a few years ago such was not the case and private schools could compensate their personnel as they saw fit.

This is an important point, one of the many which characterize the great variety of problems which face Italian education in the era of social revolution. By contrast, the storms created by the Casati Law or the Gentile Reform seem mild indeed. Private schools are important because they are the only ones which, by virtue of being slightly independent of government control, can better service education today. The world is changing, Italy is changing, but the educational programs, heavy with bureaucracy, do not change fast enough—this is the key point which needs to be resolved.

SELECTED BIBLIOGRAPHY

BORGHI, L., and SCARANGELLO A. "Italy's Ten Year Education Plan." *Comparative Education Review*, Vol. 4, No. 1, 26-30, June, 1960.

CODIGNOLA, ERNESTO. "Italia" in *Die Schulen in Westeuropa*, N. C. E., 1960.

JUSTMAN, JOSEPH. *The Italian People and Their Schools*, Tiffin, Ohio: Kappa Delta Pi, 1958.

KNELLER, GEORGE F. "Education in Italy," *Comparative Education*, eds. Arthur Moehlman and Joseph Roucek, New York: Dryden Press, 1957.

THUT, I. N., and ADAMS, DON. *Educational Patterns in Contemporary Societies*, New York: McGraw-Hill Book Co., 1964.

NETHERLANDS

N. F. Noordam, Helena W. F. Stellwag, and E. A. van Trotsenburg

The Netherlands, a small country located in Western Europe, have a land area of about 33.500 square kilometers (12.750 square miles) with 358 inhabitants the square kilometer (912 per square mile). It is a very densely populated country with a growth of 10 percent annually. The constantly improving hygienic conditions and medical care gives every newborn Dutch baby an average chance of reaching the age of 73. The density of population has made it necessary to turn large tracts of infertile ground into arable land and to reclaim land from the sea. As the supply of mineral deposits is small, it is necessary to make a most intensive use of the limited natural resources. The economic picture of this country, however, is more and more being determined by industrial activities: 42 percent of the working population is now employed in industry and 10 percent in agriculture.

As opposed to what Herodotus says about Egypt's being a gift from the Nile, the inhabitants of the Netherlands have had to conquer their country from the sea and then make a living on it. One can explain many Dutch characteristics from the fact that from olden times onward they have lived in the delta of the Rhine, which was secluded from the sea by a small line of dunes. Their first task was to make this delta habitable. One of the consequences was cooperation in the practical sphere and the growth of individualism. The agricultural area was not large, and many Dutchmen had to find a living in trade and navigation. New traits of character developed: adaptation to others, the belief that everybody has his own rights, the feeling for righteousness. And yet the Dutch were possessed of a certain superiority in finding their own way of solving problems. Sometimes this conviction led to a sense of self-sufficiency. Even in modern times the geographical position, borders on the French, German, and Anglo-Saxon civilisations, still makes its influence felt on the Dutch and they try to integrate these civilisations.

More than the result of the geographical and climatological factors, the Dutch nation is the result of its history, its struggle for freedom and independence from Spain in the eighty-year war, 1568-1648.

In the beginning of this war Calvinism was introduced from France and put its mark on the country. Calvinism was militant, fierce, intolerant, and a champion of social justice. Among the seven little states which formed the United Provinces, the province of Holland was the most influential. Holland was tolerant and moderate. In the Middle Ages its religion was never dogmatic Roman Catholic, and this did not change when Calvinism was introduced. Its economical and political supremacy held Calvinism in check. This caused a certain tension, but revolutions were never the result. Most difficulties were solved by peaceful arrangements. Dutch civilisation is typically middle-class and urban. At the end of the Middle Ages the influence of the nobility disappeared, and as a result of the Reformation influence of the Roman Catholic Church also disappeared.

Family life in the Netherlands was characterized by strong ties and intimacy. From the beginning of their history, charity and poor-relief were an example for the surrounding countries. In 1600 the city of Amsterdam, striving for humanisation of penal procedures, possessed a prison where therapeutic work was done, probably the first of this kind in the world. In the same time witch-trials disappeared, the Jews found an asylum in Amsterdam, and books forbidden abroad were printed here, *e.g.* Rousseau's *Emile* in 1762. A school for deaf-mutes already existed in the seventeenth century. Dr. Amman taught the deaf-mutes to talk. Orphans were properly cared for and were well trained in accordance with the Dutch principle that every man, rich or poor, has a right to the best possible education.

The darker side of this civilisation is a petty middle-class spirit, a lack of interest, an aversion for the unconventional, a lack of creativity and originality. These traits became evident in less prosperous periods, particularly the eighteenth and nineteenth centuries. The positive characteristics are obvious in the dynamic seventeenth century, and in the present time, which in many ways resembles the Dutch "Golden Age."

CHARACTERISTICS OF EDUCATION AND INSTRUCTION RESULTING FROM CIVILISATION

It follows that the Dutch nation produced only few great thinkers on education. The Dutch are practical-minded and a Comenius, Rousseau, or even Dewey could not have developed their theories here. Instruction has always been on a high level though it is somewhat traditional. Education pure and simple has always appealed to the Dutch as an ideal. Education often meant instruction. Its goal was learning as much as possible in the shortest time. Moralising was preferred to physical punishment. The Dutch are interested in science and its practical application. Literature and music are underestimated compared with technology. The aim of education is to raise hard-working people. Sharp business men, managers of big factories or shipyards, bright engineers and atomic experts are more highly valued than are good historians or profound philosophers.

In the Dutch schools, zeal and arduous swatting are more appreciated than brilliant ideas or originality in thinking. Owing to this, Calvinism has had a great influence also on Roman Catholics and Humanists. As a result of this and the Old Testament there is a great distance between parents and children, between seniors and juniors, between teachers and pupils. The school is an institution with a patriarchal character—the teachers give their lessons, the pupils take notes and memorise. Discussion, working with units and projects are not common and only found their way to Holland after the Second World War. Authority, though somewhat severe, is not unfair or unjust.

In the discussions about school and education the influence of Calvinism is perceptible. The Dutch like to discuss themes and topics such as the aim of education, authority, conscience, the fundamentals of punishment, the relations between school and state, school and family, school and church. Dutch parents and teachers take little interest in problems of didactics and instruction, educational problems such as socialisation and cooperation and the relation between the school and a changing society.

HISTORY OF THE SCHOOLS AND THE SCHOOL SYSTEM

Before the thirteenth century little is known of the Dutch schools, but after 1200 the towns developed and with them an extensive system of schools. At the end of the Middle Ages every parish and town in the country possessed one or more schools. Originally founded by the church, they were often taken over by the town. Apart from these schools there were convent schools and schools for the nobility. The parish school had a two-year course. The pupils, boys and girls together, went to school when they were six or seven years old. They were taught singing for church purposes (in Latin and Dutch), saying their prayers, especially the Lord's prayer, the creed, something of the liturgy, and at the end of the Middle Ages, the Ave Maria. They were taught a little reading, and sometimes even a little writing was in the curriculum. Arithmetic also became popular. The alphabet was taught by means of a wooden board with a handle. The letters and digits were notched into it, and the whole board was covered with a sheet of transparent horn: the "hornboeck."

In summer, school began at six; in winter, at eight. Lessons went on for three hours in the morning and three or four in the afternoon. There were no holidays, not even on Sunday mornings. Teaching and instruction were individual, not classical. In 1500 one may assume that every man in the country and certainly in the towns could read and write his name. After the two-year course at the Ab school (named the *Duytse* school for the instruction was in Dutch) the children in the towns went to the so called *great* or Latin school. Here the course took seven years and the pupils learned the trivium: Latin grammar, logic and rhetoric, *i.e.* the art of writing a letter and composing a speech.

In the higher grades the pupils tried to master a part of the quadrivium: arithmetic, geometry, astronomy, and music. With this, the seven liberal arts were completed. Methods of teaching were the same as in the elementary school. The classes were large: one teacher for about 100 pupils, and sometimes more than 1000 pupils in one school. Discipline was strict and punishment severe. The only university in the Netherlands was in Leuven (now Flemish Belgium). It possessed four faculties. Arts was a recapitulation and extension of the trivium and quadrivium of the Latin school and was obligatory for every student. Having finished arts, a student could study theology, law, or medicine. Teaching methods here were the same as in the elementary and Latin schools. In the morning the professor gave his *lectio*, in the afternoon his assistant held the *repetitio*. Important was the *disputatio* about a topic.

Examinations did not exist; one left the university after a successful *disputatio* on a doctor's thesis. A complete course of school training included two years elementary school, seven years trivium, two years quadrivium, three years arts, and six years theology, law or medicine.

EDUCATION IN THE MIDDLE AGES

In the Middle Ages the school was not considered an institute for education but only as an institute for instruction. The young boys and girls received their education in the family or abroad.

A young monk or village priest went to a monastery and afterwards he might go to a university if he wished to study theology. Usually he had no interest in the seven liberal arts but in the *artes mechanicae*, and so he became a carpenter or a blacksmith or an architect or he learned to brew beer and to do agricultural work. Most of the nuns did domestic work. Part of the clergy became teachers in the elementary or Latin school. They did not receive vocational training but they learned by doing. A young nobleman received his education at home until his seventh year. He played, listened to stories and nursery tales and the singing of heroic songs of primeval ages. Then he was sent to another family to serve there as a page. Here he received his education from different teachers and seniors. The disciplinarian and the maids of honour looked after his conduct, the clerical teacher taught him religion, reading, and composing music and poems. Also playing chess and singing accompanied by an instrument belonged to his accomplishment.

From age seven to twenty-one he was a shield-bearer in the service of a knight and at twenty-one, after the accolade, he was a knight himself. His seven arts were swimming, horse-riding, archery, fighting, hunting, playing chess, and composing. His education was a synthesis of Christian, Greek, Latin, and Germanic ideals. He had to fight for Christian justice and he led a life of sacrifice and courage. He promised fidelity to his master and to be a protector of the church, women, and the poor.

Inhabitants of the towns played a dominant role in the Netherlands. A boy in town received his education at home, and after another two or more years in the elementary school, he went to learn a trade in the guild or corporation. First he had to serve his apprenticeship to a handicraft or trade and then, after an examination, he was qualified to work at it for days' wages as a journeyman. To pass his examination he had to make an item such as a door, or a saddle for a horse or a statue of a saint for the church. After that he had to make his masterpiece which gained him the rank of master in the craft. Apart from the instruction in the school and the education for his trade, an educational and cultural schooling was received through the festivities the corporations organized. On these festivities, besides the Sundays, sometimes two or three a week, they saw or helped to perform a play, and took part in the processions and competitions in archery, riding, and the like. They listened to the storytellers and the singers. They could also learn how to govern a town. In this way they were constantly learning but only by following the example set by the grown-ups.

HISTORY OF THE SCHOOLS AFTER THE MIDDLE AGES

In the sixteenth century the quality of school instruction deteriorated owing to the turbulent times and the war against Spain, but in the seventeenth century the schools flourished as they had never done before.

New schools arose and new universities were founded: the first was the famous University of Leyden, 1575. The rich Dutch towns founded libraries, and the many printing offices flooded the country with Dutch books and books in foreign languages. After the beginning of the war against Spain, the nobility and the Roman Catholic clergy lost their power and this fact reinforced the influence of the citizens. The schools underwent a change. Catholicism was forbidden and instruction in religion became Calvinistic. A new book came into existence: the catechism. Humanists and Calvinists were all for a better education, and Latin, Greek, and Hebrew were among the subject matter in the Latin school. As a consequence of the invention of printing and the manufacturing of cheaper paper, the efficiency of the schools increased. The horizon of knowledge and interest expanded. Books about history and geography appeared and were read by the common man. Every Dutchman became a "theologian." Trade and navigation brought knowledge of the whole world to every little Dutch town. In every Dutch family one could find a printed Bible and a book of travels.

The high standard of instruction in schools remained throughout the eighteenth century. The French revolution brought emancipation of dissenters, Jews and Roman Catholics. Calvinism lost its preponderance and dominant position in political affairs. Centralisation took the place of the autonomy of the towns and the republic of the United Provinces became a monarchy. A national education act appeared in 1806, one of the first in world history.

The guilds disappeared, and as a result of industrialization, a new class of industrial labourers arose.

In spite of the good organization of the school system, the high level of education could not be maintained as a result of the transition from the old eighteenth-century society to the nineteenth-century society. The standard of living declined and analphabetism returned among the poorer agricultural and industrial labourers. The school sunk below the level of the late Middle Ages.

The Latin school became more traditional and did not keep up with the modern times. It gave lessons in Latin and Greek, but no modern languages nor science were part of the curriculum. In 1863 the first secondary high school was founded and soon afterwards the old Latin school was modernised into the gymnasium. In both types of schools, modern languages, history, geography, and science were obligatory for every pupil. These schools still exist. In 1901 the elementary school became compulsory.

After the French Revolution the monarchy aimed at a central state school, but the Calvinists, who could not forget their formerly dominant position, and the Roman Catholics rejected this State school. So another eighty-year war began, this time a struggle for freedom of education. Calvinists and Roman Catholics desired schools for their denominations, but ones that were paid for by the State. The struggle became even more complicated by the fact that it was coupled with a struggle for social and political emancipation of the modern industrial worker. This gave rise to three types of schools, two denominational (Calvinistic and Roman Catholic) and a school of the State. In the nineteenth century only the State school was paid for by the Government, but the Dutch found a typical solution for this problem and after 1917 the State paid for all schools, its own and denominational on an equal basis. Also trade unions, political parties, radio corporations, journals, and sporting clubs were attached to these denominations. So the Dutch people was divided into three parts: one Calvinistic, one Roman Catholic, and one neutral. School and social organizations are now founded on confessional principles. The consequences are many: For example, a strong group-consciousness has developed as has a lack of insight into the problems on a national or international level.

The tolerance of the Dutch might often be interpreted as indifference towards others and as a feeling of superiority of the group to which they belong. A positive result, however, was that in the Netherlands only few schools are based on economical or social status. Schools for the rich or schools for the poor, boarding schools, or private tutors have always been an exception.

On the whole in the Netherlands the struggle for equalization of the schools has led to a great personal interest in school and education. But this was in the first place based on confessional principles and the autonomy of every group to find its own school. The Dutch have (or had) less interest in matters of the more technical side of education and instruction. Their belief is that when the religious principles of the school are guaranteed, instruction cannot go wrong on account of the sound religious principles. This also led to lack of interest in experiments and didactics. As already mentioned, the level of instruction is high; in all junior high schools the teaching of three modern languages is a "must" in the curriculum, and after leaving school all Dutch boys and girls possess an encyclopedic knowledge of many things, but this knowledge is not always adaptable to life in state and society.

Another negative result of this school system is the difficulty for a Dutch pupil to pass from one school to another. There is little mutual contact between the schools, even between the schools of the same denomination. Therefore efficiency as a whole is not what might be expected on the ground of the great personal care of the parents and the teachers and the hard and assiduous working of the pupils.

A little before and after World War II, however, many changes took place. A new system of laws for the schools tried to break through the isolation between the divers types. Experiments in education appeared. The State offered many scholarships for poor students.

A new system of teacher-training for the elementary and secondary schools came into being. At every university in the Netherlands there is now a professor of education and didactics. Further education flourishes as never before and many technical schools have appeared. As a consequence of the new laws, the new orientation of the school, and the new types of schools, the negative results of the former system are now rapidly disappearing. This evolution is furthered as a result of the fact that the examinations are mostly under state control. Efficiency is growing because the schools of different denominations and of different types are becoming more equal and resemble each other more closely.

In the second half of the twentieth century there is a flourishing system of schools and a greater interest in the problems of education and socialization. The isolationism and traditionalism of the nineteenth century is rapidly disappearing. It is hoped that in this respect the twentieth century may prove to be a second golden age.

PRESENT STRUCTURE OF EDUCATION

National educational systems might be compared on the following two points: (1) centralisation, *i.e.* the degree of interference by the central authority in the affairs of the local authority or private enterprise; and (2) the relation between Church and State, especially the position of private or confessional education.

Centralisation

In conversations between foreigners it is often difficult to communicate even if both are proficient in the same language. This is because the content and emotional value of words given to the same concepts in the different countries are not adequately covered by translations.

This becomes very clear with words like "public" and "private," but not less so with a term like "centralisation." When it is said that the Dutch system is fairly strongly centralised, it would suggest, in American terms, that the Department of State in

Washington has the ultimate supervision and control over all education and would bear a considerable part of the expenses. Americans would see in this great disadvantages and consider themselves very fortunate that in Ohio or in California one can have the run of affairs in one's own hands. But the position would change somewhat if it is realised that this comparison is not necessarily true. The situation in the State of the Netherlands can be compared with that of Ohio or New Jersey. Then the differences would not be so great, since also in America every state makes some central regulations, such as in connection with teacher qualifications.

A different light will fall on the picture if it is borne in mind that in the Netherlands the federal phase belongs to the past; that one of strong centralisation was followed by a liberal phase and that, ultimately, under the influence of an increasingly clear democratic insight and on the basis of a stronger, conscious democratic conviction, the phase of a more pronounced centralisation followed. From this development it becomes clear that centralisation need not have an anti-progressive, anti-democratic origin, although the danger of excessive bureaucratisation and paralysis of private initiative is not illusory.

In the year 1581, when Phillip of Spain was abjured, that is, after the Dutch Declaration of Independence, when the Dutch provinces were united in the Republic of the Netherlands, the then existing provinces can be compared with the thirteen American states at the time of the American Declaration of Independence. The Federation of the seven provinces had as their highest authority the *Staten Generaal* (States General); but the provinces also had their Provincial Councils and the cities their City Councils. Of these three bodies of Government, the *Staten Generaal, i.e.* the Federal Government, was the weakest as a body of authority and in fact was neglected except when common consultation was required such as in matters of foreign affairs, defense and general finance. The strongest sovereignty was vested in the Provincial Councils, consisting of the delegates of the country districts and the cities. But the real point of gravity was to be found in the cities, which provided the funds and with it acquired certain rights. Schools were founded, governed, and controlled by the cities. City authorities made appointments, issued regulations, and had the supervision. Only occasionally did the Provincial Government act coordinately, such as in 1625 when a school ordinance was proclaimed for the whole of Holland. The *Staten Generaal* issued ordinances for only the three districts which fell directly under its authority.

With the Batavian Revolution, in the wake of the French Revolution, this state of affairs terminated. French domination brought complete centralisation in which the first king of the Netherlands, William I, brought no change, since he governed personally. The provinces had no financial means and

the cities had lost their privileges. This may seem a step backward as far as local government is concerned, but in this way a national system of education could develop and provincialism disappeared. The forerunners of the French Revolution brought the ideals of "Liberty, Equality and Fraternity" and simultaneously the modern conception that education is the object of care and responsibility of the state and that every child has the right to proper education. As a consequence education was for the first time regulated in 1806. "Public" and "private" schools were recognised. "Public" were those supported by public funds or belonging to a body by the State; "private" were those belonging to bodies not subsidised by the State. These private schools were dependent on the sanction of provincial or city governments. The state exercised supervision by means of inspectors, and controlled just about everything concerned with the public school, including the content of the curriculum.

In 1815 a national school-organization—a common school—was established. It succeeded in developing a sense of nationality. The level of education was raised considerably. After the autocratic government of the first half of the nineteenth century a period of liberalism followed which was inclined to give local enterprise greater scope for expansion.

In 1848 the Liberal Government under Thorbecke enacted a new constitution, in which the principle of freedom of education was incorporated.

About 1870 Liberalism was on the way out again. The need for stronger control from the State was again voiced on the basis of the principle that the State was responsible for the education of every future citizen.

That is why in 1870 the Central Government started giving financial aid and bore 30 percent of the expenses but formulated stricter conditions with regard to school buildings, equipment, and the like. This brought the private schools to a difficult position, since they received no financial aid. Ultimately, in 1889, the private schools received one-third of the subsidy of public education. The State also interfered rather drastically in the structure of private education. A private school could henceforth be founded only by a corporation which was recognised by law. As a consequence, after 1889 all schools run by individuals disappeared.

In 1900 compulsory education followed, which gave another motive to accommodate private education and so in 1905 public and private education were seen as composing the two parts of national education. In 1914 State interference increased but always on the basis of the democratic principle of raising the level of education for all. In 1917 the Constitution was revised and the following article included: Education is the object of continual care of the Government. In 1921 all primary education was subsidised equally. In 1956 this was realised for all secondary education. A common curriculum for private and public schools was proclaimed.

To summarise, (from 1581 onward) the following pattern emerges:

I. A federal structure was radically replaced by a central-authoritarian regime during the French occupation. Education was regarded as the responsibility of the State.
II. As a result of liberal influences, the Constitution of 1848 guaranteed freedom of education under supervision of the State. The control and administration were left in the hands of the City Councils. The finances of the City Councils being inadequate to cope with these expenses, the Central Authority increased its contribution and claimed more influence, this as the result of the necessity to provide equal educational opportunity for all. In the Netherlands the importance of a national education on equal level transcends local autonomy.

In spite of a period of strong State interference, a tendency to limit its influence and to give more scope to social organizations is at present noticeable and is laid down in the explanatory note of the Minister with regard to the ("Mammoet") Educational Act (1963).

Relationship Between State and Church

During the Middle Ages, education in the whole of Europe, including the Netherlands, was an affair of the Church. Even so, there have also been city schools, *i.e.* schools controlled and administered by City Governments. After 1581 education did not lose its religious character. The Republic of the Netherlands bore the stamp of Calvinism. City Governments appointed Calvinist head-masters who had to conduct the children to church on Sundays, just as the Catholic teachers before them had to conduct the children to Holy Communion. The clergy kept a close eye on the affairs of the schools. Apart from these there were so-called small schools, private institutions for non-Calvinists, the Roman Catholics, which existed by the grace and favour of the City Governments. These private schools were often prohibited but continued to exist in secret. Apart from these official and private schools, the need for higher schools, other than the Latin School, was felt more and more. The government had to provide secondary education for those pupils who were not destined for the university. There were also private institutions, very often French or German, belonging to immigrants.

The influence of Calvinism gradually diminished under the impact of foreign ideas such as Rationalism and the Enlightenment. The "Declaration of the Rights of Man and the Citizen" was enthusiastically received in the Netherlands. The Batavian Revolution broke with the past, but less radically than in France.

In 1806, before the annexation of the Netherlands by France, a law regulating primary education was passed. This act implied that the State would assume the cultural task of the Church. The State, *i.e.* the then existing Batavian Republic, provided the country with a national, systematically constructed educational organization.

This school was conceived as a common school with a Christian character. Article 42 of the Primary Education Act illustrates this. It reads: "School education, by the teaching of appropriate and useful skills, is made subservient to the development of the intellectual abilities of the pupils, their physical training and their training in all social and Christian virtues."

Here the foundation was laid for a general national school, a common school, on which the Central Authority exercised strict supervision by means of its inspectorate, by selection of staff and control of textbooks. To establish a school outside of this framework, the consent of the City Government was required and this was hard to obtain. Nevertheless, there were a few private schools such as the school for Jewish children. This was because the public school had a philosophy of life of its own, however vague and rationalistic it might be. The nature of the Dutch State-school at the beginning of the nineteenth century can be very well compared with the present State-school in England, which also has a Christian basis. In the Netherlands it was on just this point that a bitter controversy arose which lasted for more than eighty years.

The conception of public education was opposed by several groups. Their opposition was based on (a) the spiritual trends of public education, *viz.* its rationalistic impersonal conception of the Christian religion; and (b) the fact that they were not free to establish schools which would be in accordance with their conception of a Christian education.

From 1830-1848 the State, though adhering to the idea of the common Christian public school, had to make several concessions, that with the appointment of teachers the religious conviction of the majority of the population had to be taken into account. The liberals, however, increased their political influence during this period. They aimed at curtailing state interference and giving private enterprise more scope, although they were not opposed to the establishment of public (non-denominational) schools, should large groups of the population want them. They were supported by two groups, the Roman Catholics and some Protestants who objected to the spirit of public education.

These groups used an argument which has since been repeated often and which has acquired almost the function of an article of the Constitution in the Dutch society, namely that education is the right and duty of the parents, that it is divinely ordained and that the school is the institution to which the parents have delegated their right and duty in so far as they are incapable of fulfilling it themselves. The State, in this respect, is granted a function of service rather than that of the execution of power. One might say that this point of view is at the basis of the present Dutch school system.

During the nineteenth century, there were several possibilities to accommodate this point of view: (a) The common State school might have been maintained but would have been divided into different sections. This would have been a solution similar to that found today in some West German States, where Catholic schools are established in areas predominantly Catholic, or Evangelical schools in predominantly Evangelical areas. (b) Alternatively, the common State school might have been maintained, and during instruction the pupils might have been split up according to religious needs.

In 1848 unity was sacrificed for freedom. The article of the Constitution reads: "There is freedom of education, [except] for the control on the competence and moral behaviour of the teachers." However, the continuance of the State school was guaranteed. Everywhere in the country adequate public primary education was provided. What should be the spirit of public education? The tendency to see the state school as strictly non-confessional dominated, that is as a school in which the teacher was not only to avoid offending the convictions of others but also was to abstain from expressing his personal ideas on political and religious matters. In this respect the non-state school acted more and more as a corrective of the state school but found itself in a difficult position because it received no subsidy, while the State took measures to further public education by issuing regulations for the building of schools and equipment for classrooms.

Private education could not meet these regulations, not having the funds. And so the second phase of the educational controversy, concerning the right to subsidy for private schools, started. The first phase of the school controversy, that of freedom of education, is generally received sympathetically by a foreign audience, but it becomes somewhat difficult to make the principle of financial equality, which ended the controversy, acceptable. In this principle, according to some opinion, is lurking the danger of particularism, disruption of the national unity, and a too heavy burden on the finances of the State. It is quite understandable that such objections are brought forward, the more so because the position in the Netherlands is unique; nowhere else except in Canada does one find a similar situation, although England has gone a long way in the direction of subsidising private schools. At the outset it must be quite clear that the principle involved is: Education is the duty of the parents. There must be no discrepancy between home and school education; they are both integral parts of the process of personality formation. If, therefore, (it was argued) the State cannot offer education to a certain group of parents which would be in accordance with their beliefs, then they must not only have the right to establish schools in accordance with their convictions but also the financial possibilities must be guaranteed. This is the consequence of the principle of freedom.

In the Netherlands the right of subsidy has been acquired in stages. With every stage, however, the State held a firmer grip on private education. One of the most far-reaching regulations was that private schools could only be established by corporations sanctioned by law and not by private individuals. Owing to this all schools run by private individuals have disappeared.

In 1889 the State started subsidising salaries of the teachers of non-state schools on an equal basis.

In 1900 compulsory education was introduced, which gave weight to the argument for subsidy to non-state education. From this time onward the Socialists have strongly supported the claims of denominational education, since a large section of the working classes have demanded education for their children on the basis of a certain religious conviction.

It was considered to be socially unjust if actually only the more privileged could avail themselves of this right. In 1917 the article in the Constitution which reads: "Public education is the object of the constant care of the Government" was amended to "Education is the object of constant care of the Government."

In 1920 complete financial equalization for primary non-state education followed. If subsidies are accepted, the freedoms are limited to the appointment of staff, provided they are qualified, and in teaching aids. All the rest, such as curriculum, salaries, and legal status of teachers, are set by the government. When a private corporation with legal status requests the City Government to establish an elementary school and guarantees can be given that an adequate number of pupils will attend it (this number to be determined in relation to the size of the population), the City Government is obliged to comply with the request. In the case of secondary schools, it may be refused.

It is important to note that it is neither the Churches nor the parents but rather the executives of a corporation who submit such a request. They may be members of a Church, but they do not act in this capacity. Nor does it necessarily follow that a non-state school must bear the stamp of a particular view of life or denomination. Any corporation with legal status can submit such a request. There are in fact many private non-denominational schools.

The situation is therefore as follows: (a) private tuition at home hardly exists, and no more does non-subsidised private education. (b) The care of the

Government is extended over state and non-state education; it determines quality, salary scales, qualifications, and supervises the material needs of the schools.

Objections to the Dutch system can be summarised briefly as follows: (a) *The financial aspect*: One should not forget, however, that the educational expenses today are met fully by the State. From a financial point of view it does not make much difference. (b) *The leadership aspect*: Fragmentation of the Dutch nation might be the result. (c) State-education has no religious foundation, (d) The pupils do not learn to associate with people of other convictions.

The truth of these objections cannot be denied. On the other hand, during the past centuries a great deal has been achieved on the point of toleration, the different sections of the population are proportionately represented in the school system, freedom and variety reign, the State has a considerable control over the development of non-state schools, and last but not least, there is no section of the population which receives a private and privileged education on the grounds of a socially or materially superior position.[1]

THE SCHOOL SYSTEM

How does this country today educate the younger generation? Explaining the structure of its educational system and stating the number of pupils is not enough to give an insight in the way the Dutch people realize their educational duties and solve their educational problems.

Kindergarten Education

At the age of four, Dutch youngsters may be sent to a kindergarten (not compulsory). The modern kindergarten is an educational institute where the children get the chance to develop themselves by means of games and physical exercises, by playing, modelling, drawing, and singing for twenty-six hours a week and five hours a day. The idea is not to give formal instruction but to guide them in the process of maturing for school age. The methods differ. According to the information collected by Idenburg, 83 percent of the schools are using Froebel materials and 4 percent Montessori materials. After the age of seven the children have to leave the kindergarten, with only one exception. If there are indications, especially on medical grounds, that a longer stay in the kindergarten is desirable, continuation is possible up to the age of eight.

Primary Education

The next stage, the school compulsory age, begins at six plus and lasts for eight school years. As to primary school maturity, 11 percent of the population is not ready for schooling on primary level. Research is being done to adapt the first grade to the situation in the kindergarten by combining work and play. The primary school has a six-year course. The subjects taught are reading, writing, arithmetic, Dutch, history, geography, natural science, singing, drawing, physical education, and sometimes French or English, this however on a private basis. The methods of teaching show a great variety. The traditional teacher-centred pattern is decreasing by means of the renovation courses of the pedagogical centres, sponsored by the teachers' organisations, and also the improving teacher-training has caused a switch-over to more pupil-centred approaches. However educational work in the primary school and especially in the upper grades is hampered by the still existing rigidity in the transfer-procedures for schools in the secondary stage.

Post-Primary Education

About 86 percent of the children continue their education. Twenty years ago this percentage was only 52 percent, which shows a progress owing to the economic developments in the Netherlands after World War II. Post-primary education, or education in the secondary stage, includes: continued primary education, advanced primary education, technical or vocational education, secondary and pre-university education. Forty-three percent attend the technical or vocational schools, 30 percent the advanced primary schools, and 13 percent the pre-university schools.

Continued Primary Education

The continued primary schools are attended by pupils who are still too immature for more advanced courses or who want to start work immediately after the compulsory school-age.

Advanced Primary Education

These schools are very popular. They have three- or four-year courses. The main subjects are French, German, English, history, geography, mathematics, bookkeeping, drawing, and physical education. According to their ability and interest the pupils may choose between courses centring around the more exact subjects and those centred around languages. The leaving-certificate gives admittance to further education, such as teacher-training colleges, technical schools. Since 1957 a great deal of research has been done in order to adapt the program of these schools to the changing social situation.

1. With gratitude I acknowledge the use made of Professor Ph. J. Idenburg's instructive publication *Schets van het Nederlcndse Schoolwezen* (*Outline of Dutch Education*), Groningen 1964, in this section of the essay—Dr. H. W. F. Stellwag.

Technical or Vocational Education

Boys in the technical schools are prepared for industry, shipping, and the like. Girls in the schools for domestic science are prepared for house-craft and needlework and for several service occupations. Both school types have three- or four-year courses. In the first years, general education is combined with pre-vocational education. The pupils are admitted after finishing the sixth grade of the primary school. Craftsmanship may be learned in various supplementary courses and also under the apprenticeship-system.

Post-primary technical education may be continued in the so-called secondary technical schools and after that in the technical colleges. The technical school on the secondary level has a two-year course. It is created to prepare pupils for subordinate posts in industry. The technical college is for the training of personnel for the intermediate functions in industry and commerce.

Conditions of entry are high. Gifted pupils, holding a certificate of a post-primary technical school, however, can also be admitted, but they have to follow a preparatory one-year course.

For the girls there is a great variety of vocational courses available. The post-primary schools for domestic science have a two- or three-year course; more than one-third of the lessons is devoted to general education. An increasing number of girls, after finishing post-primary schools for domestic science, find employment in industry and office; therefore the need to evaluate the aims of this education in view of the changing social circumstances is being stressed.

Pre-University Education

About 13 percent of the primary-school population enter the higher and pre-university schools. They comprise the Latin Grammar School, called "Gymnasium," the higher school for boys (also including girls), the higher school for girls, and the lyceum. The lyceum is mostly a combination of the above-mentioned schooltypes. This phase has five-year courses with the exception of the Latin grammar school which has a six-year course. The two upper grades are streamed in A and B streams. In the A-stream Greek and Latin are emphasized, in the B-stream mathematics and physics. In the A-stream of the higher schools for boys the social sciences and the languages are stressed and in the B-stream mathematics and physics.

After passing the final examinations all these differentiations of instruction give admission to various departments of the university with the exception of the higher schools for girls. So girls who want to enter the university follow schools with programs identical to those of the boys. The commercial schools do not prepare for the university. They are oriented toward more practical studies. They give entrance to a number of specialized institutions.

Special Education

To this section belong the schools for physically or mentally handicapped pupils, the special classes for sickly children and the schools for bargees' children. Much interesting work has been done in the field of teaching-methods and organization. About 27 percent of the primary-school population attends these schools.

Not Included in the Survey

The school system is of course more differentiated than this survey shows. Only the main lines have been explained and many differentiations in schools and instruction, such as teaching methods and aim and setting, have been neglected. Vocational education shows many varieties such as schools for social work and the academy of dramatic art, schools for painters and for other craftsmen.

University education and further education for young people over compulsory age are also not included.

The Ministry of Education in the Hague and the educational division of the Dutch embassies edit booklets and pamphlets in English about these schools, *e.g. Digest* of the Kingdom of the Netherlands.

Educational Problems

The way the Dutch people are realising their educational duties is due to the specific situation in the Netherlands, although educational issues may have been influenced by the neighbouring countries. From 1840-1920 the dominating question was that of freedom of education for the non-state, mostly denominational schools and the state schools. This conflict ended with the financial equalization of the state and non-state schools, which are now financed from public funds on an equal base, however on strictly stated conditions concerning the curriculum, qualification of teachers, and the like.

The principle of freedom of education had in its wake a highly centralizing effect on school administration. The Ministry of Education is the administrative centre for all educational affairs, together with the inspectorate and the educational council, whose members are recognized experts in this field.

The Dutch are highly sensitive in questions concerning religion, and so the various religious groupings are anxiously guarding their constitutional rights. This made itself felt during the discussions about the new Education Act, the so-called Mammoth Act. Although highly important educational issues were at stake, the discussions often sanded in petty religious bias.

The Post-Primary Education Act

In 1963 the discussions about the aims and structure of Dutch education, which had lasted for more than ten years, came to an end: The Act regulating all post-primary education was accepted by parliament. However, workable solutions are still to be found, as in this Act only the design of the new Dutch educational system is laid down.

Some Main Issues

Economic development of the Netherlands after World War II has already been mentioned. The steady growth in industrial employment and the decrease of manpower in agriculture made an adaptation in education necessary. As a result, many now superfluous agricultural schools were closed, as experiments were made to combine technical and agricultural training with a view to the technological impact in agriculture. As in all Western countries, also here the technological revolution stresses the necessity of training qualified workers on all levels. Closely connected with this phenomenon is the question of how the new generation can be made familiar with the basic principles and methods by which the increasingly technical age progresses. This also includes the need for more intense social education, such as civics and knowledge of human relations.

An international phenomenon is also the greater social mobility. The structure of education however is based on rather static social divisions. It was said in an article about Dutch Education[2] that children of the lower classes were inclined to continue their education only at vocational schools for boys, at advanced primary schools for boys and girls, and at domestic schools for girls. Children of the middle-classes continued their education mostly at advanced primary schools, and at the Higher schools, the Grammar school, and the Lyceum. Children of the upper classes only attend the pre-university schools, their ability permitting.

Access to the highest forms of education, not only for the happy few but for all classes, is now generally acknowledged. The question is how to realize it. It has been remarked[3] that widening of the educational opportunities in too short a time might lead to a lowering of the standards of education. "Thus the challenge is to steer a course between the Scylla of wasting a large percentage of talented and aspiring youth and the Charybdis of lowering standards of excellence." A realization of these goals would mean a flexible transfer between the school-types, horizontally and vertically. It also would mean a replacing of the present rigid selection procedures by a guidance period and slowly increasing differentiations.

Therefore a great interest has arisen for the comprehensive school, especially in the form in which it has been realized in the American high school. It also would mean a replacing of the rather uniform and rigid system of final examinations by a more individualized system of obligatory and free subjects.

The New Structure

In the Act, a tripartite structure is introduced: preparatory university-education, general education, and vocational education. General education is planned on three levels, higher, middle and lower, which corresponds to a tripartite structure of vocational education.

Moreover, there is a vertical connection between these three levels of general education and those of vocational education. To alleviate the rigid admission procedures a so-called bridge-year has been introduced, which functions as a bridge between primary education (sixth grade) and post-primary education. By observation and psychological testing, but especially by new teaching-methods which are more pupil-centred, the ability of the pupils may come to light in this year and make it possible to transfer the child to that department of post-primary education where it has the best chances to succeed. It will take time, however, to realize these ideas by means of betterment of teacher-training, educational innovation courses, and educational research.

Teacher-Training

The bottleneck of Dutch education is the training of teachers for pre-university schools. The difficulty is how to find a working compromise between academic subject-training and professional training, between the study of a special field of knowledge and the study of methods of teaching. A positive result of the last few years is that the professional training is now generally regarded as of the utmost importance. In the other sections teacher-training is on a higher level. But also here much has still to be done to realize a more pupil-centred attitude.

Educational Reform

Sponsored by the teacher organizations and subventioned by the Ministry of Education, the pedagogical centres try to introduce renewed methods and attitudes in the schools. These activities range from conferences and courses to real curriculum-development projects.

Educational Research

The situation of educational research in the Netherlands still shows a rather diversified picture. At the

2. C. F. E. Velema. "Primary and Post-primary Education in the Netherlands," *Comparative Education Review*, 7 (1963/64), pp. 119-124.

3. J. van Lutzenburg Maas. "The 'Mammoth Law' Reforms in Dutch Education," *Comparative Education Review*, 7 (1963/64), pp. 279-285.

present moment discussions are going on to find a way to centralize and coordinate educational research, both fundamental and applied.

Some Administrative Aspects

In a country which cherishes freedom so much and which is characterized by so many diversified groupings, cooperation is a necessity. Just as the equalization of state and non-state schools had a centralizing effect, this also happened with the teacher unions and educational centres. Characteristic for Holland is its several over-covering organizations. All these boards and commissions have a controlling function. About two-fifths of the employees are organized. The teachers' organizations comprise three-fourths of the teachers of all levels.

A comparison of teachers' salaries with those of other levels of occupation is difficult because so many factors determine the salaries. Under discussion is the question of merit-rating, but this only reveals how little is still known about the function of the teacher. On questions of social prestige and social mobility some research has been done.

SELECTED BIBLIOGRAPHY

Historical

Barnouw, A. J. *The Dutch, a portrait study of the people of Holland.* New York, 1940.
Bree, L. W. de. *Het platteland leert lezen en schrijven.* Amsterdam, 1946.
Eck, P. L. van. *Hoe 't vroeger was.* Groningen, 1927.
Edmundson, G. *History of Holland.* Cambridge, 1922.
Fortgens, H. W. *Meesters, Scholieren en Grammatica.* Zwolle, 1956.
———. *Schola latina.* Zwolle, 1958.
Idenburg, Ph. J. *Education in the Netherlands.* The Hague, 1951.
Post, R. R. *Scholen en Onderwijs in Nederland gedurende de Middeleeuwen.* Utrecht, 1954.
Renier, G. J. *The Dutch Nation.* London, 1944.
Schoengen, M. *Geschiedenis van het onderwijs in Nederland.* Amsterdam, 1911, vlg.
Stellwag, H. W. F. "Problems and Trends in Dutch Education." *Int. Rev. of Ed.,* vol. 3, nr. 1, 1957.

The Educational System

Beck, Robert. "Reflections on Dutch Education." *School and Society,* 44 (1958), pp. 240-242.
Digest of the Kingdom of the Netherlands. Education, Arts, and Science, The Hague: Netherlands Government Information Service.
Idenburg, Ph. I. *Schets van het Nederlands Schoolwezen* (Outline of the Dutch School System). Groningen: Wolters, 1964. *Note:* A survey of education in Western Europe is prepared by the German International Educational Institute to replace the study of Hylla, E., and Wrinkle, W. L., *Die Schulen in West-Europa,* Bad Nauheim, Christian Verlag, 1953.

Stellwag, H. W. F. "Problems and Trends in Dutch Education." *International Review of Education,* vol. III (1957), pp. 54-67.
Thomas, J., and Majault, J. *Primary and Secondary Education Modern Trends and Common Problems,* Strasbourg: Council for Cultural Cooperation of the Council of Europe, 1963.
Velema, E. "Primary and Post-Primary Education in the Netherlands." *Comparative Education Review,* 7, (1963/64), pp. 119-124.
Verlinden, J. A. A. "Public and Private Education in the Netherlands." *The Educational Forum,* 22 (1957), pp. 51-57.
World Survey of Education II, Primary Education. Paris: UNESCO, 1958.

Act on Post-Primary Education (1963)

Gelder, L. van. "The Bridge-Year." *International Review of Education,* vol. 6, (1960), pp. 468-471.
Lutzenburg Maas, J. van. "The Mammoth Law Reforms in Dutch Education." *Comparative Education Review,* 7, (1963/64), pp. 279-285.
Stellwag, H. W. F. "Die Schulgesetze in den Niederlanden als Beispiel allgemeiner Tendenzen im Europäischen Erziehungswesen." *Pädagogische Rundschau,* 18. Jhrg. (1964), pp. 1071-1086.
Wing, R. L. "Recent Changes in Dutch Education." Thesis of the Faculty of the Graduate School of Education, Harvard University, 1959.

Teacher-Training and Educational Research

Male, G. A. *Teacher Education in the Netherlands, Belgium, and Luxembourg.* U. S. Department of Health, Education and Welfare, 1960, no. 4.
Stellwag, H. W. F. "The Attitudes of Teachers Towards Their Profession in the Netherlands." *Yearbook of Education,* London, 1963.

For Statistical Information

Central Bureau of Statistics, Oostduinlaan 2, The Hague.
F 1 — The Development of Dutch Education 1850-1950.
F 2 — Dutch Youth and its Education.
F 53 — School success and School failure in the Secondary School (generation 1949).

Addresses

The Teachers-Unions:
Dutch Teachers Organisation (NOV), Herengracht 56, Amsterdam.
Roman Catholic Teachers Organisation (KOV), Koninginnegracht 70, the Hague.
Protestant Teachers Organisation (PCOV), Madoerastraat 17, the Hague.

The Pedagogical Centres

General Pedagogical Centre (APC), P. C. Hooftstraat 149, Amsterdam-Z.
Educational Study Centre (OSC), Oranje Nassaulaan 51, Amsterdam.
Roman Catholic Pedagogical Centre (KPC), Koninginnegracht 70, the Hague.

Protestant Pedagogical Centre (CPS), Laan van Nieuw Oost-Indië, the Hague.

The University Institutes
for Educational Research

Pedagogical-Didactical Institute, University of Amsterdam, Herengracht 196 '', Amsterdam-C., Director Prof. Dr. H. W. F. Stellwag.

Pedagogical Institute of the Free University of Amsterdam, Vossiusstraat 56, Amsterdam, Director Dr. J. de Wit.

Pedagogical Institute, State University of Groningen, Oude Kijk in 't Jattstr. 41 a., Director Prof. Dr. H. Nieuwenhuis.

Pedagogical Institute, State University of Leiden, Stationsweg 25, Director Prof. Dr. L. de Klerk.

Pedagogical Institute, Keizer Karel University of Nijmegen, Berg en Dalseweg 101, Director Prof. Dr. J. J. Gielen.

Pedagogical Institute, State University of Utrecht, Trans 14, Director Prof. Dr. M. J. Langeveld.

POLAND

Waclaw W. Soroka

HISTORICAL BACKGROUND

The year 1966 marked a millennium since Poland accepted Christianity from Rome by way of Bohemia. Christianization of Poland brought this country into the sphere of permanent influences of Western thought and Western civilization.

Behind its eastern boundaries, Eastern Christianity and Byzantine Civilization spread over Kievan Rus, then over Muscovy and Russia. The Mongol domination over southern Russia from the first part of the thirteenth to the end of the fifteenth centuries brought Islam and Oriental civilization to the threshold of Poland. Tatar and Turkish military incursions deep into Polish territories began in 1241 and continued to the eighteenth century. They constituted, together with commercial and intellectual intercourse, a fabric of relations that has left traces of oriental influences in Poland.

Between Poland and Muscovy there was the pagan country Lithuania, which was exposed to the pressures of the German orders of Sword and Cross that had begun the conversion of Balto-Slavic pagans with sword and fire, early in the thirteenth century. On another side the Russian princes pushed toward the West and the Baltic Sea, toward the very core of the Gedymin's patrimony. As a result, the first Polish contacts with Lithuania were established to increase common defense capacity. Cooperation grew in the face of common enemies. In the Union of Lublin of 1569, the Polish-Lithuanian Commonwealth was organized peacefully, including Lithuanian, White Russian, Ukrainian lands and people. It was a vast state; at the beginning of the seventeenth century it was larger than France and Germany together in their 1939 boundaries. The limited power of elective kings, the weak executive and judiciary agencies of state, "liberum veto," lack of a successful program that would solve the national aspirations of the Ukrainians and White Russians, and the religious complexities, social short-sightedness of the privileged in that "Republic of the Gentry" contributed to the downfall of the Commonwealth. Exterior pressures were generated by the absolute monarchies of Prussia, Russia, and Austria. The Polish-Lithuanian Commonwealth was partitioned at the end of the eighteenth century after 400 years of successful cooperation. From 1795 until 1918, Poland and Lithuania disappeared from the face of Europe with the exception of organizations with limited freedom of action and territorial dominion: the Duchy of Warsaw (1807-1814) and the Congress Kingdom of Poland, created at the Vienna Congress.

Education in Poland, both in its organization and content, was influenced by political and social changes throughout these years. In the first period of its existence, Poland was a monarchy with a medieval representation of society in the king's Council and in the regional conventions of the estates, temporal and spiritual. The equilibrium of the estates marked that period through the thirteenth and fourteenth centuries. By the end of the fifteenth century, the Polish Parliament had acquired the characteristics of a representative legislature. The Parliament was composed of three elements: the Chamber of Deputies, Senate, and King. Since 1505 it had arrogated the position that "nothing new can be enacted without the agreement of the Diet called *Seym*." At that time, the representatives of the cities still had rights and participated in the sessions of the central Diet that convened ordinarily each second year and in the regional Dietines. However, in the middle of the sixteenth century, the peasants did not develop their political rights and this group declined economically. They lost their legal status and protection by law and became attached to the land (*glebae adscripti*). The burghers also suffered curtailment of their rights and privileges. The gentry and clergy maintained and even developed their privileged status and political exclusiveness to the second half of the eighteenth century.

Poland did not pass through the period of absolute monarchy that began in Western Europe in the sixteenth century. The kings of Poland were elective, and before assuming the throne they signed *pacta conventa,* a contract by which they committed themselves to respect the existing laws and to perform particular tasks as agreed upon in negotiations with the representatives of the Polish Diet. Since the end of the sixteenth century, all mature male members of the gentry were entitled to participate in the direct election of kings. This was the so-called election *viritim,* an attempt at introduction of direct democracy to a large country exposed to foreign intrigues and interior factions. The situation was changed at the end of the eighteenth century in the Constitution of May 3, 1791. The hereditary monarchy was introduced, "liberum veto" abolished, executive and judiciary organs improved. In the same constitution, full rights were granted to burghers. The Jews were given habeas corpus rights by that time. The protection of law was accorded to peasants.

Various ethnic groups settled on the territory of Poland, mixing into historical unity. There were Poles, Ukrainians, White Russians, Bohemians, Slovaks, and Russians of Slavic extraction. The Lithuanians added their Balto-Slavic elements as did Old Prussians. The Wallachians, Armenians, Turks, and Tatars contributed to the Polish nation throughout the centuries. Jews settled in Poland in the first centuries of its existence. Throughout the twelfth century their numbers increased as a result of persecutions in the countries of southern and western Europe and on the routes of the Crusaders. The first general statute that granted them legal protection in Poland was issued in 1264 by Boleslaw Pobożny (the Pious). The privileges were confirmed and curtailed in response to many historical factors. Poland, however, has continued to receive many Jews who were persecuted and expelled from other European countries up to the end of the eighteenth century. In the nineteenth century the Russian pogroms contributed to the settlement of Jews in central Poland. The last event of this character occurred in 1939, when the Jews were expelled from Germany just before World War II and were received by Poland among other countries.

In 1580 new privileges were extended to the Jews throughout the entire territory of Poland by King Stefan Batory. In the period of reforms initiated by the May 3 Constitution of 1791, Jews were granted "Habeas Corpus" rights, as well as the right to keep Christians as servants. The general economic factors in the country, however, did not change the difficulties encountered by masses of poorer Jews.

Germans settled in the devastated regions of Poland immediately after the first Tatar inroads. They were easily Polonized and constituted an element for urban development. Scotch, French, English, Dutch, and other ethnic groups remained in Poland as a result of religious persecutions in their countries or in the course of wars and normal migrations.

For the purposes of this study, four periods of Polish historical development will be distinguished. The first includes the period from the beginnings of the Polish state to the partitions at the end of the eighteenth century, climaxed by the third partition in 1795. The second period includes the following 123 years under the partitions and foreign domination; a time when the Polish nation existed within the foreign political organizations of Austria, Prussia, and Russia. The limited autonomy of the Warsaw Duchy and of the Congress Kingdom falls into this period. The third period began with renewed political independence in 1918, and ended with the Second World War and occupation of Poland by Nazi Germany. The fourth period began after defeat of Nazi Germany. Poland found itself then in the sphere of Soviet Russia, within the bloc of People's Republics. This has influenced the structure of Poland's educational systems, its long- and short-range goals as well as the forces shaping contemporary education. The particular stages proper to a history of education will be brought out in full detail within the frame of this general division.

POLAND BEFORE THE PARTITIONS

The first schools in Poland date from the twelfth century. These were the cathedral schools conducted for preparation of indigenous youth to the priesthood. A library at Wawel castle in Cracow existed in 1110. The parish schools appeared in the thirteenth and fourteenth centuries. Although Latin was the language of instruction, the knowledge of Polish was required from the clergy very early. The Synod of Wroclaw (Breslau) of 1248 prescribed that prayers must be said in Polish in that province. Soon, the translation of the Biblical expositions and Latin authors into Polish was recommended.

In the fourteenth century, the gentry and burghers began to enroll in the schools for the purpose of gaining useful secular knowledge, not for the priesthood. This was, however, exceptional. Among the educated secular personalities, many acquired their training abroad in Italian and French schools. The colonies of Polish students at Western universities have been traced back to the thirteenth century.

The number of local schools and students was growing. The Middle Ages ended in Poland with foundations laid for a university. It was formally established May 12, 1364, in Cracow as the second university in East Central Europe, following the Charles University of Prague. In its beginnings, it possessed three departments: Law, Medicine, Arts and Letters (patterned after Bologna and Padua). It was reorganized in 1400, adding a department of Theology. Paris was the model for Cracow University in this new period.

An increasing number of bachelor degrees produced by the University contributed to the upswing in education in the entire country. The number of schools kept growing. Monastic orders added their schools to the others in the system of education. In addition, new universities were added: Wilno (Vilnius) by King Stefan Batory in 1578, Lwów (Lviv) by King John Jan Kazimierz in 1661, and an academy-college at Zamość by Hetman and Chancellor Jan Zamoyski in 1595.

Objectives of the schools were related to the needs as they were formed by religious, social, and political forces. Recruitment and education of the clergy constituted the earliest of them. During the first years, Cracow University answered the need for lawyers and administrators. Administrators, diplomats, priests, and teachers were needed after the reorganization of the university in connection with the deepening union and growing Polish-Lithuanian Commonwealth. Pursuit of knowledge aligned the lives of nobles and burghers to streams of European thought which appeared parallel to what was visible in Western Europe, although suffering a time lag.

Poland embraced the ideas of the Renaissance and Humanism in the second half of the fifteenth century. The sixteenth century saw a general increase in the number of schools in Poland as well as increased enrollment of secular students to all schools. Two groups of schools developed in that time in addition to those from previous eras: the schools that were founded by various Protestant Churches and other religious groups that originated during the Reformation as well as the Jesuits' schools.

Protestant and other dissident schools came to prominence in Poland in the years between 1550 and 1650. The oldest in this group were the Calvinist schools. Other educational centers included the Lutheran and Arian or Anti-Trinitarian schools. They spread over the territory of Poland and into some parts of Lithuania and some parts of the Ukrainian lands. They are duly considered a factor in expanding Western Civilization in Eastern Europe. The type of Protestant high schools, patterned on the experience of Jean Sturm in Strasbourg, had prevailed in Poland in both organization and goals. It involved personal work by outstanding western Protestant educators, such as Pierre Statorius from Lausanne who learned Polish and made use of this language at his school in Pinczow (Polesie). The Protestant schools in Poland represented at that time the centers of keen thought and a high level of intellectual ability.

Jesuits came to Poland in the second half of the sixteenth century. After an initial struggle, they managed to dominate Catholic education in Poland and established their hold in national education. This was the situation until the middle of the eighteenth century with the Jesuits concentrating on high schools. Their colleges, of the uniform high school type, were established in all the provinces of the Polish-Lithu-

anian Commonwealth. As long as the Protestant schools existed, the level of the Jesuit schools was high. The competitive effort kept them from stagnation and complacency. When Protestantism in Poland yielded to the Counter-Reformation, the challenge disappeared and decay began.

Another type of school developed in the Ukrainian territories, as well as in White Russia that was attached to the Polish-Lithuanian Commonwealth. There, in addition to Roman Catholic and Protestant schools, Greek Orthodox and Greek Catholic or Uniat schools were established.

Parish schools developed in the cities and villages throughout all Poland until the second half of the seventeenth century. Then, with the introduction of the organ to the liturgy, the needs of the Church changed. This affected the school system by decreasing the effort devoted to education. Also, civil wars and devastation of the countryside in that century contributed to the decline of parish schools. The interest of peasants in these schools was curtailed by a prohibition against their sending their children to schools. This prohibition was originated by the gentry and enacted by the Diet.

By the sixteenth century, schools for girls were begun in Poland. The Protestant schools first organized special programs for the girls, followed later by numerous Catholic Convents. From the middle of the eighteenth century, commoners also placed girls at the town and parish schools.

Polish schools passed through a period of decline that coincided with the full victory of Counter-Reformation and the commanding educational position of the Jesuits. This decline was visible at the end of the seventeenth century and continued to the middle of the eighteenth century. By that time, the ideas of the Enlightenment had penetrated Poland. The ideas stimulated an intellectual revolution, bringing a re-evaluation of traditional concepts and institution, as well as powerful reform in all fields of life, especially in politics and in education.

Educational reforms began by the middle of the eighteenth century and were the work of one man: Stanislaw Konarski, a Piarist. When seventy-one, he was honored with a commemorative medal from King Stanislaw August. Konarski studied in France and Italy, and imbibed the ideas of Locke and Rollin in addition to the contemporary French educational practice. His reforms began in 1740 with the founding of Collegium Nobilium in Warsaw. This was a highly selective school for the aristocracy. It had to produce an elite of honest people and ardent patriots educated to play a role in the reforms of the country. The curricular changes included instruction of universal and national history, geography, physics, economics, and mathematics. Two years of law studies beyond the normal seven-year program were optional. Thorough teaching of modern languages was emphasized; the Polish language and literature were used in instruction. Grammatical studies of Latin were curtailed in favor of increased interest for classical literature and for rhetoric. Verbosity and flowery oratory were banished in favor of clarity and objectivity. Instruction, although improved and broadened, was considered a minor part of education, the major part being the shaping of man, his character and ability to live in and improve society.

Konarski was opposed in his own order as well as by conservative elements in the nation. Nevertheless, he was victorious. His reforms were finally accepted in all the Piarist colleges. To implement them the preparation of teachers was given special attention. Stress was placed on didactical and methodological subjects. The most promising candidates for teaching were sent to Western Universities to complete their education.

The entire system was defined in the Piarist "laws" for high schools. Their policy was aimed at encouraging further reform in the future. The new Piarist reforms were met first with resistance, then with acceptance by the Jesuit schools in their six colleges for nobles as well as in their common colleges with an enrollment of about 20,000 students including burghers and peasants.

By 1766, in the same atmosphere of daring, the king founded a secular school, the Corps of Cadets, which was led by Prince Adam Czartoryski. Among others, Tadeusz Kościuszko and Julian Ursyn Niemcewicz, later connected with the American War for Independence, were alumni.

Private efforts by two orders and from the secular Corps of Cadets were instrumental in improvement of schools and education and in strengthening the reform endeavors of enlightened citizens. The evolution moved in the direction of government responsibility for national education. Pope Clement XIV's dissolution of the Jesuit Order in 1773 precipitated this evolution. In 1773, the Commission of National Education, the first European Ministry of Education, was created by the Polish Diet. This body had to take over the closing Jesuit schools as well as all Jesuit possessions. The confiscated property of the Jesuits was assigned to national education. The Commission had also to work out a new national system of education and to administer all schools in the nation. Outstanding personalities were elected to the Commission: Bishop Michał Poniatowski, a freethinker Joachim Chreptowicz, Prince Adam Czartoryski, Andrzej Zamoyski, Ignacy Potocki, Pierre Du Pont, and others.

The Commission undertook inquiries in order to initiate projects and formulate opinions related to national education. The procedure appeared successful, and in the twenty years the Commission was active, all schools were re-organized. At the universities, research and laboratory work was promoted. High schools were unified and spread throughout all provinces. Their programs were related to the needs of the country. The burghers were given access to all educational facilities. Schools for peasants were organized and expanded. The tendencies toward equality of treatment and opportunities for peasant children were pronounced, although they had not yet risen to the challenge.

Among the goals, the education of the mind was emphasized together with moral and physical education. Responsibility for a positive stand in society was formulated and stressed. The idea of universal education was thus clearly reflected.

Seminars for teacher preparation were organized and a Society for Elementary Books was established. This Society published valuable textbooks for schools, either Polish or from foreign translations.

The work of the Commission was highly significant. It nourished the nation during the partitions, and it contributed an element of national heritage for subsequent educational reforms in Poland, after 1918.

IN THE TIME OF PARTITIONS

Polish education was damaged to varying degrees and in different ways during and after the partitions by Austria, Prussia, and Russia. Austria was the foremost in this work of destruction. Germanization of her portion of Poland was one of the essential goals of the new Austrian schools. Later, Austria reversed these policies. With the re-organization of the Austrian state into a dual monarchy in 1867, autonomy was granted to subordinate lands. By this, the Austrian part of Poland saw the re-introduction of Polish as the language of instruction and administration at Lwów and Kraków universities, at Lwów Politechnic, and at other schools. Both universities and the Politechnic soon became the centers of high scholarship and intensive national intellectual life. More children of burghers and peasants found access to university studies. Women also began to enroll in 1897. These conditions prevailed till 1918 in contrast to the strong Russification and Germanization prevalent in the other two parts of Poland.

Prussia closed most Polish schools during and after the partitions. German was then introduced in the upper classes of the middle schools as the language of instruction. New German schools were created. Polish was continuously limited and ignored, until in 1901 all instruction in the schools was done in German, and prayers had to be read in that language. The children's protest to this arrangement and their school strike in Września was cruelly broken to the astonishment of more sensitive circles of European public opinion.

In the Russian portion of Poland, after initial curtailment of Polish education, Tsar Alexander appeared the most liberal of the partitioning autocrats. All lands taken by Russia in the three partitions were organized into the Wilno School Province. Adam

Czartoryski, Jr., a friend of Alexander and Russia's Foreign Minister, became Curator of this province. The University of Wilno directed the entire system of scholastic education in the province. It soon became an outstanding center of learning and research. The province also was able to provide other schools with good teachers and professional directors.

One high school-college, the work of Tadeusz Czacki and Hugo Kołłątaj, deserves particular attention. This is the Lyceum in Krzemieniec, inaugurated in 1805. The school was open to the youth of all social and religious groups, to the gentry, burghers, and peasants; to Jews, Orthodox, and Catholics, with equality. It was based on three cycles of study. In the first four years, the memory was to be exercised through a curriculum of five foreign languages. The next six years were devoted to training reflection through study of mathematics, logic, history, geography, natural sciences, law, and literature. Drawing, dancing, music, swimming, horsemanship, and fencing were included under the best instructors. After ten years of intensive all-round education, the students could enroll for specialization in higher mathematics, mechanics, medicine, and Slavic philology. Long-range goals included practical education, civic spirit, and readiness to serve the needs of society. The Lyceum continued till 1833. Senator Novosiltsev said that "Czacki's school had arrested for a hundred years the Russification of Poland's Eastern Borderlands."

In the Duchy of Warsaw and in the Polish Kingdom, created at the Congress of Vienna, education was administered by governmental agencies. The instructions of 1808 organized elementary education as public and secular, equally accessible to boys and girls of all social and religious groups but not compulsory. By 1821, 342 elementary public schools were active in the cities and towns and 880 in the countryside, with 37,623 pupils in attendance.

The normal elementary schools were supplemented by district schools for poor children of bigger cities based on the experiments of Pestalozzi and Fellenberg as well as on voluntary private efforts as developed by Andrew Bell and Joseph Lancaster. Stanislaw Staszic, one of the remarkable personalities of that time, started Sunday schools for craftsman youth. Since 1817, the school for the deaf and dumb began to serve the handicapped. The work was accompanied with a success in the education of teachers and in publications in the field of methodology and pedagogy as well as with the organization of interest groups.

The number of secondary schools was low; there were ten high schools preparing pupils for university studies, in addition to one Piarist Collegium Nobilium. After 1816, the final exam, resembling a Baccalaureat, was introduced.

In 1818 a university in Warsaw was founded with five departments: Theology, Law, Medicine, Philosophy and Mathematics, Sciences and Fine Arts. Polish was the language of instruction with Latin being used in some courses. The professional schools included Mining, Forestry, and Technical Arts.

Already in 1823 the situation had begun to deteriorate. The discovery of secret student organizations: the Society of Lovers of Virtue and the Philomaths at Wilno University was followed by student trials, imprisonment, and deportation. Lack of financial support stunted the elementary schools. Finally, the uprising of 1830-31 resulted in submission of that territory to the Organic Statute of 1832 and to increased Russification. The short period of recurrent autonomy during the governorship of Alexander Wielopolski was followed by a new uprising in 1863. Then by 1867 Russian replaced Polish in all schools including the elementary. The University of Warsaw was closed in 1831. In 1862 the Main school was opened instead, but by 1869 it was replaced by an imperial Russian University charged with special tasks of Russification.

The situation was somewhat relaxed after the Russian Revolution of 1905, but the objectives of Russian schools in Poland had not changed. Their purpose continued to be the Russification of Poland. National aspirations in the field of education were, therefore, satisfied in private schools, tutoring systems, and in clandestine teaching.

In that period, some additional elements of education must be mentioned in this chapter: Polish works in pedagogy, professional journals and associations as well as learned societies supporting and broadening education in those areas were created. From among several names in pedagogical studies, that of Bronislaw Trentowski (1808-1869) the author of *Chowanna*, and Eweryst Estkowski (1820-1856), who edited the journal *Szkoła Polska*, are best known.

Among numerous professional organizations and learned societies related to education at that time was the Society for Assistance in Learning organized by Dr. K. Marcinkowski in 1841 at Poznań. The Society of Friends of Learning originated in Warsaw in 1800 with Stanislaw Staszic as president. In 1873 the Academy of Arts and Sciences was organized in Cracow, soon to become a center of learning and of cooperation among scholars in the country. In addition, the Society of People's Schools as well as School's Alma Mother (Macież Szkolna) exerted a deep influence on the education of that time and aided its spread over the entire nation.

AN INDEPENDENT POLAND

In 1918, a reborn Poland faced enormous war devastations, incurred by the fortunes of war in German-Russian and Austro-Hungarian-Russian front operations. The destruction capped a century of neglect and exploitation in that territory by the partitioning powers. These were the imposing factors in the background of the tasks to be undertaken by an independent nation in turbulent, post-war Europe.

In education, the most pressing need was the unification of three school systems left over from the time of partitions, Austrian, Prussian, and Russian, and to build foundations for a national education that would correspond to the needs and aspirations of the country.

A set of assumptions resulted from the discussions that were undertaken to answer the questions as to what kind of education the nation wanted and could afford. Common agreement was that education had to be considered a public matter. The central government was made principal agent to represent the public concern for education. The participation of local links of self-government, of private citizens, of the churches and professional or cultural organizations was assured in formation of educational content, in maintenance of schools, and in administrative operation of education.

Two types of schools have been adopted: public and private. Both are subject to uniform state administration and uniform requirements for accreditation based on a standard program of instruction. Public education had to be free of charge and equally accessible to all citizens. The principle of universality was combined with the compulsory character of elementary education established for children from the seventh to the fourteenth year of age. This period could be extended in some instances.

Acceptance of the principle of public education involved the important issue of religion. Public schools were to teach religion according to the creed and church affiliation of the pupil. The churches concerned were granted rights to conduct and control teaching of religion. The instructors were paid by the state. Jewish youth were freed from attending school on Saturdays.

The long-range goals of education included work on intellect as well as on moral, emotional, and physical factors to fully develop personalities. A program of character building was initiated, much like that of the English schools. French influences were reflected in the stress upon intellectual awakening and thoroughness. The peculiar situation of Poland, surrounded by menacing neighbors, Communist Russia and aggressive Nazi Germany, resulted in emphasis on patriotic values, a priority on individual obligation to the nation superior to any personal right; on a readiness to sacrifice personal life in the service of the nation.

The legal provisions for educational matters were enacted through the Decree of February 7, 1919, as well as through the Bill of July 13, 1920, and of February 17, 1922. The Law of March 11, 1932, on organization of education as well as that of March 15, 1933, on academic schools established a new educational period that grew with the first year of independence. The provisions of those laws will be followed in relation to particular problems discussed throughout this chapter. Their formal result was expressed in an administrative structure of education that was valid for the entire period. The Ministry of Religious Denominations and Public Education was set up at the top of this structure. The universities and other schools of higher education were granted autonomy that was significantly curtailed by the Law of 1932. To the end of that period, however, they were directly related to the Ministry.

In relation to the remaining schools, the country was divided into school districts headed by Curators (District Superintendents). The districts included inspectorates that correspond roughly to the counties in general public administration. The Inspectors (County Superintendents) directed the elementary schools in their regions, while high schools were out of their jurisdiction. The latter depended upon their directors and faculty acting under the supervision of Curators assisted by specialized officers.

Education developed on three levels: elementary, secondary, and higher; the last included universities and similar schools.

A compulsory seven-year period was approved for elementary education. The school obligation began at seven and ended at fourteen years if not prolonged in particular instances. A period of preschool education was proposed as desirable. An insignificant portion of the children could find a place in the kindergartens. The state left them to the initiative of local communities and private individuals. An effort was made to maintain public seminars for education of kindergarten instructors.

In spite of shortages of school buildings, teachers, and school supplies, the number of elementary schools increased rapidly as did the number of pupils and instructors. Teachers were recruited from among volunteers with sufficient general intellectual preparation. Private houses were rented and appropriated for school rooms. Table 1 illustrates that growth.

TABLE 1

Growth of Elementary Schools

Year	Schools	Teacher	Pupils	Total Number of Youth at School Age	Youth Not Enrolled in School
1910	15,133	36,637	2,227,517		
1920	21,875	40,912	2,473,646	3,900,000	1,426,354
1921					1,709,000
1924	30,381	65,665	3,395,370		
1928/29					340,000
1935/36					600,000
1937/38					512,000

Tasks of elementary education included teaching pupils to read and write, to develop their understanding of events in their lives, to increase their ability to reason, and to prepare them for life both environmentally and professionally. The basic curriculum included in the seven-year program is contained in Table 2.

The achievements of this schooling was significant. Illiteracy inherited from the partition period dropped. The general education level of the nation was raised and was expressed in a rising demand for books, journals, and professional improvement programs. The elementary education, however, failed at two points. First, not all citizens were provided equal-

phasis in literature, national and European history, modern languages and Latin. The Mathematical-Scientific stressed mathematics and natural sciences. Curricular subjects were compulsory in the frame of each chosen type. A thirty-hour, six-day week of class-work was supplemented by homework and assigned reading in the 218-day school year.

Table 3 will be used as an example of curriculum for five upper classes of humanistic-type gymnasium.

TABLE 2

Curriculum of the Elementary Schools
Poland: As Established in 1921

Subjects	Hours per week						
	Grades						
	I	II	III	IV	V	VI	VII
Religion	2	2	2	2	2	2	2
Polish	9	8	6	5	4	4	4
Foreign Language					3	3	3
Arithmetic and Geometry	3	4	4	4	4	4	4
Natural Science			2	3	3	3	4
Geography			2	2	2	2	2
History			2	2	2	2	2
Manual Training	2	3	3	4	4	4	4
Drawing	1	2	2	2	2	2	2
Music and Singing	1	2	2	2	2	2	1
Games and Gymnastics	3	3	3	2	2	2	2
Total	21	24	28	28	30	30	30

TABLE 3

Curriculum of the Upper Classes
(Humanistic Type)

Required Subjects	Hours a week by year					Total Time (i.e., 5 Years)
	IV	V	VI	VII	VIII	
Religion	2	2	2	2	2	10
Polish Language and Literature	4	4	4	4	4	20
Latin, Lang. and Lit.	6	5	5	5	4	25
French, English, or German	4	4	4	4	4	20
History	3	4	4	5	3	17½
Geography	2	2	-	-		7½
Natural History	2	2	-	-	-	4
Physics, Chemistry, and cosmography	-	-	3	4	4	11
Mathematics	4	4	3	3	3	17
Introduction to Philosophy	-	-	-	-	3	3
Physical Training	3	3	3	3	3	15
	30	30	30	30	30	150

ly with education since only in cities and larger villages were fully developed schools located. Inferior types of elementary schools operated in smaller villages and taught the children in the framework of one to four grades or one and two grades. The second point of failure is related to the function of elementary schools in preparing students for secondary education. This function could only be performed by fully equipped schools. Therefore, the children of smaller villages were limited in their chances to get to the high schools. These chances were decreased additionally by the selective character of the high schools, requiring entrance exams not easily passed without careful preparation.

Until 1938, high schools were based on an eight-year program. In 1932, another system had been introduced, composed of a four-year gymnasium and two-year lyceum. In both of the systems, the studies ended with maturity exams. They were composed of written and oral components, taken before the Governmental Examination Commission.

There were three basic types of private and public high schools: Classical, Humanistic, and Mathematical-Scientific, the last being later subdivided. The Classical type emphasized Latin and Greek languages, literature, and civilization. The Humanistic provided for a broad cultural training with an em-

As seen by this table, the total number of hours spent in five years on particular subjects is related to time devoted in the scholastic year. The time spent on modern foreign languages, for example, is equal to 20 x 31 (weeks in 218 working days) or 620 hours. In regard to history (including economic geography) it would total 775 hours for each student in the five years.

The primary goal of the high schools was to prepare students for university or other academic studies. The alumni of the high schools of general type did not, therefore, develop training of professional character. Polish high schools were selective but were accessible to all.

Vocational education was diversified and based on five or seven grades of elementary education, or on four or six years of general secondary education. These operated on lower, secondary or lyceum level. About 1,000 schools of this type operated before the last war with about 100,000 students. They were related to all fields of national economy and social need.

There were twenty-eight universities and other schools on the academic level before World War II and seven high schools without full academic character formally granted. The granting of academic status was a prerogative of the Diet performed as a legislative act.

Among the universities, Jagiellonian University at Krakow, Jan Kazimierz University at Lwów, Stefan Batory University at Wilno, and Jósef Piłsudski University at Warsaw had a long historical tradition. These schools, along with the new Poznan University at Poznan were all higher governmental schools. Additionally, three other universities were privately supported. To the last group belonged Catholic University at Lublin, founded in 1918 as a continuation of the Catholic Academy of St. Petersburg, with secular departments, intensive research, and publications. It also became a center for student organizations going beyond nationalistic to the universal. Also two free Polish Universities at Warsaw and at Łódż were private.

Other higher schools included Politechnics, and other technical academies, agricultural schools and Veterinary Medicine Academies, commercial, economic, and political science schools, teacher-training institutions, schools of dentistry, of fine arts, of music and dramatics, and also of national defense. All the major fields of human knowledge were represented at least as one of the existing higher schools.

In those twenty-eight schools of higher education, some 48,000 students studied before World War II. In comparison with total Polish population of 1936-1937, there were 1,409 students per million inhabitants, while in Germany this ratio was 1,903 per million. In Great Britain this proportion was 1,383 per million; in Sweden, one year earlier, 1,975 per million, and in Latvia 3,817 per million.

Educational facilities available for national minorities included state-supported schools and institutes as well as legal provisions for private schools of minorities that could develop in that country. This was exhibited in relation to the elementary and secondary schools. Regarding higher education, "the universities in Warsaw and Cracow provided Ukrainian scholars with five chairs in their history, literature, and language," as it was presented by Professor Stanislaw Kot in his *Five Centuries of Polish Learning.* The Ukrainian Shevchenko Scientific Society in Lwów, founded in the nineteenth century with Polish assistance and goodwill developed vigorously with monthly subsidies from the Polish government, on the same scale as its fellow Polish societies; and, apart from that, it possessed a special source of income in that all state school textbooks in the Ukrainian language were issued in its press. In 1930, a Ukrainian Institute was created in Warsaw.

In the 1930s, nearly 100 Jewish Talmudic schools (*Yeshibots*) were active in Poland as

. . . they have flourished there for centuries. . . . The Yeshibot in Lublin was the recipient of government subsidies. Intellectual works in the field of Judaic (Yiddish)

studies were taught by the Jewish Institute, with its departments of literature, language, economics, and psychology as well as the special Institute for Hebrew Studies in Warsaw. This had two sections, one for theology and one for pedagogy. It served the students of the University of Warsaw who were seeking higher education for posts as Rabbis as well as for Judaic teaching positions in the middle schools.

The period of Poland's independence was marked by the development of education in all its aspects. Pedagogical research flourished, new publications were issued, contacts with the world centers of learning were maintained through the uninhibited free initiative of individuals and through professional organizations of teachers (and other workers in education) as well as through the universities and the Polish Academy of Arts and Sciences that maintained permanent stations in Paris and in Rome.

The war of 1939-1945 brought new devastations (many libraries were used by Germans as fuel) and destruction of the educational system. In the territory incorporated by the Reich, all Polish schools and educational institutions were closed. In other parts of Poland administered under General Gouvernement, universities and general high schools were shut down, contrary to international law. In an attempt to open them, several hundred university professors, as in Cracow, were arrested and deported to concentration camps or were executed in prison, as happened at the Catholic University of Lublin.

The Polish nation organized clandestine underground schools that operated at the risk of the lives of all involved. About 2,000,000 children on the elementary level, 55,000 on the secondary level, and 10,000 on the university level were served by this method of education. The textbooks were issued by clandestine printing shops.

In July, 1944, in Polish territory to the Wisla River, freedom was gained from Nazi occupation, and education faced new realities. All types of schools, including the Catholic University of Lublin, were opened in that territory by the fall of 1944. The foundation for a new, government-operated university in Lublin was laid. The situation was characterized by pressure from Communist political objectives and by the fact that a majority of the nation supported the Polish Government in London. This government had represented Poland in the struggle against Nazi forces, and it symbolized the hope for a democratic future. It enjoyed the recognition of the Western Democracies until July 5, 1945.

The Polish Government in London gave serious attention to the wartime educational problems as well as those of the future. The Minister of Religious Denominations and Public Education maintained contacts with the leaders of the underground Polish educational system and assisted with funds provided by the government for the Resistance Movement in occupied Poland. In addition, the programs for future reorganization of education were elaborated. The plans were thoroughly democratic, conceived in compliance with the democratic platform of the government headed first by General Władysław Sikorski (until his tragic death July 4, 1943), and then by Stanisław Mikołajczyk, a leader of the Polish Peasant Party. The government and its platform was supported by four political parties: Peasant, Christian Labor, Socialist, and a fraction of the National Party. Their leaders constituted the National Council, a kind of Polish Parliament in exile that was chaired by Ignace J. Paderewski and was supplemented by a secret National Council in Poland.

Among several works in the field of education organized abroad, some produced durable effects. To these belong the Polish Pedagogical Studies established at Edinburgh in 1943, Polish University in Great Britain (with a School of Medicine), as well as The Polish Institute of Arts and Sciences in New York that joined the members of The Polish Academy of Arts and Sciences who found themselves in the United States. In Switzerland, Polish officers and soldiers, interned after the capitulation of France in 1940, organized the entire network of education that helped many inmates of internment camps in obtaining university or secondary education. This was recognized by Swiss schools.

IN CONTEMPORARY POLAND

Builders of education in Poland after the Second World War faced unusually difficult problems. A great proportion of the nation was uprooted, deported, and held to forced labor or in concentration camps, consigned to the armed forces, to the home guerillas, affected by war murders and atrocities. For five years, the youth had been deprived of normal education, some entirely and some of Polish history and geography, some in the secret education suffered because of shortcomings inherent in clandestine teaching and learning.

Nationally, more than 28 percent of the school buildings were completely destroyed and in some regions up to 76 percent of their prewar number. Library holdings were 70 percent destroyed. Over 20,000 teachers of all types of schools perished in war or in the concentration camps. This extermination was only one of the forces decreasing human resources needed for the reconstruction of education. The educational process had been interrupted for five years through the closing of high schools and universities resulting in a substantial numerical decrease in educated people. In those five years, under normal conditions and at the capability of schools as seen in 1939, 30,000 would have received university or equivalent diplomas, 70-80,000 would have finished the vocational schools, 75,000 would have obtained maturity diplomas and would be prepared for admission to higher schools. All this had been lost.

The enormous tasks in the postwar reconstruction of education were complicated by the political objectives of the Communists who took over the administration of the country. These included the establishment of Socialism in Poland, the adjustment of their own system as well as of the educational content to Marxist theory and Soviet Russian experience, and to the revolutionary transformation of the society. The entire nation met on one point: that the education had to be rebuilt immediately, had to be good and equally accessible to all. The differences between the Communists and non-Communists have been sharp on such issues as the place of national tradition in education; the concept of national independence and freedom of action; the meaning and content of democracy and of its traditional respect for individual rights; the evaluation of economic efficiency of capitalistic and socialistic systems of production, that of the individual in relation to the society, and so on.

Beginning in 1944, eastern Poland, from the Bug River to the Vistula, freed that July from German occupation, saw the opening of schools corresponding to the needs and prior structure of prewar education. The foundation of the new educational system was laid in a project of administration on May 4, 1945. They were then accepted by the All-National Educational Convention in Lódz on June 17-18 and installed by the National Council as law. The new schools were to be uniform, gratuitous (free of charge) public, compulsory (for elementary education: from seven to fourteen, and even sixteen years of age). These principles were confirmed in the Bill of July 15, 1961, that constitutes the basis of the present educational organization, as developed in three distinct periods: 1945-1948; 1948-1960; and 1961 to date. The changes worked out in those periods are reflected in particular school types.

Nursery schools were accepted as the first level of education to be developed. All children from three to six years of age had access to a nursery school that performed two duties: social and educational. Socially, by taking care of small children, they made possible the employment of mothers. Educationally, they contributed to the development of children and to increasing the effectiveness of the elementary schools. The fully developed nursery schools included quiet play, active games, calisthenics, Polish, nature study, artistic and technical exercises, music, measuring and counting, and household chores. In the methodology, this principle prevails: "From the nearest to the farthest, from the easy to the difficult." The program is divided into one, two, three, or four grades. The nurseries operate from four to nine hours a day.

The nursery schools have remained more project than achievement. Only 10-33 percent of the children have found access to one. A very small fraction of those nursery schools are fully developed.

Children that have been given the opportunities in the best nursery schools represent, therefore, an elite, in contrast to equalitarian, education. Attempts at solving this problem are hampered by difficulties in means of communication and by limited resources that do not permit the payment of expenses on educational facilities. In discussions concerning the future, the educational functions of nursery schools will probably prevail over the social ones. The older children of five and six years of age will be enrolled by the new nursery schools first.

Existing nursery schools are maintained by the state, by local authorities, by industrial establishments, social organizations, and by the parents.

Elementary education is compulsory and universal. It begins at seven and ends at fourteen years of age. The obligation to attend school at that age has been extended by the decree of the State Council of March 23, 1956, requiring that children who did not finish the seventh grade be required to attend school until age sixteen.

The universality of elementary education has many aspects: the number of children embraced by the education, equality of basic education, the same chance being given to all children to enter the high schools.

Elementary schools were made accessible to all children.

In spite of high total attendance figures in elementary education, only a portion of the children finished the seventh grade by their fourteenth or even sixteenth year, after the 1956 reforms. M. Falski calls attention to the following figures: In 1952-53—476,000 pupils left the elementary schools. From this number, 345,000 or 72.4 percent had finished the seventh grade. The remaining 131,000 or 27.6 percent finished lower grades, some the first, second, or third only. They might be considered potential illiterate material. In 1953-54, the situation worsened. The comparable figures were: 465,000 leaving elementary school; 327,000 or 70.4 percent finished the seventh grade, the remainder, or 29.6 percent, did not achieve full elementary education. The next year, 1954-55 was worse still. From 441,000 pupils only 306,000 or 69.4 percent finished the seventh grade. The remaining 30.6 percent left in lower grades.

One of the principal causes is the fact that elementary schools are not uniform in practice, although such is the theory. There are fully organized schools and schools on the lower levels of organization that are able to teach only first to fourth grades or first to fifth or sixth grades. Regional pooling schools that are to take care of children from sections with inferior schools are not adequate with existing communications to allow all children to finish the higher grades. As a result, equal access to secondary education has not been granted as yet to all children.

Meeting the needs of educational universality and equality on the elementary level is made more difficult by the ratio of children to adults, higher in Poland than in some other economically stronger nations. Under these conditions, any educational reform requires a comparatively greater proportion of national income for its implementation.

The term of elementary education was set at eight years in 1945-48. Full realization of this program appeared impossible under the prevailing conditions. The seven-year elementary schools were introduced from 1948 to 1961. The extension of elementary education to eight years was advocated by the Polish United Workers Party (Communist) and made law July 15, 1961. It became a national objective now being developed. In addition, the program of the elementary schools is being reshaped. Stress is placed upon mathematics and sciences. The practical training and professional needs are reflected in the curricula. Table 4 illustrates elementary school curriculum in this period.

Secondary schools are divided into two groups: general and vocational. The general prepares students for university studies. The vocational secondary schools train their graduates for a professional position or for further studies in higher technical establishments.

TABLE 4

Curriculum
of Seven Elementary Grade Schools Reflected
in Hours Per Week Throughout a Year

Subject	Grades						
	I	II	III	IV	V	VI	VII
Polish	9	10	9	8	7	6	6
Foreign Languages	-	-	-	-	3	3	3
History	-	-	-	2	2	3	2/3*
Biology	-	-	3	2	3/2*	2	2
Geography	-	-	-	2	2/3*	2	2/3*
Mathematics	4	5	5	6	6	6	4
Physics	-	-	-	-	-	3	3
Chemistry	-	-	-	-	-	-	2
Drawing	1	1	1	1	1	1	1
Handicraft	1	1	1	1	1	1	1
Singing	1	1	1	1	1	1	1
Physical Education	2	2	2	2	3	3	3
Total	18	20	22	25	29	31	31
Reserved for the class teacher					1	1	1
Total of teachers' hours							179

*Two hours in the first half of the year. Three, or as indicated in other cases.

In the first years of this period, the general secondary schools required six years of studies based on the six-year program of the elementary schools. These six years were divided, according to the reform of 1932, into four years of gymnasium and two years of lyceum. The structure of high schools underwent changes in this direction with the first two grades being absorbed by the seventh and eighth grades. This creates eight years of elementary and four years of secondary education.

In 1948, a uniform four-year lyceum was introduced and was based on seven grades of elementary school. In addition, a preliminary examination was required for enrollment in the general high schools. Finishing lyceum required eleven years of study.

The earlier division of general high schools into Classic, Humanistic, Mathematico-physical, and Natural Scientific types was abolished. A uniform curriculum was substituted for a diversified program. At the same time, an attempt was made to stress mathematics and natural sciences with additional emphasis on the humanistic subjects. Special attention was paid to foreign languages, particularly to Russian, English, and French. The subjects taught in the high schools are not optional but compulsory and uniform for all. As a result, the curriculum of the lyceum is heavily loaded, and the entire program difficult. The school is in session 31 to 33 hours, six days a week throughout 220 days. Table 5 will show the content of this program and its distribution.

TABLE 5

Teaching Program
in General Secondary Schools

Subject	Number of hours of class per week			
	VIII	IX	X	XI
Polish	5	5	5	5
Russian	3	3/2	3	3
Modern Foreign Languages, or Latin	3	3	3	3
History	3	3	3	3
Contemporary Poland and the World	-	-	-	2
Biology	-	2/3	3	2
Geography	2	3	2	-
Astronomy	-	-	-	1
Mathematics	5	4	4	4
Logic	-	-	-	1
Physics	4	3	3	3
Chemistry	2	2	2	-
Drawing	2	1	-	-
Physical Education	3	2	2	2
Military Training	-	2	2	2
Total	32	33	32	31

From 1948 to 1951 the private secondary schools were nationalized. They were 90 percent coeducational. Sixteen religious convent schools with their 2,000 students have remained private. The total number of general high schools in 1951 was 764; in 1960, 833; in 1963, 852. Two hundred twenty thousand students studied in these schools in 1950; 260,000 in 1960; and 339,500 in 1962. This school population constitutes eleven students per thousand inhabitants. Only a part of them completed their studies; from 1945 to 1963, about 492,000 graduated from the general lyceums. They were entitled to enroll in the

higher schools, universities, or other similar establishments. A significant portion of them, however, could not be accepted due to lack of space or failure by them in the preliminary examination.

Vocational schools underwent deep transformations and extensions both in scope and structure. The lower classes of these schools, earlier based on an incomplete elementary education, have been built on seven complete years of elementary instruction. All of them are divided into trade school (two to three years) and vocational technicums (three to five years). Teachers' training schools as well as the artistic schools also belong to this group.

The picture of vocational training must include the professional evening schools and correspondence schools as well as the in-workshop training and inter-plant schools. The total number of students in these types of vocational schools amounted to over 8,800 in 1967. The total number of students in all vocational schools and training programs was composed of 42 percent girls.

In spite of these achievements, the views of educators are somewhat perplexed by the fact that only a small portion of youth complete secondary education, either general or vocational. This fact has been more pronounced in recent years. About 57 percent to 69 percent of the graduates of elementary schools attend secondary schools. The ratio of youth at school age to the secondary school enrollment was at 56 percent in 1955-56, 39 percent in 1960-61, and was about 40 percent for 1965-66.

The number of youth who do not attend secondary schools is considerable and calls for further serious efforts to decrease. It is not only an educational problem but also social and economic. In relation to these youth, ages fourteen to seventeen, more than two-thirds are being taught nothing further and about one-fourth of this group is economically inactive, subjected to all the stresses of a lack of a societal niche.

Special schools, professional improvement programs, and an adult education system also represent a field of concern and achievement in today's Poland.

Higher education has had to shore up the five-year breach created by the occupation. The first university was opened quickly in November, 1944. It was the Catholic University of Lublin, the only private school of its type from the Elbe River to Japan, now restricted in its development. Soon, the state university, Maria Curie-Skłodowska, the second higher school in Lublin has been founded. In 1945-48, about thirty-one universities and colleges had begun functioning. Their number grew later to seventy-five. Among them, there were eight universities, ten medical academies, seven agricultural colleges, ten politechnics, seven commercial colleges, a Central School of Foreign Services, a Central School of Planning and Statistics, schools of fine arts, of physical culture, various new departments, chairs, and institutes. All featured graduate programs for study toward higher degrees. The distribution of these colleges is fair; smaller cities became centers of higher education more easily accessible to the districts' inhabitants. Candidates with a certificate of maturity may be admitted to higher studies as may those who successfully pass an entrance examination. The number of candidates is considerably higher than the number of places at the universities and other establishments. The Ministry of Higher Education oversees admissions and sets the policies that determine the social composition of the student body. The cardinal motives for this decision include the economic and social needs of society as reflected in the governmental plans, and school facilities available.

In this process, a selective attitude is maintained. The students are granted a privilege, scholarship and housing facilities. They constitute, under existing conditions, an elite, a continuation of what is called the intelligentsia.

The following scheme of the school system in Poland illustrates the interconnection of all its levels. The access to higher education was broadened by inclusion into the system of vocational schools, schools for adults, correspondence courses, and in-work training. At the same time, entrance examinations as well as shortages in classrooms limit enrollment to the schools of a higher level.

The number of students grew from 170,331 in 1956-57 to about 270,000 in 1966-67. Poland has 554 students per 100,000 inhabitants, while a social cross section of students reveals that in 1962-63 45.5 percent were the children of the intelligentsia, administrators, and white-collar workers. To the second group belong the children of workers (30 percent), the third group constitutes the peasants (19.1 percent in relation to 48 percent of peasants in the total population). Children of craftsmen comprise 4.3 percent, and 1.1 percent constitute all others.

Universities and colleges perform the following functions: They train highly qualified specialists, prepare scholars and researchers, contribute to implementation of national plans, popularize the achievements of science and technical advance.

Long-range goals set up for education in Poland include instruction as well as toning up students through character formation and the thought processes. The last goal is reflected in statements of recent educational reform acts. "The schools and other educational establishments bring up the students in the spirit of love of the Fatherland, of peace, freedom, social justice, and brotherhood with the working peoples of all countries; they are taught to like and respect labor, to maintain national property; they prepare students to active participation in development of the country, its economy and culture." The content of these values is submitted to the uniform interpretation of the Communist Party.

The instruction programs are now undergoing a deep re-evaluation in view of enormous world change and pressing need. One of the directives of the new reform is the continued extension of range in the teaching of mathematics and natural science, with an orientation toward the understanding of current technology. The humanistic subjects, particularly history, the Polish language and literature, as well as the study of current events should focus attention on the contemporary societal problems. Finally, practical training is being introduced in the elementary schools, as is technical training, and the elements of adjustment to technology are receiving implementation in secondary schools; both look toward understanding and interest for productive work.

Education has been considered a public matter from the time of the Commission of National Education. Recently, its secular character has been stressed by the administration of postwar Poland and by the forces behind the established regime. In both of its aspects, education is a matter of concern for the state and its government, central and local, of the society, acting through other organizations, and of parents. The authority and all final decisions in educational matters belong to the central government, led by the Polish United Workers' Party (Communist).

Among the central governmental agencies, two ministries hold basic responsibilities for Polish education: the Ministry of Education and the Ministry of Higher Education. Other numerous ministries are responsible for the secondary and higher schools in their fields. The Minister of Higher Education is assisted by the Chief Council of Higher Education that may act on its own initiative. Two-thirds of its members are elected from among scholars and educators from outside; one-third are appointed by the Minister of Higher Education.

In the district, county and community levels, the People's Councils are invested with authority concerning school administration. They also are responsible for material contribution to the expenses connected with construction of new schools and maintaining those already existing.

Among influential social organizations, two play an outstanding role in education: the Union of Polish Teachers and the Polish Academy of Science. The Union has a sixty-year tradition of struggle for democratic and progressive education in Poland. The Academy was founded in Warsaw in 1952, superseding the earlier, ninety-five-year-old Polish Academy of Arts and Sciences in Cracow. It has taken an important place in higher education, research and scholarly contacts on the international level, including Poland's participation in UNESCO.

Parents exert their influence over local educational problems. The periodical, *The School and the Home,* serves as a bridge between the parents and other agents of education in Poland.

SELECTED BIBLIOGRAPHY

In English

Bibliographies

APANASEWICZ, N. M. *Selected Bibliography of Materials on Education in Poland;* U. S. Office of Education, International Education Division, Washington, 1960. (Studies in Comparative Education.)

U. S. Bureau of Census. *Bibliography of Social Science Periodicals and Monograph* series: Poland, 1945-1962. Government Printing Office, Washington, D. C., 1964. (Foreign social science bibliographies: Series P-92, No. 16.)

U. S. Office of Education, Division of International Education. *Educational Systems in Poland.* Washington, 1959. (Information on education around the world, No. 12.)

The University of Chicago. Human Relations Area Files. Preliminary ed., 1955, 27: U. Chicago S-4, 5 (1954-5), 1955 EAI Pol. EAI; *Contemporary Poland; Society, Politics, Economy.* Ed. A. Iwanska. Ch. IX: Education. xxd CBT 1953-1954.

General Works

Association of Polish University Professors and Lecturers in Great Britain. *Polish Science and Learning.* London,1944.

BACH, T. *Education in Poland.* Government Printing Office, Washington, 1923. (U. S. Bureau of Education. Bulletin, 1922, No. 41.)

BARNETT, C. R. *Poland, Its People, Its Society, Its Culture.* New Haven, 1958.

BOSWELL, A. "Educational Reform in Poland." *Slavonic Review*, 3: 131-140, 1924-25.

KANDEL, I. L. ed. Columbia University. Teachers College International Institute. *Educational Yearbook.* 1st-21, 1924-44. New York, 1925-44, 21v.

DOBROWOLSKI, M. *Polish Scholars; Their Contribution to World Science.* Warszawa, 1960.

DROBKA, F. J. *Education in Poland, Past and Present.* Washington, 1927.

HANS, N. "Polish Schools in Russia, 1772-1831." *The Slavonic and EE Review,* 38: 394-414, 1960.

HEATH, KATHRYN G. *Ministries of Education: Their Functions and Organization.* U. S. Office of Education. Washington, 1962. Polish People's Republic, pp. 510-515. (Bulletin, 1961, No. 21.)

The Polish Handbook, 1925: A Guide to the Country and Resources of the Republic of Poland, ED. BY FRANCIS BAUER CZARNOWSKI. London, 1925, Education: p. 101-113, (with tables).

Poland. *Główny Urząd Statystyczny.* Poland in Figures, 1944-1961. Warsaw, 1962.

ROSE, W. J. "Stanislaw Konarski: Preceptor of Poland." *Slavonic Review* 4: 23-41, 1925-26.

———. *Stanislaw Konarski, Reformer of Education in XVIIIth Century Poland.* London, 1929.

ROSEN, SEYMOUR M., and APANASEWICZ, NELLIE. *Higher Education in Poland.* U. S. Office of Education. Washington, 1963. 2 pts. (Bulletin, 1963, No. 19, 1964, No. 22. Issued also in Studies in Comparative Education.)

Ruch Mas Pracujacych Polski. The proposed educational reconstruction in people's Poland, formulated by the Polish underground labor movement and the Polish teachers' underground convention, with an introduction by Dean E. George Paynce. New York, 1944.

TUROSIEŃSKI, S. K. *Poland's Instructions of Higher Education. . . .* Washington, 1937. (U. S. Office of Education. Bulletin, 1936, No. 14.)

———. *Secondary Schools in Poland.* Washington, D. C.: (U. S. Office of Education, Circular No. 37, 1931.)

UNESCO. *Preliminary Report on the World Social Situation.* (U. N. Economic and Social Council, Social Commission, 8th session), with special reference to standards of living. (E/CN, 5/2671/Rev. 1), New York, 1952, 180 p. Ch.: Education.

UNESCO. *World Survey of Education.* Handbook of Educational Organization and Statistics.

U. S. Office of Education. *A New International Dimension: Education and World Affairs.* 1964, Ed. 8. Education and World Affairs. The U. S. Office of Education. *New International Dimensions;* a report to the U. S. Commissioner of Education.

U. S. Office of Education. *Poland's Institutions of Higher Education.* Washington, 1936 (Bulletin, No. 14.)

WÓJCICKA, J. *Higher Education in Poland.* New York. (Mid-European Studies Center, 1954, No. 12.)

WOJCICKI, A. B. *Adult Education in Poland During the Nineteenth and Twentieth Centuries.* Cambridge, Massachusetts, 1957.

ZALEWSKA-TRAFISZOWA, H. *Foreign Students in Poland.* Warsaw, 1962.

In Other Languages

Bibliographie pédagogique internationale. Paris, (Société des Nations, Institut Intern. de Cooper. Intel., 8. T. 1-5: 1935-1939).

HARTMANN, K. *Hochschulwesen and Wissenschaft in Polen, Entwicklung, Organisation* and *Stand,* 1918-1960, Frankfurt/Main, 1962.

JOBERT, A. La Commission d'education nationale en Pologne (1773-1794) son oeuvre d'instruction civique, Paris, 1941. (Collection historique de l'Institut d'Études Slaves, IX).

O direktivakh razvitiia obrazovaniia i vospitaniia v Polskoi Narodnoi Respublike v 1966-1970 gg. (Iz doklada Pervago sebretaria TSK Polskoǐ Ob"e-dinennoi Rabochei Partii tovarishcha Vladislava Gomulki na IV s"ezde PORP) *Sovetskaiâ Pedagogika,* XXVIII, 9: 112-118, Sentiabr, 1964.

PIASECKI, E. Les écoles polonaises et leurs conditions hygiéniques, Lwów, 1910.

Pologne 1919-1939, Neuchâtel, 1946-1947, 3 v. (In v. 3 chap.: 2.: L'Instruction publique; & passim., ch. 3.: La pédagogie.)

Basic Works in Polish

BARWINSKI, E. *Bibliografia historii polskiej.* Kwart. Hist., r. 16-28, 1902-1914, ch. V.

BARYCZ, H. *Rozwój historii óswiaty, wychoyania i kultury w Polsce.* Kraków, 1949. (Historia Nauki Polskiej w Monografiach, 31.)

Encyklopedia wychowania pod red. S. Łempickiego, W. Gottliela, B. Suchodolskiego, J. Włodarskiego. Warszawa, 1933-1937. 3 v (v. 2: Bibliografia pedagogiczna.)

ESTREICHER, K. *Bibliografia polska,* 1872-1916. 1951.

FINKEL, L. *Bibliografia historii polskiej,* Lwów, 1891-1906. Dodatek, 1914.

HAHN, W. *Bibliografia bibliografij polskich.* Wyd. 2. Wrocław, 1956, ch. XVI: Kultura, Nauka, Oswiata, p. 311-343, and passim.

KRÓLINSKI, K. *Podręczny Leksykon pedagogiczny.* Poznań, 1935.

Przewodnik Bibliograficzny (Bibliographical Guide) Warsaw, 1946 (current weekly).

Textbooks

KARBOWIAK, A. Dzieje wychowania i szkół w Polsce, Petersburg, 1898-1903. 2 v.

KOT, S. *Historia wychowania,* 2. wyd., Lwów, 1934, 2 v. and its abbr. ed.

———. *Zródła do historii wychowania; wybór,* Warszawa, 1929-30, 2 v.

WOŁOSZYN, S. *Dzieje wychowania i myśli pedagogicznej w zarysie,* Warszawa, 1964 (821 p.).

PORTUGAL

Samuel Gomez

HISTORICAL INTRODUCTION

The narrow little country occupying the greater portion of the western littoral of the Iberian peninsula presents a series of cultural and historical contrasts. The Portuguese state, stretching for approximately 360 miles along the Atlantic ocean and with a population of approximately nine million, is a logical expression of a unique cultural and historical complex; and this dynamic area of interwebbed events has been manifested in education as it is conceived and operated in Portugal. In turn, these educational manifestations have had their consequences on the cultural and historical factors influencing the "lifestyle" of the Portuguese. In essence, this is the underlying, broader thesis of this study.

People here live even now to a great extent a simple existence, the majority of them still living an unbroken cultural and religious tradition. (The anticlerical republic of 1910-1926 presents a notable exception, but even this experiment, it could be maintained, was destroyed by the machinations of the cultural web of historical and social elements resulting in the failure of the Portuguese mind.) A detailed analysis of these factors is beyond the scope of this paper but any study of the facets of Portuguese life cannot escape mention of these very real phenomena.

Some of these factors are cited primarily because of their relevance to the development of the Portuguese *leitmotif* and hence their intimate connection to education.

Briefly stated, some of the historical and cultural contrasts at work are these:

1. The frontiers of Portugal are perhaps the least changed frontiers in Europe.
2. Portugal was once one of the strongest and greatest powers of the world.
3. In World War II Portugal was one of the few remaining neutrals of Europe and served as a connecting link between groups of powers. (It seems that Portugal took very little advantage of a unique role.)
4. In the fifteenth and sixteenth centuries Portuguese explorers headed by Prince Henry and Vasco da Gama helped to open up the New World but her reign of glory declined so fast and so far that until recently and because of remnants of a considerable empire the country still rules, the rest of the world almost forgot Portugal.
5. While possessing a number of beautiful and fertile valleys, the country is relatively undeveloped, living in the main by the exports of cork, fish, and wine. (A considerably wealthy business has developed in textiles of late, supported by "cheap" raw materials supplied from the Portuguese overseas provinces and foreign capital, particularly American.) Yet the poverty and the ignorance of the workers is appalling—a woman working in the fields receives daily about the price of a cup of coffee at a fashionable Lisbon hotel. (In 1961 the per capita annual income was estimated at $238; illiteracy was estimated at "nearly one-half").[1] Today the country has the lowest standard of living in Western Europe and the highest illiteracy rate in all of Europe.
6. While the governments and religion of Spain and Portugal share some similarities (they are both Catholic and fascistic, for example), some hostility exists between the two and each proudly claims its uniqueness and individuality.

Among the effective forces at work in Portugal today are the state, which means primarily one man—Salazar; the Church; the proprietorship class; and the country's relationships with its overseas provinces. The overseas holdings of Portugal are more than twenty-two times the size of the mainland state. These holdings are the Azores, the Madeiras, the Cape Verdes with their "black" Portuguese, Timor, Macao, Portuguese Guinea, Sao Tome, Principe, Angola, Mozambique, and until December 1961, Goa and two tiny enclaves in India, known collectively as the *Estado da India*. Prime Minister Salazar main-

---

1. Paul Blanshard, *Freedom and Catholic Power in Spain and Portugal*, p. 288.

tains that Portugal has no colonies but only overseas provinces which are integral blocs of the Portuguese nation. This is a moot question and one needs to ask, "When is a colony not a colony?"

Portugal was a monarchy for about 700 years. In 1910 a revolution overthrew the monarchy and a republic came to power. Between 1910 and 1926 the country experienced twenty-four revolutions and *coups d' etat*. On the verge of bankruptcy in 1928 the ruling factions invited a young and brilliant economics professor at the University of Coimbra, Dr. Antonio de Oliveira Salazar, to become Minister of Finance. Salazar immediately requested and was granted broad powers which he used to make himself Prime Minister in 1932. The financial situation was saved but the political situation was lost. The "little priest," so called because he lives an almost monastic life, established his *estado novo* (new state) which is an organic whole organized through corporations representing different phases of life. Each of the corporations is responsible for its own corporate life, like the medieval guilds. While the republic is headed by a President (at present, Admiral Americo Tomas), the country is run by Salazar who, when he came into power, returned Roman Catholicism to the country and turned the country to the right. [*Editor's note: Salazar was incapacitated by a stroke in late 1968, and Marcelo Caetano assumed his duties. However, there have been no essential changes in educational policy since then.*] Salazar executes policy based primarily on the Church philosophy as expressed in the famous encyclicals of Pope Leo XIII and Pope Pius XI. In Salazar's own words this Church sociology and political philosophy is expressed thus:

In order to have the true interests of the people nearest our heart, and to stand for their material and moral advancement, it is not necessary to believe that authority is to be found in the masses, that justice is ruled by numbers, and that the administration of the law can be carried out by the mob instead of by an elite whose duty it is to lead and to sacrifice itself for the rest of the community. . . . It is not necessary that liberty should form the basis of every political scheme.[2]

In 1933, just over a year after Salazar had become Prime Minister, "corporativism" as a national system was laid in the constitution and structure of the *Estado Novo*. Corporativism is a national system aimed at organizing and uniting the country under the banners of morality, loyalty, and work. The political doctrine and structure of the nation were set forth in the constitution and, until the promulgation of the constitution of Eire, the Portuguese constitution was rather unique in basing the New State on a direct appeal to Christian ethics.

Cultural factors, while relative and always in a state of flux, necessarily need to be analyzed in order to develop an understanding of the life-style and intellectual characteristics of a people. This brief survey is intended to offer some cues as to the structure of the characteristics of the perceptual sets of the Portuguese people. A large measure of the responsibility for what a culture has patterned entails an analysis of the process of education as conceived and implemented in that society. Discussion of some of these considerations are in the sections that follow.

Early Education

To a degree the Portuguese have adopted German methods in their technical education; in secondary education the French lycée has been their chief model. The newer universities of Lisbon and Oporto have been organized along the lines of the classical University of Coimbra. The present University of Coimbra was founded in Lisbon in 1290 by King Denis, and generations of Portuguese have pointed with pride to Coimbra as the place providing education to its greatest authors and leaders of state and as a symbolic and real stronghold of ancient Portuguese tradition. (On several occasions the University of Coimbra was moved back and forth from Lisbon to Coimbra because of dissatisfaction of rulers with turbulent students and citizens.) The University is organized around its faculties of law, medicine, letters, science, and pharmacy.

Before the founding of the University of Coimbra, Portugal had three important schools of theology operating under French influence and there were in turn a number of high church officials of French origin in the country. The development of the University of Coimbra was patterned after the great schools of theology, philosophy, and law which had sprung up at Bologna and Paris and in its early origins Portuguese culture itself was subject to the influence of France. Paris influenced the development of scholastic education in Portugal, and the Portuguese Pope John XXI (1276) was an outstanding model of scholasticism being celebrated as a theologian, a student of the Natural Sciences and of Arabic medicine. His treatment of Aristotelian philosophy, *Summulae Logicales*, was a popular textbook in logic for three centuries.

The sixteenth century has been called "the golden age" of Portugal. She lost and re-won her independence and produced one of the great poets of history, the colorful, swashbuckling Luiz Vaz de Camoens (1524-1580), author of *Os Lusiadas* (*The Portuguese*), the epic of Portugal written in imitation of Homer and Virgil. It was in this century that some contact was made between the Portuguese and the humanistic studies popular throughout all of Europe. But humanism in Portugal was short-lived and culminates

---

2. For more details about Salazar's dictatorship, see Michael Derrick, *The Portugal of Salazar;* for an ardent defense of Salazar, see Richard Pattee, *Portugal and the Portuguese World;* and for profiles of his life, see *Time*, November 16, 1953, and July 22, 1946; *Saturday Evening Post,* April 9, 1960; *N. Y. Times,* May 21, 1960.

with Camoens. Portugal ceased to enrich its intellectual contacts with the rest of Europe at a time when the rest of Europe "was going to school" with humanism. And when the Spanish Inquisition was underway, Portuguese kings actually pleaded with Rome for twenty years to be able to conduct an Inquisition of their own! The brief dawn of Portuguese glory was darkened by the Inquisition and the Jesuits. From the time that the first Jesuit schools were opened in Portugal, the Jesuits worked for complete control over education. Persecution of scholars became popular (such activities as acquaintance with foreign humanists were "un-Portuguese" activities) as well as persecution of the Jews; and humanistic scholars and teachers like Diogo de Tieve, Joao da Costa, and the Scotsman George Buchanan were arrested on the trumpery charge of eating meat on meatless days, imprisoned by the Inquisition, and prohibited to lecture at Coimbra. The Royal College of Arts at Coimbra, established to provide a pre-university education within the University setting, and its government was ordered by the king to be handed over to the Provincial of the Company of Jesus and from 1555, control of the educational machinery by the Jesuits was assured. Thereafter, Portugal became a stronghold for political and military clericism.

When things appeared to be at their worst, an element of vitalism was regenerated by the Marquis of Pombal (1699-1782), one of the most liberal ministers who ever ruled Portugal. Pombal expelled the Jesuits, weakened the Inquisition, issued new lay statutes for the University of Coimbra, and created numerous teaching posts throughout the countryside. He reformed the teaching of the Dark Ages and introduced modern elements, for example, faculties of mathematics and natural sciences were added at Coimbra and special colleges for the training of young nobility for civil services were begun, a practice that had been nonexistent in Portugal until this time. As soon as Pombal fell, however, the clock was turned back and Portugal began to insulate itself once again from the rest of the world and its ideas. The pattern of life became one composed of the elements of fear of ideas; religious faith; poverty; tranquillity; and under-education.

Contemporary Education

Since 1952 the Portuguese government has passed a number of decree-laws aimed at strengthening the system of compulsory education and it is mainly since that year that intensive and effective efforts have been made to eradicate illiteracy. Even though the illiteracy rate is the highest in Western Europe and the period of compulsory schooling is the shortest in Europe (three years), the illiteracy rate is declining fairly rapidly and according to the UNESCO *World Survey—II*, "It may be said that today most

children of school age (*i.e.*, between 7 and 13) are in school." Parents who fail to send their children to school are liable to fines but because of the poverty of the peasants, the fines cannot generally be enforced.

Pre-School Education

Pre-school education exists for children up to age seven in a number of institutions which may be private, public, or semi-public. Preprimary education is neither compulsory nor widespread; neither is there an official curriculum for these schools as there is for higher schools. Various kinds of preprimary establishments, namely *escolas infantis* (infant schools), *casas das criancas* (children's houses), *parques infantis* (infant parks), and *jardins-escolas de Joao de Deus* (school gardens of John of God, named after a Portuguese writer of some note), keep more to the national educational traditions and utilize to some extent the Montessori and Froebel methods.

Primary Education

Beginning at age seven, primary education is compulsory for at least three years and at the end of the third year pupils sit for the elementary primary school examination known as the first cycle examination, which entitles them to move up into the fourth class, where they prepare for entrance to the secondary school. Admission to secondary school and to technical schools is based on the first four years of elementary schooling. In elementary primary education the following subjects are taught: Portuguese, arithmetic, geometry, drawing, geography, Portuguese history, natural science, ethics and civics, calligraphy, manual work, physical training, and choral singing. Primary education alone is free of charge.

Secondary Education

Secondary schools comprise two types: the *liceu* and the vocational secondary school of technical studies. At this level pupils are required to pay annual fees. The course of the *liceu* is divided into three cycles. The first cycle is two years; the second cycle is three years; and the third cycle, two years. The final examination taken after completion of all three cycles of secondary schooling will admit the student to university study. Each cycle culminates in examination as well. The same textbooks are used in each subject for each year taught (called *livro unico*).

Vocational Education

Recent years have witnessed the growth and development of technical, agricultural, and commercial education being influenced to some extent by English and American developments in technical and scientific study. The framework for vocational education is this:

1. A four-year practical agricultural school (*escola practica de agricultura*) offers a course following completion of four years of primary schooling.
2. From the four-year primary school the pupil may enter a two-year preparatory cycle of vocational education.
3. Completion of the preparatory cycle leads to a four-year course at an industrial school (*escola industrial*), a three-year course at a commercial school (*escola commercial*), or a five-year course at a school for agricultural overseers (*escola de regentes agricolas*).
4. Completion of the four-year course at an *escola industrial* leads to a four-year course at an industrial institute (*instituto industrial*).
5. Completion of the three-year course at an *escola commercial* leads to a three-year course at a commercial institute (*instituto commercial*).

Teacher Education

The training course in the primary teacher-training schools lasts eighteen months and candidates (aged between sixteen and twenty-eight) must have completed the second cycle of secondary education and must have passed an entrance examination. A three-month practical course is also given on passing an obligatory final exam after the eighteen-month program. Upon completion of the entire twenty-one months the student may take the state examination for the primary school teacher's certificate. The Minister of Education decides the number of applicants to be admitted to each training school each year, and a number of tuition grants and scholarships are available.

A certain number of teachers are appointed to the *postos escolares* which are very small schools in rural districts where there are not enough children of school age to justify opening a permanent school. These teachers need only the upper primary certificate supplemented by an examination in general education and a test lesson whereby teaching ability is measured. These teachers are paid less than fully qualified teachers but nearly all are women and would probably be earning nothing at all (or much less) if they did not have these positions. Furthermore, they play a key role in the National Campaign against illiteracy.

Candidates for the secondary school teaching certificate must complete secondary education, have four years of work in the Faculty of Letters or Sciences at one of the universities, and must spend two years in the section of pedagogic studies in the Faculty of Letters. Practice teaching in the liceu is also required. On completion of the pedagogic course, students must pass a State examination in order to obtain the secondary school teacher's certificates.

Higher Education

The institutions of higher learning in Portugal are headed by the three classical universities at Coimbra, Lisbon, and Oporto. In addition to the classical universities there is the technical University of Lisbon, founded in 1930, and composed of an aggregation of a number of schools and institutes.

The universities, while conforming to the principles of centralized control, are recognized as being autonomous and each is self-governed. However, all the universities are financed and supervised by the state.

Foundations of the Universities of Lisbon and Oporto go back to the creation of the Republic in 1910 while Coimbra has flourished for over six centuries. The faculties of the University of Lisbon are letters, science, medicine, law, pharmacy, and the faculties of the University of Oporto include medicine, science, pharmacy, and engineering; two degrees are conferred: "Licenciado" and "Doutor" (corresponding to the English "Masters" and "Doctorate").

There are a number of special institutions in Portugal. Some of these are the National School of Physical Education, The Institute of Hydrology, National Conservatory of Lisbon, School of Fine Arts at Lisbon, and Oporto, Military Academy, Naval Academy. Figure 1 on page 94 diagrams the instructional pattern of the educational system of Portugal. The glossary on page 95 gives the English equivalents of the Portuguese terminology, and also on that page is a list of the university faculties.

The constitutional basis of education in Portugal makes it obligatory for children to attend schools between the ages of seven and thirteen for at least three years. The state according to the constitution is officially responsible for the maintenance and supervision of schools. In addition it is officially declared responsible for the inspection and supervision of private schools. Some of the basic aims of education are stated in the following excerpts from the articles of constitution:

The development, teaching, and propagation of the arts and sciences shall be fostered, subject to respect for the constitution, the authorities and the co-ordinating activity of the state.

The aim of the state education is not merely the development of physique and of the intellectual faculties, but the training of character, adequate preparation for a profession and the inculcation of all moral and civic virtues, in accordance with Portugal's traditional principles of Christian doctrine and ethics.[3]

The present aim of the Portuguese universities is to prepare students for the intellectual professions and to engage in scientific research while training scientists. Many times university-trained people end up holding high posts in the civil service. This is so because what often happens is that these people are the best trained for such kinds of work.

Another set of aims of education in Portugal can be inferred from the ultimate relationships that exist

---

3. UNESCO, *World Survey—II*, p. 869.

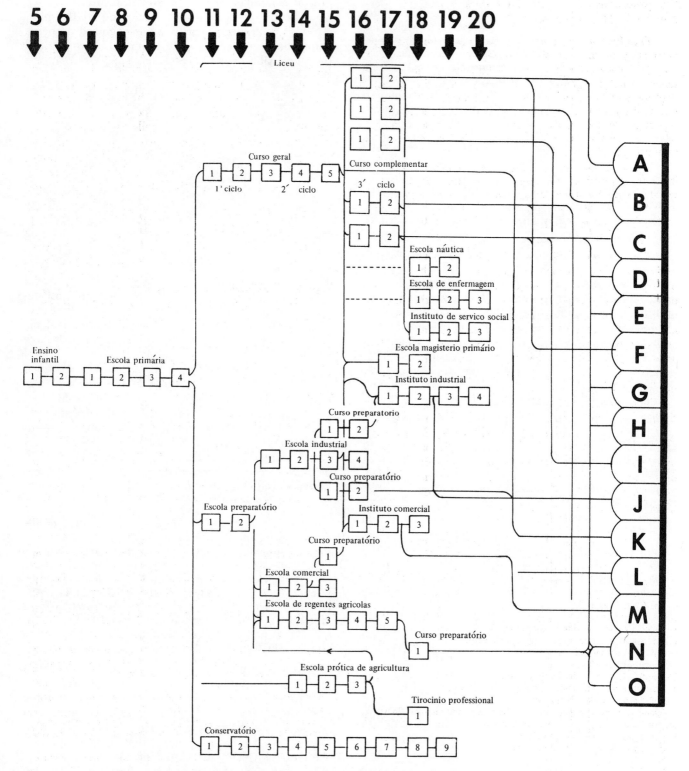

Figure 1. Instructional pattern of education in Portugal. (From **World Survey**—III, p. 977.)

between church and state. In 1940 the government and the Holy See concluded a concordat, some of the provisions of which have implications for the social role of the school:

The Portuguese Republic recognizes the juridicial personality of the Catholic Church.

The instruction imparted by the State in public schools shall be guided by the principles of Christian doctrine and morality, which are traditional in the country. Consequently the Catholic religion and morals shall be taught in the public schools. . . . to those students whose parents or guardians have made no request for exemption.

The text for the teaching of the Catholic religion must be approved by the ecclesiastical Authority, and the teachers shall be appointed by the State upon agreement with it; in no case can the aforesaid instruction be imparted by persons whom the ecclesiastical Authority has not approved as fit.[4]

Another set of objects relating to the social role of the school can be inferred from some of the aspects of the life-style of the people as it has evolved. One of the characteristics of this style is that the notion of "tranquillity" is a central feature of it. The Salazarian creed is not progress or growth but tranquil acceptance of a stable system. In a very real sense the total social system develops tranquillity and the pattern of life is not one conducive to education and intellectualism.

The objects which the school seeks to promote, then, are technical and professional competence. It is a fact that historically the tradition in Portuguese scholarship is practical rather than theoretical or humanistic as shown by the efforts of the Portuguese in navigation and colonizing, and it is in keeping with their agricultural economy that it relies to some great extent upon overseas provinces, Christian faith,

Roman Catholic ethics and morality, loyalty to the state, and tranquil acceptance of a stable cultural pattern.

ADMINISTRATIVE AUTHORITY

The Portuguese system of schools is strongly centralized. Education is the responsibility of the state, but suitably qualified persons may operate private schools subject to inspection by state authorities. There are many small private secondary schools not subsidized by the state. They follow the same program of studies as the State liceus which supervise the examining of these pupils. The Ministry is responsible for the organization, administration, and supervision of education, and the Minister of Education appoints the rectors of State and municipal liceus. The curriculum for all schools, primary and secondary, is prescribed by the Ministry.

Within the Ministry of Education there is a technical and advisory body—the National Education Board (Junta Nacional de Educacao)—which is divided into six specialized sections: moral and civic education; primary education; secondary education; higher education; vocational education; fine arts.

The Ministry contains separate directorates-general for primary education, secondary education, vocational education, higher education, school health, and sport. There are also inspectorates of secondary and of private schools within the Ministry.[5]

The Conselho Permanente da Accao Educativa (Permanent Council for Educational Action) is attached to the board, its task being to coordinate the activities of all the departments of the Ministry of

---

4. Blanshard, *op. cit.*, p. 274.
5. For more details see UNESCO, *World Survey*—I, p. 529; II, p. 870; III, p. 976.

◄   FACULDADES, ESCOLAS, INSTITUTOS SUPERIORES:
          UNIVERSITY FACULTIES OR COLLEGES

A. letras: arts (five departments).
B. direito: law
C. medecina: medicine.
D. farmacia: pharmacy.
E. ciencias: science (four departments).
F. educacao fisica: college of physical education.
G. militar: military college
H. naval: naval college
I. arquitectura: college of architecture.
J. instituto superior tecnico: college of technology.
K. belas-artes: college of fine arts.
L. ciencias economicas e financas: college of economics and finance.
M. colonial: College of colonial studies.
N. agronomia: college of agriculture.
O. veterinaria: college of veterinary science.

GLOSSARY

conservatório: vocational secondary school of fine arts or music.
ensino infantil: pre-primary education provided in institutions such as day nurseries and kindergarten.

ensino tecnico profissional: vocational education.
escola comercial: vocational secondary school of commerce with possibility of entry after second year into a preparatory class (curso preparatorio) leading to further specialized vocational training.
escola de enfermagem: vocational training school of nursing.
escola industrial: vocational secondary school of technical studies.
escola magisterio primário: teacher-training school for primary school teachers.
escola náutica: vocational training school for careers at sea.
escola pratica de agricultura: vocational training school of agriculture, at times with additional year of study (curso de aperfeicoamento).
escola preparatória: lower vocational secondary school.
escola primária: primary school.
escola de regentes agricolas: vocational training for agricultural overseers.
instituto comercial: upper vocational secondary school of commerce.
instituto industrial: upper vocational secondary school of technical studies.
instituto de servico social: vocational training school for social workers.
liceu: general secondary school with seven-year course in three cycles, the first two, of two and three years duration, providing a general course (curso geral), the last two years being specialized ("curso complementar") and preparatory to university education.
tirocinio profissional: upper vocational course in agriculture.

Education and to decide questions involving disciplinary action.

The Secretariat-General deals with all general questions of administration and with any other matters not coming within the competence of the other departments of the Ministry. The Antonio Aurelio da Costa Ferreira Institute, which deals with the problems of abnormal children, is attached to the Secretariat-General.

The Higher Institute of Culture fosters scientific research and cultural relations at the national and international levels, and provides facilities for students working for a degree in some special subject.

Primary Education

The country is divided into school districts as the administrative units. Each district has a head who superintends all his district's primary school services; he may be aided by assistants. In each municipality which is not the chief town of a district, there is a school official (a teacher) who is responsible for all the municipality's school services. Larger towns maintain a *zona* with a director responsible for his unit. These administrators are subordinate to the head of the school district. In the more remote country districts the holders of the *postos escolares* are the agents of the administration.

Primary inspectors' duties are purely educational and disciplinary. Administrative functions are discharged by the heads of school districts, in addition to their role of providing educational guidance. Primary inspectors and heads of school districts are appointed by the Ministry of Education, who can replace them at any moment.

Secondary Education

The authority of the central directorate of education is exercised in each liceu through the school director. He is chosen by the Ministry of Education from regular teachers on the general list and is appointed for an indefinite period. The administrative staff of a liceu also includes a deputy director and a secretary also chosen by the Ministry. Secondary education is divided into cycles and a director of studies presides over each cycle. (There are three cycles.)

The director of a liceu is assisted by two boards: an educational board and a disciplinary board. The function of the first of these is essentially pedagogical and it is comprised of all the teachers plus the doctor attached to the school. The membership of the disciplinary board includes the director, deputy-director, the secretary, the cycle directors, the doctor attached to the school, and the teachers responsible for religious instruction and moral education.

Inspection of secondary schools is carried out by a special department, the Inspeccao de Ensino Liceal whose duties are to determine the educational value of teaching equipment and textbooks, to give advice on schedules and methods, to assess and mark the teachers' work, to set examinations and to prepare educational statistics.

Finance

The educational budget is drawn up by the Ministry of Education sanctioned by the Finance Minister, and approved by the Cabinet. The budget is administered by the Ministry of Education and the Ministry of Public Works, the latter defraying expenditures connected with school buildings. In the municipalities, the municipalities concerned meet 50 percent of the cost of building primary schools and pay the cost of school equipment. There are no tuition fees for the primary school. With regard to private education the State makes grants to private schools considered to be important (infant schools, technical schools, art schools).

The universities are self-governed by a general faculty assembly, a senate, and a rector who represents and is selected by the Ministry of Education. While the character of each university differs, all are financed and supervised by the State.

EDUCATIONAL OPPORTUNITY

Recent years have witnessed the growth of primary schools, secondary schools, technical, agricultural, and commercial schools, and the Salazar State since 1952 has been exerting considerable effort to eradicate illiteracy. Compulsory education at state schools is free, and three years of education are compulsory between the ages of seven and thirteen. In order to enforce compulsory education various procedures, including penalties, have been adopted and are applicable to the children, parents or guardians, or to the teachers themselves. Attendance is supervised by the school authorities (heads of school districts). Fines of up to 500 escudos can be levied upon parents who do not enroll their children for school or who fail to make satisfactory arrangements for their education at home. Rather heavy fines from 500 escudos to 2500 escudos can be imposed on individuals or enterprises which admit children of school age to theaters or other places of entertainment or which employ them during school hours. As stated previously, because of the large peasant population it is difficult to enforce these fines.

Commercial and industrial enterprises have been prohibited from employing children under eighteen on their regular staff if they have not passed at least the lower primary school examination (three years) unless they have been exempted from compulsory education and, since 1954, an immigration permit has not been granted to anyone between the ages of fourteen and thirty-five unless he has at least passed the lower school examination.

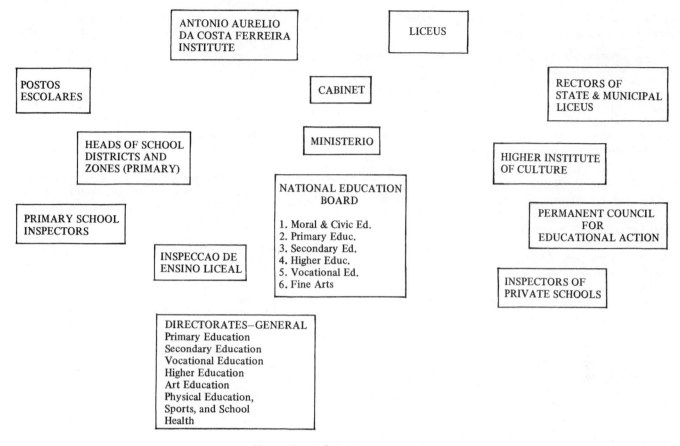

Figure 2. Administrative controls.

School attendance creates certain difficulties in the case of small farmers' children who assist their parents on the farm, and it seems to be so that what keeps the number of pupils down is not an excessively high standard nor the fees charged, necessarily (there is some alleviation of fees in the case of need), but the fact that the children will not be earning money or helping their parents while they are in school. Education and life in general is less competitive than in many countries and many people do not see the real need for formal education. (This point raises some interesting questions concerning the relationships between these factors and others such as the ever-present being of a benign church and benevolent ruler.)

Examinations are set for pupils at the end of the third year of the primary school, at the end of the fourth year of the primary school, and at the end of each cycle of the secondary school. Entrance examinations are required for entrance into vocational schools, secondary schools, and higher education. And it appears almost as though the child in Portugal goes to school to take examinations. Admission to the universities is based on the seven-year secondary school certificate as well.

The following children are exempted from compulsory school attendance: (a) children suffering from illness or mental deficiency who cannot receive instruction in special classes and (b) children living at least two miles from a State school unless free transportation is provided.

In the year 1954 10 percent of the population was enrolled at educational levels of all types. The trend seems to be for increasing enrollments creating problems in classroom shortages and teacher supply. However, school construction has been expedited and there has been an increase in graduates from teacher training schools.

A school fund is obligatory in every school providing school meals services, books and materials, opportunities for distribution of clothing, and enabling children to attend holiday camps.

Increased opportunities in adult education are being made available and the decree-law of October, 1952, provided for a two-year campaign, the National Campaign for Adult Education, the main purpose being to prepare illiterates age fourteen to thirty-five for the elementary primary examinations. While this avowedly reflects a national program with national purposes, at least it is teaching some people how to read and write.

Some mention should be made of the national youth organization, the *Mocidade Portuguesa*, to which all young Portuguese may belong. It aims at all-around development of personality, physical, moral and civic. According to Kerr:

In some respects, although it is Catholic and semi-Fascist instead of Godless and Communist, it bears a fairly close resemblance to the Pioneers of the Soviet Union—in one, the Pioneers, and the other "Lusitos" and "Infantes," 7-10 and 10-14; in one, the Komsomols, and in the other, "Vanguardists," 14-18, and "Cadetes," undergraduates. Its activities include singing, theater and film shows, camps, hostels, and a good deal of welfare work.[6]

In conclusion it might be said that educational opportunities for youth are increasing in Portugal. These opportunities are standardized and controlled by the State. It is obvious that opportunities work in two directions: the existence of opportunities as well as the presence of motivation on the part of the people to participate in them. While in the case of Portugal, educational opportunities for youth have not been unavailable, it seems as though motivation to take advantage of alternatives has not been felt and the nation remains relatively uneducated and undereducated.

BIBLIOGRAPHY

Atlantic Monthly, October 1961, p. 33-36 (editorial).

BLANSHARD, PAUL. *Freedom and Catholic Power in Spain and Portugal*. Boston: The Beacon Press, 1962.

DE BRAGANCA-CUNHA, V. *Revolutionary Portugal* (1910-1936). London: James Clarke and Co., Ltd., 1937.

DERRICK, MICHAEL. *The Portugal of Salazar*. New York: Campion Books, 1939.

HIGGINS, MICHAEL H., and DE WINTON, F. S. *Survey of Education in Portugal*. London: George Allen and Unwin, 1942.

STEPHENS, H. MONROSE. *Portugal*. New York: G. P. Putnam's Sons, 1894.

KERR, ANTHONY. *Schools of Europe*. Westminster, Maryland: The Canterbury Press, 1960.

LIVERMORE, HAROLD V. *A History of Portugal*. Cambridge, England: The University Press, 1947.

———. (ed.), *Portugal and Brazil*. London: Oxford University Press, 1953.

PATTEE, RICHARD. *Portugal and the Portuguese World*. Milwaukee: The Bruce Publishing Co., 1957.

TAYLOR, WALLACE W., and WAGNER, ISABELLE. "The Education of Physically Handicapped Children in Portugal," *Exception Children* 26: 27-28; September, 1959.

TREND, J. B. *Portugal*. London: Ernest Benn Limited, 1957.

UNESCO. *World Survey of Education. Handbook of Educational Organization and Statistics*—I. Paris: the Organization, 1955.

———. *World Survey of Education*—II: Primary Education. Paris: the Organization, 1958. p. 868-876.

———. *World Survey of Education*—III; Secondary Education. Paris: the Organization, 1961. p. 975-984.

U. S. Office of Education. *Educational Data: Portugal*. Monograph No. OE-14008. Washington, D. C.: U. S. Government Printing Office, 1959.

WELLES, BENJAMIN. "Salazar in Trouble." *Atlantic Monthly*, August, 1962, p. 57-62.

6. Anthony Kerr. *Schools of Europe*, p. 164.

SWEDEN

Wilhelm Sjöstrand

Compared with the educational systems of most of the countries on the Continent of Europe, the Swedish educational system has a relatively short history. It was not until Scandinavia had been gradually incorporated into the sphere of European culture on a Christian basis and real towns had come into existence that the prerequisite conditions existed in Sweden for the organization of special establishments for teaching and training. These conditions did not arise all at once but developed gradually from the ninth century A.D. to the twelfth century, when the Roman Catholic Church had become fairly securely rooted in the country with episcopal Sees, cathedral chapters and monasteries as its centres of spiritual power, and when the growth of permanent towns was gathering way. Moreover, these two lines of development often coincided geographically.

Consequently the development of the Swedish educational system, particularly at the beginning, has to be viewed against the background of European culture from which it derived its most important stimuli. However, this does not mean that the domestic, internal conditions played an unimportant part. No seed yields a harvest if the necessary soil is not present. But it is natural that the relative importance of these different factors should have varied in the course of time. To begin with, the seed is received from abroad and the native soil is little cultivated. Less and less need is felt to let the new seed be taken from anywhere else than from earlier crops on Swedish soil and the domestic conditions become more and more decisive as to what is to grow and ripen to harvest. Culture and thereby the educational system have an opportunity to propagate themselves by their own strength, even though ideas and assistance still come to a considerable extent from abroad and from the middle of the nineteenth century to a growing extent also from the U.S.A. At present, as a result of the intensification of international relations and the necessity of thinking in global terms, a fresh change can be discerned. Events are again being influenced more by forces outside Swedish frontiers, and their course will not be controlled from within to the same extent as before.

Another observation is closely connected with the trend just mentioned. The continual changing and remodelling can be regarded from two different aspects. On the one hand, new conditions of a spiritual and material nature have given rise to a need for reforms. On the other hand, these reforms have, as a rule, also been designed to mould and guide developments in the direction which appeared desirable under the prevailing conditions and bearing in mind the attitude of the decision-making authorities. Right up to the present century the whole of this process of transformation naturally proceeded rather slowly. It was really a question of cautious progress.

In modern times, however, Sweden is more justified in speaking of bold experimentation. The educational system has to a greater extent than formerly become a *means* of influencing developments. This is probably connected with the growth of democracy and the increased influence of politics in the community. In a world in which international and global cooperation is more and more common, the domestic conditions have provided the forces which have for the time being had the power to intervene in and influence developments, an opportunity to try to realize their own ideas with the aid of the teaching and training system. It is no longer, as formerly, a question of letting the school "tag along." The school itself is now regarded as an essential transforming factor which is there to be used. The educational reforms are thereby transformed from measures of adaptation into experiments with anticipated results in accordance with hypotheses drawn up in advance.

HISTORICAL DEVELOPMENTS TO 1809

The medieval educational system in Sweden followed foreign models extremely closely. With the bishops and the cathedral chapters as prerequisite conditions, there grew up at the cathedrals in the episcopal towns special schools (diocesan or cathedral schools), at which the pupils received, on the one hand, instruction in the *trivium* (grammar, logic, and rhetoric) and vocal music and, on the other, underwent mainly practical training as priests (liturgical and homiletic exercises). There are reliable documentary records concerning the first school of this kind (at Linköping) from about the middle of the thirteenth century. From the same period, there is information about a monastery school (at Skara) run by an order of monks, the Dominicans, which was the most important educational endeavour. Both cathedral schools and monastery schools were intended, in the first place, for religious training for the Church. The individual priests and monks needed educating for their tasks.

Those who had to teach at cathedral and monastery schools, *i.e.* the teachers and the administrators of the Roman Catholic Church were obliged to resort to the universities on the Continent, primarily Paris, Prague, Cologne, Rostock, and Greifswald, for their own training. It was not until 1477 that Sweden made its first attempt to establish a domestic equivalent in the University of Uppsala, whose initial period of activity, however, did not extend beyond about 1520. Accordingly, the apex of the educational pyramid was still, on the whole, outside the boundaries of the country.

Merchants in the towns needed a different education from that of the Church's representatives. Besides Latin and French, they found it useful to have a knowledge of law, geography, navigation, arithmetic, and the like. Attempts were made to meet this need in the municipal schools, which arose in many places in Sweden during the fourteenth century. The population of the towns, even in 1500 A.D., was only about 5 percent of the total population. A different educational ideal than the Church's was also held by the still fewer nobility, whose status as a privileged Estate was dependent on the existence of an agrarian aristocracy. This aristocracy came to be employed by the King on civil and military duties and later modelled its manner of life in accordance with chivalric ideas and activities, which came from outside Sweden. In this connection courtesy and military proficiency became more important than book learning for the upper aristocracy, which attempted to imitate this chivalric model.

Popular education was mainly under the control of the Church and was partly based on the institution of godparents. It was the duty of godparents and parents to teach the children the articles of the Christian faith (the Creed, the Lord's Prayer, and the Ave Maria). These lessons were checked by the priest at confirmation (at age seven) and at confession. The priest's task at divine service was to keep this knowledge alive by continual recital and by preaching.

In this way Christian faith and morality became in time a living reality to the people.

When the Reformation was introduced into Sweden, beginning in the 1520s, the whole educational system of the country found itself in an entirely new situation. It was now a matter of training a new generation of spiritual leaders and educating the people with their help in a different spirit than before. Uneasiness in relation to the new religion, with its interference with old beliefs and customs, reduced the influx of pupils to the old cathedral schools. These, however, were transformed relatively quickly into Protestant and humanistic schools, which were divided by the school regulations of 1571 into four classes and concentrated on teaching Latin, divinity, and vocal music. The training of ministers still took place at the Cathedral under the direction of a *lektor* belonging to the Cathedral chapter. In this respect the 1611 school regulations introduced a change by which there were to be established four-class provincial schools, whose curricula were to include Greek. In the two highest classes of the six-class cathedral schools there were, in addition, logic, rhetoric, and Hebrew, possibly also psychology, mathematics, and astronomy. Moreover, the *lektor* in theology was transferred to the school and was to look after the preaching practice and the like. Thus, while the humanistic influence increased, the training of ministers was now entirely transferred to the cathedral school.

Parallel with this development, there was an endeavour at least to shorten the time spent in studies abroad by re-establishing Uppsala University. The University received its first permanent organization in close connection with the consolidation of the Protestant Church of Sweden brought about by the Uppsala Synod of 1593. The aim now was also to train civil servants. The nobility, whose educational ideals took a more theoretical turn during the sixteenth century and were differentiated into "politics *or* the military life," were still making little use of the domestic educational system. Private tuition and then foreign travel (*peregrination*), combined with residence at foreign universities were the forms of education they preferred.

The incipient expansion of urban industries and of the citizen class led in its turn to the setting up of so-called writing and arithmetic schools in many places. The Catechism came to play a decisive part in popular education. To begin with, the minister was content with the learning of a short lesson but increased it until by and by it included the whole of Luther's Shorter Catechism with explanations. The most important occasion for instruction was still divine service. About 1600, however, the minister increasingly was required to travel about in the parish and teach people the Catechism. In addition, oral examinations in the church before divine service began were introduced. No one was allowed to approach the Sacraments without having been approved at a Catechism examination immediately preceding the Holy Communion. Parents were ultimately responsible for the children beginning to acquire the prescribed knowledge in time.

In the seventeenth century, Sweden's period as a great power began. Her position as one of the most influential powers in Europe was also reflected in the efforts made in the educational field. After a certain tug-of-war between Gustav II and (after his death in 1632) the Regency government, on the one hand, and the higher clergy on the other, there came into force the 1649 school regulations, according to which the educational system was to consist of a four-class lower school (*trivialskola*), a four-class upper school (*gymnasium*) and above that an academy or university. At the *gymnasia* the lectorships were to be well-paid posts with teaching duties in a single subject generally. In the *trivialskola* the basis of the pupil's knowledge of the classical languages was laid and in the *gymnasium* modern subjects were added (for example, mathematics, geography, and history). A so-called writer or *apologist* class was also introduced for those who did not prove to be suitable for learned studies but would have to devote themselves to commerce and the like. For this category, so-called *pedagogia* were organized in the towns and were paid for by the government or by the town concerned. The University of Uppsala was substantially expanded and after the *gymnasium* had acquired in 1649 an intermediate position between the *trivialskola* and the university, the training of the ministers was often completed at the university. The training of secular officials also became a more important aim for the university than formerly and to a certain extent the sons of the nobility also began to attend. It was especially their *galant homme* ideal that led to teachers of modern languages and physical training (riding, fencing, dancing, and the like) being employed. There was also theoretical military training (artillery, fortification). New universities were founded, among them Åbo (Turku) in Finland (1640) and Lund (1668). Because of class consciousness of the nobility, however, private tuition, concluding with a journey abroad, was still the most important form of education for the higher civil-servant class. In the sphere of popular education the standard of attainment was raised to include a real understanding of the Catechism and the ability to read. The parish clerk was to assist the minister in this teaching.

In the second half of the seventeenth century a dual process of rigidification took place: absolute rule was introduced in political affairs and orthodoxy predominated in the sphere of religion. This left its traces on the educational system in the form of fresh regulative measures. The 1686 church law made it the parish clerk's duty quite definitely to assist the minister in instructing the children in the Catechism

gratis. He was to receive payment for teaching them to read and in case of need was also to teach writing and arithmetic. The religious opposition, consisting of those of the so-called practical-piety persuasion, with their requirement of a personally dedicated and realized Christian faith, began at the same time to call for proper parish schools. The precepts in the Catechism had indeed begun to be transformed into living group standards under the pressure of the self-government which had been developed in the parishes. Under the direction of the minister, the parish meeting supervised the individual parishioner's conduct in religious and moral respects. But the result of this was, as a rule, only an external piety which did not touch the heart. For this reason it could not satisfy those who were most religious-minded.

In 1693 there were new school regulations, in which the influence of orthodoxy asserted itself in a greater concentration of the teaching on theology, Greek, Hebrew and the like. At the universities an intense struggle was going on over Cartesianism, whose rationalism and the contemporary demands for empirical scientific research sorted ill with an orthodoxy that was bound to tradition and required submission to authority. Karl XI finally decreed that Cartesianism, which asserted itself primarily in medicine and the natural sciences (anatomical dissection was introduced, the Copernician system was defended) would be allowed to be preached only in so far as it did not conflict with Christian faith and the contents of the Bible.

After Sweden lost her position as a great power about 1720, her energies were to a large extent directed to the peaceful reconstruction of the national fortunes. Technology and natural science were fostered, and the part to be played by theoretical knowledge and specialization in almost all practical work was emphasized. The importance of these views was increased by the facts that the population was increasing, that the economic situation improved in course of time, and that a well-to-do middle class was beginning to appear. To begin with, the mercantilist idea of compulsory central control was decisive, even in educational thinking, but from the middle of the century pre-liberal and then clearly liberal strains made themselves heard more and more. The problem was no longer to create a differentiated educational system in which the State could place "the right man in the right post," but to offer everyone an opportunity to realize his own potentialities in the best possible way, in freedom and in competition with others. The idea of equality led to demands for children to be educated as men and women and as citizens, while individual aptitudes and differences of ability should be taken into account and provided for.

The discussion carried on along these lines led to demands for better popular education, with permanent schools and special teachers, secondary schools with better scope for Swedish, modern subjects, and foreign languages, and the use of the university for the whole of higher education. The secularization of cultural life and its concentration on material progress made themselves strongly felt in these connections. However, the real advances fell considerably short of the demands for reform, which were opposed by the nobility and the clergy who saw in these endeavours a threat to their own powerful position. The new school regulations in 1724 involved no essential advances and even though modern subjects and foreign languages were introduced here and there into the secondary schools in the eighteenth century, there were no new school regulations until 1807. In these regulations the instruction given in the *apologist* class was extended and the above-mentioned subjects were to a certain extent provided for in the *trivialskola* and the *gymnasium*. In the middle of the eighteenth century, professional degrees for lawyers and other civil appointments were introduced at the universities and later, measures were taken to improve the training of ministers and teachers in both theoretical and practical directions. In addition there was a considerable shake-up in the spheres of economic and scientific research and toward the end of the century in the humanities also. Nevertheless, there was a decline in recruitment to the universities with a distinct trough at the middle of the century.

This fact was connected with the growth of private schools and establishments for professional training. From the point of view of both content and method, the curricula at the private schools were much more modern than those of the public secondary schools and attracted the well-to-do middle class. Alongside the universities there arose a large number of special establishments of higher education, especially in the military sphere (for example, the Cadet School at Karlskrona, 1756-92, and later the Military Academy at Karlberg Castle near Stockholm) but later also in the fields of commercial, technical, and artistic training. Characteristically enough, these establishments, as a rule, also came to give the basic, modern, general education (such as languages and science) which was a prerequisite for the specialist training. In popular education, too, the situation was improved by the creation of a series of permanent teaching appointments and schools, paid for by donations or by the parishes themselves. However, in Sweden the century of the Enlightenment appears to have been somewhat paradoxical. Heated arguments were heard in favour of a public educational system on a level with contemporary requirements, but the actual measures were taken within the framework of the private schools, the establishments for professional training and, to a certain extent, the voluntarily supported parish schools.

1809 TO THE PRESENT

Modern history of Sweden begins in 1809, when the last remnant of her seventeenth-century empire (Finland) was lost and she acquired a new constitution, becoming a constitutional monarchy with power distributed between the King, the government and the Riksdag (the Swedish parliament) and with freedom for the individual citizen prescribed by law as an aim. The personal union with Norway from 1814 to the beginning of the present century was of no essential importance in educational respects. Sweden has been at peace for 150 years and developments in this period have involved a slow process of democratization and secularization. During the nineteenth century the strongholds of the conservative and reactionary forces were the Church, the civil service and the government, while the liberal and later also the socialist reformers belonged to the opposition. This did not mean that conservative quarters said no to all reforms but that such quarters were more firmly bound to tradition and the *status quo* and wished to prevent the introduction of radical reforms unless they could have some guarantee of what these reforms would involve. The representational reform of 1866, when the old Riksdag of four Estates was replaced by a popularly elected, two-chamber Riksdag, was a turning point. Through gradual changes in the qualifications for the right to vote, this representation became in time more and more democratic. To begin with, it was the farmers and the middle class who benefited most from the reform, but from the end of the nineteenth century the working class and the women also struggled successfully for complete political freedom (universal and equal suffrage was introduced in 1921). In accordance with the principles of parliamentarianism, which are, however, sometimes difficult to apply because of the relative strengths of the parties, Liberals and Social Democrats have more and more frequently found their way to the seat of government in the twentieth century. For nearly thirty years Sweden has had a political administration which has been selected entirely or predominantly from the Social Democratic Party.

This political development has gone hand in hand with a radical reconstruction of Swedish society. In 1835 Sweden had three million inhabitants; she reached the four million mark in 1869, exceeded five million at the turn of the century and in 1960 was up to about seven and a half million. This increase took place in spite of the fact that in the nineteenth century more than a million Swedes emigrated. It was accompanied by a marked shift of population from the country to the towns in connection with the growth of industrialization, the improvement of communications, and the like. In 1800 about 90 percent of the Swedish population still lived in the country, but in 1870 this figure had fallen to 87 percent, in

1900 to 75 percent, in 1930 to 52 percent, and in 1960 to about 25 percent. Even in 1870 agriculture and its ancillary industries supported 72 percent of the population, but for the other dates just mentioned this figure fell to 55 percent, 39 percent and 17 percent respectively. At the same time industry and handicrafts increased their proportion from 15 percent to 28 percent, 36 percent and 45 percent respectively. Commerce and communications underwent a similar expansion from 5 percent to 10 percent, 18 percent and 26 percent respectively. For the public services the relative proportion was 8 percent in 1870, with a gradual change to seven percent in 1900 and 1930 and to 12 percent in 1960. The number of salaried employees per 1,000 workers in industry, however, has nearly trebled in the present century (from about 100 to about 300). There has been a very considerable growth in prosperity. The gross national product per individual, calculated in 1960 money values, was about 1,000 kronor in 1870, about 2,000 kronor in 1900, about 3,500 kronor in 1930 and about 8,500 kronor in 1960. Real wages have substantially increased. However, this has applied principally to industrial and agricultural workers, who since the turn of the century have seen their wages trebled or quadrupled, while the salaries of senior civil servants and independent professional men have stagnated. The number of persons in different income groups has at the same time undergone a striking change, so that the proportion of wage-earners earning less than 10,000 kronor and more than 50,000 kronor per year has fallen, particularly in the last 30 years, while the proportion with incomes within this range has increased correspondingly.

Changes like those just mentioned must, of course, have a decisive effect also in educational contexts. The discussion began with the introduction of the new constitution in 1809. Conservatives, the foremost of whom was Erik Gustav Geijer, the famous historian, really wanted education at the public expense only for civil servants, as representing the interests of the State. The reformers wanted better popular education, with permanent schools, municipal schools or *realskolor* (lower secondary schools) for the needs of industry and *gymnasia* (upper secondary schools) and universities, together with different kinds of higher practical schools, for civil servants and for higher education. However, in this connection opinions were divided. Some people considered having a form of school for each class of society (such as the primary school for the working population, the *realskola* or municipal school for the middle class or bourgeoisie, who pursued careers in industry). Others, even at this period, favoured a basic and comprehensive school system, *i.e.* the primary school for all children, then a *realskola or* municipal school, concentrating primarily on *realia*

(subjects such as geography, history, mathematics) and modern languages for all children who needed it, and finally a *gymnasium* and university for those who wanted it and had the necessary qualifications.

Developments from 1810-1820 ended in a compromise. The problems of popular education were pushed aside, and with the secondary school, the principle of organization by social classes won the day. On the basis of a proposal by the 1812 commission on education, the secondary school was divided by the 1820 school regulations into *apologist* schools, *lärdomskolor* (grammar school) and *gymnasia*. In the *apologist* schools the emphasis was on *realia* and modern languages. In the *lärdomskolor* Latin and mathematics predominated in a neo-humanistic spirit and in the curriculum of the *gymnasium* Hebrew and theology had a secure position. But *realia* also had a certain place in the *lärdomskolor* and modern languages could to some extent be studied in the *gymnasium*. The so-called ambulatory organization (each teacher teaching a definite subject) might also exist in the *apologist* schools and *lärdomskolor*.

However, many people were not satisfied with the educational structure which arose in this way. Demands were made for "unity and civic mind" in education and therefore the education should be common to the age of fifteen or sixteen, especially as it was only then that it was possible to say anything about the pupil's aptitudes and qualifications. The basis should be the primary school, followed by "scentific secondary schools," in which the stress should be on *realia* and modern languages, and finally on universities and higher finishing schools. As regards methods, great confidence was placed in the monitorial teaching system (Bell and Lancaster), which was being attempted in Sweden also. It was believed that this method could help both to stimulate the pupils intellectually and to educate them morally in a good civic spirit. In addition it was desired to introduce the "free promotion" system, *i.e.* the pupils were given an opportunity, by a suitable arrangement of the timetable, to progress at their own pace in each individual subject. Conservative quarters raised particular opposition to these methods. The result was that the Riksdag decided to petition for a new inquiry into the schools question and in 1825 the so-called Grand Commission on Education (thirty-five members) was appointed.

Considerable antagonisms arose within this commission. On one side there was Professor C. A. Agardh, who wanted to introduce a comprehensive-school system with full freedom of choice for the pupils in a curriculum which at the senior stage would concentrate on *realia* and modern languages and with an ambulatory organization, free promotion and monitorial teaching. Agardh's basic principle was the rights of the individual. On the other side there was Mr. Hans Järta, a provincial governor, who wanted to retain the 1820 school regulations and strongly emphasized the educative effects of the classical languages. The State's requirements for the general development of the intellectual and physical "faculties" and the need for scientific objectivity in its future officials were the main ideas with which Järta and Geijer were concerned. The result was a compromise on which somewhat more than half the members of the commission were able to agree in a final report in 1828. They wished to introduce two lines in the secondary school, one with classical and modern languages and one with only modern languages. Common instruction was to be given in all common subjects. It should be possible to pass the university-entrance examination (*studentexamen*) without taking the classical languages. The State should not support any primary schools; the parishes themselves should maintain such schools, in cases in which they proved to be necessary, primarily for poor children and orphans. Special higher practical schools, along with the universities, should receive State support. The minority of the commission wished to keep the old division into *apologist* schools, *lärdomskolor* and *gymnasia* and insisted upon the necessity of classical training for future officials and the like. In other respects they were in relative agreement with the majority. There was a unanimous decision to recommend the establishment of an experimental school to try out the new methods (*Nya Elementarskuler* in Stockholm).

The 1828 report did not lead to any definitive decision. But developments proceeded in accordance with the wishes of the majority. Thus in the 1830s, a certain group, still with Agardh at its head, presented demands for a comprehensive-school system with freedom of choice and the above-mentioned methods and organization as the most important features. These endeavours received support from Geijer's famous "defection" to the liberal camp in 1838. The background to the demands for reform in the primary school was the prevailing poverty, drunkenness and criminality and the need of general education in citizenship for all members of the community within the existing framework of the constitution. In this connection the reformers had in mind not so much the industrial workers (who were not particularly numerous yet in Sweden) as the artisans and agricultural workers and the actual farming population. In its turn education in *realia* and modern languages appeared particularly necessary for the still-increasing middle class. Reactionary forces emphasized the part played by parental instruction and classical training in popular education and higher education respectively. However, the result was that in 1831 regulations were issued for the training of ministers of religion, in which theoretical university studies were now to be a *compulsory* part, with sub-

sequent practical application at the universities. In 1832 the alternative of passing the *studentexamen* without a credit in classical languages was conceded and in 1839 teaching posts in modern languages, natural science, and physical training were introduced in the *gymnasia*. Furthermore, a number of "completely *apologist* secondary schools" were established in which the pupils might prepare for the *studentexamen* without credits in classical languages.

After a lively exchange of views a definitive solution was produced. The liberals, with Crown Prince Oscar (Oscar I from 1844) as their standard-bearer, brought into force (after a Riksdag decision in 1841) the 1842 primary-school regulations which prescribed at least one (preferably a permanent) primary school in each parish, with a teacher trained at a training college. Teacher-training colleges were to be established with State support in every episcopal town. However, parents were given the opportunity to have their children educated at home or at a private school. The parish would pay for the actual primary schools but poor local authorities would be able to claim a State grant. The basic method was to be monitorial teaching.

In the endeavours to bring a comprehensive school into existence, it was unfortunate that the primary-school question had, for the time being, been settled in this way, independently of the problem of reforming the secondary schools. Thus the idea of a comprehensive school faded into the background. The conflict continued but was now concentrated on the secondary school and the rest of the educational system. Discussion on the secondary schools was concerned partly with the curriculum and the organization and partly with the methods. In the former respect everyone began to realize the importance of future civil servants having a better training in *realia* and modern languages than before, but they were unwilling to let this come about at the expense of an organization and curriculum which would weaken the classical training, with its reputed general training of the faculties ("gymnastics for the soul"). In regard to methods, it was considered that public spirit and self-discipline were better fostered in the individual classroom under a single teacher than in the noisy, "wall-less" school, with its many different departments gathered in one and the same hall under teachers who relieved each other and their "monitors," drawn from the ranks of the more advanced pupils. Consequently, free promotion and monitorial teaching could not readily be accepted in the secondary school in the way in which the reformers desired. These reformers wanted to unite earlier schools into a single secondary school, with freedom of choice and full application of the new methods, and insisted on the need of middle-class pupils for a modern education up to the *studentexamen*. An important success was achieved in this quarter by the 1849 edict. The *apologist* schools, the *lärdomskolor* and the *gymnasia* were to be combined to form a continuous course of study with freedom of choice in the classical languages. The ambulatory timetable was introduced and free promotion was to be allowed, when the teachers and the diocesan superintendent of schools (the bishop) so decided. However, the edict contained no detailed regulations in other respects. The new secondary school therefore did not take on its final shape until the 1859 school regulations. It became a ten year school (eight classes, the last two of two years each). The first two classes are common to all pupils, with German as the first foreign language. After that the studies are divided into a modern line, with further foreign languages, and a classical line with classical and modern languages. There is still common teaching of the common subjects, but a division into quite different classes may be allowed. From grade three onward the timetable is to be ambulatory. Free promotion is allowed. However, by this time teachers had already become weary of the "well-less" school and had discovered the impossibility of working in it. The rules were again relaxed in 1865, when exemption from Greek in the Classical Line was permitted, and the so-called Partly Classical Line was introduced. In addition, the *studentexamen* was transferred in 1862 from the universities to the secondary schools under the supervision of special "censors." A significant fact is that ever since the 1830s the State had committed itself to developing the universities, as science advanced and expanded into new spheres, and had also begun to give considerable grants to a series of advanced technical schools, not only in the military sphere but also, for example, in the commercial and agricultural spheres. In certain cases these technical schools began to make it a condition of entry that the candidate should have passed the *studentexamen* or have corresponding attainments, and this was even at the time when the *studentexamen* was still being given at the universities. In other cases they contented themselves with somewhat lower qualifications or sometimes even with primary-school attainments.

Development of the primary school into an effective form of school after 1842 was jeopardized, among other things, by the possibility of establishing travelling schools or small schools with teachers not trained at a training college and by the permission to teach the children at home. Increasing doubts were also entertained as to the suitability of the Bell and Lancaster method. It was principally the primary-school teachers and Count Torsten Rudenschöld who opposed this method; he wished to introduce a comprehensive-school system which would make it possible for children in all strata of society to be assigned to suitable occupations (circulation between social classes). However, in this connection Rudenschöld himself thought of using the more advanced pupils (the elite) as teachers in infant schools. Through the intervention of Mr. P. A. Siljeström, a headmaster

whose educational endeavours were influenced by American models, the infant school came to be a *preparatory* school for the general primary school. Moreover the latter was divided into two or more classes, which were to be taught *directly* by teachers (monitorial teaching was thereby eliminated). Regulations on these points were issued in 1863 and 1864. At about the same time the State grants to the primary schools and the teacher-training colleges were increased. The colleges, at which training became a three-year course in 1865, with both theory and practical application on the programme, were opened in certain cases to women students. In 1861 the State primary-school inspectorate was established, which was a first step toward restricting the Church's supervision over the primary school, with the cathedral chapter as the most important authority concerned.

The emancipation of women was to a great extent stimulated by the contemporary social conditions, such as a surplus of women and an increasing number of unmarried women. From the 1840s liberal opinion was seeking to obtain State aid for the hitherto private schools for girls and for the training of teachers for these schools. At the beginning of the 1860s the Advanced Training College for Women Teachers (*Högre lärarinneseminariet*) was founded in Stockholm with its associated school for teaching practice and in 1875 the Riksdag voted a State grant to the schools for girls. In 1870 women gained the right to "sit for" the *studentexamen* and in 1873 the right to study for most of the university degrees except those in the faculties of theology.

In the last three decades of the nineteenth century Liberals and, in course of time and to some extent, Social Democrats took up the struggle for the increased realization of all the demands for reform presented earlier. There was now a serious desire to develop the primary school into the basic school, so that the pupils at the secondary school would also have undergone at least a part of the common schooling before going on to the higher school. In this connection Mr. Fridtjuv Berg, a primary-school teacher who later became Minister of Education and Ecclesiastical Affairs, was one of the standard-bearers. The so-called parallel-school system, the same age-groups were represented in both the primary and the secondary school, with its clear division of the pupils according to social origin would consequently disappear. At the lower level the secondary-school curriculum must be entirely disencumbered from the classical languages and, by developing more openly in the domain of *realia* and the modern languages, must also meet the educational needs of pupils who would form the lower class of salaried officials in the service of the State and the municipalities, industry and commercial life. At the same time the pupils taking the modern line must be given full parity at the universities, with the same right as other students to "sit for" different kinds of university examinations for which a knowledge of Latin had hitherto been required. The school should be freed from the influence of the Church, by setting up supervisory bodies other than the cathedral chapters. Education of girls should be improved and should receive increased State aid. In this connection arguments from Positivism and Darwinism were often used.

The opposition pointed out that the concentration of secondary-school teaching on formal training or general development of the intellectual faculties and on preparatory scientific training made it impossible to combine the primary school with the lower classes of the higher school. They also wished to meet the need for advanced general education in civics, with *realia* and modern languages, for certain members of the community by organizing, partly parallel to the primary school, independent *realskolor* or municipal schools without Latin. As regarded the retention of classical education in the secondary school, reference was still made to the formal discipline derived from the study of Latin and Greek, an idea which was increasingly clearly contradicted by associationist psychology, especially of German origin (Herbart, Beneke). These circles were likewise unwilling to abandon Latin as a requirement for a university degree.

Changes which were made were, as a rule, in accordance with the wishes of the liberal element. By a Riksdag decision in 1873, confirmed in the main in the 1878 school regulations, the three lowest classes in the secondary school were made common to all pupils. The pupils did not begin with Latin until class four and with Greek until class six (classes six and seven were two-year classes, *i.e.* the course of study lasted nine years in all). The Classical and the Modern Lines had common instruction in classes four and five in all common subjects but were then divided into different departments. In the Classical Line it was possible to drop Greek; the Partly Classical Line was retained. Attempts had been made to arrange the courses in such a way that the pupils could leave the secondary school after classes three or five with a certain rounding off of their knowledge.

In order to establish a better connection between the primary school and the secondary school, a regulation was issued in 1894 that the requirements for entrance to the secondary school were to be equivalent to the attainments of a pupil who had passed through class three in the primary school. Otherwise the conservative resistance was stronger precisely with regard to the primary school. Through a standard plan in 1874 and a new primary-school regulation in 1882, the primary school had become a six-class school and had also been enlarged by the addition of a voluntary continuation school. In a new standard plan in 1889, however, the subject of religious knowledge was strengthened and certain directions about minimum courses for poor or unintelligent children

were a severe blow to all those who wanted to make the primary school the basic school for the whole nation. However, with the 1897 primary-school regulations a new swing of the pendulum occurred. Schools for girls received increased State aid during the 1880s and 1890s. In the sphere of university education an important change took place; in that in 1891 pupils who had taken the Modern Line got the opportunity to "sit for" examinations in the arts subjects without a knowledge of Latin and without including this subject in their degree courses.

Developments during the present century have meant a complete realization of the demands for reform described above. According to the 1905 regulations, the secondary school was to presuppose the intellectual attainments which had been acquired up to and including class three of the primary school. The school was divided into a *realskola* and a *gymnasium*. The *realskola* had five classes and a finishing class, leading to the *realskola* leaving certificate. After class five it was possible to transfer to either a Classical or a Modern *gymnasium*, both lasting four years. Latin began in the first ring (the first class of the four in the *gymnasium*) and Greek could be studied from the third ring (Partly Classical Line).

In this way both the problem of the connection between the primary and secondary schools and the problem of inserting a higher examination in *realia* between the primary school and the *studentexamen* were solved. However, the State secondary schools were only open to boys. As early as 1858 the State had begun to make grants to the so-called higher primary schools, which were to enable the children from the country districts to have a higher education in *realia*, over and above the primary school. From the 1890s these establishments could also be set up in the towns. In addition there was, from 1897, a senior department in the primary school. Moreover, at above the same time small districts and communities received State grants for private coeducational schools with educational aims above that of the primary school. After the 1905 secondary-school regulations, however, an increasing need was felt to provide better opportunities for the gifted pupils in the primary school and for the young people in the country districts and the small urbanized communities as a whole to acquire the same degree of education as was signified by the *realskola* leaving certificate. In this connection the idea of basic and comprehensive schools again became topical. The result of the discussion was the decision of the 1909 Riksdag to set up a State-controlled, municipal, intermediate school, based on the six-year primary school and comprising four classes, giving an education equivalent to the final aim of the *realskola*. It was thought that higher primary schools and the earlier private coeducational schools could also be developed into such municipal intermediate schools. The grants to the former private and independent higher schools for girls would likewise be payable to schools with four classes above the actual primary school. In other words, this decision in 1909 was to a large extent a step toward realizing the demand for a basic- and comprehensive-school system, while the educational needs of the girls and the children of less well-to-do parents, particularly in the smaller communities, were provided for.

In 1909 the Swedish educational system presented the following overall picture. The primary school comprised six classes and was followed by a voluntary continuation school, a senior department or a higher primary school. In accordance with the 1905 regulations, the State secondary schools were based on class three. The same applied to all independent State-aided *realskolor* and coeducational schools. On the other hand, the municipal intermediate schools presupposed that the pupil had passed through the six-class primary school. Independent secondary schools with or without the right to hold lower certificate examinations (*realskolexamen*) and university-entrance examinations (*studentexamen*) likewise flourished. The higher schools for girls had as a rule an eight-year course of study up to the so-called "normal-school qualification." At some schools for girls *realskolexamen* or *studentexamen* could be written. There were vocational schools (presupposing primary-school attainments) for training in child welfare, midwifery, mining, bookselling, printing, public-assistance work, fishing, commercial and office work, domestic science, railway work, agriculture, dairying, lower-grade military posts, music, art, senior posts in the merchant navy, police work, nursing, forestry, tailoring, different kinds of handicrafts, technical trades and lower-grade appointments in the post office, the telecommunications department, and the customs. Special preparation was required for entry to the training colleges for teachers in the infant and primary schools. The so-called folk high schools (*folkhögskolor*) were establishments for the independent seeker for education. The *realskolexamen*, "normal-school qualification" or a similar qualification was required for entry to certain schools of mining, training schools for gymnastics teachers (female pupils), commercial schools, schools of domestic science training women teachers, training colleges for kindergarten teachers, agricultural colleges, schools of forestry, classes for training in social-welfare work, and technical schools and for senior appointments on the railways and in the post office, telecommunications department, and customs. The *studentexamen* was required for training at the Institute of Pharmacy, training schools for gymnastics teachers (male pupils), the School of Economics, training schools for surveyors, military schools for officers, the Institute of Forestry, the Institute of Dentistry, the Royal Institute of Technology, and the universities. In other words, professional training was stratified at three levels, with the primary-school, *realskola* and *gymnasium*

attainments as bases. The whole of the higher scientific training rested on the *studentexamen*.

On the basis of a proposal from the so-called commission on popular education the Riksdag decided in 1918 to introduce a system of practical schools for young people, linked with the primary school as the basic school. The continuation school became compulsory and might be general or vocational. The same was to apply to the higher primary school. The continuation school was to be followed by apprentice schools in different spheres and then by different kinds of trade schools. Alongside these trade schools, commercial schools, schools of domestic science and commercial and technical *gymnasia* were organized. These *gymnasia* presupposed as a basis approximately the level of attainment represented by the *realskolexamen*. This reform realized the idea of the comprehensive school, as regarded the lower vocational training. Uniform administration was also secured, in that the Secondary School Board, established in 1904, and the Primary School Board, which came into existence in 1914, were amalgamated to form the National Board of Education in 1920.

However, the link between the primary school and the secondary school was still not so firm as the Social Democrats in particular and various Liberals were trying to make it. A lively discussion on comprehensive schools now arose in connection with a proposal in 1922 by the 1918 educational commission. The final result was a kind of compromise, the 1927 reform of the secondary schools. The *realskola* became a four- or five-year school, presupposing either a six- or a four-year primary school. In both cases the instruction led to the *realexamen*. The *gymnasium* in its turn then became a three- or four-year course. In the same way, doubled-linked, State-aided, municipal schools for girls, with six- or seven-year courses of study, completed the system. The ordinary secondary schools were opened to girls. Arguments used to justify this reform included the necessity of giving both sexes a better opportunity for higher education, of giving the children of the financially less well-to-do a fairer deal and of facilitating the studies of country children. Emphasis was also placed on the socially levelling influence of a more uniform and coherent educational system, in which the talented children were not prevented by irrelevant external difficulties from obtaining from the secondary schools the education they desired.

Nevertheless the primary school had still not become, as a whole, the basic school for both vocational training and higher education. Further efforts were made to do this. The result was a large number of different partial reforms to the early 1960s. In 1936 it was decided to gradually lengthen the duration of the primary-school period to seven years. This reform was completed in 1948. Most of the municipal intermediate schools were taken over by the State and converted into coeducational *realskolor* in the

1930s. Many of the higher primary schools were then also transformed into municipal intermediate schools, with different lines for commercial subjects, technology and domestic science. Central workshop schools were set up in 1941. A special entrance examination for transfer to a secondary school was cancelled in 1949 and admissions were made entirely on the basis of the reports from the primary school—a change which was intended to lay the foundations for more democratic selection. In the 1940s English began to be more and more commonly taught in the primary school and the syllabus for the subject in classes five to seven was established in 1954. Two years later, a three-year *realskola*, based upon the six-year primary school with English from class five, was introduced. There was a reform of the *gymnasium* in 1953 by which a so-called General Line came into existence alongside the Classical and Modern Lines. In the last two school years each line was split into two branches: the classical and partly classical branch, the biological and mathematical branch, and the modern-languages and social-studies branch. The influx of pupils to the secondary schools has increased very substantially since the 1930s. While in 1931 the first class in the *realskola* comprised about 13 percent of an age-group and the first ring in the gymnasium about 4 percent, these figures had increased by the mid-fifties to three times as many for the *realskola* and four times as many for the *gymnasium*. The increase has continued at about the same rate during the last ten years. The number of pupils at the *realskolexamen* level rose from 18 percent of the seventeen-year-olds in 1955 to 36 percent in 1960. At the *studentexamen* level the corresponding figures were 11 percent and 13 percent. In the *gymnasium* the Modern Line has gone ahead, so that in 1960 it received about 70 percent of all the new pupils. All this increased recruitment to the secondary schools must be regarded as the effect of a series of different factors. The general increase in prosperity has made it possible for more parents than formerly to afford to give their children longer schooling. Such measures of financial assistance to pupils as the provision of free educational materials, free school meals, and different kinds of study grants and the abolition of term fees at the secondary schools have increased these opportunities and led to wider social recruitment. In addition, the transformation of society and professional life has made it more necessary for young people to acquire a better education than formerly. However, one must not stress or exaggerate the importance of this latter factor. In 1956 an important reform of the educational administration was carried out. In each municipality there are to be central school boards, instead of the separate school boards which previously existed for the primary schools and the different higher schools. County school committees also came into existence as intermediate authorities between the central school boards and the National Board of Education. The clergy and the Church (the cathedral chapters) were thereby finally deprived of the supervision of the educational system which had been theirs from the beginning.

Of course, all these changes were accompanied by some political antagonisms but there was unanimity as to the necessity of democratizing the educational system and establishing it on a basis of greater social justice. The same can be said of the actual aim of the comprehensive-school system, which became more and more clearly an important item in the programme of the Social Democrats and the liberal Left. The reforms decided on in the 1960s were prepared by the 1940 schools inquiry, the 1946 schools commission and the 1957 preparatory committee on the schools. All agreed that the pupil's personality and development in consideration for others, ability to collaborate, and democratic character as a whole should be more strongly emphasized than before, while the advance of technology and modern conditions of life would make new demands on both the basic and the higher general educational organizations in the areas of knowledge and skill. On the other hand, there was no unanimity as to *how* these aims could best be realized. The 1940 school inquiry thought of an eight-year elementary school with common teaching in the first classes and then a division on practical and theoretical lines. On the vital point, the question of *when* the division into lines was to commence, opinions differed. The majority wanted it to be after class four and the minority after class six. The 1946 schools commission suggested a nine-year comprehensive school, in which there could be a very slight differentiation in theoretical and practical directions in classes seven and eight. In class nine there would be a *gymnasium* line, a general line, and a vocational line (here the English Education Act of 1944 exerted a certain influence). The *realexamen* would be abolished and transfer to the *gymnasium* would be from the *gymnasium* line in class nine. In 1950 this proposal became the basis for a fundamental decision by the Riksdag which meant that a nine-year comprehensive school would be introduced, replacing the primary school, the continuation school, the higher primary school, the municipal intermediate school, and the *realskola*. However, the comprehensive school would only be introduced "in so far as the experimental work contemplated shows the advisability" of this reform. This experimental work on the comprehensive school outlined went on during the whole of the 1950s. However, it expanded onto such a scale and was planned in such a way that no unambiguous results could be achieved. Its results were therefore only to a slight extent decisive in regard to the final form of the comprehensive school proposed by the 1957 committee, which resulted in the decision in 1962 to set up a nine-year *grundskola* (basic comprehensive school). On this occasion a number of special investigations were conducted instead and these investigations were quoted in support of the opinions expressed.

In opposition to this victorious comprehensive-school development, with its political affiliations which have already been mentioned, there was—as is clear, above all, from the wording of the fundamental 1950 decision—a progressive but more cautious view in conservative quarters especially. These quarters did not desire to remove the earlier forms of school without having first secured a reliable basis for an assessment of the disadvantages and merits of the old school system in relation to the new. They were also more anxious to vindicate the duty of the school to impart settled knowledge and positive skills. They were willing to support *democratization* but pointed to the danger of securing this at the cost of a *levelling* process, which would in reality mean a serious deterioration especially in the education of the most talented children. However, very little attention was paid to such reasons in government quarters, though they had considerable support even among the teaching staffs.

The final transformation of the whole educational system at the beginning of the 1960s must therefore be considered the result of certain basic political concepts in which the schools and the other educational establishments were to a large extent an *instrument* for the realization of the ideas and values espoused by the persons who maintained these concepts. In the great majority of cases the reforms have meant the removal of the old and a bold experimentation with untried solutions from which those in authority believed that they could expect the results which, in their own judgment, they found desirable. The latest educational reforms have also necessarily taken place on a parliamentary basis and in statutory forms. But it would be quite wrong to think that they have been carried out unanimously. It is perhaps simply more correct to say that objections to and criticism of too precipitate reforms preponderated outside purely political circles, among the better-informed section of the general public and among the teachers in the schools. It follows from this that, with a possible change of government, one could expect, relatively soon, interventions in the educational field of a quite different kind from those in the last fifteen years.

PRESENT EDUCATIONAL SYSTEM

In accordance with the reform decided on in 1962, a nine-year *grundskola* (basic comprehensive school) for children age seven to sixteen is to be gradually brought into being before the end of the present decade. The *grundskola* is divided into junior, intermediate, and senior departments, each comprising three annual courses (grades one to three, four to six, and seven to nine). The instruction is common to all children in the same department up to and including grade six. The first foreign language (English) is started in grade four. In grade six a thorough study of the pupil's aptitudes is made. In grade seven the pupil can choose to devote five periods a week to one of five alternative courses, from the purely theoretical with five periods of German or French as the second foreign language to the purely practical with five periods of handicraft work. In grade eight there are, for seven periods a week, no less than nine alternative courses with the same kind of range and with different intermediate combinations of theoretical and practical instruction. In mathematics and foreign languages the pupil can also choose between simple and difficult courses. In grades seven and eight, however, the pupils must not be divided into separate classes according to ability or the choices they have made but are to be "kept together" for as long as possible, in accordance with the division into sections made in grade six. Not until grade nine can a re-division into new sections take place. In grade nine there are five theoretical lines (preparation for the *gymnasium*, humanistic, technical, specialized commercial, and socio-economic lines) and four practical lines (technico-practical, commercial, domestic science, and general practical lines). The *realskola*, the municipal *realskola* or intermediate school and the municipal school for girls will be gradually closed down as the *grundskola* is introduced.

In 1962 a decision was also made about the gradual establishment of a new form of gymnasial school, the *fackskola* (technical or trade school), which is voluntary, comprises two annual courses, and is divided into a general, a commercial, and a technical line. It is calculated that in its expanded form, about 1970, the *fackskola* will absorb about 20 percent of each age group. Vocational training in various spheres, for which grade nine with its four practical lines is a preparation, is calculated to need a capacity of 20 percent to 30 percent. A special committee of inquiry is currently at work on the re-modelling of the organization of vocational training. For the present it will take place in the forms which were mentioned in the historical survey (apprentice schools, vocational schools, workshop schools, commercial schools, and the like).

It is thought that about 30 percent of each age-group will be educated at the *gymnasia*. The so-called general *gymnasia* are at present organized in accordance with the 1953 regulations (see above). In addition there are commercial and technical *gymnasia*. A committee of inquiry on the organization of *gymnasia* has recently presented a report, the proposals in which will in all probability be substantially confirmed by the Riksdag and the government at the end of 1964. The general *gymnasia* and the special *gymnasia* (commercial and technical) will be combined into *one* establishment. The course of study will be a three-year one, except for the technical course, which will be four-year. After the amalga-mation the *gymnasia* will form what is called an "optional *gymnasium*." This means that all the pupils will study certain main subjects, while in other respects instruction will be given in accordance with the individual nature of the separate courses. There will be five such courses: the humanities, social science, natural science, economics, and technology. Within each of these there will be various alternatives: in the humanistic course both classical and partly classical studies; in the economics course economic, linguistic, financial, distributive, and administrative alternatives; and in the technological course engineering, building, electrotechnical, and chemical engineering alternatives. Gradually increasing specialization will make it possible for the pupils to change their courses, especially at the beginning of the *gymnasium* period. The *studentexamen* will be abolished and will be replaced by a leaving certificate, the average mark of which will decide whether the pupil in question is to be allowed to proceed to the university or not. The social-science knowledge of the average *gymnasium* student will increase while the language training will be given less prominence. It will be possible, for example, for a pupil to leave with a good knowledge of only one foreign language, preferably English. The classical languages have been pushed aside and will no longer give the humanistic alternative its special character. It is thought that the distribution of the pupils in the different courses in 1970 will be as follows: the humanities 11 percent, social sciences 15 percent, natural science 30 percent, and economics and technology each 22 percent. The general and professional *gymnasia* pupils will accordingly be as 60 percent and 40 percent (in round figures) or 18 percent and 12 percent respectively of an age group (altogether, as has already been mentioned, 30 percent of such a group). By this attempt to direct the pupils to particular studies, which is already asserting itself in the allotment of funds to the existing forms of *gymnasia*, one discerns the regard being paid to the tendency, which is connected with social grouping, to choose a profession (the lower social groups prefer the professional-training alternatives).

UNIVERSITIES, COLLEGES AND TEACHER-TRAINING

Universities also underwent radical reforms in the 1940s and 1950s. Along with the two earlier State universities at Uppsala and Lund, private colleges came into existence at Stockholm (1877) and Gothenburg (1891). In the 1950s these colleges were brought under State control and developed into universities with several faculties. A fifth university is being built up at Umeå in northern Sweden. This year (1964) a new arrangement of faculties has come into being at the universities. They now have facul-

ties of theology, law, medicine, natural science, arts, and social science, in certain cases divided into two or more sections. The teaching of the different subjects is centered at the institutes, which are combined into groups. The administrative body governing the universities and the institutes of technology is the Office of the Chancellor, headed by a Chancellor who is directly appointed by the King-in-Council (formerly the universities themselves chose their Chancellor, but now he is a civil servant in the ordinary way).

The influx to the universities and institutes has continually increased over the last few decades. In certain cases, for example, in the medical faculties and the institutes of technology, the intake has been regulated by the available resources, which has led to the relative subjects being "blocked" and to very rigorous selection of the candidates with the best credits. The faculties of arts, on the other hand, have to a large extent been open to all who had passed the *studentexamen*. The number of students passing the *studentexamen* increased between 1930 and 1960 from about 2.5 percent of the twenty-year-olds (2800 students) to about 12 percent (11,400 students). As far as the universities were concerned, this meant an increase in student numbers which differed very greatly as between different faculties. At Uppsala, Sweden's oldest and largest university, the number of students in the Faculty of Arts has increased to six times what it was in 1933 and in the Faculty of Theology it has doubled, while there are one and a half times as many law students and medical students. Altogether the total number of students has quadrupled and the most substantial part of the expansion has taken place in the last decade. An important fact is the growth in the number of women students, which became twelve times as great in the period 1933-63 and increased its relative proportion from 14 percent to 41 percent of the student body. There is a similar state of affairs at the other establishments of higher education. However, the figures largely reflect a numerical increase in the size of the age-groups, meaning that the number of twenty-year-olds increased from about 90,000 in 1957 to 124,000 in 1963. But the relative increase in the influx to the universities and institutes has been greater than this. Of those who passed the *studentexamen* at the general *gymnasia* in 1956, about 85 percent enrolled at universities and institutes, but in 1961 this figure increased to over 95 percent. Thus the same factors as have been cited regarding the recruitment to the secondary schools (see above) have also been asserting themselves as regards the universities and colleges. In this situation attempts have been made, with the aid of forecasts, to intervene in the influx and regulate it, partly by giving the "blocked" training lines definite dimensions and partly by carrying on an "information campaign" intended to influence the students' choices of career. Thus people have long spoken of a surplus of arts graduates, in spite of the fact that the shortage of teachers has grown greater and is still a glaring one. In spite of all warnings, however, recruitment to the arts subjects is increasing and with the present trend the number of persons with degrees in this sphere will quadruple from 1961 to 1971.

This serious expansion in numbers has confronted the universities with many problems. Attempts have been made to solve some of these problems by reforms in the conditions under which the students are taught. The number of teachers has been increased, especially at the lower levels (assistants and lectors), and intensified instruction in small groups has been introduced. The old platform lecture is therefore no longer the predominant form of instruction. At the higher levels the measures taken have not been equally substantial, which means that the number of students per top post (professorship) has increased enormously in certain subjects. The so-called committee of inquiry on research posts is currently studying these questions.

In the situation outlined above, in which both quantitative and qualitative angles are of current interest (*more* teachers with *different training* are required), the training of teachers has become a more and more difficult problem. After 1842 the primary-school teachers received their training at training colleges and successive reforms made the period of study four years for teachers who had no *studentexamen* certificate, two years for teachers who held a *studentexamen* certificate and two years for teachers who intended to teach in junior schools. From the 1860s a probationary year, which in course of time came to include both practical and theoretical elements, was introduced for secondary-school teachers. In 1907 a special degree (*filosofisk ämbetsexamen*) was created at the universities and the subject of educational theory was then transferred to the universities. This meant that the student had to take a one-term course in "psychology and the theory and history of pedagogics," to enable him or her to pass the *filosofisk ämbetsexamen*. This system is still substantially in force. However, in 1956 an institute of education was established in Stockholm and this was followed by similar establishments in Malmö, Gothenburg, and Uppsala. Their aim is to secure better integration of the theoretical and the pedagogical training by making the latter, with both educational theory and practice, follow *immediately* after the former. At present a special committee is working on these problems and its proposals will be to the effect that the former level of the *studentexamen* should form the basis of all teacher training, which must be based on collaboration between the universities and the colleges of education. All teachers above grade six in the *grundskola* are to acquire at the universities the necessary knowledge of their subject. However, their studies will no longer be concerned with gaining credits in well-demarcated academic disciplines but will be made up of a combination of a number of courses from different disciplines, so that they can attain the knowledge and skill which are necessary at the teacher's desk in teaching a definite subject. For this purpose the training is immediately linked with a college of education.

CURRENT PROBLEMS

Reforms in the Swedish educational system have aimed at making possible a free and gradual choice between different educational and training paths in accordance with each pupil's wishes and aptitudes, without him or her being impeded by differences in financial and social background. This aim was genuinely democratic, even from the point of view of letting the school help to make its pupils into good citizens who respect their fellow human beings.

However, it has been pointed out in various quarters that the reality is very far from corresponding to these high aims. In point of principle, it may be questioned whether it is not one thing to offer all children the same opportunities to acquire an education and quite another thing to induce them to make use of these opportunities. The democratic social structure includes and must include many varied professions, the representatives of which will create around themselves to some extent different total environments in the home and for the children. It would be presumptuous to think that the school can entirely even out these differences, which, according to some investigators, mean little in the actual acquisition of knowledge in the school but all the more in the important attitudes to education and training.

For this reason conflicting tendencies are making themselves felt in the new school organization based on freedom of choice. On the one hand, many parents and children are clearly being induced to agree with society's estimate of the white-collar occupations and accordingly to prefer courses of study that are as theoretical as possible. On the other hand, there is in many parents and children in the lower classes of society a tendency to avoid too prolonged a schooling and to react negatively to the limited opportunities for early practical training which exist in the *grundskola*. It is considered that the very critical conditions of discipline which exist at present in Swedish schools are partly due to the fact that repugnance for school is great among many pupils, especially in the final classes. Equal opportunities have been created but a kind of school has been produced in which teachers are nonplussed by the problem of stimulating the will to make use of these opportunities, which is the prerequisite condition for all pupils being able to utilize their own qualifications.

It has also been remarked that the quality has been impaired in the attempts to safeguard the ideal of equality. Of the two main principles of democracy, the equality of all men as human beings and citizens and the right of the individual to free development, the former has received so much attention that the latter may be endangered. The situation of the really gifted children in the eight-year comprehensive school may, from this point of view, be just as precarious as that of the practically minded children in the area of their special attitudes and desires with respect to education. In this connection the counter-objection is often made that many pupils with a higher average level of knowledge than before means at least as great a gain for society as an elite associated with a lower average level for the majority.

The crisis in discipline is partly connected with the above-mentioned shortage of teachers, which has become so embarrassing that in Stockholm, for example, in the 1960s hundreds of persons had to be employed who had no theoretical or practical training whatever in the teaching sphere. But the shortage of teachers is also, of course, due to the fact that measures were not taken soon enough to train the increased number of teachers which the increasing child population and the educational reform necessitated (such as a somewhat smaller number of children in each class in the *grundskola*). The financial position and prestige of the teaching profession have also worked to make it less attractive. Practically all teachers in Sweden are appointed for life after a certain number of years of service, *i.e.* they cannot be dismissed unless they have committed a serious dereliction of duty or a criminal act. A junior-school teacher in an ordinary post received in 1965 a salary of 1521 kronor per month, with an increase to 1802 kronor after a certain number of years of service. For a primary-school teacher the corresponding figures will be 1802 kronor, with an increase to a maximum of 2135 kronor. An *adjunkt* (assistant master) with the *filosofisk ämbetsexamen* begins at 2679 kronor and may rise

to 3169 kronor. A *lektor* (senior master) with the licentiate or doctorate will, as a rule, receive from 2996 to 3551 kronor (some *lektor* posts have somewhat higher salaries). In all these cases the salary scales are better if the teacher works in a so-called higher-cost-of-living area (for example, Stockholm or the most northern districts of Sweden). In 1965 a professor received a monthly salary of 4955 kronor. Though all these salaries may seem to be very good in comparison with many other countries, they are too low in Sweden to be able to compete with what industry and commercial life offer persons with similar levels of education.

From the shortage of teachers there follows another unfortunate consequence which makes the school of free choice a fine idea which is still a long way from being realized. There is not sufficient capacity at the *gymnasium* and university levels. In the 1960s thousands of applicants for different kinds of *gymnasium* education could not be admitted because of the shortage of places. At the universities many students had to be turned away from studying various subjects which were not, in principle, "blocked," because resources of different kinds were lacking. This state of affairs will probably not be remedied for several years.

Reforms in Sweden's educational system in the 1960s are a large-scale and bold experiment. What its final results will be only the future can tell. For this reason the impression given in many quarters that the battle has already been won is misleading. Whoever wishes to learn from the Swedish willingness to experiment in the educational sphere must not confuse the views and statements of those primarily responsible with the actual reality, which does not yet correspond in several respects with what Sweden has been striving to secure.

U.S.S.R.

Abraham Kreusler

EDUCATION IN PREREVOLUTIONARY RUSSIA

Kiev, Russia, the medieval Russian state that existed from the tenth to the middle of the thirteenth century, was a federation of principalities, the leading one of which was the Grand Principality of Kiev. Education in Kiev, Russia, was monopolized by the church. Very little is known about its scope and level. Kievan sources reveal a great respect for learning. Historians, however, think that literacy was limited to the hierarchy of the church and the leading princes. The bulk of the population and many of the clergy were illiterate.

In the thirteenth century, Russia was conquered by the Mongols and remained under their domination for more than two centuries. When Russia regained her freedom, the leadership passed from Kiev to Moscow which became the center of an absolute state. The rulers of this state succeeded in extending their control over other Russian lands except the Ukraine and Belorussia, which fell under Polish rule.

The Mongol conquest retarded Russian cultural development. Learning declined; the population was illiterate.

Learning returned to Russia after she acquired the Ukraine in the seventeenth century. In Kiev, while the Ukraine still was under Polish rule, Peter Mohila founded an Academy modeled on Jesuit colleges in 1631. In Moscow, in 1648-9, a boyar, Theodore Rtishchev, opened a school in a monastery and invited thirty Kievan monks to teach Slavonic, Latin, Greek, rhetoric, and philosophy. Simeon of Polotsk, a representative of the Kievan Academy, opened a theological school in 1666 which lasted only two years.

In 1687 the Slavonic-Greek-Latin Academy was established in Moscow. Its curriculum resembled that of medieval European schools. It included no study of science and technology. The Academy was given a monopoly over teaching modern foreign languages and over questions of faith. It actually exercised the functions of an inquisition.[1]

The first lay educational institutions were opened by Peter the Great. He was enthusiastic about spreading enlightenment and learning, but his approach was essentially utilitarian. Most of the schools he opened were vocational. Their object was to train men for the army, navy, and administration.

In 1701 was established in Moscow the School of Mathematical and Navigational Sciences to train officers of the Navy. In 1715 the school moved to Petersburg and became the Russian Naval Academy which exists to this day. In 1712 a school of army engineers and an artillery school were established in Moscow but were soon transferred to St. Petersburg.

Peter had also broader plans of introducing compulsory elementary education. In 1714 the establishment of two mathematical schools in each province was decreed. Students were to be drawn from the children of the local residents irrespective of their social descent. In spite of very stern measures the decree could not be carried out.

Much more successful were the parochial schools established under the provision of the Church Statute of 1721. They drew their pupils from the children of the clergy and prepared them for priesthood. Some of them enlarged their programs and changed into theological seminaries with a nine-year course of study.

Peter also founded the Academy of Science which was inaugurated after his death in 1725. Starting from scratch, it became with the passage of time the directing center of science and scholarship.

In spite of the tremendous pressure exercised by the state, the progress of education in the time of Peter the Great was very slow. It was hampered by a lack of adequately trained teachers, a lack of textbooks, a hard curriculum which overemphasized mathematics, and a very harsh discipline. The parents

---

1. William H. E. Johnson. *Russia's Educational Heritage*, p. 23.

were unwilling to send their children to school, and cases of mass desertions of students were frequent.

Some of the gentry hired foreign tutors to whom they entrusted the education of their children. They wanted schools operating on a class basis. Certain military schools, as the Military Academy founded in 1731, were restricted to boys of noble descent.

The founding of the University of Moscow in 1755 was an important step for the advancement of higher learning. But it was only in the nineteenth century that the school became an important center of scholarship.

Catherine the Great was inspired by the philosophy of enlightenment and believed that a new breed of humanity could be raised by educating children in boarding schools and protecting them from the corrupting influence of the environment.

Orphanages were opened in Moscow and Petersburg; a school for girls of noble descent was opened at the Smolny Convent in 1764; a school for girls of the non-privileged class (except serfs) in 1765 and schools for boys of the lower classes were opened. Children of noble parentage received a broad education. For all other children professional training was emphasized.

Catherine, however, realized very soon that boarding schools could not take care of all the people.

Following the Austrian example, she decided to introduce popular education. A Commission for the Establishment of Popular Schools was formed. Two-year elementary schools were to be opened in the chief county towns, and four-year high schools in provincial centers. The progress was, however, slow and disappointing because of financial difficulties, a shortage of teachers, and lack of cooperation on the part of the parents. In 1790 the total enrollment was 16,525 or only one student for 1,573 inhabitants.[2] In rural areas where the bulk of the population lived no schools were opened. This laid the ground for a permanent division of Russian society that finally led to the revolution.

The school reforms of Alexander I were of great importance for the organization of public education in Russia. In 1802 a Ministry of Education was created, and in 1803 the whole school system was reformed. The empire was divided into six educational regions, each headed by a curator. There was to be a university in every region, a four-year gymnasium in every provincial center, two-year county schools in county towns, and one-year parish schools in villages. The basic principle of this system was integration. Theoretically it was possible for students to advance from parish schools through county and provincial schools to universities.

At the beginning of Alexander's reign there were three universities: a Russian in Moscow, a German in Dorpat (founded by Emperor Paul), and a Polish in Vilna. Alexander I founded three more universities:

in Kazan, Kharkov, and Petersburg. The Universities enjoyed a broad measure of autonomy.

Because of a shortage of qualified Russian instructors, the government secured the services of foreign professors who lectured in Latin. This necessitated the introduction of intensive Latin courses in all secondary schools to prepare the students for university study. This measure became later the basis of classicism in Russian secondary schools.

Simultaneously with the state-controlled schools, a private school system subsidized by the nobility developed. The nobility resented the fact that the lower classes found their way into the schools and began to organize private preparatory institutions for nobles. These schools emphasized French and other foreign languages and such accomplishments as proper bearing in society, fencing, and dancing. Two private institutions of higher learning were also established by private efforts: the Historical Philological Institute of Prince Bezborodko in Nezhin and the Demidov Law School.

The school reforms, especially the provisions on elementary education, were not carried out as planned because of a lack of funds and a shortage of trained personnel. No school facilities were provided for the peasantry.

After the Napoleonic wars Alexander I became conservative and morbidly religious. Allied with conservative monarchies, he tried to stem the tide of rising nationalism and liberalism in Europe and suppress dangerous ideas in Russia. Education was to help preserve the existing social and political order, to bring up true sons of the Orthodox Church and loyal sons of the state. A campaign started against liberal ideas, and Russians were forbidden to study abroad. The autonomy of the universities was restricted.

Upon the death of Alexander I in 1825, the revolutionary tide of Western Europe reached Russia. The Decembrist uprising broke out against the autocratic and feudal regime of the Romanov. Appalled by this uprising and the wave of social upheavals in Western Europe, Nicholas I, Alexander's successor, was determined to stem the revolutionary tide and keep it from spreading in Russia. His political philosophy was orthodoxy, autocracy, and nationality (a belief in the devotion of the Russian people to dynasty and government). These principles were to be the basis of education. Not only dispensation of knowledge but also moulding the character of the youth, protecting it from subversive ideas was to be the purpose of education. Politically and socially Russia was to be frozen. Advancement from lower to higher schools was to discontinue. Education was to prepare the student for that station of life to which he was destined by his descent. Parish schools were

2. M. T. Florinsky. *Russia—A History and an Interpretation,* p. 596.

to be for the children of peasants and lower classes, county schools for those of merchants and lesser nobility, gymnasia and universities for the nobility.

The course of instruction was extended in county schools to three years, in the gymnasia to seven. Beginning with the fourth class of gymnasium, two sets of courses were offered: one leading to university studies, emphasized classical languages; the other, more specialized, stressed mathematics and science.

In secondary schools the office of monitor was introduced. He was to act as an adviser, keep constant watch over his advisees, be with them in class and out of class. For the purpose of supervision of the teachers' political trustworthiness and their academic competence the office of an inspector was established. At the university level, the inspector kept watch over the behavior of the students who, incidentally, were put in uniform. The Minister of Education, Uvarov, centralized and standardized the whole school system. State control was extended over all private institutions and even over private tutors.

To satisfy the craving of the nobility for exclusive schools, boarding schools were opened for boys of noble descent with a somewhat abridged program of the gymnasium. Simultaneously measures were taken to prevent the enrollment of children of lower classes in the secondary schools. However, complete segregation of children according to their social order could not be carried out because of a certain mobility in the Russian social structure. It was impossible to keep out the children of raznochintsy (people below the gentry, such as priests, petty officials, or individuals from the masses who made their way up through education and effort). However, one class of society remained practically barred from education —the peasantry. Yet, even in this dark period of reaction, education shows progress. The number of secondary schools increased from forty-eight to seventy-eight, a Russian university was opened in Kiev in 1833 in place of the closed Polish University of Vilno, and several higher technical schools were opened. Brilliant scholars appear, such as the mathematician Lobachevsky, the physicist Petrov, the embryologist Baer, and the astronomer Struve, who all made significant contributions in their fields.

The reign of Alexander II brought in its first half a period of reforms and liberalism in the field of education. The restrictions on universities disappeared; the secondary schools were reorganized and opened to all boys irrespective of faith or social status.

The reform of 1864 provided for two categories of secondary schools: gymnasia with a seven-year course and progymnasia with a four-year course. The gymnasia were of two types: (1) classical with emphasis on classical languages and (2) real-gymnasia with emphasis on mathematics and science. Graduates of the gymnasium were admitted to the university,

graduates of the real-gymnasium were admitted only to higher technical schools.

Gymnasia for girls were established by the law of 1870. They offered a seven-year course of instruction, an eighth year was added for those who wished to be trained as teachers. Women could continue their studies only at private universities which were opened in several towns.

A new university was opened at Odessa, the old Polish University of Warsaw which was for a time closed, was reopened as a Russian university.

A project for primary schools was approved, but its implementation was left to local initiative. Since education was not compulsory, it remained a monopoly of the upper and middle classes.

The attempt of a student, Karakozov, to assassinate Alexander II, ushered in a period of reaction and counter-reforms. The autonomy of the university was reduced and the police control over the students was strengthened. In the gymnasium, the program of classical languages was strengthened in the hope that 'it would protect the students from dangerous ideas and deaden their interest in social and political issues. The entire course was extended to eight years.

The new curriculum failed to achieve its purpose. Instead of checking subversion, it made the school a more fertile ground for revolutionary ideas. The classical schools were hated by most Russians. The conservative publicist Rozanov called them moral and intellectual dungeons in which gifted children suffered irreparable damage. The new revised program had one serious effect: it forced a considerable number of students to drop out before graduation.

The real-gymnasia extended their course to seven years. They discarded classical languages and stressed physical sciences, drafting, and drawing. They were meant for classes lower than gentry and were to give only professional and technical training.

The reign of Alexander III brought a revival of the philosophy of orthodoxy, autocracy and nationality, and counter-reforms in the spirit of this reactionary philosophy. The autonomy of universities was abolished and police control of the students was further strengthened. Tuition rates were raised and measures were taken to enforce at higher and secondary level segregation by social class, economic status and religious creed. Quotas were set up for Jews in secondary schools and universities. In parts of Russia inhabited by a non-Russian population, the Russian language was imposed as a language of instruction even in elementary schools.

All these inequities only fostered a craving for justice and liberty and turned the universities into centers of opposition to the reactionary policies of the government.

In the twentieth century, Russia was one of the largest and most populous states in the world. Its vast land was inhabited by numerous ethnic groups, only half of which were Russian.

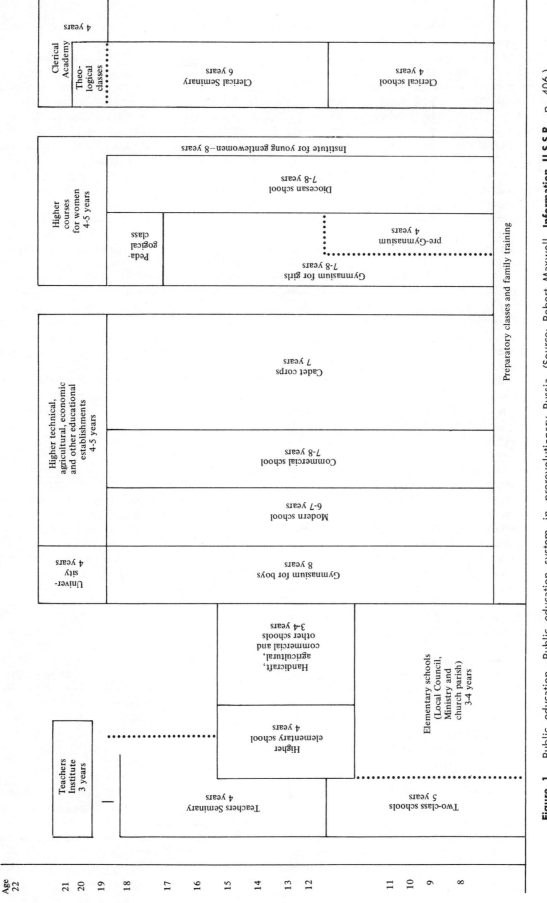

Figure 1. Public education. Public education system in prerevolutionary Russia. (Source: Robert Maxwell, **Information U.S.S.R.**, p. 406.)

116

The country was rich in mineral resources, with great potentialities for a national industry which started to develop at the end of the nineteenth century. Owing to the course of her history and to her geographic situation, Russia entered the twentieth century as a backward country with a primitive agriculture and an outmoded system of government with many social and political problems waiting solution.

In the twentieth century the Russian school system was in a stage of expansion and modernization. Universities were founded in Saratov and Rostov. The classical program of the gymnasia was considerably reduced. There were plans for gradual introduction of compulsory elementary education.

Compared with Western Europe, Russia was still very much behind in the dissemination of education. Expenditure on education was 1.20 rubles per capita. The government pursued a very oppressive policy of ruthless Russification of national minorities. Seventy-six percent of the population was illiterate.[3]

In 1914 there were 9,600,000 students; about 8,000,000 of them were attending elementary schools which represented slightly over half of the children of school age.[4] Secondary education was only for the privileged few. There were 2,000 secondary schools with an enrollment of 679,300 students; 105 higher educational establishments with an enrollment of 127,000 students. The discipline was harsh, the teaching methods authoritarian, but the education received was of a very high standard.

AFTER THE BOLSHEVIK REVOLUTION

The Revolution of November 1917 brought the Bolsheviks to power. The Bolsheviks considered education as the most important weapon in their struggle with the old order. Upon seizure of power in 1917, their first moves were directed toward the destruction of the old school system that assigned to each class of people a different type of school and toward spread of education. The school was to be secular and accessible to everybody. The rising generation was to be educated in communist ideology to secure their loyalty to the new order. A strictly defined philosophy of education was adapted from Karl Marx. It was to be a combination of general education with instruction in technology.

The Nine-Year School

Compulsory general and polytechnic education for all children to the age of seventeen was introduced. The different schools designed for different classes of society were replaced by one type of school, the unified labor school with a nine-year course of instruction divided into a five- and a four-year program. Continuity was stressed in place of division to give every child a chance to complete higher education. Admissions to universities was made open to everybody who reached the age of sixteen without submitting a secondary school diploma.

In the unified labor school, classical and foreign languages were discontinued and early specialization discarded. The school was coeducational with instruction in the native language. All children were to be provided with gratuitous hot food and textbooks free of charge. Originally, the educational plans went even much farther. All young people were to be raised in communal houses where they were to be clothed and fed at the cost of the state. The state, however, was too poor to implement such a program.

The reorganized school system was based on two principles: universalism and polytechnism. Universalism meant that education was to be accessible to everyone free of charge. Polytechnism meant that "teaching was to be closely connected with socially useful labor."

Combining labor and education is an old idea. It was proclaimed by Rousseau and Pestalozzi, and it was adopted by Marx who saw in this combination "the germ of the education of the future."

Influenced by Marx, Lenin made the combination of labor and education part of his educational program in 1917.

Neither universalism nor polytechnism could be implemented in practice. The concept of universal education had to be discarded, for after the Civil War the country needed a labor reserve in order to rebuild ruined factories and cities. The program of polytechnism failed for it was vaguely understood.

The unified labor school was a secular school in which religion was replaced by a social and political ideal. The purpose of this school was thus defined by Pinkevitch.[5]

All around development of a healthy, strong, actively brave, independently thinking and acting man, acquainted with the many sides of contemporary culture, a creator and a warrior in the interests of the proletariat and consequently in the final analysis in the interests of the whole of humanity.

As is evident from this definition, the individual was to be educated to serve the needs of the new state.

Boundless freedom was given to the pupils. Those who won the revolution believed they could capture the young generation by freeing it from the harsh discipline from which they had to suffer and they rushed to the opposite extreme. The school was turned into a republic run by the students. They decided what and how to study. The authority of the teacher declined. He was only a guide and a comrade. Corporal punishment was forbidden. Examinations and marks were abolished, homework given up, textbooks despised.

---

3. Robert Maxwell. *Information U. S. S. R.*, p. 405.
4. Florinsky. *op. cit.*, p. 1236.
5. George Z. F. Bereday. *The Changing Soviet School*, p. 62.

The traditional curriculum based on academic subjects was replaced by the project method. A selected problem, so-called complex, such as health protection, communal welfare, regional work, could become the object of investigation around which the activity of the whole group concentrated.

The meaning of polytechnism changed several times. At the beginning it was doing any kind of manual labor necessary for the upkeep of the school, such as cleaning and repair work. For a time it was self-service; then it was participation in communal affairs; and, finally, it became a course in labor combined with practice in the craft shops organized by the schools.

The effect of the experimentation was tragic. The graduates of the unified labor school were neither prepared for further study nor for active participation in building up the industry of the country. The decline of learning became a national disaster.

The Ten-Year School

Industrialization of the country forced the Soviet government to return to the traditional school, the graduates of which could continue their studies at the higher institutions and become engineers, teachers, physicians, agronomists, whom the country needed so badly.

In 1931 the Communist Party declared the unified labor school as inadequate, because it gave no preparation in the foundations of sciences, *i.e.* in academic subjects. The unified labor school was replaced by the ten-year school in which Russian tradition fully reasserted itself. The basic course of education was to be completed in three stages. The first four grades formed the primary school, grades five through seven formed the incomplete secondary school, grades five through ten constituted the complete secondary school.

The purpose of the ten-year school was mastery of knowledge. An instructional program of separate subjects, very much resembling that of the pre-revolutionary real-gymnasium, was introduced. The authority of the teacher and firm discipline were reestablished, and carefully prepared textbooks were introduced. The pre-revolutionary five-point grading scale was restored. According to this scale five means excellent, four is good, three is satisfactory, two is unsatisfactory, one is failure.

Polytechnism was frequently discussed but did not mean anything. The school shops were closed and labor was relegated to the realm of extracurricular activities. Acquisition of a firm body of knowledge of academic subjects was stressed in the ten-year school. The graduates were now more informed and were able to continue their studies at the university. A new intelligentsia was created and the foundations of a modern industrialized state were built.

ON THE ROAD TO REFORM

At the end of the thirties, the school had fulfilled its task and had become obsolete. Its main shortcoming was verbalism. Teachers limited themselves to presentation of textual material without stimulating independence of thought. The activity of the students had been reduced to passive listening and reproduction of what was given them ready-made. The worst vice of the school was an overloaded curriculum. The working day of the students lasted, on the average, twelve hours, for the homework they were expected to do occupied at least as much time as they spent in school.

After the war a new reform movement started. The growth of industry and an acute shortage of labor necessitated a readjustment of the school to the needs of a developing technological society. The concept of polytechnism revived, this time clearly defined, for Russian education advanced tremendously after the reform of the thirties. Since 1943 the Academy of Pedagogic Sciences has been in existence and has become a guiding center for theory and practice of education. The aims of polytechnism now were (1) to familiarize the student with the scientific principles of modern production, (2) to teach certain skills and working habits, and (3) to prepare for the choice of a profession.

In 1955 a new program of polytechnic instruction was introduced into the schools. The new curriculum with the program of polytechnic education was well balanced and stressed both humanities and science. Of a total of 9,857 hours, 4,653 were devoted to humanities. Compared with the former curriculum it meant a reduction of only 561 hours in the field of humanities. Polytechnic subjects occupied 528 hours or about 5 percent of the whole curriculum.

These reforms did not satisfy the Communist Party. At the Twentieth Congress of the Party in 1956, Khrushchev demanded the introduction of a course in foundations of production, the participation of senior high school students in the labor of industrial enterprises and collective farms.

The Eleven-Year School

These demands foreshadowed the coming reorganization of the school system. In 1958 a new school reform was announced.

By the reform of 1958 the ten-year school has been turned into an eleven-year school. Grades one to eight form the compulsory eight-year school. Grades nine, ten, and eleven constitute the general educational labor polytechnical school. In this school, academic work is combined with training in production. The students have four days of school work and two days of work experience at a plant. Rural schools use their farms for production training. Urban schools offer different specialties, depending on the enterprise available in the area. At the end of the tenth grade, the students take a qualification test and receive a certificate of specialization in a particular trade. Thus on graduating from the eleven-year school, the students are prepared for college entrance and are qualified workers in industry or agriculture.

Soviet educators do not identify polytechnic education with vocational. According to their opinion the difference between polytechnism and vocationalism lies in the broader background. The program is on probation and will be subject to revision on gaining new experience.

Universal secondary education has not been abandoned. Graduates of the eight-year school may complete their secondary education in a three-year general educational labor polytechnical school that offers training in production, or a technicum—a school that offers specialized semi-professional training.

Still another possibility is open to graduates of the eight-year school: if they have no desire for continuing formal schooling, they may work in industry or agriculture. In this case they are encouraged to continue secondary education in evening schools.

Underlying Reasons for School Reform

A variety of reasons, economic, sociological, and educational, was behind the school reform of 1958. The Soviet Union suffered from a shortage of labor because of a decline of birthrate in the war years. The plans of expanding agricultural and industrial production could not be carried out without an influx of millions of skilled workers and technicians. Millions of adolescents had to be made available for training and for production work. Millions of adolescents had to be placed on jobs and the school was called upon to provide fundamental technical knowledge.

The reform was also to solve a very important problem. The number of secondary-school graduates was constantly growing, but only a small percentage of them could be admitted to institutions of higher learning. The education they received made them unwilling to work in industry or agriculture. A new class of intelligentsia was beginning to emerge that had no proletarian orientation. Polytechnism was con-

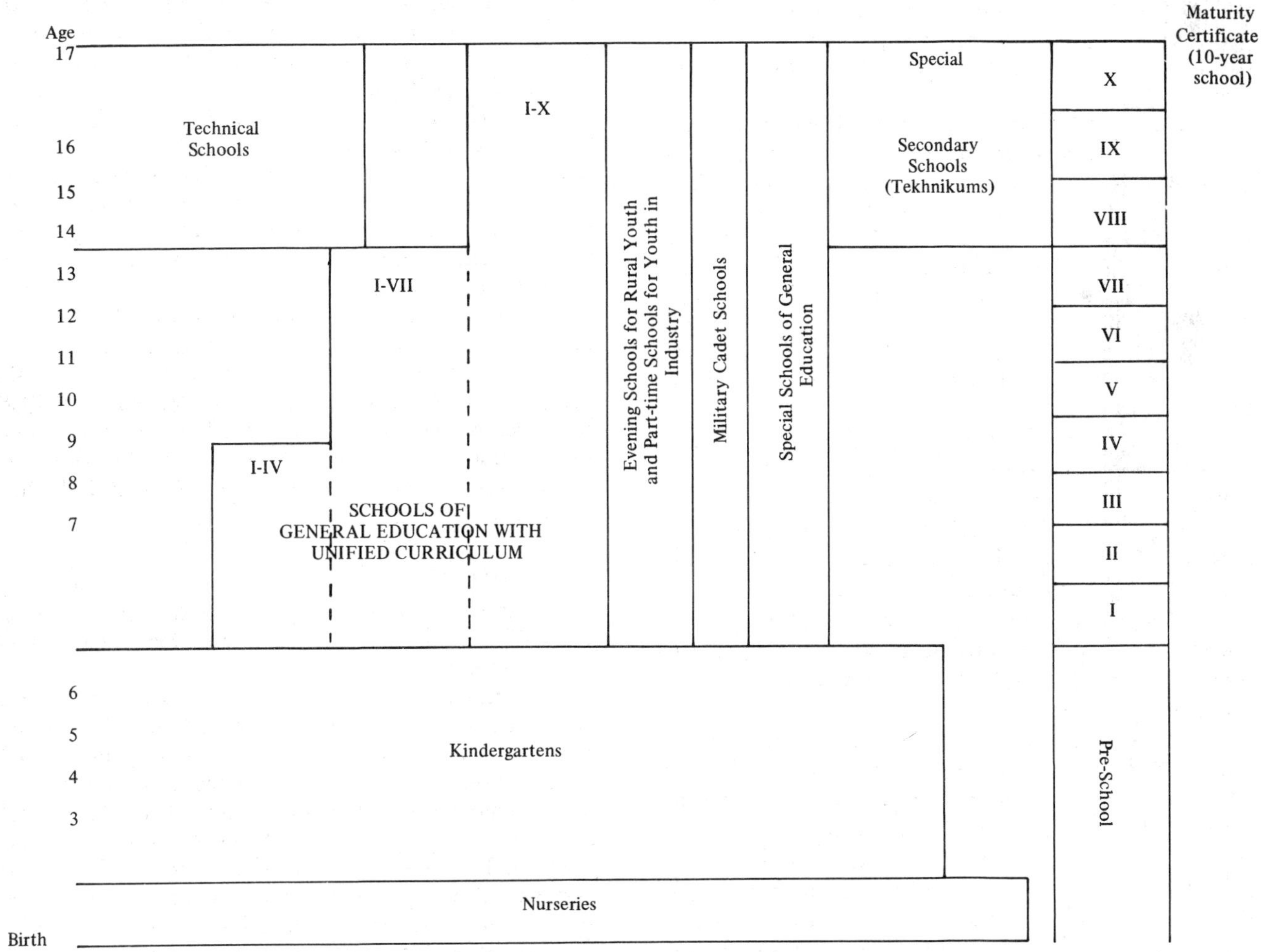

Figure 2. Educational system in the Soviet Union.

sidered the only way to remove this growing gap between education and the needs of the Soviet State. The respect for work and the working man was to be reestablished, the revolutionary spirit of 1917 recaptured, and agricultural and industrial production upgraded by an influx of a better educated youth.

Polytechnism had also an educational purpose. It was to develop habits of work and technical abilities. It had to give a professional orientation and enable the students to choose a profession suitable to their abilities.

Instruction time in the post-reform school has been increased from 9,857 hours to 12,830. Out of this 4,884 or 38 percent is devoted to humanities, 3,332 or 33 percent to polytechnic subjects, and 2,593 or 29 percent to sciences and mathematics. The fact that part of the students, upon graduating from the eight-year school, are channelled either to production or to a different type of school makes the upper division of the secondary school more selective.

Bilingualism in Soviet Non-Russian Schools

The October Revolution proclaimed the equality of all nations of the Russian Empire. At present the Soviet Union is composed of fifteen republics, called Union Republics, each of which represents a large ethnic group. The smaller ethnic groups in these republics enjoy political and cultural autonomy. That is, the native language is the language of the local government, the schools, and other institutions.

The Russian language is the official language of the Union. As such, Russian has become the medium of communication between the All-Union government and the governments of the Union Republics and the autonomous subdivisions; and it is the language of intercourse between all Soviet citizens.

The school reform of 1958 stipulates that parents have the choice of placing their children in schools conducted in the native tongue or sending them to schools where instruction is given in the Russian language. In the schools of national areas the study of Russian is elective, just as the study of the minority language is elective in the Russian schools of these areas. Though theoretically elective, Russian is widely studied in all types of schools as a required second native tongue and as the language of international communication and "socialist culture." Recently more and more schools for national minorities in the Russian Republic, the largest of the Union republics, have adopted Russian as the language of instruction instead of the native, which is taught only as a subject.

ADMINISTRATION

Education in the U.S.S.R. is controlled by the highest organs of Party and State, the Central Committee of the Communist Party and the Supreme Soviet. They supervise the overall educational policy

and have the initiative in carrying out reforms and changes on a national scale. Administration of educational activities is in the hands of the ministries of education of the individual republics.

There is no Union Ministry of Education (except for higher education and specialized secondary schools), but each of the 15 union republics and each autonomous republic has its ministry of education. At the provincial and district levels, school administration is in the hands of the provincial, city, and district boards, which act as local departments of the ministry of education. The city and district boards have jurisdiction over the school directors.

Each provincial and district Soviet has its education committee which cooperates with the boards of education in the capacity of an advisory body. The Party has its educational committees at local levels, and they supervise the implementation of educational policies of the State and Party. They take care of ideological education through the communist youth organizations, the Pioneer and Komsomol.

The boards of education maintain a staff of inspectors who are recruited from among competent and experienced teachers. Their function is to visit schools, to evaluate the work of the teachers and administration, and to help raise the standard of teaching and education.

Education is financed by the State. Usually about 14 percent to 15 percent of the total budget is allocated for enlightenment.

Though the whole system is centralized, consideration is given to local conditions. Constant experimentation in methods of teaching and educational activities is carried on and results are subject to broad discussions before any changes or reforms are undertaken. Ideas originate not only at the highest level, but very often at the grassroots level too.

PRESCHOOL EDUCATION

Right after the October Revolution measures were taken to organize preschool education. The initiators of the movement believed in the great importance and influence of preschool education. A Directorate of Preschool Education was established and an Institute to supervise teacher training opened. Originally plans were made for universal preschool education, but they had to be abandoned because of a shortage of funds.

Development of preschool education was slow in the twenties. Progress increased in the period of industrialization of the country. Since most of the Soviet women worked, child-care service had to be organized. Very often plants opened preschool institutions in which mothers could leave their children for the whole week and take them home only for week ends.

Preschool education is subdivided into two divisions: nurseries or creches for children from six weeks to three years; and kindergartens for children from four to seven years. Nurseries or kindergartens may be organized upon the initiative of any enterprise for the children of its employees or by any group of parents. Tuition is required from parents who can afford to pay. The rate depends upon the economic situation of the parents and varies from 30 to 100 rubles a month. Poor parents are exempted. The fees cover only 25-35 percent of the annual cost. The remaining part is covered by the state or sponsoring institution.

Preschool institutions differ widely in housing and facilities. A nursery or kindergarten in a collective farm may be accommodated in a thatch-roofed house; in a city it may be in a specially designed building.

At the head of a nursery or a kindergarten is a director who is assisted by teachers, a pediatrician, and a medical nurse. The domestic contingent consists of a bursar, a cook, and cleaners. The director and teachers are trained in nursery or kindergarten education. Preschool institutions may function on a full-time or seasonal basis.

Nurseries take care of the physical development of the child. A good nursery consists of a playroom, bedroom, and washroom. Children are divided into groups according to age. A mother who has a child in the nursery is required to attend courses given by the nursery.

Formal education begins in the kindergarten. It aims at an all-around development of children of preschool age, at bringing them up in the spirit of collectivism, of communist morality.

The program of education is prepared by the institutes of the Academy of Pedagogical Sciences. It emphasizes physical and mental health, the development of artistic skills, and the beginnings of academic instruction. The children are educated in the native language. They are divided into groups of twenty-five according to age. They are taught drawing, painting, singing, and dancing. Children of the senior groups learn by games, reading, simple arithmetic, and correct speech. Stories of the best classical authors are read to them and basic moral values are instilled.

Close contact is kept with the parents. The kindergarten teachers visit the parents to observe the living conditions of the child and to discuss educational policies with the parents. The parents are expected to cooperate with the kindergarten in developing certain habits. At home the children should be taught to keep their personal belongings in order and to assist in taking care of their younger brothers and sisters.

THE EIGHT-YEAR SCHOOL

The basic general educational school is the eight-year school which is compulsory. The first four grades form the primary school. In some areas inhabited by ethnic groups, a preparatory class precedes the first grade.

Elementary Grades

The main subject in the grades is the native language. Reading instruction is phonetic. The children learn at the beginning letters and sounds and very quickly pass to meaningful reading. A fourth-grader has to master a vocabulary of 10,000 words and acquire the ability of correct expression in the native language.

The basic textbooks are the same in all schools. They are prepared by competent scholars and are remarkable for their literary, cultural, and educational values. They contain material selected from great Russian writers and poets and are illustrated with reproductions of famous Russian painters.

Beginning with the third grade the native language is coupled with introductory information in science and history. The textbooks contain literary and informational sections. The literary section consists of selections from the great novelists and poets of the nineteenth and twentieth centuries. Already in the grades foundation is laid for a systematic study of native literature.

The informational section includes readings from science, geography, and history: dramatic episodes from the past and great achievements of the present.

The second subject is arithmetic. The pupils have to acquire the mastery of the four arithmetical operations and learn to work with weights and measures.

In the fourth grade, history and science coupled with geography are taught as separate subjects. In geography elementary concepts of the planet and the topography of the U.S.S.R. are taught. In history highlights of the history of the U.S.S.R. are taught. In natural science a systematic presentation of inanimate nature (air, water, mineral resources and soil) is given.

Drawing. In grades one and two, the pupils draw with crayon and water color. In grades three and four, they learn about the distribution of light and shade.

Singing. The object of singing instruction is to develop love for music and singing.

Physical Education. The program includes gymnastic exercises, walking, running, jumping, and marching.

Labor. The pupils have to acquire simple skills in the use of paper and cardboard and work with wood. They make such objects as houses, barns, and windmills from paper and cardboard. They work with clay and they sew. In grade four they also bind books and make models of machinery.

From grade three the children are expected to participate in socially useful work, such as tending public parks, raising poultry and rabbits at collective farms.

Political Education. Political and ethical education is stressed from the first grade. National pride and patriotism are inculcated, enthusiasm is instilled for great leaders of the past and present, hard work and sacrifice are glorified.

Grades Five to Eight

Native Language. A systematic study of language and literature begins in grade five. The emphasis is on the development of the ability to speak and to write correctly. Sixty-four percent of instruction time allocated for the native language is devoted to grammar. The study of literature is based on independent reading and textual interpretation. Its aim is to promote ideological, ethical, and aesthetic education.

Mathematics. Arithmetic is completed in the first half of the sixth grade. It includes fractions, decimals, percentages, and proportions. Algebra and geometry begin in the second semester of grade six. Algebra includes solution of equations of first, second, and higher degree; factorization of polynomials, roots, and powers.

The study of geometry is begun in grade six. It includes parallelism, triangles, quadrilaterals, circles, ratios, and proportions of segments, similar figures, and areas of polygons. Application of theory in practice is stressed.

History. The history program includes ancient and medieval history, introductory history of the U.S.S.R. and modern history of foreign countries.

Geography. The study of geography includes physical and economic geography of the world and of the U.S.S.R. The students are expected to be familiar with the political map and to be able to identify nations and territories. They study the natural resources of the U.S.S.R. and its economic growth.

Biology. The biology program includes botany, zoology, principles of Darwinism, human anatomy, and physiology.

Physics. Elementary notions of mechanics, heat, and electricity are taught. Application of physical laws and the underlying principles of technology are stressed.

Chemistry. Basic facts of inorganic chemistry are taught. Demonstration and experimentation are applied.

Foreign Language. The main objective is a reading and speaking knowledge. A graduate of an eight-year school should be able to (1) carry on a conversation in the foreign language he studied about the topics covered in the curriculum and (2) read without the aid of a dictionary texts based on familiar grammatical material and containing no more than four to six percent of unknown words. In most schools English, French, and German are the Languages studied.

Drawing. Classes in drawing include perspective, decorative and thematic drawing, painting, and appreciation of art.

Singing. Reading of musical notes and music appreciation are taught.

Physical Education. The program includes gymnastics, athletics, and military training.

Labor. The program includes working with wood and metal, elementary electric working and lighting, and work on the school plots. The students grow vegetables, plant trees, and help in keeping the school grounds orderly. The students receive introductory production training. Many schools cooperate with plants in mass production of various useful articles. In grade eight fundamentals of plant growing and agricultural machinery are studied.

Detailed Analysis of the Study Plan

Literature. A systematic course in prerevolutionary and Soviet literature is presented. Western European literature is given some consideration, too.

Mathematics. Mathematics includes algebra, limits, proportions, exponential and logarithmic functions, solid geometry, introductory analytical geometry, trigonometry, functions, and derivatives.

History. A systematic course in the history of Russia and the U.S.S.R. is taught. A solid body of facts is given interpreted from the Marxian point of view.

Physics. Molecular physics, heat, electricity, optics, aerodynamics, atomic structure.

Astronomy. A Survey of Astronomy including the movement, structure, and development of celestial bodies is taught.

Chemistry. The program includes a systematic presentation of inorganic chemistry and an introduction to organic chemistry.

Biology. A systematic course in biology and principles of Darwinism is given.

Foreign Language. The objectives of foreign-language study are a speaking and a reading knowledge. Graduates should be able to make oral statements, to maintain a conversation on topics covered by the secondary school and to understand with the aid of a dictionary simple scientific, political, and literary texts.

Social Science. For the first time an introductory course into Marxist philosophy has been introduced in secondary schools in 1963. The purpose of the course is to strengthen ideological education. Two hours a week are devoted to the course in grade ten. Atheism and materialist views upon the world are stressed.

Polytechnical and Specialized Instruction (Production Training). The course in fundamentals of production has an agricultural or industrial profile. In grade nine the course in the fundamentals of production has about fourteen different options, including industrial enterprise, machine building plant, electric power plant, railroads. The student selects one of the options. The training is theoretical (232 hours) and practical. The student must also spend 1,124 hours preparing for a specific trade skill such as that of a metalworker or carpenter. In rural schools fundamentals of agricultural production are studied. Practical work is done in plant growing, animal husbandry, and operation of agricultural machinery. In summer the students work on state farms.

Extracurricular Activities

An important supplement to regular school work are the extracurricular activities. They are carried on in circles organized on each subject of interest to children. There are sports circles, technical circles, circles on photography, painting, music, foreign-language correspondence, tourism, hiking, athletics. Every student may join if his marks are not too low. The activities are supervised by instructors or trained leaders. In these circles the gifted and enterprising children find areas of self-development.

Schools for Gifted Children

For exceptionally bright children special programs are sponsored by universities. In large cities are eleven-year schools for artistically gifted children. These schools are usually attached to higher institutions, to conservatories, art schools, or theaters. The ballet schools generally accept children of seven or eight years.

Schools for Handicapped

Mentally disturbed children or those with illnesses such as tuberculosis and rheumatism receive medical care and study in boarding schools situated in resort areas. These so-called forest schools follow the program of the regular schools but at a slower pace.

Special schools take care of mentally retarded children, of the blind and deaf. Vocational courses are given to prepare them for jobs and thus help them become useful members of society.

Fundamental Unit of the Teaching Process

Nothing is left to chance in the Soviet school. Each teacher has to prepare a detailed plan for the whole year and for each lesson. At the beginning of the lesson, he has to enter the subject matter of the session in the class record book. The first part of the lesson has to be devoted to recitation. The answers of the students have to be evaluated and grades entered in the classbook and in the record book of the students. The second part of the lesson should be devoted to exposition of the new subject matter, summarization or fixation in the minds of the pupils of the covered material, and home assignment.

This planning and scheduling protects from drifting into chaos and is a necessity until an army of qualified teachers has been prepared. A tendency for moving away from routine, for more flexibility in the teaching process, is already noticeable. There is also a tendency to democratize the administration. In many schools the principal is chosen by the teaching personnel.

Youth Organizations

The organizations have a powerful educative influence on the school youth. Children of primary grades are organized as Octobrists. The Octobrists are taught the elementary concepts of self-organization, such as to prepare for a holiday or to keep the classroom clean. As they reach the age of ten, they join the Pioneer organization.

Pioneer

The purpose of the Pioneer is to bring up children to be cultured, healthy, courageous, cheerful, and fearless builders of a communist society. Each school has its Pioneer brigade which is subdivided into detachments and then into links. Each of these divisions has its council and chairman chosen by the children. At the head of the whole brigade is a senior Pioneer leader, an adult specially trained for the job, a paid member of the staff.

At the appropriate age, at least 90 percent of the children become pioneers. Admission is a very solemn occasion. An oath of allegiance is taken by each candidate and the red scarf, the symbol of the Pioneer, is tied around the neck.

One of the first tasks of the Pioneer is to develop cooperation with the school. The pioneers are urged to respect their parents and teachers and to be industrious. The marks of the pioneers are carefully reviewed in the Pioneer groups. Special help is provided to those who need it.

The Pioneers are initiated into the activities of the school and the community. They look after the children of the lower grades and assist in strengthening the discipline in school. They organize brigades to help in harvesting crops, destroying insects and rodents in the fields.

A network of Pioneer palaces is maintained throughout the country. In the palaces the Pioneers take part in different clubs devoted to physical education, dancing, music, tourism, art, or technology.

A strong feeling of loyalty is developed in the Pioneer groups. Massed physical exercises, choirs, participation in local festivals with songs and dances provide an outlet for youthful energy. A slow process of socialization and indoctrination takes place and a good many of the pioneers are ready to join the Komsomol when they reach the age of fifteen.

Komsomol

The Komsomol is organized like the Communist Party and is more selective than the Pioneer. Its purpose is to train the future communist elite, to involve the young people in all activities and campaigns of the Party, to set standards of conduct, and to improve discipline among the youth. This organization plays a vital part in winning the young generation for the Soviet regime in training a reserve of future dedicated communists. They generate enthusiasm for all construction projects of the Party and volunteer to help in all great industrial and agricultural tasks. In school they help organize sports festivals and holidays. They build up the proper public opinion by publishing wall newspapers in which they criticize or praise certain practices of their institution.

Ideology

Ideology permeates all disciplines taught in the Soviet school. Each of the disciplines has a strictly defined ideological objective. Science has to develop a materialistic view of the world and undermine religious beliefs which are regarded as a remnant of capitalism. History has to impart the concept of economic determinism, the belief that the capitalist world is doomed, that the Soviet system is the best. Geography has to develop national pride by giving factual data about the size and resources of the U.S.S.R. Russian literature overemphasizes the political and social message and develops that peculiar brand of Soviet patriotism which is a blend of Marxism and Russian nationalism. Political education pervades all textbooks, all teaching materials.

The effect of this kind of education has been to develop a distorted one-sided view of the world, a world divided into an evil capitalist part of oppressors and a Soviet part, the champion of justice and equality. The close link-up of ideological education with politics, which are always divorced from morality, has wrought havoc with the Soviet youth.

Any political change in the Party line is reflected in the programs and textbooks. In the time of Stalin the programs and the textbooks held to the dominant note of class struggle, the present teaching materials reflect the policy of coexistence and building up communism.

Forced to frequent re-evaluations because of the zigzags of the party line, the individual may lose faith in the social order of his country and in its institutions. Some students had a very low estimate of Soviet reality. While working on the collective farm, they considered this institution as worse than serfdom.

Under the impact of the very harsh realities of a police state and its accompanying evils, such as purges, terror, insecurity, and corruption, the individual very often begins to see the world as a fluid one, a jungle in which the strong and the cunning have all chances to survive and prosper.

Three types are bound to develop under such pressures of school and life: an enthusiast or a fanatic blindly believing the leaders in power and always ready to follow the party line; a passive type, paying lip service to official philosophy, but in reality indifferent to everything; a self-centered cynic, immoral, and striving after his own welfare.

The war revealed the pitfalls of the type of ideological education produced in Soviet schools. Thousands of people reared in communist beliefs failed to pass the test of faithfulness and devotion to the system. Discontent at the failure in moral education was fully expressed in the Soviet periodicals before the school reform of 1958.

Realization of the shortcomings of the school has given rise to the idea of educating youth from infancy through high school in closely supervised boarding schools.

BOARDING SCHOOLS

In his speech at the XX Congress of the Party in 1956, Khrushchev advocated the opening of boarding schools to take care of the great number of children requiring proper care, such as children of war widows or of broken homes. These considerations, however, were of secondary importance. The main reason was clearly defined by Kairov, chairman of the Academy of Pedagogic Sciences. "A fundamental reconstruction of the process of teaching and educating our youth is required to bring up a young generation that by its efforts will create a society unlike the old, *i.e.* a Communist society."

Boarding schools are increasing, but are beset with many problems. Such schools require a proper material basis which takes years to develop. An ideal boarding school should be opened in the countryside, in a healthful wooded area. It should be a kind of children's village with gardens and a farm of its own. It should have a library, laboratories, workshops, a gymnasium, and a medical center. The number of such schools is growing. Many of the existing boarding schools have been hurriedly opened in buildings adapted from old schools and lack even such necessities as bath and laundry facilities. The very regulations and instructions of the Ministry of Education on how to preserve food, how to prepare drinking water, how to use oil lamps, point to extremely primitive conditions. Some boarding schools are located in peasant huts. In a few of them the children have to prepare their own food. In some of them two-thirds of the students are day students, since there is no place to accommodate them in the dormitories. Some complain of not being provided with adequate food and clothing and of poor medical service. All of them struggle with educational problems, principally with a shortage of adequately trained educators. Boarding schools require highly qualified educators, able to organize both work and play.

Building up boarding schools for all the youth, as it is planned by the government, will be a very slow process. For one thing, they are expensive. The parents are expected to pay only for board and clothes, and even this rule has exceptions. In the Far North, in mountainous regions, and districts inhabited by nomadic people, the pupils are exempted from any fees. Children of needy parents are exempted wherever the boarding school is located. The contribution of the parents who pay toward the maintenance of the schools is very slight compared with what the state has to spend. These schools have to be very heavily staffed. Besides the teaching personnel there are for each forty pupils two educators, a cook, a cleaner, an accountant; for each eighty, a supplier of provisions. The school has to provide food, clothes, shoes, and textbooks for the children. Even the government considers the realization of the plan a long process.

Each boarding school has a patron, an industrial enterprise, or a collective farm of its area. Often the patron provides necessary equipment for laboratories, workshops, industrial and agricultural training and practice for the students. There are reports of boarding schools engaging in productive activities that become a source of income used for the benefit of the whole collective.

Common to all the boarding schools are the efforts to organize a self-governing student body and through it to educate the individual. The main group organization is the Pioneer. Teams are formed of individuals both of the same and different ages to provide supervision of older pupils over the younger ones, to create a homelike atmosphere. The youngsters are cared for by their patrons at meals at the table, and from them they acquire the habits of cleanliness and proper behavior. Both are supervised by their educators.

A boarding school has ideal conditions for combining general education with productive labor, for training patterns of behavior, and inculcating certain ways of thinking. Self-government gives the youngsters the illusion of freedom of any restraints which a child may resent at home. The pressures of the group are not questioned. On the contrary, the approval of the group is sought for as the greatest reward; disapproval is avoided as the greatest punishment. Under subtle leadership the children get conditioned to behave and to think according to a pattern. The possibilities of political indoctrination in such a group are enormous. The boarding school is therefore looked upon as the ideal Soviet school of the future.

Lengthened day programs are substitutes for boarding schools. Children involved in this program stay in school after classes are over. They get a hot lunch, rest, do their homework, and play games under the supervision of teachers.

EIGHT-YEAR SCHOOLS

The eight-year school suffers from many shortcomings. Its teaching personnel and equipment are inferior to that of the secondary school. Raising the standard of knowledge is considered an urgent matter. The school continues to be plagued by the problem of repeaters, children who are kept two years in the same grade. Some teachers who feel that they are under pressure of advancing to the next grade pupils with poor achievements practice a certain liberal attitude in grading, a thing which is considered a great vice.

Secondary Schools

Inadequate preparation for higher studies is the main shortcoming of the secondary schools. To be admitted to a university, an applicant has to pass a highly competitive examination. Each year 50 percent of the applicants fail in mathematics and physics and a good many in Russian language, literature, and history. The extension of the high school program has failed to secure vocational preparation. Many high school graduates do not work in the special field for which they have been prepared.

Vekua, professor of the Novosibirsk University and member of the Academy of Science, attacked one of the fundamental principles of the secondary school—the striving for an all-around development.[6]

According to his opinion the school programs are inordinately overloaded. Even the brightest students cannot master the syllabus. He thinks the program should be disburdened.

Another evil that he sees is the inadequate preparation which the secondary school teachers receive in the pedagogical institutes. Many of these higher schools suffer from a shortage of highly qualified specialists and a lack of modern teaching equipment.

There are still secondary schools staffed with teachers without higher education.

The Party and the school authorities complain of shortcomings in ideological education. Intensification of atheistic indoctrination is planned.

The criticism often voiced by parents and scholars of the overcrowded program of the eleven-year school finally led to action. In August, 1964, The Central Committee of the Communist Party and the Council of Ministers issued a decree on reducing the secondary school program to two years, to grades nine and ten. In the new program, 2100 hours have been allocated for general educational disciplines and 708 hours for polytechnic subjects. The production training program has been shortened to two years. This reduced program should provide sufficient theoretic and practical preparation for one of the mass professions in industry, construction, or agriculture. Schools are advised to choose such a specialty for

6. *Pravda*, July 20, 1964.

which preparation is possible in the course of two years. A qualification test should be taken at the end of grade ten and specialty certificates issued. In areas in which there are no conditions for providing professional preparation, production training should be given only in school shops and habits of work in a certain special field developed.

PART-TIME SCHOOLS

The general educational schools enroll the largest number of students in the Soviet Union. Though the upper grades are not compulsory, many students continue their studies in these grades. Those who are not interested and those who have to work for their support enter vocational schools or go to work and study part time in evening schools or correspondence schools.

Evening Schools for Working Youth and Rural Youth

It was the intention of the school reform of 1958 to make the evening school the main educational establishment in which young workers and farmers should complete their secondary education. The enrollment in these schools was in the Russian republic according to the Minister of Education in the RSFSR, about 3,000,000 in 1966-7. The organization of these schools is still in its beginning stage. They have no proper accommodation, are ill-equipped with teaching aids and teaching materials. The situation in correspondence schools is not much better.

Teachers of evening schools encounter difficult problems. The preparation of the students is uneven. Large numbers enroll at the beginning of the year, but a considerable percentage drops out. Attendance of those who continue is very irregular. Working under pressure to keep their students, the teachers are forced to a liberal attitude. The administration of institutes complains that students who have received the certificates of maturity in evening schools are not prepared for entering a higher institution.

Vocational Schools

In 1940, by a decree of the Council of the People's Commissars (Ministers) an Administration of Labor Reserves was set up. This agency is charged with training labor reserves for different industries and is given the power to draft rural and urban youth to be trained in vocational schools.

The following schools have been opened.

1. Factory apprentice schools (F.Z.O.) offering six-month to one-year courses to train youths between sixteen and nineteen years of age as mass production workers.
2. Trade schools offering a two-year program for training metal workers, chemists, miners, and transport workers.

3. Railroad schools offering a two-year program to train machinists, helpers, boilermakers, and fitters.

The vocational schools are tuition-free. The trainees are provided with room, board, uniforms, and work clothes. Graduates of these schools are considered as mobilized and are bound to work for four years with guaranteed wages in accordance with the general regulations.

In this way large numbers of rural and of urban youth that dropped out from schools were channelled into industry. Between 1940 and 1958 more than 10,000,000 workers were trained in the schools of the Labor Reserve. Metal and textile industries have their own schools, the plant and factory schools, in which about a 100,000 persons receive their training annually.

In the fifties the number of graduates of ten-year schools was so large that only 30 percent of them could be accepted by the higher educational institutions. The rest had to be channelled off to industry to satisfy the needs of the country for skilled workers. In 1954 vocational schools were opened for graduates of ten-year schools who were not admitted to higher institutions. These schools offered free training for different industries and dormitory accommodations for out-of-town students.

Many economic enterprises offer on-the-job-training.

Agricultural Production

Three-year on-the-job courses in agronomy and animal husbandry were organized in 1950. In 1953 courses were set up by the Administration of Labor Reserves to train machine operator personnel. In 1953 two types of schools offering vocational training in agriculture were set up by the Administration of the Labor Reserves.

1. Trade schools for the mechanization of agriculture offering two-year courses to train combine operators, tractor drivers, and mechanics for farm machinery.
2. Schools for mechanizers of agriculture offering one-year courses for training tractor drivers and combine operators. The schools are financed by the USSR Ministries of Agriculture and State Farms. In 1955 schools were opened offering one-year courses for tractor-driver mechanics. Trainees were provided with room, board, uniforms, and stipends. In 1959 vocational technical schools were established for agriculture to train graduates of ten-year schools as general mechanics, electromechanics, electricians, or agricultural laboratory assistants. Trainees are provided with room, board, uniforms, and stipends.

TECHNICUMS

Technicums belong to the category of secondary special educational institutions training middle-grade specialists. They are set up and financed by different ministries which are in need of specialists, and supervised by the ministries of education. They may be roughly divided into three types:

1. Schools training semiprofessional personnel in public health—nurses, medical assistants, dental and laboratory technicians.
2. Schools preparing semiprofessional personnel in education, music, and arts.
3. Schools training technicians for industry, transportation, and agriculture.

Two kinds of programs are offered by the technicums:

1. Three- and four-year courses for graduates of the seven-year school.
2. Two- and three-year courses for graduates of the ten-year school. Admission for full-time study is granted to persons in the ages between nineteen and thirty-five.

The number of technicums has been constantly growing to satisfy the needs of the country for skilled labor. Still admission is granted to only a part of the enormous number of applicants. There are technicums which have ten applications for each vacancy. Honor students are admitted without any examination. All other eligible applicants have to pass a competitive entrance examination. In certain schools the entrance examination is preceded by a specialty examination, the purpose of which is to determine the preparation and the abilities of the applicant for the chosen field.

The curriculum is overloaded. It usually comprises general educational courses (for graduates of the seven-year school), general courses in the special field, specialized courses, laboratory work, practice, military and physical training, and political education. The school is in session six hours a day. The number of instruction hours in 1200-1300. Before graduation the students are required to present a diploma project or to take a State examination. A serious problem for the students is a short supply of adequate textbooks caused by a necessity of constant revisions due to the constant change of specialties. In 1958, the technicums prepared for 275 different specialties. The demanding curriculum also presents great difficulties, especially to graduates of the seven-year school. According to estimates, only 60 percent of students graduate. Still the number of students is constantly growing; for example, in 1958, there were 2,011,000 students enrolled in technicums, as many as in the higher institutions in the same year.

HIGHER EDUCATION

Higher education in the USSR is highly specialized. Its purpose is to prepare specialists for all branches of national economy and culture, dedicated builders of communism. The following types of higher educational institutions are distinguished: universities, technical institutes, pedagogical institutes, foreign language institutes, medical institutes, institutes of fine art, academies, and conservatories of music. At present there are over forty universities and over seven hundred institutes.

National supervision of higher education is conducted by the USSR Ministry of Higher Education which takes care of the curricula in all institutions of higher learning. Local control is exercised by the republican ministries of education. Certain institutes are under the jurisdiction of the ministries concerned with the profession for which they prepare. So, for example, the medical institutes are under the jurisdiction of the Ministry of Health. The curricula, however, are supplied by the USSR Ministry of Higher Education.

Universities

A university is headed by a rector who is responsible for the whole institution. He is a member of the Communist Party, a distinguished administrator, not necessarily a scholar. He is assisted by a prorector who is always a prominent scholar. The prorector organizes instruction, supervises the academic program, the research carried out by the staff members and students, and the postgraduate program. In administrative and financial affairs, the rector is aided by a deputy who is in charge of buildings and grounds and all economic affairs of the institution.

The universities are divided into faculties (departments) representing the fields of specialization. Usually there are faculties of mathematics and physics, chemistry, biology, geography, history, and philology. Each faculty is headed by a dean and is in turn divided into "chairs" (sections), each headed by a professor. The dean is charged with the administration of his department. In addition to his normal load of teaching six hours a week and research, he has to spend three hours in his office, for which he is paid 50 percent of his salary.

The executive organ of the university is the academic council which is chaired by the rector and consists of the deans of the faculties, heads of sections, prominent professors, representatives of the Party, trade union, and the responsible ministry. It deals with the general problems concerning the whole institution.

The Teaching Staff

The teaching staff of a university consists of professors, docents (associate professors), senior instructors (assistant professors), instructors, and assistants. A docent and a professor have to have the degree of a candidate of sciences. A professor is also expected to hold a doctor's degree. Not all professors, however, have this degree. All of the teaching staff are expected to do independent research.

Professors and docents are elected by the Academic Council by secret ballot and are confirmed by the Ministry of Higher Education. After five years they are subject to reappointment. A competition is announced for their position and everybody who is qualified has the right to apply. This arrangement is designed to stimulate the professors and docents to constant research in their field.

Admission

In theory, any graduate of a secondary school under thirty-five may apply for admission. To be admitted, an applicant has to pass a competitive entrance examination based on the material covered in secondary schools.

In practice, however, there are other considerations which influence the admission policy. Each year there is an enrollment quota for higher and specialized secondary education which is determined by the needs of the state.

According to the recent regulations of the Ministry of Higher and Special Secondary Education, priority in admission will be given to applicants with at least two years of work experience and to demobilized soldiers. Directly from general school will be admitted only about 20 percent, in the first place, honor students and students with special aptitudes in the chosen field.

A student receives a stipend which enables him to cover the expenses for room, board, and other necessaries of life. Students usually live in hostels, men and women in different wings of the same building. A student may forfeit his stipend if he does not maintain his grade average.

The curriculum is very demanding and specialized. In the course of five years the student has to take 5,000 to 5,400 instruction hours. The only general educational courses included besides the foreign languages, are the courses in the socio-political disciplines: in Dialectical and Historical Materialism, in Political Economy, and in Marxist-Leninist Philosophy. At present the whole program is being intensified. A new course in Foundations of Scientific Communism has been introduced in many schools.

Dialectic materialism is considered the only scientific view upon the world, since it is supposed to be based on the achievements of all sciences. It is accepted by the Soviet educators just as a religious code might be accepted and is not subject to discussion from any other point of view than that approved of in the USSR. In the courses on Political Economy and the Foundations of Scientific Communism a tremendous body of facts is given interpreted only from the Soviet point of view. The purpose is a wholehearted unquestioning acceptance of the Soviet version of communism as absolute truth, of the Soviet system as the best.

The student is expected to attend all lectures, laboratories, and seminars. He is to pass in the course of the semester a great many quizzes and examinations at the end of each semester. Some examinations are written, most of them are oral before a panel. Every year the student is expected to write a term paper and before graduation a diploma thesis based on independent research. On completing the thesis, he has publicly to defend it before a commission.

On graduation, the student receives a diploma specifying his specialty. No special degrees are awarded. Students who graduate with honors may enroll in a postgraduate training program, called *aspirantura,* which prepares either for university teaching or research.

The *aspirantura* is a highly specialized three-year program at the end of which the student has to submit a thesis and publicly defend it. On completing the program the postgraduate receives the title of candidate of sciences.

The highest degree, the doctor's degree, is achieved by relatively few people. It requires many years of study and an original contribution in the special field. It is in its scope and requirements higher than the doctor's degree in Western Europe or America. In 1961-62 the Higher Attesting Commission confirmed 818 doctor's degrees. The age of the people who received the degree is very characteristic (Information source: *Pravda,* July 26, 1962).

AGE	NUMBER OF PEOPLE
Before reaching 30	2
Between 30-39	10
Between 40-50	291
Between 50-60	300
Above 60	125

Job Assignments

Before graduation the students are informed of job openings in their field of specialization. Conditions of work are discussed and consideration is given to the wishes of the student. Upon graduation the student receives a job assignment and is expected to remain at his place of work for three years and thus repay the state for his education.

Correspondence Courses

About 530 institutions of higher learning have their correspondence departments. There are twenty-three special correspondence institutes which have their consultation centers and branches. Enrollment in correspondent departments is constantly growing. Over 40 percent of students study at present in correspondence programs.

The requirements for admissions to correspondence courses are the same as for full-time study, except that there is no age limit. To be admitted the applicant has to pass the entrance examination. After the examination a ten-day enrollment course is given in which the curriculum and methods of independent study are explained and introductory lectures are given.

In the course of the year the correspondent student has to spend thirty days in the summer and ten days in the winter at the institution. During the residence period the student does his laboratory work, attends review lectures, introductory lectures for the following term, and passes the required tests and examinations.

Correspondence institutes have consultation centers in places where there are more correspondent students. At the center students may obtain help and attend lectures. The student has to submit written assignments which are the only way of checking his progress. Correspondence study lasts one year longer than a regular program. The training of correspondence students is on a much lower level than that of regular students. The dropout rate is very large.

Secondary school graduates who have been forced to take a job are constantly encouraged to complete their higher education in evening courses. Evening students cover the same syllabus but study one semester longer. They are allowed a paid leave for ten days to take the examinations. In the final semester, they are given a four-month leave to prepare the diploma thesis and to pass the state examination. During that time the student receives a stipend.

More than half of the students in higher education study in part-time programs.

Teacher Education

The program of training teachers has been constantly lengthened in the USSR. At present kindergarten and primary school teachers are trained in pedagogical schools offering two-year programs for graduates of the complete secondary school. Secondary school teachers are trained at the universities or in pedagogical institutes, with a five-year program for graduates of the eleven-year school. University graduates are considered as better qualified teachers, even if they have no pedagogical training, for they are very well grounded in their special fields.

Pedagogical Institutes

Pedagogical institutes are divided in faculties (departments) of related subjects, such as mathematics and physics or Russian language literature and history. Candidates for admission must be graduates of a secondary school and have to pass a highly competitive entrance examination. Accepted candidates receive stipends which cover room, board, and a minimum for clothes and entertainment.

The students are required to choose two majors, two related specialties in which they receive intensive training. The lecture load of the students is heavy. It ranges from 4,110 to 4,818 hours during a five-year course. The students are required to pass an average of about thirty-five examinations, about fifty minor quizzes, and a state examination before graduation. The curriculum stresses subject matter, professional and ideological education, practice teaching, and familiarity with extracurricular activities.

Besides having to cope with an unusually heavy load, the students are expected to participate in social activities, such as local or republican Soviet elections and youth organization. As future teachers, they are closely watched. Each pedagogical institute has its secret department reporting on the political reliability of the students and teachers.

Graduates of pedagogical institutes do not compare favorably with university graduates who have less professional training but more schooling in subject matter and familiarity with the techniques of independent research. Nor are pedagogical institutes staffed with highly qualified teaching staffs as universities are nor is their equipment up to date.

Job assignment presents no difficulties. Before graduation the district boards of education send in their requirements to the Ministry of Higher Education and the students choose the school they like and apply for a job. In a recent year the pedagogical schools and institutes graduated 135,000 teachers. Most of them were assigned jobs. The army of primary and secondary school teachers is at present 2,500,000 men.

In the hierarchy of Soviet Society the teacher occupies a respected and responsible position. Appreciation of his work and responsibilities is often expressed in the press. Twenty-seven teachers are deputies of the Supreme Soviet. Thousands of teachers are deputies of local Soviets.

In certain districts it has become tradition to organize receptions for the new teachers, to prepare living quarters, and to make them feel at home in their new place of work.

A teacher is secure in his job if he is competent and carries out conscientiously his duties. Very rarely is he dismissed without exhausting all means of helping him. After twenty-five years of service he may retire, drawing a pension for the rest of his life. He may stay in service if he chooses, drawing his retirement pay in addition to his regular salary.

A teacher is paid for class guidance, correcting of papers and any additional teaching he may perform above his normal load of twenty-four hours in the elementary grades and eighteen hours in the secondary school. The new scale of teacher salaries is slightly above that of the physicians. This salary can secure only a very moderate life. The teacher is required and expected to be an idealist and enthusiastic about his work and mission in society. The satisfaction derived from his prestige and public recognition should compensate for the hard life he has.

Elementary school teachers with secondary education receive a much lower pay than those with higher education. They may continue their education in evening or correspondence courses which are organized by each pedagogical institute.

BIBLIOGRAPHY

BEREDAY, GEORGE Z. E. *The Changing Soviet School.* Boston: Houghton Mifflin Co., 1960.

BUTJAGIN, A. S., and SALTANOV, JU. A. *Universitetskoe Obrazovanie.* V SSSR: Izdatelstvo Moskovskogo, Universiteta, 1957.

COUNTS, GEORGE T. *The Challenge of Soviet Education.* New York: McGraw-Hill Book Company, 1957.

DEWITT, NICHOLAS. *Education and Professional Employment in the USSR.* Washington: National Science Foundation, 1961.

———. *Soviet Professional Manpower: Its Education, Training, and Supply.* Washington, D. C.: National Science Foundation, 1961.

FLORINSKY, MICHAEL T. *Russia—A History and an Interpretation.* New York: The Macmillan Company, 1959.

GALKIN, K. T. *Vysshee Obrazovanie.* Moscow: I Podgotovka Nauchnyky, Kadrov V SSR, Sovetskaja Nauka, 1958.

GANELIN, S. I. *Ocherki Po Istorii.* Moscow: Srednej Shkoly, 1954.

GONCHAROV, N. K. *Perestroika Sovetskoi Shkoly.* Moscow: Izdatelstvo Znanie, 1959.

GONCHAROV, N. K., and KOROLEV, F. F. *Novaja Sistema Narodnogo, Obrazovania V. CCR.* Moscow: Akademia Pedagogicheskix Nauk, 1960.

JOHNSON, WILLIAM H. E. *Russia's Educational Heritage.* Pittsburgh: Carnegie Press, 1950.

KAIROV, I. A. *Sovetskaja Shkola Na Sovermennom Etape.* Moscow: Akademia Pedagogicheskix Nauk, 1961.

KING, EDMUND. *Communist Education.* London: Methuen & Co., 1963.

KONSTANTINOV, N. A. *Ocherki Po Istorii.* Moscow: Srednej Shkoly, 1954.

KONSTANTINOV, N. A. and STRUMINSKY, V. JA. *Ocherki Po Istorii.* Ychpedgiz: Nachalnogo Obrazovania, V Rossii, 1949.

KREUSLER, ABRAHAM. *The Teaching of Modern Foreign Langues in the Soviet Union.* Leiden: E. J. Brill, 1958.

MAKARENKO, A. S. *O Vospitanii Molodezhi.* Trudrezervizdat, 1951.

———. *O Vospitanii Vsemie.* Moscow, 1955.

———. *Problemy Shkolnogo Sovetskogo Vospitania.* Uchpedgiz, 1963.

MAXWELL, ROBERT. *Information USSR.* New York: The Macmillan Company, 1962.

ROSEN, SEYMOUR M. *Higher Education in the USSR.* Washington, D. C.: U. S. Department of Health, Education, and Welfare, 1963.

SPIRIN, L. F., and SHAGOVA, A. JA. *Shkola Internat.* Moscow: Uchpedgiz, 1958.

TRACE, ARTHUR S. *What Ivan Knows that Johnny Does Not.* New York: Random House, 1961.

U. S. Department of Health, Education and Welfare. *Education in the USSR.* Washington, D. C., 1957.

———. *Soviet Commitment to Education.* Report of the First Official U. S. Education Mission to the USSR. Washington, D. C., 1959.

———. *Soviet Education Programs.* Washington, D.C., 1960.

Periodicals

Doshkolnoe Vospitanie
Inostrannye Jazyki V. Shkole
Nachalnaja Shkola
Narodnoe Obrazovanie
Semja I Shkola
Sovetskaja Pedagogika
Uchitelskaja Gazeta
Vestnik Vesshej Shkoly

Part Two

Education in Asia

AREA ESSAY: ASIA

Carlton E. Beck

Development and problems of Asia are too vast for unified treatment in any single essay. The geographic distances and topography, the religious and political differences, the racial and historical factors militate against such an essay. The nations must speak for themselves because their own perceptions of the past three or four thousand years have made more difference in their development than any sort of objective truth concerning that period. Fortunately, the authors of the essays in this section have done so.

Nonetheless, there are certain commonalities in outlook and certain events which have colored nearly all of Asia in some manner, with the influences depending upon many factors within each nation. Those who would understand Asia might begin with the three volumes edited by Charles A. Moore, entitled *The Chinese Mind, The Japanese Mind,* and *The Indian Mind,* published in 1967 by East-West Center Press, Honolulu, Hawaii. In it the three nations which have dominated the history of Asia more than any other eastern lands are examined by men who are of those nations, but who dispassionately delve into the views of the people and the origins of their thinking.

There are several good histories of Asia as a whole, but these are better done area by area, and the scholars have chosen to consider the areas primarily by historical period. Also, the fate of so many nations in Asia is so closely involved with that of three or four Western powers that complete understanding presupposes a knowledge of *their* "mind," to use Moore's term once again, juxtaposed with the Asian nations involved.

Among the important commonalities found in the East are the following:

An overriding concern with spiritual matters in all aspects of life.

An interest in ethical relationships among men, far more than in material wealth.

An attitude of the small importance of individual human *existence.*

A belief that those who see transcendent reality most clearly contribute far more in that role than by doing mundane work ("A scholar shall not carry a basket. . . .").

An acceptance, especially by the common people, that the spectre of hunger and disease shall be ever-present in their lands.

A distrust of neighboring groups, bordering almost on national paranoia in some cases, but based on historical grounds.

Fierce courage in the face of danger and trial.

A tendency generally to view life in dichotomies, as thesis-anti-thesis.

A faith in sacred or classic writings of the past for the resolution of present difficulties.

A reliance on the speculative rather than the empirical.

A sincere attempt to live one's philosophy or religion.

A class structure or caste structure which survives even most severe attempts to repress it.

A stoic acceptance of suffering in life as necessary, but an optimism about "freeing oneself" after this life.

Unswerving loyalties and sense of duty in the face of the most extreme hardships.

Preference for the abstract over the concrete.

A search for inner peace in a world of turbulence.

The immediate reaction of those knowledgeable about any specific area of the East may be "Yes, but . . ." or "How can one generalize for *all* of the East?" Let the listing stand as *propositions* rather than as *axioms* for any one nation. They are the listing of the editor rather than footnotes from other authors and editors. It is believed that they may aid in an understanding of the individual essays dealing with education. If some or all of the above apply to a nation, then that nation will show the effects in its views and practices in education and general culture.

Rather than delay the reading of the individual essays on education in the various selected nations of the East by recounting the well-explored dynasties, lives, periods, sacred books, and gaps in recorded history, let it be said only that he who would understand the East must immerse himself in it. It is not possible to understand it from slogans, from the accounts of Western "evaluators," or from a knowledge of military or regent successions. In the latter two cases, one must look not to sequences, but to consequences. What did they *mean* in the lives of the people and to the world?

As to the intrusion of Western explorers and colonial powers and their influence in the East, one can say only that their effect has been great in some respects and almost unnoticed in others. No one can deny the great effect that Marxist-Leninist doctrine has had on the China mainland, for example. This is a situation which at this point is so confused that prediction or evaluation becomes sheer guesswork, but undeniably the introduction of that brand of ideology will color Asian history—and world history—for decades. No one would seriously deny the great influence of Western technology upon the Far East, especially in Japan. But who is to say that Western religious thought has really permeated the East, all missionary efforts to the contrary? And who can say that Western ethical ideals or views of man have altered seriously the views of the East in these matters? These are only a few examples.

"East is East. . . ." Perhaps that should be the *end* of the quotation. But in the ever-shrinking world, it cannot be.

CAMBODIA

Mildred S. Kiefer

EARLY PERIOD (802-1863)

Cambodian education began in the days of the pagoda schools when Buddhist monks brought literacy to small groups of boys assembled for the purpose of receiving religious instruction.

Pupils' days were spent in chanting the Holy Scriptures and in copying passages extracted from the *Pali Canon* or *Tripitaka*, which had been inscribed and preserved on slender, palm-frond "pages." The activities were as repetitive as the stone faces of the "God-King" who looked down from the towers of Angkor Wat and upon whose power and benevolence the people depended.

The use of the pagoda itself as a classroom was followed in some instances by construction of separate school buildings within the pagoda compound. Parallel to the physical development there evolved a somewhat more comprehensive curriculum, although the major objective of the pagoda schools continued to be the provision of religious instruction.

FRENCH COLONIAL PERIOD (1863-1946)

In addition to the pagoda schools, which continued to exist and develop, were those organized by the French Colonial Government. Called "Franco-Khmer" (French Cambodian), these schools fulfilled a twofold purpose: (1) they made available to children of French nationals the same education they would receive in the mother country and (2) they educated whatever number of Cambodian youth the colonial government deemed necessary to meet its needs for minor functionaries.

CAMBODIAN INDEPENDENCE (1946-1953)

Cambodian independence was achieved by stages. On January 7, 1946, she was accorded autonomy by the French Government. Steps toward complete independence resulted in the surrender by France of all the attributes of sovereignty on November 9, 1953.

Laudably, the Cambodian government did not await complete sovereignty before attacking the problems of education. Ministry of Plan statistics revealed the following enrollments existing in 1951:

Elementary school enrollment:	176,000 pupils
Secondary school enrollment:	3,000 students
Total enrollment:	179,000

These findings resulted in the expressed concern of the government for more educational opportunity. This was matched by that of the Cambodian people for whom school, irrespective of kind or quality, was the symbol of achievement, and all that many parents asked was permission for their children to squeeze into the crowded, poorly-equipped, palm-thatched classrooms.

Few vocational opportunities existed for those children completing the six years of elementary school. Their hopes lay in being selected for secondary education. For those successful enough to graduate from the *lycée*, the coveted opportunity to enter government employment offered the primary means of escaping the harsh limitations of their rice-culture environment.

In 1951, governmental decrees were enacted which greatly affected education. In and of themselves the decrees were important, as they stipulated certain changes which were to occur; even more significant is the fact that they marked the beginning of Cambodian self-direction as evidenced by the replacement and revision of existing regulations, many of which had been decreed by the Indo-China Union in 1917.

Two of the most important developments were (1) the reorganization of the inspectorate of primary schools and (2) the reorganization of the Ministry of National Education. (See Figure 1, p. 136.)

A significant accomplishment of the former placed the supervision of the pagoda schools, renamed "Khmer-Primary" (actually the public schools of rural

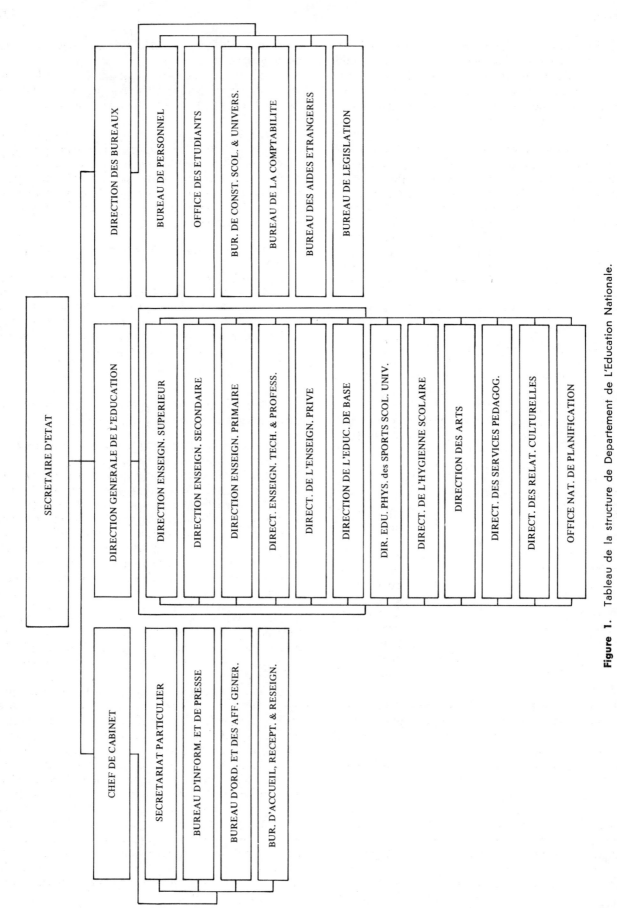

Figure 1. Tableau de la structure de Departement de L'Education Nationale.

136

Cambodia) under the direction of the provincial primary school inspector. This gave encouragement to a more liberalized curriculum, even though these schools were now looked upon only as a provisional solution of the shortage of teachers and classrooms, due to be progressively replaced by "Franco-Khmer" schools.

Accomplishment of the latter placed upon the Ministry the responsibility for the development of the following departments, as well as the training requirements of teachers in designated categories:

Primary Education, grades 1-6, called "Enseignment Primaire," and designated as grades twelfth through seventh after the French system, was undertaken by the above-mentioned Franco-Khmer and Khmer-Primary Schools. Upon completion of each level of schooling, appropriate certificates were awarded.

For the Franco-Khmer Schools the following qualifications were established:

1. *Teachers* were required to hold the secondary school certificate and, in addition, the teacher training-school certificate which could be obtained after a year's supplementary course devoted to professional training. Available records do not reveal the name or source of this supplementary year's training, but it is presumed to be the forerunner of The National Pedagogical Institute which operates at the present time.
2. *Assistant teachers* were required to hold the complementary school certificates, earned after six years of elementary schooling, and completion of an intensive short course in teacher training. They were recruited by competition.
3. *Pupil teachers,* "moniteurs," were employed chiefly at the first levels of primary education. They were recruited by competitive examination from candidates holding one of the three following qualifications: Higher Bonze (Buddhist monk) teacher's certificate granted at the end of a two-year course at the Bonze Higher School; a traditional education teacher's certificate from a modernized pagoda school; or the Diploma of Higher Pali Studies.

In the Khmer Primary Schools, most of the teachers, all of whom were monks, held elementary school certificates, awarded upon completing three years of primary school, and had taken an additional year of training in a school of instruction established especially for them.

Headmasters and Inspectors of Khmer Primary Schools had usually completed a two-year course in a higher school of instruction.

Secondary Education, grades 7-12, "Enseignment Secondaire," designated as grades sixth through first, after the French system, was undertaken by one government school, *Lycée* Sisowath, and by a few private secondary schools. Upon graduation, students were, and still are, awarded the first baccalaureate, *Baccalaureate 1 er Partie.*

Students successfully completing an additional thirteenth year, *Classes Terminales,* were and are awarded the second baccalaureate, *Baccalaureat 2 ieme Partie.*

Because the new education law adopted the French certification system, secondary school teachers were required to have the same preparation as those in France. It therefore remained necessary to import nearly all of the country's secondary school staff from France. This ensured the Cambodian secondary schools of two values:

1. It provided qualified teachers for secondary schools, and
2. It provided, under a treaty agreement with France, that secondary school graduates would be admitted without examination into French universities. On the negative side, the annual round trip from France was very costly to the Cambodian government, and the drive for nationalization, or *Khmerization* desired by the country's leaders was retarded.

Vocational and Technical Education. In this department four courses were provided:

1. *Apprenticeship Centers* offering two years of work in shoemaking and dressmaking
2. *Workshop Centers* providing two-year courses for the training of local craftsmen who, until then, had had no training opportunity whatsoever
3. *Technical Colleges,* secondary schools, offering one to three years' training in the skills of pipefitting, copper-smithing, electronics, and carpentry
4. *The School of Cambodian Arts* for the training of craftsmen in such traditional arts as goldsmithing, enamelling, lacquering, silk weaving, and sculpture

It is unclear as to the qualifications of the instructors of these classes. They were quite likely native craftsmen who, in turn, had been taught by other craftsmen in a kind of informal guild-type organization.

Higher Education. Organized in this division was the *National Institute of Legal and Economic Studies,* open to holders of the baccalaureat and of the secondary certificate, who, after a two-year course could take a diploma, *bacchelier endroit,* or the qualifying law certificate. In 1952, the year following the decrees, a third year was added, which allowed bachelors of law to become licentiates in law. The Institute thus became a law faculty which was placed under the patronage of the Dean of the Paris Faculty of Law. Its principal objective was the training of civil servants for positions in legal, administrative, and financial departments of the government. As in the case of secondary schools, the faculty members were imported from France.

Specialized Schools. A number of Ministries met the need of providing training for staff members by appropriating funds for this purpose:

1. *Public Health* organized a four-year course for health officers.
2. *Public Works* provided a two-year course for training foremen to become assistant engineers.
3. *National Economy* developed two types of schools: *The National School of Agriculture and Stockbreeding,* a three-year course for the vocational training of inspectors of agriculture, animal diseases and stockbreeding, and of agricultural technicians. *The School of Forestry,* a three-year course for training inspectors of rivers and forests.
4. *National Defense* trained officers for the Khmer National Army.
5. *Public Worship* organized two schools: A Buddhist Institute for the study and research of Buddhism and the Higher School of Pali, for the advanced study of Pali, the specialized language of the monks, principally with a religious objective.

Available records fail to indicate the source or qualifications of the instructors of Specialized Schools. It is assumed they were educated in France, with the exception of those in the Public Worship category, obviously trained in Buddhist institutions by Buddhist professors.

Private Schools. Minority groups, notably Chinese and Vietnamese, organized and supported their own schools.

There were also other private schools usually with a Roman Catholic affiliation which served principally the children of French nationals, as did the Franco-Khmer government schools of the colonial period. Cambodian students were also admitted to these schools.

CONTEMPORARY CAMBODIA (1953-   )

Operational aspects of the decrees were paralleled, if not implemented, by the advent of foreign aid, the first of which was actually begun in 1951. The next few years saw the development of cooperative efforts of such international organizations as United Nations (UNESCO, WHO, FAO), the Colombo Plan, and the assistance of individual countries, including Australia, Czechoslovakia, Japan, France, The People's Republic of China, The Soviet Union, The United States of America, and West Germany. Since French Aid had its inception in the colonial period, its activities are more properly described as continuing rather than initiatory.

Comprehensive surveys were now undertaken by the Ministry of Education, in order that the needs of the country might be projected against the resources of foreign assistance.

It was to be expected that the extension of educational opportunity received priority. Between 20 and 24 percent of the national budget was allocated to this project. In addition, private funds accounted for still more schools.

The Ministry of Plan statistics for 1961 revealed remarkable gains at the end of the first decade of independence: more than threefold at the elementary level; an excess of nine times the 1951 figure at the secondary level.

1951	1961	
Elementary pupils 176,000	Elementary pupils 540,000	
Secondary students .. 3,000	Secondary students 28,000	
Total enrollment 179,000	Total enrollment ..568,000	

By 1966-7, Cambodian education enrolled about 850,000 students at primary level; 90,000 at secondary level; and about 8,000 in higher education and technical-vocation education combined. Paradoxically, the expansion aggravated rather than ameliorated the problem of the unemployed graduate. Secondary school curricula, still largely classical, ill-fitted him for the demands of business and industry for skilled workers, and he was as reluctant as ever to face the prospect of life as a rice farmer.

This fact was cause for grave concern not only on the part of the Ministry but government officials as well, headed by His Royal Highness, Prince Norodom Sihanouk.

Popularization of working with one's hands was the motivation for organizing Work Days when government officials headed by Prince Sihanouk put in a day's labor on such projects as the building of schools and roads. Even the construction of the railroad between the capital city and the seaport was initiated on such a day.

Action programs designed to change attitudes and to provide training which would alleviate this situation resulted in the development of the following:

1. Five model *collèges,* grades six to nine, were built, each with a department of vocational education offering such courses as typing, industrial arts, and home economics.
2. The newly created Bureau of Pedagogical Services began the development of its Industrial Arts Section, first by the training of a chief and assistant chief who, in turn, trained others and placed them in Pilot Shops. At the end of 1962, 400 such shops had been established in elementary schools throughout the country.
3. Work was begun on the expansion and construction of new facilities in a vocational high school, L 'Ecole des Arts et Métiers, grades 7-12, designed to accommodate 1500 students. In 1964, four classroom wings had been completed and work had begun on the shop areas.

Concurrent with secondary school activities were those at the elementary level, the two main features being the construction of fourteen Model Schools throughout the provinces and a college, Le Centre du Préparacion Pédagogique à Kampong Kantuot, grades seven to ten, for the education of elementary teachers, the first of its kind in the country.

The fourteen Model Schools were organized on the community-school concept, whereby problems of the community became the subject-matter of the curriculum. Emphasis was placed upon health education, gardening, practical science, cooperatives, home economics, and industrial arts. The methodology, functional and pragmatic, constituted changes from the repetitive exercises of an earlier period and facilitated the coordination of subject-matter with related activities outside the classroom walls—the school compound and the community.

The schools were "Model," not in the narrow sense of providing curriculum design to be copied *in toto* by their neighbors, but rather in the example they furnished. Their willingness to forego the security of repeating old patterns in the search for meaningful solutions to problems was dynamic and contagious. An earlier generation would not have identified these problems, much less accept them as appropriate curriculum content.

Development of the Teachers College saw the modification of old customs and the introduction of totally new ones. Freshmen students were accepted on a fifty-fifty ratio for boys and girls, thus markedly extending the opportunity of women for education and for professional advancement. The status of, and the desire for, education was demonstrated by the fact that for every group of 200 freshmen admitted, more than 5000 applications were received for these coveted positions. As in the Model Schools, there was also the trend toward the acceptance of a more pragmatic philosophy and curriculum. Coupled with this was the changed attitude of the graduates regarding the villagers in whose schools they taught. For some, it meant the acquisition of a totally new set of human-relations skills. Rural folk were now linked in partnership in the new enterprise of school and community development, rather than enduring the isolation and rejection of the uneducated, an accepted practice of earlier days.

Other institutions mentioned earlier underwent change and expansion. The National Institute of Legal and Economic Studies became the Royal Khmer University, embracing departments whose forerunners were the training courses in the Specialized Schools category, identified now as colleges of medicine and medical science, law, arts and humanities, science and technology, and, for professional education, The National Pedagogical Institute.

The National College of Agriculture, a separate institution, is under reorganization. Plans include the awarding of a diploma at the end of a four-year course.

RECAPITULATION

Cambodia's history of education, begun when monks assembled groups of boys for religious instruction, proceeded to the colonial period where it was influenced by the French classicists, then moved on to independence which period also contributed its share of obstacles, problems and achievements.

In summary, the following topics are extracted as being particularly relevant to the total situation:

1. *Goals:*

Short-range goals were expressed almost wholly in terms of need for increased educational opportunity, meaning simply, more classrooms and more teachers.

Long-range goals, while continuing to stress opportunity, defined education qualitatively in terms of personal development in relation to the needs of the country.

2. *Obstacles:*

Carried over from the early period has been the persistent power of tradition, the greatest single deterrent in the movement toward change; the transmission solely, of religious instruction by the monks, the long adaptation of a subject people to colonial authority and the prestige value of classical education are obstacles still to be overcome in terms of goal achievement.

3. *Major Problems:*

Cambodia's greatest problem is caused by its geographical location. Even though she succeeds in maintaining political neutrality, the inherent limitations and anxieties are of no small consequence.

If peace and stability are achieved in Southeast Asia, economic expansion in business, industry, and agriculture necessary to the support of education will likely follow.

4. *Assets:*

Of the six million inhabitants, about 87 percent live in the rural areas. Rice farming accounts for about 80 percent of the tillable land, 3,080,000 acres, the balance being planted to rubber, cotton, and a variety of other crops as corn, edible beans, sesame, peanuts, kapok, pepper and tobacco. Tree and shrub crops yield palm sugar, coconut, citronella, coffee, a number of native fruit trees notably mango and papaya, and a few imported varieties.

Rice yields have increased due to agricultural extension programs, and while yields are still too low, the country exports a surplus of from 100,000 to 300,000 tons annually.

Rubber exports amounted to more than 39,000 tons in 1961, and in the same year cotton production amounted to almost 30,000 tons.

In addition to agriculture, stock-raising, fishing, and forestry are being developed. Present livestock estimates include 1,300,000 cattle, 450,000 sheep, and 650,000 pigs.

Another important item of revenue is the exportation of freshwater fish, the Great Lake being the most productive area of its size in the world.

Forests cover more than 45 percent of the land and include low-cost species which are consumed locally, as well as several varieties classified as precious woods, valuable for export.

Local handicrafts supplement the income of the rural and village population who engage in silk spinning, embroidery, basket-making, pottery, and the manufacture of agricultural implements, boats and carts.

Private industry since 1953 has made notable gains boasting a distillery, wineries, rice mills, and a few factories producing assorted articles. A latex mill, developed in the French Colonial period, is still in operation. State-owned industries account for a cotton mill, plywood factory, paper mill, and cement works.

Economic expansion is also urgent from the standpoint of providing opportunity for the schools' graduates to secure employment. While students would probably be satisfied with the continuation of traditional curricula if employment were guaranteed upon graduation, recent demonstrations would seem to indicate a growing disillusionment with traditional education. The state of unrest, of which Ministry and government officials are aware, is of a minor nature and could be redirected if business and industrial development are achieved and secondary curricula revised to satisfy the expectations of the learners.

5. *The School System:*

Education, in its lowest terms, must still be conceived of as the three-year primary school, either inside or outside the pagoda compound, deriving its character and *raison d'etre* from its religious source, repeating the same chants that have persisted since the time of the Prophet Buddha, more than 2500 years ago.

Progressing qualitatively are the six-year schools, usually in provincial centers and the capital city, and, at the apex, if functional learning is the criterion of achievement, the 14 Model Schools.

Secondary school education has at its lowest qualitative level, the remote *collège*, grades six through nine, which is still unrelated to the needs of the people, and whose graduates possess no salable skills. *Collège* in its more modern form offers such practical subjects as typing, industrial arts, and home economics in addition to the classical curriculum.

The *lycée*, still almost entirely classical, includes grades nine to twelve or thirteen, if the second baccalaureate is achieved. From it go those who are fortunate enough to secure government positions and

those for whom secondary diplomas are the entrance requirement for higher education.

At this level, students may choose among the several courses offered as listed above in the paragraphs describing the evolution of the law school to the university.

Statistics indicating the number of years of education which the Cambodian people receive are unavailable. Generally speaking, in the densely populated areas as provincial centers and the capital city, few children lack access to a three-year school and most have access to a six-year school. In the remote areas where the large percent of the population lives, the picture is far less encouraging. It will probably be many years before all the children in these areas have the opportunity of attending even a three-year school.

The 1961 Annual Report of the Ministry of Education indicates for the seventeen provinces now organized for the purpose of education a range from 1.9 percent to 11.5 percent of pupils of elementary school age in school attendance, the national average being 8.6 percent.

This still does not tell anything about the high attrition rate which characterizes both elementary and secondary enrollment. (A typical educational pyramid is reproduced in Table 1.)

TABLE 1

Typical Educational Pyramid

Between Grades		Percent
11 and 12	*	30
10 and 11	*	80
9 and 10	**	10
8 and 9	***	20
7 and 8	***	40
6 and 7	*****	60
5 and 6	**********	10
4 and 5	************	25
3 and 4	****************	30
2 and 3	************************	30
1 and 2	********************************	50

****

NOTE: Sources other than the Ministry of Plan have presented these statistics which may be considered representative of the drop-out rate at the present time.

Coupled with this is the question of literacy. Always a relative term, criteria must be established if conclusions are to be drawn. If defined in terms of those who can write their names or chant religious passages and phonetic sounds, the number is comparatively high. The criterion of functional literacy, in the sense of being able to read with comprehension a newspaper, government poster or pamphlet, and to use simple arithmetic processes in life situations, sharply reduces the number.

School age entrance is set at six years according to the custom of many oriental countries. Inasmuch as a child is considered a year old at birth, he would be considered five years old in Western societies. Since many parents believe that the earlier the child enters school the more he learns, children are often admitted at age four, and one sometimes sees children who appear even younger.

Public schools are supported by national funds. In the year 1959, 22.54 percent of the total national budget was allocated to education. This represented an increase of 11.4 percent over the previous year. Contributions from foreign aid added approximately 11 percent of the expenditure of national funds for education.

6. *Teachers:*

At the present time teachers' qualifications are the same as those established by the 1951 decrees, described in detail earlier in this account.

Graduates of the national schools are assigned positions immediately following the awarding of the teaching certificate. Since these students are educated at government expense, they are required to teach ten years in order to compensate for their schooling. Those who resign before the service period ends are required to remit to the government the cost of their education.

All of the professions, including teaching, are held in high esteem. If purchasing power is the criterion used, teachers are somewhat above government clerks, comparable to skilled tradesmen or professionally trained government workers such as agricultural extension agents; they are considerably below the level of doctors, dentists, and lawyers.

Within the profession, teachers are somewhat below the level of principals and other school officials. Elementary teachers are at a disadvantage because housing is not provided them by the government as is the case with secondary and university teachers. As a consequence, there is considerable effort exercised by them to be assigned to schools in their native village, since living with one's family is greatly to be preferred to living in a strange household. The amount of mobility and jockeying for assignments before one is placed in his home village accounts for the loss of continuity in service, a distinct disadvantage in the development of quality teaching.

Another factor which contributes to the high rate of teacher mobility is that elementary positions are sometimes used as stepping stones to those which command higher pay, either within the profession or in the business world.

Teachers' organizations are widespread, their function being almost wholly professional, although recently they have begun to exercise some influence in the matter of salaries and conditions of employment. Since teachers are civil service employees, tenure is automatic.

Recent developments (1966-7) include the training of thirty pre-school teachers, an increase in salaries, and a concern for reforming secondary education.

Although change is slow, there are practices in Cambodia which indicate that for some, the proof of one's devotion to country is no longer wholly measured in terms of his ability to copy faithfully in stone or on paper or to repeat through life-acts the values of a glorious past.

BIBLIOGRAPHY

CAMBODIAN MINISTRY OF INFORMATION, ED. *Cambodia Today and Yesterday,* Phnom Penh. Cambodia 1963, 38 pp. (Both English and French texts are included.)

LE MINISTERE D L'INFORMATION DU GOUVERNMENT ROYAL DU CAMBODGE. Cambodge 1962, 307 pp., Phnom Penh, Cambodge French text.

UNESCO. *International Yearbook of Education,* Vol. XXII, 1960, 512 pp., Place De Fontenoy, Paris. English text.

———. *World Survey of Education.* 1954, Place De Fontenoy, Paris, 943 pp. English text.

UNITED STATES AGENCY FOR INTERNATIONAL DEVELOPMENT. *Survey of United States Technical Aid to Cambodian Education,* Cody, Peter, ed., 1963 (unpublished). Washington, D. C. English text.

———, KIEFER, MILDRED S. *End of Tour Report,* 1960 (unpublished). Washington, D. C. English text.

———, LOFER, W. HAROLD. *End of Tour Report,* 1960 (unpublished). Washington, D. C. English text.

CHINA

Stewart Fraser

The history of Chinese education has an unbroken line of some four thousand years. The present rulers of China have shown that they are at once both proud and critical of their ancient heritage. The Communist regime has compressed, if not "fitted in," the feudal period of Chinese history crudely into the story of education, illustrating it with references to the famed examination system and decrying it by reference to the exploiting bureaucracy which controlled the masses for the imperial houses that came and went.

HISTORY

A study of Communist philosophy and practices in education today is difficult to comprehend without an introduction to Chinese educational history. The closely followed pronouncements on education today by the regime's political philosophers, ranging from Mao Tse-tung, Lu Ting-yi, Chou En-lai, and Liu Shao-ch', are shored up with historical references. Mao Tse-tung's famous polemic against Communist party formalism in 1942 was couched as an attack on "The Party's Eight-legged Essay," an allegoric reference to the eight formalized steps so necessary in writing a classical essay in imperial times. The often-quoted phrase in Chinese Communist Ideological discussion, "a hundred flowers blooming, a hundred schools of thought contending," refers historically to a period of intellectual ferment in the warring states, a period over two thousand years ago.

Reliable records would suggest that education as a formal and national institution began before 2000 B.C. The most permanent and well-known of these institutions can be identified as an interlocking system of schools and a hierarchical form of civil service examinations. During the Chou dynasty from B.C. 1122 to 249, these institutions flourished. They illustrated both psychological and sociological aspects of educational theory in conceiving education as a process of transmitting the accumulated treasures of civiliza-

tion without dissipation to succeeding generations. The intricate conventions of Chinese social order, the overpowering reverence for the past, and the dominant theme of filiality as the transcendental virtue were the cardinal elements in the theory of education codified rigidly into a formal and accepted process of transmission. Today the Chinese Communist elites are concerned with formalizing a process of Marxist transmission. It is one of the dilemmas of the regime as to how it can best transmit the zeal for revolutionary activity from one generation to the next. No longer is filial responsibility held at a premium unless it pertains to the paternal wisdom of Mao Tse-tung, whose political and educational pronouncements become more pontifical and revered as he becomes deified in the Communist world, at least in the orthodox and eastern branch of it.

The historical elements of education as a process of transmission in classical times were maintained for over one thousand years following the Chou period with little modification. This was followed by the great intellectual developments of the medieval period of China's great achievement during the T'ang and Sung dynasties (A.D. 620-1200). The Chinese scholars placed their nation in the foremost ranks of the civilized nations. They were responsible for refining literature and philosophy and they imprinted their critical judgment and forms of thought upon the literature that generations following accepted unquestioningly as the most infallible interpretation of the wisdom of the ancients. Confucius himself consciously fostered this tendency of veneration for the ancients, and his example was followed faithfully by scholars during the succeeding centuries. Chinese educational thought was transfixed, mesmerized and held captive in the bonds of a perfected classicism such as has not been known since the pinnacle of Greek scholarship. The seven centuries until the nineteenth century accordingly saw a highly developed, logically consistent and scholarly educational format which satisfied

China until the barbarians penetrated during the middle of the nineteenth century.

The institutions of education and the theory of educational transmission performed faithfully and correctly not only from one generation to another but from dynasty to dynasty irrespective of the revolutionary changes or how alien were the races which seized the imperial throne.

The Chinese Imperial System of Higher Education

Much has been made of the Mandate of Heaven theory whereby the dynasty which ruled was legitimate and any rebellion against it was not only wrong but treasonable and wicked (unless a rebellion proved to be successful). Under the changed circumstances the "mandate" was deemed to have been altered and the successful rebel became the legitimate ruler in China. The right of rebellion, also referred to as the "Chinese Constitution," was of some importance to the scholarly class in Imperial China and allowed them to play a continuing unbroken role in the vicissitudes of Imperial politics. C. P. Fitzgerald has succinctly described the role of the scholar, stating:

The Confucian scholar was certain that whatsoever king might reign, he would be the Vicar of Bray for he was essential to government; he was not merely the Vicar of the Chinese Bray, he was also the squire and the magistrate too. A Chinese change of dynasty was not a revolution; it was a change of government sometimes carried out by force, more often by the constraint of superior power without bloodshed. Rebellions rarely overthrew dynasties, and when they did the scholars hastened to enlist under the banner of the victorious rebel and assure him of the Mandate of Heaven—provided he in turn was willing to use them to carry on the system of government they understood and served.[1]

The Imperial scholars and the rigorously intellectual court administration, who in reality ruled China, were products of an educational system already well established many centuries before Marco Polo made his celebrated journey to China. Victor Purcell, writing on Chinese education, quotes from the Book of Rites, which describes the ancient order in education, stating:

For the purpose of education among the ancients each village of twenty-five families had its school, each district of five hundred families its academy, and each department of 2,500 families its college. . . . At the beginning of the Chou Dynasty (1122 B.C.) all candidates for official employment were required to give proof of their acquaintanceship with the Five Arts—music, archery, horsemanship, writing, and arithmetic—and to be thoroughly versed in the rites and ceremonies of public and social life, an accomplishment that ranked as a sixth art. . . . by imitation and parental precept. Teachers, when they appeared, had the double function of teachers and ministers of state.[2]

Tradition of bureaucratic scholars and literary teachers playing a major role in the government of China has been well founded and shows a continuity of more than two thousand years. But of greater importance is the foundation offered by Chinese scholarship during the past millennium and its influence in the ultimate development of a modern educational system. The institution of the educated elite playing the leading part in the administration of the Chinese Empire has given a well-established body of precedent upon which other civilizations have modeled their civil services.[3] A soundly established school system for an educable elite was acknowledged to be the basis of the higher examination system upon which successive Imperial administrations were founded. Schools were in the main divided into primary, where recitation, imitation, and calligraphy were taught; middle, which specialized in the learning of canonical works; and classical, where composition was the principal activity. For the most part, private endeavors were responsible for the maintenance of schools and most of the larger families or clans supported their own schools. At the primary and secondary levels the state did little to support, organize, or encourage schools.

In the Sung Dynasty (960-1279), however, there came into being institutions generally called as Provincial Colleges, or Shu-yuan. The colleges in actual fact were neither very grand nor particularly pretentious in accommodation but provided a gathering place for students preparing for higher examinations as well as a place of residence for well-known scholars. The Shu-yan were, at worst, cram colleges preparing students for the rigor of Imperial civil service examinations and, at best, represented the embryonic schools of higher learning which ultimately became fully established in China.

No lectures were given in the academy; the function of the professor was only to advise the students as to their reading and to criticize the results of their research. Occasionally a professor or some outside scholar would lecture on some selected topic, but on the whole the Shu-yuan was a place of self study and a center of research under expert guidance.[4]

---

1. C. P. Fitzgerald. *Revolution in China.* New York, Frederick A. Praeger, 1952, p. 12. It is fruitful to analyze Professor Fitzgerald's thesis regarding the role of the scholar and intellectual and see how far it is applicable to the latest of the dynasties which has seized power in China, namely the Chinese Communist Party.

2. Victor Purcell. *Problems of Chinese Education.* London, Kegan Paul, French, Trubner and Company, Ltd., 1936, p. 2, citing Legge, *Sacred Books of the East,* Vol. XXVII, p. 346.

3. See E. A. Kracke, Jr. *Civil Service in Early Sung China 960-1067: with particular emphasis on the development of controlled sponsorship to foster administrative responsibility.* Cambridge, Massachusetts, Harvard University Press, 1953, for a detailed account of the Chinese Civil Service Examination and recruitment system during the years it achieved the form maintained until the twentieth century.

4. Purcell, *op. cit.,* pp. 24-25, citing from T'ang Leang-li, *China in Revolt.* London, 1927, p. 33.

The system of examinations for the civil service included practical, artistic, and academic subjects. Originally the examinations were confined to the various "arts" with the addition later of examinations in civil law, revenue administration, agriculture, military science, and Imperial geography. There are indications that by the twelfth century or during the T'ang and Sung Dynasties (618-1126), the Chinese public examination system had reached the peak of its development and remained stabilized in form and content for a further eight centuries until the "Old System" ended between 1905 and 1911. With the advent of the written word, candidates were no longer required to be proficient in all the arts, and for over a thousand years scholars merely wrote odes in praise of music and essays on the archery and horsemanship of the ancients, where formerly they had to demonstrate their equestrian skill and shooting proficiency, as well as indicating their accomplishments as musicians.[5]

The examination system itself was complicated, hazardous, and discriminating. In fact, toward the end of the nineteenth century over two million candidates were examined each year, of whom ultimately 1 or 2 percent passed all the various examination stages, and of these it is said only 10 percent received preferment for official appointments in the civil service.[6] The first examination was taken at the subprefectural level, the second before the prefect, and the third before the provincial examiner. The third examination step was in reality the basis for further testing in order to classify successful candidates for bachelors' degrees, and to retain the status of the baccalaureate, a candidate was compelled to attend triennial examinations or face the risk of being degraded. The result of the triennial examinations allowed the examiner to classify the bachelors into ten different grades. If a candidate persevered and his category was sufficiently high, he was permitted to sit for the master's degree. But the attainment of this status was not sufficient for his employment in the higher grades of Imperial civil service, and he had to journey to Peking where he took further examinations for the degree of Doctor of Literature. Even at this stage of the man's academic career, employment was not certain and vacant posts were distributed by lottery, thus preserving to the last the aurora of competition and strict impartiality which surrounded the whole civil service system.[7]

Such was the vista of honor that stretched up before the ambitious Chinese. No one was excluded from the public examinations except the immediate descendents of play actors, executioners, Yamen torturers, or separated by three clear generations, and the descendents of barbers, priests, nail cutters, and scavengers.[8]

There were about fourteen thousand bachelors' degrees added to the graduate list each year and by the turn of the twentieth century there were approximately 700,000 graduates living. The fact, however, still remained that to obtain a government position, instruction in classics and history was of major importance until "Western education" was introduced in the latter part of the Imperial Regnum.

A criticism of Chinese education at its highest level would have to indicate the disregard by the Chinese for most branches of study which were practical, and therefore was a narrowing of culture in its widest sense. Of primary importance were the rites and duties of the government and of the individual to other members of society. The Confucian system of dependent and subordinate values and the unchanging role of the school in educational instructions were of such importance that criticisms were unthinkable. The principal end of teaching in Imperial China required teachers to develop quiet and orderly citizens. The most educable were to be steeped in classics, taught to conform, and to become protagonists rather than critics of the system which held the scholar in such high esteem.[9]

The system of higher education in China at the end of the nineteenth century was virtually a volun-

---

5. See W. A. P. Martin, *The Chinese, Their Education, Philosophy and Letters.* New York, Harper and Brothers, 1881, pp. 39-84, for a description of the Imperial examination system and higher education in China.

6. See Justus Doolittle, *Social Life of the Chinese: with some account of their Religious, Governmental, Educational and Business Customs and Opinions,* Chapters 15, 16, and 17. An excellent account is given of the higher educational system during the middle part of the nineteenth century.

7. The system, however, according to various authorities was riddled with corruption, nepotism, impersonation, cheating, and in reality negated many of the beneficial aspects of the examination system. See Doolittle, *op. cit.,* Chapter 17, for a detailed account of the measures taken to prevent cheating and substitution. Few writers on the Chinese examination system have failed to comment adversely on the extent to which bribery, falsification, and cribbing were a feature of the exercises. However, it is with some surprise that Herbert Giles, Professor of Chinese at Cambridge University, is noted to have said that "their system of competitive examinations has indeed served the Chinese well. It is the brightest spot in the whole administration, being absolutely above suspicion. . . . The Chinese who make no attempt to conceal or excuse, in fact rather exaggerate any corruption in their public service generally do not hesitate to declare with striking unanimity that the conduct of their examinations system is above suspicion and there appears to be no valid reason why we should not accept this conclusion." Herbert A. Giles, *The Civilization of China,* p. 118.

8. Purcell, *op. cit.,* p. 36.

9. Prior to the study of the classics, four major books were the educational fare at the intermediate or secondary level of schooling. These were the books of Confucian Analects, Great Learning, Doctrine of the Mean, and Mencius. After these the classics were taken up and formed the core of the senior secondary studies. The classics were "The Spring and Autumn and the Books of Poetry, History, Rites and Changes." They were held in particular reverence and constituted standard form for behavior and conduct from which there was no appeal. The style of examination was highly formalized and at the higher level a stereotyped essay plan based on eight logical steps (the "eight-legged essay") was expected of all candidates. The language of instruction and textual publications were in Wen-li, that is, Classical Chinese, and would today be equivalent to expecting all students to utilize Latin or Greek as their academic language.

tary system of nationwide public examinations of a severely formal character. These were encouraged by the Provincial and Imperial administrations in order to recruit a literate class of officials chosen on an intellectually democratic basis. As a combination of a democratic "examinations system, and intellectual elite," in the civil service on such a vast scale, it is perhaps unique in the history of public administration and political science. The use of education for mass indoctrination was unthinkable. Instead, an intellectual elite to which all could aspire was established. The use of education to introduce new or revolutionary ideas and to provide scientific and cultural advances was likewise unthinkable, instead the classics, tried and true formats, were adhered to and Chinese scholars stubbornly refused at a most critical period of their history to accommodate their intellectual capacities to a changing world, soon to be dominated by barbarians from the Occident.

It is only becoming increasingly clear during the middle of this, the twentieth century, that many Western writers of a hundred years ago, in analyzing Chinese education, believed that the absolute values of the West and its material superiority were of paramount and exclusive importance. By Western standards education in China did not lead to inventiveness but merely to the acquisition of knowledge. Progress, the dominant if not historical value of the West, had little place in the outcomes of Chinese education. The European visualized himself as moving forward progressively with the conviction that his educational system would assist social and political betterment. The whole value of Chinese education, however, was based on the premise that perfection lay in the past and scrupulous imitation or emulation was the procurer of virtue. This was the heritage of Chinese classical education that both the Nationalists and Communists had to contend with and adapt to their own *modus operandi*. Much of the writing that has been done on the Imperial system of education was undertaken at a time of decline in Chinese history, and the contrast with the "progress" and "scientific" achievements of the West has screened out many of the more important contributions and significant features of Chinese education. The Imperial system suffered from convulsions, discredits, and degenerated into chaos with the introduction of Western learning and educational institutions, particularly under the Republicans.

Possibly during the past hundred years of China's history there has been only a decade or two of "comparative internal stability" throughout the entire country such as that imposed by a totalitarianism regime of the communist type. Thus the contrast between the Communist structure of higher education and that established by those who fell heir to the Imperial administration, namely the Republicans, may be especially glaring. But the groundwork and experimentation was the labor of a multitude of educational

groups, some Imperial, some Republican, some Nationalist, and some Western. Without their monumental achievement the present Regime, in spite of its ruthless, scientific efficiency, would have been hard-pressed to show the spectacular gains it has been able to show after ten years of control.

These antecedents are important, valuable, and go far to explain the burden of transition and the inherent difficulties facing Chinese education today. Undeniably there are many Chinese educators today who wish to see their country both preserve its Imperial glory and compete successfully with the foreigners who once controlled the destinies of China. Thus there is a problem of nationalism which continues to dominate education in China, irrespective of which regime is in power. It is a current that runs through the endeavors of pedagogy and provides one of the more "stable" and continuing factors encountered in Chinese education.

New Forms to 1895

In spite of the depredations and the invasions of the European nations who encroached on China's sovereignty from 1840 on, changes in the higher educational structure of Imperial China were slow to be manifest and what was done appears to be ineffectual from the standpoint of preserving China's independence. The challenge of Western education and scientific ideas was not taken up either by the Manchu rulers or scholars in any determined or vigorous manner until it was too late. The Chinese intellectual continued to regard foreigners as barbarians and hired special soldiers of fortune or specialized teachers on an *ad hoc* basis. They did little to mobilize resources of the empire and train Chinese on a large scale to do these things themselves. One writer sums up the picture of decay in Imperial educations, stating:

Confucius says the best way to govern the people is to enrich them and having enriched them, educate them. The precept was not fulfilled. The house of the scholar was too often a windowless hovel, he sat for his examinations in little cells which a Westerner would think of as slums, the great Hanlin itself (a symbol of a system though not in actual use) was in ruins and its courts grass grown for centuries. Public works like the Grand Canal or the Great Wall touch the reader's imagination; one is not prepared to find that they are in no sort of repair, that education has not succeeded in producing enough public spirit to maintain in good report a highway of any length, the capacity to deal effectively with flood, famine or afforestation, or enough official integrity to secure any appreciable portion of the revenue for national purposes. The standard of living has always been low and the literary system did nothing to raise it. As a cultivation of the mind the literary system of China was impressive; as a creator of tangible wealth, at the end of its days, that is, it was scarcely so.[10]

---

10. Purcell, *op. cit.*, p. 41.

These criticisms are particularly pertinent if one considers educational aims from a Western point of view, but unfortunately Chinese education was essentially a vehicle to preserve the *status quo* and bring tranquility to the largest nation on earth. But in defense of this system of specific education it is important to realize that the system was one of China's own making, and one that owed virtually nothing to the outside world. It was autocratic, entirely a creation of China's rulers, administrators and scholars, concerned with the efficient administration of a kingdom of 400 million or more people.

This system had its grave faults and it was often evaded by bribery; but it was founded on a wise enduring principle. It created an aristocracy of learning, which excepting for temporary setbacks, has been more powerful than the military class. It has prevented the rise of a hereditary ruling class and has checked the development of a caste system, both of which institutions have been the deadliest enemies of democracy in Europe and in other countries of Asia.[11]

Deficiencies of the system as presented by Westerners were either unrecognized or unknown to the Chinese until their empire was breaking up. Then their educational efforts of previous centuries were derided cruelly by the practical and scientifically educated barbarians from the Occident. The fact that this system had functioned successfully for two millennia and could have done so for another two if left alone was insufficient to deter the impressment of Western forms of education on the Chinese by their rulers and by Europeans. In fairness to the system, it would be of greater validity to criticize the examinations themselves and note their degeneration rather than to criticize the principle upon which they had been established. Unfortunately, time passed them by and because they were based entirely on texts, treatises and books written in a dead language unknown and foreign to the common people, there was little opportunity to re-evaluate their contents and apply them in the light of current events. The Chinese intelligentsia were thus involved in a classical web of their own making and because of the content and methods used in higher education they were unable to adapt to changing conditions and profit from the experience of the scientifically advanced Western countries. Until the West became determined to "open the door" into China, the scholars' ideas and institutions had gone unchallenged, and they themselves were in no position to challenge the educational format in which they were well entrenched, as it would have destroyed their own positions.

Chinese education at the end of the nineteenth century was decaying, incestuous and corrupt—in some respects undoubtedly unable to cope with the educational prowess of the West. While it was decadent in comparison with European education, it was still faithfully reproducing the acts and culture of the past; its excellence in transmitting its cultural heritage and classical spirit of Confucianism was unexcelled. But within two decades came sweeping changes which shook and finally toppled the Empire setting free new developmental forces. The short-lived disastrous war with Japan (1894-1895) had its effects on the Chinese, especially those who had received a Western education. They pushed forward their ideas for educational and political reform with vigor. The defeat at the hands of Japan enabled the Chinese reformers to come out in the open. This led to the short reform movement of 1898, the savage reactionary movement of 1900, and the educational reforms of the succeeding decade. The thoroughgoing revolution of 1911 finally weakened the classical bonds which united and held an emerging China with her great past.

Twentieth-century changes in education included a 1903 commission appointed to prepare plans for a new educational system; these plans bore a close resemblance to Japan's new educational system that itself had been largely manufactured in the West. In 1905 an Imperial edict ended the two-thousand-year-old examination system. This meant that both the school system and mechanics for civil service appointment through examinations were abruptly put aside. The new educational system was hardly operative when the far-reaching revolution of 1911 swept away more of China's cultural heritage, at least that part which had been desperately retained by the classicists. The revolutionary party manifested intolerance and impatience toward ancient traditions and cared little for the transmissions of cultural heritage. Western theories and systems of education were eagerly sought, not only secondhand from Japan but directly from the United States, Britain, and France. Many students went overseas to Japan, later to Europe and North America to study. When they returned, these scholars played an increasingly important role in both education and government.

During the Republican period from 1911, especially after 1927 with the establishment of a nationwide Nationalist government, educational innovations were often patterned after American prototypes. The visits of American professors, such as John Dewey, Paul Monroe, George Lewis, E. D. Burton, W. A. McCall, and L. M. Terman, were all part of the movement to update Chinese education as well as to provide a scientific basis upon which it will be built.

After 1928 when the Nationalist regime consolidated its hold, a new era was ushered in which implemented as well as exploited the famous Three Peoples Principles of Sun Yat-sen. Education thus emphasized civic, social, and rural interests as well as military and labor service for the benefit of the

11. See Peake, *op. cit.*, Chapter 1, *passim*, and Purcell, *op. cit.*, Chapter 2, *passim*.

state. The new Kuomintang-dominated regime contained many who were honest, devoted, and intelligent and saw education as a vehicle for social reform. The Kuomintang was also ultranationalistic and socialistic, both in its theory and initial practice of government. Much was done for education though more was needed. Compulsory education in the lower school grades was introduced and the more practical and applied courses such as the natural sciences and technological subjects were stressed at the expense of the Confucian classics which were no longer a mandatory part of the curriculum. Illiteracy which had been as high as 85 percent was attacked systematically, and adult schools were established in rural and city areas for propagating the mass education movements.

The education of illiterates was a failure because of political instability and the Chinese shortage of teachers. It is still a problem with the current regime which has to cope with an illiteracy rate of over 40 percent.

Educational progress during the Nationalist period was substantial, particularly at the elementary level and by the end of the Second World War nearly 70 percent of the children were in school. During the First World War barely 20 percent of elementary school children were able to attend school.

Within half a century of abandoning the traditional and classical forms of education China had a modern though rudimentary educational system. During the period from 1911-1949, western educational thought, politics and practices had played a predominant role in shaping the future direction of Chinese education. But in terms of a nation of over 700 million and the needs of this expanding population this was insufficient. The national conditions and appalling poverty after seven years of constant warfare coupled with a devastating civil war of four years had sapped both will and courage. The social and educational machine of the country had run down.

COMMUNIST CHINESE EDUCATION

It has been said that China has had a long history of despotic and absolutistic government broken occasionally with only short periods of democracy.

The contemporary phase of China's development under the Communist regime embodies both traditional patterns of control and certain extreme western forms of organization. The interlocking of totalitarian ideas, both Classical and Communist, can be ascribed to the pervading forces of tradition. The Communist rulers followed and practiced the same techniques of educational control practiced by the Nationalists as well as by rulers in Imperial times. The elaborate and complex system of educational supervision established by the Nationalists in propounding Sun Yatsen's three principles were applicable and transferable to the Communist ethos. The development of state

controls, whether imperial or national, has allowed the Communist to inherit a system of education and cultural transmission par excellence.

Communist Philosophy of Education

There is an intimate and special relationship between the state and education in Communist countries. This relationship in China can be identified in its durability as the relationship between theory and practice or the Marxist philosophy of education as interpreted by leaders such as Mao Tse-tung, and the actual implementation of these theories by the cadres or grassroot communist activists working in schools, universities, and among Chinese youth. Chinese Communist educational literature rarely approximates or discusses what the western non-Marxist would define as educational theory per se. Their educational theory is an extension and application of dialectical materialism to educational theory and practices as interpreted by Marx, Lenin, Mao and more recently by Lu Ting Yi and Liu Shao-ch'i. Communist education is intimately concerned with both politics and economics and whenever their goals are adjusted the changes are directly related to education. Chinese Communist educational theory is extraordinarily adaptable within limits, and any particular educational policy or stricture can be either implemented or abandoned in the name of adjusting the proper relationship between theory and practice. This has its corollary in the attitude toward propagandist indoctrination and for the Communist, education is not merely an elucidation of ideas, rather it is the persistent propaganda which changes thinking and conditions thought processes along strictly defined channels. The formal institutions of education, the schools, universities, and teachers' colleges have been supplemented by part-time schools, half-work half-study institutes, people's university, "red and expert" colleges. Irrespective of their titles the psychological theories of intellectual Pavlovism are applied here—and are the underpinning techniques used for indoctrination.

Mao Tse-tung in 1957 briefly stated his views on education explaining that "Our educational policy aims to enable the educated to develop normally, mentally, and physically, and to become Socialist conscious and cultured laberers."[12] The Chinese Communists have as a cardinal principle of their educational philosophy the total eradication of the social and political gap between the worker-peasant and the intellectual.

The theoretical and perhaps earliest legal basis upon which to seek a philosophical basis of educational goals can be found in 1949 at the start of the regime's establishment. The following provisions re-

12. Mao Tse-tung. *Problems as to the Correct Ways of Dealing with Internal Contradictions Among the People.* Peking: Peoples Press, 1957.

garding the new regimes cultural and educational policies are to be noted in the *Common Program*, adopted in September, 1949. The relevant educational provisions are as follows:

Article 41. The culture and education of the Chinese People's Republic shall be the culture and education of the New Democracy, that is, nationalistic, scientific, and popular. The cultural and educational work of the People's Government shall deem its principal tasks those of raising the cultural level of the people, training of personnel for national construction, eradication of feudalistic, compradorish and fascist ideologies, and promotion of the idea of serving the people.

Article 46. The educational method of the Chinese People's Republic shall be to integrate theory and practice. The People's Government shall systematically, and by stages, reform the old educational system, the contents of education, and the methods of pedagogy.

Article 47. It [the People's Government] shall systematically, and by stages, carry out universal education, strengthen secondary education and higher education, emphasize technical education, consolidate the spare-time education of laborers and the education of cadres now on duty, and give revolutionary political education to the young intellectuals and old intellectuals, so as to satisfy the widespread needs of revolutionary work and national construction.[13]

Chinese Communists have derived their educational philosophy from their political activities and theories. They have in part broken with their Confucian tradition and are significantly reshaping their nation through a cultural-political policy based on Marxism-Leninism as interpreted by the highly skilled intellectualization of Mao Tse-tung. In reality, many of the Communist principles of education are being evolved, in response to the Western impact and pressure on Chinese life. Science and technology and the capacity for sophisticated nuclear research are the results through Western education of these changes. The forces of Western liberalism have certainly been dampened by the philosophy of dialectical materialism, while it is European, and it is being rapidly absorbed into the Chinese stream of educational philosophy.

Chinese leaders are selective in their xenophobia toward Western or non-Communist education. The break with a Confucian past has been made but this does not negate the possibility to draw upon China's rich heritage or encompass foreign teachings if they suit the aims of contemporary Chinese Communism.

Mao Tse-tung in 1945 in his discourse *On Coalition Government* succinctly stated this view:

With respect to foreign cultures, the policy of xenophobia is wrong. Progressive foreign cultures should be absorbed as much as possible, in order to serve as the model of the Chinese cultural movement. The policy of blind-folded obedience is also wrong. The actual needs of the Chinese people should be used as the yardstick, so as to absorb foreign cultures with discrimination. As regards the an-

cient Chinese culture, this should be neither discarded nor blindly obeyed. It should be adopted with discrimination, in order to facilitate progress of the culture of the New Democracy of China.[14]

TEACHER TRAINING

The need for trained competent teachers in a mass educational system are nowhere felt as strongly as in China today. Yet, in discussing the production of teachers in the numerous teacher training establishments to be found in China, it should be noted that an enormous number of teachers have no professional training in pedagogy far less possessing a minimum scholastic record to suit them even for college-level work. The Chinese Communists boast both that trained teachers are not necessary and a true "socialistic consciousness" is more important, and at the same time lament their inability to graduate adequate teachers fast enough from the normal schools.

A great number of academically qualified teachers have been required to go directly into high school and university positions without the benefit of professional training. Part-time, summer, and correspondence courses are meant to eventually remedy these defects.

There has been some experimentation in the structural organization of the teacher training institutions, however, a three-level hierarchy still appears to predominate consisting of the higher normal university or college, normal school, and junior normal school.

The junior normal school only prepares kindergarten through fourth grade elementary teachers. The normal school prepares teachers for all the grades of elementary school, and the various higher normal universities and colleges train instructors for the secondary schools.

The higher normal institutions are considered critical in the regime's plans for mass education and there is a premium placed on the development of facilities for higher normal education. Yet, they are able to satisfy only a modest portion of the demand for their graduates. Normal schools find it difficult to recruit sufficiently prepared students into the teaching profession.

The curriculum content in normal education will vary intellectually with the level of the institute. It is advanced at the higher normal college which requires a full secondary education to enter and it is distinctly lower at the junior normal school which

13. "Kung-t'ung, Kang-ling" (Common Program), Chapter V in Chiao-yu tsu-liao ts ung-k an She (Collected Educational Materials Society), (ed.), Tang-ch ien chiao-yu chien-she ti fang-chen (Policies of Present-Day Educational Construction) (Peking: The Society, 1950), p. 1-2.

14. Mao Tse-tung, "Lun lien-ho cheng-fu" (On Coalition Government), in Mao Tse-tung hsuan-chi (Mao Tse-tung's Selected Works), end ed. (Peking: People's Press, 1952), Vol. II, p. 1083-84.

admits those who have only completed higher elementary schooling.

The major curriculum divisions are: (1) political education, (2) academic subjects, (3) pedagogy and psychology, and (4) practical work and practice teaching.

The specific goals of teacher training would include the following: (a) the production of efficient politically loyal and ideologically "correct" teachers for the schools of China and (b) the production of competent subject-oriented teachers, who are not only masters of their subject but able to relate their subject matter to the contemporary Chinese scene as determined by the Communist Party.

EDUCATIONAL ADMINISTRATION AND POLITICS

The Communist Party decides, initiates, and debates educational policy, and a highly centralized educational administrative structure is theoretically and informally meant to carry out its decisions efficiently and quickly. In actual practice the Party, though initiating discussion on administrative policies, requires all the Ministerial functionaries as well as teachers throughout the country to be cognizant of new programs and changes in the Party line. The Party needs mass support and understanding of its programs and it requires "controlled criticism" for both an understanding of its designs as well as a critical response to avoid errors. Yet, the Communist Party does not play a formal or legal part in the administrative structure of Chinese education from the Ministerial level down through provincial, county, town, and village levels. The link between Party and educational administration is unofficial, personal, but total. "Policy is decided in the first place by the Party leaders, who then proceed by virtue of their other offices held within the state to translate the policy into action."[15]

Decision-making, execution of policies, and the administration of education in China has certain apparent virtues of speed and effectiveness. Absent are many of the parliamentary and public scrutiny agencies one finds in Western non-Communist society. There are no constitutional provisions requiring checks and balances and the virtual mono-party structure allows for instant nationwide implementation without the possibility of effective and widespread protests. Protests there are, but with a firm grip on all the communication media, teachers' unions and other pedagogical associations, it takes time, courage, and a very just cause to openly hamper the administrative processes. In theory, therefore, the Chinese may display an efficient and all-embracing administrative system which concentrates entirely on questions of application, not political philosophy. In practice, the enormous bureaucracy of functionaries refuse to accept responsibility which hampers the structure in its

smooth working. There have been token attempts to decentralize educational administration, to combine and then separate and to combine again ministries of education and ministries of higher education.

Provincial initiative in establishing universities enrolling students and in adopting localized curriculums have been in and out of vogue. That the Chinese are not educational pragmatists in their administration of schools is to be denied, but to say that they have developed a highly efficient system of administration is to ignore the results. Criticism as to inefficiency and faulty planning as well as revelations as to improper coordination of manpower needs illustrates the fact that a mono-party all-embracing through informal control of administrative policy-making powers is no guarantee of an efficient school system, although it is the largest and one of the most impoverished in the world.

CONCLUSION

The fifteen-year-old record of educational enrollments and general progress in providing school facilities has been significant. Major progress was made during the first five years of the regime's tenure but it can be only viewed against the devastating conditions which preceded it. The next five years leading up to the *Great Leap Forward* program of 1958 showed a settling down and an attempt to chart the long-range plans for educational development concentrating on first primary and then secondary education. This phase was abruptly ended and in 1958 there was an attempt at all levels and in all phases of educational and political life to surge ahead. The enrollment in schools reached a peak in 1960, especially in higher education, and may have approached one million full-time students. Some nine years later it was doubtful if this figure had been maintained and in all likelihood has decreased. The extraordinary attempt to expand China's economy was officially regarded as defunct by 1961, and the years after have seen only a cautious attempt to return to a high qualitative level of student enrollment rather than a quantitative one. It has, however, clearly counteracted the antagonism between "manual and mental" workers. A successful attempt has been made to place greater stress on science and advanced technology in the curriculum. Practical work and theoretical studies are at last better integrated and the intellectuals' disdain for manual labor has been most forcibly overcome. The regime has a long way to go before it can achieve universal elementary education which now stands at approximately 75 percent, with secondary education still catering to less than 40 percent of the high school population. The development of a universal system of higher education is even

15. K. E. Priestley, "The Peoples Republic of China," in Theodore L. Reller and Edgar L. Morphet, *Comparative Educational Administration*, Englewood Cliffs, New Jersey: Prentice-Hall, Inc., 1962, p. 279.

further from the grasp of educational planners, though it has been promised during the next fifteen years. Citizens who are both "red and expert," that is, both communistically oriented and technically proficient, are still few and far between. The present and ultimate goal of Chinese Communist education is to produce a nation of "red and expert citizens." There are obviously more than there were when the regime took over in 1949, but in relation to the grandiose plans of the regime, even more are demanded of the educational system before China can truly offer herself as an example to Asia of a mass-educated nation which can even approach the educational standards of Japan, far less the USSR or the United States of America.

SELECTED BIBLIOGRAPHY

Chinese History, Culture, and Philosophy

Bodde, G. *China's Cultural Tradition*. New York: Holt, Rinehart & Winston, Inc., 1959.

Fung Yu-lan, *A History of Chinese Philosophy*. Translated from the Chinese by Derk Bodde. 2 vols. Princeton, N. J.: Princeton University Press, 1951 (Vol. I), 1953 (Vol. II).

Hu, Chang-Tu. *China: Its People, Its Society, Its Culture*. New Haven, Conn.: HRAF Press, 1960.

Legge, James. *The Philosophy of Confucius*. Mount Vernon, N.Y.: Peter Pauper Press, n.d.

Chinese Education: Classical and Imperial

Biggerstaf, Knight. *The Earliest Modern Government Schools in China*. Ithaca: Cornell University Press, 1961.

Chiang, Mon-lin. *A Study in Chinese Principles of Education*. Shanghai: Commercial Press, Ltd., 1924.

Fairbank, John King (ed.). *Chinese Thought and Institutions*. Chicago: University of Chicago Press, 1957.

Galt, Howard Spilman. *History of Chinese Educational Institutions*, Vol. I. London: Arthur Probsthain, 1951.

Hsiao, Theodore Encheng. *A History of Modern Education in China*. Peking: Peking University Press, 1932; Shanghai: Commercial Press, Ltd., 1935.

Kuo Ping-wen. *The Chinese System of Public Education*. ("Teachers' College Contributions to Education," No. 64.) New York: Teachers' College, Columbia University, 1915.

Chinese Education: Modern and Republican

Becker, C. H.; Langevin, P.; Falski, M.; and Tawney, R. H. *The Reorganization of Education in China*. Paris: League of Nations Institute of Intellectual Cooperation, 1932.

Chow Tse-tung. *The May Fourth Movement: Intellectual Revolution in Modern China*. Cambridge, Mass.: Harvard University Press, 1960.

Chuang Chai-hsuan. *Tendencies Toward a Democratic System of Education in China*. Shanghai: Commercial Press, Ltd., 1922.

Hu Shih. *The Chinese Renaissance*. 2nd ed. New York: Paragon Books, 1963.

Kuo Ping-wen. *Higher Education in China* (*Bulletins on Chinese Education*, Chinese National Association for

the Advancement of Education, II, No. 10.) Shanghai: Commercial Press, Ltd., 1923.

Purcell, V. *Problems of Chinese Education*. London: Kegan Paul, Trench, Trubner and Co., Ltd., 1936.

Sun Yat-sen. *San Min Chu I: The Three Principles of the People*. Translated by Frank W. Price; ed. L. T. Chen, Chungking: Ministry of Information of the Republic of China, 1943.

Twiss, George Ransom. *Science and Education in China: A Survey of the Present Status and a Program for Progressive Improvement*. Shanghai: Commercial Press, Ltd., 1925.

General Survey and Background

Brandt, Conrad; Schwartz, Benjamin; and Fairbank, John King. *A Documentary History of Chinese Communism*. Cambridge, Mass.: Harvard University Press, 1952.

Fitzgerald, Charles P. *Flood Tide in China*. London: Cresset Press, 1958.

Tang, Peter S. H. *Communist China Today*. 2 vols. New York: Frederick A. Praeger, Inc., 1957 (Vol. I: Domestic and Foreign Policies); 1958 (Vol. II: Chronological and Documentary Supplement).

Communist Ideology and Educational Philosophy

Lu Ting-Yi. *Education Must be Combined with Productive Labor*. Peking: Foreign Languages Press, 1958. See also Lu Ting-yi "Education Must be Linked to Productive Work," in *Soviet Education*, I, No. 4 (February, 1959), 57-64; (originally translated by V. Z. Klepikov from Hung ch'i [Red Flag] for *Sovetskaya Pedagogika*, December, 1958). See also "Education Must Be Combined with Productive Labour," *Peking Review*, I, No. 28 (September 9, 1958), 5-12.

———. *Let a Hundred Flowers Blossom: A Hundred Schools of Thought Contend*. (A speech on the policy of the Communist Party of China on art, literature, and science delivered on May 26, 1957.) Peking: Foreign Languages Press, 1958.

Mao Tse-tung. "On 'Letting a Hundred Flowers Blossom,' 'Letting a Hundred Schools of Thought Contend,' 'Long Term Co-existence and Mutual Supervision'" (chap. 8) and "The Question of Intellectuals" (chap. 5) in *On the Correct Handling of Contradictions among the People*. Peking: Foreign Languages Press, 1957.

———. *Oppose the Party "Eight-Legged Essay."* Rev. ed. (originally published in 1942). Peking: Foreign Languages Press, 1955.

———. *The Orientation of the Youth Movement*. Rev. ed. (originally published in 1934). Peking: Foreign Languages Press, 1960.

———. *Reform Our Study*. Rev. ed. (originally published in 1941). Peking: Foreign Languages Press, 1960.

———. *Talks at the Yenan Forum on Art and Literature*. Rev. ed. (originally published in 1942). Peking: Foreign Languages Press, 1956.

General Survey of Education

Cheng, J. Chester. "Basic Principles Underlying the Chinese Communist Approach to Education," *Information on Education Around the World Series*, No. 51,

OE-14034-51. Washington, D. C.: U. S. Office of Education, 1961.

CHI TUNG-WEI. *Education for the Proletariat in Communist China.* 2d ed. Hong Kong: Union Research Institute, 1956.

HU, CHANG-TU. *Chinese Education under Communism.* ("Classics in Education" No. 7.) New York: Bureau of Publications, Teachers' College, Columbia University, 1962.

JOHNSON, CHALMERS A. *Communist Policies Toward the Intellectual Class.* Hong Kong: Union Research Institute, 1960.

LINDSAY, MICHAEL. *Notes on Educational Problems in Communist China, 1941-47,* with supplements on 1948-1949 by Marion Menzies, William Paget, and S.B. Thomas. New York: International Secretariat, Institute of Pacific Relations, 1950.

ORLEANS, LEO A. *Professional Manpower and Education in Communist China.* Washington, D. C.: National Science Foundation, 1961.

PRIESTLEY, KENNETH E. *Education in China.* Hong Kong: Dragonfly Books, 1961.

Elementary and Secondary Education

BARENDSEN, ROBERT D. "Planned Reforms in the Primary and Secondary School System in Communist China." *Information on Education Around the World,* No. 45 (August, 1960). Washington, D. C.: United States Department of Health, Welfare, and Education; Office of Education (Government Printing Office), 1960. (See also "The 1960 Educational Reform," *China Quarterly,* No. 4 (October-December), 55-65.)

Higher Education

CHEN, THEODORE HSE-EN. "The Popularization of Higher Education in Communist China," *Information on Education Around the World,* No. 24, OE-14002 (August, 1959). Washington, D. C.: United States Department of Health, Education, and Welfare; Office of Education (Government Printing Office), 1959.

———. *Teacher Training in Communist China* ("Studies in Comparative Education Series," No. OE-14058). Washington, D. C.: United States Office of Education, 1960.

CHUNG SHIH. *Higher Education in Communist China.* Hong Kong: Union Research Institute, 1953.

SHIH CH'ENG-CHIH. *The Status of Science and Education in Communist China: And a Comparison with That in the U.S.S.R.* Hong Kong: Union Research Institute, 1962.

WANG-CHI. *Mainland China Organizations of Higher Learning in Science and Technology and Their Publications: A Selected Guide. Washington,* D. C.: Government Printing Office, 1961.

Part-Time and Half-Time Educational Programs

BARENDSEN, ROBERT D. *Half-Work, Half-Study Schools in Communist China: Recent Experiments with Self-Supporting Educational Institutions.* Bulletin No. FS5.214, OE-14100 (1964). Washington, D.C.: Government Printing Office, 1964.

HARPER, PAUL. *Spare-Time Education for Workers in Communist China.* Bulletin No. 30, OE-14102

(1964). Washington, D. C.: Government Printing Office, 1964.

Thought Control and Ideological Reforms in Education

CAO CHUNG and I-FAN YANG. *Students in Mainland China.* Hong Kong: Union Research Institute, 1956.

CHEN, THEODORE HSI-EN. *Thought Reform of the Chinese Intellectuals.* Hong Kong: Hong Kong University Press; and London; Oxford University Press, 1960.

CHOU EN-LAI. *Report on the Question of the Intellectuals.* Peking: Foreign Languages Press, 1956.

HOUN, FRANKLIN W. *To Change a Nation: Propaganda and Indoctrination in Communist China.* Glencoe, Ill.: Glencoe Free Press, 1961.

HUNTER, EDWARD. *Brainwashing in Red China: The Calculated Destruction of Men's Minds.* New York: Vanguard Press, 1951.

JOHNSON, CHALMERS A. *Freedom of Thought and Expression in China: Communist Policies toward the Intellectual Class. Hong Kong:* Union Research Institute, 1959.

LIFTON, ROBERT J. *Thought Reform and the Psychology of Totalism: A Study of "Brainwashing" in China.* New York: W. W. Norton & Co., Inc., 1961.

MU FU-SHENG. *The Wilting of the Hundred Flowers: The Chinese Intelligentsia under Mao.* New York: Frederick A. Praeger, Inc., 1962.

YEN, MARIE (*pseud.*). *The Umbrella Garden: A Picture of Student Life in Red China.* (Originally published as *College Life under the Red Flag.* Hong Kong: Union Press, 1952.) New York: The Macmillan Co., 1954.

Educational Aspects of Science, Technology, and Economic Development

GOULD, SIDNEY H. (ed.). *Sciences in Communist China.* Washington, D. C.: American Association for the Advancement of Science, 1961.

NEEDHAM, JOSEPH. *Science and Civilization in China.* 3 vols. Cambridge: Cambridge University Press, 1954 (Vol. I), 1956 (Vol. II), 1959 (Vol. III).

Sino-Soviet Relations and Educational Cooperation

MAYER, PETER. *Sino-Soviet Relations since the Death of Stalin.* Hong Kong: Union Research Institute, 1962.

NORTH, ROBERT C. *Moscow and the Chinese Communists.* Stanford, Calif.: Stanford University Press, 1952.

International Relations in Education

BAGCHI, P. C. *India and China: A Thousand Years of Cultural Relations.* Bombay: Hinds Kitab, Ltd., 1950.

FRIED, M. H. (ed.). *Colloquium on Overseas Chinese.* New York: Institute of Pacific Relations, 1958.

HEVI, EMMANUEL JOHN. *An African Student in China.* New York: Frederick A. Praeger, Inc., 1964.

LU YU-SUN. *Programs of Communist China for Overseas Chinese.* Hong Kong: Union Research Institute, 1956.

Motherland: Four Overseas Chinese Students Tell the Stories of Their Welcome in China. Hong Kong: Union Press, 1956.

PYE, LUCIAN W. *Some Observations on the Political Behavior of Overseas Chinese.* Cambridge, Mass.: Massachusetts Institute of Technology, 1954.

INDIA

Rajendra Pal Singh

India is one of the most ancient of living civilizations. The long continuity of her history is at once her bane and her blessing. If, on account of this, changes in the outlook of Indians have not kept pace with the times, their past has never failed to receive admiration from others. The modern Indian is as unlike his distant and cultured forbears as a modern American is from the early settlers. The missionary fire, the spiritual outlook, and the humble pride of having reached a certain high status in culture is almost entirely missing now. Still, he has an unmistakable stamp of the past on him. The modern Indian stands at a crossroad, as it were, undecided and a bit confused. The choice, however, because of his distinct history, traditions and mixture of races cannot be an easy one.

India is a country of teeming millions. It is a place where innumerable races, religions, and traditions have combined to make it a hotchpotch sociologically and historically. Her size and variety are confusing. Nevertheless, her charm is indescribable. Behind her crumbling social superstructure, changing patterns of life and evanescent ancient values lies something that has defied change so far and continues to do so even now. That is the soul of this country, bright and eternal.

It is common knowledge that South and North India have separate histories and, but for short intervals, mutual political contacts have been rather meagre. The multifaced undercurrent of Indian social life, however, despite the passage of centuries and long distances within the country has shown singular homogeneity. The credit of making South and North India one political unit must go to the English. Therefore, the reader is warned against making generalizations of any sort.

India's history, though divided into several periods, maintains a continuity that is unique. Neither the foreign invasions nor the swift political changes within the country ever succeeded in disrupting the social life of the people.

Perhaps a brief mention of India's greatest of wonders, her caste-system, is also necessary. Now rigid and outgrown, it was once the mainstay of Indian society. It represented a rational division of labour, and consequently it gave rise to a system of education that was patterned on the functions and duties of the members of the different castes. The Hindu mind is still conditioned by this division of society. Like many other facets of this society, the castes also have survived the onslaught of time and criticism.

The history of known ancient India and her education begins with the people of Indus Valley. This civilization flourished about five to six thousand years ago. It is still undecided whether these people were really Aryans or not. But their rich and varied life, their complex culture and high standard of civilization, their material well-being and artistic pursuits, learned from recent excavations, are sufficient to indicate that some form of education and training in various professions must have been fairly common. Sir Mortimer Wheeler believes that a college building is to be seen among the ruins of Mohenjodaro.

Of the times starting from the Rig-Vedic Aryans (*circa* 4000 to 1500 B.C.) clearer knowledge is available. All villages had a form of elementary education. The average rural professions transmitted their skills from father to son. The education for the rest was mostly religious in character and was given in the families of teachers or Gurukulas. Renowned teachers attracted more and better students. They also offered several subjects. Sometimes many teachers combined to offer various branches of study and thus provided a system parallel to modern universities. This system prevailed both for religious training and for the study of secular subjects. Secular subjects consisted, of course, of medicine, law, warfare, logic, and metallurgy.

In a short time India became known as a prosperous and learned country. But learning was never treated as an end in itself. It was regarded as a part

152

of religion. "It (learning) was sought as the means of salvation or self-realization, as the means to the highest end of life, *viz.* emancipation."[1]

This system of education remained almost unchanged for several centuries. Before the beginning of the Christian era this country built several big universities of the modern type with numerous faculties. Of these Nalanda, Taxila, and Vallabhi flourished for many centuries with undiminished glory. To these temples of learning came seekers of wisdom both from distant countries and nearby areas. Mostly foreign students came to learn about Buddhism, an offshoot of Hinduism. Not only were the sciences of astronomy, astrology, and mathematics developed to a considerable extent, but also other subjects such as philosophy, logic law, engineering, and medicine.

This continued until the death of last glorious Hindu-Emperor, Harsha. But by then, India had enjoyed signs of exhaustion and decadence. India did not see a single century of perfect peace after Harsha. From the eleventh century A.D. Muslim invasions became a regular feature. By the beginning of twelfth century, the last of Hindu Emperors of Delhi was defeated and killed by the Muslims and thus ended a long chapter of peace and prosperity. Now the treasures of India were ransacked and her schools of learning thrown into the background only to be supplanted by an alien system. The sonorous Sanskrit was replaced by polished Persian. The Court favour was denied to the Hindu schools and colleges. They languished because of deliberate neglect.

The Muslims kings of Delhi until the time of Akbar were not interested in the cause of education. The reason for this is not difficult to understand. It has been pointed out by Sir Jadunath Sarkar that until Akbar

state and society retained its original military and nomandic character—the ruling race living merely like an armed camp in the land. It was Akbar who, at the end of sixteenth century, began the policy of giving to the people of the country an interest in the state, and making the government undertake some socialistic functions in addition to the mere police work it had hitherto done. Down to Akbar's time the Muslim settlers in India used to be *in* the land but not *of* it.[2]

Considering that this state of mind prevailed until Akbar, the neglect of education is not at all surprising. Perhaps one cannot blame these rulers. They lived in an alien country whose people they could never completely understand. Perhaps for the first time India faced a people who refused to identify themselves with the natives.

Notwithstanding these facts, the rulers were fickle-minded in regard to everything they did. If one king started giving grants to certain institutions of his choice, his successor would invariably stop these and start giving grants to other institutions. In fairness, however, one can say that not a single king opposed the cause of education, and for Muslim boys schools of primary and higher education were opened in the capital towns or where the Muslims were the majority. Their character, curriculum, and methods of teaching were different from those of the Hindu schools. Therefore, a parallel system came into existence, one for the Muslim classes and another for the Hindu masses. Whereas the former was proselytising, intolerant, and limited in character, scope, and curriculum, the latter was insufficient, dull, and a spent force by then. The renowned Hindu teachers and their famous centres of learning were a thing of the past now. No longer could the Hindu and Buddhist scholars roam about freely discussing their newly acquired learning and expect rewards for their labour.

For the Muslim boys and girls, Maktabs or primary schools and Madresahs or higher institutions of learning were opened by both the king and philanthropically-minded noblemen. Primary classes were normally held in the precincts of Mosques where the Muslim priest acquired the small children with the principles of Islamic theology and required them to memorize the Koran. Some history and geography were also permitted. But the real standards of education were to be witnessed in the schools of higher learning where scholars of renown taught. Here again the emphasis was on the Islamic studies, but some secular subjects were also taught. Primarily, the scholars were of foreign origin. The ruling Muslim community was not very large, and a fresh supply of men of learning and arms was obtained from other Muslim countries. The local converts were never treated with the same respect as the foreigners.

As for the majority of Hindus, their ancient pattern continued to serve them. But as noted earlier, it was now neither so vigorous nor so universal. Its days of glory were over. Most of the Hindu scholars of renown left the North for the South and Rajasthan where they could still receive some sort of court favour because there the Hindu kings ruled in relative peace and prosperity.

Writing of the influence of Muslims on ancient pattern of education, A. L. Mudaliar says that the ancient systems of education were not influenced or affected except that in certain parts, due to the impact of Moslem invasion, some of these seats were adversely affected and had to be closed down. The reason for this is none other than the intolerance of the ruling class.

Under the rule of Great Moghuls the conditions improved noticeably. The intolerance had by now lessened. The majority of the ruled were accepted as part of the social and political system. Some help and encouragement were given to the Hindus to im-

---

1. Dr. R. K. Mookerji, *Ancient Indian Education*, Macmillan, London, 1951, p. 21.
2. J. Sarkar, *India Through the Ages*, Calcutta: M. C. Sarkar & Co., 1960, p. 42.

prove their lot. Even some of the highest jobs in the kingdom were offered to them. But this was done to win them over. And this could be done because the Hindus were willing to be won over. They had learned to talk in the Muslim Court languages. They had adopted very largely the Muslim court practices and manners. Even the dress was modified to please the rulers. In some of the Hindu schools, foreign languages were being taught, especially Persian and Arabic. If exigencies of administration required the cooperation of the Hindus, economic necessity compelled the Hindus to accept the foreigners as their rulers.

After the death of the last of Great Moghuls in 1707 India lost all signs of political order and prosperity, not that they were always manifest under the Moghuls. It was during this most turbulent period that the British entered India for trade. The situation was tantalizing enough and if the British exploited it for their benefit, they can hardly be blamed. Their genius for diplomacy, statesmanship, and trade was fully exhibited in this period and gradually gave them mastery over the whole of the sub-continent, the competitors having been driven into the background.

By the beginning of the nineteenth century the British started showing interest in the cause of education. Even if the motives for this great favour were suspect, the fact remains that they brought Indians for the first time in contact with industrial and economically advanced Europe.

If the early East India Company period is characterized by missionary activities, the later period should be known for marked disfavour toward them. In any case, while India was still undecided about the type of education she would require in the future, yet another pattern of education was introduced. Undoubtedly, it was done at the request of a few brilliant Indians and zealous British who were not particularly interested in the betterment of Indians as such. They were establishing the superiority of their school subjects over the existing languages and sciences. The ready-made system was introduced. Gradually, because of the fact that knowledge of English was helpful in getting relatively lucrative jobs, Indians studied it.

Socially a carbon-copy of the English gentry was the ideal. Educationally, then, European knowledge and languages were coveted accomplishments. This time both the Hindu and Muslim systems of education suffered equally. Nevertheless, their schools and colleges continued to exist, helped by philanthropically-minded Hindus and Muslims operating educational facilities for those who preferred the flow of Eastern knowledge to the dazzle of the Western. Almost all villages had schools for primary education but this extensive indigenous system soon fell into disuse for numerous reasons, one being their out-of-date curriculum. Efforts to revive it were made, but somehow they proved unsuccessful.

By 1857 the English finally had established themselves as rulers of the entire subcontinent. The first War of Independence had ended in a fiasco. The Queen through Parliaments had taken over and in her first message to India on this occasion she declared her intention to treat all Indians as equal, without any prejudices or bars. Whether this promise was kept or not is a moot point. Nevertheless, it became the solemn duty of the English to provide facilities of education in India. Until then they could escape the responsibility by putting forward arguments.

Once the fate of the country was decided the Indian students came forward in even greater numbers than before to join schools and colleges run by missionaries and by the government. Even the voluntary bodies did not lag behind. Among the upper classes, the flaunting of European manners and dress became unusually common.

Before the turn of the century, universities had been opened in the big cities of the country. A demand for universal education was made by one of the most eminent of Indians. Mr. Jawahar Lal Nehru in his book *The Discovery of India* says,

... the British Government, in spite of its dislike of education, was compelled by circumstances to arrange for the training and production of clerks for its growing establishment. ... So education grew slowly and, though it was a limited and perverted education, it opened the doors and windows of the mind to new ideas and dynamic thoughts.

And at another place in the same book Mr. Nehru says,

English education brought a widening of the Indian horizon, an admiration for English literature and institutions, a revolt against some customs and aspects of Indian life, and a growing demand for political reform.

Whatever impact Western education had on the minds of the Indians, it was all foreseen by people like Macaulay. Much though Indians may blame the British government and people for bringing what they brought, India shall forever remain grateful to them for their Oriental scholars who not only revived India's ancient languages and values, but also salvaged many of the great books from oblivion. They gave Indians pride in being Indians, something that long since had been forgotten. This pride brought back a sense of mission, a sense of duty, and a will to act not only for self-benefit but for the country. For the first time perhaps Indians received, in the form of this alien education, lessons in patriotism.

This period also witnessed the revival of the ancient Gurukulas and institutions of Oriental learning. It must be admitted that they never proved very successful although they did have their votaries.

Perhaps another result of this Western contact was the rise of a middle class in India. With the passage of time it grew in strength and number. This education produced a class that lay great store by the Western languages and culture. They were not all even reasonably well-off, but they had a vested interest in this education, so they were responsible to a great extent for its success in this country.

Early decades of the twentieth century saw yet another impact of this education. Fierce nationalism brought in its train a new philosophy of education, and that too from unexpected quarters. Mahatma Gandhi put forward an educational scheme that was both simple and highly practical. It was rightly named Nai Talim or New Education. It was new for it was based on a new principle of education, *viz.* on craft. Around a simple craft was woven the whole fabric of this education. It was new in the sense that it required the early education to be conducted through the medium of mother tongue. It attracted attention, but since it was associated with Mahatma Gandhi and Mahatma Gandhi was associated with the activities of the Congress Party, it could not become popular at all. There was another reason for its unpopularity. The products of this system could never get lucrative jobs under the government where the official language was English which was not to be taught, at least as efficiently as in other schools. For the time being, it did not cross the boundary line of the Asrama of Gandhiji. Only when Congress formed its ministries in several provinces in 1938-39 was it really implemented sincerely. But soon the differences between Congress Party and the Government resulted in the abandoning of provincial autonomy and hence of this scheme.

Paradoxically enough, the ones who were opposed to the English system of education were those who had had a course in it and, vibrant with emotion, waxed eloquent in the language which they condemned vehemently as the medium of instruction. But this should not be construed as a reflection on their sincerity.

On the eve of Independence in 1947 India had inherited innumerable problems born out of the protracted contact with the West. Politically divided yet free, socially uprooted yet hopeful, and educationally backward yet potentially strong and eager, India launched plan after plan of education to cure herself of the ills that appeared temporarily incurable.

It could be said that in 1947 India was left an educational system that was neither national nor comprehensive. If she inherited about a dozen universities and about two hundred colleges, their courses and curricula were a curious mixture of Eastern and Western subjects. These were institutions like Shantiniketan started by Nobel Laureate Tagore for the purpose of bringing about synthesis in Eastern and Western cultures, Gurukalas to promote ancient wisdom of the East, Maktabs for the perpetuation of Islamic knowledge, and the characteristically Western colleges and universities for the large-scale production of Middle-grade Indians to fill subordinate vacancies

in the British Empire. The rate of literacy in India was as low as 12 percent of the total population with minor variations in various provinces in 1947. If for all this the Second World War and political unrest are partially responsible, the British rulers are no doubt also to blame. They have been variously blamed for being short-sighted, aimless, anti-national and haphazard in their efforts.[3] They also have been praised unduly for their work. Therefore, one might be tempted to conclude that whatever the British did had a humanitarian motive behind it all, although perhaps the plan was defective and the aims much too restricted. Despite the Sargent Report, education was never very well-planned, and the stock-taking never very accurate and effective.

It must be said to the credit of these alien rulers that perhaps for the first time in the history of India seeds of a national pattern of education were sown. If the growth has not been lush and luxuriant the reason does not lie so much in the insincerity of the motives as in the short funds made available for the purpose.

EDUCATION TODAY

Under the provisions of the Indian constitution education is the responsibility of the states. It has been further established that "the Government of India is authorised to give grants in aid to the states to develop their educational programmes." Because of the concurrent responsibility in economic and social planning, the central government and the states are bound to work for educational planning, since the latter is part of the former. The vast sums required for financing education are beyond the limited resources of the states to provide. The central government cannot, by its very nature, remain indifferent toward the progress of education. India is professedly a welfare state, and education is the prime requisite of such a state. Further, by choice, India is also a democratic country which, once again, requires an enlightened citizenry. But the provision of even rudimentary knowledge to all is not a matter to be taken lightly. A rough estimate has shown that over $10,000,-000 are required to provide free, compulsory and universal education for the age group six to fourteen. It is a colossal sum and a country like India cannot even imagine affording this expenditure. With a population of over 500 million people and a rate of literacy lower than 32 percent, the task the Government has set for itself appears impossible. However, it could be said that the job is being attempted nobly.

The Minister of Education is responsible to the Parliament. He is assisted by a Deputy Minister and a Parliamentary Secretary. The Minister is responsible for the national policies in education. He is also directly responsible for the administration of centrally

3. Nurullah & Naik, *A Student's History of Education in India*, London: Macmillan, 1951, 356-366.

governed universities and institutions of all types in the Union territories.

In his work he is assisted by fifteen advisory bodies, the oldest of them being the Central Advisory Board of Education of which the Central Minister is ex-officio President, the Educational Adviser to the Government of India works as its Secretary, and all State Education Ministers are its members. The Ministry of Education at the Union level is composed of nine divisions, *viz.* Administration, Elementary, Basic, Secondary, University, Physical Education and Recreation, Hindi, Scholarships, Research and Publications, and Social Welfare.

As noted earlier, the Union Minister of Education works as a coordinating agency between the States and the Central Government and the States themselves. The Central Government works also as a clearing house for educational information. Both of these functions have been inherited from the British. Another important work that the Central Education Ministry does is regarding the promotion of Hindi, the official and national language of India. The State governments in consultation with the Central Government and the Planning Commission prepare educational programmes; this is described as a "working partnership" among the three.

The "Centre" (or Central Government) through its various bodies works in all the branches of education. While it promotes basic education, it also helps universities of the country receive grants through its university Grants Commission patterned on the English U.G.C. A recent autonomous creation of the Ministry is the National Council of Educational Research and Training, a body responsible both for teacher training at graduate and post-graduate levels and research in all areas connected with education. It gets all its funds from the Ministry but maintains an autonomous status. This body has the Union Minister as its ex-officio chairman. Having the opening of multi-purpose schools throughout nation as a policy, the training of teachers is a job that the Centre has undertaken through this body.

Besides these functions the Union Education Ministry finances the indigent, the exceptionally talented, and the physically and mentally handicapped; it also gives grants-in-aid to numerous educational institutions spread all over the country. It maintains the National Archives along with Archaeological departments containing priceless documents of past centuries and also the modern works on history and culture.

It is stipulated that the other Ministry, *viz.* Ministry of Scientific Research and Cultural Affairs—responsible for the Technical education and cultural affairs—be merged with the Education Ministry. This Ministry has so far maintained a chain of National Laboratories which conduct high-level research work in various advanced fields. This Ministry also collects scientific knowledge from other countries and circu-

lates it in this country. It also does pioneer work in the field of technical education, such as planning, financing, and providing it at different levels. Also, it provides scholarships to students going abroad for studies in those fields, the facilities for which are lacking in India. To save foreign exchange and avoid other complications, the government has opened three Technological Institutes in the country. One of them is assisted entirely by the United States.

At the Central level other Ministries are also engaged in the training and educational work, for instance, the Ministry of Home Affairs is concerned with the training of Indian Administrative officers, Hindi teaching and education in the Union territories including Delhi; and Ministry of Health, with training doctors and nurses. In brief, education is the concern of all Ministries and therefore a wide variety of institutions are a natural corollary.

State Roles in Education

Education, as pointed out earlier, is the responsibility of the states. It is for the states to plan and finance education in their respective jurisdiction. Unlike the United States, however, the educational standards are more or less uniform throughout the country. The Central Government sees to it. This means that although states are independent of the "Centre" in so many respects, they are obliged to have a national outlook in all matters. Education is one field in which national standards are to be rigorously maintained. This is done through annual conferences of Ministers of Education, Directors of Education, Vice-chancellors of the universities, and others.

At the state level, again there is an Education Minister assisted by Parliamentary Secretary and a permanent staff consisting of various ranks of officers. The states have a permanent Directorate of Education, headed by a Director of Education who is in turn assisted by numerous Deputy Directors and Assistant Directors. There is, however, a separate Directorate of Technical Education with an entirely separate and specialized staff. Selections are made for the ranks of District and Subordinate officers through an open competition under a Public Service Commission.

The states are divided into districts, counterparts of the English "counties." All districts have District Inspectors of Schools assisted by junior office assistants and officials. The interests of the minorities are protected by their own set of inspectors. For the education of girls, once again, there is a separate arrangement headed by Regional Directresses in place of Inspectors.

At all levels the states finance education. The Governor of the state is ex-officio Chancellor of all Universities in his state, except of the Central Universities.

The Minister of Education in the state finally bears the responsibility of encouraging, assisting, and guiding education. He is the real policy maker of the state; the others only assist him in carrying out the projected work.

Local Roles in Education

In the urban areas, for the promotion of primary and Nursery education only, (the former being compulsory) municipalities or corporations are responsible. Municipal Councils have an educational branch made up of elected people assisted by a permanent Education Officer and other subordinate officials. They have both men's and women's branches. These educational councils are guided by a Deputy District Inspector of Schools who belongs to the State's educational cadre and is assisted by Sub-Deputy-Inspectors of Schools. This system is repeated for rural areas where the nomenclature of the elected body is "district board."

Now that these have been grouped under Block Development Boards, educational responsibility is being shifted from District Boards to the Development Blocks. Here also a gazetted officer is in charge of all work, including education.

So what is planned at national level is gradually passed on to the village level. The curriculum of all levels of state is planned at the state level. This does not apply to the universities. Whereas this system is helpful in maintaining a uniformity throughout the state, it necessarily leads to an unnecessary rigidity. There is lot that could be said against the State's prescription of textbooks. Had it been otherwise, perhaps the defects of too much freedom also might have become obvious.

In India, people are increasingly becoming conscious of their rights. Therefore, the slipshod way in which primary education is being managed and provided has recently come in for heavy criticism. A strong segment of the population feels that education should be completely taken over by the state governments. This does not mean that all locally elected bodies are defective.

Pre-Primary Schools

Like most other countries this country also has pre-primary schools. They are patterned on the Montessori or kindergarten system. Since the children of pre-compulsory age go here, these institutions are restricted in number. Barring exceptions, these schools are meant only for rich and urban people; for rural areas this education is as yet a dream. Some of these charge very high fees and in return provide education that falls far short of expectation. In some, the medium of instruction is English, but the majority content themselves with the mother tongue. In some, the teachers are exceptionally qualified and get good salaries, whereas in others if the teachers get even regular salaries they should be described as fortunate. In short, all types of institutions exist at this level

ranging from very good to decidedly bad. Private bodies and even profiteers have invested money in these schools. In some cases the municipalities run such schools or give incentive grants. Even the states are not indifferent toward them. Here, the teachers are invariably women. Training facilities for such teachers also exist, though they cannot be described as adequate.

These schools have become a necessity for working mothers. Therefore, in the industrial areas the government operates them. These schools cannot compete with the good private institutions.

What prevents this education from being universally available is lack of teachers, buildings, finances, and even children. Their future is, however, bright, as the need for pre-primary education is being increasingly felt.

Primary Education

Despite the three five-year plans primary education is not as yet free, universal, or compulsory. There exist remote corners in the country where the light of education is as far away as spaceships are from the distant stars. Even in the midst of such cities as Bombay, Calcutta, or New Delhi children of school-going age roam the streets, unmindful of the benefits and laws concerning education. People who fail to realize the value of education are not rare to meet.

But the wind of change is noticeably strong. The attitudes of the people are fast changing. The barriers of class and caste are gradually breaking down. A nation is emerging—hopeful, strong, and multitudinous.

At this stage, India has two parallel systems of education: one, "primary, lower secondary, higher secondary" system; another a "junior basic, senior basic, higher secondary" system for the age group six plus to sixteen plus. The age breakdown is as follows: Six plus to eleven plus, eleven plus to fourteen plus, and fourteen plus to sixteen plus. This age breakdown is common to both systems. There could be schools with primary and secondary classes or exclusively for either.

The percentage of single-teacher schools is high. Normally the teacher-pupil ratio is one to thirty-five. The reason for two nomenclatures lies in the fact that the "primary, secondary" system was given by the British, but as soon as the Congress Party took control they adopted "basic" education as their national educational policy. The characteristic feature of "basic" education is its insistence on making education craft-centered. Its philosophy is "earning while learning." The scheme of "basic" education has undergone several changes, having been first put forward in 1937 by the "Father of the Nation." The present "basic" education resembles in name only the original plan, for no one seriously takes the view that education can be made economically independent of state or local grants. Gandhi wanted to see education pay for itself, hence productive work was the cornerstone of his scheme. His plan of education was simple: teach through mother-tongue whatever you have to teach; allow children much freedom; make education craft-centered; the products of the craft will pay for the cost of education; make this system universal, compulsory, and free. India is a poor country and its population lives for the most part in villages. This scheme is suited to her needs.

Discussing the merits of the plan is not the task of this essay. Here, concern is with describing the first rungs of the educational ladder.

The aims of primary and "junior-basic, senior-basic" obviously differ. The plan, philosophy, and nature of "basic" education have already been discussed. Primary education is what "basic" education is not. Its major purpose is to prepare children for secondary education. For those who will finish their education at the primary stage, this will enable them to learn rudiments of knowledge, such as reading, writing, environment and home. Gradually the children shall understand their social order and learn to react properly toward it. The sole distinction between the aims of ordinary primary education and "basic" education lies in the fact that whereas in the former the information is given without any reference to craft, in the latter the whole system is so evolved that craft becomes its centre. To be more explicit, depending upon the social environment a craft would be selected for teaching in a particular area; afterwards, the economics, the arithmetic, and the accountancy of the same shall be taught enabling the child to learn simple economics, arithmetic, and the like through it.

Because the plan is felt to be fundamentally sound, the Government of India decided to adopt "basic education" for its future educational endeavours. It decided to convert all the primary schools into "basic" schools. In the year 1960-61, 23.3 percent of the total children were involved "in all classes" in "basic" schools. The lack of trained teachers, craft equipment and, to a large extent, vision has made the conversion very slow and in certain states nothing has been changed except the name plates of the schools. Whether this indicates insincerity or not is difficult to say.

In most cases the schools of primary stage, whether "basic" or otherwise, get government or local aid. But there are some that do not take help from either. They are private schools, exclusively for the rich. They charge very high fees, provide boarding and lodging facilities, and have English as their medium of instruction. It would not be wrong to say that, like any other country, India practices class distinction. If the practice is crude and obvious, it signifies only that this country is not as yet a socialist country.

In these primary schools including "basic" schools the teachers are relatively well-trained. Speaking relatively, they are very low-paid people. Even now, the teachers of primary schools get lower salaries than peons in the state or central government. School buildings are not always attractive. The equipment is often inadequate. The laws of compulsory education are law. Especially in the villages, the children of school age fail to come regularly. The rate of wastage is considerable. The textbooks are not always scientifically graded. They are not, however, expensive. Unlike European policies, the children have to pay for their conveyance, clothes, and books. In some advanced states of India, mid-day meals are provided free.

Girls, especially among the lower classes beyond the ages of 9 and 10, are real bread-earners and can hardly be spared for such an apparently unproductive and uneconomic activity as education. Early marriages are another important reason for girls not being able to attend primary classes beyond ten plus.

There are signs that in near future significant changes will occur in both the equipment and the personnel of primary education. All states are going to have state colleges of Elementary (Primary) Education where researches in this field will be conducted. In certain states that already has been implemented. The salaries of the teachers have been revised and will soon be revised again. New schools are being built with good buildings and better equipment. The future holds great promise.

Secondary Schools

Somewhat similar to other countries in the world, Secondary Education in India bristles with numerous problems but holds out tremendous possibilities.

India has two types of schools: one, "higher secondary schools," and the other, "high schools." The student enters class IX at the age of fourteen plus and that is the actual beginning of "high school" education. If he passes a public examination conducted by state departments of Education after the end of class X, he is awarded a high school diploma and if he passes the examination after XI education, he receives a diploma of "higher secondary." The distinction lies in the fact that the former gives the student an opportunity to enter a two-year course of "intermediate education" at the end of which he can take an examination, which is also conducted by the State Department of Education; after that examination, the student can enter a three-year university degree course without undergoing an "intermediate" course of study. A state follows one pattern or the other. It is not possible by law to have both patterns in the same state. Of course, there *are* exceptions and these shall be explained later.

Before 1947, *i.e.* in the pre-Independence days, India had only one pattern, the "High School—Intermediate" pattern. Afterwards, secondary education was made an end in itself. It was assumed that very few students would go to the universities or colleges. Therefore, after obtaining "higher secondary" diplomas, students should be able to assume junior posts in the country. After "high school" this was not possible. For an "intermediate" diploma, one had to study for two years more and had to take another public examination. Thus "higher secondary" was an improvement in both senses. It would give students minimum qualification to enter jobs and would also require them to take only one examination.

Because education only in liberal arts subjects was found to be highly unsatisfactory, a plan of opening multi-purpose schools was devised and implemented. Therefore, India now has multi-purpose schools, with diversified courses, running alongside the above two. They offer several training opportunities, after which the trainees can enter vocations following a year or two of apprenticeship. These schools are not narrowly conceived as to curriculum. They give students as many opportunities to learn and to play as any of their counterparts do. To date the number of multi-purpose schools does not exceed 2500. These schools have so far been ill-equipped, and well-trained teachers for them have not been easy to find. But it is perhaps the first bold educational experiment attempted by the government of India.

India has "All India" Secondary Schools as well, distinguishable from state secondary schools. These schools are meant for the children of Central Government employees whose posts are transferable, so that the children do not suffer educationally. This plan is centrally sponsored and is entirely supported by the central government.

India has forty-two public schools patterned on the public schools of England, catering almost exclusively to the rich. Their role in the country's education has been variously praised. One of the recent admirers of these schools has been the President of India. The medium of instruction in these schools is primarily English. The curriculum is being oriented to "basic" education, following recommendations of a central committee. Of all secondary school teachers, the teachers in public schools receive the highest salaries. They are typically well trained, but a good graduate or post-graduate degree is all that is needed to enter these schools. Of course, the Indian Public Schools do not play exactly the same role as in England; neither has their "tie" the same attraction or value; even so, they provide a coveted form of education and constitute a privilege.

The curriculum at both the "high school" and the "higher secondary" stages has several streams, *e.g.* Science, Arts, Commerce. A student in any of the streams is expected to elect four subjects from the many offerings. The teachers at this stage are post-graduates with a teaching certificate of one-year

duration. English, except in convent or public schools, is no longer the medium of instruction. Its place has been taken by fourteen regional languages. Still, English is taught to all children, at all levels, in all schools and in all states. In fact, English is not offered here as a *foreign* language. It is a second living language in India.

Secondary education has undergone a complete transformation since independence. Before 1947, it was a single pattern: high school—intermediate. Secondary is now no longer regarded as a mere ladder leading on to University education. It has been made in most cases a terminal education after which students follow vocations of their choice. The number of streams has also increased. The multi-purpose schools will soon revolutionize the system. Science, because it leads to better vocations, is the most desired stream.

Students with good science marks can enter medical, scientific, engineering, and technological careers. These professions are relatively well paid. Therefore, at the secondary stage the greatest rush for admissions is to be seen in science courses.

High School or Higher Secondary examinations are conducted by State Departments of Education through their own machinery known as Boards of High School and Intermediate Examinations. If the state offers the High School—Intermediate pattern, a student has to take public examinations twice, but if it has a higher secondary system, the public examination must be taken only once. In regard to years of schooling for secondary education, uniformity is entirely missing. Nevertheless, an Intermediate student of one state can seek admission or job in another state without losing a single advantage. This uniformity of standards throughout the country, though kept at the cost of variety and imagination, is extremely convenient.

Coeducation in secondary schools is normally avoided. The teachers are therefore either male or female depending upon the sex for which an institution has been created. The secondary schools in certain states are run entirely by the State Governments but in most cases voluntary-aided schools are a rule. Voluntary-aided schools are operated under the private management within the supervision of the District Inspector of Schools. All types of management exist ranging from excellent to decidedly poor. In certain voluntary-aided schools the working conditions of the teachers are as good as in the government schools, but in certain others their lot is far from being enviable.

University Education

Universities are not new to India. But the modern universities are different from their ancient counterparts. Created by Acts of State legislatures or Parliament, the modern universities—a product of Western influence—are the highest institutions of learning in India. They are financed by States and also by the Union Government, through a body, *viz*. University Grants Commission, patterned on the English U.G.C. There are, however, a few centrally administered universities as well, chartered and entirely financed by the central government. The U.G.C. is a specialized committee which offers advice to the Central Government but which is autonomous. Its major functions are to determine grants for all universities, whether state or central, and to consider the merits of opening new universities and the extension of the old ones. It is responsible for carrying out policies of the Central Government regarding higher education. Distinguished men of letters serve on this commission as chairman, members and secretary, all for a fixed term. In case of the Central universities, the President of India and in case of the State Universities the Governor are the highest ex-officio officers. In a way, therefore, Indian universities are government institutions. In common with the universities elsewhere, Indian universities offer varied courses of higher learning and grant graduate and post-graduate degrees. Doctoral work is also one of their major functions.

Those students who have taken the Intermediate certificate are allowed to take the first university degree after two years of work and examination; otherwise three years is the required minimum. Except in certain subjects where there is very high demand, students are admitted on the strength of their past academic record, consisting mainly of the higher secondary examination or Intermediate examination. But that is not the only consideration and therefore others not really well qualified also get admitted.

Besides the categories to which all universities belong (*viz.*, Central or State) the Indian universities are mostly of three types, based on their organization and administration. They are: Unitary-residential or teaching universities; teaching and affiliating universities; and merely affiliating universities. Where the universities provide teaching facilities for their degrees, the universities are called "teaching" or "unitary-residential" universities. Where they do both teaching and affiliating work they have a distinct name to show their character. And by merely affiliating type is meant the universities that do not undertake to teach students but grant degrees to those who received education in the colleges affiliated to them. These colleges could be government as well as private or aided, depending upon the nature of the sponsoring body.

A university is headed by Vice-Chancellor (counterpart of the President of the U.S. universities) who is nominated by the Governor of the state or President of India on the advice of the Minister of Education, usually from a list of three names sent from the university court or Senate. In academic matters, the Vice-Chancellor is assisted by an Academic Council consisting of senior Heads of the Departments (or Chairman) where he makes important decisions regarding courses of study, standards, and the like. Normally he carries out the policies of the Executive Council, consisting of representatives of University teaching staff, alumni, the court, the Academic Council, and the Government. For each subject the university has a Board of study which prescribes its courses and textbooks subject to the approval of the Faculty, the Academic Council and the Executive Council.

The real administrative and office work is carried on by the Registrar, who is a permanent official; many busy clerks assist him.

Although the number of years required for the first degree course are different in different universities, they are all regarded as equivalent. This fact obviates the need for an independent accrediting agency. For a post-graduate degree a student has to take an examination after two years of work and only after a post-graduate degree can he seek admission to a course leading to a Ph.D. degree which, if a student is industrious, can be obtained within two academic sessions, one session being equal to nine calendar months.

The conflicting claims of India's mixed culture have produced universities whose counterparts are difficult to find elsewhere. One such university is Shant-ni-ketan, started by the Nobel-Laureate, Rabindra Nath Tagore, which is regarded as a bold experiment in international understanding. By laying stress on the fine arts, languages and culture, the aesthetic side to the students is developed in addition to their other facets. There is also a Gurukul university, reminding Indians of their rich heritage, cultural resilience, eternally puritanic values, and glorious past. In past centuries Gurukulas were institutions of higher learning where teachers allowed a certain number of students to live with them and learn reverently at their feet both secular and religious subjects. Times have changed, but not for Hindus whose time-sense is neither affected nor fettered by the mundane laws of calculations. As for the preservation of Muslim religion and culture, India has four universities. The secular nature of the Government of India has not prevented it from patronising all these institutions.

The life of the Indian university is considerably different from life in the European universities. Indian students are invariably harassed by financial difficulties. Government stipends are few, as are philanthropic contributions.

University students have to pay for their tuition, books, clothes, and conveyance. But the opportunities for earning during this period are indeed lamentably few, hence the common dependence on parents. If university students are lacking in force of conviction, originality, academic work, and brilliance, they have in the recent years compensated for these qualities by acquiring notoriety in other fields, notably politics. An almost universal complaint against them is their participation in politics. Senior professors recently have been accused of living life remote from both students and society.

The universities hold their own examinations for each class every year. These examinations are held at the end of the session's work, and success and failure in them decide the fate of the students. A number of examination papers are prepared by internal examiners (the regular teachers of the universities). Some are sent to universities elsewhere. The examination papers are then sent to a set of moderators, who assess the standards of academic achievement. Lately the examination system has come in for a great deal of criticism. But like all other things in India, it has survived the onslaughts and continues to evoke admiration from eminent people.

Preparation of Teachers

A typical western importation, preparation of teachers has acquired a place of considerable importance in Indian education.

A hierachy of cadres is maintained. Teachers for pre-primary, primary, secondary, and technical schools are prepared in different institutions. Emphasis is equally pronounced on in-service training for all these teachers.

Educated people in India realize the importance of trained teachers; still, not all schools require trained teachers, and where they are required not all succeed in getting them. Nursery, kindergarten, and public schools are institutions that do not normally insist upon having fully trained teachers.

Hundreds of teachers with degrees annually leave the profession. Opportunities for better pay in government service and other pursuits often offer better pay and working conditions.

Training institutions are generally voluntary institutions receiving grants-in-aid from the state and union Governments. University departments of Education either offer the course for secondary teachers themselves, or delegate their responsibility to affiliating post-graduate colleges. State Governments also run their own colleges for secondary school teachers through their Education Departments.

The latest entrant in the field is the Union government. The Education Ministry of the Union Government through an autonomous body, *viz.* National Council of Educational Research and Training, has opened four Regional Colleges in the country with a view to preparing teachers for multi-purpose schools. Here the prospective teachers are taught for four years in an integrated program, including pedagogy. For the first time in India teachers are being specially prepared to teach agriculture, commerce, and technical skills. In addition, one-year courses leading to the B.Ed. degree and the diploma in education are also offered in regional colleges to prospective teachers of science and technology. These colleges are regarded as a great experiment. Incidentally, teachers in these institutions enjoy the same benefits as those of a university staff.

At all levels training colleges are either coeducational or separate, with the former type the rule and latter the exception. Recently, an emphasis is being placed on preparing teachers for rural areas specialized in "basic" education. The distinction between rural and urban areas is carried to the extremes. Many educationists believe that these have to remain and develop along entirely different lines. In their opinion "basic" education is suited to village children alone. Consequently, a "basic" oriented teacher is supposedly the only competent teacher for villages.

The aims and objectives of teacher training for rural areas are as follows:

1. To give the student-teachers practical experience of the life of a community based on cooperative work for the common good. (Dr. E. A. Pires distinguishes between rural and urban education by stating that the function of the former is to prepare rural children for rural life by teaching them crafts and trades of the locality; and of the latter to prepare urban children for urban life in its complexities. He feels that the second factor that distinguishes the village school and the village teacher from their urban counterparts is the nature and extent of the contribution they will make to the entire life of the community.)

2. To help them to understand and accept the social objective of ["Basic" Education], and the implications of a new social order based on truth and non-violence.

3. To encourage the development of all the faculties (physical, intellectual, aesthetic and spiritual) of each student-teacher toward the achievement of a well-integrated, harmoniously balanced personality.

4. To equip the student-teacher professionally for his work, *i.e.* to enable him to understand and meet the physical, intellectual, and emotional needs of children.

In all colleges, student-teachers are required in their training period to learn certain essential principles of educational psychology, experimental psychology, history of Indian education, principles of school administration, methods and principles of teaching school subjects, health and hygiene, and the theory of education. The number of years required for undergoing training decide the content and level of the above subjects. For a single-year course all the above subjects are so compressed that the student-teachers acquire only bare acquaintance with each. Student teachers teach in schools for a varying number of days. They are required to prepare notes for lessons for each period they take. Each lesson is supervised by training college staff who give their opinions both during and after the period. In the "basic" schools, also, this process is repeated, but in addition students study the principles of "basic" education and practice teaching crafts.

Fees are charged in most institutions; only the government institutions are free. In the Regional Colleges, large stipends are given to students in addition to other benefits. As compared to European countries, fees charged are low, the maximum being about four dollars a month, but the average income of an educated man in India is not high.

Selection procedures vary from institution to institution and state to state. In the state of Uttar Pradesh state officials select teacher candidates in all state institutions. In the case of voluntary aided institutions the procedure of selection is laid down by the state department of education. The universities and colleges adopt their own procedures.

The selection tests range from very difficult to an open-to-all invitation. Normally the procedure consists of an interview and a written language and aptitude test. Past academic records are invariably considered for the selection of candidates. They are the sole criterion of selection in state colleges, but not in voluntary-aided institutions where other factors are as significant as the past records.

The life of a student-teacher is very busy throughout the session. He has to work hard to pass the examination. The "practice of teaching" examinations are given by external examiners. The written papers are set by State Department of Education or by the universities in their respective academic jurisdictions.

Specialists in education are produced at the university level where courses toward the Master of Education and Ph.D. in education are offered. Pioneer work in educational research is being done by the National Institute of Education at Delhi. The need for producing such specialized people is great.

There is a growing realization that training of teachers is an important step in raising educational standards. Cheaper and better techniques must be developed for training teachers who did not attend training colleges for pre-service instruction. Correspondence courses are being considered for this purpose.

TECHNICAL EDUCATION

India is on the threshold of the technological age. The present government has encouraged this development. Much remains to be done, however, before this country becomes "technologically advanced." Whether the direction is right and proper has yet to be ascertained.

Today technical education is given at all levels. Junior technical schools admit students at the age of fourteen-plus for three years. After this training and education these boys go to industries as skilled personnel.

After the junior technicals, India has polytechnical schools. Here the minimum qualification required for admission is matriculation. The training period spreads over three years. During this time students learn the applied side of technical sciences. Soon another year will be added; then it will be possible to teach both the principles and applications of various technical subjects of study. In "polytechnics" the commonly offered branches are mechanical, civil, and electrical engineering. There are about 200 polytechnical schools in India. After completing their studies, polytechnical students take jobs such as junior technical assistants and overseers.

The polytechnics generally are state controlled but some are run by the universities as well.

All states have their own Directorates of Technical Education, assisted and guided by an All-India body, and thus a coordination is achieved in the standards and courses. The State and the Union Governments give liberal grants to these institutions, and the salaries offered here compare favorably with the universities.

Equivalent to the Polytechnic diplomas are diplomas in textile technology and leather technology. Institutions offering these courses are not called polytechnics, although the type and period of education in these is identical with the polytechnical schools.

The next rung of the ladder in technical education is the degree in civil, electrical, mechanical, chemical, mining, and agricultural engineering. The minimum qualification for admission to these courses is the "Intermediate." Here a student undergoes a training of four years before he takes the final examination to earn the degree. These degree courses are offered in the universities or in the National Institutes of Technology. Certain affiliated colleges of the universities also provide opportunities for this training.

India did not have a single Institute of Technology until 1947. The four present Institutes now offer opportunities for graduate, post-graduate, and research work. Graduates of these Institutes are a pride of the nation. Each of the Institutes has an intake capacity of over 1600 at the undergraduate level and 300 at the post-graduate level. One of these Institutes is patterned after the Massachusetts Institute of Technology in the United States and was opened with American assistance.

Hundreds of Indian scientists are receiving their training abroad. Of these, the majority are in the United Kingdom and the United States. Hopefully, India will soon reach a point when she will no longer find it necessary for her students to go elsewhere for training in scientific subjects.

Other Problems

India has many adult illiterates. Several attempts have been made to teach them simple reading and writing. But the teaching of some 75 percent of all adults is not an easy task. The value of literacy is recognized universally. Therefore, a program of adult education was planned at the Union Government level.

A National Centre for Fundamental Education has been established in New Delhi to train higher grade personnel for social work, to develop suitable techniques, to carry out research on selected problems, and to serve as a clearing house of information for "Social Education." A "Social Education" Institute for workers is functioning at Indore. People's Colleges and Rural Institutes are doing a great service in rural areas by providing educational facilities there.

There are also a number of institutions for physically and mentally handicapped children all over the country, but their number is quite small as compared to the task.

All of the measures mentioned above are vital to the full development of India.

THE EDUCATED MAN

For an Indian an educated man has to present a living synthesis in his personality of the so-called Eastern and Western values. Not only has he to learn and exhibit democratic behavior, but he has to have faith in socialism. This synthesis in life and outlook would result from a deep understanding of ancient traditions and values, a clear knowledge of history and a wish to combine material prosperity with spiritual pursuits. Only a passionate believer in the destiny of Man can live up to this ideal; for it would require freedom from prejudice, transcending barriers of caste and color, and having a respect for all faiths. Democracy entails a faith in the equality of all; it means leading a life that is economically, socially, and politically free, one in which each individual has an opportunity to make decisions for himself. Nations and individuals must not be at loggerheads with each other. Earning a respectable salary, understanding the basic issues of life, living at peace with others, realizing the interdependence of men and nations, contributing toward the betterment of all are, among others, the attributes of an educated man that an Indian would like to regard as his national ideal.

GOALS OF EDUCATION

India has accepted a socialistic pattern of society as her ideal. For the success of democratic socialism, educated, conscientious, and law-abiding democratic citizens are essential. All these qualities are dependent upon the type of education the country provides.

India is not near the achievement of her goals in education. Unlike more advanced countries of the world, India has not succeeded in providing even minimum education to all. Universal, free, and compulsory education until the age of fourteen plus is as yet a dream. Provision of ancillary services which is regarded as an important part of the plan of education is merely a cherished ideal. The atmosphere in which children could learn well the most basic tenets of democracy is missing. Not only does India suffer from the malaise of economic and social inequality, but there is no unanimity regarding the national objectives of education. The views of the political majority party in regard to education have been challenged. The once-hallowed pattern of "basic" education has withered. The hesitation in its implementation, the acceptance of it as a gospel, unpreparedness to introduce variety into its program, and the belief that education can be made self-supporting at all stages have contributed toward its withering.

EQUALITY OF OPPORTUNITY

Equality of educational opportunity is an avowed policy of the government. But where fees are changed at all stages, where entrance into institutions is decided by "pulls and pressures," and where politicians interfere in the working of educational administration, equality of opportunity must remain a remote ideal. This should not be taken to mean that the government is not sincere, or that the people responsible for running the educational institutions are not aware of their responsibilities. Castes are another hindrance in the achievement of this cherished ideal. Denominational institutions that abound in the country are run for the protection and betterment of particular denominations.

Economical inequality tends to influence adversely educational equality. There are two types of institutions in this country: one for the classes and another for the masses. If the poor succeed in reaching the top, their success should not be attributed to the benevolence of others. Sheer merit coupled with the will to succeed can sometimes show wonders. Good Montessori schools leading to rich private schools provide excellent educational opportunities to the sons of the rich. The United Kingdom and the United States are not distant lands for a rich man's son. Foreign degrees are still prized. They show quicker results than anything else, hence the scramble for them.

PROBLEMS OF EDUCATION

There could hardly be an educational system entirely free from problems. Even the most advanced countries have problems to deal with. The nature and extent of problems that exist in India are obviously different from those of other nations.

The most important problems of this system of education lie in the confusion of aims of education.

India has not decided what type of country she would like to become. A materially prosperous country, taking her humble place amidst the advanced countries of the world? One leaving material prosperity alone for the achieving of spiritual superiority over others? Or a synthesis of both? There is no single policy of education. There are many.

One does not know whether the work of a rural primary school should be identical with or different from the work of an urban school. Of late, numbers of students have been taken as an index to progress. Besides, no one appears to know the distinction between a "basic-oriented" and "non-basic oriented" primary school; the curriculum of both in certain places is almost the same.

The state of secondary education is still more confusing. Whether secondary education is to be a terminal education for the majority of children or merely a rung on the educational ladder leading to higher education is undecided. Whether "High School, Intermediate, College" pattern should be considered a national pattern or instead the "Higher-Secondary, College" pattern, India has not decided. Even the number of years considered sufficient for a secondary education diploma have been a point of controversy among the Directors and Ministers of Education.

Higher education provides the greatest evidence of indecisiveness in aims and objectives. Innumerable students pass in and out of the institutions of higher learning annually without realizing in the slightest degree the value of the education they have had. There exists a great disparity between the value of arts and science subjects. Arts subjects are held in lower esteem than those in science.

For a foreigner the variety in the types of institutions of higher learning must be baffling. Gurukulas and universities are put in the same category, although their function and historical traditions are different.

Working conditions and facilities vary from institution to institution. A good private institution may offer the same salary and other benefits as a government-run institution, but not as a rule.

The question of the medium of instruction still remains undecided. The evolution of a three-language formula, a Soviet importation, has not been helpful. In the heat of defending one language against the other there has been bloodshed. The question of the medium instruction is related to a wider problem of safeguarding political interests. Therefore, a purely academic issue has taken on political overtones.

The lowering of standards has followed the expansion in education. It is felt that the standards of education were once high but that they have gone down because of the negligence, badly equipped institutions, and an unprecedented expansion. These changes are said to apply especially to higher education.

Today the accent in Indian education is on science and technical studies. Problems and problem-solving are an eternal process and evidently a sign of the living. That the Indian educational system is very much alive, no one can deny.

SELECTED BIBLIOGRAPHY

ALTEKAR, A. S. *Education in Ancient India*. Bombay: Asia Publishing Co., 1960.

ASHRAF, K. M. *Life and Conditions of the People of Hindustan*. Delhi: Jiwan Prakashan, 1960.

FILHO, M. B. L. *The Training of Rural School Teachers*. New York: UNESCO, 1953.

KEAY, F. E. A *History of Education in India and Pakistan*. London: Oxford University Press, 1959.

MUDAHIAR, A. L. *Education in India*. Banaras: Nand Kisore & Brothers, 1948.

NEHRU, J. L. *The Discovery of India*. London: Meridian Books, 1956.

PANIKKAR, K. M. A *Survey of Indian History*. Bombay: Asia Publishing Co., 1962.

JAPAN

Toshiyuki Hara

A BRIEF HISTORY OF EDUCATION IN JAPAN

Two important events are prominent in the progress of Japanese education covering more than one thousand years. The first is the Meiji Restoration in 1868, and the second is Japan's surrender in the Pacific War in 1945. The former was new Japan's point of departure for her rapid development as a modern nation. This was made possible by establishing diplomatic and commercial relations with advanced Western countries after the fall of the Tokugawa Shogunate which had adhered to the policy of seclusion for the preceding 300 years. The latter was the starting point for Japan's rebirth as a new democratic country following the devastation caused by the War into which she had recklessly plunged. Therefore, it seems to be appropriate to divide the history of education in Japan into three periods: (1) before the Meiji Restoration, (2) after the Meiji Restoration, and (3) after the Pacific War.

Education Before the Meiji Restoration

Education in the Aristocratic Era

It is not yet scientifically established when and how the Japanese immigrated from southern islands or the Asian Continent and became an integrated race. However, about the middle of the fourth century, a clan state was founded under the single authority of the Tenno family (the Emperor's clan), which was the strongest clan at that time. The tenno family built the capital of Nara in the main island of Honshu. About the fifth century, some of the people were supposed to be able to read and write Chinese characters and they began to absorb the Chinese civilization after some Chinese classics and Buddhist texts were introduced through Korea. From the sixth to the twelfth centuries, the Tenno government remained comparatively stable and gradually expanded

the sphere of its influence to the west and the east, although at times there were political crises.

It is worth mentioning as an educational event that the Daigaku (a national college) and the Kokugaku (provincial colleges) were established about the beginning of the seventh century taking the T'ang school system as a model. The Taiho Ritsuryo (Taiho Code) which was completed in 701, stipulated that a Daigaku in the capital and a Kokugaku in each provincial capital should be established. However, it is not certain whether a Kokugaku was really built in each province except for one, that is, the Fugaku or Kokugaku at Dazaifu in Kyushu, the largest provincial capital in Western Japan at that time.

Moreover, in the capital there were several Shigaku (private schools) which were affiliated with the Daigaku and were maintained by some leading aristocratic clans for the purpose of educating their sons. However, needless to say, there were no schools for the common people. The rule, common to all countries in the world, that the school is at first introduced merely for educating the children of the privileged class, also applies to Japan. Therefore, various aspects of cultural heritage known today, for instance, Horyuji temple, the oldest wooden building in the world, Daibutsu (a colossal bronze statue of Buddha) at Nara, Waka (Japanese poem), Kana (the Japanese alphabet), and so on, were all created in connection with the aristocrats' religious, cultural and recreational life. There was nothing special to be regarded as culture or education in the life of the common people in those days.

Culture and Education in the Era of Feudalism

Toward the end of the twelfth century, the Kamakuru Bakufu or Shogunate was founded by Bushi (the warrior class). Political power was taken over by the warriors from the hands of the Emperor and aristocrats, and then the capital was moved from

Kyoto to Kamakura, about 300 miles east of Kyoto. The 400 years that followed were marked by continuous internal wars, large and small, fought by many Daimyo (feudal lords) who were competing among themselves for political leadership.

Buddhism, since its introduction to Japan, had caught the minds of the succeeding Emperors and aristocracy and had been protected by them. However, around the twelfth century, its several sects had gradually become too ritualistic and formal to be of any help to the people who were ardently seeking consolation in religion. From among the young Buddhist priests who were really discontent with such a tendency, there emerged religious reformers, Honen, Shinran, and Nichiren. They founded new sects one after another by reinterpreting the Buddhist Sutras and bringing religion nearer to the daily life of the common people. This was a kind of Reformation in Japan and the origin of what is known as native Japanese Buddhism.

At the same time, the Zen sects were brought into Japan by Dogen and Eisai from China and their doctrines were accepted by the warrior class. The Zen sects became popular since they laid more stress upon practising Zen than upon the pursuit of academic studies of the Sutras or the formal performance of religious ceremonies. In short, the mind of the warrior who valued a simple and ascetic life could easily conform to the rigidness of the Zen sects. Sado (Tea ceremony) and Nogaku (No play) were characteristic cultural expressions created by the warrior class in those days.

As for education, there were no schools for the common people or for those of the common warriors, because in those days of wars and disturbances most feudal lords had scarcely any time or desire to care about the education of their own children or those of others. Only certain Buddhist temples used to give a sort of secular education on the elementary level for a limited number of the children of aristocrats and upperclass warriors. As the Zen sects spread among the warrior class, more and more upperclass warriors sent their sons to Zen temples to have them learn the fundamentals of the Chinese classics and Zen doctrines.

Education in the Era of the Tokugawa Shogunate

EDUCATIONAL POLICY OF THE TOKUGAWA GOVERNMENT. In 1603 Ieyasu Tokugawa founded the Shogunate Government in Edo (now Tokyo) atfer conquering all the other feudal lords and bringing the country under his power. He said, "I have come into power *on horseback* (this means with the sword), but I cannot govern the people on horseback." He encouraged the Bushi or Samurai to study Confucianism as he thought it most suitable for qualifying the warrior class as the rulers and administrators of the feudal

society. He invited Razan Hayashi, the greatest Confucianist of the day to become his political consultant. The library and school established by Razan in Edo was later taken over and run by the government as a special institution for the training of the vassals of the Shogun, general commander.

As Razan was a scholar of the Chuhsi school, a unique sect of Confucianism which laid great stress upon the hierarchical system in a feudal society, the government considered Chuhsism most convenient for fixing people's social status in four classes, *i.e.* the warriors, the farmers, the craftsmen, and the merchants, with the warrior class on top and the other three classes subject to the warrior class. Thus, Chuhsism gradually came to be treated as official learning.

Following the policy of the Shogunate to encourage learning, other feudal lords invited eminent Confucianists and set up special schools for the warriors and their sons at the capital cities of their domains. But about the eighteenth century, there arose some groups of scholars of Confucianism other than Chuhsism. Moreover, many private schools were established by such scholars as Buddhist priests, Shinto priests, medical practitioners and so on in order to meet the gradually increasing needs of the people of non-warrior status to receive education. Some of those scholars began to criticize the policy of the government on the basis of their different academic viewpoints. To check this tendency, the government prohibited all other schools of Confucianism except Chuhsism in 1789.

However, toward the end of the Tokugawa Shogunate Era, the political systems of both central and local feudal lords became unstable because of their maladministration and financial difficulties. The progressive and critical schools of Confucianism as well as the schools of Kokugaku (national classics) and Rangaku (the study of the Dutch learning) became active and later their criticism served as the theoretical basis for the anti-Shogunate movements.

THE TERAKOYA—SCHOOLS FOR COMMONERS. In the feudal society, the commoners were strictly discriminated by, and suffered under, the tyranny of the warrior class. The Shogunate government was at first indifferent to the enlightenment of the commoners and believed in the Confucian tenet that the common people should only be trained to be obedient, rather than educated.

But toward the end of the seventeenth century, when the political system of the Shogunate became stable and industry and commerce gradually developed, the common people wanted to learn the fundamentals of reading, writing, and calculation. In Edo, Osaka and other big local cities increasing numbers of merchants were very serious about giving education to their children. Moreover, even some of the clan governments themselves began to take interest in educating commoners so that they might understand and obey the governments' orders. In answer to those needs, there appeared the Terakoya (*Tera* means a Buddhist temple, *Ko* means a child, and *Ya* means a house), the only schools for the commoners.

As explained before, around the sixteenth century some of the children of upper-class warriors and wealthy merchants were being given lessons by learned Buddhist priests. Accordingly, the Terakoya was used as the name of the schools for commoners. One cannot overlook the fact that the rapid increase of the Terakoya from the beginning of the nineteenth century correspond with the economic prosperity of the common people, particularly of the mercantile and industrial classes.

Until the middle of the eighteenth century, most of the Terakoya teachers were Buddhist or Shinto priests and Ronin (dismissed or unemployed Samurai or Warriors). However, from the end of the same century common teachers rapidly increased. This was because of the policy of the central and local clan governments to let wealthy commoners open the Terakoya. Usually they were appointed village officials who were given a quasi-warrior status. In this way, the governments tried to win the support of the common people by spreading the government-oriented education among them lest they should become critical of, or antagonistic to, the government policies.

The subjects taught at the Terakoya were mainly confined to elementary reading and writing. The materials used were mostly Oraibon (wood-engraving books in the form of collections of letters), excerpts of laws or regulations enforced by the governments concerning the commoners' daily life, and some elements of Confucian ethics. It was about the beginning of the eighteenth century that arithmetic came into the curricula of the Terakoya and it became an independent subject around the beginning of the nineteenth century.

There were, of course, no fixed rules about the age of admission, the time for admission, and the length of school years at the Terakoya. Though the enrollment of the Terakoya ranged from only a few pupils to more than one hundred, usually one teacher taught about twenty pupils. The teaching method was similar to that of the English Dame school in the eighteenth century, that is, teachers used different subject matter according to individual pupils and taught them personally. It was a far cry from the progressive methods of today.

It is hardly possible to show authentic data about the rate of school attendance at the Terakoya, because there are no exact records preserved. But many researchers assume the rate to be about 30 percent in the middle of the nineteenth century.

Needless to say, the Terakoya exhibits no features of modern schools, such as the grading system, the theory of curriculum construction, the individualization of teaching, and so on. Nevertheless, it is evident that the Terakoya satisfied the commoners' urgent need to enlighten their children by training them in the three R's and other subjects.

The wide diffusion of the Terakoya, which had been closely connected with the rise of the commoners' standard of life caused by their gradual economic prosperity, pioneered the road to the elementary school system after the Meiji Era. This peculiar form of education for the common people in a feudal society was really unique. It is one which we cannot find in any other country and it facilitated Japan's transition from feudalistic to modern school system.

Education After the Meiji Restoration

The starting point of the modernization of Japan was the Meiji Restoration in 1868. During the course of about seventy years from that time to the outbreak of the Pacific War, there were three epoch-making events: first, the enactment of "Gakusei" (Code of School System) in 1872, second, the proclamation of the Imperial Rescript on Education in 1890; and finally, the issue of "Kokumingakko Rei" (National School Ordinance) in 1941. These three events are the milestones which mark the different stages in the development of modern education in Japan.

"Gakusei" and the Change of Japanese Education

FIVE ARTICLES OF THE IMPERIAL OATH. After destroying the Tokugawa Shogunate, the new Japanese government under the reign of the Emperor Meiji began actively to have diplomatic and trade relations with Western countries. It set as its goals the rapid development of industries and the consolidation of military power in order to catch up with the level of the advanced Western countries. The principles of the new government were most clearly expressed in the Five Articles of the Imperial Oath declared by the Emperor Meiji at the start of the government in 1868. These were as follows:

1. The opportunities of conferences of all sorts shall be open to everybody and all measures of government and administration shall be decided by public opinion.
2. All classes, high and low, shall unite in vigorously carrying out the plan of government.
3. Officials, civil and military, and all common people shall, as far as possible, be allowed to fulfill their aspirations so that there may not be any discontent among them.
4. Unenlightened conventions of former times shall be broken through, and everything shall be based upon the just and great law of Universe.
5. Knowledge shall be sought throughout the world, so that the foundation of the Empire may be solidly established for future prosperity.

The government thus strove to enlighten the people by diffusing education and to train many capable leaders needed in various fields of national life by quickly establishing higher educational institutions.

"GAKUSEI" AND ITS SIGNIFICANCE. In 1871, when the government introduced the prefectural system by abolishing the former feudal lords' domains, the Ministry of Education was established in the government and it took the responsibility of administering nationwide education. Therefore, within the Ministry a committee was set up immediately to begin the study of the education in Western countries and to make a plan for a new educational system in Japan. This plan was promulgated as "Gakusei" in 1872. As the preamble to "Gakusei," the government issued "Dajokanfukoku" (Decree of the Grand Council) in which the government encouraged the people to receive education without any discrimination as to class or sex and recommended that no house have uneducated children.

"Gakusei" adopted three stages of school education, namely, "Shogaku" (elementary schools), "Chugaku" (middle schools), and "Daigaku" (universities) as the basis of its organization. It divided the whole country into eight "Daigakuku" (university regions) with the aim of establishing one university in each Daigakuku. One Daigakuku was further divided into thirty-two "Chugakuku" (middle school divisions) with one middle school in each division. Moreover, one Chugakuku was subdivided into 210 "Shogakuku" (elementary school sections), each having one elementary school. Thus, "Gakusei" expected to have 8 universities, 256 middle schools, and 53,760 elementary schools in all.

When comparing "Gakusei" with the school system of today, one notices many defects. Nevertheless, it had several progressive practices unseen in the education of contemporary Western countries. For instance, it adopted a single ladder school system of four-four-three-three in elementary and secondary education, each of the elementary and secondary schools having two divisions, lower and upper, respectively, and the promotion of pupils in schools was done by the half-year. Besides these facts, one cannot forget the important role played by the Terakoya in the rapid materialization of "Gakusei" in all Japan. It is a surprise to know that the number of elementary schools opened in 1874, only two years after the start of "Gakusei," was 20,014. This was mainly due to the efforts of prefectural governments which endeavored to convert existing "Terakoya" into new elementary schools by faithfully following the educational policy of the central government.

Shortly afterwards, a new type of teaching, the recitation method, began to be used in classrooms. It gradually took root among most schools with the introduction of blackboards, chalk, and other instructional aids unknown in the days of "Terakoya." A year before the promulgation of "Gakusei," the Ministry of Education established the Tokyo Normal School and intended to train many capable teachers to promote new education. Most of the graduates of the School were appointed as teachers of the pre-fectural normal schools later set up in each prefecture and they greatly contributed to the rapid diffusion of new education.

The School Ordinances and the Imperial Rescript on Education

THE CODE OF EDUCATION AND ITS REVISION. The central government suffered severely from the financial weakness common to a newly established government. It was hardly able to give sufficient subsidies to prefectural governments to enable them to enforce the provisions of "Gakusei." In financial resources, the prefectural governments were even weaker than the central government, so they could not afford to spend much money for the new education. In addition, it was quite difficult for most people, who had just become free of exploitation by feudal lords and therefore were still poor economically and culturally, to pay school fees for their children. In this respect, one must recognize that the monthly elementary school fee was to be fifty sen per pupil, while the price of two litrs. of rice, sufficient to feed two adults and a child for one day was only 2.5 sen at that time. As a result, the rate of school attendance in 1877 was only 39.88 percent for boys and girls.

The Ministry of Education was worried about this tendency and began to correct the conditions, especially by softening the strict control of educational administration by the central government. They realized that too much centralization in educational administration would never bring the expected results. Accordingly, the Ministry issued "Kyoikurei" (Code of Education) in 1879. It was compiled by Mr. F. Tanaka, then Vice-Minister of Education, with help from Mr. D. Murray, then special adviser to the Ministry. The former had been in the United States for many years studying the actual conditions of educational administration there. The latter had gained much exact information about Japanese society and education by visiting many schools and communities in the country.

The Code's purpose was to decentralize the educational administration to a great extent, correcting the defects of "Gakusei," which rather forced prefectural governments to carry out the orders from the central government. It had even a provision for the school committee to be elected by popular vote in each school district, a type of school board system similar to that in the United States.

Unfortunately, the Code invited the misunderstanding that the central government had lost enthusiasm for diffusing and developing education. Therefore, most people stopped sending their children to school and the percentage of school attendance rapidly dropped. Alarmed by those circumstances, the Ministry decided to return to the centralized control of educational administration by issuing "Kaisei Kyoikurei" (Revised Code of Education) in the following year.

In the meantime, under the influence of the political and social ideas pouring into Japan from Europe and the United States, the intellectuals began to demand that the government inaugurate a parliamentary system and criticized severely the dictatorial policies of the government. Worried by this political offensive, the government decided, on one hand, to introduce a constitutional monarchy and, on the other, to make the people be united in their thought by educating them to worship the Emperor and to be loyal to him.

THE SCHOOL ORDINANCES AND THE IMPERIAL RESCRIPT ON EDUCATION. This policy of the government resulted in the issue of "Gakkorei" (The School Ordinances) by Mr. A. Mori, then Minister of Education, in 1886 and the proclamation of the Imperial Rescript on Education in 1890. In those days, the Japanese industries were progressing gradually and consequently the country could be equipped with fairly modernized military forces. The Ordinances were thus enforced when the objective of the policy of "National Wealth and Military Strength," pursued by the Meiji government at its start, was being considerably well achieved.

Exactly speaking, the School Ordinances consisted of four separate Ordinances, that is, the Elementary School Ordinance, the Middle School Ordinance, the Normal School Ordinance, and the Imperial University Ordinance. The Ordinances clearly aimed at educating the Japanese people on the basis of nationalism and also made four-year elementary education compulsory for all children. Steps were taken for the proper training of competent elementary school teachers by the Normal School Ordinance, and in spite of the reorganization and improvements of the teacher training system in later years, the basic principles clarified by the Ordinance had never been changed until the end of the Pacific War.

The School Ordinances laid the foundation of the legal structure for the Japanese school system later on, while the Imperial Rescript on Education, which put great emphasis upon ancestor worship, loyalty to the Emperor, filial piety, devotion to the country and so on, based on Shinto and Confucian ideology, gave the moral orientation for the development of Japanese education in the following half century. In other words, education in Japan, from elementary to higher levels, has since then been conducted solely on the basis of the Rescript.

EDUCATION AFTER THE SINO-JAPANESE WAR. After that, the increase of the industrial as well as military power enabled Japan to win the Sino-Japanese War (1894-1895) and the Russo-Japanese War (1904-1905). As new territories, Japan gained Formosa (now Taiwan) and south Saghalien, and she extended her sphere of influence to South Manchuria. Annexing Korea in 1910, Japan became one of the great Powers in the world. Moreover, Japan entered World War I on the Allied side, and during and after the War she actively competed with other Powers in acquiring rights and interests in China.

In accordance with the rise of the country, education also greatly progressed. Various important Ordinances concerning education were issued during the period. For instance, the Girls' High School Ordinance and the Industrial Middle School Ordinance were introduced in 1899 for promoting secondary education for girls and vocational education for boys, respectively. The term of compulsory education was extended to six years by the revision of the Elementary School Ordinance in 1907. Here one must especially take notice of the fact that the state-compiled textbook system came into existence in 1903.

Before that, all the textbooks of elementary and secondary schools were compiled by private publishing companies and they were subject to the official approval of the Ministry of Education. However, about 1902 and 1903, several scandals concerning the adoption of textbooks came to light in a few prefectures. Corruption was found among prefectural officials, school principals, teachers, and publishers. Those incidents called forth violent criticism by general public against those people, and the Minister of Education was severely attacked by the Opposition party in the National Diet for his lack of oversight. Taking advantage of the scandals, the Ministry decided to cancel the textbook authorization system and began to compile textbooks for most subjects of the elementary schools. The actual use of them in schools was begun in 1904.

This meant that the curriculum of elementary schools was put under the control of the government, and as the state-compiled textbook system was later expanded to include secondary schools, the governmental control of the school curricula continued to be tightened until the end of the Pacific War.

Promulgation of the National School Ordinance

POLITICAL, ECONOMIC AND SOCIAL UNREST AFTER WORLD WAR I. Japan made steady progress as a capitalist country conquering the economic difficulties caused by inflation after World War I. The labor movements and the movement for popular suffrage became increasingly active under the impetus from the Russian Revolution along with the spread of liberalism, socialism, and democratic thought among the people. In addition, the damage caused by the big earthquake in Tokyo area in 1923 exerted great influence upon the life of the whole nation. Consequently, there appeared chaos in the people's thought. In order to suppress the bad effects of such social trends, the government began to intensify the regimentation of people's ideology by taking recourse to the Imperial Rescript on Education again.

In 1925, the Ordinance was issued to assign an army officer to each middle school, college and university, irrespective of whether it was a national, a public, or a private institution. The officer took charge of military training of all boy students. Moreover, young people from sixteen to twenty who did not attend secondary schools were forced to receive military training in Youth Training Schools by the Ordinance issued in 1926.

On the other hand, in 1924, the Ministry of Education newly set up the Section of Social Education and it became the Bureau of Social Education in 1929. This office mainly exercised control over public libraries, museums, other social educational institutions, and also gave guidance to women's and youth organizations. The establishment of the office signified that the government became very active in controlling social education as well as school education.

The economic crisis of 1929 which broke out in the United States caused serious damage to the Japanese economy, and consequently Japanese laborers and farmers greatly suffered from the ensuing economic depression. Accordingly, tenancy and labor disputes took place in many parts of the country. Many leftist students spurred by Marxism were arrested because of dangerous thoughts in and out of school.

In the meantime, the Manchurian Incident occurred in 1931. In the next year, some young chauvinistic army and navy officers, who stood firm for holding the Japanese rights and interests in Manchuria, assassinated the prime minister, several other cabinet members, and a leader of the Zaibatsu (the big business concerns). The assassinations were carried out in an unsuccessful *coup d'etat* staged in conspiracy with fanatic rightists who opposed the weak-kneed foreign policy adopted by the government at that time. After this incident, the government essentially fell into the hands of the Army and Navy leaders. Entering into an alliance with Fascist Italy and Nazi Germany in 1939, Japan openly came to support totalitarianism.

THE NATIONAL SCHOOL ORDINANCE AND THE PACIFIC WAR. It was under these circumstances that the government enacted the National School Ordinance in 1941 with the aim of radically reorganizing the Japanese educational system.

The first Article of the Ordinance says: the National School shall aim at the training of the people basically by giving them elementary general education following the way of the Imperial Polity.

This clearly aimed at promoting ultra-nationalism which laid great stress on the reinforcement of Emperor worship. The content and method of elementary school education was completely changed to conform to this aim. Moreover, the education in secondary schools, normal schools, and colleges was also revised following the pattern of National Schools. The recollection by a young teacher cited below will help the reader understand the real situation of education in those days. After finishing his compulsory education during the Sino-Japanese Incident, he was trained at a normal school and then became a teacher of a National School.

. . . The life at school was just a miniature of barracks life. As grades progressed, the contents of textbooks were centered around Emperor worship and were full of Japanese mythical tales, episodes of heroes of loyalty to the Emperor and stories glorifying militarism. "Morals," which mostly stressed loyalty to the Emperor and filial piety, as well as another subject, "Japanese National History" compiled on the basis of the Shintoist historical viewpoint, greatly contributed to casting innocent younger generations into the model of militaristic and Emperor-worshipping subjects.

Thus, Japan rushed headlong along into the catastrophe of the Pacific War toward the end of the year when the National School Ordinance was proclaimed. As the war situation became unfavorable to Japan, the production of munitions suffered a decrease because of intensive air raids and the shortage of the working population resulting from mobilization. Therefore, the Ministry of Education issued an order to reduce the school years of the students above the secondary school level for the purpose of mobilizing them into various munitions factories. The number of the students mobilized in this way totalled over three million or 70 percent of all students.

Eventually, in 1943, the government recruited college and university students in order to replenish the front-line forces. As the damage caused by air raids in big cities grew larger and larger, the mass evacuation of elementary school pupils was carried out in every city by the government order. At last, by the War Education Ordinance issued in 1945, the Student Troop was formed at every school unit for the purpose of resisting the landing of the Allied Powers. As the time of the defeat drew nearer, the education in all schools, from elementary schools to universities, came to a complete standstill. Thus came August 15, 1945, the day of Japan's unconditional surrender.

STRIVE FOR NEW EDUCATION. From the above description, it might be assumed that the education of Japan before the end of the Pacific War had mainly been under the strong governmental control and had always been imbued with powerful nationalism. However, there were many educators or administrators who strove to modernize education in the true sense of the word immediately after the Meiji government started.

Several educators, for example, who went to study the education in the United States early in 1880s, were deeply impressed with the Oswego Movement there and they brought back the educational thought and method of J. H. Pestalozzi to Japan. Thus, the teaching method of object-lesson became rapidly popular among elementary school teachers at that time and Pestalozzi has long been respected as a model of the teacher in Japan since then.

About 1890s, Mr. E. Hausknecht, then visiting lecturer at the Tokyo Imperial University, gave lectures to students on the pedagogy of J. F. Herbart and Herbartians, and Herbartian educational thought and method soon diffused among Japanese educators through the efforts of the young scholars taught by him.

The idealistic and speculative way of study on education which prevailed later in Japan seemed to have stemmed from the Japanese educators' affinity with German idealism in those days. In the meantime, a number of progressive educators and scholars also appeared and started to criticize the reactionary aspects of Japanese education in defiance of the current of the times.

Moreover, as democracy and liberalism widely spread among the Japanese people after the World War I, the new educational thoughts and practices in Europe and America were soon introduced into the educational world. For instance, so-called neo-Rousseauism advocated by Ellen Key and the new theory of education or psychology as well as new teaching method developed in the United States called attention of the teachers of those days. It is to be noted that in those years Deweyan philosophy of education was also discussed actively among teachers or university professors of education and some of the progressive teachers of public elementary schools experimented to teach their children by the Dalton Laboratory Plan free from the control of the Ministry of Education.

Therefore, those days are called the first period of liberal education in Japan. This new and democratic education appeared to take root and develop for a time, but it failed to gain strength under the increased oppression of the government as was explained in the previous section.

However, Japan could be proud of the fact that it had a number of excellent educators who were really democratic, liberal, and experimentally-minded to promote Japanese education even though their experiments and proposals could not necessarily prevail as a general trend. It may fairly be said that it owes much to the efforts of those progressive-minded people that the new education after the Pacific War was so rapidly and fruitfully reestablished in Japan as will be described later.

Education After the Pacific War

Education Policy of the Occupation Forces

The program of educational reform under the occupation was started by the successive directives issued by SCAP (the Supreme Commander of the Allied Powers) to the Ministry of Education from September to December in 1945.

First of those directives was about the administration of educational system of Japan. This demanded that militarism and ultra-nationalism should be rooted out of all school curricula, textbooks, and all other instructional materials. The second ordered the removal of militarists and ultra-nationalists from schools and educational administrations. The third ordered the withdrawal of state protection of the Shinto religion and prohibited the teaching of Shinto doctrines in all educational institutions. The fourth was concerned with the abolition of the subjects of "Shushin" (Morals), Japanese history and geography. The state-compiled and state-authorized textbooks of other subjects were approved for use after erasing particular passages with black ink in accordance with the directives.

The teachers, who were permitted to return to classrooms after their long, toilsome wartime activities in or out of the country, began to work again with a hope that education would become the foundation for the reconstruction of Japan, notwithstanding the serious shortage of schoolhouses, educational facilities, materials, and so on. The Ministry of Education itself could find no other way than to make an effort to prevent the deterioration of education by faithfully following the directives issued successively from the General Headquarters of the Occupation Forces.

The Report of the United States Education Mission to Japan

In response to the demand of the G.H.Q., which wished to get useful suggestions from a group of outstanding educators for democratizing Japanese education, the United States government dispatched the United States Education Mission to Japan in March, 1946. The Mission, consisting of twenty-seven eminent scholars with Dr. George D. Stoddard as chairman, worked energetically, having conferences and visiting many schools with the cooperation of a specially formed Japanese committee. After one month's careful investigation, the Mission presented its report to the SCAP.

Here are a few quotations from the report. As for the aims and content of Japanese education it says as follows:

a highly centralized educational system, even if it is not caught in the net of ultra-nationalism and militarism, is endangered by the evils that accompany an entrenched bureaucracy. Decentralization is necessary in order that teachers may be freed to develop professionally under guidance, without regimentation. . . . To this end, knowledge must be acquired that is broader than any available in a single prescribed textbook or manual, and deeper than can be tested by stereotyped examinations. . . .

Morals, which in Japanese education occupy a separate place, and have tended to promote submissiveness, should be differently construed and should interpenetrate all phases of free people's life. . . . Books in the fields of geography and history have to be rewritten to recognize mythology for what it is, and to embody a more objective viewpoint in textbooks and reference materials. . . .

Concerning administration of education, the report suggests as follows:

the principle is accepted that, for the purposes of democratic education, control of the schools should be widely dispersed rather than highly centralized as at present. . . . In order to provide for greater participation by the people at local and prefectural levels, and to remove the schools from the administrative control by the representatives of the Minister of Home Affairs at the local level, it is proposed to create educational agencies elected by popular vote, at both local and prefectural levels. . . . There is proposed an upward revision of compulsory education in schools to be tax-supported, co-educational and tuition-free, such education to cover nine years of schooling, or until the boy or girl reaches the age of sixteen. It is further proposed that the first six years be spent in primary school as at present, and the next three years in a "lower secondary school" to be developed through merging and modifying the many kinds of schools which those completing primary school may enter. These schools should provide general education for all, including vocational and educational guidance, and should be flexible enough to meet individual differences in the abilities of the pupils. It is proposed further that a three-year "upper secondary school" be established, free of tuition costs, in time to be co-educational, and providing varied opportunities for all who wish to continue their education. . . .

Start of New Education

The new Japanese Constitution, which replaced the old Emperor-centered Constitution, was promulgated in November, 1947. The Constitution, which was based on the respect of fundamental human rights and on the principle of the people's sovereignty, was intended to serve as the foundation for complete democratization of Japan.

Pursuing the spirit of the Constitution as well as the suggestions of the U.S.E.M. report, the "Fundamental Law of Education" and the "School Education Law" were issued in March, 1947. The program of democratization of Japanese education was thus started, in spite of the difficult social and economical conditions after the War.

The principle of equal opportunity of education implied in these two laws put into effect by the introduction of the single-ladder school system based on the American six-three-three plan, coeducation in most public schools, part-time upper secondary schools, correspondence courses, and so on. The term of compulsory education was extended from the former six years to nine years (six-year elementary and three-year lower secondary school education).

As for secondary and higher education, most of the former middle schools were reorganized into new coeducational upper secondary schools. The former three-year higher schools, industrial colleges, normal schools, and three-year universities became new four-year colleges or universities. Two-year junior colleges were also established. A limited number of graduate schools with master and doctor courses were soon set up in the former national, public, or private universities.

The curricula of elementary and secondary schools were wholly revised in accordance with the School Education Law and its enforcement regulation. Social studies, a new subject, came into existence in both elementary and secondary schools. Especially in elementary schools, this subject was taught by integrating the former history and geography and was expected to be the driving force of new education in Japan. In 1947, the Ministry of Education published the courses of study of all subjects and began to authorize textbooks compiled by publishing companies following the courses of study. The system of the state-compiled textbooks which had lasted as long as forty-five years was thus abolished.

Being strongly influenced by American practices, most teachers came to lay much emphasis upon pupils' life experiences in guiding their learning. Thus, in many schools, the experimental study of curriculum construction was actively taken up by teachers themselves with the cooperation of professors of education. The curriculum construction was for a time a catchphrase among teachers. Moreover, new teaching methods such as project method, problem-solving method, unit method, discussion method, and the like, as well as extracurricular activities and guidance theory were introduced from the United States and were earnestly practised in many schools.

Because most of the teachers had been trained in the pre-War period, a series of refresher courses and workshops, on the national or local level, were held at colleges and universities under the supervision of the G.H.Q. in order to re-educate those teachers. Especially, the Institute for Educational Leaders (IFEL), held from 1949 to 1952 at four leading universities, that is, the Tohoku, Tokyo, Kyoto, and Kyushu Universities under the co-sponsorship of the C.I.E. (the Division of Civil Information and Education) in the G.H.Q. and the Ministry of Education, greatly contributed to the training of many excellent leaders in education. At these Institutes, the new educational theories and practices were introduced into the Japanese educational profession by many American professors and educators who were invited as lecturers by the C.I.E.

The "Board of Education Law" was issued in July, 1948. This meant that the principle of Japanese educational administration shifted from centralization to decentralization. According to the law, each prefectural board consisted of seven members, and each municipal board of five members, elected by popular vote in each election area, respectively. The board supervised and administered education under its jurisdiction with the advice of a superintendent appointed by the board.

The first election of the board members was held in October, 1948, in each prefecture and several large cities. All local municipal boards were started in

November, 1952. And the "Ministry of Education Establishment Law" was enacted in 1949 in accordance with the principle of democratization of educational administration. Most of the administrative powers the Ministry had long been holding in its hands were transferred to the hands of prefectural boards of education.

However, the progress of reorganization of Japanese education had not necessarily been carried out smoothly. It was just a fairly long, thorny path for the Japanese people to follow, but they were all struggling through difficult social and economic conditions in the post-War years with a hope of realizing the goal of historic reform in education. Particularly, many small towns and villages which were financially hard pressed, had to make great sacrifices in order to build schoolhouses for newly-established lower secondary schools. Many a tragedy was reported in which several mayors of small towns or villages committed suicide on failing to get a sufficient budget for the new school buildings.

Reconstruction of Japanese education, even though it has not been completed yet, was the result of the combined efforts of all the Japanese people who had cooperated with the educational policies of the central and local governments with the firm conviction that the basis for the renovation of Japan could be found only in educational reconstruction as stated in the preamble of the Fundamental Law of Education.

THE LAND AND THE PEOPLE OF JAPAN

Geography

Japan is located to the east of the Asian Continent and consists of four main islands, Hokkaido, Honshu, Shikoku, Kyushu, and more than 3,000 smaller islands including the chain of islands of Okinawa which are still occupied by the United States. Her area covers 369,661 square kilometers. As she is located within a long range from 45 to 25 N. Lat. and Honshu largely consists of ranges of mountains from north to south, her climate is full of variety; land utilization is extremely limited.

Population

Japan is a nation largely consisting of homogeneous stock; the Japanese race. Her population is nearly 95,180,000 and the density of population is about 258 persons per square kilometer in 1962.

Industry and Economy

Rapid economic growth made in the past ten years in Japan is evidenced by the fact that the index of industrial production in 1962 was almost three times as large as that of the year 1950.

Living Standard of the People

Several statistics are suitable for showing the living standard of the Japanese people. In 1962, they consumed 1,135. K K.W.H. of electricity per capita and 195.1 Gal. of city gas per capita. Their daily calorie intake was 2,080 cal. per capita. One out of 125 persons owned a motor car. They used 7.7 kg. of clothing per capita a year. Forty-two percent of the population was subscribing to daily newspapers. They saw movies 8.8 times per capita a year. The National income was ¥15,783 billion ($43 Billion) and the national income per capita was ¥165,901 ($455) in 1962.

Level of Education of the People

Already in 1902, the percentage of school attendance of compulsory school age children was over 90 percent and it reached 99.0 percent in 1920. It was 99.82 percent for boys and girls put together in 1962. Accordingly, there is no problem of illiteracy among the people today.

Religions of the People

It would be interesting to note that Shinto believers surpass Buddhist believers in number and the sum total of both believers is more than the total population. This is a unique phenomenon in Japan which stems from the custom that the Japanese people usually believe in both Shintoism and Buddhism without taking the matter of religious faith too seriously. For instance, most of the people do not care if they send their children to a Christian school or college even though their family religion is Buddhism or Shintoism.

GOAL OF EDUCATION

Fundamental Law of Education

The goal of education in present Japan is clearly stated in the "Fundamental Law of Education." If one calls the "Gakusei" (Code of School System) of 1872 the first Education Manifesto in Japan which gave an orientation for the modernization of Japanese education, then the Fundamental Law of Education may be called the second Education Manifesto which laid the foundation for democratizing Japanese education. The Law reads as follows: "Fundamental Law of Education" (Law No. 25, 31 March, 1947)

Having established the Constitution of Japan, we have shown our resolution to contribute to the peace of the world and welfare of humanity by building a democratic and cultural State. The realization of this ideal shall depend fundamentally on the power of education. We shall esteem individual dignity and endeavor to bring up people who love truth and peace, while education which aims at the creation of culture, general and rich in individuality, shall be spread far and wide. We hereby enact this Law, in accordance with the spirit of the Constitution of Japan, with a view to clarifying the aim of education and establishing the foundation of education for new Japan.

Article I. Aim of Education. Education shall aim at the full development of personality, striving for the rearing of a people, sound in mind and body, who shall love truth and justice, esteem individual value, respect labor, have a deep sense of responsibility, and be imbued with an independent spirit, as builders of a peaceful state and society.

Article II. Educational Principle. The aim of education shall be realized on all occasions and in all places. In order to achieve the aim, we shall endeavor to contribute to the creation and development of culture by mutual esteem and co-operation, respecting academic freedom, having regard for actual life and cultivating a spontaneous spirit.

Article III. Equal Opportunity in Education. The people shall all be given equal opportunities of receiving education according to their ability, and they shall not be subject to educational discrimination on account of race, sex, social status, economic position, or family origin. The state and local public bodies shall take measures to give financial assistance to those who have, in spite of their ability, difficulty in receiving education for economic reasons.

Article IV. Compulsory Education. The people shall be obligated to have boys and girls under their protection receive nine-year general education. No tuition fee shall be charged for compulsory education in schools established by the state and local public bodies.

Article V. Coeducation. Men and Women shall esteem and co-operate with each other, co-education, therefore, shall be recognized in education.

Article VI. School Education. The schools prescribed by law shall be of public nature and, besides the state and local public bodies, only persons prescribed by law shall be entitled to establish such schools. Teachers of the schools prescribed by law shall be servants of the whole community. They shall be conscious of their mission and endeavor to discharge their duties. For this purpose, the status of teachers shall be respected and their fair and appropriate treatment shall be secured.

Article VII. Social Education. The State and local public bodies shall endeavor to attain the aim of education by the establishment of such institutions as libraries, museums, citizen's public hall, and others, by the utilization of school institutions, and by other appropriate methods.

Article VIII. Political Education. The political knowledge necessary for intelligent citizenship shall be valued in education. The schools prescribed by law shall refrain from political education or other political activities for or against any specific political party.

Article IX. Religious Education. The attitude of religious tolerance and the position of religion in social life shall be valued in education. The schools established by the state and local public bodies shall refrain from religious education or other activities for a specified religion.

Article X. School Administration. Education shall not be subject to improper control, but it shall be directly responsible to the whole people. School administration shall, on the basis of this realization, aim at the adjustment and establishment of the various conditions required for the pursuit of the aim of education.

Article XI. Supplementary Rule. In case of necessity appropriate laws shall be enacted to carry the foregoing stipulations into effect.

School Education Law

Based upon the long-range goal of education in the Fundamental Law of Education, the "School Education Law" enacted in the same year clarifies the short-range goal of Japanese education on each level of the schools. These are as follows:

Kindergarten

Article LXXVII. The Kindergarten shall aim at bringing up young children and developing their minds and bodies, providing suitable environment for them.

Article LXXVIII. In order to realize the aim in the preceding Article the Kindergarten shall endeavor to attain the objective in each of the following items:

1. To cultivate everyday habits necessary for a sound, safe, and happy life and to effect a harmonious development of bodily functions.
2. To make children experience in the kindergarten a group life and cultivate willingness to take part in it as well as the germs of the spirit of cooperation and independence.
3. To cultivate the germs of the right understanding of and the right attitude towards surrounding social life and events.
4. To guide the right use of language and foster an interest in fairy tales and picture books.
5. To cultivate an interest in creative expression through music, dance, pictures, and other means.

Elementary Schools

Article XVII. The elementary school shall aim at giving children elementary general education according to the development of their minds and bodies.

Article XVIII. In elementary school education efforts shall be made to attain the principles mentioned in each one of the following items in order to effect the aim stated in the preceding Article:

1. To cultivate right understanding, the spirit of cooperation and independence in connection with relationship between human beings on the basis of children's experience in social life both inside and outside the school.
2. To develop a proper understanding of the actual conditions and traditions both of children's native communities and of the country, and further, to cultivate the spirit of international cooperation.
3. To cultivate basic understanding and skill on food, clothing, housing, industries, etc., needed in everyday life.
4. To cultivate the ability to understand and use correctly words and expressions of the Japanese language needed in everyday life.
5. To cultivate the ability to understand and manage correctly mathematical relations needed in everyday life.
6. To cultivate the ability to observe and dispose of natural phenomena met in everyday life in a scientific manner.
7. To cultivate habits needed for a sound, safe, and happy life and to effect a harmonious development of mind and body.

8. To cultivate basic understanding and skill in music, fine arts, literature, etc., which make life bright and rich.

Lower Secondary School

Article XXXV. The lower secondary school shall aim at giving pupils secondary general education according to the development of their mind and body on the basis of education given at the elementary school.

Article XXXVI. In secondary school education efforts shall be made to attain the principles mentioned in each one of the following items in order to realize the aim stated in the preceding Article:

1. To cultivate the qualities necessary as members of society and the state, securing the objectives of the elementary school education more thoroughly.
2. To cultivate fundamental knowledge and skill in vocations required in society, the attitude of respect for labor, and the ability to select their future course according to their individuality.
3. To promote their social activities in and out of school, to guide their emotional stability, and to foster their fair judgment.

Upper Secondary School

Article XLI. The upper secondary school shall aim at giving the students higher general education and technical education according to the development of their mind and bodies on the basis of the education given at the lower secondary school.

Article XLII. In upper secondary school educational efforts shall be made to attain the principles in each one of the following items in order to realize the aim stated in the preceding Article.

1. To cultivate the qualities necessary as able members of society and the state by further developing the results of the lower secondary school education.
2. To make students decide on their future course according to their individuality and on the basis of their consciousness of a mission in society to cultivate higher general culture, and to make them skilled in technical arts.
3. To cultivate broad and deep understanding and sound critical judgment regarding society, and to attempt to establish their individuality.

Universities

Article LXXI. The university, as a center of learning, shall aim at teaching and studying higher learning and technical arts as well as giving broad general culture and developing intellectual, moral, and practical abilities.

Education for the Handicapped

Article LXXI. The school for the blind, the school for the deaf, and school for the handicapped shall aim at giving education respectively to the blind, deaf, and mentally and physically handicapped such as the mentally and physically weak, etc., on the same level as the kindergarten, the elementary school, the lower secondary school, or the upper secondary school, and at the same time,

giving necessary knowledge and skill to supplement their infirmities.

Besides the School Education Law, there are many laws enacted in close relation with it. These are "School Library Law," "Law for Promotion of Science Education," "Law for Promotion of Education in Isolated Areas," "School Lunch Law," "School Hygiene Law," "Vocational Education Promotion Law," "Private School Law," "Social Education Law," "Law for Promotion of Youth Classes," and others.

SEVERAL ASPECTS OF EDUCATION TODAY

Organization of School System

The school ladder of pre-war Japan was originally assumed to be a single-track system in principle, but exactly speaking, it could be called a quasi-single-track system, for the doors of colleges or universities were not usually opened to the graduates of vocational middle schools. Also, those graduates, even if they tried, could hardly pass the entrance examination of "Kôtôgakkô" (Higher Schools) which like English Grammar Schools or French Lycées, were primarily preparatory schools for a few Imperial Universities. The curricula of vocational middle schools and those of middle schools were different, the latter being preparatory schools mainly for "Kôtôgakkô" or colleges. The course for the elite was, no doubt, limited. Moreover, the education above elementary school level was conducted by strictly separating boys and girls except at the colleges of fine arts or music. The present school, however, is a perfect single-track system as already explained.

Administration and Finance of Education

By the Ministry of Education Establishment Law enacted in 1949, the main functions of the Ministry are, first of all, the determination of the basic standards for education as well as the elevation and diffusion of education. Second, great importance is attached to the Ministry's surveys and statistics of education compiled and published for the benefit of schools throughout the country. Third, it has a great part to play in providing necessary funds and materials for the development of education and culture.

Curricula of Elementary and Lower Secondary Schools

Curriculum standards for elementary and lower secondary schools are established by the Ministry of Education. The course of study published by the Ministry outlines the basic framework for curricula the aim of each subject, and the aims and contents of teaching in each grade. Each school organizes its own curricula in accordance with the course of study with due consideration to local community conditions and to the pupil's stage of mental and physical development and experience. The curricula should cover the following four areas: regular subjects, moral instruction, extracurricular activities, and regular school events. Extracurricular activities include pupil assemblies, homeroom and club activities. Regular school events include ceremonies, athletic meetings, literary exercises, the school journey, summer colonies, camping, and others. The following is an outline of the curricula of elementary and lower secondary schools (compulsory education) explained according to the official publications of the Ministry of Education.

1. JAPANESE LANGUAGE. In elementary and lower secondary school, children are expected to learn to read, speak, and write in Japanese and to understand the language when spoken or read orally. Generally speaking, the Japanese letters consist of Kanji (Chinese characters or ideographs) and Katakana or Hiragana (unique characters invented by simplifying the Kanji ideographs). The course of study prescribes the minimum number of Kanji characters to be taught in each grade. At the compulsory education level, 1,850 characters are required to be taught, and 881 of them are to be taught at the elementary school level.

2. SOCIAL STUDIES. Social studies include the studies of history, geography, and civics. In elementary schools, these subjects are not taught separately. Children must acquire a basic understanding of Japanese history and geography before they leave elementary school. In lower secondary schools, pupils, in principle, should be taught geography in the first grade, history in the second grade, and political, economic, and social studies in the third grade, but teachers are permitted to integrate these subjects.

3. MATHEMATICS (ARITHMETIC IN ELEMENTARY SCHOOLS). In elementary schools, basic calculation, measurement, and figures are taught in the lower grades, and calculation of fractions, etc. are taught in the upper grades. In lower secondary schools, arithmetic, geometry, and algebra are taught integratedly. In the fourth and subsequent grades, elementary school children learn how to use the abacus, which is a traditional calculating instrument still commonly used in Japan. Children learn how to use the slide rule from the first grade of lower secondary schools.

4. SCIENCE. Science includes the study of biological, physical, and natural phenomena. In elementary schools, stress is placed upon observation in the lower grades, and simple principles are taught in the upper grades. In lower secondary schools, science instruction includes in one grouping an introduction to physics and inorganic chemistry and in another grouping the basic elements of biology, organic chemistry and earth science.

5. MUSIC. In elementary schools, both vocal and instrumental music are taught. Rhythm training, music appreciation, singing, and reading and writing of music are taught in all grades. In the upper elementary grades, instrumental music, musical expres-

sion and music appreciation are stressed. In lower secondary schools, musical expression is stressed in the first grade, appreciation of music in the second grade, and both of these in the third grade. Some melodies are required to be taught in all elementary and lower secondary schools throughout the country, such as folk songs and traditional popular songs of Japan and other countries.

6. HOMEMAKING. In elementary schools, basic knowledge about clothing, food, and homemaking are given to both boys and girls in the subject "homemaking." In lower secondary schools, girls are taught cookery, dressmaking, mechanical drawing, household appliances, handicrafts, and infant care in the required subject "industrial arts or homemaking" and in the elective subject "homemaking."

7. FINE ARTS. In elementary schools, drawing, wood-cutting, engraving, design and handicrafts are taught as well as appreciation of fine arts in the subject "art and handicrafts." In lower secondary schools, the subject "fine arts" includes drawing engraving, design, and appreciation of Japanese, Asian, and Western fine arts.

8. INDUSTRIAL ARTS. In lower secondary schools, boys learn mechanical drawing, woodwork, metalwork, horticulture, mechanics, and electricity, while girls are taught domestic mechanics and electricity, in the subject "industrial arts or homemaking."

9. PHYSICAL EDUCATION. Free exercise is given in all grades. Besides free exercise, apparatus exercise, rhythmic gymnastics, and the like are stressed in the lower grade of elementary schools, and field, track, and team games are stressed in the upper grades. Health education is also given in the upper grades of elementary schools. In lower secondary schools, health education is given as well as physical training in the second and third grades. Of the total physical training hours in lower secondary schools, 30-40 percent includes team games, 15-20 percent apparatus exercise, and 40-50 percent other physical training activities.

10. FOREIGN LANGUAGE. One foreign language selected from English, German, French and other modern languages is offered in lower secondary schools as an elective subject. The aim of this subject is to give basic knowledge of speaking, reading, and writing in the foreign language. English is taught in almost every school. In the course of study for English, a standard list of 500 words is used as the minimum requirement in lower secondary schools.

11. MORAL EDUCATION. Moral education was introduced into all grades of elementary and lower secondary schools in 1958-59. The purpose of moral education is to develop in children an awareness of basic moral principles in their daily life, a creative attitude in life, and an appreciation of those qualities which are recognized as representing good character and leading to habitual right conduct. Teachers are required to help children acquire the moral atti-

tudes needed by good citizens of a modern democratic country. Moral education is also expected to be imparted in the teaching of other subjects. In private schools, moral education may be replaced by religious education.

12. EXTRACURRICULAR ACTIVITIES. Extracurricular activities include pupil assemblies, homeroom and club activities. Club activities are cultural, physical, and productive activities conducted by pupils independently without limitations of grade or class.

National Scholastic Achievement Survey

Since 1956 the Ministry of Education has been conducting an annual nation-wide scholastic achievement test in several subjects for the pupils of elementary and secondary schools by either census or sampling survey method. The main purpose of the test is to acquire necessary data for improvement of educational conditions which seem to have effects on pupil's scholastic achievement.

Teacher Training, Certification of Teachers, Social Status of Teachers

Teacher Training

Before the War, the training of elementary school teachers was exclusively in the hands of the prefectural Normal Schools (all became three-year National Normal Schools in 1943) and that of secondary school teachers mainly in the hands of several Higher Normal Schools. After the War, in 1949, all National Normal Schools were reorganized into either Teachers' Colleges of four years or schools of education in the new universities and they took charge of the training of both elementary and secondary school teachers. Moreover, in order to train specialists in pedagogy and educational psychology at teacher training institutions, the faculty of education, to which a graduate school was added later, was established at Tokyo, Kyoto, Kyushu, and six other universities.

Teacher Certification Law

Provisions of "Law for Certification of Educational Personnel," enacted in 1949, are similar to those practised in most states in the United States. In accordance with different categories and levels of certificates, the candidates must acquire more than 124 credits covering such subjects as general education, professional courses, and educational courses. The same law also gave, for the first time, the provisions for the certification of superintendents, school principals, and supervisors. Introduction of those certificates was expected to have a great significance viewed from the standpoint of the sound development of teaching profession. However, after a few years, because of various difficulties accompanying the enforcement of the provisions, it was revised, and the certificates of superintendants, principals, and supervisors were abolished.

Procedure of Appointment

The teachers of national schools are national public officials appointed by the Minister of Education and those of prefectural or municipal schools are local public officials appointed by the respective prefectural boards of education. The total number of public school teachers was about 780,000 in 1963.

Salary Scales

Salary scales prescribed by prefectural and municipal by-laws are usually based on the national salary scales for teachers. Consequently, the salaries for teachers in each local public body are very similar.

Social Status of Teachers

In Japan, the teachers, regardless of whether they are elementary or secondary school teachers, have been held in fairly high respect, in spite of their being paid a low salary. According to a survey conducted by Professor K. Odaka of Tokyo University in 1953, the rank of an elementary school teacher was not so low as was found in the results of similar surveys done in the United States. However, since this survey refers back so many years ago, it is quite possible that the social status of teachers has now become considerably lower.

Organizations of Teachers

There are many educational personnel organizations with different purposes. The Japan Teachers' Union (membership is about 560,000), the Japan Upper Secondary School Teachers' Union (membership is about 35,000), and the Japan Federation of Teachers (membership is about 13,000) are major welfare organizations. Though these are not labor unions as defined in the Labor Union Law, the Japan Teachers' Union is affiliated with the Japan General Council of Trade Unions. Besides these unions, a number of organizations for professional research and study have been formed since the end of the War. For example, there are the Japanese Society for the Study of Education, the All Japan Council of Prefectural Superintendents, the National Federation of Prefectural Boards of Education, the National Federation of City, Town, and Village Boards of Education, the National Federation of Elementary School Principals Association, the All-Japan Lower Secondary School Principals Council, the National Association of Upper Secondary School Principals, and others.

MAJOR PROBLEMS IN JAPANESE EDUCATION

Over two decades having passed since the end of the War, education in Japan has progressed in all fields and its various features have changed remarkably when compared with those before the War. But, frankly speaking, the main defect of Japanese education seems to be the disharmony between the form and the substance in the course of its democratization. Apparently this stems from a lack of public democratic consciousness which ought to support the growth of a democratized system in education.

For instance, at the start of the prefectural boards of education, most of the board members were elected from among teachers or former teachers recommended or backed by respective prefectural teachers' unions and PTA's. Thus, the prefectural boards turned out to be made up mostly of the representatives of the groups of professional educators, contrary to the principle of lay control in educational administration.

After a few years, the system of boards of education elected by popular vote was changed to another system in which all board members were appointed by the heads of local public bodies. This is merely one of the examples which explain the immaturity of the Japanese people's consciousness of democracy. In short, they are usually too impatient to improve matters step by step. The writer would like to discuss several urgent problems with which all Japanese people, to say nothing of educators, are now confronted.

Inadequate Educational Budgets and Increase of Parents' Expenditure on Their Children's Education

The national income of Japan in 1960 reached about ten times as much as that of 1905. Moreover, the national income per capita in 1960 was about two and a half times as much as that of 1950. Accordingly, people's desire to have their children receive higher level education has risen markedly. Such a trend shows the increase of public educational expenditures of both the national government and local public bodies.

Nevertheless, about 20 percent of elementary schools and about 40 percent of lower secondary schools are today still suffering from outworn schoolhouses as well as a shortage of classrooms and laboratories.

Though caution is urged in comparing the data of several countries which differ socially or economically, a comparison of the public educational expenditures per pupil in Japan with those of some other leading countries shows the inadequacy of the educational budgets of the national and local governments of Japan. Consequently, the parents' share in their children's educational expenses in Japan seems to be larger than that of parents in other countries.

It is quite natural that parents' share in the increase of their children's educational expenditures keeps pace with the rise in their income. However, judging from their unreasonably large share, it is an urgent need to attain a drastic increase in the educational budgets of the national and local governments.

Entrance Examinations for Colleges and Universities

"The Entrance Examination Hell" has been for many years a cliché in Japanese journalism. The entrance examinations are a kind of malady in present-day Japan, from which both young students and their parents suffer.

There are many stages of entrance examinations from the lower grades to the following high-grade schools. But the entrance examination conducted by colleges and universities for applicants from upper secondary schools is the most competitive, and, consequently most controversial, one. Generally speaking, the procedure of the entrance examination to colleges and universities is characterized by the following two tendencies.

In the first place, colleges and universities, regardless whether they are private or national institutions, conduct their own special scholastic achievement test for a limited number of subjects announced to the public in advance. In the second, the determination of successful applicants is made mainly or exclusively on the basis of examination scores, and two other factors, the upper secondary school principal's report about the applicant and the health examination, perfunctorily conducted by the institutions, are taken into account only in some special cases.

Moreover, with respect to the date of the entrance examinations, seventy-two national colleges and universities are divided into two groups of nearly equal number, of which the first group holds examinations at the beginning of March and the second at the end of the same month. Further, more than 500 public and private colleges (including junior colleges) and universities conduct their entrance examinations at their own choice and convenience on such dates, usually ranging from the end of January to the beginning of April.

Consequently, the applicants can take as many examinations as they choose by considering the date, the subjects required, the examination fee, and their travel expenses. To make the matter worse, thousands or more than ten thousands of applicants usually rush to take the entrance examinations for a few particular colleges and universities, traditionally regarded as "first-rate" ones by the general public.

Accordingly, the competition of the applicants to obtain admission to these famous institutions has become astonishingly bitter. In many cases, unsuccessful applicants to a certain "first-rate" college or university try the next year's examination at the same institution after one year's hard preparation. There are quite a large number of applicants who try the entrance examination of the same institution two, three, four, or even more times. They are generally called "Ronin Students." The term Ronin means "a warrior out of employment in the feudal days." A few years ago, an applicant for Tokyo University did get admission finally after seven years' Ronin life full of arduous preparation.

In consequence, in big cities like Tokyo, Osaka, Kyoto, and others, there are many private preparatory schools for those Ronin students, established for the sole purpose of providing them with preparation courses for entrance examinations of higher institutions. The number of those schools is now estimated at about 300 and their enrollments are said to be over one hundred thousand in all. Several preparatory schools in Tokyo usually conduct their own entrance examinations because of the excessive number of Ronin applicants. This is surely an abnormal phenomenon in Japanese education today, more to be regretted than laughed off.

In addition, about 2,500 upper secondary schools, which mainly provide academic courses, are always making efforts to adapt their curricula and instructions, more or less, to the needs of the entrance examinations of colleges and universities in order to get their students admitted to as many higher institutions as possible. In public opinion, the prestige of a particular school is usually measured by the number of students whom it sends to the higher institutions.

As a sort of chain reaction, the admission to such "high prestige" upper secondary schools is now becoming more and more difficult for lower secondary school graduates especially in urban districts. Recently it has been reported that there seems to be a lot of "Ronin" graduates of lower secondary schools with the intention of trying to pass the entrance examination of particular famous upper secondary schools once more.

How can such a phenomenon, unknown in other countries, happen in Japan? Of course, there are many reasons for it. But the most essential one is the so-called "Labelism," which evaluates a person not by his real ability or merits, but by the length of his schooling, and especially by the name of the college or the university from which he graduated. Labelism has so strongly taken root among the older generations that today most people are eager for their children to enter and graduate from well-known colleges or universities. This is the reason why so many applicants rush into a few famous institutions.

Another evil brought by the "Entrance Examination Hell" originates in the method of examination itself. At present, most upper secondary schools or preparatory schools tend to teach their students to conform to the requirements of the entrance examinations. It is not too much to say that the education in upper secondary schools, especially in those college-bound schools, is now extremely distorted by the huge pressure of the entrance examination of higher institutions.

The greatest problem in Japanese education is, to be sure, the improvement of the method and system of the entrance examinations of colleges and universities. Many thoughtful people, to say nothing of educational people, are now aware of the seriousness of the problem and are beginning to discuss proposals for its fundamental solution.

One of the steps taken is the establishment of the "Noryoku Kaihatsu Kenkyu-sho" (the Research Institute of Developing Human Ability) similar to the Educational Testing Service in the United States under the sponsorship of the Ministry of Education in 1963. Its aim is to investigate the possibility and make necessary preparations for introducing a nationwide achievement test for upper secondary school students which could take the place of the entrance examinations conducted by colleges and universities themselves. Japan has the highest hopes for the future success of the Institute.

Antagonism Between Educational Administration and Teachers' Union

It is no exaggeration to say that the most serious problems of education in Japan mainly originate in the continuous antagonism between the Ministry of Education and the Japan Teachers' Union on the national level, and consequently the similar antagonisms between local educational authorities and local teachers' unions in most prefectures or municipalities.

Those antagonisms began in 1953 when the Ministry of Education revised the course of study for social studies. And then, in 1954, the government enacted the Law Governing Provisional Measures for Securing Political Neutrality of Compulsory Education. From that time on, the state of affairs became aggravated year after year.

In 1957, the Ministry tried to guide prefectural boards of education toward enacting a regulation concerning teacher evaluation on the plea of normalizing education. The Japan Teachers' Union, in response to the trend, quickly directed each prefectural teachers' union to develop a strong protest movement to check the enactment of the regulation. For instance, in June, 1958, a confused fight took place between the members of the union who picketed in order to stop the board members attending a meeting and the policemen who protected the board members as they entered the office in Wakayama city. Struggles like this continued to occur in many prefectures in the same year.

Eventually, the antagonism attained its peak when the Ministry issued a regulation to introduce a new subject "Morals" in the curricula of elementary and lower secondary schools in 1958. The Ministry planned to hold a series of workshops for the explanation of "morals" in cooperation with the prefectural boards of education in some representative regions of the country, but the Japan Teachers' Union and local teachers' unions opposed the introduction of "Morals" on the ground of its reactionary character. First of all, the unions took action to dissuade the teachers and supervisors from attending the workshop. Second, when this was found ineffective, they demonstrated around the house at which the workshop was held, roaring against the meeting together with many local labor unions' members and students of the "Zengakuren" (Japan Students' Union).

Further, the Japan Teachers' Union decided to oppose the national achievement test which the Ministry wanted to conduct for elementary and secondary school pupils in 1956. This opposition movement took on a violent aspect when the Ministry tried to let prefectural boards of education hold the tests for lower and upper secondary school students in July and October, 1961. At that time, some active members of several prefectural teachers' unions were arrested for obstructing official business which the principals and prefectural officials, non-members of the unions, had to carry out. The cases regarding those teachers' violation of the Local Public Service Law are still pending in court.

Why did this antagonism inconceivable in many countries occur in Japan? There seem to be several reasons. First, the Liberal Democrat Party (the Conservatives) in power, which has held a majority in the House of Representatives for many years, refused to negotiate with the opposing parties (the Progressives), that is, the Socialist Party and the Democratic Socialist Party, concerning important educational problems. On the other hand, the Liberal Democrat Party has been trying to enforce anti-progressive policies in education on the strength of its majority in the Diet.

Second, as the Japan Teachers' Union has the most influential member organization of the Japan General Council of Trade Unions and has had particularly close relations with the Socialist Party since its formation, it has always opposed every educational policy enforced by the government of the Liberal Democrat Party.

Thus, the Japan Teachers' Union, which regards all educational policies of the Ministry as aiming to maintain capitalism, to protect the interests of the group of free nations and to force the Japanese people to prepare for war by the Japanese-American Security Pact, has developed strong political movements in order to oppose the enforcement of all educational policies of the Ministry.

Accordingly, the most regrettable phenomena in Japan's education really exist in the fact that all important problems of public education, in spite of the clear statement of non-partisanship in public educa-tion in the Fundamental Law of Education, are involved in the furious partisanship struggles between the government and the opposition parties.

Without any prospect of intelligent compromise between the Ministry of Education and the Japan Teachers' Union concerning national or local level problems in education, it would scarcely be possible to expect further development or improvement in Japanese education.

BIBLIOGRAPHY

ANDERSON, R. S. *Japan: Three Epochs of Modern Education.* Washington, D. C.: U. S. Office of Education, 1959.

ISHIKAWA, KEN. Nippon-shomin-kyoikushi (*History of Education for Common People in Japan*). Tokyo: Toashuppansha, 1948.

————. Nippon-gakkoshi-no-kenkyu (*Study on History of Japanese Schools*). Tokyo: Shogakkan, 1960.

IWANAMI, KOZA. Gendai-kyoikugaku (*A Series of Modern Pedagogy*), Vol. 5. Tokyo: Iwanamishoten, 1962.

KAIGO, TOKIOMI. Nippon-kindai-gakkoshi (*Modern History of Japanese Schools*). Tokyo: Seibido, 1936.

KARASAWA, TOMITARO. Kyokasho-no-rekishi (*History of Textbooks*). Tokyo: Sobunsha, 1956.

KEENLEYSIDE, H., and THOMAS, A. F. *History of Japanese Education.* Tokyo: Hokuseido, 1937.

MONBUSHO (Ministry of Education). Nippon-no-kyoiku-kyujunen (*Ninety Years of Japanese Education*). Tokyo, 1962.

————. Gakusei-kyujunenshi (*Ninety Years of Japanese School System*). Tokyo, 1964.

————. *Education in Japan: A Graphic Presentation.* Tokyo, 1964.

————. *Education in 1962.* Tokyo, 1964.

————. *Japan's Growth and Education.* Tokyo, 1963.

————. *Progress of Education Reform in Japan.* Tokyo, 1950.

————. *Revised Curriculum in Japan.* Tokyo, 1960.

————. *Youth Education in a Changing Society.* Tokyo, 1961.

SANSOM, G. *History of Japan,* 3 vols. Stanford: Stanford University Press, 1958, 1961, 1963.

The Second U. S. Education Mission to Japan. *Report of the Second U. S. Education Mission to Japan.* Washington, D. C.: U.S.G.P.O., 1950.

STORRY, R. *A History of Modern Japan.* New York: Pelican Book Co., 1960.

TAKAHASHI, SHUNJO. Nippon-kyoiku-bunkashi (*History of Japanese Education and Culture*). Tokyo: Dobunshoin, 1933.

U. S. Education Mission to Japan. *Report of the U. S. Education Mission to Japan.* Washington, D. C.: U.S.G.P.O., 1946.

UNESCO. *World Survey of Education. Handbook of Educational Organization and Statistics.* Paris, 1955.

————. *World Survey of Education, II. Primary Education.* Paris, 1958.

————. *World Survey of Education, III. Secondary Education.* Paris, 1961.

NEW ZEALAND

John E. Watson

Elemental facts of New Zealand's thousand years of human history may be stated briefly: a group of islands, two of them quite large, remote, rugged, but offering a hospitable habitat; two races of men arriving from the north at different times; two sets of social usages and economic demands carried by adventuring peoples in search of new homes. First, the Maori, making minimal demands and growing slowly in numbers; then the European, coming much later, multiplying more rapidly, and asserting dominance over the land and the Maori. In becoming an appendage of Europe, its history turned at once to a story of interaction between a Polynesian people and another race bringing customs, beliefs, and appetites shaped by British nineteenth-century experience. Adaptation and improvisation became the recurring themes; contradictions have been plentiful. Ideas and habits brought from the homelands were transformed, sometimes to satisfy old demands, sometimes because they no longer seemed relevant; new usages have been evolved to utilize or to understand the new environment. Nothing has remained just as it was when it crossed the seas, neither political institutions nor social customs, nor literary nor artistic forms. Equally there is little that has not retained something of the character of its original source. The shaping continues, inherent, endemic. Since most of its people have continued to be Europeans, and because life continues to come to these islands from the north, New Zealand continues to be a country looking across the sea for nourishment. But it is possible that the first adversaries encountered by the Europeans, the land itself and the Maori, have still to make their full impact upon a society that has achieved full control of its own affairs only within living memory. In another century, the land and its earliest men, subdued but still resilient, may have stronger demands to make.

It might easily be assumed that a small, new, homogeneous country like this would have a comparatively simple system of public education with few of the administrative complexities that beset great federal nations like India, the United States of America or the U.S.S.R. For some things, methods of financing or the size and number of administrative units, for instance, this assumption would undoubtedly be true. The system of public schooling that New Zealand has evolved is indeed simple in the sense that it is a single entity catering for only two races instead of a hundred or more. But the complexities inherent in such an intimate expression of human aspirations and frailties as a school system are not invariably a product of size or ecological diversity. Indeed, for a student of comparative education, the precise value of a study of New Zealand schooling may lie in the fact that in this small community, remote if not isolated, a comprehensive range of problems has been encountered in a brief space of time and a variety of solutions have been attempted. A revolutionary nerve has never been too far below the surface: tradition has been more nostalgic than coercive. Shifts in professional outlook and responsibilities, as well as administrative manner have at times been sudden, significant, even profound. The problems that have puzzled educational administrators in other parts of the world have usually had their counterparts in this microcosm too, either in the present or the recent past.

DISTINCTIVE FEATURES

Two ideals, both parental gifts, have lain at the foundation of New Zealand's state. When the British extended their dominion to these islands over one hundred twenty-five years ago, they were anxious to promote better race relations than had hitherto characterized European expansion. The ideal of racial harmony has continued to exert an immense, expanding, and generally benevolent influence. The tradition of generous state activity in providing schools and welfare programmes, for instance, began for the

Maoris before it was applied to the Europeans, and a comparable concern persists. True, the ideal is, as yet, imperfectly achieved, and faces a challenging future, but it has been accomplished sufficiently to serve as a mark of distinction and promise.

The second objective of colonization perceived the possibility of creating in these salubrious islands a fresh expression of English civilization through transplanting a carefully selected cross-section of English society complete with an elite class of land-owners to provide leadership and inspiration as "persons of cultivation and refinement." High-minded notions of this kind soon went astray, perhaps inevitably. But before a generation had passed, a new breed of men had begun to speculate on a more revolutionary concept, the possibility of establishing here a civilization that was "no mere lacquer on the surface." In choosing the ideal of educational opportunity as their foundational principle these men were determined to bring into being a social order more truly equalitarian than the nineteenth-century Britain that they had left behind.

This was to be simply a condition, however, not an end, for the things they valued, their aspirations and nostalgia, were still governed by the intellectual and the ethical traditions of their exclusivist home-land. And with these they soon linked objectives presently labelled social welfare. Thus, before the seed had sprouted they prepared to take seriously Samuel Johnson's advice that "a decent provision for the poor is the true test of civilization." Many societies, large and small, have now chosen similarly, but in the late nineteenth century these choices were still rare. Within the limits of geography, time, and a shortened social spectrum, these ideals became the lodestars of the school system that emerged.

Administratively, there seem to be at least three reasons why this school system might be of interest to the contemporary student of comparative education. First, despite its short history, small size, and population, New Zealand has already had experience with a variety of administrative forms and methods. This is not the result of political instability or temperamental fickleness, but of a pragmatic determination to gain the best of both worlds in a situation where neither complete centralization nor complete decentralization of control would be acceptable or workable. The general motive at different times and varying contexts has been to retain a capacity for pursuing national policies with vigour and economy while offering ample scope for local public participation and a proper respect for professional autonomy. This deversity of the experience seems to have reinforced the pragmatic temper and encouraged a capacity for questioning the degree to which the resourcefulness of a school system is determined by the form of its administration.

Second, its history is a rare but many-faceted demonstration of the argument that local participation and responsibility need not be endangered by centralized financing. The first schools were set up, controlled and financed by local districts, but over the past three-quarters of a century New Zealand has turned to a system of providing from national taxation all of the finance required for building and maintaining schools, teachers' salaries, operating costs, and specialized services. The system of allocation has become highly centralized, not only at the point of contribution but also, with minor exceptions, at the point of disbursement. There are no local taxes, and the total amount donated directly to schools by parents amounts to less than 1 percent of the total educational budget. The distributional benefits of these policies are evident and accepted. More significantly the readiness of men and women to give voluntary help in organizing, planning, and administering the system, and their numbers, seem little different from the situation in countries where funds are actively raised locally. It has been estimated that the numbers of citizens serving on school boards, and various educational commissions or committees are as numerous as full-time teachers and administrators.

A third reason for interest may lie in the sequence of reform and the consequences of the national passion for equalizing educational opportunity in a bi-racial community of limited resources, scattered population, and improvising temperament. Given the sentiment of the new settlers and the imperatives of the habitat, a continuing effort to remove obstacles, geographical, financial, social or personal, standing in the way of a better schooling for any child is hardly exceptional. To begin it was necessary to populate a raw environment with classrooms and teachers, and a series of sequences are discernible in this quantitative expansion of opportunity: primary, secondary, university; the general need first and then the increasingly specific; the majority, the unwanted, the exceptional. The recognition of the implications for school organization, curriculums, and teaching methods came more slowly, and more unevenly, but again in familiar sequence. Now, with the quantitative expansion virtually achieved (one-fourth of the nation is enrolled at an educational institution) the emphasis turns more to the qualitative problem of finding better ways for developing men and women with integrity, with open minds and inner resources, and with some appreciation of the graces and excellence of civilized human experience. What is possible now is determined in large part by phases of growth already passed, by past achievements and failings.

HISTORICAL SHADOWS

In preliterate Maori society, institutional learning was a privilege of an elite. Certain superior priests or *tohungas*, who served as the living repositories of tribal knowledge and belief, received an arduous training at a *whare wananga*, house of learning. Although without the advantage of a written language, they learned by remarkable feats of memory to transmit the history of tribal lore, genealogies and a well-populated pantheon. The love of war, of oratory, and of the decorative arts were especially prized. Unfortunately, as one historian remarks, their epic attracted no Homer. Although some of their deeds have been sketched in chant and song, they are now generally beyond the scholar's grasp, however vivid they remain in historical imagination.

The earliest settlements of Europeans, coming much later, were far apart and of varying origin. Each had to make its own provision for schooling, often slowly and sporadically. In some places they were established by the churches, in others by private citizens, entrepreneurs, or public associations. Not surprisingly they closely resembled the schools of the homelands, England, Scotland, Ireland, and used similar books and syllabuses. Provincial governments, established in 1852, set about the task more systematically, but they, too, varied greatly in wealth and circumstance. Good teachers were not easy to attract, and it could hardly be claimed that the clamour for more schooling was as yet universal. But public opinion in the societies that the settlers were leaving behind had already been awakened to the idea of education as a public responsibility, and increasing numbers of the new settlers began to recognize schooling as a social necessity rather than a charity. From the outset a sprinkling of humanitarians wanted elementary schooling to be both universal and compulsory. Before this could be established the prior issue that had to be resolved turned on the respective roles of the Church and State in the field of education even though, in the absence of an established church, all sects of the Christian faith enjoyed equal status before the law. For twenty years the provincial governments experimented with various approaches toward denominational involvement. All proved unsatisfactory in one way or another, and by the seventies each province had adopted policies of religious neutrality in providing elementary schooling.

Meantime, with improving communications and a deepening sense of national unity, sentiment in favour of universal elementary schooling grew steadily; the movement toward secularism was, perhaps, simply an incident toward its realization. Many influential leaders had, by this time, become convinced that the provision of schooling would have to be a responsibility of the central government if the evils of apparent inequalities were to be avoided. In 1876, the abolition of the provincial governments offered the opportunity. Soon after its election to office, and on the eve of a decade of increasing economic and political gloom, the new central government introduced an education bill, which laid the foundations of a national system of free, secular and compulsory primary schooling. In amended form this became known as the Education Act of 1877.

National school systems do not come into being simply by passing acts of parliament, of course, and the embryonic nation, now numbering just over half a million, fell upon hard times almost immediately. Export prices tumbled disastrously and more people left than arrived. The big issues were land settlement, taxation, and social welfare; temperance, prohibition, electoral reform, the emancipation of women and the expansion of secular schooling were lesser themes. Nonetheless, within ten years of the passing of the Act, the primary school population had doubled, and it was soon growing at twice the rate of the general population. Attendance, it is true, continued to be a major problem, some children escaping altogether, while others attended only irregularly. Step by step, however, the causes of poor attendance were overcome; school rooms became more accessible, teachers were recruited more successfully, and administrative enforcement became more consistent. By the turn of the century the majority of parents had begun to appreciate the positive advantages of better schooling. Official reports were quick to proclaim the young nation's lead on the old homelands, and they openly accepted the oldest of the new nations as their standard. The benefits to economic and social order were not long delayed. Within forty years, universal primary schooling was both an accomplished and accepted fact.

The foundation Act had made no comprehensive provision for secondary schooling however. Indeed, by allowing primary and secondary schooling to develop separately, as much an accident as an act of deliberate policy, this legislation set up barriers between the two levels that have persisted to the present day. As in the case of primary schools, the earliest secondary schools began as imitations of overseas models, importing teachers, curriculums and methods of organization, catering for the children of the well-to-do and a small number of highly-selected scholarship pupils. Sponsored locally, they grew up as isolated units. When the national system of primary schooling was established, there were no more than a half dozen of them in the whole country, but within twenty years they had multiplied fivefold. Before the end of the nineteenth century every town centre of importance had its secondary school.

And yet they continued to be a privileged group, endowed from public funds, charging fees, restricting admittance, free of control by the State, and determined to stay out of its orbit. Their curriculum bore little relationship to that of the primary schools (many indeed maintained their own quite large preparatory divisions) or to the immediate needs of the community. When they felt the need in the 1880s for some kind of external examination as a goal for their select group of pupils, they deliberately avoided the possibility of state intervention by placing themselves in the hands of the university through adopting the university entrance examination as the hallmark of a completed secondary education. For a time, while enrollments remained restrictive, the results seemed beneficial; but as soon as the state began liberalizing opportunities for secondary schooling through a series of "free place" measures, the situation became increasingly intolerable. The history of secondary schooling in New Zealand in the present century may be read as a continuing effort to reverse that decision in order to gain the freedom required to develop more comprehensive functions of little concern to the universities.

At the same time the pillars maintaining the separation of the secondary schools from the primary school system had begun to crumble. Faced with the growing efficiency of the primary schools, the preparatory departments of the older secondary schools had atrophied, for example, and before the end of the century many had begun to receive the bulk of their pupils from the primary schools in their districts. The immense significance of this fact was hardly noticed. Now, with the contemporary hindsight, it is easy to see that it represented yet another emphatic rejection of the European (and English) tradition of two parallel systems of schooling, one for the classes and the other for the masses. Private decisions of this kind in the homes of the community, based on geographic reality as much as sentiment, foreshadowed an early commitment to an end-on system of comprehensive schooling in which the primary and secondary levels would form part of a continuous whole. The decades that followed became increasingly occupied with attempts to remove structural impediments to its realization.

As in other countries, the task of recasting the curriculum of secondary schools with an exclusivist history proved notoriously difficult. It was attempted first, without much success, through a series of financial inducements, aimed at introducing more science, agriculture, and commercial work. Then, in an oblique attack on the conservatism of the older schools, provisions were made before World War I to establish technical high schools in every city and town and to expand the secondary "tops" to primary schools in country districts.

Untrammeled by the external examinations the new co-educational technical schools soon led the way in providing more vocationally oriented objectives for non-academic pupils. Rather perversely, public popularity soon persuaded them to also parallel their new practical courses with others barely distinguishable from those of the older secondary schools. But, being pre-vocational, these schools never became technical in the European sense, and they have remained strongly committed to diversifying the choices open to pupils and parents. There is little doubt that, with the comprehensive high schools later established in small towns and suburban areas and the secondary departments associated with primary schools in country districts, these technical high schools offered a

unique contribution to the development of the omnibus type of school that is now characteristic of the New Zealand approach to secondary schooling.

An integral view of primary and secondary schooling has developed only haltingly however. As elsewhere, a great many of the tensions and conflicts associated with further democratization and unification have centred upon the point of juncture between each level. In particular, since the 1920s, the efforts to introduce a transitional form of junior secondary schooling (known as intermediate schools) became especially contentious. Traditionally, the pattern of schooling in New Zealand, as in the United States of America, consisted of an eight-four system. Almost immediately following the achievement of universal primary schooling, and as a result of pressure for a more effective introduction to secondary schooling, a beginning was made in the twenties on restructuring this pattern to a six-six system. Even though they enjoyed public and political support at the local level, these reforms had a checkered history until after World War II when dramatic changes in school enrollments created a much more propitious climate for their widespread introduction. Owing to historical, administrative, and geographical circumstances, they have been accomplished most successfully so far in urban areas, in the form of a six-two-four sequence. Still, it is an interesting commentary, perhaps, that although intermediate schools in New Zealand have adopted objectives and forms of organization that are virtually identical to the comprehensive, non-selective junior secondary schools of other countries, they have not yet been commonly accepted as part of the secondary system.

Meanwhile, the type of spiritual pioneering more recently evident in the adult community has been foreshadowed perhaps by the vast transformation that has taken place in the spirit of primary and intermediate schooling over the past thirty years and which more recently has also begun to revitalize secondary schooling. In broad perspective these changes are similar to those of other progressive school systems. First, teachers, more worldly, better educated, more professionally alert, have become more sensitive to the tangible and intangible differences among children, more responsive to their active and creative powers, more appreciative of the need to balance intellectual, emotional, and physical growth. Second, the value of schools in promoting a common, liberal culture has become more widely accepted. In other words, their central purpose is no longer interpreted as simply that of equipping children with the tools of learning or spreading literacy but more importantly of offering the advantages of growing up in a civilized and culturally rich environment. They are happier and more expansive places than they used to be, more receptive to parents and the world of art, music and good books and more spirited and self-conscious.

No single reform has been as significant in providing scope for this transformation as the abolition in 1936, after forty years of agitation, of a national external examination that was formerly applied universally at the end of the primary course. This action, by liberating the primary (and intermediate) schools, and at the same time by removing the last organizational barrier to universal secondary schooling, confirmed the country's commitment to comprehensive schooling, and served as an immediate incentive for its enrichment. The changes in the theory and practice of primary schooling that have followed have not always had an easy passage to be sure. Some critics have seen them as a sacrifice of the 3R's to non-essentials, others have been uncomfortable with contemporary attitudes toward authority, some have feared that increased emphasis upon the expressive arts is detrimental in some way to the formation of character. Such disputation is of course a surcharge upon democracy. The one thing that is certain is that there are not many parents who, when comparing their schooling with that of their children, would wish to have the old order restored.

University education was also founded in much the same way in the same period as primary and secondary schooling. The dispersal of its institutions and opportunities, its non-residential character and plebian associations, were also greatly influenced by a metropolitan conception of the role of a university common in England in the late nineteenth century. The first university was established in Dunedin in 1869, by Scottish Presbyterians. If size and community need had been the only considerations, this might have been sufficient for a century. But the English Anglicans of Christchurch had other ideas and an alternative vision of a university. Within four years they, too, had established a university college and set in motion the events that led eventually to a federal university system to be known for over eighty years as the University of New Zealand.

The University of London provided the administrative model for the liberal admissions policies favoured by the controlling authorities of this colonial university; the standards and values of scholarship honoured by the teachers of its constituent colleges, on the other hand, have more often been those of the exclusive, full-time, residential universities of the Old World. Thus a pervasive state of tension between the attitudes of the community as a whole and the aspirations of some sections of its academia became perennial and accentuated by the fact that higher education remained relatively undifferentiated. Invariably, the community has had its way in extending opportunities broadly, but it has shown rather less concern about the implications of its decisions. Added to this the smallness of the total university enrollment, its geographical dispersal and economic significance has meant that these choices have been expensive, and

that they will become more so if quality is to be preserved.

The original federal system of university education has now been dissolved however, and in its place six autonomous universities compete for support and esteem. Contrary to common belief, New Zealand is not a wealthy country, even though wealthier per capita than many and even though it spends heavily on the material appurtenances of modern life. But over the years it has allowed itself to develop a habit of spreading thinly among its universities no more than it spends on subsidies for bread or milk. Old habits like this succumb only slowly. Recent appraisals of the unique importance of the universities for national growth and development have been accepted phlegmatically, but with neither open exhilaration nor public protest. It is too early yet to assess the civilizing potential of the new order.

It has already been noted that the founders of New Zealand's system of public schooling, like their colonial brothers elsewhere, were resolved to avoid the denominational connection with education responsible for the duality or pluralism of many European systems. This decision has never been acceptable to the adherents of the Roman Catholic faith, who now comprise about one-eighth of the community. As a result, there has grown up alongside the State system another extensive system of primary and secondary schools, built, staffed, and supported by the Catholic Church. Organizations such as the Anglican and Presbyterian Churches and others have also seen fit to set up schools of their own outside the state system, but these are not numerous. Eight out of ten private primary schools, and two-thirds of private secondary schools are Catholic, and they account for one in ten of the total school enrollments. Most of the private secondary schools are small, and two-thirds of them are girls' schools. In educational practice it is the state schools that generally set the pace.

The scope and size of its school system is at once a source of justifiable pride to the Catholic community and the cause of its long-standing grievance against the State. Ever since that national system was established, Catholics have contended that their system is entitled to financial assistance from the State, although their claim has not been supported by other organizations administering private schools. Many of the advisory services and facilities that have been set up for the State services are already freely available to all private schools. Their pupils benefit from transport and boarding allowances offered by the State, and they are also offered a variety of subsidies in purchasing equipment, books, and aids. But no state assistance has yet been offered toward the cost of purchasing school sites, erecting or maintaining school buildings, or for teachers' salaries or the operating costs of private schools. Despite strenuous canvassing by the Catholic community, there seems little likelihood of any departure from these policies. The deeply felt desire for community that fashioned the public school system as an instrument for creating and strengthening the bonds of common citizenship in this new society has remained alert and viable. There are no indications that the public is ready to accept proposals that could conceivably undermine the sense of unity regarded as basic to a stable, working democracy.

THE ORGANIZATIONAL LADDER

Children normally begin their primary schooling in New Zealand earlier than those of other nations. At the age of five and at the discretion of parents, they may (and 98 percent do) enroll at one of the 2,500 public or private primary schools; they are not obliged to do so, however, until they have reached the age of seven. As three- and four-year-olds, before they have enrolled at a school, an expanding proportion, now about a fifth, will have spent some mornings or afternoons at a kindergarten or play centre. These two broadly similar and parallel pre-school services are organized by two major voluntary associations with the help of government subsidies.

Half a century ago a large proportion of children began their more formal schooling in small one- and two-teacher schools set in the open country. To attract young and enterprising teachers to these schools a variety of incentives were introduced and the quality of schooling available in rural areas became one of New Zealand's more distinctive contributions. The special incentives are still effective. Now, however, rapid urbanization, vastly improved roads, and a continuing policy of centralizing small schools have greatly changed this picture. Small one- or two-room schools at present comprise fewer than 40 percent of the total, and they enroll only a very small proportion of the total primary school population. Nowadays, the more common school is suburban, set in several acres of playing fields, housed in glass-fronted, single-storied, wooden buildings attended by three to four hundred children, staffed by ten or a dozen teachers and serviced with a full-scale dental clinic and other ancillary facilities. Many country children also travel by bus today to a similar type of centrally placed school. Extensive school transportation services are indeed a striking feature; more than a sixth of all pupils, primary and secondary, public and private, are at present receiving some form of assistance in this way.

The curriculum of primary schools comprises all the English language subjects such as reading, writing, composition, spelling, literature; social studies; arithmetic; nature study; music; art; handicraft; and physical education. After passing through the "infant" classes, children progress through the four "standards" normally taking six years in all. Promotion from class to class is, in the main, based upon the age of pupils rather than upon fixed standards of attainment. Pro-

visions for individual differences normally take the form of flexible class-sectioning or syllabus differentiation rather than rapid or delayed promotions. A wide array of services for those with special needs, the physically or intellectually handicapped, those with speech defects or undergoing hospital treatment, and others, have expanded greatly during the past two decades. The extent to which these services are provided by educational authorities, frequently in the form of clinics and special classes within ordinary neighbourhood schools, is notable reflection of a deeply felt national attitude. Generally speaking, New Zealanders are very reluctant to set any group of children apart from their fellows any more than is necessary.

After six years of primary schooling, at about the age of eleven years, a steadily increasing proportion of children, now over 40 percent, transfer to a two-year intermediate school. As stated earlier, these have been set up so far mainly in urban areas, but plans to extend a comparable reorganization in rural areas are now being stepped up. In the districts where such schools do not at present exist, children continue in the traditional eight-year primary school without prejudicing in any way their opportunities for secondary schooling.

New Zealand's intermediate schools are non-selective area schools, continuously associated with the same group of four or five primary schools from which they enroll all their pupils; three-quarters of the teachers in each school are also normally primary teachers. Their pattern of internal organization and many features of their corporate life are clearly transitional, however, between the patterns traditionally associated with primary and secondary schools; moreover, they have generally brought about a very considerable improvement in the articulation of these two levels. The core of their curriculum is essentially the same as that provided for the same age group in eight-year primary schools, but their workshop activities are more systematically developed, and in recent years a considerable revitalization has been occurring in the introduction they provide to foreign languages, elementary mathematics, and physical science.

In principle, every child, whatever his ability, is free to go to the secondary school of his parents' choice and to remain there without cost, until he is nineteen years of age. At all stages from kindergarten to the senior secondary level transfer is virtually automatic; opportunities for higher education or employment are not affected in any direct sense by the particular secondary school a child has attended. All secondary schools therefore cater for a wide range of pupils. If, for reasons of size, tradition, or location they are not all equally comprehensive, they do at least all provide a sufficient measure of common studies to preserve equality and flexibility of opportunity. Publicly they are known by many names, high schools, grammar schools, colleges, technical high schools, district high schools, agricultural colleges, but this does not indicate any real difference in function. They recruit from the same force of teachers, provide the same length of schooling, prepare pupils for the same public examinations, receive advice from the same group of professional officers, and are financed and administered in very similar ways. It would be easy, however, to overstress the importance of the uniformities that have been the price of the increasing democratization of the past twenty-years. For most of its history New Zealand's pattern of secondary schooling has been highly fragmented. In spirit and organization there is still much more variation than would first appear, and some concern with keeping open the possibilities for local innovation and distinctiveness.

This comprehensive pattern of secondary schooling enables New Zealand to escape altogether the problems of selection that bedevil educationists in most European countries, but, as a result, it has to face in acute form the difficulties of providing within one, often relatively small, institution courses that are suited to the needs and abilities of a complete cross-section of the community. If the solutions adopted are in some ways unique, governed as much by geographic realities as the equalitarian temper of its people, the general problem is common to all countries that have reached the stage where they can contemplate providing secondary education for every child. A realization of the implications of this objective in New Zealand became really explicit only a little more than twenty-five years ago.

Despite the changing character of the secondary school population, their curriculums up to that time had remained academic and geared to the needs of university admission, even though less than a tenth of their entrants eventually began a university course. The situation was aggravated further by the abolition in 1936 of the only examination that feebly screened entrants from the primary schools. Large numbers of their pupils were terminating their secondary schooling within a year or two of enrollment and with courses vaguely incomplete, and this appalling waste of effort threatened to become worse if the school-leaving age was raised. A major reorganization of secondary schooling was clearly called for, and it was evident that the community was in no mood for any re-imposition of a system of selection.

All of the major reforms that have set the tenor of the present pattern of secondary schooling were taken while the country was at war. The first bold step was taken by the universities in 1944, when they raised the standard of their entrance requirements by a year and at the same time introduced a system giving the secondary schools power to "accredit" those pupils whom they considered fitted to undertake university studies. This sudden release of bonds that had shackled the secondary schools for half a century threatened to leave them bewildered and without a

compass. To give them a sense of direction it was decided, after exhaustive discussions, to introduce a flexible senior examination to be administered by the State and designed to serve as a filter as well as a terminal qualification. Known as the School Certificate Examination this gained quick acceptance from employers and the public, and during the initial phases of reform it doubtless gave shape and form to the curriculum of secondary schools. Since that time its monolithic assumptions have proved disquieting to many and the trend now is toward more individualized measures of a completed secondary schooling.

It is common practice for secondary schools in New Zealand to offer courses rather than a collection of isolated options to be chosen at will. Great ingenuity is often exercised in arranging timetables to cater to the needs of small groups or even of individuals, but there is really no opportunity for pupils to select a collection of subjects having no inner cohesion. Each course has a fairly definite pattern comprising a majority of compulsory subjects (English, mathematics, general science, social studies, music, an art or craft, and physical education) and a limited number of options such as foreign languages, commercial practice, engineering or workshop activities. Pupils are expected to take their interests and vocational ambitions into account in choosing courses, and teachers commonly offer informal but effective guidance when students appear to be in danger of making unrealistic choices. The structuring of the curriculum means that the number of choices to be made is not often large and the issues are usually fairly clear-cut. In the initial selection of their secondary school courses few pupils seem to require the specialized help offered by school psychologists or vocational guidance services.

Almost all children now complete ten years of schooling (five to fifteen years) and three-quarters continue beyond the minimum leaving age of fifteen. The trend toward prolongation is very pronounced. Of each hundred pupils beginning intermediate schooling (Form I) nearly 60 percent now enter Form V (eleventh year) and more than a fifth enter Form VI (twelfth or thirteenth year) to prepare for admission to a university. These proportions increase yearly for both boys and girls.

All universities in New Zealand accept a common entrance qualification, and more than 80 percent of those who qualify for admission have been accredited by their schools. University education is available at a low cost to every person who meets these requirements of entrance and studies successfully as a full-time student. As a consequence, the number of secondary pupils who ultimately become university students is relatively high, at least an eighth of each age group. If students attending teachers' colleges, special training schools, and technological colleges are included, it may be said that about one-sixth of each age or grade group enroll at an institution of higher education sometime after completing a secondary course.

Many others enroll in private business colleges, of course, or in industrial or retail courses, or the training schemes associated with public utilities and departments of state, and so on. More than a third of the boys, for instance, take up an apprenticeship contract. Arrangements for these vary from trade to trade, but most require young tradesmen to continue workshop lessons at a technical college as an integral part of their training and to complete the appropriate qualifying examinations. Many young tradesmen outside the major metropolitan centres are able to fulfill these requirements with an enterprising and pivotal national Technical Correspondence School, which enrolls more students than any other institution in the country. At a higher level, below but sometimes parallel or alternative to university training, broadly similar arrangements are at present being developed for training technicians at both regional and national institutes of technology. A major construction programme for these institutes that has recently been launched is indeed one of the most notable of contemporary developments, and symbolic of significant shifts in the economic and industrial structure of the country.

New Zealand's system of higher education thus consists of six universities, ten teachers' colleges, and four technological institutes, all of which are located in widely separated urban centres. The four older universities, founded in the nineteenth century, all offer a variety of courses leading to degrees in arts, science, law, commerce, and music. In addition, each includes some specialized professional schools: Auckland, engineering, architecture, fine arts, obstetrics and gynaecology; Victoria, public administration, social science, and a language institute; Canterbury, engineering, fine arts, and agriculture; Otago, medicine, dentistry, theology, mining, physical education, and home science. One of the newer universities which has evolved from an agricultural college of some considerable international reputation (Massey) has special schools of veterinary science and food technology. Teachers' colleges, which hitherto have been administered by the state employing authorities, are now in the process of becoming relatively autonomous institutions, but the expectation is that they, too, will eventually become associated with an institute of education in each university.

Consistent with its general outlook, New Zealand has been generous in offering opportunities for enrollment at a university. Two-thirds of its students receive some degree of state aid, and the proportion of young people of superior ability, who possess the appropriate qualifications and who do not enroll at a university, is considered low. As elsewhere, a quick switch in demographic circumstances, a rapid build-up in the demand for graduates, and a marked improvement in the proportion of able students continuing their education have all been responsible for a sharp acceleration in enrollments, almost certainly a doubling within the present decade. Equalitarian sentiment, allied with the urgent need for more highly qualified people, has in turn brought about strenuous efforts to accommodate all qualified entrants without restriction. The resulting pressure upon facilities and staffing has brought about a host of difficulties that are not likely to be fully overcome for some years, and in the meantime they may impede urgent internal reforms. A major national programme of university construction is underway, but the problem of finding enough staff of sufficient calibre in a highly competitive international market is not likely to be solved so easily. Even if the universities do manage to avoid those dangers of "rationing educational poverty" which threaten whenever new commitments are undertaken with inadequate finance, staff, and facilities, more pervasive challenges lie within.

The shape of New Zealand's future universities is, for this reason, not yet discernible. Their major problems for some years ahead lie undoubtedly in the area of curriculum rather than in selection or admission, and the basic issue is somewhat similar to that which has already faced and transformed the secondary schools. In brief, it is to provide courses and facilities suited in both general content and special professional emphases to the needs and interests of the whole range of able young people who now qualify for admission to them. Wastage rates at present are high, whether measured in terms of scholastic failure, drop-out, or a graduation rate of less than fifty per head of admissions, and some part of the explanation seems to lie with a feeling among many young people that what is offered is not closely-enough related to their needs and interests. The generous admission policies of the universities now have to be matched by greater diversification of their curriculums. This, however, will not be easy to achieve in a small country far removed from the world's great centres of learning, and the time for dalliance seems short. If the universities decide that an omnibus role is inconsistent with their values and traditions, it is almost certain that the mounting pressure of the community's insatiable demands for highly educated people will accomplish the differentiation by setting up alternative institutions.

CONTEMPORARY CONCERNS

In the last twenty years New Zealand has doubled both the proportion of its national income, and of its gross national product, that is devoted to education. In this same time the enrollments of its primary schools have doubled, those of its secondary schools and teachers' colleges have trebled, its universities have entered upon a programme of unprecedented expansion, and a start has been made in introducing higher levels of technological training.

All these developments reflect, as they do in other nations, a remarkable change in demographic circumstances, rising expectations on the part of both parents and employers, and widespread provision of equality in educational opportunity. When compared to some of the newer nations, New Zealand enjoys certain advantages, of course, in coping with contemporary demands, but this has not spared the administrators, teachers, or citizens who share in the organization of its school system from the need for care and precision in considering priorities for development. To assist with the clarification of needs and objectives, a range of commissions, councils, and committees has been set up during the past decade to review nearly every aspect of education.

In broad perspective, the contemporary prescription is similar to that of other nations at a comparable stage of development: intelligent leadership; a well-informed citizenry capable of appreciating excellence in all fields; larger infusions of knowledge and discriminating power; wider diffusions of trained ability and skill. The needs, therefore, are essentially intellectual. Fortunately, an appreciation of the critical role of the education system in developing the country's intellectual resources now seems to be fairly widespread, one benefit, perhaps, of the frustrations and dislocations accompanying the rapid growth of the past two decades. The protracted shortage of teachers at all levels, primary, secondary, and now university, has demonstrated, as never before, how intimately the whole community is affected by what happens to the children in its schools. Not only has the function of the teacher become a matter of deep public concern; in addition it has been subjected to increasing professional scrutiny. Both the community and the teaching profession have come to see more clearly the level of personal culture, skill, and sensitivity that teachers require to cope adequately with contemporary objectives. Viewing the national aspiration and the public temper, a recent major Commission concluded that only a radical and expensive answer would meet the need: a complete revision of the existing pattern of training teachers, and a thorough-going re-evaluation of their status and rewards.

The initial steps in implementing the recommendations of that Commission have already been taken, although the full reform will require more than a decade. Until now, the main source of initiative in the national programme for recruiting and educating teachers has been in the hands of the central Department of Education, and in the case of primary teachers, the basic forms of professional preparation have remained unchanged for half a century. They were provided in two-year colleges, with some concurrent part-time university study for a minority, followed by a year of probationary service in the schools. Professional training for secondary teachers, a much more recent development, has expanded at unprece-

dented scale and has become increasingly diversified during the past twenty years. In addition, many other training programmes have sprung up over the past decade to prepare people for a wide range of special services.

In re-ordering these diverse programmes the intentions of the reforms now being implemented are fourfold. They are first, to give the profession more say in its own preparation; second, to promote regional diversification in the avenues for training; third, to bring about a more organic relationship between various training programmes and the universities; and fourth, to establish a system of preparation that has, within itself, a capacity for growth and development. The powers formerly confided in the control of the Department of Education for the determination of over-all policies have been transferred to a national advisory council. Within a year of its appointment, this body has set out a detailed scheme for lengthening the training of primary teachers, drawn up a national programme for preparing secondary teachers, developed a plan for establishing more teachers' colleges, and made suggestions for a realignment of the academic and administrative relationships of up-graded teachers' colleges. In each university district it is anticipated that an Institute of Education located within the university will eventually exercise a general oversight of courses in each of the teachers' colleges associated with it. These Institutes, controlled probably by representatives of the university, the teaching profession, and employing authorities, are expected to become the focal point in the future for professional stimulus, refreshment, research, and publication in each region.

These fundamental reforms in the education of teachers are but one component of the contemporary proposals for revaluing the teaching profession, however. Others have to do with conditions of service, remuneration, and recruitment. External observers, knowing the circumstances of comparable countries, would perhaps be justified in concluding that New Zealand teachers already occupy a position of some strength. They receive generous financial assistance to prepare for teaching, undergo no direction of service, enjoy security of tenure, benevolent retirement pensions, considerable scope for influencing the direction of educational policy, and a fair measure of freedom in deciding what, where, and how they teach. But the inescapable fact is that, despite these widely appreciated benefits, the morale of the teaching profession has suffered grievously in coping with the spectacular expansion of the post-war period. Further, the capacity of the profession to attract sufficient recruits of good calibre to teach one-fourth of the population and to demand from them the exacting commitment required in contemporary circumstances has been seriously weakened. Faced with these facts, the major Commission already referred to concluded that the professional rewards for teaching, when compared with other professions, have become incompatible with the status needed to discharge its trust. It recommended setting up machinery for continuing re-evaluation. This price would have to be paid, it warned, if the prospect of national decline was to be avoided.

However, in a world increasingly swayed by the views of people whose skins are coloured, the respect and influence that New Zealand earns may be determined more by the promise of another of her foundational principles. It would not be impossible for New Zealand to become a mediator between the potential adversaries who inhabit her northern horizon. Geographically she belongs to the east, culturally to the west. With Australia she is admirably suited to develop intimate contacts both with the emerging nations of Asia and the older nations of the west. Moreover, she has the potential advantage of a bi-racial heritage. If, within her own borders, social attitudes and legal formulations can be brought to greater harmony, this potential may yet become a critical qualification.

With the passing of the turmoil of the nineteenth century a fair measure of racial harmony has in fact developed, mainly because the Maori people have first been too few in number to offer any precise threat, and second, because their own qualities—intelligence, dignity and good humour—have equipped them to demand and obtain the respect on which equal status rests. But the future is less certain. Already a vast transformation in the ecology of Maori people is underway and the unstated assumptions of the agreement by which Maori and European have lived in tranquility are now being called to question. Both races have begun to recognize rather anxiously that all aspects of their contemporary dilemmas meet within the field of education.

This does not mean that the community has failed to offer all of its basic equalities, educational and legal, to Maori youth or that they have failed to prove their capacity for taking advantage of them. Mostly they sit together in the same schools, all schools serve both races, and there is a long history of administrative concern. The Maori people are by no means impotent politically. But a lag in Maori achievement is painfully evident and if allowed to persist will almost certainly offer a deeper threat to racial harmony than anything yet encountered. The problem is not so simple as that of merely ensuring that the Maori youngsters are fitted to capitalize on their undoubted talents. The more subtle task is to find what it means to be a Maori contributing distinctively to the commonweal while at the same time receiving its just rewards. In broad perspective, the national promise seems now to demand sufficient diversification of the Maori component to ensure that general verdicts and racial labelling become impossible. Increased capacity for self-scrutiny and the feeling of urgency presently associated with public interest in the issues of Maori schooling give some grounds for hoping that the worst possibilities of the future may be avoided. Here perhaps, in the courtship of Europe and Polynesia, the distinctive contribution of New Zealand's school system is in the making.

SELECT BIBLIOGRAPHY

Beeby, C. E. New Zealand. "An example of secondary education without selection," *International Review of Education*, 2, 1956, pp. 396-409.

Campbell, A. E., and Parkyn, G. W. *Compulsory Education in New Zealand*. Paris: UNESCO, 1952.

Ewing, John L. *The Origins of the New Zealand Primary School Curriculum 1840-1878*. Wellington: NZCER, 1960.

N. Z. Department of Education: Report of the Minister of Education, E-1. Wellington: Government Printer. (Annual publication)

———: *School Enrolment Projections for the Years 1959-72*, Wellington: Government Printer, 1959.

Parkyn, G. W. *The Consolidation of Rural Schools*. Wellington: NZCER, 1952.

Parkyn, G. W. ed. *The Administration of Education in New Zealand*, Wellington, 1954.

Report of the Committee on New Zealand Universities (Chairman, Sir D. H. Parry). Wellington, 1960.

Report of the Commission on Education in New Zealand (Chairman, Sir George Currie). Wellington, 1962.

Richardson, Elwyn S. *In the Early World*. Wellington: NZCER, 1964.

Roth, Herbert. *A Bibliography of New Zealand*. Wellington: NZCER, 1964.

Watson, John E. *Intermediate Schooling in New Zealand*. Wellington: NZCER, 1964.

PAPUA-NEW GUINEA

Penelope Richardson

Everyone has the right to education. Education shall be free, at least in the elementary and fundamental stages. Elementary education shall be compulsory. Technical and professional education shall be made generally available and higher education shall be equally accessible to all on the basis of merit.

from *Universal Declaration of Human Rights*

The number of total illiterates in the Territory of Papua and New Guinea is in excess of 80 percent of the population, and more than 65 percent of the school-age children do not go to school. The Australian Administration of the Territory has pursued a vigorous policy of educational advancement during the last decade, but much remains to be done. Opportunities for schooling at the primary level have been greatly increased, but the number of Papuans and New Guineans who have completed secondary education is pitifully small; to date none has qualified for a university degree. For many years the Papuans and New Guineans will need assistance from Australia or from other more highly developed countries if they are to maintain a modern educational system on their own.

EARLY HISTORY

The island of New Guinea is divided into West Irian, the Territory of Papua, and the Trust Territory of New Guinea. West Irian, which was formerly Netherlands New Guinea and is now part of Indonesia, lies outside the area to be discussed. Papua became a British Protectorate in 1884, a British Colony in 1888, and an Australian Territory in 1906. New Guinea was a German Protectorate from 1884 until an Australian military administration assumed control in 1914. The Council of the League of Nations granted Australia a mandate to govern New Guinea in 1920, and since then it has been under Australian control. Papua and New Guinea were administered separately by the Australian government until the Japanese invasion in 1942, when a wartime administration was set up to govern both Territories jointly. Although the Territory of Papua is strictly an Australian possession and the Territory of New Guinea is a United Nations Trust Territory, they have been formerly combined as the Territory of Papua and New Guinea for purposes of government since 1946. Accordingly, education in Papua developed independently of education in New Guinea.

PAPUA

Missionaries from the London Missionary Society, the Methodist Overseas Mission, the Anglican Mission, and various orders of the Roman Catholic church first brought education to some coastal areas of Papua and nearby islands in the last quarter of the nineteenth century. They established schools primarily to further their religious objectives. The early schools were generally of a low educational standard. They emphasized religious instruction and aimed to make their pupils literate in the vernacular. Sir William McGregor, administrator of British New Guinea from 1888-1898, arranged a "gentlemen's agreement" whereby the London Missionary Society, the Methodist and the Anglican Missions were allotted specified areas in which to work. The Roman Catholics, who arrived after this division was made, refused to recognise the agreement. Because of this tradition the three Protestant missions are still localised, whereas the Roman Catholics operate in all areas.

During his long term as lieutenant-governor of Papua (1909-1940), Sir Hubert Murray raised money for education through a Native Taxation Fund and used it to subsidise and to give grants-in-aid to mission schools in preference to establishing government schools. He was opposed to the creation of a Papuan intelligentsia and considered that diffusion of an elementary education, including a knowledge of English, over as wide an area as possible was desirable. In his words, "It would be unwise to give the Papuan a first-class education unless the way to advancement is to be fully opened to him."[1] During these years the government's contribution to education remained very small. In the year 1939-1940, for instance, the government's total expenditure on native education in Papua was £5,316, made up of grants to missions (£3,130) and examination expenses (£785), agricultural training (£1,075), publication of a school newspaper the *Papuan Villager* and a school reader (£276), and clerical expenses (£50). The number of children enrolled in mission schools in 1940 was estimated to be 25,000. At the government examination held in that year, ninety-one children secured certificates for standard V (primary level), the highest standard of education then available.

NEW GUINEA

The first missionaries to arrive in New Guinea were Lutherans and Roman Catholics on the mainland, and Methodists and Roman Catholics on the islands and, as in Papua, the first schools were set up shortly after their arrival. The German Administration of that time showed little interest in education, but it did encourage literacy in German by giving subsidies to those missions which taught in German. It also established one school near Rabaul for training government servants.

When Australia was granted the mandate to control New Guinea, she acknowledged her responsibility for education, but once again there was little action. In 1927 the missions declined to accept an offer of government subsidies for education because they feared that they might lose control of their activities. Progress in education was very slow. Although the government acknowledged that the education of the native people should not be left solely as the responsibility of the missions whose schools, as in Papua, concentrated on religious teaching and on the ultimate selection and training of mission catechists and teachers, yet it did not fulfill its aim to establish at least one school in every District. In the year 1940 there were 65,598 pupils attending 2,566 mission schools in New Guinea; and the government had established six primary schools (four of which were within a six-mile radius of Rabaul) and one technical school, with total enrollments of 491 and 97 pupils respectively. Government expenditures on native education, which was met from the general revenue, was £8,274 in that year.

POST-WAR DEVELOPMENT

One of the first actions of the Provisional Administration of the Territory of Papua and New Guinea, set up to restore order after the Second World War, was to establish a Department of Education. This Department was to implement a policy of education and to maintain control of education. It had virtually no pre-existing basis from which to work. It began building schools, providing them with teachers, drawing up a Territory syllabus and establishing its own examination standards. Most mission schools had closed during the war and all missionaries from alien countries had been interned. The Department of Education assisted the missions in post-war rehabilitation and established a system of grants-in-aid to mission schools because it was clear that the missions would, for many years, provide the bulk of the education facilities. The grants-in-aid also partly ensured that the government would control standards and syllabuses in the mission schools. By 1950 there were 718 mission schools with an enrollment of 41,471 indigenous pupils and nine government schools with an enrollment of 438 pupils in Papua; while in New Guinea there were 2,303 mission schools and 35 government schools with enrollments of 85,467 and 2,204 indigenous pupils respectively. In that year government expenditure on native education was £178,249 in Papua and £282,669 in New Guinea. Although these sums were thirty times those spent on education in 1940, they still remained small in terms of the needs of the country.

Education in the Territory is now governed by the Education Ordinance of 1952-57 (which came into operation in 1955) and subsequent Education Regulations. The broad objectives of educational policy, as stated by the former Minister for Territories, the Honorable Paul Hasluck, are

a. the political, economic, social and educational advancement of the peoples of Papua and New Guinea;
b. a blending of cultures;

   and, in the absence of any indigenous body of religious faith founded on native teaching or ritual,
c. the voluntary acceptance of Christianity by the native peoples.

The steps necessary to attain these objectives, as expressed yearly in the Annual Reports, are to

a. achieve mass literacy, *i.e.* to teach all indigenous children to read and write in a common language;
b. awaken the interest of the indigenous people in, and assist their progress towards, a higher material standard of living and a civilised mode of life;
c. teach the indigenous community what is necessary to enable it to cope with the political, economic, and social changes that are occurring throughout the Territory;
d. blend the best features of indigenous culture with those of civilization so that the indigenous groups will be able to manage their own affairs and regard themselves as a people with common bonds in spite of tribal differences; and
e. provide within the Territory, as a means of encouraging the above, a full range of primary, secondary, tertiary, technical and adult education for both sexes for all classes of the community.

1. Commonwealth of Australia, *Annual Report on the Territory of Papua*, for the year 1937-38, p. 21.

LANGUAGE FOR LITERACY

Before the war the missions had aimed at literacy in whichever vernacular they had selected as the mission language of the area, *i.e.* the language into which the Scriptures were translated and in which services were held. Thus school instruction was in Motu along the coastal area near Port Moresby, in Yabem in the area around Lae, and in Kuanua on the Gazelle Peninsula and the Duke of York Islands near Rabaul, to name only three. This meant that some children were being taught in a "foreign" language other than English. There is no predominant language group in the Territory, and a recent count of mutually unintelligible languages is in excess of five hundred. There are two fairly widespread *linguae francae* in the Territory, Police Motu in Papua and Melanesian Pidgin (Pidgin English) in New Guinea, but neither is a wholly satisfactory medium of communication for instruction in schools. Missions which have used Melanesian Pidgin in their schools have had varying degrees of success, in spite of its inadequacy.

The Department's aim is to achieve mass literacy in a common language, English. It maintains not only that English should be taught as a major subject in the schools, but also that it should be the language of instruction at all levels from the lowest class. However, the Department permits mission schools to give instruction in the local vernacular in the early years with a transfer to English by standard III primary level. Departmental policy on language has been adopted wholly in some mission schools near towns and mission headstations, but the majority of mission schools are continuing to give instruction in the vernacular to the lower classes. In 1959 the Department issued a statement that all schools that taught children in a vernacular other than their own would be closed in the following year, but this threat was not carried out. However, the missions are gradually accepting the fact that the change to instruction in English, although regrettable, is a necessary expedient because of the need to accelerate the development of Papua and New Guinea. English is the language of instruction in all departmental schools from the lowest class, but the government allows visiting mission pastors to give religious instruction in departmental schools in whichever language they consider the children understand best. And so, as regards mass literacy, in the remote areas to-day native peoples who have been recently contacted are stepping straight from illiteracy in their own vernacular to literacy in English in the same way as they move from transport on foot or by canoe to transport by airplane.

PRESENT STRUCTURE

In October, 1961, the then Minister for Territories, the Honorable Paul Hasluck, M. P., introduced a Five-Year Plan whereby total school enrollments were to increase from 195,436 in 1961 to 350,000 over the five-year period 1962-1966, and further to 750,000 by 1975, by which time all children of school age would have access to schools. Although emphasis was to be placed on increasing opportunities for primary education, secondary schools and technical and professional training were to be developed in proportion to the numbers capable of proceeding to a higher level of education. The following were the expected increases in enrollments:

		1961		1966
Primary Schools	from	189,574	to	336,000
Post-Primary and Secondary Schools	from	4,564*	to	10,000
Technical Schools	from	662	to	2,000
Teacher Training Schools	from	636	to	2,000

*This figure included 2,100 adult students studying through the Auxiliary Training Branch of the Administration.

Table 1 is included on page 194 to illustrate the rapid growth that has taken place in education.

Formal schooling in Papua and New Guinea today ranges from pre-schools (run by the Department of Public Health) for children from three to five years through primary and secondary schools (run by the missions and the Department of Education) to Leaving Certificate or matriculation level. There were eight indigenous students attending university courses in Australia in 1964. The commission appointed to report on higher education in the Territory has recommended "that the early establishment of a fully autonomous University is essential."

PRE-SCHOOLS

In addition to those pre-schools which follow the Australian pattern and which are attended mainly by expatriate children, there were in 1964 sixteen pre-schools which provided special training for indigenous children. These schools, all of which were in urban or semi-urban centres, had an enrollment of more than 700 Papuan and New Guinean children and were staffed by thirty female indigenes who had been, or were being, trained as pre-school teachers and who worked under European supervision.

PRIMARY SCHOOLS

A total of approximately 230,000 children between the ages of six and fourteen years were attending primary schools in 1964. This represented nearly 35 percent of the estimated total of children in this age-group. In spite of the rapid growth of the Department of Education, the missions are still carrying out the bulk of the work in primary education. Mission primary schools fall into two categories: "registered and recognized" schools and "exempt" schools. "Registered and recognised" schools use the same syllabus as departmental schools and English is officially the

TABLE 1

Growth in Education from 1959 to 1964

	MISSION				GOVERNMENT			
	1959		1964		1959		1964	
	Papua	New Guinea	Papua	New Guinea	Papua	New Guinea	Papua	New Guinea
Primary 'A' Schools	6 schools 635 pupils	10 schools 568 pupils	3 schools 291 pupils	10 schools 759 pupils	8 schools 675 pupils	21 schools 1,261 pupils	14 schools 1,213 pupils	24 schools 1,899 pupils
Primary "T" Schools	288 schools 24,694 pupils	329 schools 29,239 pupils	429 schools 34,820 pupils	1,016 schools 84,037 pupils	78 schools 6,498 pupils	153 schools 10,409 pupils	131 schools 18,613 pupils	263 schools 31,561 pupils
Exempt Schools*	728 schools 32,136 pupils	2,413 schools 81,612 pupils	286 schools 13,614 pupils	1,489 schools 47,520 pupils	- -	- -	- -	- -
Secondary Schools†	5 schools 265 pupils	11 schools 376 pupils	11 schools 776 pupils	21 schools 1,655 pupils	11 schools 467 pupils	12 schools 550 pupils	8 schools 1,608 pupils	13 schools 1,845 pupils
Technical Training	1 school 30 pupils	1 school 36 pupils	2 schools 82 pupils	3 schools 131 pupils	2 schools 149 pupils	2 schools 269 pupils	14 schools 703 pupils	14 schools 669 pupils
Teacher Training	5 schools 120 pupils	13 schools 311 pupils	3 schools 58 pupils	12 schools 255 pupils	2 schools 51 pupils	1 school 28 pupils	1 school 240 pupils	2 schools 116 pupils

*These are of a very low standard and are not recognised by the government.

† The figures for 1959 include "post-primary" schools as well as secondary schools.

194

language of instruction, although the government still permits them to teach in the vernacular in the early years and transfer to English by standard III level. These schools receive grants-in-aid from the government for every certificated teacher and for equipment. "Exempt" schools generally have only lower primary school classes. The teacher has no recognised qualification and often plays the dual role of teacher and pastor, and instruction is in a vernacular or *lingua franca*. These schools receive no subsidy from the government, and it is in the interest of the mission to raise their standard.

The main objective of the Territory primary school syllabus is to teach children to use English as a means of communication, both spoken and written, by the time they complete primary schooling. Major emphasis is placed on English, both oral (through language drills, oral composition, story telling and speech training) and written (through sentence construction and composition, spelling and dictation and, in the higher standards only, poetry and grammar). The syllabus, specially designed to attain the objectives as stated by the Honorable Hasluck includes eight subjects as well as English. The hours per week recommended for instruction at the standard IV level give some indication of the emphasis given to each.

Oral English	3 1/3 hrs
Written English	7 2/3 hrs
Arithmetic	3 2/3 hrs
Social Studies	1 3/4 hrs
Health	1/2 hr
Natural Science	1 hr
Music and Singing	1/2 hr
Physical Education	1 1/2 hrs
Art and Craft	2 3/4 hrs
Ethics and Morals	2 hrs

Apart from the mission "exempt" schools, the missions and the Department of Education run two types of primary schools, primary *T* schools which use the specially devised *T* (Territory) syllabus and which concentrate on the teaching of English as a foreign language, and primary *A* schools which use the New South Wales (Australian) syllabus. In 1964 the missions had 118,857 children enrolled in primary *T* schools and 1,050 enrolled in primary *A* schools; and there were 50,174 children enrolled in primary *T* schools and 3,112 enrolled in primary *A* schools run by the Department of Education. In addition there were 61,134 children in mission "exempt" schools. Some Papuans and New Guineans who have taught their children English at an early age prefer to send them to *A* schools; 156 indigenous pupils were attending *A* schools in 1964. However, the required language facility and the cost of clothing and other sundries limit the numbers of indigenous children at *A* schools.

Class enrollments at primary *T* schools in 1964 were:

	MISSION	GOVERNMENT	TOTAL
Preparatory	34,668	10,239	44,907
Standard I	30,564	9,076	39,640
Standard II	23,016	8,843	31,859
Standard III	13,895	8,378	22,273
Standard IV	8,799	6,373	15,172
Standard V	4,970	4,209	9,179
Standard VI	2,945	3,056	6,001

SECONDARY SCHOOLS

Secondary education is provided for children of all races by schools in the Territory and by a subsidy scheme which assists children to go to schools in Australia. In actual fact most expatriate children go to Australia under the subsidy scheme and most indigenous children attend schools in the Territory. There are, however, multi-racial high schools at Port Moresby, Rabaul, and Lae. The numbers of students who received subsidies for secondary schooling in Australia in 1964 were

European	1,105
Asian	237
Mixed Race	120
Indigenous	90

The number of indigenous students in secondary schools has increased significantly only in recent years. Although the missions have some secondary schools, the government provides most of the secondary education. Most of the secondary schools are boarding schools and draw their pupils from many parts of the Territory. Of necessity the development of secondary education follows, rather than parallels, that of primary education, and in the next few years the number of children in secondary schools will increase as the number of children completing primary education increases.

At present all Territory secondary schools follow the New South Wales (Australian) syllabus leading to the Leaving Certificate at matriculation level; formerly some followed the Queensland (Australian) syllabus. They are transferring from a five-year to a six-year course to conform with the changes in the New South Wales system of education. High schools and junior high schools provide secondary education for indigenes; previously there were also post-primary schools which taught standards VII to IX. The few students who satisfactorily completed standard IX in these schools qualified to proceed in two years to the Queensland (Australian) Junior Certificate, and fewer still went on to the Senior Certificate or matriculation level. Standard VII was still in existence in 1964 as a transition year between primary and secondary schooling for those who had gained a low level pass in standard VI.

The small number of indigenous students in the upper standards of secondary schools in Papua and New Guinea during 1964 are shown in Table 2.

TABLE 2

Secondary School Students in 1964

	INDIGENOUS			ALL RACES*		
	Boys	Girls	Total	Boys	Girls	Total
Standard VII	1,088	310	1,398	1,088	311	1,399
Form I	1,840	488	2,324	1,911	577	2,488
Form II	1,041	258	1,299	1,085	324	1,409
Form III	337	38	375	372	73	445
4th Year†	60	6	66	76	16	92
5th Year	36	-	36	45	6	51

*Includes Europeans, Asians, Mixed Race and indigenous persons.

†The differing terminology is due to the current change in New South Wales secondary education.

HIGHER EDUCATION

Although there are no educational institutions at a tertiary level in Papua and New Guinea, some professional training is offered in medicine, agriculture, and administration. Technical education and teacher training are discussed later in this chapter. Since 1959 the Papuan Medical College in Port Moresby has offered a five-year course for Papuans and New Guineans who have reached a standard roughly equivalent to three years of secondary education. It follows lines similar to the Fiji School of Medicine in Suva. In 1965 the Department of Agriculture will offer a three-year diploma course to students of intermediate certificate level of education at Vudal Agricultural College near Rabaul. The Administrative College, which opened in Port Moresby in 1963, gives full-time classes to matriculation level and administrative training to selected indigenous public servants, as well as providing some clerical training. The Department of Posts and Telegraphs offers a five-year course for technicians and three-year courses for communications officers and postal assistants at its Training College in Port Moresby.

TECHNICAL SCHOOLS

The Department of Education's division of technical training conducts three technical schools and twenty-five junior technical schools as well as providing instruction through the Native Apprenticeship Scheme introduced in 1955. The technical schools at Port Moresby, Rabaul, and Lae have as a minimum entry requirement the successful completion of primary schooling (standard VI level). Technical drawing, woodwork, and metal work are among the subjects taught, but approximately 75 percent of the school time in the first two years is devoted to academic subjects which include English, arithmetic, social studies, and general science. After the satisfactory completion of two years of training, students can either become apprenticed for five years or they remain at the school for an additional two years for training in carpentry, joinery, boatbuilding, automotive or diesel mechanics, plumbing, and welding.

Under the Native Apprenticeship Scheme, which is controlled by an Apprenticeship Board, apprentices who complete their indentures and pass the final trade examination are awarded certificates as skilled tradesmen. Twenty-two trades have apprenticeship agreements under this scheme, and through it 177 apprentices have become fully qualified. In 1964 there were 193 apprentices under training in Papua and 252 in New Guinea, all of whom were taking a five-year course.

The twenty-five junior technical schools accept boys with about five years of schooling, many of whom are too old to continue at primary schools. These schools offer a two-year course, and instruction time is divided evenly between ordinary school subjects and training in such skills as brickmaking and bricklaying, carpentry and building, plumbing, painting, elementary mechanics, auto-servicing and driving, and boatbuilding. On completion of this course, the best students can enter an apprenticeship, but the majority become assistant tradesmen or semi-skilled workers.

At a lower level the government runs a few community technical schools which aim at making some specific improvement in living conditions by teaching people to use local materials and resources in a variety of ways. Due to pressure from the village people, there is a tendency for these schools to grow into junior technical schools.

The missions also participate in technical education, but not to any great extent. In 1964 there were two mission institutions in Papua and three in New Guinea which gave instruction similar to that at government junior technical schools and which were recognized by the government. Training in manual arts at a lower level and on-the-job training in carpentry and joinery were given by some missions. In many instances the missions expect the students trained in their technical schools to work for them when they complete their training.

ADULT AND COMMUNITY EDUCATION

Radio broadcasts are used extensively as a medium of community education. The Australian Broadcasting Commission has transmitters at Port Moresby and Rabaul, and the Territory Administration's Department of Information and Extension Services broadcasts from Rabaul, Wewak, Kerema, and Goroka. Programmes such as the news are broadcast in Simple English, Melanesian Pidgin, and some local vernaculars. In addition there are special school broadcasts, "Let's Speak English," "Listen and Learn," "Health and Hygiene," and "Know Your Territory." The Department of Information and Extension Services also produces a fortnightly newspaper in three languages, *Our News* in English, *Iseda Sivarai* in Motu, and *Nius Bilong Yumi* in Pidgin, publishes simple instructional pamphlets, and has a 16-mm. film service which screens educational films throughout the Territory.

A number of other government departments contribute to adult and community education. Women's clubs organised by the Department of Native Affairs play a large part in adult educational activity for women and girls. These clubs teach sewing and cookery and give instruction in hygiene, nutrition, and home nursing. They help to raise the general standard of living in the villages and to improve the social status of women in the towns. The Department of Public Health teaches hygiene, sanitation, and the prevention, treatment, and control of disease. The Department of Agriculture conducts extension programmes to introduce new food crops and to promote cash cropping and animal husbandry. English classes for adults, started in 1964 by the Department of Education to teach oral and written English, met with a very enthusiastic response. There were ninety-nine groups throughout the Territory with an enrollment of about 4,000, the majority of whom were illiterate.

Other organisations which contribute to adult and community education include the Boy Scout and Girl Guide Associations, the Young Women's Christian Association, and Savings and Loan Societies.

TEACHER TRAINING

Four different teacher training courses are available in Papua and New Guinea, the *E* course for expatriates (conducted by the Department) and the *A*, *B*, and *C* courses for indigenes (conducted by the Department and the missions). The *E* course, which is available to both departmental and mission teacher trainees, accepts for enrollment mature expatriate adults with the Australian Intermediate (or Junior) Certificate level of education who have usually had some other training since leaving school. It is of six-months' duration and concentrates on methods of teaching English as a foreign language. The *E* course, which is essentially a "crash" training programme, started in November 1960 and has been highly successful. It has done much to provide staff for the increased number of primary schools.

Teacher training for indigenes is now at three levels. There is the one-year *A* course for those who have completed primary schooling (standard VI), the two-year *B* course for those who have completed Form II at secondary level (or the old standard IX), and the two-year *C* course for those who have completed the Intermediate (or Junior) Certificate level of education. The Department of Education has Teachers' Colleges at Port Moresby, Goroka, and Madang; and the missions have fifteen teacher-training institutions, nine of which are controlled by the Roman Catholics, two by the Seventh-Day Adventists, and one each by the Lutherans, Methodists, Anglicans, and London Missionary Society. The 669 indigenous teacher trainees during 1964 were placed as follows:

	MISSION		GOVERNMENT		TOTAL	
	MALE	FEMALE	MALE	FEMALE	MALE	FEMALE
A Course (1 year)	149	58	116	28	265	86
B Course (2 years)	71	18	134	11	205	29
C Course (2 years)	17	–	34	15	51	15
plus "Technical" (2 years)	–	–	10	8	10	8
	237	76	294	62	531	138

Shortage of teachers has always been a problem in Papua and New Guinea, and the problem is in no way diminishing as the modern system of education expands. The Department and the missions alike employ expatriate and indigenous teachers. Expatriate teachers, who are mainly Australians, are either trained teachers who are recruited or seconded from one of the Australian state education departments, teachers who are trained specially for the Territory at the Australian School of Pacific Administration in Sydney, European teachers with the necessary qualifications who are local residents, or locally trained diplomates from the *E* course.

Most departmental indigenous teachers have at some stage undergone a course in teacher training, but some started teaching before any formal courses were in existence. For all practical purposes the untrained teachers are equated with *A* course graduates, consideration being given to their years of experience in teaching under supervision. In contrast, the majority of indigenous mission teachers have had little or no training as teachers, and in addition their standard of formal education is often very low. A "Permit to Teach" certificate is required for teachers at all "registered and recognised" schools; but many teachers at "exempt" schools do not have even this low qualification. The numbers of mission and departmental teachers in 1964 were as follows:

	MISSION		GOVERNMENT	
	EXPATRIATE	INDIGENOUS	EXPATRIATE	INDIGENOUS
at primary *A* schools	33		115	
at primary *T* schools	668	2,960	411	1,118
at "exempt" schools		2,179		
at secondary schools	144	6	153	13
at technical schools	11		68	42

Thus it is seen that the ratio of indigenous teachers to expatriate teachers in mission primary *T* schools

(4.4:1) is higher than that in Departmental primary T schools (2.7:1).

FINANCE AND TEACHER SALARIES

The government is bearing most of the cost of expansion of educational facilities, which has been mainly at the primary level. However, the number and capacity of secondary and technical schools are also increasing to provide places for the increasing numbers of students demanding this type of education. The size of the government grants for education has increased steadily in recent years. In the financial year 1963-64 the Territory Budget allowed £4.1 million for education, with an additional £1.6 million for capital works, out of a total budget of £38.3 million. Teachers' salaries, allowances and travel expenses accounted for half of the education vote; other large items of expenditure were for equipment, maintenance of capital assets, grants-in-aid to missions, and for subsidies paid for children (both expatriate and indigenous) at present at secondary schools in Australia. Grants-in-aid to missions include subsidies for every qualified teacher, for all secondary school students, for teacher and technical trainees, and for equipment for schools.

Departmental teachers receive much higher rates of pay than mission teachers. Like other workers in the mission field, mission teachers receive low salaries. The few material benefits which they receive satisfy most, but a few feel that the mission has pressured them to become teachers with the mission when they could have entered more remunerative occupations elsewhere. Moreover, in the Protestant missions a person often performs the dual function of teacher and pastor or teacher and evangelist. Departmental teachers, on the other hand, are well paid by Territory standards.[2] By June 1963 a total of 1,053 indigenes had qualified to join the Public Service. These people had either completed Form II at secondary school (or its equivalent) or had taken at least a three-year course of training following the completion of primary schooling or had been appointed under special circumstances. The Department of Education employed 426 or 40 percent of this more highly educated (and consequently more highly paid) group, followed by the Department of Public Health with 172 or 16 percent, the remaining 455 being distributed among the other twenty-two departments and branches of the Administration. Thus the Department of Education is tending to consume its own product (a criticism previously levelled at the missions) to the detriment of other government departments whose services are also vitally necessary in a developing country. Expatriate teachers receive salaries and allowances which compare with those of teachers in Australia and which are far higher than those of indigenous teachers.

FUTURE PROSPECTS

When he announced the five-year development plan in 1961 the Minister for Territories expressed the hope of providing universal primary education in Papua and New Guinea by 1975. No one has repudiated the Minister's statement, but it now does not seem at all likely that this target will be achieved. Moreover many more places in secondary and technical schools will be needed to absorb the students now enrolled in the lower classes of primary schools who wish to proceed to higher education. It is one thing to reach a position where all children have access to primary schools and quite another to supply adequate opportunities for education at advanced levels. With limited staff and finance the Department must decide whether it will establish primary schools in new areas or consolidate the education system in old areas. The Commission on Higher Education[3] considered that a 50 percent primary enrollment, with an appropriate development of secondary and tertiary education, was a more realistic target for 1975.

As regards equality of educational opportunity, for the minority of children who are fortunate enough to be within reach of schools from an early age and who have ability, the possibilities are unlimited. All education is free, there is nothing to prevent the intelligent child from going ahead. To date there have been insufficient numbers of pupils requiring secondary education rather than insufficient places in schools for them. Steps must be taken now to see that this position is not reversed over the next few years as the mass of children who are now receiving primary education reach for something more.

In contrast to the government, the missions have no single stated policy on education. The major aim of Christian education, as expressed by one of the missions, is the imparting of Christian truths and knowledge and the "betterment" and raising of the standard of living and way of life of the indigenous people. Through their schools the missions have a very effective instrument for spreading Christianity among the people within their area of influence. Moreover, schools are needed to train church leaders if strong autonomous churches controlled by indigenes are to be established within the foreseeable future. In 1963 twenty-four different missions were conducting schools in Papua and New Guinea.[4] The main denominations were as follows:

---

2. It seems likely that teachers will not be so well paid when the Public Service Ordinance 1964, which provides for the re-organisation of the Public Service, takes full effect.

3. G. Currie, J. T. Gunther, and O. H. K. Spate, *Report of the Commission on Higher Education*, p. 31 .

4. Further, the work of one denomination is not always co-ordinated within the mission itself; the Roman Catholics, for instance, run schools through the Divine Word, Sacred Heart, Holy Ghost, Holy Trinity, Franciscan, and Marist Missions.

	Papua	New Guinea
Roman Catholics	142 schools	1,373 schools
Lutherans	6 schools	865 schools
Methodists	106 schools	137 schools
Seventh-Day Adventists	50 schools	174 schools
London Missionary Society	216 schools	—
Anglicans	126 schools	29 schools
Others	79 schools	120 schools

Under the auspices of the Department of Education, an Education Advisory Board of eleven members, including four mission representatives, holds conferences twice a year. Policy recommendations are forwarded to the Minister for Territories for his consideration. The Department's area inspectors visit mission schools throughout their Districts and its Mission Relations Section at Headquarters controls payments for grants-in-aid and maintains statistics and records of mission education activities.

The two main obstacles preventing the spread of education are shortage of teachers and shortage of money. Since there are many more indigenous teachers than expatriate teachers, most of the teaching is done by indigenous teachers, many of whom do not have a high standard of education. However adequate is the course given in teacher training, the teacher is handicapped if he lacks a broad basic education. Until sufficient numbers of indigenes are educated to a higher level, there will be increasing calls on expatriates to teach in secondary schools and in the higher standards of primary schools. The missions' problems in financing education are not so acute as the Department's, since the missions receive grants-in-aid and are able to make a little go a great deal farther than the Department can; but their staffing problems are just as serious. The indigenous people now want education; it is to be hoped that the Department of Education and the religious missions will be able to provide it in sufficient quantity and quality for the children of the future.

BIBLIOGRAPHY

Australian School of Pacific Administration. *Report on Education by the No. 3 Senior Officers' Course, Territory of Papua and New Guinea, October, 1958.* Unpublished paper, Sydney, 1958.

Brown, H. E. *A Survey of Educational Trends in Four South Pacific Territories.* Thesis submitted to the Ohio State University, 1962.

Bunker, A. R. *The Development of Secular Education in Papua-New Guinea 1946-1959.* Thesis submitted to the University of Sydney, 1961.

Commonwealth of Australia. *Annual Report on the Territory of Papua.* Canberra: Commonwealth Government Printer, annually.

———. *Report to the General Assembly of the United Nations on the Administration of the Territory of New Guinea.* Canberra: Commonwealth Government Printer, annually.

Currie, George; Gunther, J. T.; and Spate, O. H. K. *Report of the Commission on Higher Education in Papua and New Guinea.* Canberra: Union Offset Company, 1964.

Essai, Brian. *Papua and New Guinea—A Contemporary Survey.* Melbourne: Oxford University Press, 1961.

Frerichs, A. C. *Anutu Conquers in New Guinea.* Columbus: The Wartburg Press, 1957.

Groves, W. C. *Native Education and Culture-Contact in New Guinea.* Melbourne: Melbourne University Press, 1936.

Hasluck, P. *Australian Policy in Papua and New Guinea.* George Judah Cohen Memorial Lecture. Sydney: University of Sydney, 1956.

Mair, L. P. *Australia in New Guinea.* London: Christophers, 1948.

Murray, J. K. *The Provisional Administration of the Territory of Papua and New Guinea: Its Policies and Problems.* John Murtagh Macrossan Memorial Lectures, 1947. Brisbane: University of Queensland, 1949.

Reed, S. W. *The Making of Modern New Guinea.* Philadelphia: American Philosophical Society, 1943.

Robson, R. W. *Pacific Islands Year Book and Who's Who.* Ninth Edition, edited by Judy Tudor. Sydney: Pacific Publications, 1963.

Rowley, C. D. *The Australians in German New Guinea 1914-1921.* Melbourne: Melbourne University Press, 1958.

Territory of Papua and New Guinea. *Annual Report to the Minister of State for Territories from the Public Service Commissioner.* Port Moresby: Government Printer, 1963.

———. *Syllabus for Primary T Schools.* Port Moresby: Department of Education, revised 1962.

———. *The Second Camilla Wedgwood Memorial Lecture and Seminar.* "The Education of Women and Girls" by Richard Seddon. Port Moresby: Government Printer, 1960.

United Nations Trusteeship Council. *Report of the United Nations Visiting Mission to the Trust Territories of Nauru and New Guinea, 1962.* New York, 1962.

Wilkes, J. (editor). *New Guinea and Australia.* Prepared under the auspices of the Australian Institute of Political Science. Sydney: Angus and Robertson, 1959.

Williams, F. E. *The Blending of Cultures: An Essay on the Aims of Native Education.* Territory of Papua Anthropology Report, No. 16 of 1935. Port Moresby, reprinted 1951.

PHILIPPINES

Bonifacio E. Pilapil

THE LAND AND THE PEOPLE

The Philippine archipelago is approximately 500 miles from the southeast coast of Asia. It stretches about 1,100 miles from northern Borneo to Formosa. There are estimated to be around seven thousand one hundred islands and islets that comprise the archipelago but only 462 of these islands are more than a mile in area. The Philippines is divided into three regional groups, namely: Luzon, Visayas, and Mindanao. South of Luzon are the Visayas comprised of the islands of Panay, Negros, Cebu, Masbate, Samar, Leyte, and Bohol. The total land area of the Philippines is 115,739 square miles. The temperature varies from seventy-five to eighty-five degrees Fahrenheit.

The Filipinos trace their origin from the Indonesians and the Malayans, from Southeast Asia. From this group 90 percent of the Philippine population is comprised today. About 34 percent of its population is Catholic. Other religious groups are Protestants, Aglipayans, and Iglesia ni Kristo 9 percent, Mohammedan 6 percent and Buddhist and other religions 1 percent. There are at least eighty-seven different kinds of languages spoken by the people. Commonwealth Act No. 134 was passed enjoining the adoption and development of a common language for the country which is now officially called Pilipino. Together with English and Spanish language, Pilipino is offered in the schools from kindergarten to the university level.

EDUCATION UNDER SPAIN

Although the Philippines was "discovered" by Ferdinand Magellan in March 16, 1521, it was not until 1595 when settlements of more permanent nature were established. King Philip II, in answer to petitions sent to him, issued a decree in 1585, ordering Governor Santiago de Vera and Bishop Salazar to discuss measures for the founding of a college. By virtue of this decree the College of San Jose was

founded in 1601. This college, by a royal decree in 1875, became a part of the University of Santo Tomas. The University of Santo Tomas, founded in 1611 by His Excellency Fray Miguel de Benavides, started to organize departments in Philosophy (1645), Theology (1645), Canonical Law (1734), Civil Law (1734), Jurisprudence (1820), Humanities (1850), and Institute (1871). Liberal Arts, Natural Sciences, Secondary and Elementary education were begun years later.

Schools on the secondary level were next organized. The majority of the secondary schools were located in Manila and in the various theological seminaries, namely, in Vigan, Nueva Caceres (now Naga City), Cebu, and Iloilo. The aims of higher and secondary education were largely determined by the ideal set by the aristocratic society of the time. College and secondary education was for the upper classes. The distinction of belonging to the *gente ilustrada* was very much sought by the well-to-do students. A *titulo* (degree) was considered a badge of social standing and prestige.

The system of primary instruction was not established until after the middle of the seventeenth century. In 1778 when Don Jose de Basco y Vargas assumed the governorship of the Philippines definite steps were taken to organize schools. Every possible inducement was offered to make the Filipinos learn the Spanish language. Those who could read, write, and speak Spanish were given preference in government employment. Attendance was compulsory between the ages of seven to twelve years. Parents were fined if they failed to abide with the law. The subjects taught in the elementary schools were (a) religion, consisting primarily of Christian doctrine, sacred history, and principles of ethics; (b) reading; (c) writing; (d) practical instruction in Spanish, Spanish grammar, and orthography; (e) principles of arithmetic, comprising the four fundamental operations, common fractions, decimal fractions, metric systems and its equivalents in ordinary weights and measures; (f) general geography and history of Spain; (g) rules of deportment; (h) vocal music; and (i) pratical agriculture as applied to the products of the country. Although there was a prescribed curriculum, the school had no fixed program, was strictly sectarian, ungraded, and had no definite standards for each year to accomplish.

EDUCATION IN THE REPUBLIC, 1896-1898

The Revolutionary Government which eventually supplanted Spanish rule created a Department of Education. The Constitution of Biac-na-Bato in November, 1897, provided for education. Filipino revolutionists established a university known as the Literary University of the Philippines. This university offered courses in medicine, law, pharmacy, and notary public. The revolutionary government also provided for the establishment and continuance of secondary schools, vocational courses, a military academy, and primary education. Title III, Article 5, of the Biac-na-Bato constitution specified the separation of the church and the State, a provision which put an end to church control over education in the Philippines.

PRESENT EDUCATIONAL SYSTEM

Passage of Act No. 74 by the Philippine Commission on January 21, 1901, marked the beginning of the present educational system of the Philippines. This Act created the now Department of Education. The period from 1901 to 1910 might be considered the period of organization and orientation. Public schools established curricula of instruction based on the American pattern of education, English was the medium of instruction and religious instruction was prohibited in all the schools. The main purpose of education was to prepare the people for self-government.

Under the Department of Education more schools were established. This period brought about rapid growth and expansion in enrollment, attendance, and promotion of pupils.

Two major problems faced by the school system during this period were (1) the lack of trained teachers not only in the subject-matter field but also in methods of teaching and (2) the construction of adequate as well as sanitary school buildings to house the increasing school population. The first problem was partly solved when on September 1, 1901, the Philippine Normal College was opened in Manila to train teachers for the elementary level. A few months later the Philippine College of Arts and Trades was also opened. The PCAT took the burden of training teachers in industrial arts. In April 10, 1907, Executive Order No. 10 of the Governor General promulgated the reservation of fifty-seven hectares for the use of the Central Luzon Agricultural University. This university, together with the College of Agricul-

ture of the University of the Philippines, trained teachers in agriculture. This promulgation is a milestone in the development of vocational education in the Philippines. It was also during this period that the Philippine Nautical School was placed under the administration and supervision of the Bureau of Public Schools. By 1908 the University of the Philippines was founded.

During the early American occupation the teaching load was first shouldered by American teachers who came to the Philippines in the United States transport ship named *Thomas*. These American teachers were assigned to organize schools in the *barrios* (villages) and *poblaciones* (towns). At the beginning they numbered about a thousand, but this decreased as more and more Filipino teachers became trained to take over the job. Table 1 shows the proportion of American and Filipino teachers from 1900 up to 1960:

TABLE 1

Proportion of American and Filipino Teachers in the Public Schools of the Philippines 1900-1960

Year	American Teachers	Filipino Teachers	Total
1900	889	2,167	3,056
1905	826	3,414	4,240
1910	773	8,275	9,048
1915	589	9,308	9,897
1920	385	17,244	17,630
1925	353	25,241	25,594
1930	307	25,279	28,586
1935	160	27,755	27,915
1940	97	43,682	43,779
1945	14	46,996	47,010
1950	8	85,396	85,404
1955		101,150	101,150
1960		120,110	120,110

The problem of school building was partially solved with the passage of Act No. 1801, known as the Gabaldon Act, by the Philippine Commission. This Act set aside the amount of one million pesos for the construction of standard school buildings.

The period following 1910 until 1935 was generally called the period of school reforms, adjustments, and evaluation. During this period the country saw a tremendous growth in enrollment, accompanied by increase in the number of teachers. Widespread interest in education had been aroused among the people. Schools were established in areas that years before were considered inaccessible. Attention was focused on the development of the elementary school program.

At this time it was felt that the public schools had been fully established, and a type of education at least partially adapted to the needs and conditions of the Philippines was achieved. The school planners then turned their attention to the revision of the courses of instruction. When Frank R. White became Director of Public Schools in 1909 his first act was to put emphasis on industrial instruction. Vocational courses were introduced in grades. Vocational curricula such as farming, trade, business, household arts, agricultural education, and farm management were offered. As teacher supply became acute, the two-year normal curriculum was opened in selected provincial high schools.

Efforts were also directed toward the preparation and adaptation of textbooks to Philippine needs. Advisory committees were formed from time to time and members were appointed for this purpose. In order to systematize the adoption of textbooks for the public schools, Act No. 2957, approved by the Legislature in 1921 and subsequently amended by Acts Nos. 3185 and 3402, created a Board on Textbooks to take charge of the selection and approval of books to be used in the public schools.

In March 8, 1924, the Philippine Legislature enacted a law to create a Board of Educational Survey to study and survey all educational institutions, facilities, and agencies in the Philippines. The purpose of the survey was to assess and make recommendations on the results of twenty-five years of "educational experiment to prepare the people for self-government." the entire survey staff consisted of twenty-three prominent Filipino and American educators headed by Dr. Paul Monroe, Director of the International Institute and Professor of Education, Teachers' College, Columbia University.

Members of the survey staff gathered data for certain definite phases of school activity. The survey team made a thorough investigation of every aspect of the school system covering such things as secondary education, primary education, teacher training, industrial work, health education, higher education, finance, administration and supervision, testing, and others.

This educational survey submitted its report to the Legislature of the Philippines in 1925. The findings of this survey became the basis for changes in the educational system. Another educational survey, often referred to as the Swanson Survey was made in 1960. Its aims and objectives were similar to the Monroe Survey.

With the establishment of the Commonwealth Government in 1936, an orientation of educational plans and policies became necessary to conform to the requirements of the Constitution. The framework of the educational system, however, remained the same.

During the short-lived Japanese occupation of the Philippines in 1941-1945, the school curriculum was revised in order to weed out any Western content and to gear the curriculum to the objectives of the Co-Prosperity Sphere envisioned by the Japanese for Asia. The Japanese system was immediately abandoned when Japan lost the war.

The Philippines were granted independence by the United States on July 4, 1946. During this period the enrollment in the schools almost reached the saturation point. By 1960 the total school attendance was 4,541,775 which showed that one of every four Filipinos was in school. Much emphasis was directed toward the development of community schools in the primary and elementary level. Many changes took place from 1946 as the Republic tried to meet the challenge of a complicated as well as expanding educational system.

IMPORTANT EDUCATIONAL LAWS

The Constitution of the Philippines gives the state the power to supervise and regulate all educational institutions. Article XIV, Sec. 5, of the Constitution provides that

all educational institutions shall be under the supervision of and subject to regulation by the state. The Government shall establish and maintain a complete and adequate system of public education, and shall provide at least free public primary instruction and citizenship training to adult citizens. All schools shall aim to develop moral character, personal discipline, civic conscience, vocational efficiency, and to teach the duties of citizenship.

Act No. 74 passed by the Philippine Commission in 1901 created the Department of Instruction under a General Superintendent of Public Instruction. This law laid the foundation for the organization of the Philippine educational system. Subsequently Acts Nos. 477, 672, 1137, 1407, and 1698 were passed by the same commission between the years 1902 to 1907 which resulted in several modifications in the educational system the most important of which was the creation of the Bureau of Education headed by a Director and an assistant under the Department of Education.

Legislative Act No. 2782, passed in 1918, extended the facilities for free elementary education to all children of school age; provided increases in the salaries of municipal teachers; and abolished the tuition fees in the intermediate grades for grades five to grades seven.

Act No. 3050 created the Teachers' Pension Fund. This Act was replaced by Commonwealth Act No. 186 which established the Government Service Insurance System. This law was later amended by Republic Act No. 660 which provided for life and retirement insurance for teachers and other government employees.

Act No. 3377 provided for the construction of buildings and the equipment of trade and agricultural schools. In addition, Commonwealth Act No. 313 authorized the establishment of regional trade and agricultural schools.

Commonwealth Act No. 381 gave the National Government the responsibility for the support of the first four grades. The local government became responsible financially to the other grades in the elementary school. At the present, however, all public elementary schools are supported by the National Government.

The Educational Act of 1940 (Commonwealth Act No. 586) reduced the elementary school course from seven to six years. This law also established the two-single-session plan for the primary grade (one to four) and the one-teacher-one-class plan in the intermediate grades (to six).

Republic Act No. 842, otherwise known as the Public School Salary Act of 1953, provided for automatic salary increases for public school officials, teachers, and other government personnel according to experience, educational qualifications, and civil service eligibility.

The Elementary Education Act of 1953 (Republic Act No. 896) authorized the revision of the elementary school system by restoring Grade seven and the double-session plan.

Although most of the laws passed were directly concerned with public education, some laws were also passed specifically for private education.

Act No. 74 of 1901 provided that "nothing in this Act shall be construed in any way to forbid, impede, or obstruct the establishment and maintenance of private schools." In 1910 the office of Superintendent of Private Schools was created for better supervision of private institutions.

In 1917, Act No. 2706 provided that the Secretary of Education shall have authority to supervise, inspect, and regulate all schools and colleges in order to determine the efficiency of instruction given in them and to prepare and publish from time to time the minimum standard required of school courses.

In 1926, the Office of Private Education was created, as recommended by the Monroe Commission. In 1936, Commonwealth Act No. 180 was passed to implement the provisions of the Constitution of the Philippines regarding the administration and supervision of private schools. This law placed a Director in charge of the office of private education.

THE DEPARTMENT OF EDUCATION

The Department of Education is administered and supervised by the Secretary of Education, assisted by an under-secretary. They are appointed by the President of the Philippines with the consent of the Commission on Appointments. The Secretary is vested with powers and duties to carry out general policies regarding education.

The Office of the Secretary is composed of the Administrative Division, Physical Education Division, and the Board of Textbooks.

Under the Department of Education are several bureaus:

The Bureau of Public Schools. Headed by a director, this bureau is in charge of the administration and supervision of all public schools. In 1947, adult education in the Philippines became a part of its responsibility.

The Bureau of Private Schools. Headed by a director, this bureau is in charge of supervising and regulating the operation of private schools, colleges, and universities. The bureau also inspects private educational institutions to determine whether such schools, colleges, and universities meet the standards set by the Department of Education.

The Bureau of Vocational Education. Formerly a division under the Bureau of Public Schools, vocational education became a separate bureau in 1964. It is headed by a director. The bureau is in charge of the administration of all public vocational schools and colleges in the Philippines including schools of fisheries and agriculture.

The Bureau of Public Libraries. The Bureau of Public Libraries is headed by a director. The following are some of the important functions of this office: (a) to preserve all books, library materials and equipment belonging to the bureau and those under its care, (b) to provide reading facilities to the public and especially extension of such facilities to all parts of the country, (c) to acquire books, library and other materials and equipment, and (d) to prepare, print, and publish pamphlets, monographs, manuscripts, scientific and literary works deserving to be published in the interest of the government, of the public welfare, of the history of the Philippines, or of science and arts in general.

The Institute of National Language. This office was created to carry out the provision of the constitution enjoining the adoption and development of a common national language based on one of the existing native languages of the Philippines. The Filipino language is now taught in all schools. The institute prepares materials for instruction and also undertakes linguistics research.

The Philippine Historical Committee. This body is headed by the Chairman of the Committee who is appointed by the President of the Philippines. The duties of the committee are the following: (a) identification and appropriate marking of historical landmarks of ancient and present Philippines, (b) acquiring by donation or purchase old relics owned by private persons, and (c) prescribing or repairing important old papers and documents owned by the Republic of the Philippines or any of its political sub-divisions.

The National Museum. Formerly a part of the National Library, the National Museum was transferred to the Department of Education by virtue of Executive Order No. 94. The museum is headed by a director who is appointed by the President of the Philippines with the consent of the Commission on Appointments. The main function of the museum is to preserve and exhibit objects of permanent interests in one or more of the arts and sciences and to prepare, print, and publish manuscripts or literary or scientific works deserving to be published in the interest of the government, of the public welfare, or of the science and the arts in general.

PRE-PRIMARY EDUCATION

Several public and private universities and colleges have provided kindergarten departments similar to those of the United States in organization, curriculum, and method of instruction. Much emphasis in the kindergarten program is geared toward the development of social as well as art activities. Children enrolled in kindergarten schools are between the ages of five and six. The instruction in the classroom is in the English language.

ELEMENTARY EDUCATION

The Educational Act of 1940 reduced elementary education from seven to six years and made school attendance compulsory from the ages of seven to thirteen years. Grades one to four consist of the primary and Grades five and six are considered the intermediate grades. The national government provides for free public elementary education. In the primary school, the child gains fundamental knowledge, habits and skills, and ideals of thought and action which are desirable for practical citizenship.

Table 3 shows the minimum time allotments for the elementary school curriculum.

TABLE 3

Minimum Time Allotments for the Elementary
School Curriculum

Subject Area	Number of Minutes a Day		
	I-II	III-IV	V-VI
I. Social Studies	40	50	50
II. Work Education	40	60	80
III. Health and Science	40	40	50
IV. Language Arts	110	110	120
V. Arithmetic	40	40	50
VI. Arts and Physical Education	40	40	50
TOTAL	310	340	400

The following are suggested contents for each area of the curriculum:

a. Social Studies includes character education, geography, history, civics, community problems, good manners and right conduct, and Filipino family customs and traditions. Religious instruction is optional in accordance with law and existing regulations.

b. Work Education includes those phases of work in agriculture, home making and family living, industrial arts and retail trade and other activities designed to develop knowledge, attitudes, proper work habits and skills, and wise utilization of resources.

c. Health and Science includes personal hygiene, community health, elementary science, and safety education.

d. Language Arts includes language, spelling, reading, phonics, and writing skills in the native language, Filipino and English.

e. Arithmetic includes the development of skills in the fundamental operations and the solution of problems related to community life.

f. Arts and Physical Education include such subjects as music, drawing, painting, modeling, physical education, clubwork, and hobbies.

Although the elementary school curriculums are prepared in the Central Office in Manila and prescribed for all classrooms in the Philippines, they are merely intended for uniformity of minimum requirements for each grade. Teachers and local school administrators are given a free hand in suiting curriculum materials to the needs of the children and the local conditions of the community. Classroom instruction places emphasis on the functional, social, as well as the economic values of the subject matter taught.

There are two other types of elementary curriculum, namely, the agricultural and settlement farm. The agricultural curriculum which is only for grades five and six contains the same subjects included in the general intermediate curriculum with the addition of ninety minutes daily farm work which includes gardening, farm crops, and agricultural club work, drawing, carpentry, woodworking, and repair work.

The settlement farm curriculum includes the same subjects included in the general intermediate curriculum for both primary and intermediate grades, with the addition of sixty minutes of daily field or farm work in grades one to four and half of the school day in grades five and six.

SECONDARY EDUCATION

The secondary curriculum was designed to furnish the background for college work as well as to prepare the student for definite occupational pursuit.

There are five types of secondary curriculum offered in Philippine schools, namely: (a) general secondary, (b) secondary trade, (c) secondary fishery, (d) secondary vocational, and (e) secondary agriculture.

The general secondary curriculum accounts for 78 percent of the total population in the secondary schools. The minimum number of forty-minute periods per day required for completion of the secondary general courses under the 2-2 plan is presented in Table 4.

The general secondary curriculum which is prescribed in all public secondary schools is partly aca-

TABLE 4

Minimum Numbered of 40-Minute Periods a Day
Required for Completion of the
Secondary General Courses Under
the 2-2 Plan

Subjects	Common 1st and 2nd Years	College 3rd Year	Preparatory 4th Year	Total	Vocational	
					3rd Year	4th Year
English	2	2	2[b]	6[b]	1	1
Filipino Language	2	1	1	4	½	½
Social Science[a]	2	1	1	4	1	1
Mathematics	2	2	2	6	1	1
Science	2	2	2	6	1	1
Health, Physical Education and PMT	2	1	1	4	½	½
Work Experience or Vocational Education for Boys or Home Economics for Girls	4	-	-	4	4	4

1. Where possible all academic classes shall be given in the morning and work experience or vocational education in the afternoon or vice versa. PMT may be given on Saturdays if desired.

2. There should be a guidance program in every school under a trained guidance counselor.

a. In the first and second year, science will be one period of 40 minutes. In the third year and fourth year of the college preparatory it should be double period; in the third and fourth year for vocational it should be a double period every other day. The science courses should be balanced between biological sciences and physical sciences.

b. These two periods may be English, social science or mathematics. For those who intend to pursue non-technical courses like Law, Education or Business, etc. in college they should be electives in English or social science. For all others, they should be in mathematics.

demic and partly vocational. Exploratory vocational courses are offered in the first year from which the student may later select the vocational subject that he wants to pursue for further study. For those students contemplating entering the university, optional subjects, such as mathematics or physics, may be taken in lieu of vocational courses.

In the trade curriculum different courses are offered to provide training to the student for some specific occupation. Proficiency in actual performance of a task is the primary consideration in promoting students to the next grade. This means that the student should have a high degree of workmanship training on the different projects that the school provides for him.

The agricultural curriculum was envisioned by the planners to provide experiences for the students who enroll in high schools located in areas where the main occupation of the people is farming. The curriculum provides courses for both boys and girls. The girls are given practical training in gardening and orchard care, poultry raising, animal husbandry, dairying, handicrafts, and marketing farm products.

Considering that the Philippines has a coastline of 10,850 miles and is endowed with rich fishing grounds, the fishery curriculum was designed to provide students with experiences in the area of fishing. Subjects in Fishery and Practicum ranging from forty minutes in the first year to two hours in the third and fourth years are required by all students enrolled in the fishery curriculum.

Secondary schools are supported either by the national government or by the provincial government. Roughly 75 percent of public secondary schools are supported by the provincial government. Almost all of these schools offer the general secondary curriculum. The remaining 25 percent or less, mostly trade, agricultural, fisheries, and schools offering special courses which are secondary in nature are supported by the national government.

HIGHER EDUCATION

As of 1962, there were forty-six public colleges and universities in the Philippines. The University of the Philippines which was founded in 1908 had for its aim to provide advanced instruction in literature, philosophy, sciences, the arts, and to give professional and technical training. The university charter also provided that no student shall be denied admission to the university by reason of age, sex, nationality, religious beliefs, or political affiliation. The University awards the doctor of philosophy in addition to the bachelor and master's degrees.

Just as important as the University of the Philippines are the colleges and universities located in Manila, Central Luzon, Visayas, and Mindanao. The Philippine Normal College in Manila and eight other teacher-training institutions in the provinces offer courses towards the bachelor of science in elementary education. Graduate study leading to the master's degree are also offered in these institutions with majors in guidance and counselling, administration and supervision, home economics, English as a Second Language, Filipino, and teaching of the blind. Many of the graduates take positions of leadership in the school systems of the Philippines.

The Philippine College of Commerce and the Philippine College of Arts and Trades train students for business and industry. The Philippine Nautical School provides trained officers for the shipping and trade industry of the country.

Financial support of public higher education is derived mainly from two sources: (a) from congressional appropriations and (b) from tuition fees. Except the University of the Philippines and the University of Mindanao which generally receive larger appropriation from Congress, the institutions derive more than half of their income from tuition fees.

PRIVATE EDUCATION

A private school in the Philippines may assume the name of school, institute, academy, junior college, college, or university. The name "technology," however, may not be used unless the school operates a four-year collegiate course in technology which requires for admission, graduation from a four-year secondary course. Section 3 of Commonwealth Act No. 180 also limits the term university to those institutions that possess the following: (a) the operation of a four-year undergraduate course in liberal arts and sciences, (b) the operation of a recognized postgraduate course in liberal arts and sciences or in education, leading to the master's degree, (c) the operation of at least three professional colleges, (d) the possession and maintenance of a professionally administered library of at least ten thousand volumes of collegiate books; provided, however, that the operation of a recognized post-graduate course in liberal arts and sciences or in education, leading to the master's degree shall not be required of universities recognized as such prior to the approval of the Act.

The "Manual of Information for Private Schools" in 1953 also requires private universities to include ownership of adequate and suitable grounds and buildings, and maintenance of a faculty at least 60 percent of which hold professorial ranks and are on full-time basis.

The Secretary of Education is given the power to revoke the recognition granted to any private school or college if in the judgment of the secretary such school or college had failed to keep up to the standards of instruction.

During the school year 1962-63 the total number of students who graduated from colleges and universities was 59,239. Of that number 50,680 were graduates of private colleges and universities which is roughly 85.5 percent of the total graduates.

PREPARATION OF TEACHERS

Teacher-training institutions train one or more of the following types: (a) pre-elementary or kindergarten level, (b) elementary level, (c) secondary or high school level, (d) vocational and technical, and (e) higher learning, collegiate, professional.

In the pre-elementary level the Baguio Vacation Normal School of the Bureau of Public Schools has for many years been offering courses in pre-elementary education to graduates of the four-year general elementary teacher-education curriculum or to selected holders of Bachelor of Science in Elementary Education degrees. The regional normal schools also provide some training to teachers in the pre-elementary level.

Length of teacher preparation programs in the elementary level increased from two to four years leading to the bachelor of science in elementary education degree which is required of all teachers entering the teaching profession. For teachers in the non-Christian Schools, however, the completion of a two-year normal school curriculum is still allowed

in order to carry out the national policy of attraction and integration of the non-Christian groups.

The teacher-training curriculum for prospective elementary school teachers provides for two types of courses: (a) those that fall under general education and (b) those that come under the professional preparation. During the past few years the Philippine Normal College undertook a curriculum revision program wherein an increase in the number of liberal arts courses was offered.

The requirements for teaching in the secondary school is the completion of the four-year course leading to the degree bachelor of science in education with major or minor in specific fields of specialization. The curricula for the bachelor of science in education are the same for both public and private institutions. The courses offered can also be divided into two types, namely (a) general education and (b) professional preparation. Lately, there have been several moves to include more humanities and/or liberal arts courses in the curriculum.

Steady measures are taken by the Bureau of Vocational Education to raise the quality of vocational and industrial arts teachers so that their education and training can be comparable with those required for the general education subjects. This means that a full-college diploma is required for elementary and secondary school teachers while a graduate degree would be necessary for instructors of college subjects. The bureau also initiated the training and preparation of industrial arts and vocational teachers in regional schools of arts and trades and in state colleges of agriculture. To give the graduates more rounded training the bureau intends to recommend amendments of the Apprenticeship Law.

Teacher-training courses offered in the private vocational schools are the bachelor of science in industrial arts, bachelor of science in industrial education, and bachelor of science in commercial education. These courses as followed in the private schools are the same as those prescribed in the public schools because the graduates from these courses are usually employed by the public schools to fill positions now filled by unqualified teachers.

APPOINTMENTS, QUALIFICATIONS, AND TENURE OF TEACHERS

It has been the practice to appoint teachers who are holders of academic degrees related to the subject or subjects they will teach. As a general policy, public school teachers are appointed from the list of eligibles, as certified by the Bureau of Civil Service.

Public school teachers enjoy tenure of office as provided in the constitution and by Commonwealth Act No. 171. Since teachers are civil service servants they cannot be removed or suspended from the service except for cases provided for by law. Teachers are also protected by law against assault and physical injuries by parents, students, and other persons while in the performance of their school duties. In addition teachers enjoy special privileges, such as vacation pay, maternity leave, sick leave, reduced medical fees, study leave, and compulsory insurance. They are entitled to a retirement from the government service upon reaching the age of sixty-five or at fifty-seven if the teacher had rendered at least thirty years of service.

Although school officials and teachers in private schools, colleges, and universities are not covered by tenure laws enjoyed by public school teachers, the Social Security Act of 1954 provides that all teachers employed in private institutions be members of the Social Security System. The system gives the private school teachers protection against disability, unemployment, sickness, old age, and death. The bureau of private schools requires all private schools to have the teachers under contract and that teachers cannot be dismissed from the service without just cause.

In the Philippines teachers are recogized as leaders and are accorded respect that is due to them as members of the profession.

PROBLEMS AND GOALS
OF PHILIPPINE EDUCATION

The Philippine educational system is faced with several problems. They are discussed briefly in the following paragraphs.

A HIGHLY CENTRALIZED ORGANIZATION. Mass education was introduced by the Americans in 1901. Since then growth in school population has been phenomenal. One of the most important problems that the schools now face is that of modernizing the system itself. At the time when the present educational system was established there were no duly established local government units that could support the schools. The schools were administered and supervised from the central office in Manila. Today there is a need for decentralization so that local units can be given some responsibility for the operation of the schools.

COMPETENCY OF THE TEACHING STAFF. During the school year 1959 in the elementary schools, 68.41 percent of the teachers were eligible and 31.59 percent were ineligible. In the secondary level, 48.50 percent were eligible and 51.50 percent were ineligible. In the vocational schools, 30 percent were eligible and 70 per cent were ineligible. Since civil service examinations are not conducted frequently, the Bureau of Public Schools has to resort to its own competitive examinations in order to select teachers for employment from among those who are ineligible. Steps have been taken to up-grade the lot of the teachers, such as scholarships, seminars, workshops, and in-service training.

SCHOOL PHYSICAL FACILITIES. The causes for lack of school buildings seem to stem from several factors: (a) lack of adequate appropriation for additional classrooms to meet the ever-increasing enrollment, (b) lack of appropriations for repairs, and reconstruction of old or destroyed school buildings, (c) unsystematic faulty and haphazard allocation, distribution, and release of public funds for school buildings, and (d) losses caused by natural calamities. The government recognizing these grave shortcomings has passed a bill during the last session of Congress providing specifically for construction of school buildings.

STUDENT POPULATION AND ITS WELFARE.

(a) Oversized classrooms. The oversized enrollment per class in most Philippine schools in the elementary level is not conducive to effective teaching and learning. Some of the classes have been filled to fifty or more pupils which is beyond the physical facilities of the classroom to the detriment of efficient teaching. Studies on effective teaching seem to indicate that thirty-five to forty pupils per class in the elementary grades would be just right if not ideal.

(b) Lack of textbooks. In many of the schools there is an apparent lack of textbooks. Many of these textbooks are also outdated. Textbooks in physics, biology, and other natural sciences are many years behind such that their contents are no longer authentic in the light of modern discoveries and advancement. The last war destruction, the ever-increasing school population, and the slow governmental support for purchases of new textbooks seems to prevent the public schools from supplying the pupils with enough textbooks. In 1959 it was estimated that the public schools had a ratio of one textbook to every twenty pupils.

(c) Restoration of Grade Seven. The Educational Act of 1940 reduced the number of grades in the elementary school from seven to six. In the United States and other countries the length of the elementary schooling is eight years. It is very important that the seventh grade be restored in the school system of the Philippines.

(d) Multilingual problem. The dialect in the locality (vernacular) is now used in the public schools for grades one and two. The Filipino national language and the English language are taught as separate subjects. The English language becomes the medium of instruction from grade three and upward to college. Filipino language is taught as a subject from grades three up to college. Spanish language is taught as a subject starting with the high school and also in college. And yet in the United States, James Conant reported that the American six-three-three-four system is not doing satisfactorily to produce good and useful graduates, in spite of the fact that English language was uniform in all schools as language of instruction.

(e) Large number of dropouts. In a study on the number and percentages of pupils surviving each grade level, conducted by the bureau of public schools and confirmed by a similar survey by the national economic council in 1959, it was revealed that of every one hundred pupils who started in grade one in the public schools, forty-five finish grade four, nineteen finish grade six, and only four finish high school. The reasons given for this poor attendance is either that the parents saw no progress in the children or that the latter lost interest in their schooling.

NATIONALISTIC TRENDS IN EDUCATION. In addition to carrying out the constitutional as well as congressional mandates, the schools are taking the initiative in inculcating nationalistic ideals starting in the early grades. Steps have been taken to secure or microfilm documents all over the world on Philippine materials that may help historians to revise textbooks on history in accordance with the true facts supported by original documents so that students will be presented a true picture of their past and present. Textbooks in other subjects are constantly being revised in order to include Filipino facts and data with the aim of developing among the students better knowledge of the Philippines.

GEARING THE SCHOOL CURRICULUM TO THE NATIONAL PROGRAM OF ECONOMIC DEVELOPMENT. In consonance with the national program of economic development the department of education adopted the following: (a) revision of state colleges' curricula, giving more emphasis and coordinating programs on expanded vocational courses and activities without prejudice to basic education which is essential in democratic way of life, (b) revision of the curricula of the different vocational schools, such as, agricultural, fishery, arts and trades, and other vocational activities, and improving the types of instruction adopted to meet the demands of local community life as well as the demands of national economy, and (c) intensification and coordination of the home industries program.

Since 1966, some major concerns have been better teaching of sciences, reducing the dropout rate, especially at the secondary level, providing more qualified teachers, and providing better physical facilities for education.

The schools have to provide the necessary know-how and the required manpower to conduct, continue, and bring to fruition the government's effort toward economic sufficiency.

REFERENCES

ALDANA, BENIGNO V. *The Educational System of the Philippines.* Manila: University Publishing Company, Inc., 1949.

Bureau of Public Schools. *The Revised Philippine Educational Program.* Manila: Division of Adult Education, 1958.

GALANG, ZOILO M., and FLORO, Exequiel. *Encyclopedia of the Philippines,* Vol. IX. Manila: McCullough Printing Company, 1950.

GREGORIO, HERMAN C. *School Administration and Supervision.* Manila: R. P. Garcia Publishing Company, 1961.

ISIDRO, ANTONIO. *The Philippine Educational System: Its Foundation and Practice.* Manila: Manila Educational Enterprises, 1947.

―――. *Principles of Education Applied to The Philippines.* Manila: Alemars, 1952.

LIM, MANUEL. *Shortcomings of the Philippine Educational System, Remedial Measures Adopted, and Proposed Solutions.* Manila: Department of Education, 1959.

ORATA, PEDRO T. *Education for Better Living.* Manila: University Publishing Company, Inc., 1953.

Philippine Board of Educational Survey. *A Survey of the Educational System of the Philippine Islands.* Bureau of Printing, 1925.

UNESCO, Philippine Educational Foundation. *Fifty Years of Education for Freedom, 1901-1951.* Manila: National Printing Company, Inc., 1953.

UNESCO. *World Survey of Education 1950-1954.* Berichthaus, Zurich: 1958.

U. S. Operations Mission to the Philippines. *A Survey of Public Schools of the Philippines, 1960.* Manila: Operations Mission, 1960.

THAILAND

T. S. Turbyfill

The Thai (or Siamese) are descendents of a people who about 2000 years ago lived north of the Yangtse River in the comparatively small area which today constitutes Szechwan Province in western China. Through successive migrations and conquests of indigenous populations, primarily the Khmer, they gradually occupied the central portion of the present country, and in 1257 founded a center of government at Sukhothai. During the Sukhothai era the Thai alphabet was developed largely from Khmer script, borrowing a large number of words from Pali. In 1330, the ruling King founded Ayudhya as the capital city. Ayudhya was completely destroyed by an invading Burmese army around 1767, and in 1782, Rama I of the present dynasty established Bangkok as the capital. Unlike other countries of Southeast Asia, Thailand was never colonized by European powers.

Thailand was an absolute monarchy until a bloodless *coup d'etat* of June 24, 1932, converted the nation to a constitutional monarchy under a provisional constitution. The first Constitution was proclaimed on December 10, 1932. On May 11, 1949, a Declaration of the Council of Ministers changed the name of the Kingdom from Siam to Thailand (Freeland). With only some minor changes in fundamental laws, the constitution of 1932 lasted until March 8, 1952, at which time a new constitution was adopted based largely on that of 1932. On October 20, 1958, a bloodless *coup d'etat* led by army officers took over the government, abolished the constitution, declared martial law for the country, and began to draft a new constitution patterned somewhat after a parliamentary type of government. This situation exists at the present time.

In theory, the King is Head of State, exercising legislative power by and with advice and consent of the Interim Legislature, executive power through the Council of Ministers headed by the President of the Council (Prime Minister), and judicial power through Courts established by law. In actual practice, since 1958, the Prime Minister has virtually dictated the government and assumed extraordinary powers under provisions of martial law. The draft of the new constitution is continuing, provisions of which receive wide publicity as they are agreed upon by the constitutional committee.

Thailand at present extends from the 5th to the 21st degree north latitude and from the 97th to the 106th degree east longitude. Thus, the country is rather long and narrow with an overall length of 1,020 miles, a coastline of 1,300 miles, and an area of 200,198 square miles, thus comparable in size to the state of Texas. The population is approximately thirty million people.

On the east and northeast, the Mekong River forms much of the boundary with Laos and Cambodia. A mountain range, densely forested, separates the Kingdom from Burma on the west and northwest. The extreme northern part of the country consists of mass mountain ranges, from which rise four rivers which unite in the north central area of the country and form the Chao Phya (river), the country's largest river, flowing southward through the center of the country. The valleys of the tributary rivers are highly suitable for cultivation of rice, tobacco, soy beans, and contain large stands of teak. Central Thailand is a vast flat alluvial plain on either side of the Chao Phya, is inundated during the rainy season, and thus is admirably suited to the growth of rice. Rice is Thailand's chief product and chief export. The eastern part of the country is a plateau, with insufficient moisture for rice cultivation, and is largely a cattle grazing area, supplemented by a silk-weaving industry. Southern Thailand is a long, narrow peninsula extending from the head of the Gulf of Thailand to Malaysia, and it abounds in fruit, rubber, and tin.

A large part of the country is still underdeveloped although comparatively fertile. Only slightly more than 15 percent of the country is under cultivation, and consequently economists consider that it could support a considerably larger population. Some 80 percent of the population engage in farming, but the country is making a concerted effort toward industrialization. Industries being developed include cement, tobacco, silk, steel, canneries, plywood, glassware, paper, sugar, gunny-bags, galvanized sheet metal, clothing, and various other minor endeavours. Hydro-electric power is also developing extensively, and tourism has become a major source of foreign exchange.

About 95 percent of the population is Buddhist, which is the state religion. The social, intellectual, and political life of the country is greatly influenced by Buddhist philosophy, and most literature and art are based upon Buddhist history, thought, and traditions. However, there is complete freedom of religion and religious beliefs, and two other religious groups practice freely in the country—Christians and Moslems. Buddhism is a part of the curriculum in all schools except Moslem and Christian missionary schools. The Moslem population is concentrated in the southern provinces bordering Malaysia.

EDUCATIONAL HISTORY

Prior to 1851 there was no formal system of education or established schools in Thailand. Except for members of the royal court, education was strictly a family affair, and all training was of an apprenticeship nature. Parents who wished to have their children, primarily sons, learn to read and write, would send them to live in a *Wat* (Buddhist temple) to be taught by the monks and priests. After learning the basic skills in formal education, they would return home to be trained by the father in the family trade. Only those children whose fathers were in a trade or profession which required the ability to read and write were so educated. The subjects taught in the Wats were reading, writing, Thai, Pali, elementary arithmetic, morality, and manners.

Generally, the ability to read and write was not considered necessary in most professions. Thus, most people, including painters, moulders, carvers, architects, and farmers, were illiterate. Reading and writing was regarded as a trade just as other trades, and it apparently did not occur to the Thai that these abilities were the key to other branches of knowledge and therefore should be considered universally desirable.

Thailand became acquainted with the western system of education during the reign of King Rama IV of the present dynasty (1851-1868), who prior to gaining the crown, had served almost forty years in a Wat, during which time he had learned English. In attempting to establish friendly relations with countries in Europe and America, he engaged a number of Europeans to teach his children English and other subjects and also arranged for the first Thai scholars to study in Europe. His son, King Rama V,

succeeded him, and early in his reign commanded that an announcement be made persuading princes and courtiers to send their sons to a school established within the precincts of the Royal Palace. The new school was divided into two courses, a first course and a second course. Subjects taught were reading, writing, arithmetic, bookkeeping, and civil service, with English added for more advanced students.

During the same period public administrative development was greatly accelerated. Many ministries and governmental departments were established and created a substantial demand for educated officials to serve in various capacities. All students who passed the final examination of the new school were admitted to positions in the Civil Service (a tradition which has affected the attitude of school graduates to the present time), and consequently the school was very popular among the courtiers and people.

During the early part of the present century, government, private, and church schools expanded slowly, and grammar, science, geography, algebra, and geometry were added to the curriculum. King Rama VI initiated the first system of free public education when he issued a proclamation in 1921 requiring all children between the ages of seven and fourteen to attend school until they had completed grade four. Many free government schools were established, but the quantity was much too small to provide for all the children of the Kingdom. Usually, schools were established only in centers of large population.

When the 1932 revolution changed the form of government from an absolute to a constitutional monarchy, one of the new constitutional principles was the establishment of universal general education. An educational Council was established to prepare a national plan for education. When completed, in 1936, the plan provided for a four-year compulsory primary school, and contingency for students to then enter either a three-year lower general secondary school or lower vocational school, after which they could proceed to a three-year upper general or vocational school. These upper secondary schools led to a two-year pre-university school for those wishing to enter universities or to a technical school for those wishing to become more skilled in vocational trades. Secondary education was provided in both government and private schools. Pre-university education was arranged primarily by universities.

In 1951 the government introduced a new national education plan which was a revision of the 1936 plan, the primary feature of which was the introduction of an alternate three-year program after primary school which placed less emphasis on general subjects and concentrated more on manual skills. In 1960, a new Scheme of Education was announced and is the basis of the present school system. In addition to curriculum changes at all levels of education, the new scheme added three grades to compulsory elementary education and reorganized secondary education.

ADMINISTRATIVE STRUCTURE

Thailand is governed by a Council of Ministers chosen by the Prime Minister and constitutionally responsible to the King. Within a general policy framework laid down by the Council, the Minister of Education determines the detailed policy for the public school system and for private schools in the Kingdom and is responsible for administering the school system. Intermediate between the Ministry of Education and the Council of Ministers is the National Council for Education which was established in 1959 and has been assigned some responsibility for the planning of education. This Council, of which the Prime Minister is president and the Minister of Education chairman of the executive committee, also has a specific administrative relationship to the universities in Thailand, and its budget is a part of that of the Prime Minister's Department. The actual authority exercised over the Ministry of Education is still somewhat tenuous, but becoming annually better defined.

The Minister of Education is assisted by a Permanent Under-Secretary of State who is the chief administrative official for the Ministry of Education. The Ministry is divided into Departments with individual responsibility for different levels or types of education, and the Departments are divided into divisions with responsibility for specific aspects of the educational program. Each Department is headed by a Director-General with certain autonomous powers defined by law, making them in some respects independent of the Under-Secretary's office.

In addition to this ministerial organization is a somewhat separate administrative structure which is partly a heritage from the absolute monarchy overthrown in 1932 and partly a means of decentralization of control. The country is divided into seventy-one provinces (Changwads), each administered by a Governor who is an officer of the Ministry of the Interior and possesses considerable legal power within his province. Service Ministries, like Education, are represented at this level by a senior officer who is responsible for technical matters to the Minister of Education (specifically to the Under-Secretary), but administratively to the Governor, making them in a large measure autonomous of the Ministry of Education.

Provinces are further divided into districts (Amphurs), districts into communes[1] (Tambols), communes into hamlets (Mubanes), each with a chief administrative education officer. For education, a third administrative structure is beginning to increase in importance—the municipalities. The capital town of each province, together with a few large district towns, have been given a special municipal status which implies some central budgetary grants, some local revenue rights, and varying degrees of responsibility for local government, including in many instances the control of elementary education.

For supervisory purposes, the educational system is divided into twelve regions, each region consisting of from five to seven provinces. Each region has a Regional Education Officer (Commissioner of Education), whose duties are largely supervisory or inspectorial.

GOALS OF EDUCATION

The *National Scheme of Education,* proclaimed in 1960, became effective at the beginning of the 1961 school year. The aims of education were declared therein to be as follows: (Free translation)

1. The Thai people shall be educated according to their individual capacities, so they will be good moral and cultured citizens, with a sense of discipline and responsibility; good mental and physical health, and with a democratic outlook. They should attain knowledge and the ability to engage in an occupation useful to their country and nation.
2. Boys and girls should receive education in school up to the age of fifteen, at least.
3. Boys and girls should strive to gain knowledge and experiences that will serve useful purposes in their lives.
4. Education should be carried out to serve the needs of the individual as well as those of society, in harmony with the economic and political systems of the country. It shall comprise, *inter alia* [sic]:

   a. Moral education—that aspect of education which deals with ethics and refinement, moral responsibility, and with the spirit of service.
   b. Physical education—that aspect of education which deals with the promotion of good health, mental and physical, and a sporting spirit.
   c. Intellectual education—that aspect which deals with the improvement of thinking, and with the acquisition of knowledge, techniques, and principles conducive to a useful and happy life.
   d. Practical education—that aspect of education which deals with habits of industry and perseverance and with the training in manual skills that are basic to good living and a useful occupation.

THE SCHOOL SYSTEM

The school system is organized under a unified Ministry of Education. The Ministry of Education is divided into Departments which are further subdivided into Divisions, and Divisions into Sections. Each Department is responsible for a particular type

---

1. Groups of villages or hamlets.

and level of education. Specific organization and basic responsibilities are as follows:

1. Office of the Secretary to the Minister, with responsibility for political relations, educational policy, and public information.
2. Office of the Undersecretary, which exercises administrative control over Regional, Changwad (provincial) and Amphur (district) Education officers, and also has responsibility for external affairs, public relations, and cultural activities.
3. Department of Secondary Education, responsible for secondary schools (public and private), textbooks, curriculum, and in-service teacher training.
4. Department of Elementary and Adult Education, responsible for nursery schools, kindergartens, public and private elementary schools, and adult education.
5. Department of Vocational Education, responsible for vocational and technical schools.
6. Department of Teacher Training, responsible for teachers' colleges, teacher certification, intensive short courses for in-service training of teachers, and in-service training of teachers' colleges teachers.
7. Department of Physical Education, responsible for national stadium, training teachers and supervisors of physical education, Boy Scouts Brigade, and Junior Red Cross activities in the schools.
8. Department of Educational Techniques, responsible for preparation of educational materials, educational information, educational research, and vocational guidance.
9. Department of Religious and Cultural Affairs, responsible for monasteries, board of priests, religious culture, and teaching priests.
10. Department of Fine Arts, responsible for preserving and promoting national art and culture in Thai tradition.

The administration of schools is somewhat complex, and rests upon tradition as well as legal bases. In the provinces, both public and private schools are under the administrative control of the provincial "superintendents" (called Education Officers). Theoretically, these superintendents work under the supervision of Regional Education Officers. Actually, since regional education officers are not members of provincial staffs, they at best can only act as coordinators between the ministry and the provinces.

Each provincial superintendent has nominal control of all teachers and principals in his province, but principals and teachers are also responsible to the Division of Government Schools in the Ministry of Education, as well as to their respective Departments. In the final analysis, the greatest authority rests with the Director-General of each Department.

The school system is organized into three levels—pre-school, elementary, and secondary, basically a two-seven-five pattern.

PRE-SCHOOL EDUCATION. Pre-school education consists of two types of kindergartens. The first is a two-year kindergarten attended by children age three to five. The second is a one-year kindergarten, usually attached to a primary school, which children ordinarily enter at age five. However, these schools are a comparatively unimportant part of the school system since less than 3 percent of children entering grade one have attended pre-school classes. Thus, for practical purposes, the education system is a seven-five one, except for some vocational schools which provide six years of secondary education.

ELEMENTARY EDUCATION. Elementary education is divided into two levels—four junior grades and three senior grades. The first four grades are compulsory, and the aim of the Kingdom is to as rapidly as possible extend compulsory education through grade seven. There were in 1966-67 over 23,000 elementary schools in the Kingdom which enroll over 4,000,000 students; approximately one-eighth of the total population. It is estimated that some 90 percent of all children of primary school age are in school, and that 96 percent of all children attend school at one time or another. However, a large number of students never achieve functional literacy because of a number of problems.

Primary education advanced so rapidly after World War II that a critical shortage of schools, teachers, equipment, and instructional materials exists throughout the system.

Curriculum: The curriculum of the elementary school with the subjects and hours of instruction per week is generally as follows:

Lower Elementary School (Grades 1-4)

SUBJECT	HOURS PER WEEK
Thai	7
Social Studies	6
Elementary Science	3
Mathematics	3
Physical Education	3
Art Education	3
Total	25

Upper Elementary School (Grades 5-7)

SUBJECT	HOURS PER WEEK
Thai	4
English	3 (5)*
Social Studies	4
Elementary Science	3
Mathematics	4
Physical Education	2
Art Education	2
Practical Arts	8 (6)*
Total	30

*School choice

SECONDARY EDUCATION. Secondary education, enrolling in 1965 about 200,000 students, is divided into two streams—academic and vocational. Each type of school admits students who have completed grade seven and successfully passed a secondary entrance examination.

1. Academic High Schools: The academic high school is divided into two levels, the lower school consisting of grades eight to ten and the upper school consisting of grades eleven and twelve. The upper two grades are commonly called "pre-university" which indicates their purpose of preparing students to enter the universities. Of the total public high schools in the Kingdom, approximately 70 percent have only the lower three grades, and the other 30 percent contain all five grades.

Approximately half the secondary students in the country attend private secondary schools, due primarily to the lack of seats in the public schools. Private secondary schools ordinarily encompass only the lower three secondary school grades.

Less than 30 percent of the students completing grade ten go on to grade eleven, and approximately 55 percent of these eventually complete grade twelve.

Curriculum: The subjects and weekly allocation of time in class instruction hours of the lower secondary school is as follows:

SUBJECT	HOURS PER WEEK
Thai Language	4
English Language	4 or 6
Social Studies	4
Science	3
Mathematics	5
Health Education	2
Art	2
Practical Arts	4 or 6
Total	30

There are no electives except in the fine and practical arts areas. The upper secondary or "pre-university" school is divided into two courses, pre-university arts and pre-university science. Subjects and weekly allocation of time is as follows:

PRE-UNIVERSITY ARTS		PRE-UNIVERSITY SCIENCE	
Thai Language	5	Thai Language	3
English Language	8	English Language	6
Social Studies	5	Social Studies	3
General Science	4	Physics, Chemistry, and Biology	8
Mathematics	2	Applied Science	2
Arts or Trades	2	Mathematics	6
Electives*	2	Arts or Trades	2
Total	30 hours	Total	30 hours

*Mathematics or a second foreign language.

A third "general" course is planned for this level, the curriculum to be as follows:

SUBJECT	HOURS PER WEEK
Thai Language	3
English Language	4
Social Studies	3
General Science	4
Mathematics	2
Arts or Trades	2
Commerce	4
Vocational Subjects	4 or 8
Electives from any of the areas	4
Total	30

2. Vocational Secondary Schools: Vocational Secondary Schools are divided into two levels, a lower vocational level providing a three-year curriculum (grades eight to ten) in such trades as building and construction, cabinet-making, masonry, painting, blacksmithing, metal work, leather craft, small-boat building, weaving, tailoring, home economics, auto mechanics, and agriculture. This type of school is diminishing. Higher vocational level (grades eleven to thirteen) provides a three-year curriculum in carpentry, building construction, commercial, secretarial science, engineering trades, tailoring, arts and crafts, agriculture, welding and sheet metal, radio and telecommunications, electrical, machine shops, and auto mechanics.

The curriculum of the lower vocational schools consists of seventeen hours of regular academic studies and a minimum of thirteen hours of vocational training weekly. In the upper vocational schools, vocational subjects comprise eighteen to twenty-four hours weekly of student time, and academic subjects comprise twelve hours weekly.

In addition to these vocational schools, the Department of Vocational Education is responsible for six Technical Institutes of junior college level, grades fourteen and fifteen. The Technical Institute in Bangkok is much more extensive and has a more comprehensive program than the five others located in the larger provincial towns. Students enter the technical institutes after completing the higher vocational schools, and can pursue two-year courses in auto mechanics, radio, electricity, building construction, carpentry, metal works, machine shop, secretarial training, accounting, retailing, tailoring, home economics, surveying, printing, photography, industrial arts, and vocational teacher training.

There are 198 vocational schools in the country. However, except for the technical institutes, most of them are specialized secondary schools with only 90 preparing skilled workers for industry, and a large number of these offer only agriculture or carpentry.

As in most Asian countries, vocational training is seldom the first choice of students and consequently for the most part vocational students are unsuccessful applicants for academic training. The condition is further aggravated by the fact that most of the schools are poorly equipped, have too few and poorly trained teachers, and materials for instruction are in short supply. A major effort to change these conditions has been planned by the government. Of the total number of students in secondary schools, approximately 15 percent are enrolled in secondary vocational schools.

TEACHER TRAINING. Except for the College of Education and the Faculty of Education, Chulalongkorn University, the twenty-six teacher-training colleges of the Kingdom are of either two-year or four-year curricula (approximately half of each type). Students enter the teacher-training colleges after completing grade ten. However, they can enter the last two years of the four-year colleges after completing pre-university secondary school. Generally, those who complete the two-year program are trained for elementary schools, and those completing the four-year program are trained for secondary schools. Unfortunately, students entering teacher-training schools represent the low average of the graduates from the lower secondary schools since the ablest students seek pre-university training with the aim of gaining admission to the universities.

Teacher-training colleges graduate each year approximately 5,500 students, which represents about half of the yearly demand for teachers. There is universal recognition of the need for a concerted effort to expand both quantity and quality of teacher graduates in order to meet the demands for trained teachers at all levels of education in Thailand.

The College of Education is a degree-granting institution with a regular four-year program of studies leading to the bachelor's degree and also trains a small number of students for the master's degree, a further two-year program. Also granting degrees in Education is the Faculty of Education, Chulalongkorn University. In addition to teachers graduating from this four-year program, students graduating with degrees from other faculties in this and other universities can achieve a teaching certificate after a one-year program of studies in the Faculty of Education.

HIGHER EDUCATION. The universities of Thailand are all state institutions (no private universities are allowed), financed and controlled as a part of the Office of the Prime Minister. Coordination of policy and budget is effected in principle through the Secretariat of the National Council, whereas in fact each university has a large degree of autonomy exercised through its own particular governing body. This condition is further amplified by the tradition of appointing high government officials (usually ministers) as chancellors of the universities. The universities are patterned generally after British institutions of higher learning.

There are seven universities in Thailand: *Chulalongkorn University,* with Faculties (schools) of Education, Commerce and Accounting, Political Science, Engineering, Architecture, Arts, and a graduate school. *Kasetsart University,* with Faculties of Agriculture, Fisheries, Forestry, Veterinary Science, Eco-

nomics and Cooperative Science, and Irrigation Engineering. *Thammasat University,* with Faculties of Liberal Arts, Law, Political Science, Economics, Social Administration, Commerce and Accountancy, and Public Administration. *The University of Medical Science,* consisting of nine faculties and a graduate school of medicine. Three of the faculties are faculties of medicine at different teaching hospitals. The other six are: Faculty of Dentistry, Faculty of Pharmacy, Faculty of Public Health, Faculty of Tropical Medicine, Faculty of Medical Technology, and Faculty of Medical Science. *Silpakorn University,* with Faculties of Painting and Sculpture, Thai Architecture, Decorative Art, and Archaeology. *Chiengmai University,* (opened in 1964), with Faculties of Humanities, Natural Science, and Social Science. The Faculty of Medicine, Chiengmai Hospital will later be transferred to this university, and other faculties will be added in the future. *The University of the Northeast* (Khonkaen), initiated in 1965, with Faculties of Agriculture, Engineering Science and Arts.

Universities in Thailand enroll approximately 17,000 students with some 2,200 graduating annually.

ADULT EDUCATION. The Ministry of Education initiated a program of adult education in 1940, now carried on by the Division of Adult Education in the Department of Elementary and Adult Education. This division is responsible for adult schools and adult education programs below university level, public libraries, and operates a training center for community development workers. Although adult education training facilities are not very extensive, optimistic estimates by the government give present adult illiteracy as 30 percent (1960) as opposed to 68 percent in 1940. There is a concerted opinion among those best informed that functional illiteracy is considerably higher than 30 percent as all persons who have attained some degree of schooling are considered as being literate, whether or not they can actually read and write the Thai language.

TEACHERS

The teaching profession is highly respected in Thailand, as evidenced by the fact that the highest form of address is to call an elderly respected person "teacher."

All teachers, including university staffs, are civil servants, and consequently their salaries, ranks, and privileges are based upon education and experience and are comparable to other government employees. Thus, their salaries equate to salaries in other public service professions. Upon retirement from the civil service at age sixty, or at an earlier age for specified reasons, they receive a pension for life based upon past salary and years of service.

All public and private teachers under the Ministry of Education are required by law to belong to the Teacher's Institute, a quasi-official organization set up by the Teachers' Act of 1945. The objectives of the Teacher's Institute are to "protect the interests of teachers and to promote their education and welfare." It also organizes training courses for teachers and maintains a teachers' hostel in the capital city, Bangkok. All teachers pay annual dues.

The executive committee of the institute consists of the Minister of Education as Chairman, the Undersecretary of State for Education as Deputy Chairman, and all the Directors-General as *ipso facto* members. Other members are teachers with at least ten years service elected at an annual conference for four-year terms. Consequently, it is closely allied in all respects to the wishes of the Ministry of Education. The Executive Committee also acts for the Civil Service Commission with respect to public teachers in the matters of discipline and promotion.

Of the total teaching force in the elementary school, 73 percent are men and 27 percent women. In the secondary schools, 55 percent are women, and 45 percent men. By the Ministry of Education's definition for a qualified teacher, approximately 70 percent of the elementary teachers, 49 percent of the vocational teachers, and 35 percent of the secondary and teacher training teachers do not hold minimum qualification credentials. Slightly less than 4 percent of the entire teaching force hold college degrees. This comparatively low status of qualification for teachers is due largely to the rapid expansion of the educational system after World War II, particularly since the early fifties.

The average work load for elementary teachers is twenty-five hours per week and for secondary teachers, eighteen hours per week. Average class size for elementary schools is 40-45, for secondary schools 35-40, and for vocational schools, 32-37. Average teacher-pupil ratios respectively are 1-32, 1-29 and 1-18.

Teachers are hired on a yearly basis, and are on duty in the schools for 204 calendar days. Including sick, annual, and "business" leave, teachers are allowed up to seventy days absence from their duties annually, exclusive of holidays. They also may be granted educational leave, during which time their salary is continued, and they either must work toward obtaining degrees or raising their qualifications. Usually, educational leave is for one year, but in many instances it is granted for longer periods of time. The teaching profession has exceptional holding power, and teacher attrition from all causes is estimated at slightly over 3 percent annually.

FINANCING OF THE EDUCATIONAL SYSTEM

All government schools in Thailand, including the universities, are financed from the national budget. No revenue for schools is raised from local sources, although in many instances a local community will contribute, largely in kind, to the construction of a new building. Each department in the Ministry of Education obtains an annual budget, approved by the Budget Bureau, for the purposes of salaries, equipment, buildings, subsidy, and miscellaneous expenditures.

All government schools are theoretically free up to the higher secondary level (pre-university). At this level students are charged fees which are primarily used for school equipment, libraries, and sports.

Private schools, owned and financed by private individuals or groups, receive small subsidies from the Ministry of Education for the purpose of helping pay the salaries of properly qualified teachers. At the secondary level, almost half of the total student population attend private schools, and consequently are charged tuition sufficient to cover the cost of their education. The number of private schools at the elementary level is insignificant. Generally, students enter private schools because there are not sufficient "seats" in Ministry of Education schools to accommodate them. Private schools at the secondary level are encouraged by the government to help relieve the financial burden of the rapidly expanding secondary system.

Universities in Thailand are financed entirely from the National budget and, since no private universities are allowed, the entire cost of university education, exclusive of student tuition charges, is borne by the government.

From 18 percent to 20 percent of the national budget annually is appropriated for educational purposes. The government declared its intention (in 1964) to increase the total budget for education 10 percent annually for a minimum of ten years. Even at this rate of increase, there is serious doubt as to whether the education system can expand rapidly enough to satisfy the demands for education, particularly as compulsory education is being raised from grade four to grade seven, hopefully to be accomplished by 1970.

MAJOR PROBLEMS IN EDUCATION

The most critical problems of the schools of Thailand are directly related to the complementary effects of rapid population growth and rapid expression of the educational system since World War II. Taken together, these conditions would strain the resources of a country which already had a well-established educational system, with a major portion of the students of school age enrolled in school. Since the country had a comparatively small system, partly due to lack of normal growth during the war years, all problems have been compounded during the last decade.

Foremost among the most critical problems is the shortage of qualified teachers. This shortage is likely to continue for some years as expansion of teacher-training facilities, also handicapped in progress by a shortage of qualified teachers at this level, is too slow to keep apace with the expanding elementary and secondary school systems. Since the teacher-training schools at the present time annually graduate only approximately half the teachers needed each year, the gross number of unqualified teachers will continue to increase for the foreseeable future, although the ratio of qualified to unqualified teachers will improve slightly.

Related problems also exist in classroom shortages, equipment, instructional supplies and textbooks. Taken together, these problems have manifested themselves in an extraordinarily high failure rate at all levels and grades in the school system. The situation is worst in grade one where 40 percent of the pupils fail annually. The "chain reaction" effects of such a condition are obvious for a system which already has a shortage of all elements needed for conducting a school system.

Despite the relative rapid expansion of graduates from all the levels of the educational system during the past decade, there is a pressing need for even greater acceleration of the system due to the gradual evolution from an almost completely agrarian society to more emphasis on industrial development. Vocational and technical schools in the Kingdom are too few, and those which exist are poorly staffed, equipped, and housed. To further aggravate this situation, traditionally, students do not aspire to vocational training but much prefer academic training with the expectation that this will lead to civil service jobs. Since civil service jobs are limited in most sectors and opportunities for higher education are relatively few, a growing surplus of graduates from the academic secondary schools constitute a corps of restless, dissatisfied adults with resulting implications for social and political unrest within the country.

At the university level, a need exists for many more graduates in the fields of teaching, engineering, medicine, and agriculture. In other fields, graduates are equal to or exceed demands. Although great efforts are being made to expand university education, this level is also greatly handicapped by a shortage of teachers. Since highly trained technicians command from two to four times the civil service salaries earned as university teachers by taking positions in private industries, no practical solution to the university staffing problem has been devised.

Other problems relate to lack of schools in rural areas, the reluctance of teachers to go to rural areas, the reluctance of parents to send their children to school after grade four, poor school attendance, and problems inherent with low standards of living.

The government of Thailand recognizes all of these problems and is earnestly striving to solve them as soon as possible. One obvious obstacle is the lack of the financial resources needed for rapid development. Another is the lead time needed for increasing the effectiveness and efficiency of lower levels of education due to the necessity of first developing teacher training colleges, which in turn depend on university graduates for faculty, and the universities are already seriously understaffed.

Consequently, a number of decades will be needed to attain universal elementary education and develop the desired standards in higher levels of education.

BIBLIOGRAPHY

Reports and Publications of the Royal Thai Government

Brief History of Education in Thailand: Department of Educational Techniques, Ministry of Education, 1960.

Educational Statistics, Ministry of Education, Published Annually.

Annual Report of the Ministry of Education, Ministry of Education.

Reports and Publications of International Agencies

Level of Education: Thailand, 1960, Statistical Study No. 2: UNESCO Bangkok, January, 1963.

Educational Developments in Thailand, 1949-1962 Reports to the International Conferences on Public Education Organized by UNESCO and the International Bureau of Education: Ministry of Education, 1962.

A Changing Secondary Education in Thai Culture: by Temsiri Panyasingh and Maurice A. McGlasson. UNESCO 1963-64.

Documents

Education in Thailand, Abhai Chandavimol, Thailand, 1963.

Education in Thailand, External Relations Division, Ministry of Education, Bangkok, 1960.

A Study of the Role of Secondary Level Education in Human Resource Development in Thailand, Ministry of Education, Office of the Undersecretary, Educational Planning Office, March, 1964.

Preliminary Assessment of Education and Human Resources in Thailand, Joint Thai-USOM Human Resource Study, 1963.

Universities in Thailand, Kamhaeng Balankura, Bangkok, Thailand, 1964.

The National Education Council of Thailand, Kamhaeng Balankura, National Education Council, Bangkok, Thailand, 1964.

General

BUSCH, NOEL F. Thailand, An Introduction to Modern Siam. Princeton, N. J.: Van Nostrand Press, 1959.

VIETNAM

Nguyen-Dinh-Hoa

Vietnam is a land where scholarship is highly respected, and education has always been encouraged by the state. Education traditionally has been a sure means to fame and success, and knowledge is greatly sought after by everyone who is able to obtain it.

In the past, education in each village was provided in private schools, and private tutors were often hired individually and sometimes for a group of better families. Mastery of the Chinese Classics let the students through regularly held civil service examinations which opened an official career to the rich and the poor alike.

Apart from strictly Buddhist examinations, the national dynasties of Ly (1009-1225), then of Tran (1225-1413), held a set of competitive examinations known as *tam giao* examinations aimed at checking on the candidates' mastery of all three religious doctrines—Confucianism, Buddhism, and Taoism. After deliberate attempts by the Minh conquerors (1414-1427) to impose Chinese civilization, reforms in education were carried out under the independent Lê Dynasty (1428-1527) to give particular recognition to successful candidates in the Confucian-oriented state examinations. Throughout modern times marked by strife and division, struggle (1527-1592) between the Lê and the Mac usurpers, then between the rival families of Trinh and Nguyen (1674-1774) followed by the emergence in 1765 of a third family, the Tay-Son who succeeded in destroying the Trinh but later lost to the Nguyen, classical education continued to be dispensed until Chinese studies finally had to yield to Western scholarship.

The foundation for a Western-oriented educational system was laid soon after the French colonial rule began. Attempts were made to expand formal schooling, and a program of French-Vietnamese education was inaugurated. But the system was inadequate in many respects, its progress rather slow, and the rate of illiteracy very high.

Since Vietnam regained independence, however, the bulk of national efforts have been concentrated on extending the frontiers of knowledge to the most remote corner of the land, and mass education has been promoted on a par with formal education given in ever-increasing public and private institutions.

TRADITIONAL EDUCATION

Early Chinese Studies

Vietnamese began to study Chinese characters in the early days of Chinese domination, and probably as early as in the time of Trieu-Da (207-137 B.C.) the founder of the Kingdom of Nam-Viet (Nan-yueh). Education was, however, first formally organized only since the days of Si-Nhiep (Shih Hsieh), who was Governor of Giao-Chi from 187 to 226 A.D. and whose efforts to encourage Chinese studies and spread Chinese techniques were both successful and appreciated.

The early system of education was very rudimentary. The standards of education were not very high, either, and all famous native students at that time studied in China (Ly Tien, Ly Cam, Truong Trong). The independent Ngo (939-965) and Dinh (968-980) dynasties did not last very long and were more preoccupied with military reorganization and government reforms than with education. Instruction was indeed carried on only in Buddhist monasteries, after the first emperor of the Dinh dynasty created a hierarchy of priests and built several temples.

Formal education in Vietnam in those days had the objective of preparing for the two main learned professions—the Buddhist priesthood and government service.

Buddhist Education

Training for the Buddhist clergy was conducted in temples and monasteries through the medium of Chinese written characters. Ly Cong-Uan, the founder of the Ly Dynasty (1009-1225) was raised in the Co-

Phap Temple by a monk named Ly Khanh-Van, and was instructed by another monk, Ly Van-Hanh. Nguyen Hien, a famous scholar, also spent all his youth in a Buddhist temple. Under the Ly (1009-1225) and the Tran (1225-1413), although Confucian ethics and rites dominated government activities, Buddhism itself contributed to the popularization, or at least expansion, of Chinese studies. Missions were sent to China for sacred texts, and Buddhist monks were honored as teachers as well as doctors and astrologers.

Aside from the rigorous training for the novitiate which led, through an involved hierarchy, to membership in a monastic community, Buddhist teachings were dispensed through several writings of great value.

There was, of course, some instruction which Buddhist monks gave the laity, and there were also Buddhist masses, Buddhist services held on different occasions, and a rather extensive Buddhist literature.

Confucian Education

Other type of education, which, in theory at least, led to the civil service examinations, constituted the principal concern of State schools as well as that of private schools, and at the same time contributed to a considerable development of Confucian culture. Private schools were kept in villages or market-towns by scholars variously called *thay-do, thay khoa, thay tu, cu do,* and *cu nghe.* Most of the teachers were retired officials, all of whom had received full academic titles. Many teachers had thousands of students. Such famous scholars as Chu Van An, under the Tran, Phung Khac Khoan, Nguyen Binh Khiem, Le Qui Don, under the Lê and Vo Truong Toan, Nhu Ba Sien, under the Nguyen, had the credit of having trained generations of good citizens.

As the end of feudal revolts and threats of invasion from the north enabled the development of arts and letters, Emperor Ly Thanh-tong (1054-1072) established the Van-mieu or Temple of Literature at the southern gate of Thang-Long in 1070. It housed the statues of Confucius and of his four principal disciples as well as the images of seventy-two sages. But it was also a school reserved for princes and children of high-ranking officials.

Emperor Ly Nhan-Tong (1072-1127) created the National College, called Quoc-tu-giam in 1076, and the first literary examination was held then for the recruitment of mandarins.

Under the Tran dynasty (1225-1413) new schools were opened at the capital and other important centers. The National College was opened to the youth while famous scholars taught Chinese classics in private schools. At the end of the fourteenth century, the usurper Ho-Qui-Ly ordered elementary schools created in every administrative unit of the nation in order to make education available even to needy children.

With the Lê dynasty (1428-1527), Chinese studies reached their fullest popularity. Existing schools were reorganized, and new ones were opened. Curricula were revised. During the reign of Emperor Le Thanh-Tong (1460-1497) libraries were set up, and specialists were appointed to the task of teaching Chinese classics in institutions of higher learning. The National College was expanded by adding new classrooms and facilities to accommodate recipients of scholarships. With a view to encouraging learning, officials decided to have names of successful candidates in doctoral examinations engraved on stone slabs displayed in the Van-mieu courtyard.

Beginning with the sixteenth century, Chinese studies spread from Tonkin and North Annam to Central Annam and Cochinchina due to Vietnamese and Chinese scholars attracted by the Nguyen dynasty.

Once he had unified the country, Emperor Gia-Long (1802-1819) followed the Lê system of civil service examinations in its rough outline. His successors all contributed structural reforms. Emperor Minh-Mang (1820-1840) gave classical education both great development and strong organization, which explains why during the entire nineteenth century Chinese letters still enjoyed the prestige which they had known under the Lê.

Much of the education—technical and ethical—was imparted outside monasteries and schools. Members of trade guilds through their apprenticeships ran their own varieties of vocational education, which provided skills in handicrafts and in commercial methods as well as in Chinese calligraphy. Farming techniques were transmitted from fathers to sons. Women, although not eligible for public office and therefore not admitted to the schools which prepared for the civil service examinations, were by no means uneducated. Private tutors were hired in better families to initiate their daughters into the mysteries of the printed page. Mothers taught their girls how to manage a household, how to behave in courtesy and propriety and how to prepare for their duties toward their future husbands and mothers-in-law.

School Life

Teaching in the old days was a serious business, the teacher remaining very dignified and the students extremely respectful. Confucian ethics placed the teacher above the father and second only to the emperor. When a teacher died, his students wore mourning for three years. Students of the same school usually were members of a *hoidong-mon,* formed either by the teacher or the students themselves. The most successful, or the oldest among the students, would be chosen by the teacher as headman (*truong-trang*) to look after his condisciples with the assistance of a *giam-trang* or a *can-trang.*

When the teacher needed some help, the students offered it to him. At his death or at his wife's, the students would help his eldest son with the funeral. At the funeral the students had to wear white turbans and white clothes and follow the hearse to the cemetery. The period of "heart mourning" (tâm-tang) was three years. On anniversaries of death of the teacher or of his wife, the students made contributions to finance the ceremonies. If the teacher died heirless, the students would gather at the house of the *truong-trang* to offer sacrifices on the anniversary of the teacher's death every year until the *truong-trang* died.

In some areas the students even contributed money to build a hall for the worship of the teacher's soul, or to acquire rice fields whose income would be used for the same purpose, thus allowing the perpetuation of the cult in the memory of their teacher and his wife.

There was complete freedom in instructional procedures, and the relationships between a teacher and his students were very close and informal. The results of such an education should have been very good, but actually the level of education was very low despite the high percentage of literacy among the masses. One reason is that the teacher received no formal training in pedagogy and tended to follow the same methods by which he had been taught himself. Beginning children were taught a few primers, the purpose of which was to make them commit to memory quantities of maxims and proverbs in rhyme or clichés about Chinese history. The deep meaning of the texts was beyond the pupil's comprehension, and he was expected only to understand the meanings of individual Chinese characters and be able to count the strokes, recognize the 214 "radicals" and distinguish the "even" and "uneven" tones, then match one sentence with another in parallel couplets. After those few primers became known by rote, the teacher would start to teach books about Chinese history, the Four Books and the Five Classics—repertoire of the Sung scholars. The teacher would merely give the meaning of each written symbol, making sure to follow the orthodox interpretation. In an essay the students were expected to use all the set phrases taken from the prescribed books.

COLONIAL EDUCATION

As soon as South Vietnam (Cochin-China) became a colony the government abolished literary examinations and schools for Chinese characters. A system of French-Vietnamese schools was instituted. The reform program in North Vietnam (then called Tonkin) and Central Vietnam (then called Annam) was slower. In 1908 there appeared a Council for the Improvement of Education. The program of studies comprised four levels.

The primary level consisted of two parts: an elementary part, where the medium of instruction was Vietnamese, and the next higher level, where French was used more extensively. The teachers, all

Vietnamese, were controlled by French inspectors and by native educational officials called *doc-hoc* and *giao-thu*.

The "higher primary" level of instruction was given in such schools as were created in Saigon, Hue, Hanoi, Haiphong, and Namdinh, where teachers were graduates of the Higher School of Pedagogy or holders of the *licence*.

Secondary education proper was dispensed at the Lycée du Protectorat in Hanoi, the Khai-Kinh Lycée in Hue, and the Petrus Ky Lycée in Saigon.

In the beginning, local degrees were awarded: the Certificate of Elementary Primary Studies which may be acquired at the end of the third year, the Certificate of Primary Studies, at the end of the sixth year, the Diploma of Higher Primary Studies, at the end of the tenth year, and the French-Vietnamese *Baccalauréat*, at the end of the thirteenth year. Later, the same schools prepared the students directly for the metropolitan *Baccalauréat*. A number of privileged Vietnamese students were admitted into the French lycées in Hanoi (Albert Sarraut), Saigon (Chasseloup Laubat), and Dalat (Yersin).

A School of Medicine was created in Hanoi in 1902, and since 1917, the University of Indochina developed around this nucleus. Next to such technical schools as the School of Agriculture and the School of Public Works, there were a School of Fine Arts, a Faculty of Law, and a Faculty of Medicine and Pharmacy, where from 1933 Vietnamese students could prepare for the M.D. degree.

A Directorate of Public Instruction was responsible to the French Governor-General for the technical control of all the public and private schools in the colony and for the development of educational policies to be applied to Vietnam, Cambodia, and Laos.

EDUCATION SINCE INDEPENDENCE

When Vietnam came into existence as a free and independent nation, the Vietnamese had inherited an educational system which was traditionally bookish, theoretical, and therefore antiquated. All forms of practical skills were looked down upon, and science and technology were much neglected. The vast majority of the population was illiterate. The French-borrowed system of education had little relevance to the needs of a developing country determined to establish itself among the nations of the modern world.

Efforts to change the inadequate system at the beginning were limited, but the past twenty years tell a story of steady educational development.

Today, free education, with modern methods and approaches, is being expanded in the cities and spread deep into the hamlets. Responding in many directions to the demonstrated yearning of the people, especially the humble, to achieve schooling for their children, the government maintains high priority for education despite the demands of a war of self-defense against Communist aggression.

In 1966-1967, there were 1,957,310 children attending primary school, over three times the figure for 1954, the year of partition.

There were more than 31,000 elementary teachers. With building continuing, there were more than 6,500 elementary schools in the nation, with nearly 31,500 classrooms.

In 1970, elementary enrollment is expected to reach more than 2.8 million, and to grow from there.

The Problem of Language

The medium of instruction at the primary level and in the 621 secondary schools continues to be Vietnamese. The problem of language poses itself in an imperious manner. During the first cycle of secondary education, students are required to take only one foreign language for four years (six hours per week for the first two years, then five hours per week for the following two years). But beginning with the fifth year, a second foreign language is added to the first one so that graduates of Vietnamese high schools will be equipped to follow full lectures in foreign universities where either French or English is the language of instruction. On the other hand, the use of Vietnamese as the vehicle language throughout university courses is being intensively promoted through translations and publications of textbooks and glossaries, thus readying the Vietnamese language for handling even medicine and other advanced sciences.

Levels of Instruction

After kindergarten, a student in the Humanities ordinarily follows the five-seven-three program. The seven-year secondary program is sanctioned by examinations at the end of the fourth, sixth, and seventh years (or ninth, eleventh, and twelfth grades). Slight specialization begins after the first cycle (four years) of secondary education: the teenager then can elect to follow for three years either a science education (natural science or mathematics) or a liberal arts education (languages). The high school graduate is eligible to enter university courses.

High school enrollment for the year 1966-67 was 431,171 as compared to the 1954 figure of 55,000 students. The fourteen-year period since Geneva has also seen an increase in the number of secondary school trained teachers to 10,212.

Five universities are presently operating in Saigon, Hue, Dalat, and Cantho. Three of them are national universities whereas Dalat University is a private Catholic institution and Van-Hanh University, located in Saigon, is Buddhist-endowed. Each college or faculty within a university offers a different program. At present, over thirty thousand students are taking courses in Law, Medicine, Pharmacy, Dentistry, Sciences, Letters, Architecture, and Education. Degrees granted include the licentiate and the doctorate.

Technical and vocational training, mass education and adult education receive due attention from the authorities. The Phu-tho Complex called the National Technical Center, and the College of Agriculture, Forestry and Animal Husbandry will help the expansion of the industrial sector and the modernization of agriculture. A National Institute of Administration trains administrative officers and government workers for all echelons. Private schools, where both elementary education and secondary education are given, lend a helping hand to the government. The campaign against illiteracy is in full swing, and the ultimate aim is to add another million or so to the ranks of literate citizens, who incidentally can take advantage of numerous opportunities for post-school education through evening classes.

Success of an overall educational program, of course, depends largely on the number of teachers trained each year. Several normal schools and the Faculties of Education, of Sciences, and of Letters will continue to feed trained teachers and professors into all educational institutions in the nation.

Future plans necessarily have to be conceived in terms of basic needs on the primary level although the secondary and tertiary levels are constantly kept in mind. If the needs of three million school children are to be fulfilled, teacher-training institutions should turn out a large reinforcement contingent of some 35,000 to assist those presently on the payroll. A model high school has been operating in Thuduc right on the new campus of the University of Saigon. The Faculty of Medicine now has a new site in Cholon where a teaching hospital will be built. Students and faculty members are being sent abroad, mainly to the USA, Canada, England, Australia, and France to receive further training.

The role of Vietnamese women in the educational picture has always been important. Women's greatest contributions remain in the domain of family education in the home, and kindergarten (the Vietnamese equivalent for which is, incidentally, "mothers' education").

A National Education Council was set up in 1964 to make recommendations for the re-orientation and reorganization of the educational system. Education was to make a more direct contribution to the achievement of national objectives of economic, social, political, and spiritual progress.

Behind the program of educational reforms is the concept that education is a vital national investment, a major determinant of economic growth. The government is now putting special emphasis on science and technology at all levels. The secondary curriculum offers a wide range of elective subjects in technical and commercial studies, home economics, agriculture, and industrial arts—subjects unknown in the past.

Much remains to be done, but as the National Education Conference held in Saigon in 1964 enunciated it, Vietnamese education has to be humanistic, national, and scientific. Vietnamese are determined to create favorable environments and opportunities for every citizen to make progress according to his ability and aspirations, and to train the technicians needed by the nation.

BIBLIOGRAPHY

Department of National Education, Republic of Vietnam. *Secondary Education Curriculum.* Saigon: Department of National Education, 1960, 158 pp.

Education in Vietnam. Special Edition published by the Review Horizons Saigon: Review Horizons, n. d. 16 pp.

Education in Vietnam 1965. Saigon: Ministry of Education, Department of Research and Planning, 1965, 47 pp.

Embassy of Vietnam. *Education in Viet-Nam.* Washington, D. C.: Embassy of Vietnam, 1959, 9 pp.

FALK, CHARLES J. *Educational Survey in Central Viet-Nam.* Saigon: U. S. Operations Mission to Vietnam, 1956, 78 pp.

———. *Higher Education in Viet-Nam.* Saigon: U. S. Operations Mission to Vietnam, 1956, 89 pp.

"The Growth of Education in Viet Nam." *Vietnam Press Bulletin,* No. 2742, July 14, 1963, pp. 5-8.

HICKEY, GERALD C., and VO HONG PHUC. *Research Report on the Department of Education.* Saigon: Michigan State University Vietnam Technical Assistance Project, 1957, 86 pp.

HICKEY, GERALD C., and others. *Report on the Organization of the Department of Education.* Saigon: Michigan State University Vietnam Technical Assistance Project, 1956, 26 pp.

KEATLY, ROBERT. "Vietnam Universities vs. Reformers." *The Wall Street Journal,* October 6, 1967.

LAVERGNE, D. C. and SASSANI, ABUL H. K. *Education in Vietnam.* Washington, D. C.: U. S. Department of H. E. W., Office of Education, 1955, 23 pp.

LE QUANG HONG. "Compulsory Education in Viet-Nam," *Compulsory Education in Cambodia, Laos and Viet-Nam.* Paris: UNESCO, 1955, pp. 115-154.

National Education Study. *Education Vietnam: Proposals for Reorganization (Elementary, Secondary, Vocational, Technical, Adult),* 322 pp.

NGUYEN DINH HOA. *Higher Education in the Republic of Vietnam.* (Vietnam Culture Series No. 6) Saigon: Directorate of Cultural Affairs, 1963.

———. *Higher Education in Viet-Nam from the Early French Conquest to the Japanese Occupation.* Ms. 1951.

NGUYEN KHAC KHAM. *The Acceptance of Western Cultures in Viet-Nam* (from the 16th century to the 20th century). Saigon: Directorate of National Archives & Libraries, 1966, 39 pp.

NGUYEN VAN THUAN. *A Survey of Vietnamese Occupational Prestige and Aspiration.* Saigon: Michigan State University Vietnam Advisory Group, 1962, 41 pp.

PHILPOTT, GLADYS. "Vietnamese School Gongs Sound," *NEA Journal,* September, 1967, pp. 22-23.

PIKE, EDGAR N. "Adult Education in Vietnam." *Program Bulletin of The Asia Foundation.* San Francisco: The Asia Foundation, 1959, pp. 1-3.

Public Universities of the Republic of Vietnam. Report of the Wisconsin State University-Stevens Point, Foundation, Inc. in contract with the United States Government, Agency for International Development, USAIS/Saigon. April 1967, 85 pp.

Saigon University Bulletin. 1966. Saigon: Republic of Vietnam, Ministry of Education.

Secondary Education in Asia. Bangkok: UNESCO, 1961. (Reprinted from World Survey of Education: III. Secondary Education.)

SHAFFER, H. L., JR. "Literary Examinations in Old Viet-Nam," *Viet-My,* Vol. 8 (March 1963), pp. 38-45.

THOMPSON, VIRGINIA, and ADLOFF, RICHARD. *Cultural Institutions and Educational Policy in Southeast Asia.* New York: Institute of Pacific Relations, 1948, 86 pp.

Vietnam Press. "1967 year of gain for Vietnamese National Education Program." Bulletin No. 4392, Morning Edition, January 22, 1968, pp. A-1 to A-5.

VU TAM ICH. "A Historical Survey of Educational Developments in Vietnam," *Bulletin of the Bureau of Social Service* (University of Kentucky), 32 (Dec., 1959), pp. 1-135.

WCOTP. *Impact on Education of Terrorist Activities in Viet-Nam.* (Report of WCOTP Commission of Inquiry, May 18-26, 1962, Vietnam.) Washington, D. C.: World Confederation of Organizations of the Teaching Profession, 1962, 22 pp.

Part Three

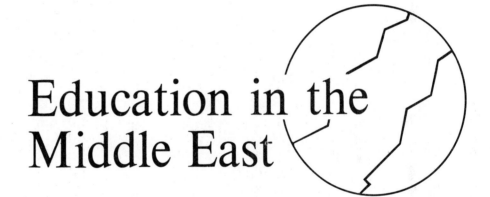

Education in the
Middle East

AREA ESSAY: THE MIDDLE EAST

Patricia Lei Alzobaie

An area as old as civilization itself, a land rich in oil and fertile land but poor from deserts and rocky mountains, the countries of the Middle East are a study in contrasts. Skyscrapers stand side by side with remains of civilizations which were rich in culture while Europe lay asleep. Hand weavers, goldsmiths, and donkeys are neighbors to modern oil refineries, factories, and late-model car import agencies. Passing by the old and the new are women in veils and those dressed in the latest Parisian styles, men in ancient tribal dress and doctors and professional men schooled in the latest western technology, and children who seem at home being a combination of the old and the new.

The people in this area are usually Arabic and usually Moslem, although substantial unassimilated minorities may be found in several countries in the area. There are large numbers of Christians in Lebanon, Kurds in Iraq, and a sprinkling of Persians, Turks, devil worshippers, Sabians, and a multitude of other groups in many of the countries.

After centuries of domination by foreign powers, the Arab countries of the Middle East are currently in a period of strongly developing Arab and nation-centered pride and nationalism, of revolt against the status quo, and of an eager seeking of the knowledge and technology of other countries.

The result of these forces has been a separation of generations. The leading doctors, professors, and other professional men in a country are often the western-educated children of illiterate parents. They leave their countries hoping to acquire the skills of other nations of the world to further the aims of Arab nationalism. They return to find that their absence, itself an attempt to help nationalism, has separated them from the forces of the movement.

Parents and children fail to understand one another, and so do the religious and non-religious, cultural conservatives and liberals, and Western and non-Western oriented Arabs.

The Moslem religion permeates all facets of the lives of the majority of the people in the area. Religion is not a once-a-week event but is so embedded in the culture as to make a definition of what is a part of the Arab culture and what is Islamic an impossibility. The dedicated follow Moslem tenets dedicatedly, and the modern reject them, while both groups mirror the attitudes, values, and linguistic manifestations of the religion.

Such a setting has created many educational problems in this part of the world. Education indigenous to the area consisted of religious schools, whose sole function was to teach the tenets of Islam, the ability to read the Koran, and very basic skills. The modern educational system, as it exists today, is largely an importation. It is often one that does not fit the Arabic Moslem culture of the area.

The Arabic countries of the Middle East have wide differences between the farmers and other members of the working classes and the wealthy landed classes. There is a growing middle class composed of teachers, lawyers, doctors, and small businessmen. The lower classes have discovered that education is the key to social mobility, and they are sending their children to school in numbers that the existing educational structure is straining to accommodate. Anti-illiteracy campaigns are under way, aiming to reach the parents as well as the children. Night classes for workers, groups of college students and teachers sent into rural areas, and attempts at Bedouin education programs are under way. However, the budget and human resources of the countries are taxed, often beyond endurance, to keep pace with the growing interest in education and the population expansion.

Elementary education in particular is faced with problems arising from class differences. It is faced with having to meet the needs of the lower classes for basic health, economic, and practical education, along with providing a program of value to the middle- and upper-class children.

The Arabic language presents educational problems. Vast differences exist between written classical Arabic and the language spoken by the people. It is as though American school children were asked to learn to read, write, and speak the language of Chaucer, and to use this language as a vehicle of instruction for acquiring other subjects in school. This is the language that is used in newspapers, on radio and TV, and by educated people in conversation.

An attempt has been made to expose unassimilated minorities to the Arabic language of the cultural majority. Such attempts have been faced with strong opposition. Each minority group strives to preserve its national and linguistic entity. Many solutions to this problem have been tried, with varying degrees of success.

Faced with the problem of education for numbers of people beyond what the educational system can handle, these countries have often adhered to a system of public examinations to determine who shall be allowed to continue on to higher levels. While not accepted in America, such a system may be justified in the context of a country that has need for large numbers of highly educated people, but which has facilities for providing an education for only a limited number of students.

This program of government examinations has resulted in a more rigid curriculum than might be desired. The needs of various groups in each of the countries are not met as they might be under a more flexible system. Teachers teach for the examinations, not for the needs of the students. However, faced with the need for trained people, with space for limited numbers, even the critics are unable to propose an alternate solution.

Vocational education as an alternative to academic preparation has not generally met with a great deal of success. With education viewed as the means to social mobility, the emphasis is on reaching a level of education that will enable the child to hold a white-collar job, generally government-sponsored. There is a stigma on doing even skilled labor among the classes with a minimum of education. The goal of education is viewed as being an escape from such a fate.

Education of women in the Arab Moslem culture presents another problem. A wide gap exists between the modern women and those who are tradition-oriented. Efforts are being made to make special provisions for the education of women, with special encouragement being offered.

Elementary education is often coeducational, secondary seldom, and a choice of higher education on a coeducational or segregated basis is often offered as a solution. The structure for the education of women exists, but not all levels of society are culturally ready to avail themselves of the structure. However, there is a growing body of professional women in all of the countries of the area.

The contrast between city and country life presents still another problem peculiar to the area. In some countries, there exists a surplus of teachers in large cities and an acute shortage in rural areas. Once educated, the typical person is reluctant to return to the area from which he comes. Attempts are made in some countries to accept students from all areas of the country into teacher-training institutions, in the hope that a percentage of them will return to their native areas as teachers. The problem remains, however, of the best teachers remaining in the big cities, with the less capable teachers going to the very areas where the best teachers are needed.

The Arab countries of the Middle East remain an area of contrast and problems, where both are accentuated rather than solved by education. It is an area where much is being done to try to solve the problems that exist. The problems are unique to the area, a result of historical and social forces, and require creative solutions. They are problems that have been a long time in developing, and they will require a long time for solution.

Education in Arab countries of the Middle East has the advantage of being enthusiastically supported by society and of having men and women who are eager to help solve the problems of the nations and people to whom they have a strong loyalty, with whom they have a firm identification, and with whom they have an even stronger and firmer pride.

BIBLIOGRAPHY

Dodge, Bayard. *Al-Azhar; A Millennium of Moslem Learning.* Washington: Middle East Institute, 1961.

"Iraq." *International Yearbook of Education,* Vol. XXV, 1962-63, pp. 186-188.

Hans, Nicholas. *Comparative Education: A Study of Educational Factors and Traditions.* London: Routledge and Kegan Paul Limited, 1958.

Mallinson, Vernon. *An Introduction to the Study of Comparative Education.* London: Heinemann, 1961.

Reller, Theodore L. *Comparative Educational Administration.* New Jersey: Prentice-Hall, Inc., 1962.

Rugh, Douglas. "Education in Arab Countries of the Near East," *Comparative Education,* Arthur Henry Molhiman, ed. New York: Henry Holt and Co., Inc., 1951.

Thut, I. N., and Adams, Don. *Educational Patterns in Contemporary Societies.* New York: McGraw-Hill, 1964.

U. A. R. Ministry of Education. *Report on Development of Education in the U. A. R. in 1959-60.* Cairo, U. A. R. Education Documentation Center, 1960.

AFGHANISTAN

Clarence Linton

Afghanistan is a landlocked mountainous country surrounded, on the north, by the Union of Soviet Socialist Republics; on the east, by the Peoples' Chinese Republic, Kashmir, and West Pakistan; on the south, by West Pakistan (Baluchistan); and on the west, by Iran. Its total area is about 250,000 square miles, roughly the size of the state of Texas and in approximately the same latitude. Kabul, the capital city, is about the same distance east of Greenwich as New York City is west, the difference in time between Kabul and New York City being nine and one-half hours.

The entire country is dominated by the Hindu Kush Mountains and their subsidiary ranges, which form a part of the great Asian highland extending from Turkey to eastern China. The Hindu Kush take off from the Pamir Knot ("Roof of the World") and extend about 600 miles southwestward through the heart of the country forming the divide between Central and Southern Asia.

From prehistoric times until the thirteenth century A.D., nomadic or seminomadic peoples from the steppes of Central Asia have migrated into the Oxus Valley (valley of the Amu Darya) which is shared by the U.S.S.R. and Afghanistan. After establishing themselves here these peoples moved westward into Iran and southward across the Hindu Kush into southern Afghanistan and northern India. Chronology for the earliest invasions is not precise but the sequence is known. First the Aryans took possession of all this area becoming the basic ethnic element in Afghanistan, Iran, and northern India. They were followed by Iranians (People of the original Aryan element whose name is a derivative of "Aryan"), Greeks, Scythians (Saka) Parthians, Yue-chi (Kushans), Ephtlalites (White Huns), Turks, Arabs, and finally by Mongols.

Afghanistan was a crossroads of migration, trade, and cultural diffusion for more than two thousand years. The great silk route between China and India

and to the western world passed through Afghanistan. It was by this route that Buddhism entered China and the Far East. It was principally through northern Afghanistan and its ancient city of Balkh that East-West caravans passed.

People of Afghanistan today, officially estimated to total 13,500,000, being principally of Caucasoid and Mongoloid races, representing a score or more of ethnic groups, and speaking more than a score of different languages, are, nonetheless, united by common patterns of family and tribal life and by religion. All the peoples who have become part of the present population either had or acquired similar values and ways of life. The extended family was and still remains the basic social and economic unit in all ethnic groups. Fully two-thirds of the total population is still tribally organized. About one-seventh of the population is either nomadic or seminomadic. Approximately four-fifths of the people live in villages and at least 85 percent earn their living by agricultural pursuits. More than 99 percent of the people are Muslims, about 80 percent being Sunni and 18 percent Shia.

Afghans are proud of their past, of having been a part of several great empires of Central and Southern Asia, of having on occasion the center of power within her borders, and of having cities which were at times world famous, particularly Balkh, Ghazni, Herat, Kandahar, and Kabul. But Afghans are also prone to find excuses for their present illiteracy, poverty, and backwardness in forces beyond the control of their forebears or themselves, and therefore assumed to be the will of Allah (or fate). They tend to think too much about the destruction and devastation of Genghis Khan and his Mongol hordes in the thirteenth century; about the negative effects of the extinction of the East-West overland trade routes beginning in the sixteenth century; about the rivalries between European powers with respect to Afghanistan, particularly between the British in India and Czaristic Russia in Central Asia in the nineteenth century; and about the injustice and chagrin as well as the impoverishment caused Afghanistan by the three Anglo-Afghan Wars in the nineteenth and twentieth centuries.

People of Afghanistan today are facing many of the same problems faced by other developing countries in their present-day aspirations to play a dignified and effective role among modern nations.

PRE-ISLAMIC EDUCATION

There are no historical records bearing directly on education in Afghanistan prior to the beginning of the Islamic period, about the middle of the eighth century, but one may assume that some kind of education of the young did exist and that it was similar to that prevailing in neighboring countries. Most children and youth received only informal education by means of family membership, village life, and occupational activities. There may have been some rudimentary schools which provided a modicum of formal education for children of the elite as a necessary preparation for positions of leadership, as is known to have been true in Iran, with which country Afghanistan had close cultural and political ties prior to the Islamic period.

ISLAMIC EDUCATION FROM 750 TO 1900

Since the Arab conquest of Afghanistan was not completed and Islam was not firmly established until the middle of the eighth century, the pattern of formal Islamic education, which became similar in all Islamic countries, could not have been introduced into Afghanistan before that time.

Religious motivation for learning the teachings of the Prophet, on the part of the people in general, and for becoming religious teachers and scholars on the part of a few, gave rise to "mosque" schools (also called "Koranic" and "mullah" schools) throughout the Islamic world. Such a school, when it existed, was usually conducted in a mosque or in some other available place by a mullah (religious teacher), or other "learned" person, for young boys of varying ages. The students sat on the floor or ground in front of or around the teacher. The primary purpose was to teach the boys to read the Koran orally in the Arabic idiom with approved pronunciation, accent, and intonation. This was accomplished by having the students first listen to the teacher as he read aloud a verse or two, then the students repeated in chorus a word or phrase at a time in immediate imitation after the teacher. This process might be repeated many times, after which the students were required to practice aloud individually until they had memorized the assigned passage. Each student was then required to recite for the class what he had been assigned. Interpretation of the meaning of the verses read was given by the teacher, but grammar

was delayed until some proficiency in reading and writing had been attained. Practice in writing was usually done on a small smooth board with a reed pen and a white fluid made by mixing water with chalk or white clay. Models of writing were set by the teacher and copied by the students. When utensils were not available, students sometimes copied the models in sand or soil with their fingers or any available instruments. To reading and writing, elementary arithmetic, particularly as related to almsgiving and inheritance according to Islamic teachings, was sometimes added.

In mosque schools there was no prescribed amount of work to be accomplished nor any common standard of proficiency. Occasionally an able student was given private instruction and, in some instances, might travel to distant places, even to other countries, to study under famous teachers. It is not known how many mosque schools there were in Afghanistan or what percentage of boys attended them, but it is believed that only a few attended for a short time and that those who became scholars were exceptions.

For the preparation of mullahs and other religious scholars there were a few special religious schools at the secondary-school level (though they often contained primary school classes as well) in cities. These schools were called "madrasa." These institutions were sometimes famous because of learned instructors and many students. Samarkand (across the Oxus to the north of Afghanistan) in the ninth century, Ghazni in the eleventh century, and Herat in the fifteenth century (both in Afghanistan) were noted centers of Islamic learning. In addition to religious studies, mathematics, astronomy, philosophy, history, geography, and sometimes vernacular languages were taught.

Private instruction of children (both boys and girls) of the wealthy at home seems to have occurred in Afghanistan as elsewhere from very early times.

STATE EDUCATION FROM 1900 TO 1964

The first state schools were established by Amir Habibullah Khan in 1004. These were one combination primary-secondary school and a military school. The former, called Habibia College, was intended for the preparation of boys for government service. There were at that time very few persons literate enough to serve as clerks or in administrative positions. School administrators, teachers, and textbooks were imported from Muslim India. While the Koran and theology were also taught, Habibia College was the first school in Afghanistan to emphasize secular studies. It was necessary for most boys for many years to enroll first in the primary classes (grades 1-6) and many students remained in school only a short time. It was not until 1931 that the first seven boys were graduated from the twelfth (highest) class.

In 1909 the first primary school, as such, was established. It is said that the first primary schools were much like the present day village schools (described below), with one or two teachers who had been trained privately or in mosques. These schools at first were held in mosques but were later housed in rented or government-owned buildings. The main purpose of these schools was to teach reading, writing, arithmetic, fundamentals of Islamic religion, and civics.

The first steps toward the establishment of a teacher-training institution were taken in 1912 in the capital. Apparently at first this was little more than a school providing primary education for boys with some attention given to methods of teaching. The demand for teachers was greater than this institution could supply. At times boys who had completed the work of class six were allowed to teach in the lower primary classes. At other times those who had completed class nine were allowed to teach in any of the primary classes. Eventually students were required to complete the work of class twelve in order to graduate, but always it has been necessary to permit persons to teach in primary schools who have not graduated from this teacher-training institution.

After the Third Anglo-Afghan War and the attainment of Afghanistan's independence from British control of its foreign relations by Amir Amanulla Khan in 1919, a new impetus was given to state education. The first school for girls was opened in Kabul in 1921, and a considerable number of boys and girls were sent to Turkey, France, and Germany to study. Three additional primary-secondary schools were established in the capital: Esteklal Lycée, with the assistance of French administrators and teachers in 1921; Nedjat Oberrealshule, with the assistance of German administrators and teachers in 1924; and Ghazi College, with the assistance of British administrators and teachers in 1926.

Progress was retarded for a number of reasons. There was an acute shortage of qualified Afghan teachers, textbooks were inadequate or nonexistent, and instructional equipment and supplies had to be imported at great expense. All schools were closed for a time during the disturbances following the abdication of King Amanullah in 1929. Afghanistan was neutral during World War II but was handicapped educationally because some foreign teachers had to leave the country and it was difficult to obtain instructional materials from abroad. Despite these and other obstacles, the Ministry of Education from 1929 on began to open schools in provincial cities. By 1932 there were a total of twenty-two state schools (apart from military schools) with a total of 1,350 students and 105 teachers.

Immediately after the end of the second World War, Afghanistan began to seek the help of other countries in solving her educational problems. In 1949 a mission of the United Nations Educational, Scientific, and Cultural Organization was invited to study the situation and make recommendations to the Ministry of Education. UNESCO sent a specialist in teacher education in 1951 and has continuously maintained specialists and teachers in Afghanistan since that time. In 1952 the United States of America, through a contract with the University of Wyoming, began to send specialists and teachers in agriculture, engineering, and related subjects. In 1954 a similar contract with Teachers' College, Columbia University, provided a team of teacher-education specialists to supplement the assistance of the University of Wyoming and UNESCO. During the intervening years the United States has renewed and expanded these contracts and arranged with several other universities for the assistance of special missions and for members of the regular staff of the Education Division of the USAID Mission in Afghanistan. Other countries also have provided assistance in education through bilateral agreements with the government of Afghanistan, including foreign lecturers in Afghanistan and study grants for Afghans in the respective countries.

In 1956-57 the First Five-Year Plan of Economic and Social Development was inaugurated by the government of Afghanistan. The Second Five-Year Plan was completed in 1966-67.

A new constitution was adopted in September, 1964, which stresses the responsibility of Afghanistan to provide primary education for all children.

The Ministry of Education is drafting a basic education law, which, for the first time, attempts to bring into one statute all the pertinent decrees, orders, and regulations under which state education is conducted.

GOALS OF EDUCATION

Today the immediate or short-range goals of education in Afghanistan, as viewed by both the people and their government, are conceived principally in terms of individual aspirations, such as: (1) to become a good Muslim; (2) to become an effective member of family and village (or city); (3) to become literate; and (4) to qualify for a good position. These are traditional goals and they remain basic. In addition, educated persons and especially government leaders are thinking today in terms of social, economic, and political goals which embrace the well-being of the state as well as the individual. These are more remote or long-range goals, such as: (1) to qualify for advanced education in order to qualify for positions of greater responsibility and leadership; (2) to improve the economic and social status of the individual and thereby of the nation; (3) to increase equality of opportunity and thereby social mobility; (4) to increase loyalty and commitment to national goals; and (5) to prepare the people for increasing participation in the determination of public policy.

Since only about 10 percent of the boys and 1 percent of the girls of school age are now in school, formal education still plays a minor role in the lives of most Afghans. However, there is a large measure of agreement among educated and uneducated Afghans alike on the characteristics of the good Afghan. Despite ethnic differences, there is a basic unity in Afghan society. There is almost universal agreement that a good Afghan must first of all be a good Muslim, meaning that he must believe the tenets of the faith and observe its ritual to the best of his ability, and behave in a manner becoming a good man. Modesty, sobriety, bravery, honesty, truthfulness, piety, loyalty, hospitality, and self-respect are inculcated in the home, and children in school are admonished to work hard to acquire these virtues as well as skills and knowledge.

Unfortunately, there is as yet little equality of opportunity for formal education, and there cannot be until primary education is available to all.

Obstacles to the Achievement of the Goals of Education

The first and perhaps the most difficult obstacle to the achievement of the goals of education until recently has been insufficient motivation. Until about 1950 this was undoubtedly the major obstacle. Widespread illiteracy (defined as inability to read a newspaper or write a letter—at least 90 percent), ignorance, superstition, and indifference, on the part of most of the people, and fear, on the part of many religious leaders, that secular education would make the young irreligious, kept most boys and nearly all girls out of school. This is said on the assumption that if there had been a desire for education, the government would have found the means of providing teachers and schools. Even today, sixty years after the establishment of the first state school, only one boy in ten and one girl in a hundred are in school. Persistent effort on the part of the government since 1950 is beginning to create a stronger motivation for education as evidenced by the increase in schools and enrollments. By 1961-62, there was a total of 1,426 schools of all types and 233,314 students below university level. Today, in some areas, the government is hard pressed to provide buildings, textbooks, and teachers as rapidly as requested by the people.

It is the belief of the writer that the major obstacle to the achievement of the goals of education today is the lack of a clear and adequate design for the entire educational system. As in other developing countries, Afghanistan is faced with a very difficult problem of needing to do everything at once but without sufficient means. As a consequence, the school system has grown by adaptation and imitation of various features of French, German, British, and American education with too little attention to integration. Serious defects are, in part, the result of failure to come to grips with and find solutions for a number of persistent problems. The most important of these problems is undoubtedly the failure thus far to reinterpret Islam in relation to the demands of modern science and social progress. Inconsistencies between religious and secular education will increase to the detriment of both if this problem is not solved by cooperative efforts of religious and educational leaders. There is at present no comprehensive plan for the education of the children of nomadic groups, estimated to constitute about one-seventh of the total population. Introduction of vital, functional subject matter and modern methods of instruction are largely thwarted by the lack of plan, equivocal sanction by the Ministry of Education, and inadequate professional preparation of teachers. Higher education in Afghanistan will be limited both quantitatively and qualitatively until there is a firm decision with respect to the language or languages of instruction at the university level. Language instruction in the primary and secondary schools should be made to conform to that decided upon for the university. At present Pushtu, Persian, French, German, English, Russian, and, on occasion, other languages are used as the languages of instruction in Kabul University.

This multiplicity of languages presents both instructors and students with a problem beyond their solution. The inevitable result is the perpetuation of memoriter learning of extremely limited amounts of subject matter which students can manage to get into their notebooks. At present almost no reference work can be required of students because either appropriate books are not available or the students cannot read them. In most instances a foreign instructor is limited in what he can present to students by the necessity of pausing often so that his remarks can be interpreted. The questions of the students and the answers of the instructor must also be interpreted. This greatly limits the possibilities of communication between instructor and students and perpetuates the lecture method of instruction. Qualified interpreters and translators are few. It is almost impossible to obtain copies of translations of instructor's notes in time or of a quality to make the effort worthwhile. It is the writer's estimate, based on much experience with such matters, that about one-fourth as much can be accomplished by an instructor under such circumstances as he could accomplish if the students could read, write, and speak the language in which he teaches. This is also a problem for Afghan instructors and for Afghan students when one of their two national languages is used, because very few people are really proficient in both Pushtu and Persian. This latter defect suggests the need for more effective instruction in these languages in both primary and secondary schools.

An acute shortage of qualified teachers and school administrators is a third major obstacle to the achievement of the goals of education. There is at present keen competition among the ministries of government, Kabul University, business, industry, and other employers, including the United Nations and other foreign agencies in Afghanistan, for the very limited number of graduates of the secondary schools each year; and teaching ranks near the bottom of the preference list of careers. There are too few able secondary-school graduates wanting to prepare for teaching and many of those who do enter teaching drop out when opportunities for other employment arise. Among those who meet the present minimum standards are some superior persons and dedicated teachers, but at least half of these teachers need additional professional preparation. It is the estimate of the writer that fully one-half of all the teachers now in service are really unqualified by reason of lack of interest, low ability, or inadequate professional preparation. Fortunately there is general recognition of this problem. The Ministry of Education, with the assistance of UNESCO, UNICEF, and the Teachers' College, Columbia University, Teacher Education Team, is taking the following steps to overcome this obstacle:

First, considerable work is being done to improve the quality of professional preparation of primary- and middle-school teachers in the original teacher-training institution in the capital, which provides a three-year program in classes ten to twelve.

Second, three additional teacher-training institutions similar to the one in Kabul are in process of development in provincial cities, and it is planned that others will be established when qualified instructors are available.

Third, to meet the rising tide of public interest in education, an emergency teacher-training program is now in operation, whereby most of the graduates of the middle schools throughout the country are sent to the four teacher-training institutions for a one-year professional program in class ten, after which they are expected to teach in the primary schools. It should be understood that, even with such limited preparation, these emergency teachers are better prepared than many of the teachers now in service. The gradual upgrading of these emergency teachers through inservice and full-time study, or their eventual replacement by teachers with higher qualifications, is contemplated.

Fourth, a faculty of education has been established in Kabul University, providing four years of professional preparation beyond the secondary school. Its primary purpose is the professional preparation of school administrators, specialists, and members of the staffs of the provincial directorates of education and the Ministry of Education.

Fifth, an academy of teachers is being developed in the capital primarily to train staff for the teacher-training institutions throughout the country. This institution, for the next several years, will be staffed principally by foreign instructors, each of whom will have five Afghan counterparts whom he will train in an on-the-job program and, after foreign study for one or two years, these Afghan counterparts will be assigned as instructors in the existing or newly established teacher-training institutions. This academy will train both men and women counterparts. A second purpose of the academy is to train primary-school teachers. A two-year professional program is provided in classes ten and eleven.

Sixth, a higher teachers' college is being developed in Kabul to train graduates of secondary schools in classes thirteen and fourteen, that is, at the university level, as teachers in middle schools.

There are no teachers' organizations in the country, principally because the government has not permitted them. It is anticipated that such organizations will be encouraged and facilitated under the new constitution. Teachers' salaries are slightly higher than the civil service scale, but the income of teachers is generally lower than that of doctors, engineers, interpreters, translators, and business employees. Indeed, many Afghan domestic servants in the homes of foreigners are paid more than are teachers. The efficiency and interest of many teachers is lowered by the necessity of supplementary employment in order to make a living. The government is attempting to make teaching more attractive by increasing salaries, introducing more democratic procedures in administration and supervision, and by rewarding merit. An annual teachers' day has been established when special programs are given at the schools and the King awards money prizes to outstanding teachers. There are indications that these and other measures are proving effective in raising morale and developing professional loyalty.

In common with most developing countries, Afghanistan is handicapped by lack of sufficient money for education. Despite recognition by the government that education should play a very important role in the social and economic development of the country, as evidenced by the allotment of an estimated 12 percent of the total national income to education, many desirable advances cannot be made, or must progress slowly, until additional money for education is available. The Five-Year plans have been directed toward the development of the economy of the country in the expectation of obtaining more money for education as well as for other purposes.

Among major obstacles to the achievement of educational goals is the preparation of adequate teaching and learning materials, especially textbooks and reference books. This obstacle is made greater by the policy of the government requiring two languages of instruction in the primary and secondary schools, thus necessitating two sets of books at all levels, and by the indefiniteness of policy with respect to the language of instruction at the university level.

At present most graduates of the secondary schools have had six years of English, but a considerable number have had French and a few have had German instead of English. There are a considerable number of foreign instructors at the university level, most of whom must teach in their own language— French, German, English, Russian, or other—and depend on interpreters for communication with students in classes, seminars, and laboratories. Some students are always at a disadvantage, particularly when translations of textbooks, reference books, and lecture notes are not available in the language in which they are most proficient. There is need of a definite and firm decision with respect to (1) languages of instruction at all levels; (2) a plan for the preparation of textbooks and reference books; (3) the training of interpreters and translators; and (4) the translation of textbooks, reference books, lecture notes, and other necessary teaching and learning materials into both Pushtu and Persian. Fortunately, the Ministry of Education has taken an important step in this area by contracting with the Franklin Press, a nonprofit publishing organization with much experience in such matters in Iran, to assist in the training of staff of the Press of the Ministry of Education, in planning programs of production of text and reference materials, including the preparation of translators, and in printing the needed books and other materials. Since 1955 the Institute of Education, the institution through which the Teachers' College, Columbia University, Teacher Education Team, has worked to assist the Ministry of Education and Kabul University, has prepared experimental mimeographed and offset press editions of more than 100 textbooks and supplementary reading books for the primary and secondary schools, including a complete series of textbooks for the teaching of English in classes seven to twelve.

Education in the future in Afghanistan will undoubtedly depend in considerable degree on the solutions found for at least three additional problems. The first is the basic education of the general population, including a marked reduction of the percentage of illiteracy. An extensive community development program and renewed efforts in the promotion of literacy classes for adults, which are in progress, should improve this phase of education markedly. The second problem in this category is the provision of greater equality of educational opportunity for women and girls. The benefits of this may prove greater than many other things deemed necessary. The third problem of great importance to the future of education in Afghanistan is the introduction of democratic ideas and procedures into all aspects of life. There is at present a cautious commitment on the part of government to the solution of these and related problems. Fortunately, certain elements of democratic human relationships are a part of the tradition and practice of Afghan family and tribal life. These elements are reinforced by the Islamic concept of the equality of all men before Allah. The government is giving much thought these days to the goals and methods of democracy. Programs for citizenship education are being prepared for all levels of the educational system.

DESCRIPTION OF THE EDUCATIONAL SYSTEM

Responsibility for the administration and supervision of all aspects of formal education is vested in the Ministry of Education, which consists of the Minister of Education, two deputy ministers of education, presidents of the several departments, and directors of numerous bureaus and offices. The provincial directors of education and their staffs are responsible to the Minister of Education through the respective provincial governors. In addition to the regular school system, certain educational societies and organizations are under the administration and supervision of the Minister of Education but not the Ministry. These include the Society of Ariana Encyclopedia, the Boy and Girl Scouts societies, The Afghan Historical Society, the Public Library, Kabul Museum, the Pushtu Academy, and the Women's Welfare Society.

Religious and secular education, with few exceptions, are combined in the sense that both are financially supported and administered by the state. Islam is the state religion and as such is taught in all state schools. Most of the former mosque schools, which before 1949 were exclusively religious schools, are now village schools, combining religious and secular instruction with some financial support from the state and under the administration of the Ministry of Education. Likewise, the madrasa and the faculty of theology of Kabul University receive some financial support from the state and are, at least nominally, under the administration of the Ministry of Education, or in the instance of the faculty of theology, under the Minister of Education through the Rector of Kabul University.

The new constitution authorizes the conduct of private schools by Afghans—mosque schools, madrasa, and Arabic schools (for memorizing the Koran); and by foreigners, exclusively for their own children. The number of the latter is insignificant. It appears that the government is not prepared at this time to authorize the conduct of secular schools by Afghans for Afghan children.

State education, as distinguished from exclusively religious education, is wholly supported by the state and its control is highly centralized in the Ministry of Education. The authority delegated to provincial directors of education and local school administrators is very limited. In general, textbooks, timetables, methods, length of school year, holidays, and the rules and regulations under which the schools operate are prescribed by the Ministry of Education. The Ministry of Education is presently drafting basic education laws which it is anticipated the new parliament will enact soon. It seems probable that some cautious steps will be taken toward greater participation of parents, teachers, and local school administrators in policy-making and administration. It also seems possible that the people will be invited and facilitated in making contributions to the cost of education through gifts of labor, land, buildings, and materials. This now happens occasionally. Textbooks, equipment, and necessary school supplies are provided by the Ministry of Education. In boarding schools, room, food, uniforms, medical service, and pocket money are also provided by the Ministry of Education free of cost to the students.

There are two national languages of instruction throughout the entire school system from primary school through the university. These languages are Pushtu, which for political reasons is made the official language, and Persian, which for linguistic and cultural reasons must be taught as if it were a second official language. The following policies govern the language of instruction in the primary and secondary schools: (1) The language of instruction is Pushtu in areas where the majority of the people are Pushtu speakers. Instruction in Persian as a second language in such areas is begun in class four. (2) The language of instruction is Persian in areas where the majority of the people are Persian speakers. Instruction in Pushtu as a second language in such areas is begun in class four. (3) In case of doubt about whether the majority of the people of a given area are Pushtu or Persian speakers, the language of instruction shall be Pushtu. Some children in most areas are disadvantaged with respect to the language of instruction because their mother tongue is one of the more than twenty languages other than Pushtu or Persian, and the children of the minority language group are always at some disadvantage. Few people learn Pushtu as a second language voluntarily but most Afghans understand and speak Persian. Pushtu is the language of the dominant ethnic group from which the ruling family comes and the government has taken steps to require all teachers and government officials to learn Pushtu, if it is not their mother tongue. Classes are provided for this purpose, but the requirement is resented by Persian speakers. Pushtu is a more difficult language than Persian, its literature is limited, and few for whom it is a second language become proficient in its use. Lack of interest and inferior teaching result in a low level of proficiency in Pushtu as compared with Persian.

The educational system provides a total of sixteen (eighteen) years of schooling, including six years of primary education (or a combination of village-school and primary-school education), six years of secondary education, and four (six) years of university education (the faculty of medicine requires six years).

Since there is considerable variation in climate because of altitude, the country is divided into warm areas and cold areas. In warm areas the long vacation is taken in the summer and in cold areas, including Kabul, the long vacation is taken in the winter. Because of the shortage of wood for fuel and the cost of oil, which must be imported, most school buildings are not heated.

Primary Education

There are two types of schools at the primary level: village schools, which provide instruction for the first term of primary education, which embraces classes one to three, and the regular primary school, which provides for both the first and second terms of primary education, classes one to six.

Ages of students in primary schools vary. The Ministry of Education offers the following guide but suggests that exceptions may be made by provincial directors of education:

Class 1— 6 to 9 years
Class 2— 7 to 10 years
Class 3— 8 to 11 years
Class 4— 9 to 13 years
Class 5—10 to 15 years
Class 6—11 to 17 years

Subjects taught and the number of periods of instruction for each subject and each class each week in village schools are indicated in Table 1.

TABLE 1

Village School Subjects Taught Per Week

Subjects	CLASSES		
	1	2	3
	Periods per Week*		
Holy Koran	2	2	2
Theology	2	2	2
Pushtu†	5	5	5
Arithmetic	4	4	4
Caligraphy	5	5	5
Total	18	18	18

*Throughout the primary and secondary school classes are normally 45 minutes in length. In the university they are 50 minutes.

†Persian is substituted for Pushtu in areas where a majority of the people are Persian speakers.

There are now more village schools than all others combined. This is in large part the result of an effective attempt of the Ministry of Education to enlist the cooperation of religious teachers in the mosques in providing a modicum of secular instruction in addition to the religious instruction. This has stimulated interest in state education. It is estimated that about half of the students completing the first term of primary education in a village school go on for the second term in a regular primary school. It is significant that the greatest increase in the number of schools for girls is now occurring in this category. In 1956-57 there were 384 village schools for boys but none for girls, whereas in 1960-61 there were 693 for boys and 95 for girls.

The subjects taught and the number of periods of instruction for each subject and class each week in the first and second terms of the regular primary schools are indicated in Table 2.

TABLE 2

Regular Primary School Subjects Taught Per Week

	CLASSES					
	FIRST TERM			SECOND TERM		
	1	2	3	4	5	6
	Periods per Week					
Holy Koran and Theol.	4	4	4	5	5	5
Pushtu*	12	12	12	5	4	5
Persian**	-	-	-	5	5	5
Arith. and Geom.	4	4	4	4	5	5
History	-	-	-	2	2	2
Geography	-	-	-	2	2	2
Natural Science	-	-	-	2	2	2
Drawing and Handcfs.	3	3	3	2	2	2
Caligraphy	4	4	4	2	2	1
Physical Tr.	1	1	1	1	1	1
Total	28	28	28	30	30	30

*Persian is substituted for Pushtu as the language of instruction in areas where the majority of the people are Persian speakers.

**The study of the second national language is begun in class 4.

Instruction in the first term of the regular primary school, as is usually true also in the village schools, is given by one teacher, whereas in the second term it is departmentalized.

The Ministry of Education is attempting to facilitate differentiation in handicrafts, natural science, and other subjects in relation to agriculture, other occupations, and environmental conditions where schools are located. Unfortunately, most teachers are poorly prepared for such adaptation and tend to limit their teaching to the textbooks.

Secondary Education

Secondary education also is divided into two terms: the first term embracing classes seven to nine is called "middle school"; and the second term embracing classes ten to twelve is called "lycée." Often in the initial stage of development, middle-school classes are added to a primary school and later lycée classes may be added to the combined primary-middle school to make a combined primary-secondary school. With increased enrollment in cities the primary classes may be transferred to other quarters to establish a new primary school, leaving the original building and grounds for the exclusive use of secondary-

school classes. Usually vocational and technical school classes are housed separately.

In order to provide advanced schooling for graduates of primary schools in villages and towns where no secondary school exists, a few boarding schools have been established in provincial cities as well as in the capital. These schools usually begin with class seven and add higher classes as students advance. No boarding schools have been established for girls to date.

The maximum age for admission to the seventh class is fifteen.

The subjects taught and the number of class periods for each subject and class each week in the middle school and the lycée are indicated in Table 3.

In the city of Kabul where progress in secondary education for girls is more advanced, girls have the choice of pursuing the regular middle-school and lycée programs, as indicated in Table 3 below, or a

TABLE 3

Middle School and Lycée Subjects Taught Per Week

Subjects	CLASSES							
	MIDDLE SCHOOL					LYCEE		
	7	8	9	10	11			12*
						Sc.	Math.	Phil.
	Periods per Week							
Holy Koran	1	1	1	-	-	-	-	-
Theology	2	2	2	2	2	-	-	-
Religions	-	-	-	3	-	-	-	-
Pushtu†	3	3	3	4	4	3	3	5
Persian‡	3	3	3	3	3	3	3	4
Arabic§	2	2	2	-	-	-	-	-
Foreign Lang. ‖	6	6	6	6	6	4	4	4
Physics	2	2	2	3	3	3	4	2
Chemistry	2	2	2	3	3	3	3	2
Biology	1	2	2	-	3	3	4	2
Geology	-	-	-	3	-	-	-	-
Mathematics#	5	5	5	7	7	7	9	3
History	2	2	2	2	2	2	2	2
Geography	2	2	2	2	2	2	2	2
Civics	1	1	-	-	-	-	-	-
Economics	1	1	1	-	-	-	-	-
Philosophy	-	-	-	-	-	-	-	5
Logic	-	-	-	-	-	2	2	2
Drawing and Handcfs.	1	1	1	-	-	-	-	-
Sports**	1	1	1	1	1	1	1	1
Total	35	36	35	38	36	33	37	34

*Differentiation in relation to academic interest to be pursued in the university

†The language of instruction. See notes on Tables 1 and 2.

‡The second national language.

§Principally grammar, necessary for understanding the Arabic element in Pushtu and Persian.

‖German in one school, French in two schools, and English in all the others. Russian will undoubtedly be the foreign language in a new technical school at the university level.

#Includes arithmetic, geometry, algebra, trigonometry, and calculus.

**Physical education is usually referred to as "sports." Primary attention is given to team games, particularly soccer and basketball.

regular middle-school program followed by either of two vocational two-year programs in the lycée as indicated in Table 4.

TABLE 4

Two-Year Vocational Subjects Taught Per Week

Subjects	PROGRAMS			
	HOME ECONOMICS		TEACHER-TRAINING*	
	Class		Class	
	10	11	10	11
	Periods per Week			
Holy Koran	-	-	2	2
Theology	3	3	-	-
Pushtu†	3	3	5	4
Persian‡	3	3	4	4
Foreign Lang.	4	4	6	1
Physics	2	2	2	2
Chemistry	2	2	2	2
Biology	2	2	2	2
Mathematics	2	2	4	4
History	-	-	2	2
Geography	-	-	2	2
Child Care	2	2	-	-
Housekeeping	3	3	-	-
Tailoring and Knitting	4	3	2	1
Cooking	3	3	-	-
Child Psychology	-	2	1	1
Teaching Methods	-	-	-	2
Drawing and Handcrfs.	3	2	1	1
Total	36	36	35	30

*This represents the first attempt to offer a modicum of professional preparation of women primary-school teachers.

†The language of instruction. See notes on Tables 1 and 2.

‡The second national language.

Vocational and Technical Education

The Department of Vocational Education of the Ministry of Education is responsible for the administration and supervision of all vocational and technical schools, including trade schools, religious schools, and teacher-training institutions below university level. There are a few trade and vocational schools at the middle-school level and there are two teacher-training institutions at the university level—the faculty of education and the advanced teachers' college, both in the capital.

University Education

Kabul University, located in the capital, was established in 1946, the faculty of medicine having been established in 1932. It now includes the following faculties: agriculture, economics, education, engineering, home economics, medicine, pharmacy, law, letters, science, and theology.

Admission to any faculty except medicine is based on the *baccalaureate* awarded to graduates of lycées, or its equivalent for graduates of vocational and technical schools. The faculty of medicine requires applicants to take a preliminary year of physics, chemistry, and biology in the faculty of science before beginning professional studies. The normal program of the faculties is four years in length. Successful graduates are awarded the *license*. The faculty of medicine requires a one-year internship after the completion of the basic four-year program, a total of six years after graduation from the lycée.

The university is administered by a rector who is elected by the university senate with the approval of the Minister of Education. The university senate is composed of the dean and two elected members of each faculty. Its actions are subject to the approval of the rector and the Minister of Education.

A second faculty of medicine is in its ninth year of development at Nangrahor (Jalalabad). It is now under the administration of the university senate and rector of Kabul University. Eventually it will become part of a second university.

Examination System

Generally throughout the primary and secondary schools oral and written examinations are administered three times a year at the end of the first three months, at the end of the first six months, and at the end of the school year. For classes nine and twelve teachers submit questions and the Departemnt of Secondary Education of the Ministry of Education selects those to be used at the end of the school year. The provincial director with the approval of the Ministry of Education designates proctors for these examinations. All students of class twelve are assembled in central places for their final examinations. For all other classes examinations are largely under the control of local school administrators and teachers. There is now some experimentation with objective-type examinations in place of the older essay questions. In a few vocational and technical schools, and generally in the university, examinations are administered twice rather than three times a year. In some instances oral examinations are omitted. Under this system teachers tend to teach with the examinations in mind and students try to get important bits of information in their notebooks which they memorize before each examination.

Table 5 (p. 236) indicates the increase in enrollment in the different types of schools and in the faculties of Kabul University during the First Five-Year Plan (1956-57 to 1961-62).

The increase in enrollment at all levels has been dramatic. For example, in 1966-7 the following numbers of students were enrolled at the various levels: primary, 402,000; middle schools, 36,000; secondary schools, 8,000; technical and vocational schools, 7,000; teacher-training, 6,000; and higher education, 3,300.

TABLE 5

Enrollments in Various School Types, 1956-7 to 1961-2

	NUMBER		
Type	1956-57	1961-62	% Increase
Village Schools	16,421	44,122	169
For Boys	16,421	39,463	140
For Girls	———	4,659	——
Primary Schools	99,672	168,976	70
For Boys	89,660	145,241	62
For Girls	10,012	23,735	137
Middle Schools	4,586	11,179	144
For Boys	3,705	8,748	136
For Girls	881	2,431	176
Lycees	1,088	2,915	168
For Boys	900	2,287	154
For Girls	188	628	234
Vocational and Tech.	3,451	6,122	77
For Boys	3,451	6,122	77
For Girls	———	———	——
University Faculties	874	1,987	127
For Boys	830	1,751	111
For Girls	44	236	436

SELECTED BIBLIOGRAPHY

Afghanistan, Ministry of Education, Kabul: *Education in Afghanistan During the Last Half-Century*, c. 1956.
> *Education in Afghanistan*. Revised and enlarged. To be published in English, Pushtu, and Persian.
> *Manuals and Syllabi* for primary, secondary, and vocational education. Various dates.
> *Proposed Manual of the Department of Supervision and Inspection*, 1964.
> *Draft of Proposed Basic Education Law*, 1964.
———. Ministry of Planning. Kabul: *Survey of Progress* (1961-1962).
> *Second Five-Year Plan* (March 1962–March 1967).
———. Royal Afghan Embassy (London). *Afghan Progress in the Fifth Year of the Plan*, 1961.
ALI, MOHAMMAD. *A Cultural History of Afghanistan*. Karta Char, Kabul. Afghanistan: Published by Mohammad Ali, 1964.
American University. *Area Handbook of Afghanistan*. Prepared by Foreign Area Studies Division, Special Operations Research Office. Richard V. Weeks, Ed. Washington, D. C.: American University, 1959 (Multilithed).

DODGE, BAYARD. *Muslim Education in Medieval Times*. Washington, D. C.: The Middle East Institute, 1962.
ELPHISTONE, MOUNTSTUART. *An Account of the Kingdom of Caubul and Its Dependencies in Persia, Tartary, and India*. London: Richard Bentley, 1842. 2 Vols.
Encyclopaedia Britannica, 13th ed. Consulted on many topics.
FRASER-TYTLER, SIR W. K. *Afghanistan: A Study of Political Developments in Central and Southern Asia*. Revised. London: Oxford University Press, 1960.
GUILLAUME, ALFRED. *Islam*. Baltimore: Penguin Books, 1954.
HERODOTUS. *The Histories*. Translated by Aubrey de Selincourt. Baltimore: Penguin Books, 1954.
HITTI, PHILIP K. *History of the Arabs*. 7th ed. New York: The Macmillan Company, 1960.
International Bureau of Education. *International Yearbook of Education*. Geneva: International Bureau of Education. From 1951-52 to present.
KHAN, MIR MUSHIN SULTAN MOHOMED, ed. *The Life of Abdur Rahman, Amir of Afghanistan*. London: John Murray, 1900. 2 Vols.
LAURIE, S. S. *Historical Survey of Pre-Christian Education*. London: Longmans, Green, and Company, 1902.
MARKHAM, CLEMENTS R. *A General Sketch of the History of Persia*. London: Longmans, Green, and Company, 1874.
MONROE, PAUL. *A Brief Course in the History of Education*. New York: Macmillan Company, 1905.
PAZHWAK, ABDUR BAHMAN. *Aryana* (Ancient Afghanistan). Hove, England: Key Press, c. 1954.
PICKTHALL, MOHAMMED MARMADUKE, Translator. *The Meaning of the Glorious Koran*. New York: The New American Library, 1953.
SASSANI, ABDUL HASSAN. *Education in Afghanistan*. Washington, D. C.: U. S. Office of Education.
SHAH, SIRDAR IKBAL ALI. *Afghanistan of the Afghans*. London: The Diamond Press, 1928.
———. *Modern Afghanistan*. London: Sampson Low, Marston Company Ltd., 1938.
SHALABY, AHMAD. *History of Muslim Education*. Beirut, Leanon: Dar al-Kasashaf, 1954.
SYKES, SIR PERCY M. *A History of Afghanistan*. London: The Macmillan Company, 1940. 2 Vols.
TCCU Team (Teachers College, Columbia University, Team). *Six Months' Reports*. 1954 to the present. *Terminal Reports of Specialists*. 1955-to the present.
ULLAH, NAJIB. *Islamic Literature: An Introductory History With Selections*. New York: Washington Square Press, 1963.
UNESCO (United Nations Educational, Scientific, and Cultural Organization). *Report of the Mission to Afghanistan*. Paris: UNESCO, 1952.
WILBER, DONALD N. *Afghanistan: Its People; Its Society; Its Culture*. New Haven: The Human Relations Area Files, 1962.

ISRAEL

Randolph L. Braham

HISTORICAL BACKGROUND

History of modern education in Israel is the remarkable story of great achievements and persistent problems. It dramatizes the determining role played by education in the national renaissance of an ancient people and the founding of a new State. Indeed, perhaps in no other country has education been so interwoven with the historical tasks of national rebirth and cultural survival as is the case of Israel.

Although education experienced a phenomenal development in Israel only after the achievement of national independence in 1948, its roots can be traced to the educational experiments undertaken by the pioneers who settled in the then Turkish-occupied Palestine during the second half of the nineteenth century. Before that date, the education of the indigenous Jewish population was almost exclusively ecclesiastical and offered in the *Talmud Torahs* ("Study of the Law"; traditional community-maintained schools), *Heders* ("Room"; one-teacher one-room schools) and *Yeshivot* (institutions of higher Jewish studies) that were concentrated primarily in the four "holy cities" of Hebron, Jerusalem, Safad, and Tiberias. The language of instruction was Yiddish in the *Ashkenazi, i.e.* the German and East European Jewish communities and either Ladino, a Spanish dialect, or Arabic in the *Sephardic, i.e.* the Spanish and "Oriental" (Arabic) communities.

Beginning with the first *Aliya* (influx of immigration) of 1882, however, the religious motivation of the indigenous Jewish population was gradually supplemented by the national aspirations and Zionism of the new settlers. With the change in the composition of the Jewish population, the exclusiveness of ecclesiastical educational institutions gave way to the establishment of a variety of types of schools financed and maintained by Jewish philanthropic and Zionist organizations the world over. By far the most important of these were the *Alliance Israélite Universelle* (France), the *Anglo-Jewish Association*

(Great Britain), the *Hilfsverein der deutschen Juden* (Germany), and the *Hovevei Zion* (Russia and Eastern Europe).

Although the programs of these organizations varied in terms of emphasis, they were all dedicated basically to the defense of the civil and religious liberties of persecuted Jewish groups and the advancement of the economic and cultural well-being of Jewish communities the world over. Among the first modern educational institutions established in the Holy Land was the Mikveh Israel ("The Hope of Israel") Agricultural School. Built by the Alliance near Tel Aviv, the school trained a large number of experts in various fields of agriculture and animal husbandry. These experts were to play a leading role in the subsequent establishment of the collective (*Kibbutzim*) and smallholders' (*Moshavim*) settlements. These, in turn, played a determining role in laying the foundations of the renascent State. With the passage of time the number and types of schools built by these national and international organizations increased. The *Hovevei Zion* was particularly active in the revitalization of Hebrew and the establishment of the Hebrew national school system. Its distinguished leader, Mr. Menachem Ussishkin, visited Palestine in 1903 and was instrumental in the organization of the Hebrew Teachers' Association, perhaps the most important single factor responsible for the development of modern education in the country.

In addition to the establishment of collective settlements and the propagation of Hebrew, the *Hovevei Zion* was also active in the development of Hebrew post-primary education. In 1906, it brought about the establishment of the first Hebrew secondary school in Palestine—the Gymnasia Herzlia of Jaffa—which since its transfer to Tel Aviv in 1908 has been among the most respected educational institutions of this type. The *Hovevei Zion* also built a secondary school in Jerusalem and Haifa, and in 1913 it founded the first Hebrew Teacher-Training School for Girls in Jaffa.

Impressive as these educational endeavors of the various Zionist and philanthropic organizations may have been, however, they merely laid the foundation of the secular and mixed secular-ecclesiastical education system which emerged and developed during the British Mandate in Palestine.

The Mandate Period

Shortly after the entry of British forces into Palestine in 1917, the Jewish school system underwent a number of fundamental changes which were to lay the foundation of the present system of education in Israel. The expansion of educational facilities and the concomitant increase in enrollment, together with the vision of establishing a Jewish National Home in Palestine in accordance with the stipulations of the Balfour Declaration of 1917 led to the gradual development of a well-crystallized Jewish National School System.

During the three years of British military rule (1917-20), the Jewish school system, which included about ninety institutions and some 10,000 pupils, was placed under the jurisdiction of a commission of the World Zionist Council. Following the establishment of British Civil Administration in 1920 and the subsequent approval of the Palestine Mandate by the Council of the League of Nations (1922), the Jewish Community (*Knesset Israel*) claimed and in fact exercised the right to maintain its own schools in accordance with the provisions of Article 15 of the Mandate.

Although *de jure* supreme responsibility for education resided in the Palestine Government, its Department of Education had direct, complete, and exclusive jurisdiction only over the Government schools, which in reality meant only the Arab schools. The Department's relationship with the Jewish public school system was to a large extent only indirect and formal. The Jewish schools continued to operate under the auspices of the Zionist Council until 1929 when they were taken over by the Jewish Agency for Palestine. In 1932, general responsibility for the administration of the Jewish school system was entrusted to the *Va'ad Leumi* (the General Council of the Jewish Community in Palestine). Although an autonomous body exercising delegated governmental or quasi-governmental functions, the *Va'ad Leumi* cooperated closely with the Government Department of Education on matters of budgeting, licensing of teachers, and inspecting of schools. The Government Director of Education was usually kept informed about developments in the Jewish sector of the educational system by his Jewish Assistant Director and five Jewish inspectors who constituted the Jewish branch of the Department.

The *Va'ad Leumi* operated through a well-organized network of executive and administrative organs whose powers and responsibilities were delineated in the Education Code.

Aside from its cooperation with the Government Department of Education, the *Va'ad Leumi* worked closely with the local education authorities (Municipal Councils, Local Councils, and Village Authorities) concerning the construction, maintenance, and administration of schools. Depending on their wealth, size, and importance, the local education authorities maintained the buildings, supplied the equipment, and participated in the appointment of the teaching staff. The lack of centralized authority, however, often resulted in confusion as to the location of new schools, the assignment and remuneration of teachers, the nature of the curricula and syllabi, and other educational matters.

During the Mandate period, the Jewish public school system was neither free nor compulsory. It included those kindergartens, elementary and secondary schools, and teacher-training institutes (seminaries) which were controlled and financed by the *Va'ad Leumi* and various statutory authorities. In fact, one of the primary factors responsible for the autonomy the *Va'ad Leumi* enjoyed during the Mandate was the financial burdens it assumed in the educational sphere. While until 1922 the Government provided no assistance to the Jewish school system, between 1922 and 1925 it offered small annual per capita grants based on the number of pupils enrolled in the Community schools. From 1926 to 1933, the Palestine Government allocated 20 percent of its education budget to the Jewish school system calculated so as to reflect the ratio of the Jewish population to the rest of Palestine's population. Beginning with 1933 the formula was again changed with grants envisaged to reflect the proportion of Jewish and Arab children in the five to fifteen age group. In reality, however, the Government grants to the Jewish school system averaged only about 10 percent per year. Approximately 80 percent of the cost of Jewish education was covered by local Jewish sources. Of this, about half was in the form of school fees paid by the children's parents or guardians.

The "Trend" System

Differences in the historical and cultural backgrounds of the two major national and religious groups inhabiting Palestine and their conflicting political aspirations led to the establishment of what in reality became two separate educational systems: the Arab (Government) and the Jewish. The separatist tendency that prevailed in the country as a whole became particularly acute in the Jewish school system by the evolution and flourishing of the so-called "trend" system. Because of the virtual autonomy the Jews enjoyed in the field of education, the diversity of the Jewish population, and the different social and political philosophies of the major Zionist parties reflecting the predominant socio-political trends of the Jewish community, the Jewish educational institutions failed to develop into an organically unitary system. The educational philosophies, the curricula, and general programs of the schools tended to reflect the different outlooks of the three major Zionist parties (trends) supporting them: (1) the General Zionist; (2) the *Mizrahi* ("Spiritual Center"); and (3) Labor.

The General Zionist schools were national-Zionist in outlook with emphasis on the development of Hebrew culture and the appreciation of national values. Although secular, they reflected a positive attitude toward the principles of Jewish religion. The schools supported by the *Mizrahi*, an orthodox-Zionist political movement representing the religious segment of the Jews, offered a religion-oriented program with emphasis on the inculcation of religious beliefs and the observance of rituals. The Labor schools were affiliated with the *Histadrut* (General Federation of Jewish Labor) and attached less importance to Jewish-religious subjects than did the General Zionist or *Mizrahi* trend schools. Although they devoted considerable attention to Bible studies, the subject was usually approached from the historical and literary point of view. Many of the Labor schools paid special attention to the development of skills in both industrial handicrafts and agriculture.

The separatist tendencies inherent in the trend system were further aggravated in the pre-1953 period, when the *Agudat Israel*, an ultra-orthodox movement established in the 1930s, was given co-equal status with the other trends. Moreover, with the formation of splinter parties within the labor and Zionist movements a number of "sub-trends" developed, which were particularly noticeable in the *Kibbutzim* and *Moshavim*.

During the British Mandate, the three trends that operated within the framework of the *Va'ad Leumi* system had enjoyed virtual autonomy in the determination of the curricula and syllabi, the hiring of teachers, and the inspection of the schools. Each trend was administered by a Trend Schools Council whose head, the Chief Inspector, represented it in the Department of Education of the *Va'ad Leumi*.

The party political and administrative divisions notwithstanding, the Jewish school system developed at a rapid rate. By 1944-45, of the close to 529,000 Jews that lived in Palestine 99,469, or 19 percent, were in schools. Of these, 79,441 were enrolled in the Jewish public school system: 12,490 in kindergartens, 55,471 in elementary, 9,527 in secondary, 1,067 in vocational, and 886 in teacher-training schools. Of the trends, by far the most powerful in terms of educational influence was the General Zionist. Of the 79,441 children in the Jewish public school system, 42,311 were enrolled in the General schools with the rest almost equally divided between the two other trends.

Weaknesses of the Jewish school system were revealed in a detailed report prepared in 1946 by a Commission of Enquiry appointed at the request of the High Commissioner for Palestine by the British Secretary of State for the Colonies. The report criticized especially the determining role played by the parties and the subordination of educational policies and administration to political considerations.

The Commission made a number of constructive recommendations designed to streamline the administrative structure and the educational system of the Jewish Community, but the intervening historical changes prevented their immediate implementation. Some of the proposals were adopted by the Ministry of Education and Culture of the newly established State of Israel and implemented in light of the conditions and requirements of the new State.

THE POST-INDEPENDENCE PERIOD

The Provisional Government which was established upon the attainment of national independence on May 14, 1948, was confronted with a series of urgent tasks related to the military and economic survival of the new State. It, therefore, was content to let the Department of Education of the *Va'ad Leumi* continue to exercise supreme authority over the educational system, now including not only the schools it administered during the Mandate but also those that were outside the system, both Jewish and Arab. The Department of Education continued to function in this manner until March, 1949, when a permanent Government was formed on the basis of the parliamentary elections held two months earlier. The new Government also included a Ministry of Education and Culture headed by a full-fledged cabinet member.

Although overall responsibility for the policies and affairs of the Ministry lies with the Minister, the staff operates under the immediate guidance of the Director General who is appointed with the approval of the Cabinet. He is assisted by a Deputy Director General and five Assistant Directors General in charge of administration, elementary, post-elementary, teacher training, and examinations and teacher affairs, respectively. In addition, the Ministry includes a number of departments, offices, and sections—each with well-defined tasks and responsibilities in various spheres of education and culture.

For purposes of administration and efficiency, the Ministry brought about the establishment of twelve district offices of education and culture in the six regional administrative units of the country. Six of the district offices operate in the sphere of elementary education, three in post-elementary education, and three in the field of culture. Each district office is headed by a District Inspector who is appointed by, and acts in behalf of, the Minister.

In addition to the Ministry of Education and Culture, which has overall control and policy-delineating powers in the educational sphere as a whole, responsibility over the nature and content of education, especially in the post-elementary school system, is also shared by other ministries, agencies, and local governmental units. The latter are especially active in the construction, equipment, and maintenance of schools and the assuring of a variety of school services, including those related to the health and feeding of the children.

An important role in the educational process of Israel is also played by a number of national and international organizations, including the AMAL (Labor), ORT (Organization for Rehabilitation Through Training), Hadassah (Women's Zionist Organization), WIZO (Women's International Zionist Organization), MW (*Mizrahi* Women's Organization of America), and the *Alliance Israélite Universelle*. Working in cooperation with the central ministries and the local governmental units, these organizations are particularly active in the nursery-kindergarten and post-elementary education. They own, maintain, and operate a considerable number of kindergartens, academic, vocational, and agricultural secondary schools, and provide material and financial assistance to the institutions of higher learning.

EDUCATIONAL REFORMS

Introduction of Compulsory Education

In its efforts to streamline the educational system of the new State, the Ministry relied to some extent on the proposals made by the British Commission of Enquiry in 1946. Aware of the importance of education for the survival and flourishing of the nation, the Ministry initiated a series of reforms of which perhaps the most important one was the introduction of free and compulsory primary education.

The Compulsory Education Law was adopted by the *Knesset* (Parliament) on September 12, 1949. It provides for the free and compulsory education of all children from five to thirteen years of age and of those adolescents aged fourteen to seventeen who have not completed their elementary education. The nine years of compulsory schooling include one kindergarten year for the five-year-olds. The adolescents who have not completed elementary education are required to attend educational institutions for "working youth," which usually offer afternoon or evening classes.

Abolition of the Trends

Conscious of their responsibilities, the Israeli leaders recognized at an early phase of the new State's life that the trends constituted a potential danger to national unity. Although they realized that the trends had played a useful role during the Mandate period in bringing about virtual universal primary education through their competitive efforts, they were also convinced that by the 1950s the trends had outlived their usefulness. After considerable public debate and wrangling on the *Knesset* floor, the Israeli parliament adopted the State Education Law on August 12, 1953. Concurrently with the abolition of the trends, the Law also provided for the establishment of a unified "State Education" and "Religious State Education" system to operate under the control and guidance of the Minister of Education and Culture.

"State Education," as defined by the Law, is "education provided by the State on the basis of the curriculum, without attachment to a party or communal body or any other organization outside the Government, and under the supervision of the Minister or a person authorized by him." "Religious State Education" is defined as "State education with the distinction that its institutions are religious as to their way of life, curriculum, teachers, and inspectors."

Overall policy delineating powers under the Law are exercised by the Education Committee composed of at least fifteen members, who are appointed by the Minister with the approval of the Cabinet. On matters dealing with religious State schools, the Minister acts in conjunction with the fourteen-member Council for Religious State Education.

Upon the abolition of the trend system, the Labor and General Zionist schools merged and became part of the "State Education" system, while the schools of the religious wing of the Labor trend merged with the *Mizrahi* institutions to constitute the "Religious State Education" system. An exception was made with the *Agudat* schools, which under the 1953 Law were allowed to opt out of the official State school system. They acquired, however, the status of "officially recognized" schools eligible for State subsidies by agreeing to include in their curriculum basic minimal programs prescribed by the Ministry of Education and Culture. With elimination of the trends, teachers and employees of the educational system in general were prohibited from further engaging in propaganda activity in behalf of any party or other political organization.

Scope of Education

The scope of State education in Israel is defined in Article 2 of the 1953 Law, which states that it is based on

the values of Jewish culture and the achievements of science, on love of the homeland and loyalty to the State and the Jewish people, on practice in agricultural work and handicraft, on *khalutzic* (pioneer) training, and on striving for a society built on freedom, equality, tolerance, mutual assistance and love of mankind.

Financing Education

Financial burdens of the State in the sphere of education tended to increase with the expansion of the total and school population. Between 1948 and 1964, the country's population tripled, but its school enrollment expanded sevenfold, from about 100,000 to 700,000. The overwhelming majority of the school population is enrolled in the free and compulsory educational system of the State.

The budget of the Ministry of Education and Culture is the second largest in the national budget, surpassed only by that of the Ministry of Defense. In 1964-65, it amounted to about 255,000,000 Israel Pounds, representing an increase of 23 percent over the 1962-63 budget. In addition to the financing of the public school system, the State is also active in supporting the institutions of higher learning. In 1964-65, the State's subsidy to higher education amounted to close to 38 million pounds, representing about 50 percent of the regular budget of these institutions. The State has also assumed full responsibility for the remuneration of the teachers employed in the public school system.

The Ministry's financial burdens in school constructions and post-elementary and higher education are shared by the local governmental units and a number of agencies, including the Jewish Agency for Israel, and by various international Zionist and/or philanthropic organizations. Total educational expenditures, consequently, are much higher than the budget of the Ministry may imply. In 1963-64, for example, it amounted to around 500 million Israel Pounds.

Secondary education in Israel is neither free nor compulsory. The schools are owned and operated by private individuals or organizations and local governmental units. The level of the tuitions and fees varies, generally speaking, with the caliber of the program offered. It normally ranges from 500 to 750 pounds per year. Nevertheless, no child who meets the academic requirements is denied the opportunity to attend a secondary school merely because of the inability of the parents or guardians to pay the tuition fees. For the advancement of secondary education, the State adopted a generous scholarship and graded tuition system in 1957. The fees are graduated on the basis of the child's ability, the economic status of the parents or guardians, the size of the family involved, and the number of children in secondary schools. Originally planned for the academic secondary schools only, the graded tuition system has been gradually expanded to the agricultural and vocational post-elementary schools operating under the supervision of the Ministry of Education and Culture as well. To qualify for the tuition allowance, a pupil desiring to enter an academic secondary school must pass the so-called *seker* examination which is given to all pupils at the completion of the eighth grade.

The number of students entitled to the graded tuition allowances increased from year to year. In 1961-62, 49,453 secondary school students (grades nine to twelve) were entitled to such allowances. Of these, 44,199 were enrolled in the academic and agricultural schools and 5,254 in the vocational schools.

By 1963-64, their number increased to 72,300 (41,000 academic, 16,000 vocational, and 15,300 agricultural) students.

As a result of the measures initiated by the central and local governmental units, the burden on the parents has eased considerably. The cost of secondary education in 1963-64 was shared as follows: parents, 55 percent; Ministry of Education and Culture, 25 percent; and local authorities, 20 percent.

TYPES OF EDUCATION AND TRAINING

Types of education provided in Israel in the 1960s and the various age levels covered are illustrated in Figure 1 on p. 242. Technically, Israel's structure of education is not different from that of any Western country. Israel is unique, however, in the sense that although all schools tend increasingly to follow the policies laid down by the Ministry of Education and Culture, they differ in terms of ownership and, to a lesser degree, in objectives. Thus, there are nursery-kindergarten, primary, and post-primary schools owned and operated by the *Kibbutzim* and *Moshavim*, the *Aliyat Hanoar* (Youth *Aliya* or Immigration), the central and local governmental units, Zionist and philanthropic organizations, and private individuals.

The *kibbutz* schools offer the best possible conditions for the physical and mental development of the children. The educational requirements of the *kibbutz* community receive a priority second to none.

Kibbutz children are divided into groups and normally they advance from one level of education to the other or from class to class as members of the same group. In most *kibbutzim* the first grade is skipped, with the six-year-olds learning the three *R's* within the framework of the kindergartens. The curriculum is broad and flexible reflecting the political and socio-economic conceptions and requirements of the respective *kibbutz*.

The *Aliyat Hanoar* schools operate under the auspices of the Education Department of the Jewish Agency for Israel. Originally, these schools included the children who were rescued from the Third Reich and Nazi-occupied Europe. In the post-independence period, however, these schools tended to include an increasing number of children coming from Eastern Europe and the North African and Middle Eastern countries. A large percentage of these are from broken families and the economically disadvantaged groups. In addition to its own schools, which are inadequate to meet the educational requirements of the children under its care, the *Aliyat Hanoar* also places its wards in *kibbutzim*, children's villages, and special institutions, depending upon the specific requirements of the children. Although the curriculum includes the standard subjects taught in all types of schools, special emphasis is placed on vocational training.

Aside from these specific characteristics of the *kibbutz* and *Aliyat Hanoar* schools and of the special,

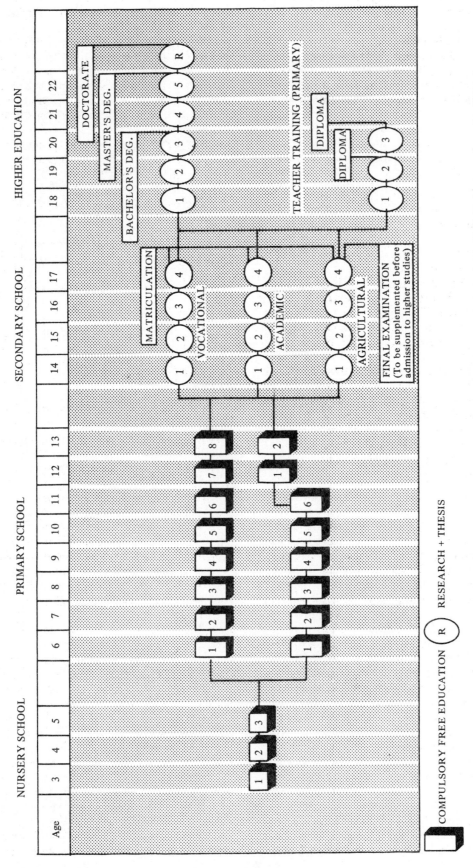

Figure 1. The structure of education in Israel: 1963-64. (Source: **Report on Educational Developments in 1963/4 Presented at the 27th International Conference on Public Education, Geneva, July 1964.** Jerusalem: Ministry of Education and Culture, [1964], p. 3.)

religious institutions of learning, the institutional framework of Israel's system of education is fairly standard. The number of educational institutions, both Hebrew and Arab, tended to increase with the passage of time. While during the 1948-49 academic year Israel had only 1,342 educational institutions (excepting the institutions of higher learning), by 1962-63 their number increased over threefold to 4,146.

Nurseries and Kindergartens

The nursery and kindergarten system is highly developed, especially in the collective and cooperative settlements. The nurseries (*ganon*) are usually designed for children ranging from two to four years of age. They were originally conceived to fulfill two basic needs of great importance to both the older and the younger generation of immigrants: the propagation of Hebrew and the satisfaction of child care requirements of working mothers. The kindergartens (*gan yeladim*) provide pre-primary training for four-to six-year-old children. They place no emphasis on formal studies; they aim primarily at the physical and emotional development of the children within the social atmosphere of the institutions. Although many of the nurseries and kindergartens are owned by private individuals charging fees commensurate with the services offered, most of these institutions are built and maintained by voluntary women's organizations, often in cooperation with local governmental units. In terms of their function and scope, Israel has five types of kindergartens: public, *kibbutz*, all-day, boarding, and private.

Primary Education

Under the terms of the Compulsory Education Law of 1949, primary education is free and compulsory for all children between the ages of five and fourteen. There are several types of primary schools: eight-year, six-year, and four-year institutions. By far the most prevalent type is the eight-year institution. Irrespective of their structural differences, these schools are often combined with secondary schools, *i.e.* schools offering combined primary-secondary education. The school year normally begins a few days before the Hebrew New Year (but never before September 1) and ends in the last days of June providing about 210 days of schooling. The schools are open six days a week, Sunday through Friday in the Hebrew system; in the Arab and Christian schools, the school week is adjusted to the religious practices of the respective communities. Classes begin at 8:00 A.M. and continue to 12:00 or 1:00 P.M.; in overcrowded communities afternoon sessions are also held from 12:00 or 1:00 P.M. to 4:00 P.M. In terms of size, the schools vary from very large ones in the cities to very small ones in the villages. The average number of pupils per primary school increased from

217.2 in 1951-2 to 319.7 in 1962-63. The average class size increased during the corresponding period from 27.5 to 30.2.

Primary responsibility for the registration of school-age children lies with the parents and guardians. The choice of whether to register the child in a State school, religious State school, or a "recognized" school of the Agudah is left entirely up to the parents or guardians. By far the most popular type of schools are the State schools. In 1963-64 they accounted for 63.2 percent of the primary school enrollment while only 28.7 percent attended the religious State schools, and 8.1 percent the "recognized" schools.

The curriculum is established under the auspices of the Minister of Education and Culture, with primary responsibility for its formulation and implementation vested in the Assistant Director General in Charge of Primary Education. With the exception of specifically Jewish and biblical studies, the Israeli primary school curriculum is fairly standard. The religious State schools and the "recognized" institutions allot more time to Jewish, talmudic and biblical studies and are especially concerned with the training of children for a religious way of life. With this aim in mind, these schools emphasize the observance of rituals, the recitation of prayers, and strict adherence to talmudic law.

The examination and promotion procedure is not uniform. The general assessment of the children's progress is normally based on the teachers' direct observations and occasional oral or written examinations. The pupils' grades are stated in numbers, ten being the highest and equivalent to excellent, and one the lowest. The passing mark is usually six. Except in the most severe cases, promotion is automatic. After completing the eighth grade, the children are given a country-wide examination known as *seker*. It is administered not only to determine the knowledge of the subjects taught but also to guide the parents and teachers in the choice of secondary education and vocational orientation. The grades received in these examinations are considered in the determination of eligibility for tuitional support in secondary schooling.

In addition to the regular primary schools, Israel also has special "schools for working youth." These are educational institutions for adolescents ranging from fourteen to seventeen years of age who have not completed their elementary education as provided by the Compulsory Education Law. These are primarily attended by children of immigrant families from the Moslem world and by those coming from low-income or socially and culturally deprived families. The teaching methods employed in these institutions are highly flexible due to the great differences in the background, age, and education of the students. Classes are usually held in the late afternoons or evenings three or four times a week. The curriculum provides for nine to twelve hours of class work per week evenly allotted to language, Bible, arithmetic, and citizenship (including history, geography, and nature).

The education of the handicapped is the responsibility of the State. Overall guidance and control are exercised by the Special Education Section of the Ministry of Education and Culture. Handicapped children are assigned to special institutions in accordance with the results of the medical and other special examinations performed under the auspices of the local education authorities. Depending upon the nature of their disabilities, handicapped children are taught either in the regular public schools, in "special classes," or in "closed" institutions. The tendency, especially in smaller communities, is to integrate the handicapped children with the other pupils. Children requiring prolonged medical treatment or supervision are usually placed in "closed" institutions.

Secondary Education

Unlike primary education, secondary education in Israel is neither free nor compulsory. Although the secondary schools are not part of the central public school system, the Ministry of Education and Culture is actively involved in their affairs. It is particularly active in the preparation of the curricula and syllabi, the revision of textbooks, the preparation and administration of the matura (*Bagrut*) examinations, and the partial financing of secondary education. Within the Ministry, immediate responsibility in the sphere of secondary education lies with the Assistant Director General for Post-Primary Education.

Israel has three major types of secondary schools: academic, vocational, and agricultural. These may vary in terms of the number of years of schooling offered (eight-year, four-year, or two-year), sessions available (day and/or evening), and ownership or sponsorship (*kibbutz, moshav, Aliyat Hanoar,* organizational, and governmental). All of these, in turn, may be either secular or religious. And there are, of course, secondary schools for the Arab and Christian communities.

In terms of their schedule of operation and grading, the system is basically the same as in the primary schools.

Irrespective of their type, the academic secondary schools aim to impart general education and help develop the character and personality of the students. In contradistinction to the vocational and agricultural secondary schools, the academic schools emphasize the preparation of the students for the matura (*Bagrut*) examinations offered at the end of the twelfth year and for their entry into the institutions of higher learning. The curriculum is fairly uniform up to the tenth grade, when the students are differentiated in terms of their aptitude, interest, and intended field of specialization. Accordingly, in the

eleventh and twelfth grades they may be registered in one of several "trends," *i.e.* areas of concentration, depending on the facilities and offering of the respective school. The major areas of concentration are: Humanities (with or without a second foreign language), Social Science, Mathematics and Physics, Oriental Studies, Agriculture, and Biology.

Although the *Bagrut* examinations are normally taken only by the graduates of the academic secondary schools, they may also be taken by individual graduates of the other type secondary schools as "external" (correspondence) candidates. External candidates, however, must either prove evidence of ten years of schooling or pass a preliminary comprehensive examination. Beginning with the 1964-65 academic year, the *Bagrut* examinations are conducted in seven subjects. Of these, five are obligatory subjects with uniform examinations administered throughout the country; in the two additional subjects, the individual schools administer "internal examinations." Of the five obligatory subjects, one is given at an "expanded level" depending on the student's area of concentration.

In spite of the complexity and difficulty of the *Bagrut* examinations, the number of successful candidates increased from 802 in 1948 to 4,431 in 1962. Of the latter, 3,903 were graduates of the Hebrew academic secondary schools, 453 were "external" candidates, and 75 were graduates of Arab-Christian secondary schools. Secondary school graduates who fail or elect not to take the *Bagrut* examinations are given a "secondary school certificate" testifying to their completion of high school. The "certificate" is not accepted, however, for purposes of admission into the institutions of higher learning.

Vocational education is offered in workshops, factories, vocational-technical schools, and comprehensive academic-vocational schools. Although most of these schools are owned and operated by a variety of public and private organizations, ultimate jurisdiction over the educational process proper is exercised by the Department of Vocational Education of the Ministry of Education and Culture. Mindful of the requirements of an increasingly technological society, the Government adopted a series of measures in recent years to discourage the gravitation of elementary school graduates toward the academic secondary schools. One of the most important of these was the establishment of "comprehensive" schools offering a combined vocational-academic education. The vocational schools vary in terms of their specialization and the number of years of training offered. By far the most prevalent type are the three-year and four-year vocational-technical schools. In contradistinction to the one-year and two-year institutions, which are almost exclusively trade schools devoted to full-time practical training, the three-year and four-year schools devote from twenty-one to twenty-six hours a week to theoretical secondary school subjects. The curriculum varies in terms of the nature, ownership, and offerings of the respective schools. The school day is normally divided between practical work and theoretical subjects.

Agricultural education has been intertwined with the establishment and flourishing of the Jewish communities in the Holy Land. In light of the early pioneers' conceptions about the "return to the soil" and the great emphasis placed on agricultural training, it was no accident that the first modern Hebrew secondary institution was an agricultural one—the *Mikveh Israel*—founded in 1870. In terms of ownership and jurisdiction, agricultural education is similar to vocational education. The agricultural institutions developed to a large extent in response to the various and changing needs of the farm population. In the course of time the following six types of agricultural schools evolved: agricultural secondary schools; agricultural boarding institutions; secondary continuation classes in *kibbutz* settlements; *Aliyat Hanoar* schools; multi-purpose youth centers; and vocational agromechanics schools.

Higher Education

In addition to the many research and professional institutes of non-university level, Israel has five major institutions of higher learning: the Hebrew University of Jerusalem; the Technion—Israel Institute of Technology of Haifa; the Bar-Ilan University of Ramat Gan; the University of Tel Aviv; and the Weizmann Institute of Science of Rechovot.

Although autonomous from the academic and administrative point of view, the institutions of higher learning operate under the general provisions of the Council of Higher Education of the Ministry of Education and Culture. Established in 1958, the Council has exclusive powers in the sphere of recognizing institutions of higher learning and is the chief State authority in all matters pertaining to higher education. Presided over by the Minister of Education and Culture, the Council is empowered to determine the type of degree or academic titles a recognized institution may confer.

The Hebrew University of Jerusalem is the country's oldest and largest institution of higher learning. Officially opened in 1925, it experienced a phenomenal development in the post-independence period. From a student body of 871 in 1948-49, enrollment increased to 12,000 by 1968; the increase in the number of faculty members and degree recipients during the corresponding period was phenomenal.

Located in Technion City, in the outskirts of Haifa, the Technion—Israel Institute of Technology is one of the best schools of its type in the world. Its courses are offered in six faculties—Architecture, Chemical Technology, Civil Engineering, Electrical Engineering, Mechanical Engineering, and Physical Sciences—and the following departments: Aeronauti-

cal Engineering, Agricultural Engineering, Industrial Design, and Mining and Metallurgy. The Technion is also engaged in a vast research program, with the projects either initiated by the institution itself or sponsored by other private and governmental agencies in Israel and abroad, including some from the United States. Its student body increased from around 700 in 1948 to over 4,000 in 1968.

The Bar-Ilan and Tel Aviv universities were established in the 1950s, the former, modelled after Yeshiva University in New York, to serve the needs of religious students, the latter, developed under the auspices of the Municipality of Tel Aviv, to serve the needs of Israel's largest metropolitan area.

The Weizmann Institute of Science was originated in 1946 through the reorganization of the Daniel Sieff Research Institute, which was founded in 1934 by the late Dr. Chaim Weizmann, the first President of the State of Israel. Originally devoted only to research in organic chemistry and microbiology, by 1963-64 the Institute had a scientific and technical staff of over 1,000 engaged in over 200 projects conducted within the framework of eighteen research units. The Institute also has a Graduate School since 1958, which offers three-year courses leading to the doctoral degree for students already in possession of the Master of Science degree.

Teacher Training

Kindergarten and primary and some special vocational school teachers are trained in two- and three-year teacher-training institutes (seminaries); the secondary school teachers are trained in the schools of education or special teacher training programs of the institutions of higher learning. In 1962-63, Israel had forty-two teacher training institutes. Of these, twenty-three were State, fifteen religious State, one Arabic, and three independent. In terms of their scope and function, these institutes were of the following five types: (1) institutes for the training of kindergarten and primary school teachers for the State and religious State schools in the cities and towns; (2) institutes for the training of village teachers; (3) institutes for the training of vocational school teachers, (4) institutes for the training of teachers for the "independent," *i.e. Agudat Israel* schools; and (5) institutes for the training of *Aliyat Hanoar* instructors. Overall responsibility for teacher training lies with the Assistant Director General for Teacher Training. The administrative and the teaching personnel of the institutes are appointed and paid, as are the State primary school teachers since 1953, through the Ministry of Education and Culture. The Ministry also has the power to issue rules and regulations concerning the admission of students, the curriculum, and the qualifications of the faculty.

Theoretically, the teacher-training institutes require that the applicants have a matura (*Bagrut*) diploma or an equivalent foreign certificate. However, exceptions are made with applicants for the village teacher-training institutes and those taking certain special admission examinations. With minor variations to fit the specific requirements of the respective institutes, the curriculum is fairly uniform and established under the auspices of the Ministry.

Enrollment of the teacher-training institutes increased from 1,470 in 1948-49 to 7,700 in 1966-7. As is increasingly the case in most other countries, a large percentage of these students are girls. Overfeminization is but one of the many serious problems confronting teacher education in Israel. The failure of the system to produce a sufficient number of qualified teachers is due to many causes, including the phenomenal expansion of school enrollment, the relative decline in the social and economic status of the teachers and the teaching profession, and the lure of other fields. The shortage of qualified teachers is particularly felt by the secondary schools whose increasing requirements cannot be met by the present programs of the institutions of higher learning.

The problem of teacher training, like that of education in general, is intertwined with the complexity of problems Israel has been compelled to deal with since the attainment of national independence in 1948. A small country of less than 8,000 square miles with five-eighths of the land barren and devoid of natural resources and surrounded by hostile neighbors bent on its destruction, Israel, with an original Jewish population of only 650,000 in 1948, witnessed by 1965 the ingathering of almost one and one-half million exiles. The immigrants, many of them survivors of the Nazi concentration camps, speaking more than seventy different languages and dialects and bearing the stamp of the most varied cultural background, confronted the new State with formidable social, cultural, and economic problems. Conscious of their great responsibilities, the Israeli leaders recognized at an early phase of the new State's life that education represented the master key for the successful solution of all these problems. Through their dynamism and farsightedness they brought about a rapid development of education at all levels. By 1964-65 there were more people enrolled in schools than there were Jews within Israel's boundaries when the State was established. The close to 700,000 people enrolled

in Israeli schools during that academic year constituted one-third of the nation, the highest proportion of any national population involved in an educational process. The rise in enrollment between 1948 and 1964 represented a sevenfold increase in the school population in comparison with only threefold expansion of the total population. The phenomenal development of education in Israel reflects the conviction of the leaders and the people that a nation's greatness depends primarily on the excellence of the individuals composing it.

Recent increased tensions with Arab states have heightened nationalistic feeling.

Developments in education since 1966-7 have included increased enrollments at all levels: preschool, 100,000; primary, 460,000; secondary schools, 143,000; teacher training, 8,000; and higher education, 30,000. More attention is being given to nomadic groups and other culturally distinct peoples.

BIBLIOGRAPHY

The Educational System: The Pre-State Period

Great Britain. *Colonial Office. The System of Education of the Jewish Community in Palestine. Report of the Commission of Enquiry Appointed by the Secretary of State for the Colonies in 1945.* London: His Magesty's Stationery Office, 1946, 119 pp.

NARDI, NOAH. *Education in Palestine, 1920-1945.* Washington, D. C.: Zionist Organization of America, 1945.

The Educational System: The Post-Independence Period

AVIDOR, MOSHE. *Education in Israel.* Jerusalem: Youth and Hechalutz Department of the Zionist Organization, 1957, 179 pp.

BENTWICH, JOSEPH S. *Education in Israel.* Philadelphia: The Jewish Publication Society of America, 1965, 204 pp.

BRAHAM, RANDOLPH L. *Education in Israel.* Washington, D. C.: U. S. Department of Health, Education and Welfare, Office of Education, 1965, app. 200 pp.

HYMAN, ABRAHAM S. *Education in Israel* (A Survey). New York: Israel Education Fund, 1964, 106 pp.

SMILANSKY, MOSHE; WEINTRAUB, SHOSHANA; and HANEGBI, YEHUDA, eds. *Child and Youth Welfare in Israel.* Jerusalem: The Henrietta Szold Institute for Child and Youth Welfare, 1960, 334 pp.

JORDAN

Huda J. Nasir

Jordan lay dormant for many years and only recently has moved to develop its human and natural resources. Therefore, in discussing education in Jordan it is necessary to point out that its true educational history is extremely limited.

Jordan gained its status as an independent nation after World War I. The government of Jordan from the date of its independence 1946 has been in the hands of a monarchy.

Today, the king has the sole responsibility for developing and modernizing an ancient land with deep-seated customs and traditions.

Prior to World War I, education in Jordan was primitive. There was little educational effort.

The history of education in Jordan could be said with some justification to have started with the partitioning of Palestine in 1948.

In that year, a large number of refugees from Palestine came to Jordan. With its primitive educational system, it was impossible for Jordan to accommodate the large number of school-age children. The refugees almost flooded Jordan with pupils; they exceeded 50 percent of the normal school population.

Schools that were available, public and private, tried to meet the demand for education, but they were inundated. This condition existed until 1950 when the United Nations moved to assume major responsibility for education of the refugees.

The United Nations Relief Works Agency entered into an agreement with the government of Jordan to permit it to maintain and operate schools. In accordance with this agreement, UNRWA now develops plans and programs which are executed under the authority of the United Nations General Assembly.

The director of UNRWA works closely with a Jordanian Advisory Committee and submits reports and recommendations to the General Assembly only after full consultation with this committee.

UNRWA deals with the Jordanian Ministry of Development and Reconstruction on all matters per-

taining to the improvement of internal educational plans. In the initial planning stages of the UN work in Jordan, it was decided that all educational plans and programs would be under the direction of the UNESCO while all matters pertaining to the administration of schools would be governed by UNRWA. Under this division of responsibility UNESCO inspects schools, prepares reports, and supervises the curriculum while UNRWA supervises the purchase and distribution of school equipment and teacher salaries.

It should be stated at this point that final authority for all educational matters rests with the Ministry of Education. The UN educational program exists only with the full understanding that the Ministry of Education is the final arbiter of any difference of opinion that may arise. UNESCO and the Ministry of Education, however, have worked well together in improving Jordanian education.

GOALS OF EDUCATION

Short-range goals of education in Jordan emphasize elementary education. The increase in school population in the last decade has been mainly in elementary enrollment. Plans have been developed to avoid dropouts and to improve the use of human resources in the elementary school program. It is recognized that before a good secondary and higher educational program can be developed, a sound elementary education base should be laid. Thus the enrollment in secondary schools in proportion to the eligible school population is still small.

The present educational program and the law provide for compulsory, universal, and free education in government schools. This program seeks to provide education for all and does not ignore the fundamental educational principles of mental, physical, and emotional well-being. Thus Jordan is deeply concerned with education of the whole child, the child who will be a worthy and capable citizen of a newly developing nation.

A basic philosophy of education in Jordan is expressed well in the simple statement, "A tree which grows tall and sturdy must plant its roots deep." Thus the goal of education in Jordan is centered around the development of an intelligent and responsible citizen who has his roots planted in a sound elementary school program.

In 1964 an Educational Law provided for the development of the 9-3 system instead of the 6-3-3 system. Jordan is the first Arab nation to take the step of combining the preparatory and the elementary education.

Since Jordan is an emerging nation, it is increasing the secondary subject-matter program by 85 percent to meet the demands for needed technical training. Jordan seeks to improve vocational education through industrial training, agricultural research, and commercial skills. Jordan is opening a new vocational school for women.

In all of the educational goals, Jordan seeks to develop uniformity of purpose and administration throughout the nation. This is to be done under the direction of the Ministry of Education.

OBSTACLES TO ATTAINMENT OF THESE GOALS

Main obstacles to attainment of these goals center around a few principal points. These are discussed briefly in the following paragraphs.

The major obstacle to Jordanian education is lack of government funds for adequate school plants and facilities. Funds available are quite inadequate to provide necessary educational facilities. There are consequently serious problems of overcrowded classrooms and schools with inadequate instructional equipment. Library facilities and modern audio-visual aids are woefully inadequate; all of these shortages make the teacher's job a particularly difficult one in Jordan.

Educational philosophy and instructional methods are not always developed in a spirit of cooperation. Supervisory personnel do not always understand clearly their task. Therefore, there is some inefficiency in school administration because of vague understanding of individual responsibility and lack of clear lines of authority below the level of the Ministry of Education. There is some over-lapping of duties which results in waste and inefficiency. Jordan is now moving to clarify lines of authority and administrative duties.

Under the Ministry of Education, the curriculum is planned by experts without consultation with teachers, who are expected to be docile and to follow plans of their superiors. To accomplish optimum results, the teachers should have a part in planning the curriculum and in selection of textbooks. The Ministry

of Education is aware of this problem and is seeking greater teacher participation in curriculum planning and textbook selection. Committee work is one route by which the Ministry of Education seeks to increase teacher responsibility and participation in curriculum planning. It is hoped that in time this will bring about greater flexibility throughout the educational system. There is a present attempt to increase the in-service education of teachers.

Another problem confronting the Jordanian Ministry of Education is a complete dearth of an educational guidance and counseling program. The need for such a program is clear to the Jordanian educators.

A counseling service would be a great help in dealing with emotional problems of pupils. For example, there appears to be a need for dealing with feelings of inadequacy in many pupils; this feeling appears to cause a large number of dropouts.

The Ministry of Education is concerned about these problems. One of the ways that Jordan seeks to meet them is through better organization of teacher-training courses. Many inadequately trained teachers are now employed. They lack the necessary professional educational training to meet the needs of pupils and schools—elementary and secondary—to which they are assigned by the Ministry of Education.

Jordan is engaged in a massive effort to increase the professional training of those who conduct teacher-training courses. Many of Jordan's best qualified professional educators are encouraged to study in the United States and other countries.

It is too early to tell how much influence may be exerted by students who have attained various degrees in foreign colleges and universities, but Jordanian leaders and professional educators have high hopes and expectations.

Another obstacle confronting Jordanian education is the inflexible elementary and secondary school curriculum. The tendency to uniformity makes it almost impossible at present for the school or the teacher to provide for individual differences of pupils.

At present all students are subject to rigid, uniform goals and educational environment. Many pupils do not achieve full educational development and potential because of this traditionalism. Presently, curriculum planning is carried out by the Ministry of Education without consultation with teachers.

THE SYSTEM OF EDUCATION

As previously mentioned, the 1964 Educational Law provides for the 9-3 educational structure in lieu of the 6-3-3. Formerly, the educational system comprised six grades which became part of the nine-grade cycle in 1965. Pupils enter school at age six; at age twelve they formerly entered a preparatory cycle of three grades which is also included in the nine-grade cycle since 1965. At age fifteen the pupils enter a senior secondary cycle of three grades. Each cycle is completed with the pupil's taking the public State Examination. Those who pass this examination are eligible for the next educational cycle. Those who successfully complete the Senior Public State Examination may enter the Teacher-Training Colleges or the University in Jordan or institutions of higher education outside of Jordan.

There are five government teacher-training schools in Jordan and two UNRWA teacher-training institutions, three for women and four for men, each supporting two-year programs.

In the past, education has not been coeducational in Jordan. The number of boys enrolled now in public schools is about twice that of girls. This is accounted for, in part, by a culture that has built up the position of man and diminished the status of woman in society. Coeducation started in the University of Jordan, which was founded in 1962 and which had a total enrollment of 166 students in 1962-63. In 1964-65, there were 447 pupils enrolled. Jordan is enlarging the University facilities at present. In July 1966, the University of Jordan graduated its first class of 165 students.

TYPES OF SCHOOLS

There are several types of schools in Jordan:

1. Government public schools are financed and supervised by the Ministry of Education.
2. The Ministry of Defense has established schools for children of its troops stationed in the isolated areas of Jordan.
3. The Ministry of Social Welfare supervises two detentional schools, a reformatory supporting a school for juvenile delinquents, and a school for the blind.
4. The Ministry of Health has established a nursing school and an institute for midwifery, both of which are free and which maintain boarding facilities. Nominal salaries are paid during training to student nurses who are willing to sign contracts to serve the Ministry of Health for a specific period.
5. The Department of *Wakfs* (religious endorsement) and Muslem affairs maintains an orphanage which operates an elementary school and preparatory vocational school. This department also maintains a secondary school which follows the stipulated curriculum of the Ministry of Education with the exception of the religious courses offered in the senior year.

All these Ministries have their own administration which includes financing for schools under their direction. It is to be noted, however, that the Ministry of Education supervises all aspects of education including that administered by the other Ministries.

Private school education, the oldest type in the nation, existing when Jordan was under control of The Ottoman Empire, was left to individuals and community initiative for centuries. The Muslem *Kuttab* (lower elementary school) provided all the elementary education that was offered in Jordan. These private schools were operated by teachers who charged fees to maintain the schools. The primary goal of these schools was to teach people of all ages the Koran plus some arithmetic and writing. The Ministry of Education has now incorporated many of these schools into its system. The Kuttab as it formerly existed has been entirely eliminated.

Prior to Jordanian independence, religious missionaries operated schools where the Christian minority lived. These schools maintained an open-door policy for all pupils regardless of their age or religion.

Foreign agencies were granted full freedom by the Jordanian government to administer and operate such educational and philanthropic institutions. In pre-independence times these schools followed foreign methods and programs of teaching and emphasized the respective foreign language of their sponsor countries.

Today, private schools continue to exist, but they are under the official eye of the Ministry of Education. They adhere to the State curriculum and prepare students for public examination. The Ministry of Education encourages private schools with nominal subsidies, but as the public school grows, the importance of the private school system in Jordanian education is rapidly waning.

Another type of school is the UNRWA/UNESCO school. Even with the present massive Jordanian effort to meet a growing demand for education, it cannot hope to handle the large number of refugees who have entered Jordan from Palestine.

In order to meet the need for refugee education, the United Nations set up under its agency UNRWA agreements with Jordan providing for educational financing and other forms of assistance. UNRWA also extends further educational aid to refugees.

In the beginning the United Nations program was conducted in overcrowded and poorly equipped tents. Teachers were inadequately trained and poorly paid. But UNRWA has overcome many of these difficulties by erecting permanent school buildings and raising teacher salaries. Summer seminars provide for in-service training and increase the emphasis on elementary education. All such educational efforts are supervised by the Ministry of Education.

UNRWA also provides grants for refugee children attending government or private schools. The actual cost of the child's education is not covered by the grants.

UNESCO provides experts in teacher training and modern techniques to carry out a major pre-service and in-service training program.

Twice a year UNRWA conducts workshops for representatives of Ministries of Education in countries where the United Nations program is provided. At these meetings educational innovations are discussed and are then placed in practice in the various countries.

Jordan hopes that in time UNRWA will be able to handle all of the education needed by refugee children from Palestine. If this work were done, over 30,000 additional places would be provided for Jordanian children who cannot attend schools now because of lack of educational facilities.

There are more than 170 UNRWA/UNESCO schools in Jordan, with separate schools for boys and girls.

In the rented schools there are about two-thirds the number of students as in UNRWA-built schools.

SELECTING TEACHERS

There is a difference between theory and practice in teacher selection in Jordan. Ideally Jordan seeks, wherever possible, to find and employ teachers who have been adequately trained in teachers' colleges. In reality, however, only a very small percentage of teachers are professionally trained.

In a recent school year, of 6994 teachers working in Jordan, only 1381 had had any training in teachers' colleges or universities. In fact, a very large number of elementary school teachers have had little formal education.

All teachers in Jordan are appointed and promoted by the Ministry of Education. There is a uniform salary scale. Promotion to the senior level in Jordanian public schools requires a minimum of six years of successful teaching and in-service education. All teachers are civil servants. The civil service Law Number I of 1958 governs the recruitment, probation, classification, promotion, and retirement of all civil servants including teachers.

An insurance fund was initiated in 1960 into which the teachers of the Ministry of Education pay a small percentage of their monthly salaries. The accumulated amounts are spent on the needy families of deceased teachers or on the families of teachers whose service is terminated without their being qualified to receive a pension.

The number of teacher-training institutions remains about the same, but they have doubled their enrollment since 1960, without significant improvement in curricula or method of training.

There are no teacher unions in Jordan. All the work normally handled by such organizations is handled by the civil service commission.

Major laws which have influenced Jordanian education started with the General Educational Law of 1955 establishing basic purposes and objectives of education. These objectives centered around the following principles:

1. The basic task of education is . . . to develop the personality of the citizen, to bring up a generation sound in body, creed, mind and character which rec-

ognizes its duties toward God and the motherland, and works for the well-being of the country. . . .
2. The objective of the Kindergarten is to guide children toward the acquisition of good habits and activities, develop their interests, habituate them into discipline, and prepare them for admittance to the elementary schools.
3. The objective of elementary education is the preparation of the pupil to become a good citizen.
4. Secondary education aims at the preparation of the student for worthy adult life and for the achievement of a certain academic standard which enables those with aptitude and readiness to specialize.[1]

The same law mentioned the importance of strengthening Jordan's communication with other Arabian states.

The next Law was Civil Service Rule Number I of 1958, mentioned previously.

In 1962, the Ministry of Education, in cooperation with the Council of Education, founded Jordan's University. The law provided for a site on 150 acres of land northwest of Amman, the capital of Jordan. This law further declared the University was to be controlled by ten trustees who administer and direct the policies of the University.

As previously noted, a law of 1964 provided for the 9-3 instead of the 6-3-3 system of education. It is to be noted that the whole Jordanian Education system provides the initial steps of Jordan's effort to join the twentieth-century community of nations, by recognizing that a prime step in this direction is universal and free education for all citizens. Jordan has made significant progress in a very short time. The progress of Jordan in education is even more noteworthy considering its isolated location and size. There were nearly 2,000,000 people in Jordan in 1965. With an area of only 37,740 square miles, most of which is desert, it is difficult for Jordan to support the demand for education.

Prime industries of Jordan are a large and growing tourist trade, cement, petroleum, tobacco, and phosphate establishments. Agriculture centers around the production of olives, grapes, citrus fruits, pears, peaches, figs, and other fruits. The economy is geared for the most part to dry farming methods since the River Jordan is dry and irrigation facilities are almost nil. A great portion of the land is uninhabitable.

Because of the agrarian economy and problems of educational administration, the teachers of Jordan receive about one-third as much salary per month as other professional workers such as doctors and lawyers. On the whole, teachers receive less than skilled merchant tradesmen. Although the teachers' salaries are lower than those of other professions, teaching is highly respected in Jordan. Therefore there is much desire on the part of the young people to enter the teaching profession.

---

1. The Jordanian Embassy. *Education in Jordan,* a report, Washington, D. C., 1964-65, p. 3.

Religious education is required in every school cycle; pupils are divided into groups according to their religious affiliations. Each group has its own teacher of religion.

The majority of the people adhere to Muslem. There are other religions in Jordan, with Christians the second largest religious group.

Jerusalem is Jordan's main tourist attraction. [Ed. note: Not currently in Jordan's possession.] Most of the world's ancient holy temples are centered in this city.

Today, educational opportunity in Jordan is much greater than in the past. Universal education has made remarkable progress in a very short period of time under the able leadership of King Hussein, who himself visits schools and takes real interest in the Jordanian educational system and its future. One can look forward to steady and continued progress in Jordanian educational effort.

If education is to have direction in Jordan, aims are all-important. These aims must be flexible and adaptable to meet the needs of an evolving society. Since 1948 when the area was divided into Jordan and Israel, the aims of education have been concerned with a broadening conception of the duties, responsibilities, and rights of the citizen in supporting and maintaining this new society.

The qualities of the educated man in Jordan are intimately concerned with improving the quality of communication in society, and with distinguishing between truth and falsehood (the development of logical thinking). It is expected that the educated man will be aware of the role of critical thinking and inquiry in improving man's basic understanding of the importance of differences in personality and the dignity and worth of the individual in an emerging society.

A major problem confronting the nation is the present tense political situation existing between Jordan and Israel. The distrust and inbred hatred between the two nations is not easily understood by those who have not lived in an atmosphere of fear and despair for over two decades.

An amicable settlement of the situation could do much to enable Jordan to devote to education time and money that is now being spent on arms for defending its borders. It would appear that a prime way of resolving the difficulty would be more education on each side of the border in fundamental principles of tolerance and mutual understanding.

BIBLIOGRAPHY

AFIFY, S. MOHAMED. *A Comparative Study of Supervision of Secondary Instruction in the United Arab Republic and the United States. Dissertation.* Lawrence: The University of Kansas, 1962, pp. 200-305

Jordanian Embassy. *Education in Jordan* (a report). Washington, D. C.: 1964-65, pp. 1-17.

The Ministry of Education. *The Annual Report Book.* Jordan: The Triple Press Co., 1962-63, pp. 58, 63, 85, 143.

———. *Jordan* (annual book). The General Press of Information, 1961-62, pp. 206-222.

The Ministry of Information. *Jordan* (annual book). The General Press of Information, 1964, pp. 41, 61, 180, 193.

UNESCO. *International Yearbook of Education.* The International Bureau of Education and UNESCO, Vol. XXIV, 1962, pp. 206-28.

KUWAIT

William Graves

The name of Kuwait implies a struggling country scarcely able to survive economically, but this land area no larger than New Jersey and situated on the Persian Gulf is a land of contrasts where the Tribes of Abraham, the Greeks, the Persians, and even Alexander give it a historical link with antiquity as far back as time is recorded. Kuwait's modern history dates back to settlement by the first of the Sabahs just prior to the American Revolution. The Bedu arrived in the Ottoman Empire and laid a begging claim to this backwater of desert Nejd, a land where shade temperatures reach 110 degrees F. and under the glaring sun 160 degrees F. This was the land; the people were the Bedu tribes or families, the Anizas and the Amarats, which included the Sabahs, Khalifas, Salehs, Jalahimas, Zayids or Ghanims, Shamlans, and Maawidas, all still flourishing in Kuwait today. The leading family today is the Sabahs who were headed by the "richest man in the world," Abdullah Al-Salim Al Sabah, until his death in 1965. Abdullah claimed the land on an internationally accepted thesis that the Sabahs and Khalifas begged the Turkish Governor in 1756 to allow them to "eke out a living in Kuwait" and that they "meant no harm." That they "meant no harm" was no doubt true, as Kuwait today expends its great wealth for the whole Arab world. However, the Sabahs' claim to "nobility" and "purity" of family line as claimed by Abdullah could be questioned historically and possibly should be questioned for the educational benefit of Kuwaiti citizens.

Each family group in this small area should be appraised in the context of its history, *i.e.* the Hadar who live in houses or huts and the Araibdar who live with and harass the Hadar in the heat of summer but take to the wilderness in their tents when the winter rains arrive.

Students of Comparative Education might well ask what impact tribal conflicts have on this oil-soaked "desert Switzerland," the benefactor of the Middle East. After reading Arab history, one could well ask what kind of educational system would evolve in an enormously wealthy country, which is accepted in the family of nations, but historically believes that: (1) *herds* and loot are the true wealth of the Bedu; (2) earned money is degrading and carries no social status; and (3) trade smacks of *usury*, is despised by the Bedu and forbidden by the Koran.

The Kuwaiti are a generous, easy-going people enjoying and sharing their affluence under a paternal despotism.

Although the above are generalizations, they gain credence in the anthropological, historical, and sociological context of Kuwait's past and present.

Before the Sabahs, Kuwait was a base of operation for the Khalid Tribe who used the wells and grazing for their herds. The Rahma bin Jabir pirates roamed the Persian Gulf from Qurain Island off Kuwait. When the British defeated the pirates and secured free entry into the Persian Gulf, they received special treaty relations with the Sabahs. In return, Kuwait received the protection of the British Empire.

To the Kuwaiti, slave trade was a necessity. Historically, the proud Bedu looked upon manual labor as beneath them; therefore, the labor was done by women and slaves. In order to pursue the activities of piracy, gun running, and some legitimate trades (fishing and pearling), manpower was required; slaves were necessary. Slavery was not legally abolished until 1950, and there were still a half million slaves in Saudi Arabia in 1962. In addition, concubines (slaves) were imported for the harems. It is relatively common yet to hear veiled women speaking fluent German or other languages in the market places—presumably imported concubines.

All nations have truth sayers who band together to "stamp out evil." The Arab world is no exception and was beset by fanatical and marauding tribal sects. The Wahabis, followers of Muhammad Abdul-Wahab, the Oliver Cromwell of the Middle East, made a lasting impression on desert Arabia. Their mission was to purify and unify the Arab world through "faith, felicity, and good works." The sword and the inevitable brutality of a holy war were the means by which the Wahabis spread The Word. Internecine warfare was then added to the more mundane activities of camel stealing, woman stealing, smuggling, slaving, and attacks on the Nazarany and Jews. The unsettling influence, the nemesis and the demise of the Wahabis comprise a spectacular chapter in modern Arabian history.

The nemesis of the Wahabis was a Scotsman who was captured and enslaved when his crack British troop was defeated. He and other survivors were forced to march from Alexandria to Cairo carrying the severed heads of comrades under their armpits for the entire trek. The fittest British survivors were sold in the slave market.

The Saud-Wahab vision of a great Mogul or Sultan who could maintain authority over the "hoards of brigands and petty chieftans of the Bedu," enforce observance of the Ramadan Fast, abolish prostitution, piracy, drinking of wine, and opium eating collapsed at Dariya at the enslavement of the Scot and a gifted eighteen-year-old General, Tusoun, son of Turk Muhammad Ali.

The puritanical but ruthless Saud-Wahab alliance ran head on into the treacherous brilliance of the Turks. Tom Keith, the Scot from Edinburgh, unshaken by his "adopted land" became a "Muslim" and led the Turks on the Wahabis at Medina, the Prophet's burial place, where a thousand Wahabis were butchered in the streets. Tom Keith became Ibrahim Aga, Governor of Medina.

The easy-going Kuwaitis, never sanctioning mass murder or brutality, nevertheless were thankful for deliverance from the Wahabis. Perhaps it is that if a geographical territory is welded into an Empire under the guise of purification, it will culminate in fanatacism—a superimposed unity sacrificing freedom and enslaving the minds of its captives for an unattainable goal. The story of the Wahabis is typical of the violence and fanaticism, which have recurred throughout Arab history. On the other hand, Kuwait's stability dates as far back as the American war for independence without, of course, the American geographic advantages, i.e. oceans and multiple resources, to protect her. Although influenced at various times by the English, the Ottoman Turks, and the Egyptians, the Kuwaitis have retained their Bedu identity. Nor has Kuwait succumbed to religious fanaticism. Led by the Sabahs, Kuwait has survived many vicissitudes and has provided a haven for refugees from all warring factions. Kuwait's survival has not depended on puritanical austerity but on generosity, or where necessary, on payment of tribute.

By 1756 the Sabahs were the leading family of Kuwait. They were grazers, traders, and raiders. Although they were not the richest family, their ability and character singled them out as leaders. The Sheik was Sabah, son of Salim Ahmad Suleiman, grandson of the original Sabahs, who arrived in Kuwait looking for fresh grazing and water. The original Sabahs allied themselves not only with the British but with the Turks headquartered at Basra. The Turkish Govenor accepted these ". . . poor settlers who were trying to eke out a living and meant no harm to anyone." He did not insist on payment of tribute or on a Turkish representative in Kuwait. Kuwait's Arabian relations in Iraq and the Khalid family were enemies of the Turks, but Kuwait lived in relative peace with the Turks and the surrounding Arabs.

As already noted, the attitude of the Kuwaitis extended to relations with England, whose East India Company was a major Kuwait financial ally in the late nineteenth and early twentieth centuries. They arrived as "useful guests" and later became protectors and finally business partners. The British were assimilated in the Arab world without much conflict, even though they represented a Christian power. One British objective in the Middle East was to persuade the Shah to join the Christian powers of Europe against the Turks. In return they instructed the Shah Abbas of Persia on military techniques and supplied arms. As a result the Shah Abbas opened his domains to all Christian people and guaranteed their safety from persecution by military and religious leaders and excused them from paying custom duties. Thus, the British influence in the Middle East laid the groundwork for other Western/Christian countries to deal with the Arab World.

Kuwait has more millionaires than the United States. The Bedu attitude toward wealth—a fair share for all after the Chief has taken his share—was hammered into a national policy by the late Sheikh Abdullah Al-Salim Al Sabah. The artisans and laboring class are given every opportunity for remunerative occupations or to be trained for them. There is no problem of unemployment, relief, or pensions for the aged. Per capita income, excluding the ruling family,[1] averages close to $3,000 (per family head). This income is high by any national standard but is only a part of the picture. Fringe benefits as noted above are standard. In many instances food and shelter are additional benefits. Even the telephone service is virtually free. Other welfare states may boast of as many benefits, but they *cannot* claim, as the Kuwaitis can, that these marvels are performed entirely without personal income taxes.

For its achievements, Kuwait deserves every superlative. Dating from 1950 when Sheikh Abdullah became ruler, its achievements have been sensational. Kuwait City has grown from a typical walled Arab coast town to a modern metropolitan city. However,

---

1. Incomes of the ruling family are "classified." They *are* the State and hold all Secretarial positions.

the growth of its educational system is one of its most remarkable achievements.

Egyptian scholars perhaps have been the most influential in curriculum changes of the Kuwait educational system based on the admission of Kuwaiti secondary school graduates for study in Egyptian universities. The present system is divided into three four-year stages. The curriculum emphasizes primary and intermediate-level reading, writing, arithmetic, and mental and physical development. Separate but equal plants and curriculum have been established for both sexes. The secondary education is academic or vocational. The first two years of the academic curriculum are general; during the last two years the students follow either a literary or a scientific course.

If a student is tracked vocationally, he may follow a technical or a commercial course. There is one Commercial Evening School, which parallels the general secondary school curriculum. A second type is commercial, primarily for government and private employees, which specializes in bookkeeping, typing, and accounting. Ability to read and write are the only entrance requirements to these schools.

Kuwait's only technical college was established in 1954 for graduates of the primary school and offered a curriculum limited to carpentry. This college was constructed at a cost of approximately $12,-000,000 and had an enrollment of eight students during its first year. Its present curriculum offers twelve branches of study including electricity, auto mechanics, drafting, tool and die making. There are two teacher-training colleges, established in 1961 and 1962, one for men and one for women, for those students who have received intermediate school certificates. The increase in enrollment at the technical and teacher-training colleges from 1960 to 1964 were phenomenal, as shown below:

TEACHERS SCHOOLS		TECHNICAL COLLEGE	
YEARS	STUDENTS	YEARS	STUDENTS
1960-61	75	1960-61	185
1963-64	400	1963-64	384*

*There were sixty-four teachers for these students at a ratio of six students to one teacher.

Other schools include the Al-Mahad Al-Dini theological school where the curriculum parallels the primary and intermediate school curriculums but stresses Arabic, the Koran, and Islamic Law on the secondary level. On graduating, the students continue their education at Al-Azhar University in Cairo or at the newly-opened University of Kuwait (initiated in 1966 with 440 students, 370 from Kuwait).

The Kuwait education system provides schools for the deaf, the blind, and the mentally retarded. In addition, a center for combating illiteracy for men has been established.

Education in Kuwait is free. Books, supplies, food, and lodging are all provided, and at the teacher-training schools some clothing is supplied free. There is a liberal scholarship program for those completing secondary school. Before 1959 all graduates of secondary schools were sent abroad for further study. At present, 80 percent of the male science students and 70 percent of the male art students receive scholarships to study abroad. To encourage female graduates, 100 percent of them are offered scholarships. These scholarships include transportation, tuition, clothing allowance, general allowance, supplementary book allowance, and a holiday allowance. These scholarships, on an exchange basis in the United States, amount to a total of about $3,600 per year each.

School health services, from the elementary through the secondary schools, include students, faculty, administration, and maintenance personnel. There are 127 schools, with a clinic and a physician for every five schools. Each clinic has a laboratory, a pharmacy, and an X-ray unit. A general physical examination is given to all those new to the school. Vaccination against smallpox and whooping cough is compulsory before registration. Students are periodically examined for tuberculosis, trachoma, dental cavities, skin diseases, and congenital defects. Health education is promoted through radio, TV, and student-operated radio.

Another outstanding feature of Kuwait education is the school kitchen, which prepares food daily for the students, faculty, and school personnel. All students' needs are provided. The dirty, infected, infested child of an illiterate tribesman will graduate professionally trained and in good health. All tuition is free, and, as previously mentioned, meals and health services are provided. The students at the technical and teacher-training schools receive pay.

It is no wonder that the school population has increased under such liberal policies. In 1957 there were approximately 100 students per 1000 population; by 1963 this figure had doubled. The education of girls started much later than that for boys because of the cultural lag caused by purdah. In 1936 there were no girls in Kuwait schools; at present, through intermediate school, there is approximately an equal number of boys and girls.

Kuwait employed 3,575 teachers in 1962-63. The overall ratio of pupils per teacher is enviable—around twenty-two for grades K-8, fourteen for secondary, and seven for vocational and special schools. Approximately 50 percent of the teachers are women, but 95 percent of the teachers come from other countries. The weakest link in the educational system, no doubt, is the supply of trained teachers, of which only 30 percent are college graduates and less than 60 percent have had training in education.

Although Kuwait has not closed the gap in the training of her teachers, her building program for educational institutions has been phenomenal in construction, size, equipment, and facilities. The high schools look like small modern cities, comparing in plant size and acreage to some American universities. One secondary school has a 400-acre campus that boasts five botanical gardens, an assembly theater seating over 2,500, a dining hall with an electronically operated kitchen, a library, five well-equipped science labs, a student union, an Olympic-sized swimming pool, three regulation football fields (one floodlit), three handball courts, three hockey fields, four volleyball courts, a running track, four basketball courts, a huge grandstand seating 1,500, and a marine club for rowing and sailing. In addition there are six apartment buildings, each of which can accommodate 200 students (each having his own room).

Amid all this affluence, the teachers have not been forgotten. There are forty bachelor dwellings, each separate and having a garden patio; forty-two villas for married teachers; thirty rooms for servants; a faculty union equipped with its own swimming pool. It is estimated the complete high school and staff facilities cost between $25,000,000 and $30,000,000. At present, the school is providing an education for 1,400 boys from age fourteen through eighteen.

The plants and facilities of all schools in Kuwait are spectacular by any educational standards. There are twenty-four kindergartens, each uniquely built. For example, one is decorated entirely in blue mosaic. All kindergartens are equipped with miniature swimming or wading pools, the latest in playground equipment, and a small farm where the children care for rabbits, ducks, chickens, pigeons, and the like. The kindergartens are provided with dormitories in which each student has his own bed, marked, as is all his equipment or property, by some art work created by him. Twenty parents visit the school once a week on a rotation basis for parent conferences. The intermediate schools are comparably well equipped according to needs, and all have regulation-size swimming pools.

Kuwait, true to Muslim generosity and tribal practice, has accommodated her less fortunate Arabic neighbors, thus mitigating their envy. By 1961 there were sixteen schools built in the gulf sheikdoms, primary, intermediate, and secondary, with a student enrollment of 3,886. Teachers' salaries, books, stationery, food, medical services, and all other expenses are born by Kuwait. She also provides scholarships for the students to study either in Kuwait or abroad at the expense of the Kuwait government.

Beneath the surface of the educational system's glittering modern facilities, there is much to be done. Literacy had increased to only 35 percent by 1957. There are few who write of the success of the Kuwait student abroad. In his book *A Golden Dream*, Ralph Hewins claims that of 400 students who went abroad in 1960, less than ten graduated by 1963.

The dichotomies referred to herein plus the pace for change set by Abdullah are the core of Kuwait's problems. Her generosity cannot help but attract more and more of her less fortunate neighbors, thus expanding the population and increasing the need for skilled labor.

The size of the enrollment from primary to secondary schools would indicate statistically that there are many failures. Perhaps the types of examinations used should be examined and updated.

Kuwaitis are not inclined to follow the teaching profession, possibly because in their opinion it is somewhat related to being a servant. Present scholarship statistics indicate that teaching ranks fourth in choice of career. In view of the fact that 95 percent of the teachers are non-Kuwaiti, it would appear that they do not see the need for Kuwait teachers as urgent or that it is a less desirable profession to the Kuwaiti student. There are a great many statistics regarding the benefits of teacher-student ratio, plant facilities, and the like; however, there is little detailed information on salaries or organizational structure for the teaching staff.

Kuwait plans for a university seem premature, particularly in view of the shortage of Kuwait teachers for the elementary and secondary schools. There cannot help being some problems in importing 95 percent of the teaching staff if for no other reason than many will eventually wish to return to their homelands and must be replaced. It might be well to consider some training on a junior college level to help equip the students for study abroad, but with present teacher training and supply, it would not seem judicious to try to staff a university with all foreign teachers. In a country of 600,000 with only 4,000 secondary students, it would appear that elementary and secondary education would be the prime concern. In 1966-67, there were just over 5,600 teachers and 115,000 students in 190 government schools.

Under the Ministry of Education, the educational system is a loosely structured paternalistic one. The hierarchy of the various Ministries are, in almost all instances, made up of members of the Sabah family or close relations, assisted by imported functionaries and specialists. The Sheikh, of course, appoints the heads of the various Ministries and keeps in close touch with the projects of each. This method of administration is paternalistic and not institutional. Therefore, the educational system is the private philanthropy of a very rich family rather than a community institutional endeavor.

The schools have operated on a stepped-up educational pace for only a decade, so that the hypothesis that a concentration on eliminating adult illiteracy is desirable might perhaps be premature. In fact, such a concentration might eradicate much that is desirable in the culture. It should be recognized that Allah and the Koran give the people their identity—not progress. The adult population should not be forced into the mainstream of Western ways, but it should act as a brake. One writer proclaims that the aim should be to draw the attention of the people to "shortcomings" in their respective "communities."

It is doubtful that in the Arab idiom there is a concept of community. There are family, neighbor, and tribe, with the very personal connotation of blood lines, but not community with its connotation of institutionalization.

The people of an area where temperatures reach 160 degrees F. will certainly have much leisure time, even without wealth. With the advent of wealth and the introduction of technological and labor-saving devices, there is now more leisure time than ever before. Through their educational system the Kuwaitis should preserve and promote their forms of recreation and leisure as well as adapt some Western forms.

In the field of general culture, the Ministry of Education might well encourage the translation of Arabic books and manuscripts and promote markets for their sale throughout the world for the benefit of the Western world. A commission of scholars could be formed, to whom the choice of books and manuscripts for translation would be entrusted. The same could be done for Arabic arts and music. Arab artists and musicians should be introduced into the Western world, for these people have preserved something of the past from the cradle of civilization, and the world should not cut the umbilical cord of history that gives all mankind its identity.

BIBLIOGRAPHY

DICKSON, H. R. P. *Kuwait and Her Neighbors.* London: George Allen & Unwin, Ltd., 1956.

FREETH, ZAHRA. *Kuwait Was My Home.* London: George Allen & Unwin, Ltd., 1956.

HEWINS, RALPH. *A Golden Dream, The Miracle of Kuwait.* London: W. H. Allen, 1963.

MIELCHE, HAKON. *Lands of Aladdin.* London: William Hodge & Co., Ltd., 1955.

Ministry of Guidance & Information, Department of Culture and Publicity, Division of Tourism, State of Kuwait, *Kuwait Tourist Guide.*

Ministry of Guidance & Information of Kuwait, *Kuwait Today, A Welfare State.* Nairobi: Quality Publications, Ltd.

Report of Missions Organized by the International Bank for Reconstruction and Development at Request of the Government of Kuwait, *The Economic Development of Kuwait.*

LEBANON

Farouk Mourad

BACKGROUND

"On September 1, 1920, [The Commander-in-Chief of the French Armed Forces in Syria and Lebanon, General Henri Gouraud] proclaimed in Beirut the restoration of Grand Liban."[1] In April, 1920, the Western Allies partitioned the lands which had constituted the Ottoman Empire. France was given the right to Syria and Lebanon; this action was endorsed two years later by the League of Nations. France was in charge of the affairs of Lebanon until the Day of Independence, November 26, 1941. However, the last foreign troops left on December 31, 1946.

Formerly, under the Ottoman Empire, dating back to the establishment of the Islamic State, Mount Lebanon, a part of Syria, as well as Al-Hijaz, Yemen, and other regions were administrative provinces, whose rulers paid allegiance to the Calif (Al-Khalifah). Historical sources refer to the relative autonomy which Mount Lebanon enjoyed throughout history. This may be attributed partially to the topography of the land and partially to the tribal and feudal lines on which the people were organized. Historical references also point to the heterogeneity of the people in terms of faith and cultural orientation. The lands east of the Mediterranean and north of Arabia had experienced a series of invasions, each invader leaving some elements of its own people and culture.

Under the power of the French Mandate, Lebanon was to go through some critical developments which left an enduring mark. Although political independence was gained almost three decades ago, Christian missionaries and certain subtle measures exercise influence on the cultural orientation of Lebanon.

Original inhabitants of Lebanon were the Phoenicians who themselves were a composition of Arabian Semites and other tribes. In the words of Dr. Barmaki:

About 3500 B.C., a new Semite Folk, the first of a series of waves of Semites which periodically overflowed from the overpopulated, sparsely cultivated and underwatered Syrian and Arabian deserts, burst into Egypt by way of the Red Sea and perhaps overflowed into (what is consequently called) Phoenicia.[2]

The Phoenicians contributed one of the earliest, most advanced civilizations in man's recorded history.

In contemporary Lebanon, the sectarian influences which were sustained by missionary schools and universities have left their mark on the political life of the country. The Lebanese republic is uniquely structured on sectarian lines, with proportionate representation for every minority religious group.

The history of educational development in Lebanon is a history of a subtle struggle for domination in the political arena among the different religio-political factions. Furthermore, the resultant growing attitude toward national unity, which became even more urgent after the summer of 1958, is in line with the trends in educational policy.

Lebanon now comprises an area of 3,470 square miles, is inhabited by "a population of approximately 1,000,000."[3] It occupies a strategic position in the Arab world, and Lebanon's leadership in the contemporary Arabian culture is a profound one.

Early Educational Development

Education in society performs two major functions: one is that of perpetuating the culture and the other is that of developing leadership. Early educational attempts in Lebanon could very clearly illustrate the role of leadership toward some prescribed ends. At the same time, societal conditions at different historical stages had created either a favorable attitude or resistance, depending upon what segment

1. Philip K. Hitti, *Lebanon in History: From the Earliest Times to the Present* (London: The Macmillan Company, Ltd., 1957), p. 489.
2. Dimitri Barmaki, *Phoenicia and the Phoenicians* (Beirut: Khayats, 1961), p. 6.
3. Hitti, *op. cit.*, p. 497.

of society was involved, and what the prescribed goals were. In order to understand the present educational system in Lebanon, a review of some major historical developments in the field of education in Lebanon becomes necessary. The prevailing pattern of private and sectarian education in Lebanon may be traced back into the history of the country, where the system of public education is of relatively recent development. The earliest patterns were found to have been the clergy schools. Some of these were established by the Maronite Church with the support of the Roman Church and the European Catholic missionaries. This relation between the Maronite Church in Lebanon and Europe proved to be of particular significance in the history of education in Lebanon.

"It was in the late twelfth century, while the Franks were in occupation of coastal Syria[4] that the Maronites, as their allies, became formally attached to the Roman Catholic Church. After 1291, when the last of the Crusaders were expelled from Syria, the ecclesiastical union between the Maronites and Rome tended to weaken,"[5] Franciscan missionaries to Syria during the fourteenth and fifteenth centuries wished to strengthen the ties with Rome. This was a starting point for the flow of support from Europe[6] to establish the Christian schools in Lebanon. A number of village primary schools were established by Maronite clerics; Ihdin was one such village. Other more advanced schools were also established by Maronite monasteries as early as 1624.

One such school was founded in the village of Huqa in the north and another in the village of Bqarqasha. In 1728, a school was opened in the village of Ayn Toura, which at the present time is run by the Lazarist Fathers. The importance of education for lay boys became quite apparent to the Maronite Church by the first half of the eighteenth century. The schools at that time taught the children reading, writing, and arithmetic, besides the instruction in religion. The medium of learning was the Arabic language.

The first institute of higher learning was a clerical seminary established at Ayn Waraqa in 1787. Two years later it was converted into a semi-secular school. Another such institution was established by Greek Catholics at Ayn Traz in the same period. By the end of the nineteenth century the only schools providing secondary education were those serving well-to-do Christian families. Few Druze boys were sent to such schools. Some families who could afford to hire private tutors at home did so. It had been customary to do this among the Moslem families up to the early twentieth century. This method also was employed to provide education for girls. Most common elementary education was provided for boys only in schools connected with the Mosques. In some cases, rooms were established adjoining the Mosque for the purpose of teaching. Ibraheem Pasha's reforms in Syria and Lebanon in the nineteenth century particularly inspired the Moslem community in Lebanon, resulting in a strong desire to overcome their passive role in the educational development of their country.

EDUCATION IN THE NINETEENTH CENTURY

It has been indicated earlier that educational efforts by missionaries in Lebanon were aimed at restoration of religious ties with Europe. These efforts were particularly effective later in the nineteenth and twentieth centuries by orienting Lebanese culture toward the West. This was furthered by the following developments:

1. There had spread throughout the Ottoman Empire during the nineteenth century a general reform movement aimed at some measure of Westernization. Nations turned to the West for new ideas and techniques. The Lebanese took a share in this movement.
2. Mohammad Ali's vast educational reforms in Egypt extended into Syria and Lebanon through the efforts of his son, Ibraheem Pasha, beginning in the third decade of the nineteenth century.
3. "The presence in the country of a large group of Maronite and other Uniate Christians, who maintained regular contact with Europe, was also important."[7]
4. France, through its mandatory powers, exercised great influence in Syria and Lebanon. The diffusion of the French language and other culture patterns are evidences of this influence.

As a result, the Western orientation of the people was accomplished, and the French system of education was adopted in Lebanon.

Historical records of nineteenth-century Lebanon refer to the active work of missionaries in the field of education, inspired in particular by the arrival of the first Protestant Mission in 1820. The American Mission opened classes for girls, one at Beirut and another in the mountains for Druze girls. In 1835 a boarding school for boys was established in Beirut and another at Abey in 1843. By mid-century there were between three and four hundred pupils in the schools conducted by the Syrian Mission (as the American Protestant Mission in Beirut was then called). By 1860, a chain of schools including one for girls had been established in Lebanon backed by American missionaries. These were known as the Lebanon Schools. Before the end of the century a number of boarding schools for secondary education were in existence; these schools were for girls or boys

---

4. Of which today's Lebanon is a part.
5. Kamal S. Salibi, *The Modern History of Lebanon* (New York: Frederick A. Praeger, 1965), p. 121.
6. [And eventually America.]
7. Salibi, *op. cit.*, p. 120.

and were located in Sidon (1862 and 1881),[8] in Tripoli (1872), and Brummana (1877). But most important of all was the establishment in Beirut in October 1966,[9] of the Syrian Protestant College, operating at the present time under the name of the American University of Beirut.

Roman Catholic missionaries followed the example and founded Jesuit schools in Beirut (1839), in Ghazeer (1843),[10] in Zahlah (1844), and subsequently in Bikfayya, Tanaqil, Jazzen, Bayr-al-Qamar, and Sidon.

By 1914 Maronite nuns operated thirty girls' schools, and Maronite and Greek Catholic schools for boys were enjoying considerable success.

Of special importance was the École Patriarche, founded in 1865, and the École de la Sagesse, in 1874, both in Beirut. The College Oriental was founded in Zahleh in 1898.

Other schools were established by Greek Orthodox followers, such as the one near Tripoli (1833), Souq-al-Gharb (1852),[11] and at Beirut in 1880, the latter a school for girls.

On the other hand, a "Moslem society"[12] established a series of schools in Beirut, Sidon, and Tripoli. A Druze school also was founded at Abey in 1862.[13]

CONTEMPORARY EDUCATION

The present system of education in Lebanon is to a large extent the product of certain major developments of the past. These may be summarized as follows:[14]

First, there were missionary schools; Catholic, Protestant and Orthodox, established by German, American, English, Italian, Russian, Greek, and Swiss missions, and each following to some extent its own system and curricula. These schools can be classified in two categories: Anglo-Saxon and Latin. Second, there were the Ottoman schools, which followed systems and curricula based on the French model. These schools were abolished by the fall of the Ottoman rule of Lebanon. A system of schools was established under the Ministry of Education, with leadership of the French administration in Lebanon, and following the French model. Third, there were private national schools, bound to follow the French system.

Dr. Nashabah[15] maintains that the French administration made sure to spread its influence throughout Lebanon and to create a cultural attachment between that country and France. Differences between the missionary schools were encouraged,[16] which proved to favor those missionaries using the French model in their schools. All schools were required to include instruction in French; the French Government provided French instructors for private schools, if necessary.[17]

Since 1922, the French Baccalaureate was official in Lebanon, but in 1929 appeared the Lebanese Baccalaureate, with its two parts, which became equal

to the French and gradually gained in importance in the country.

Missionary schools in the country were particularly responsible for the relatively high literacy rate in Lebanon.[18] Furthermore, they offered the only institutes providing secondary and higher learning in the country. However, Dr. Nashabah notes that this was part of an overall plan enforced by the French administration to exclude other national efforts from this important educational sphere,[19] because of lack of appreciation and consent to their aims and objectives.

The Ministry of National Education and Fine Arts faced serious difficulties when, after independence, it attempted to provide national educational guidelines and put limitations on the absolute freedom which foreign missionaries enjoyed in the conduct of their schools. The result was that the Legislations of 1946[20] supported the French enforced system of education. Subsequent legislations aimed at regulation of these schools were ineffective because of lax enforcement.

As late as 1952 the Ministry of National Education established Secondary Schools and in 1953 regulated school inspection in Lebanon. In 1955 the Secondary Service came into existence.

Educational Organization

Much has been said about the system of private education in Lebanon. The national efforts in the field of education merit greater attention. Because of growing concern over the role of education in the modern world, considerable pressure has been developed in Lebanon favoring deeper involvement in this field on a national scale. There is increasing evidence that the State is abandoning its previous passive attitude regarding this issue. Five years of primary education have become compulsory since the 1957-58 school year. School inspection has also become more active and effective.

---

8. Under the name of the Gerard Institute.
9. Incorporated by the Legislature of the State of New York.
10. Later transferred to the Universite of St. Joseph.
11. Later transferred to Beirut as the College des Trois Docteurs.
12. Jamiyyat al-Mauasid al-Khayriyya al-Islamiyya.
13. Al-Madrasa al-Dawoudiyya.
14. Hashem Nashabah, "Evolution of School in Lebanon," Beirut, *The Review of Education*, No. 6 (April, 1963), p. 24.
15. Nashabah, *op. cit.*, p. 24.
16. Refer to the Lebanese Constitution of May 23, 1926.
17. Eucine, Chapman. *Lebanon: A Study of Educational System of Lebanon.* Hastings, World Education Series, AACRAO, 1964, p. 5.
18. Estimated at 87 percent. See "Education in Arab States," *Information Paper,* No. 25. New York: Arab Information Center (Jan. 1966), p. 114.
19. Including Ministry of Education.
20. Under No. 6989 and No. 7001.

There are five administrative branches in Lebanon: Beirut, Al-Biqa, South Lebanon, Mount Lebanon, and North Lebanon. However, they enjoy little local autonomy and operate on the basis of policies and orders furnished by the Central Body. Education in Lebanon tends to be highly centralized.

In 1966-7, the Educational Budget constituted 3.2 percent of the gross national income. In the same year public schools enrolled 164,500 primary pupils, being taught by 10,000 teachers, as compared with 13,800 primary teachers instructing 274,500 pupils in 1500 private schools. In the academic year, 1965, the enrollment at the Lebanese University was 4,836, in the Arab University 4,745, in the Universite of St. Joseph, 2,184. Enrollment at the American University was 3,260 for the year 1965-6.

Public secondary education enrolled about 6,000 students in 1966-7, while private secondary schools had about 18,200. About the same numbers applied also to higher education.

The Structure of Education

Despite the apparent French touch in the existing system of education in Lebanon, there still exist many differences, due in part to the relative lack of material resources and to the unique circumstances in that country, some of which were noted at the beginning of this essay. Many reforms have been introduced in the French model in France and currently some serious consideration is being given to these reforms in Lebanon. Two years of preschool education is provided only in a few private schools; elementary education starts at age six. The primary school offers five years of instruction, the completion of which permits pupils passing the examination to receive a Preparatory Studies Certificate.[21] The program includes religious instruction, reading, recitation, essay-writing, grammar, dictation, history, geography, and mathematics. A foreign language, either French or English, is included. Beginning with the second year, two and one-half hours weekly instruction is given in drawing, handicrafts, music, and gymnastics. Public schools start on the first Monday after October 5 and continue until July 1. The school year is nine months or 160 school days.[22]

Students holding the Preparatory Primary Studies Certificate may proceed to a seven-year secondary school or to four years of higher primary school, where they may take advanced courses in the same subjects, plus physics, chemistry, biology, and mathematics. Or the student may go to a three-year vocational school which prepares assistants in engineering, building, management, mechanics, and industrial chemistry. Pupils who choose Higher Primary School may, upon passing the examination, receive the Higher Primary Studies Certificate (Brevet d'Etudes). They may then proceed to the School of Arts and Crafts (three years) or to Teachers' Training School[23] (three years), or

they may join the upper division of the Secondary School (three years). At the latter, upon completion of the two years before the final one,[24] and by passing the examination, students receive the Baccalaureate Part I. During those two years the students have specialized either in Literature or Science. In the final year, they study philosophy or mathematics and receive, upon passing the examination, the Baccalaureate Part II.

Higher education is offered at the American University (Beirut), Universite Saint Joseph, the Lebanese University (1951), and the Arab University (1960). These four universities offer a variety of subjects and are coeducational. Instruction at the American University is in English; at the Universite Saint Joseph, French; and in the other two, in Arabic. There is also an American Junior College for women, sponsored by the Presbyterian Church, attached to the American University in Beirut. Another of the institutes of higher learning is the Near East School of Technology (Evangelical Church).

A growing number of teachers' colleges are being established, reflecting concern over the qualifications and status of teachers. Both governmental and private colleges are preparing teachers for the elementary and higher elementary and secondary levels. Teachers in the public schools are civil servants and work for the Central Ministry of National Education; teachers in private schools sign contracts on an individual basis, though the Teachers' Union in Lebanon is of growing importance.

Examinations

Major certificates are given upon passing certain public examinations. These examinations are the responsibility of the Ministry of National Education and are administered simultaneously through the country. These examinations are given special national concern, particularly the Baccalaureate.

A growing concern is felt in educational circles about Lebanese education and is attested by many pages in professional journals dealing with the subject. Clues are presented concerning the major problems facing education today and reforms are being demanded that will help Lebanese education to meet the needs of the people, education consistent with national aspirations and goals. A need for more active leadership on the national level is strongly felt, and it is hoped that the Ministry of Education will assume this role.

21. Certificate d'Etudes Primaires Preparatoires.
22. See Abu H. J. Sassani, "Educational Data: Lebanon," (Washington: Information on Education Around the World, No. 42-NE [March, 1960]).
23. For primary school instruction.
24. These are the fifth and sixth grades in seven years of secondary school.

BIBLIOGRAPHY

AL-SAYED, ABD AL-AZIZ. "The Message of the University," *Review of Education, No. 1,* (October-November, 1964), pp. 10-13.

BARMAKI, DIMITRI. *Phoenicia and the Phoenicians.* Beirut: Khayats, 1961.

BOGARDUS, EMORY S. "Social Change in Lebanon," *Sociology and Social Research,* Vol. 39, No. 4 (March-April, 1955), pp. 254-260.

CHAPMAN, EUNICE. *Lebanon: A Study of the Educational System of Lebanon.* Hastings, Nebraska: World Education Series, AACRAO, 1964.

DIDGE, BAYARD. "History of Education in the Arab World," Information Paper No. 21, New York: Arab Information Center, 1963.

GRASSMUCK, GEORGE, and SALIBI, KAMAL. *A Manual of Lebanese Administration.* Beirut: American University, 1955.

HITTI, PHILLIP K. *Lebanon in History: From the Earliest Times to the Present.* London: The Macmillan Company, Ltd., 1957.

KHOURI, SALAM. "Girls' Education Movement in Lebanon: College Graduate Girls and Education in Lebanon," *The Review of Education,* No. 637. June, 1964, pp. 36-44.

NASHABAH, HESHAM. "Evolution of the School in Lebanon," *The Review of Education.* No. 6, April, 1963, pp. 22-27.

NOUR AL-DEEN, MOHMOUD. "Curriculum in Lebanon," *The Review of Education,* No. 435, March, 1966, pp. 13-17.

RASHED, ALI. "The President's Address First Graduation Day, Arab University," *The Review of Education,* No. 1, October, 1964, pp. 14-17.

SADAQAH, NAJEEB. "Education in Lebanon," *Review of Education,* No. 3, January, 1963, pp. 3-26.

SALIBI, KAMAL S. *Modern History of Lebanon.* New York: Frederick A. Praeger, 1965.

SASSANI, ABU H. K. "Educational Data: Lebanon," *Information on Education Around the World,* No. 42-NE (March, 1960).

SAUDI ARABIA

Wadie Farag

One of the most amazing episodes in the study of history was the birth of the new faith, Islam, that took place in the seventh century of this era in the Arabian Peninsula. About A.D. 570 Muhammad, the prophet of Islam, was born in Mecca, which has now become a flourishing commercial city in Saudi Arabia. Today, Mecca, with its famous sanctuary of the Ka 'bah, is the holiest city in Islam. It is toward Mecca that some 350,000,000 Muslims face at prayer. Mecca, to about one-eighth of the world's population, is what Bethlehem is to a Christian.

Saudi Arabia occupies about four-fifths of the Arabian Peninsula with a total area of approximately 830,000 square miles. For administrative purposes, the Kingdom of Saudi Arabia is divided into provinces. Most important of these are Najd, the Hijaz, and the Eastern Province. North of Najd is the district of the Northern Frontiers, while south of the Hijaz are the three districts of Tihamah, 'Asir, and Najran. These three districts, though administered separately, are often treated as a single geographical unit by the name of 'Asir.

THE PEOPLE

The population of Saudi Arabia is estimated to be about six and a half million people. More than half of the people of Saudi Arabia live in oases and till the soil. The majority of the other half are Bedouins roaming the desert with their camels, flocks, and herds. People are employed in such varied pursuits as working in the oil industry, engaging in government work, pearling, and engaging in the different commercial lines.

Saudi Arabs are known to have two major common characteristics: they speak Arabic and are Muslims. While several other Arab countries have among their population a minority of adherents of other faiths, for example, the Christian Copts of Egypt, the Arabs of Saudi Arabia are all Muslims. Adherents of other faiths are only to be found among the foreigners who are employed in the different industries, most famous of which is the Aramco Oil industry.

Life of the Bedouins differs greatly from that of their settled countrymen. Their occupation as herdsmen keeps them moving about the country to take advantage of rain-filled wells and pastures for their animals. Moving the way they do, though in a planned and deliberate manner, makes the problem of opening schools for them rather acute. A large number of Bedouins, however, are today in the regular Army and the National Guard and several choose the settled life and seek employment in the different companies.

THE GOVERNMENT

His Majesty King 'Abd al-'Aziz ibn 'Abd al-Rahman Al Faisal Al Sa'ud, who was the first king of Saudi Arabia until his death in 1953, was the founder of the present kingdom of Saudi Arabia. In 1953 his son, His Majesty King Sa'ud ibn 'Abd al-'Aziz Al Faisal Al Sa'ud, began to reign. He continued to rule over the kingdom up until November 2, 1964, when his half brother, King Faisal ibn 'Abd al-'Aziz Al Faisal Al Sa'ud, began his reign. His name indicates that his father was the late King 'Abd al-'Aziz and that he comes from the Faisal branch of the House of Sa'ud. It is the House of Sa'ud that gives its name to the Kingdom of Saudi Arabia.

The King of Saudi Arabia both reigns and rules. To help him, the Council of Ministers began functioning in 1954. Prior to 1950 only three ministries were known, namely, the Ministry of Foreign Affairs, the Ministry of Finance, and the Ministry of Defense and Aviation. The Ministry of Education was organized in 1954. Before that time there was a Department of Education that took care of the educational interests of the nation.

THE MINISTRY OF EDUCATION

The Ministry of Education has been making remarkable growth since the time it was organized in 1954. Prior to that time there were few public and religious schools. A few private schools existed. In these schools, however, the teachers were unacquainted with modern methods and were unqualified for the teaching profession. This situation continued until the Raqia School and other private schools, such as As-Sawlatiya, Al-Fakhriya, and Al-Falah, were established and registered some improvement.

The Ministry of Education under its first Five-Year-Plan ending in 1963-1964 brought about a most outstanding growth. It is expected that in the second Five-Year-Plan, which began in 1965, even a more remarkable progress will be registered.

It is interesting to note, for example, that while the first elementary school was established in 1925 and a number of primary schools with elementary classes were opened in 1936 and developed to full elementary schools in 1939 with a total enrollment in these schools of 2319, the situation today gives a totally different picture. In the year 1962-1963 alone, 100 elementary schools were opened, all of which were properly equipped with teaching facilities, textbooks, and teachers. Today, the school system includes elementary, intermediate, and secondary schools, agricultural schools, commercial schools, industrial schools, night schools, and training schools for teachers. A student in Saudi Arabia can begin his studies in the elementary school and continue his studies until he can obtain a Ph.D. degree from the King Saud University at Riyad.

Tremendous growth made in the Ministry of Education can be clearly seen from the study of its budgets which are increased substantially from year to year.

The Elementary Cycle

Since the Ministry of Education was organized in 1954, special emphasis was given to elementary education in order to provide at least a basic minimum of education to as many children as possible.

The first modern elementary school was established in 1925. By 1939 several schools were opened with a total enrollment of 2,319. By 1949 the number of schools had risen to 182 with a total enrollment of 21,409. In 1951 there were 210 schools and 28,317 students, increasing in 1953 to 326 schools with a total enrollment of 43,774.

In 1954, when the ministry was first established 120 schools were opened, bringing the total number of pupils to 49,740. The number of both schools and pupils began to grow steadily. In 1956 there were 581 schools with a total enrollment of 79,274; in 1960, there were 712 schools with 104,203 pupils; in 1961, 834 schools with 122,955 pupils; and in 1962, there were 938 schools with a total enrollment of 139,328.

The figures for the school year 1962-1963 (see bottom of page) show the progress reached in the elementary education.

While the number of girl pupils is comparatively low, it shows a substantial effort made by the state on the vital issue of education for girls which will be discussed later.

It is important to note, however, that by the school year 1962-1963, elementary school enrollment throughout Saudi Arabia had risen to 168,223 as compared with 57,841 only seven years earlier.

The Intermediate Cycle

In 1958, the Ministry separated the three intermediate years from the secondary cycle. The schools thus separated numbered 34 with an enrollment of 3,912. In 1959, the number of schools increased to 36 with an enrollment of 4,466. In 1960 the figures were 50 schools and 5,477 pupils; in 1961, 84 schools and 9,240 pupils; and by 1962, the number of pupils in the intermediate schools had risen to 11,636.

For the 1962-1963 school year, the figures (p. 264) mark the growth in the intermediate schools.

To every fifteen students in the elementary schools there is only one in the intermediate. It is hoped that this ratio will improve in the years to come.

Until recent years the intermediate stage consisted only of theoretical studies which led the student to the theoretical secondary stage and later to the university stage. However, the country was in dire need of people with a vocational training in the fields of both agriculture and industry and also in need of

ELEMENTARY SCHOOLS 1962-1963

			GOVERNMENT SCHOOLS	PRIVATE SCHOOLS	TOTAL
Number of Schools			998	63	1061
Number of classes			6573	361	6934
Number of teachers			8150	359	8509
	Men	7568	170	7738	
	Women	582	189	771	
Number of Students			158208	10015	168223
	Boys	139328	5307	144635	
	Girls	18880	4708	23588	

INTERMEDIATE SCHOOLS 1962-1963

		Government Schools	Private Schools		Total
Number of Schools		65	16		85
Number of classes		323	78		401
Number of teachers		620	102		722
	Men 620	80		700	
	Women	22		22	
Number of students		9125	1892		11017
	Boys 8866	1582		10448	
	Girls 259	310		569	

skilled employees in accounting, typing, shorthand, and business administration. For this reason the Ministry established model intermediate schools taking into account the diversification of studies in this stage such that it embraces all these stages, namely, the theoretical intermediate stage—Intermediate Industrial Training, Intermediate Business Training, and Intermediate Agricultural Training. These stages will be considered separately.

Intermediate Trade Schools

The first trade school was opened in 1949 with an enrollment of 30. In 1954 two more schools were opened with an enrollment of 174. One of these schools opened at Medina, the famous city which has the tomb of prophet Muhammed. The other school opened at Riyad, the capital. In 1956 the Eastern District witnessed the establishment of a new industrial school and in 1958 the Ministry opened a second school at Riyad bringing the total enrollment to 641. Two more schools were opened in the Western District and in el-Qassim in 1959, thus raising the number of industrial schools to seven with a total enrollment of 867. By 1960, the number of students reached 1,200; then it increased to 1,562 in 1961. In 1962 the figures for the Intermediate Industrial Schools show considerable growth.

INTERMEDIATE TRADE SCHOOLS 1962-1963

Number of Schools	7
Number of classes	82
Number of teachers (all men)	267
Number of students (all boys)	2173

Intermediate Commercial Schools

To meet the increasing demands in business offices, companies, and banks, four Intermediate Commercial Schools were opened in 1959 with an enrollment of 214. By 1960 the number of students rose to 507 and then to 720 in 1961. The growth in the Intermediate Commercial Schools in 1962 is indicated by the figures at top of next column.

The Ministry in preparing each syllabus for these students consulted the offices and firms in which these students were later expected to work. The Ministry intends to increase the number of commercial schools considerably.

INTERMEDIATE COMMERCIAL SCHOOLS
1962-1963

Number of Schools	2
Number of classes	36
Number of teachers (all men)	62
Number of students	940

Intermediate Agricultural Schools

In 1960, the first Intermediate Agricultural Schools were opened in Saudi Arabia. That year five schools were opened with a total of 198 trainees. In 1961 the enrollment rose to 362 students and then the enrollment almost doubled in 1962 when the trainees numbered 618. Although the number of schools did not increase from 1960-1962, the following figures for the school year 1962-1963 show definite improvement in the Intermediate Agricultural Schools:

INTERMEDIATE AGRICULTURAL SCHOOLS
1962-1963

Number of Schools	5
Number of classes	23
Number of teachers (all men)	43
Number of students (all boys)	618

From the statistics given above, it is to be noted that all the intermediate trade, commercial, and agricultural schools are

1. Government-owned schools,
2. Taught by men teachers only,
3. Opened for boys only.

This situation is different, however, in the theoretical intermediate schools where there are 102 private schools that employ other than eighty men teachers, twenty-two women teachers. In these theoretical intermediate schools are to be found students from both sexes in both the government and private schools.

Secondary Cycle

Secondary Institutes

Secondary education was started mainly with the purpose of training teachers for the elementary schools. In 1926, under the Saudi reign, the first secondary institute was started in Mecca with 41 students.

In 1948, two other secondary institutes were opened, one at Medina and the other in 'Oneiza. The enrollment in all three schools was 257. In 1952, the figures rose to 335. In 1953, the 'Oneiza institute was closed and by 1956 the students in the other two institutes numbered 965. In 1958 when the Ministry expanded its teacher training program, it started liquidating the two institutes at Mecca and Medina. These were completely liquidated by 1961.

Secondary Schools

In 1937, the first secondary school was opened with the object of preparing students for higher studies in Arab and foreign universities. The enrollment in 1937 was only 41. By 1944 there were four of these schools with a total enrollment of 368. In 1950, the number of schools rose to eight with an enrollment of 723. By 1953, there were twelve schools with 1,617 students. The Ministry started an expanded secondary school program in 1954. This was done to raise the educational standards of the country, to meet the pressing demands for education, to train teachers for the elementary cycles, and to produce better-educated citizens. By 1955, the number of secondary schools had risen to twenty-three with a total enrollment of 2,394. By 1956, there were thirty-five schools and a total enrollment of 4,912.

Separation of the intermediate cycle from the secondary cycles caused the number of secondary schools to drop to eighteen in 1958. Of these schools, fourteen were combined secondary-intermediate schools. In 1961, the number of secondary schools were increased to eighteen with 2,176 students and by 1962 the figures for the secondary cycle were as follows:

SECONDARY SCHOOLS 1962-1963

	GOVERN-MENT	PRIVATE	TOTAL
Number of Schools	17	4	21
Number of classes	109	12	121
Number of teachers (all men)	249	12	261
Number of students (all boys)	2770	257	3027

Here again all the students are boys with only men teachers teaching the 121 classes.

Dar et-Tawhid

Emphasis on religious training is to be naturally expected in the Saudi Kingdom that prides itself on having the most important holy sites of Islam within its territory. In 1943, Dar et-Tawhid school was opened at Taif with an enrollment of 21 students. The object of the school was to train the students to specialize in the Muslim religion and to prepare themselves for work as Shari'a judges, teachers of

Arabic, and preachers. In 1949 the enrollment rose to 91, then to 207 in 1953 and to 304 in 1958. In 1960, this one school had 413 students. The enrollment rose to 429 in 1961 and by 1962 the figures for Dar et-Tawhid school, showed considerable growth as can be seen from the following:

DAR ET-TAWHID 1962-1963

Number of classes	18
Number of teachers	28
Number of students	497

Post-Secondary Schools

The Department of Education in 1949 started the Shar'a (Jurisprudence) College to enable secondary school and Dar et-Tawhid graduates to continue their higher studies. The school was to serve as the nucleus for a Saudi university. From 5 students in 1949, enrollment rose to 51 in 1951, to 55 in 1952, to 126 in 1958, to 229 in 1960, to 242 in 1961, and to 259 in 1962. This College of Jurisprudence now entails a period of four years and confers the degree of Bachelor of Theology on its graduates.

Teacher-Training Institutes

Along with the accelerated growth of the elementary schools came the increased demand for Primary Teacher-Training Institutes. Three elementary teacher-training schools were established in 1953 with an enrollment of 71. The newly-formed Ministry of Education, previously only a Department of Education, opened two more schools in 1955 bringing the enrollment to 252. In 1956, another school was opened and the total enrollment reached 399. In 1957, however, 21 new schools were opened and the enrollment in all 27 schools reached 1,052. In 1959 the number of schools increased to 32 with 2,687 enrolled. In 1960 there were 35 schools and 3,467 students, and in 1961, 37 schools and 4,395 students. By 1962 the figures were as follows:

Number of classes	194
Number of teachers (all men)	387
Number of students (all boys)	5575

THE HIGHER TECHNICAL INSTITUTE

The first higher technical school was established in Riyad to train instructors for the intermediate trade schools and to meet the requirements of the different industrial establishments in the kingdom. The students of this institute are given practical training in workshops and factories to better fit them for their future work. This High Institute of Technology, like the Teacher-Training College and the Administrative Institute, covers a period of four years of studies and awards degrees similar to those of the College of Jurisprudence.

It is important to mention that education is not only free in Saudi Arabia, but, as an incentive for students to enroll, the government awards a subvention to each student ranging from 100 Saudi Riyals to 250. This is besides giving the students their textbooks, medical care, and transportation free of charge.

Other institutions that are maintained by the government are schools for the blind and retarded children, for elimination of illiteracy, for adult and fundamental education, and for athletics and social welfare.

Education for the Blind

Training of the blind has become an integral part of the socio-educational structure of the Kingdom of Saudi Arabia. Several centers were opened for the teaching of the blind where specialists and experts carry out their task of training a group of instructors to teach the blind according to the most modern methods and techniques. From 1962-1964 three new centers were opened which followed the pattern of training which was already well-established in the capital Riyadh. Statistically the picture is indeed illuminating:

Year	Provided Training for
1959	60
1960	100
1961	150
1962	270
1963	450
1964	600

Thus there are the following annual increases:

Year	Increase Over Previous Year
1960	40 (66%)
1961	50 (50%)
1962	120 (80%)
1963	180 (66%)
1964	150 (33%)

Both primary and intermediate education at the blind schools follow curricula identical to those of the normal Saudi schools. Results so far show no difference whatsoever in the respective times taken to reach the same academic levels.

The basic pattern continues of teaching boys and youths on normal academic lines, with vocational training for men over twenty. The proportions at each center now are

	Primary	Intermediate	Vocational	Total
Riyadh	130	11	119	260
Mecca	35	—	60	95
Hufuf	72	—	88	160
'Onaiza	30	—	55	85

The Saudi blind have equipment on a generous scale. In addition to modern and very spacious build-

ings for their training, a wide range of equipment has been purchased from the R. N. I. B., London. This includes the purchase of maps and globes in relief, special instruments and tools for measurement and joinery, specialized games, tactile educational aids, and writing and drawing aids.

A complete Braille printing press of adequate capacity has been purchased and installed in Riyadh. This makes it possible to produce within the organization's own headquarters all textbooks, magazines, and other publications for their own use.

It is pleasant to note that the proportion of instructors to students is high. Although recruiting staff seemed at first very difficult, success has been greatly achieved because of the generous salary scale decided by the government. Now there are eighty-nine members who comprise the staff, sixty-nine of whom are Saudi by nationality.

Not only are high salaries given for those who work with the blind, but there are student grants given to all blind who are regularly attending the institutes. The last six budgets show the rise in expenditure caused by the continual progress made in the work for the blind:

	Rials	Dollar Equivalent
1959	10,000	2,220
1960	232,000	52,700
1961	1,300,000	290,000
1962	1,600,000	359,000
1963	2,500,000	555,550
1964	3,500,000	777,778

Adult Education

The Ministry of Education, realizing that illiteracy disturbs the equilibrium of society, has started illiteracy combating centers. These centers were generally set up in existing school buildings, and arrangements were made for evening classes so that students who work during the day can attend. In 1955, 1,713 students attended 23 "literacy" schools. In 1957 the number of schools increased to 57 with 5,270 students attending. By 1960 there were 8,220 students attending 87 "literacy" schools.

The following table shows the increase in the number of adult students attending the different Illiteracy Combating Centres in the years 1961, 1962, 1963.

ILLITERACY COMBATING CENTRES IN 1961, 1962, 1963

Year	No. of Centres	No. of Students	No. of Classes	No. of Teachers	No. of Administrative & Technical Staff
1961	87	9,220	323	329	107
1962	183	16,843	598	578	196
1963	259	22,788	879	775	210

It is indeed remarkable to note that special curricula and books were devised for the adult-students in keeping with their intellectual levels, vocational aptitudes, and mentalities. This step proved to be a real step forward and much more practical than using the curricula of the early years of the elementary education stage.

Evening Schools for Training Teachers

In 1952 the Department of Education opened evening schools to provide elementary teachers with the opportunity to improve their qualifications. These elementary teachers are taught the principles of pedagogy as well as a number of academic subjects to improve their general knowledge. In 1952 the enrollment in these evening schools was 170. Other schools for the same purpose were opened bringing the total number of students to 279 in 1955 and to 777 in 1959.

Education for Girls

Education of girls was largely neglected until 1960. Prior to that date their education had been conditioned by the wishes of their parents and their attitude toward education. Until 1960 there were some private schools which offered education for girls, but these were not sufficient to meet the pressing need.

In 1960, the State, for the first time in history, allocated a budget for the education of girls. Although the budget was 2,000,000 Saudi Rials (about $450,000 U. S.) it was certainly a start in the right direction. That year, fifteen schools for girls were opened of which three were teachers' training schools. In addition thirty-nine private schools became subject to government supervision. The number of girls in government schools in 1960 totalled 5,204.

The 1961 budget more than doubled. The State that year allocated the sum of 4,400,000 Saudi rials (about a million dollars) for girls' schools. Of that sum 910,000 rials were paid as subsidies to private schools.

The figure for the 1962 budget was 7,164,400 rials (about $1,600,000). The subsidy for private schools, however, remained the same. Because of this increase in budget, sixteen new elementary schools and three teachers' training schools were opened. The total enrollment by that time was 11,714.

The 1963 budget increased to 12,415,480 rials (about $2,750,000) and the total enrollment for girls was 19,139. In addition to the regular academic courses the syllabus for girls included the teaching of practical subjects as home economics, needlework, dressmaking, and cooking.

The General Presidency of Girl Schools that supervises both government and private schools for girls released the following tables that indicate the progress made in the education of women in the year 1962-1963:

ELEMENTARY STAGE

	SCHOOLS	CLASSES	STUDENTS
Government	60	546	19,119
Private	24	168	5,117
Total	84	714	24,236

INTERMEDIATE STAGE

	SCHOOLS	CLASSES	STUDENTS
Government	—	—	——
Private	8	18	284
Total	8	18	284

TEACHERS' TRAINING INSTITUTES

	INSTITUTES	CLASSES	STUDENTS
Government	7	15	261
Private	—	—	——
Total	7	15	261

The above figures are a clear indication of the progress made toward the education of girls in the kingdom. A large number of Saudi girls have graduated from Arab universities and have returned home to help in the education of the girls in their own home country. These Saudi women-teachers number only 164 as compared with 117 Egyptians, 179 Jordanians, 224 Palestinians, 25 Syrians, and few others from other nationalities.

In 1962 the government singled out approximately 20 million rials for its two seats of higher learning, namely, King Saud University and the Islamic University that are in Riyadh and Medina respectively. In this connection it is of interest to note that the Saudi Arabian government grants scores of fellowships to be awarded annually to African students to further their education in all the Saudi Arabian institutions of higher learning, specially King Saud University and that of the Islamic University in Medina. Not only are fellowships granted to citizens of other countries, but the government annually sends missions abroad to further their education. The number of students sent every year on study missions abroad for undergraduate and postgraduate work (Master's and Doctor's degrees) is steadily increasing. About 1,800 students studied abroad at these levels in 1966-67.

King Saud University

One of the most outstanding accomplishments of the Saudi government in the field of education was the establishment of King Saud University in Riyad in 1957. The university admits applicants who hold the General Secondary Education Certificate or other equivalent certificates. In addition to Saudi students, the university admits students from other Arab countries. In 1963 the university offered sixteen scholarships to foreign students from Nigeria, the independent African states, and countries of the Arab South.

Those who receive such scholarships must not only be Moslems but must know the Arabic language. The university comprises four colleges. These colleges are

1. The College of Arts and Literature. This is the oldest college in the university. When it started its first academic year in 1957-58 it had only twenty-one students. Today the college has several departments, namely, History, Geography, Arabic Language, Literature, English Language, and Literature. The first group of fifteen students graduated from the University in 1960-61 with a Bachelor's degree in Arts from the Department of History and Geography. The following year another twenty-seven graduated from the same college.

The figures for the College of Arts and Literature that can award the B.A., M.A., and Ph.D. degrees are as follows:

YEAR	REGULAR STUDENTS	EXTERNAL STUDENTS	PROFESSORS, LECTURERS, AND INSTRUCTORS
1960-61	133	62	30
1961-62	117	171	28
1962-63	207	154	28

2. The College of Science. This college was opened in 1958-59 and can confer the General B.Sc., Special B.Sc., M.Sc., and Ph.D. degrees. This college has several departments, namely, Physics, Chemistry, Mathematics, Botany, Zoology, and Geology. Following are the figures from 1960-1963:

YEAR	NO. OF STUDENTS	PROFESSORS, LECTURERS, AND INSTRUCTORS
1960-61	65	24
1961-62	80	34
1962-63	102	34

In addition to the thirty-four professors, lecturers, and instructors, there are fifteen laboratory heads in charge of the different well-equipped laboratories.

3. The College of Pharmacy. This college was established in 1959-60 and can confer the degrees of Bachelor of Pharmacy and Pharmaceutical Chemistry as well as the Master's and Doctor's degree in Pharmacy. Included in the curriculum for the Bachelor of Pharmacy degree are the following subjects: Zoology, Botany, Physics, Natural Chemistry, Organic Chemistry, Inorganic Chemistry, Classification of Medical Plants, Raw Drugs, Analytical Chemistry, Raw Drugs Chemistry, Pharmaceutics, Galenic Pharmacy, Pharmaceutical Chemistry, Applied Pharmacology, Toxicology and First Aid, Bacteriology, Public Health, Pharmacy Legislation, Bookkeeping, Pharmacy Administration, and a modern European language.

Again the figures for 1961 and 1962 show definite progress in the College of Pharmacy. In 1960-61 there were nineteen students and six professors and associates. In 1962-63 there were thirty-seven students

and ten professors and associates. This is besides seven laboratory technicians.

4. The College of Commerce. This college was established in 1959-60. Other than the M.A., and Ph.D. degrees in commerce, the college can confer a B.A. in commerce in either Accountancy and Business Administration or in Economics and Political Science. The subjects taught in the College of Commerce include Accountancy, Business Administration, Economics, Public Finance, Legislation, Law, Statistics, Mathematics, Insurance, Economic Geography, Political Geography, Political Science, and a modern European language. In 1962-63 there was a staff of twenty professors, lecturers, and instructors teaching 454 students as compared with only 388 students in 1961-62 and 274 students in 1960-61.

The Islamic University of Medina

Another very important institute of advanced learning was inaugurated in 1961 in Medina. The scope of studies in this university covers a period of four years at the end of which the successful student receives the degree of Bachelor of Arts in Muslim Theology. This University, like the Al-Azhar University of Egypt, the oldest university in the world, is intended to be a great citadel of learning in Islam.

THE GENERAL DIRECTORATE FOR LIBRARIES

The Directorate for Libraries has under its supervision several important libraries that are of vital importance to the educational interests of the nation. These libraries are

16 General Libraries containing 74,550 volumes and 6,450 manuscripts

12 Specialized Libraries containing 41,500 volumes

20 Private Libraries containing 60,000 volumes and 2,000 manuscripts

One University Library containing 60,000 volumes

135 School Libraries containing 77,500 volumes

The National Library in Riyadh

This properly designed and equipped library cost 1,221,000 Saudi rials to build. This is one of seven sister libraries decided for each of Mecca, Jiddah, Medina, Riyadh, Tayif, the Eastern Region, and el-Qasseem.

SUMMARY

In conclusion it must be said that Saudi Arabia drew on the experiences of the other Arab states in the formation of its curriculum and has made great strides in its endeavor to bring education to its masses. It has recruited instructors from neighboring countries to help in the six years of study in elementary education, the three years of instruction in the intermediate schools as well as in the three additional studies in the secondary schools. It did the same thing to help in the establishment of the King Saud University. Today it could be said that the Kingdom of Saudi Arabia, that was in a dormant stage prior to the advent of the Saudi reign, is now standing at the threshold of a new era of cultural and intellectual reckoning. The feats so far achieved should be measured against the limited time allowed for their accomplishment. Certainly the progress effected in the past few years will open new vistas and wider horizons in the dissemination of science and learning among every level of the Saudi Arabian society in decades ahead.

The magnitude of the progress made in the development of the educational program in the Kingdom of Saudi Arabia is now proceeding at a geometrical pace.

BIBLIOGRAPHY

Arabian Nights (Many editions. Most famous translations by Burton and Lane)

BURTON, SIR RICHARD F. *Personal Narrative of a Pilgrimage to Al-Madinah and Meccah*. London: Bell, 1898, and other editions.

CHEESMAN, R. E. *In Unknown Arabia*. London: Macmillan, 1926.

DOUGHTY, C. M. *Travels in Arabia Deserts*. New York: Random House, 1946.

GUILLAUME, A. *Islam*, 2nd ed. Harmondsworth, England: Penguin Books, 1956.

HITTI, P. K. *History of the Arabs*, 6th ed. London: Macmillan, 1956.

———. *The Penetration of Arabia*. London: Alston Rivers, 1905.

PICKTHALL, M. *The Meaning of the Glorious Qur'an*. New York: New American Library, 1953.

LAWRENCE, T. E. *Seven Pillars of Wisdom*. Garden City: Doubleday, 1935.

LEBKICHER, ROY; RENTZ, GEORGE; STEINEKE, MAX, with contributions by other Aramco employees. *Aramco Handbook*. The Netherlands by Arabian American Oil Company, 1960.

Ministry of Education Saudi Arabian Kingdom, *A Brief Report on the Ministry of Education for the year 1962-1963*.

———, *Report on the Progress of Blind Training and Education*.

Ministry of Information Saudi Arabian Kingdom. *Education for Girls* (Book II).

———, *Education in Saudi Arabia* (Book IV).

PHILBY, H. ST. JOHN B. *The Heart of Arabia*. London: Constable, 1922.

THOMAS, BERTRAM. *Arabia Felix*. New York: Scribner's, 1932.

VILLIERS, ALAN. *Sons of Sinbad*. New York: Scribner's, 1940.

WILLIAMS, KENNETH. *Don Sa'ud*. London: Cape, 1933.

WILSON, SIR ARNOLD. *The Persian Gulf*. London: Allen & Unwin, 1954.

YALE, WILLIAM. *The Near East: A Modern History*. Ann Arbor, Mich.: University of Michigan Press, 1958.

SKEIKDOMS AND PRINCIPALITIES OF PERSIAN GULF AND ARABIAN PENINSULA

Patricia Lei Alzobaie

Until comparatively recent times, the numerous sheikdoms and principalities of the southern Arabian peninsula and the Persian Gulf lay slumbering, little disturbed for hundreds of years. Agriculture provided a living of sorts for the majority of people, agriculture on land almost too poor to support it. Pearls, fishing, and shipping augmented farming in some places. The whole area was one to which few people came but many left in an attempt to find a better way of life.

Education was available to few of the people. Only Koranic schools existed, providing instruction in the Koran, basic literacy, and simple arithmetic.

The dramatic discovery of oil in some of these areas and the hope of finding it in others has changed the picture rapidly. Oil revenues have become available to provide for a variety of educational programs. Oil-rich areas have helped their less fortunate neighbors in starting such programs.

Rapid development in countries aided by oil has resulted in a gap that precludes consideration of them as a single group with areas where oil has not been found. Some places have but a single school, others have the structure for the development of an excellent modern educational system. In most of the area, few secondary schools exist; education for girls is just beginning; and problems of expansion, buildings, and native staff and curriculums present tremendous difficulties.

SOUTHERN ARABIAN PENINSULA

In the Aden Protectorate, the curriculum was entirely Indian previous to 1937. After that date, it became British in structure and outlook, with the London G. C. E. the desired outcome of a secondary education.

In other parts of the Federation, each area maintained its own separate non-native, curriculum until 1963. East African, Sudanese, and other books and methods were used.

With the formation of the Federation, the curriculum became standard throughout the area, centrally determined by a Minister of Education.

The structure is now one of four years of primary school, three years of intermediate for boys and four for girls, and then secondary school. The academic secondary school leads to the Cambridge certificate.

Following the academic four-year secondary school, students receive aid while studying for an additional two years to prepare them for study abroad. Entrance to all levels beyond the intermediate school is determined by competitive examinations.

A second type of secondary school is the two-year technical school, leading to skill in office work. A third type is the technical institute, leading to specialization in public technical education, fine arts with a possibility for study in London upon completion, teaching in public schools, health, and government and industrial employment.

The standard school year is from 180 to 190 days long. In remote areas, time out for fishing and farming reduces this figure somewhat. Many schools are on double shifts in an attempt to meet the increasing demands upon education.

Education at all levels is free, with boarding facilities and financial support available from the intermediate level on. All levels of education are available to girls, with secondary school attendance being in Aden.

Little of the curriculum and texts is native to the area. Books at the primary level are generally East African translations with only a very few locally written texts.

At higher levels, books from several sources are used, depending upon suitability and availability. At no level are teachers' guides and resources provided, though an attempt is being made to supply some instructions and other help.

Adult education programs exist, and private educational institutions supplement the efforts of the public system.

In Hadhramaut, modern education began in 1939 with the adoption of the Sudanese curriculum, in total. This system was greatly opposed at first but is now preferred to the Koranic schools.

In the time since, the system has changed in two ways. First, it changes as the Sudanese curriculum changes. This is reinforced by having many teachers trained in Sudan. Second, changes have been made to adjust the materials to the culture of Hadhramaut. Religious instruction has been made to fit the religion of the area, local units of measure are included in mathematics instruction, local history is taught, and children in story books are children of Hadramaut rather than of Sudan.

The elementary, intermediate, and secondary schools are each four years. Beyond elementary school, admission is based on competitive examinations.

Instruction at the intermediate and secondary levels is in part in English, as in Sudan. However, some Egyptian books are used because of their availability and because of the fact that many students from this area attend college in Egypt.

Again, education is free at all levels, with boarding facilities available.

Education for girls exists, but social tradition makes progress difficult. A further problem is the lack of trained native women teachers. This is being solved by hiring teachers from other countries, notably Jordan.

The secondary school is only now graduating its first class. Founded in 1962, it is still operating on a very small scale.

TRUCIAL STATES

Information on the Trucial States is scarce. Little has been published on educational developments in any but a few of these small areas.

In Qatar, the educational system has benefited tremendously from oil revenues. Money is now available to try to place a primary school of six years in every village with enough students to support it.

Examinations provide the basis for entrance to intermediate and secondary schools. Students are provided with free tuition, books, meals, clothing, medical care, transportation, bursaries, and boarding facilities when needed.

In addition to the academic secondary school, with the possibility of further study abroad, teacher training and technical education provide additional opportunities. The oil companies also operate training centers for their employees.

As in the rest of the area, the curriculum is imported from other Arabic countries. The educational pattern is 6-3-3 for academic education and 5-3 or 6-3 for technical and industrial education.

In Muscat and Oman, education is limited to the main towns, except for Koranic schools. There are no higher educational facilities and a bare mention of secondary schools is made in the literature.

Bahrein is similarly progressive in having a relatively old educational structure, dating from 1925. The 6-5 system is followed. The student population has increased tremendously due to added interest in education and increased available money from oil production.

COMMON PROBLEMS

All of the countries of this area are faced with grave educational problems. For those countries not fortunate enough to have oil, money is the first of these. Manufacturing is virtually non-existent, natural resources are few, and only a small percentage of the land is arable. The United Kingdom and other Arabic countries, notably Kuwait, have provided support in terms of texts, clothes, and grants.

Lack of educated native-born citizens to serve as teachers presents another problem. Other Arab countries provide the bulk of the teachers, with some being recruited from other parts of the world. However, few of the other Arab countries have a surplus of teachers large enough to meet their own increasing demands for education and those of this area.

A great deal of public education is needed to convince the ordinary illiterate citizen of the value of schooling for the young people of these countries. The pattern for generations has been for the boys to help their fathers and for girls to marry at an early age. Education is not viewed as necessary nor particularly desirable, especially for girls.

The public attitude toward education, combined with the severe lack of staff and facilities makes a consideration of compulsory education premature. A long period of meeting demands for education must precede concern for compulsory education.

The lack of any facilities for higher education presents another problem. While training people abroad is a costly method, there are at present no human resources to staff local colleges. The increasing need for teachers at all levels will soon serve to compound the problem.

A second facet of the problem of lack of facilities for higher education is the fact that in many parts of this conservative Moslem Arabic area, few families are willing to send their girls abroad to study. The culture is oriented toward the seclusion and protection of women. College attendance alone outside the country is unthinkable in a conservative family.

The heavy reliance upon teachers from the United Kingdom and systems that are often oriented toward British certificates of completion and scholarships abroad are apt to cause education to meet with even stronger opposition from the uneducated majority. The trend throughout the Arabic-speaking world is toward Arab nationalism. The externally oriented schools of the area are at odds with this trend. Recent attempts have been made to meet this problem by including the Arabic language, history, and culture in the program and examinations at all levels.

Industry, in those places where it has begun to develop, is competing for the services of the few educated people. As it is able to pay more than the government can offer teachers, this serves as a drain on potential teaching staff.

No country of the southern Arabian peninsula has a national curriculum nor nationally devised texts. Arabic texts from other countries are used, and the curriculum is either similarly adopted or is British in orientation. An adopted curriculum and materials cannot hope to best serve the needs of each of the several countries in the area.

Technical education is not popular. In the eyes of those with even a minimum of education, this is for people unable to achieve higher educational levels.

The numbers of people leaving some of the countries of this area to seek employment elsewhere is a drain on the potential human resources. It is probable that many of these people are the very ones with the initiative their country needs.

Education in the sheikdoms and principalities of the southern Arabian peninsula and Persian Gulf is just beginning to develop. Oil revenues and help from other countries has spurred the development. Severe problems of finance, staff, public acceptance, materials, lack of higher education facilities, lack of nationally oriented goals, competition for educated people by industry, non-acceptance of technical training and manual labor, and an exodus of people from the area exist. When these problems begin to be solved, equally pressing ones of mass education to meet increasing demands will appear.

Time is against an easy solution of the educational problems of this area. Before the public education structure has a chance to develop, demands from industry, government, and an increasingly aware public will provide the structure with more problems than it will be readily able to meet.

BIBLIOGRAPHY

Abu Shehry, Esa Mahmood. *Atta Lim el Ibtidi*: *Wal Mutawassit fil Kuwait* (*Elementary and Intermediate Education in Kuwait*). Beirut: The Regional Center for Training Senior Arab Educators, 1964-65.

Al Mazuree, Ahmed Yousef. *Manahig Atta-liem al Thanawi fil Kuwait* (*Secondary Curriculum in Kuwait*). Beirut: The Regional Center for Training Senior Arab Educators, 1964-65.

Al-Saeed, Yousef. "Sa-heefit A 'Tukhteet A-Terboree fil Bilad Al-Arabic Shibat." (Intermediate and Secondary Education in the South Arabian Federation), *Magazine of Educational Planning in the Arab Countries*: Vol. 4, No. 10 (1966).

Anabaki, Said Yislam. *Tukreer An Al Menahij Al Talimiya Wa Idara Aterbowea Fe Dowla Al Qaetia fe Hadramat* (*Report of Curriculum and School Administration in the Qaeti States of Hadramat*). Beirut: The Regional Center for Training Senior Educators in the Arab World, 1964-65.

Fedda'q, Khalid Aideroose. *Tuqreer An Menahij Al Marhalla Al Iptidiaya Bitlihad Al Jenoub Al Arabic* (*Report on Elementary Curriculum In South Arabian Federation*). Beirut: The Regional Center for Training Senior Educators in the Arab World, 1964-65.

"Middle East Education Survey, 1961," *Statistical Yearbook*, 1961. New York: United Nations, Department of Economic and Social Affairs, 1961.

SYRIA-U.A.R.

Lily Stewart Methven

Syria's state system of education as it is today is comparatively new, dating only from 1946 when Syria became an independent republic after over twenty years under French mandate. Prior to this, the Province of Syria had been part of the Ottoman Empire for four hundred years, except for a few years of annexation to Egypt, and had included not only present-day Syria, but also Lebanon, Palestine, and Transjordan.

After many valuable contributions to the ancient world, including the invention of the alphabet, the first three hundred years under Ottoman domination found Syria in decline. Education was almost entirely religious and consisted largely of memorization of the Koran. Some light was shed on the otherwise dark educational scene by the presence of some Catholic missions, one of which, the Lazarist Catholic mission, founded a school for boys in Damascus in the late eighteenth century.

It was not until the last century of Turkish domination that there was some progress in the field of education. The period during the 1830s when the Province of Syria was annexed to Egypt proved noteworthy as Ibrahim Pasha, whose father, Muhammed Ali, ruler of Egypt, had made cultural contacts with the West, allowed both European and American missions to establish schools. Not until the early 1860s, however, did the slaughter of Christians in Lebanon and the spread of unrest to Damascus, together with the opening of the Suez Canal, cause greater European and American interest in the area and lead to the establishment of a number of mission schools. Schools were founded also by a lay mission, the French Mission Laique, and by the British Syrian Mission. American educational influence was particularly great and resulted in establishment of an institution of higher learning as well as schools at lower levels.

This higher institution, the Syrian Protestant College, was founded in 1866 by the American Presby-terian Mission and later became the largely non-sectarian American University of Beirut. It was followed by another institute of higher learning, a Jesuit college, which was originally established in Ghazir in 1843 and was moved in 1875 to Beirut where it later became the Universite de St. Joseph. These institutions are representative of the English-speaking and the French-speaking influences on education. The former used English as the language of instruction but also gave courses in Arabic and was not affiliated with a Western government. The latter used the French language and was to some extent subsidized by the French government.

Those boys who did receive an education usually went to mission schools, which, at first, were attended mainly by Christians. Other schools had been established during the nineteenth and early twentieth centuries by the Ottoman Turks as several of the Sultans admired the administrative and particularly the military skill of the West and believed these could be achieved through education. The schools they established were attended mainly by the sons of Turkish officials and, in some cases, by sons of leading Arabs. Turkish, not Arabic, was the language of instruction.

The years after World War I saw division of the lands of the Ottoman Empire, France being given the mandate over Syria and Lebanon. Between this time and the granting of Syrian independence, little was done toward developing education with Arabic as the language of instruction. The prime aim was the development of French culture.

But there was a growing desire among all classes of society that their children should receive an education that would enable them to enter the professions or government service. Among the urban middle class there was also a desire that girls as well as boys should be educated, something unthought of a few years earlier.

By 1938 there were four main types of school.[1] These were as follows: official schools, maintained by the Syrian and Lebanese governments; "national" schools, which did not give religious instruction; schools maintained by religious communities; and foreign controlled and subsidized schools. Of these the third and fourth groups were largely maintained by Christian organizations, and the third group was the largest.

Problems at this time were the lack of common intellectual ground caused by the diversity of schools; that of teaching Arabic and making it an adequate language of expression for modern scientific concepts while not neglecting European languages; that of peasant illiteracy; and that of producing farmers and technicians rather than government officials and lawyers.

World War II saw the emergence of Syria as an independent republic, which it became officially in 1946. From this time to the present, attempts have been made to solve some of the problems mentioned in the previous paragraph and to develop a system of education suited to Syrian Arab needs and aspirations.

Syria today has a population of some five million people, over a third of whom are city dwellers. Most are Moslem, but about 14 percent are Christian. Farming is the chief economic activity with some industrial development, which is helped by foreign aid.

The main aim in education is the creation of an Arab nation and emphasis is placed on the study of Arabic. A complete system of public education exists, although for many students elementary education is the first and last stage, and it is therefore designed to meet the needs of both terminal students and those who will go on to further stages of education.

Primary education is compulsory. It lasts for six years usually beginning at the age of six. This stage must be completed by the time the student is fourteen years of age. The elementary curriculum places the greatest emphasis on Arabic which is followed in importance by arithmetic. Drawing, religious education, and music are also studied, with the principles of science and hygiene (replaced by agriculture in rural schools) added from the third year. Extra time is given to agricultural education in rural schools. Athletics also have a place in the curriculum. Upon successful completion of the sixth grade, students are awarded a scholastic certificate. Books are free only in cases of financial need.

Teachers at this level are selected from graduates of male and female Elementary Teachers' Training Institutes. Emergency teachers must be used to fill vacancies and they must have the Certificate of General Education or at least the Preparatory School Certificate. Special teacher-training courses and seminars are given by the Ministry of Education during vacations to provide teachers to meet the needs of the expanding educational system.

Those students who pass the governmental general competitive examination at the end of their primary school years may begin three years of preparatory school which are free, but not compulsory. The preparatory curriculum still places emphasis on the study of Arabic, but the study of a foreign language is given almost as much time, followed by mathematics, social studies (including national education), general science and hygiene, practical studies (for boys, handicrafts and agricultural training; for girls, needlework and home economics), religious education, athletics, drawing, and music.

Students are selected for three years of secondary education, also free but not compulsory, according to their success in the general preparatory examination. Places are limited so they go to students with the highest grades. Those who pass the examination, but for whom there are not places may go to private schools, if they can afford to do so. After the first year of secondary education, students enter either the literary or the scientific stream for their final two years.

Arabic language and literature still have an important place in the curriculum, but time spent on them may be equalled or even slightly exceeded by time spent on other subjects. After the first year the curriculum also differs according to stream. Arabic language and literature are studied by both streams each year, as are a foreign language, religious education, and history. Time is also devoted to athletics and military education. Other subjects studied by one or both streams are a second foreign language, Arab society, geography and geology, philosophy, sociology and economics, logic and ethics, mathematics and geometrical drawing, physics, chemistry, and biology. After three years a general examination supervised by the Ministry of Education is given and those who are successful are awarded the Secondary Certificate.

There are four types of teachers at these levels. First, there are the graduates of Damascus University with the licentiate degree of B.A. or B.S. or equivalent from other accredited institutions. Second, there are the graduates of Secondary Teachers' Training Institutes who hold the licentiate or bachelor's degree plus one year of training in the theory and practice of education. Third, there are those whose qualification is experience. Fourth, there are graduates of Elementary Training Institutes who are allowed to teach in preparatory and secondary school to help meet the need for teachers.

Technical preparatory and secondary schools provide another form of education to that described previously. These schools are almost all free governmental ones. The preparatory technical school may be entered, upon successful completion of primary education, by means of a competitive examination.

1. A. H. Houran, *Syria and Lebanon* (London: Oxford University Press, 1946), p. 94.

Scholarships may be awarded to outstanding students in financial need to cover or help cover cost of room and board. The technical preparatory school provides three years of training in industry for boys and in handicrafts for girls. The industrial curriculum includes training in blacksmithing, molding, surveying, combustion engines, engraving, electricity, wireless, textiles, tailoring, and carpentry. Handicrafts include sewing and embroidery. Success in a general examination at the end of the course qualifies the student for the Certificate of Technical Preparatory Education.

Holders of this certificate or of the General Preparatory Education Certificate may begin three years of training in a technical secondary school. At this level commercial training is also offered. Agricultural schools exist only at this level and all expenses of students attending them are paid by the Ministry of Agriculture.

Higher education is offered by the University of Damascus established in 1919 and the University of Aleppo established in 1958. Both institutions are autonomous and are in the process of expanding. To enter one or other of them a student must hold the secondary education certificate or its equivalent. Graduates of commercial, agricultural, and industrial schools may be accepted by the faculties of commerce, agriculture, and industry respectively, if they pass the entrance examination given by these faculties. Four-year courses are given except in the faculties of medicine, dentistry, and pharmacy where studies are of longer duration.

Higher technical education is offered in four institutes, all established in 1960. These are the High Commercial Institute in Aleppo, which offers four-year courses leading to a bachelor's degree in commercial and financial sciences to students selected from holders of the General Secondary Education Certificate, the Technical Secondary Education Certificate (commercial section) or an equivalent qualification; the High Institute of Agriculture in Damascus, which offers a four-year course leading to a bachelor's degree in agriculture sciences to students selected from holders of the Certificate of Secondary Education (scientific section), the agricultural certificate or an equivalent qualification; the High Institute of Fine Arts in Damascus, which has three branches, architectural engineering, decorational engineering, and fine arts, and offers a four-year course leading to a bachelor's degree to students selected from holders of the appropriate secondary education certificate or an equivalent qualification; and, finally, the Institute of Industrial Education in Aleppo, which offers regular two-year courses to students holding the appropriate secondary certificates, leading to the institute's diploma, and also offers practical courses of three months or more.

Private schools, which have played such an important part in Syrian education, continue to do so. Since the 1940s, however, their character has been somewhat different. Until this time even local private schools had followed the French or the American pattern. With the drive toward the development of a Syrian Arab nation, private schools were required to accept government control and inspection and to use the government curricula and textbooks. Some deviation from the prescribed curricula may be allowed with permission. This may allow the introduction of a foreign language at the primary level, which is otherwise forbidden. At this time all kindergartens are private. Aid may be given by the government to private schools. The importance of private education may be seen by the fact that there are almost as many preparatory and secondary school students in private schools as in government schools.

Syria has many problems of other Arab nations. Some of these were cited in 1955,[2] some ten years after independence, and it is interesting to examine them now, after more than fifteen years, in the light of those educational developments previously mentioned. First cited was the fact that, although an increasing number of children were attending school, some were probably prevented from attending by economic pressure. Second was the problem of increasing educational opportunity while maintaining quality and of adapting education to the needs of the country. The curriculum was criticized as being too academic and general with not enough emphasis on sciences, economics, and civics. More vocational education was recommended, with emphasis on agriculture in rural areas and great stress on creative manual work. It was thus hoped to improve living standards and to bring about more respect for manual labor. Third, teaching methods were criticized as being too greatly influenced by examinations and too reliant upon memorization. More discussion and intellectual initiative were thought to be needed. Fourth, vocational education was considered to have been neglected and to lack prestige. Fifth, adult education was also thought to have been neglected.

Bold attempts have been made subsequently to meet problems such as those cited. Many new schools have been built, some of them for vocational and adult education. Education is also being adapted to meet the needs of the country with more stress on vocational needs and on agriculture in rural areas. Educational opportunity is still limited by financial considerations and there is still considerable reliance on selection by competitive examinations, but this is to be expected while educational places remain scarce.

Yet another problem is that of school premises because money which could be used for building must be used to rent accommodations for immediate needs.

Plans have been made for a continuing program of school expansion. Much remains to be done, but

2. *The Economic Development of Syria*, International Bank for Reconstruction (Baltimore: The Johns Hopkins Press, 1955).

giant strides have been made in the last twenty years toward realization of the aim of the Ministry of Education to create a new Arab generation.

SELECTED BIBLIOGRAPHY

The Economic Development of Syria. International Bank of Reconstruction. Baltimore: The Johns Hopkins Press, 1955.

Education in the Arab States. New York: Arab Information Center, 1966.

HARBY, MOHAMMED K. *Technical Education in the Arab States*. UNESCO educational studies and documents, No. 53, 1965.

HITTI, PHILIP K. *Syria: A Short History*. New York: The Macmillan Co., 1959.

HOURANI, A. H. *Syria and Lebanon*. London: Oxford University Press, 1946.

YEMEN

Stanley Weinstein

Yemen has clearly delineated boundries on only three sides. There is no eastern frontier. The total land space is estimated at 75,000 square miles. A 300-mile Red Sea coastline forms the western limit of territory. On the north is Saudi Arabia. Toward the northwest is the Asir Provence of Saudi Arabia. To the south is the Aden Protectorate. Yemen is essentially mountainous. Most of the country is composed of fertile highland plateaus rising from 4,000 to 10,000 feet in height. The highest point in the land is Jobal Hadhur which rises 12,336 feet above the Red Sea coast.

CLIMATE

Extreme humidity combines with high temperatures (as high as 130 degrees Fahrenheit in the shade) to produce a stifling, hot climate. Winds blowing northwest in summer and southwest in winter bring little rain but cause severe sand storms. During the months of January and February temperatures average 68 degrees. The climate in the highlands, however, is considered to be the best in Arabia. In this area the summers are temperate and the winter is cool with some frost. The temperatures reported in this area range from 71 degrees in June to 57 degrees in January. Rainfall in the highlands ranges from 16 inches in San'a', the capital city, to 32 inches in the Monsoon area of the extreme southwest, San'a''s average year-round temperature is 63.5 degrees Fahrenheit.

POPULATION

On July 1, 1949, the government of Yemen estimated the population to be four and a half million. Other estimates put the population at five million. The principal towns are San'a', the capital, with about 60,000 people; Ta'izz, about 75,000; al-Hudaydah, with 40,000 people is the chief port; Bayt-al-Faqih, 12,000; Zabib, 8,000; Dhamar, 8,000; Ibb, 7,000; al-Luhayyah, 6,000; and Yorim, 5,000. There is overpopulation as the birth rate is very high and the death rate low. This condition has been attributed to the fact that the climate is considered to be so healthful, although the temperature is often 130 degrees Fahrenheit. Another explanation for the high population rate can be explained by the decree introduced in 1938 by the Imam, which forbids emigration.

ETHNIC GROUPS

Many ethnologists contend that the purest Arab stock is to be found in Yemen. Classified as Joktanic Semites, they claim descent from Himyar, great grandson of Joktan, who descended from Shem, the son of Noah. Veddoid and Negrito blood and a strong Negroid strain are detectable in the people. A cosmopolitan population lives in the coastal towns and villages. Somalis, Danakil Ethiopians, African Negroes, Parsis, and Hindus make up this group. In 1949 practically the entire population of Yemenite Jews, who had been living in their own secluded communities, left Yemen for Israel, en masse, with minor exceptions. Today there exists within the country a small minority group of jews.

LANGUAGE

Arabic is spoken throughout Yemen. The script is composed of twenty-eight consonants plus other marks and is used in all Arabic-speaking countries as well as Iran and Pakistan. In vocabulary and other features there is considerable difference between the classical language used for writing and formal speaking and the spoken dialect used for ordinary discourse.

RELIGION

Islam is the dominant religion of Yemen. The ruling class are the Zaydis, a sect of Shi'i Islam. They comprise less than half the population. The main religious group in Yemen are the Shafi'i's, a Sunni sect. Antagonism between these two communities has had serious repercussions in the nation's internal and external affairs. There are also about 50,000 Isma'ilis, members of another Shi'i' sect, who owe allegiance to an Imam in India.

COMMUNICATIONS

Postal, telegraph, and telephone services are limited in this country. A radio station was built in 1947, but broadcasting is irregular. Yemen maintains contact with the outside world through a two-way radio.

HISTORY

In Classical times Yemen prospered as part of one of the three regional divisions of Arabia. It prospered as it was the site of a great trade route. The wealthy kingdom of Sheba was the best known of the South Arabian kingdoms. Their prosperity (tenth century to second century B.C.) was based on the profitable incense trade. Other trade routes and development of commercial navigation began to undermine its prosperity. The land was invaded and the rulers changed. The religion of Islam was accepted in the seventh century. Yemen very early showed signs of the religious tension and seclusion that still exists today.

In the ninth century Zaydi imam Yahya al-Hadi ila'l Haqq founded the Rassid dynasty which has survived, with some interruption, to this day.

Since that day Yemen has been under the control of the Ottomans, the Egyptians, the British, the Idrisis, returning from time to time into the hands of the Zaydis.

During World War I Yemen tried to extend control over the Aden Protectorate and the R.A.F. was often called on to effect Yemen withdrawal. In World War II Yemen was neutral and therefore was not a charter member of the United Nations, gaining admittance in 1947. In 1953, 1955, and in 1959 the more liberal Yemenis led uprisings as they desired economic reforms and equality of opportunity. However, Imam Ahmad was able to suppress them.

In 1945 Yemen joined the Arab League. In 1958 they formed a federation, called the United Arab States, with the newly established United Arab Republic. In December, 1961, the federal connection with Egypt was severed and in September, 1962, after the death of Imam Ahmad, the Imamate was overthrown by revolutionary forces led by Brigadier 'Abdallah al-Sallal, who appointed himself prime minister and commander-in-chief of the army. He set up a republican council of four to carry through his revolutionary policy. In September of 1966 Sallal returned to Yemen after spending ten months in Cairo to find that his strife-torn country was still engaged in a four-year-old civil war. Yemen is divided into three republican camps, each a warring faction. The

United Arab Republic has much control in Yemen and its supporters are one of these factions. The other groups are the Royalists who are supported by Saudi Arabia and led by a deposed Imam and the Independent Republicans. Most political observers feel that the largest number of people would like to be independent republicans but are dependent on the UAR to maintain the regime against the Saudi-supported factions.

Due to the backwardness of this country it is difficult to assess public opinion in any way, to inform the people, to get and analyze information of any sort. The country has always been and continues to be war-torn and unstable.

It must be remembered that until 1962 Yemen was little known to the outside world and the ruling Imam represented the last example of Islamic medieval absolutism. Upon his death in September, 1962, his successor ruled for only one week before being deposed by the military group led by Sallal, who proclaimed Yemen a republic and set himself up as President. Although a provisional constitution has been set up and free elections promised, it is felt that Yemen will have difficulty functioning as a democracy. The reasons for this point of view are as follows: (1) There is a tradition in Yemen for settling issues by tribal warfare; (2) There exists a long-established system of feudalistic government based on the allegiance of tribal chiefs who are suspicious of central authority and have to be paid for their support; (3) There seems to be a struggle within the new regime based more on rivalry within Muslim sects than on political issues; (4) the Arab demands of Egypt in its battle for power with the Saudi monarchy (both controlling factions within Yemen); (5) the present and intense competition between the Chinese and the Soviet Union to acquire a foothold in Yemen which will serve as a stepping stone to Africa.

In addition, observers of the situation in Yemen feel that many psychological barriers will have to be overcome before the Yemeni people will be ready to accept Western ideas. It is pointed out that modern ideas and education are essentially antagonistic to the archaic conception of a one-man government. It must be understood that the idea of individual initiative is an alien concept in a society where the son traditionally submits to the father, the father to the family head, the head of the family to the local authority, who in turn seeks counsel from the central government. The Yemeni individual learns at an early age to submit to authority and the adult typically resists creativity and change. In many areas, particularly among the poorer classes and among the rural groups, suspicions of the motives of government are quite prevalent. The government not only plans changes but upholds the laws, collects taxes, supports military conscription, and performs tasks which are regarded as interference by the masses. Many regard the government and government officials as agents of imposition and control and government institutions are feared and avoided. Innovations do not command respect or prestige and individuals do not derive satisfaction out of being identified with technological change. Combining these with the traditionally prevalent philosophy of fatalism, the development of a technological awareness, and an atmosphere of creativity becomes extremely difficult.

ECONOMY

Yemen is traditionally agricultural and largely self-sufficient in the production of foodstuffs. Ninety percent of the people are engaged in farming. Coffee is the principal export crop, but the cultivation of qat, a narcotic, is gaining in importance. Qat is exported only to neighboring countries because it must be used within a few days after it has been harvested or it loses its narcotic qualities. Yemen also produces fine craft work. At present, modern industry is practically non-existent and, therefore, Yemen must import textiles, matches, oil, and manufactured items of all sorts. Plans are being formulated that call for establishment of textile manufacturing facilities that would use domestic cotton. With the assistance of Syria and Communist China, several weaving and spinning mills have been established together with a small munitions plant. The Soviet Union has constructed a deep-water port, recently completed an international airport, and has agreed to provide agricultural machinery, to erect factories, and to supply road-building equipment. Oil exploration concessions have been granted although oil has, as yet, not been discovered. Geological explorations indicate that there exists within Yemen potential wealth in coal, gold, silver, and other minerals. A power plant and a glass factory is scheduled to be built in San'a'. A cement factory and a hydro-electric station are planned for al-Hudaydah. Traditional industries flourish, however, as they have for millennia. Almost all clothing, jewelry, shoes, implements, and even weapons are made by hand in Yemen from domestic materials.

FOREIGN TRADE

In 1926 a treaty of Commerce and Friendship was drawn up between Italy and Yemen. This treaty was concerned with development of trade between the two countries and was to employ Italian technology and financing. In 1934 a Treaty of Friendship and Mutual Cooperation was drawn up for the same purposes with England. This agreement was to last for forty years. In March of 1956 a trade treaty with the USSR was signed. This provided that Yemen would send to the USSR hides, coffee, and foodstuffs in exchange for machinery, petroleum products, wheat, and rice. During this same year, trade agreements with Czechoslovakia and East Germany were also completed.

EDUCATION

The importance of educating the people of the Middle East cannot be overemphasized since the illiteracy rate is so high as to be practically universal. In Yemen about 5 percent of the total population is literate.

Traditional education is provided mainly by the "kuttab" and the "madrasah" which are the traditional religious schools. This kind of educational institution still provides the children with a knowledge of the Qur'an (Koran) and the fundamentals of the three R's. Since the location of the religious schools is usually in the mosques, this type of school is widespread over the whole country.

Students planning on continuing their studies proceed to religious colleges, which are also located in the mosques. Most important of these religious colleges are in the towns of Bir Al Azab, Zabid, and Dhazar. The subjects taught include Arabic, Philosophy, Commentaries on the Qur'an, Muslim Law and Tradition, and History. Graduates of these colleges are normally appointed to government posts and to the courts as judges.

After the withdrawal of the Ottoman Turks in the 1920s, education was reorganized. In 1925 the Imam established the 25,000-volume library of the Great Mosque at San'a'. The library consists mainly of religious texts and old Arabic manuscripts. In the same year the school of Bir Al Azab was founded. This period marked the beginning of rapid expansion of the educational system which has taken place over the past thirty years.

Public secular education in Yemen is a new concept and at this time is not highly developed. Recently a modern grade-school system has been introduced in addition to the traditional religious training institutions. This new system provides a primary course of six years, an intermediate course of three years, and a secondary course of three years. In these schools modern subjects are being introduced and emphasis is no longer placed on the rote memorization of the Qur'an.

Since higher education could be received only in the religious colleges, students wishing to pursue studies of another nature began to leave Yemen to go abroad in 1936. At about this same time (with the onset of World War II) the Imam recognized the importance of exchange between nations and Yemen recruited teachers and technicians from other Arab countries. At that time Iraq sent 100 teachers to assist with education in Yemen.

On June 16, 1963, a Republican Decree was published establishing a Ministry of Education whose task was the assumption of the responsibility for the organization of schooling throughout the country. The United Arab Republic was called upon to assist in the initial stages and sent a number of experts who were authorized to serve as general education advisors within the Ministry.

The primary school enrollment in 1954 included 40,000 children out of 655,000 children of primary school age, according to UNESCO's estimate. (It must be pointed out that because of government restrictions and other problems, some of which have been mentioned previously, estimates emanating from Yemen vary widely.) It is said that in 1956 there were 2,155 primary schools with 93,099 pupils, four secondary schools with 296 students, eighteen technical schools with 1,252 students, and one teacher-training school with an enrollment of 50. There are six vocational schools and an agricultural school. In 1955, 250 Yemenis were studying in Egypt, thirteen in Italy, thirteen in the United States, and four in the United Kingdom.

Today there are three high schools, located in the cities of Sana, 'a Ta'iz, and Hodeidah. The number of students enrolled in secondary schools in 1956 was as follows: 296 students taking general high school courses and 1,252 taking a vocational high school course. The number of teachers in Yemen teaching on the high school level in the same year was sixty-nine in general education and two hundred and nineteen in vocational education; of these nineteen came from the UAR in 1959, twenty in 1960, and fourteen in 1961, and the others came from the other Arab countries and Yemen.

A teacher-training college has been established in Yemen. In 1956 it had a staff of sixteen teachers and there were fifty students attending classes. In *Education in the Arab States*, published by the Arab Information Center, 757 Third Avenue, New York City, it is stated that some of the Yemeni youth, looking for modern education which was not available at home, left to study abroad. There were seventy secondary pupils and three university students in Egypt in 1953, two in West Germany, two in Italy, and two in the United Kingdom in 1959. There were thirteen Yemeni students in the USA in 1960 studying as follows: one in agriculture, one in business administration, two in medical science, two in physics and natural science, five in social science, and the rest unspecified.

Since the Yemeni revolution on September 26, 1962, the UAR government has supplied Yemen with most of its needs and sent a total of forty-six teachers in 1963.

At the same time the government opened several boarding schools for orphans and destitute children and supplied them free of charge with room and board, books, and the other materials needed.

The revolutionary government of Yemen, realizing that there was a very serious lack of schools in the country, did its best to open as many schools as possible all over the country and it is planning to start more schools in the future. It is important to note here that three of these schools are girls' schools which established modern education for women. In 1963 the enrollment of girls in these schools was rec-

ognized to be one of the aims of the new educational system. It is the hope of the Revolutionary government to overcome this great loss of educable manpower which is being sustained by the traditional Arabian unwillingness to educate females.

The revolutionary government of Yemen realized that it was very important to transform the traditional school system into a modern one by introducing the modern subjects into its curriculum and by adopting the modern textbooks used in the rest of the Arab League countries, adding the relevant books describing the history and geography of Yemen written by Arab scholars.

At the same time the new Yemeni government is trying to modernize religious education in the country following the pattern established by Al Azhur University in Cairo. This should have a great effect on the religious leaders of the future.

The revolutionary government started its program to transform the traditional schools into modern ones by applying the new method of teaching and introducing modern subjects in thirty-six kuttabs:

6 in the Sana'a district	6 in the Al Beidha district
6 in the Aab district	6 in the Hodeidah district
6 in the Ta'iz district	6 in the Sa'da district

These schools are on the elementary level and will supply the future modern junior and senior high schools with students. These primary schools admit students at the age of six or seven and education is now compulsory between the ages of seven and seventeen. Primary education covers six years of schooling except in the villages where primary schools usually offer only four courses, or are still of the traditional Qur'anic school type. The primary school is followed by a three-year intermediate or lower secondary school and the successful students can proceed to the three-year upper secondary school.

At the post-primary level a number of other types of schools exist. There is the three-year teacher-training school, the school of agriculture, and the religious colleges. The primary and secondary schools are provided for the people at the expense of the state. The curriculum includes the teaching of the national language Arabic, Modern Languages, Literature, and Science. English is compulsory at the preparatory and secondary levels and is taught for six years, from about twelve to nineteen years of age. French is taught only on the secondary level in the literary section for about two years, from fifteen to seventeen years of age.

Aims of the modern language program in the primary schools are to enable pupils to understand spoken English, to speak correctly, to read with understanding, and to write a few sentences about daily life with relative facility. At the end of the third year the pupil is expected to know enough to continue in school or to embark on a vocational career.

The language program in the secondary school aims to develop civic responsibility, appreciation of cultural heritage, general culture, an attitude of critical thinking, and an appreciation of aesthetic values. The specific aims of this program are to increase the pupil's language skills in speech, reading, and writing.

Except for the religious colleges there is no higher education in Yemen. As mentioned before, students wishing to pursue their studies at this level have to go abroad. In 1963 there were some 300 such students enrolled in the Universities of the Arab states. Many of them had, in fact, followed their secondary studies, and in some cases their primary schooling, in countries outside of Yemen. For the past thirty years a student-exchange program has been in operation. Students from Yemen have been sent to other countries in the Middle East as well as to Europe and the United States. The Egyptian University in Cairo has provided scholarships for Yemeni students wishing to study in Egypt and for Egyptian students going to Yemen.

The number of students studying abroad in 1964, mainly on grants from other Arab governments, reached 587. Before 1962 there were about 340 students studying abroad on their own. The revolutionary government decided to support them in order to facilitate their studies and to hasten their return to Yemen, where their services are needed.

In order to qualify teachers to staff the schools which have been recently started and to implement the new system of modern education, the Yemeni government is planning to establish new teacher-training schools in every district. This program was begun in 1964 and at this time there is no complete or reliable information available regarding the status of this program. These schools were to have 150 students each and admitted first-year students for the academic year 1964-5.

These teachers' colleges will also admit teachers from the traditional schools to night classes to raise their standards and the standards of their schools, which are in the process of being transformed into modern schools.

The Ministry of Education in the new Yemeni government is planning to open seven junior high schools in every district, including an industrial school in Sana'a, a commercial one in Hodeidah, and an agricultural school in Ta'iz.

The Ministry is also planning to open seven girls' schools, one in each district, which will be staffed by teachers from the UAE and other Arab countries. Already, with the help of teachers recruited from other Arab countries, a school of agriculture and an experimental station have been established at Sana'a to instruct farmers in the use of modern agricultural techniques and methods of crop improvement. In addition, Yemen now has six vocational schools, a military academy, a college of aviation, a college for radio and telecommunications, and the previously mentioned agricultural school.

In 1964, statistics indicate that there were approximately 75,000 students as compared with 64,000 in 1963. In 1964 there were about 1900 teachers in Yemen and the number of teachers now in teacher-training schools is still unknown.

In 1964 the budget of the Yemeni Ministry of Education reached 2,286,648 Yemeni rials (a rial is about one dollar). This may not sound like a large expenditure, but it is a tremendous improvement over the situation before the revolution when there was no budget for education at all and the schools had to depend on the privy purse of the Imam or on waqf (money left in trust for religious purposes), which was neither regular nor fixed.

The Yemeni government hopes that with this foundation the people will be put on the right path toward putting much needed emphasis on education. It is their hope that they will be able to raise the standard of living for this generation and for generations to come through the development of their country's resources.

An interview with Dr. Moshe Perlman at UCLA revealed that he believes any statistics emanating from Yemen are highly questionable since there is no census taken. The country is so backward and war-torn, the government so unstable, that the possibilities of reaching the people are remote. Any statistics pertaining to the school "system" (which he believes to be nonexistent) are just fantasy.

The republican government tried to institute a system of schooling and in September, 1966, the cabinet resigned in protest of certain political issues. This leaves only the question again as to what will happen next. It must also be pointed out that with the population as small as it is and with the small number of children there, Dr. Perlman asks, "What kind of system can there be?"

There are no museums in Yemen, and archeological remains found at ancient sites still are unclassified in Sana'a. Artifacts of great civilizations of early Yemen are present in many parts of the country, but the Imam did not allow foreign scholars to survey and excavate them.

Furthermore, visits of foreigners to Yemen as tourists have been forbidden by the government.

BIBLIOGRAPHY

Education in the Arab States. New York: Arab Information Center.

MARCO, ERIC. *Bibliography on Yemen.* Coral Gables, Florida: University of Miami Press, 1960.

The Middle East and North Africa: 1965-1966. London: Europa Publications, 1966.

World Mark Encyclopedia of the Nations, 1963.

Part Four

Education in North
America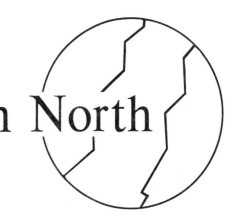

CANADA

F. Henry Johnson

THE ESTABLISHMENT OF THE SCHOOL SYSTEMS. The basic fact about the culture of Canada is that it is largely derivative. The original ethnic groups which came to Canada seeking refuge and opportunity on its coasts, in its lush valleys, and on its boundless prairies sought to retain and perpetuate the cultural traditions and institutions of their home lands. In contrast to the "melting pot" of the great industrial United States, transforming the varied types of immigrants into the ideal of a homogeneous "one hundred percent" American society, the Canadian environment has been more permissive to ethnic minorities. There has been no Canadian melting pot but rather, as John Murray Gibbon termed it, "the Canadian Mosaic." Each racial group has contributed its colour and pattern to the design but, as a mosaic is more than the sum of its parts, the environment of Canada has also been a formative influence.

So with Canadian education its beginnings are seen in the attempts of pioneer forefathers—French, British and American—to reproduce the educational institutions of their home lands in the Canadian backwoods. What finally developed was a structure made in Canada to Canadian specifications but with certain imported materials.

NEW FRANCE. When French colonists settled in Acadia and along the shores of the St. Lawrence River in the seventeenth century their missionary priests lost no time in establishing the typical French *petit école,* the parish school, wherever possible. The Abbé Gosselin claimed the existence of thirty-two such schools during the French regime. There were also schools established by French teaching orders. The Ursulines arrived in Quebec in 1639 and opened what became a famous school for girls which is probably the oldest girls' school in North America. An order founded in Canada by Marguerite de Bourgeoys in 1659, the Sisters of the Congrégation de Notre Dame, established schools for girls in Montreal, Trois Rivières, Quebec, and Louisbourg as well as in some of the parishes. Boys' schools were opened by some of the male teaching orders, notably the Jesuits.

Secondary teaching in Canada began in Quebec when the Jesuit elementary school there by 1635 expanded into a college offering Latin. Bishop Laval in 1663 established a seminary for training priests and in 1668 founded a *Petit Séminaire* to give secondary schooling to boys, most of whom were destined for the priesthood. By the eighteenth century this had become a typical Jesuit College following a curriculum similar to its many sister institutions in France. It was the prototype of numerous *colléges classiques* which were established in Quebec by teaching orders in the nineteenth century and which still offer almost the sole academic entry to the French-speaking universities of Canada. The original vocational school in Canada was one established by Bishop Laval in 1668 at St. Joachim below Quebec. Here, on an experimental farm, boys were taught agriculture and practical arts in addition to the rudiments of education.

In the colonial period of New France, elementary education was possibly as widespread as in the mother country. Scholars' estimates of the extent of literacy in the colony before the British conquest vary widely from about one-third to four-fifths. Judged by the standards of the seventeenth and eighteenth centuries the education of girls was good and fairly widespread.

Significance of these French colonial beginnings is evident in the twentieth century when one realizes that the parish is still the administrative unit for elementary education in Quebec, that church orders still operate the *colléges classiques* and that the Roman Catholic church has until 1964 continued to control the public educational system of its communicants through a Roman Catholic Committee of the Quebec Department of Education.

THE ATLANTIC COLONIES. The earliest British settlements in Canada were in the Atlantic Provinces. Although Nova Scotia had become a British possession by the Treaty of Utrecht in 1713, little British colonization took place until the establishment of Halifax in 1749. The first efforts at education here were private venture schools or classes held by itinerant schoolmasters. The colonial government of Nova Scotia did nothing to foster education in the colony before the outbreak of the American Revolution, its only educational enactment being of a restrictive nature designed to limit the issuance of teaching certificates to adherents of the established Church of England. This church, through its philanthropic educational societies, chief of which was the Society for the Propagation of the Gospel in Foreign Parts (S.P.G.), sponsored some of the earliest schools in the Atlantic colonies.

The monitorial schools which were so popular in the industrial cities of England in the early nineteenth century were introduced to Nova Scotia at the same time. Here, and in the neighboring colony of New Brunswick, this type of school enjoyed a long life.

The real beginning of public education in the Atlantic colonies dates from Nova Scotia's *General Education Act* of 1811 which introduced a typical American educational tradition, the local school district with its annually elected board of school trustees. Between 1755 and 1775 large numbers of American settlers had come into Nova Scotia from the New England colonies. By 1767 they constituted more than half the population and their attachment to the New England common school tradition accounts for the introduction into Canada of a distinctly American institution. The Act of 1811 left the initiative for establishing a school with the local inhabitants, offering government grants only after a school had been built. The trustees hired and paid the teacher.

The democratic process was viewed with suspicion by officialdom of the time with the result that limitations were imposed on the election of school trustees. At first, although six trustees were to be elected, the governor's magistrates were to select only three of these to form the school board. By 1850 this restriction on the elective principle had been withdrawn.

In New Brunswick locally controlled common schools were also set up by legislation as early as 1816. Here, too, the government was loath to place the schools in the hands of democratically elected trustees. At first the school boards were appointed by the Justices of the General Sessions. Not until 1858 were the New Brunswick local boards fully elective.

Eastern colonial governments were in the beginning perhaps more interested in the establishment of secondary and higher education than in common schools. Nova Scotia's first legislation to create a Latin grammar school was in 1780, predating government-supported elementary schools by thirty-one years. New Brunswick authorized the establishment of grant-aided county grammar schools in 1816 concurrent with its first common school Act. It was perhaps understandable that the governments of pioneer colonies might be more concerned with grammar school education for an elite class of leaders, civil servants, and professional men than with the general spread of literacy.

Nova Scotia's first grammar school was established at Windsor in 1788 and developed into King's College (1802), Canada's oldest English-speaking institution of higher learning. To support its second grammar school (in Halifax) in 1789 the Nova Scotian government imposed a tax on imported wine.

The smallest Canadian colony, Prince Edward Island, passed its first education Act in 1825 providing government grants to assist districts in erecting schools and paying teachers.

Establishment of free school systems, based on local assessment rather than on the traditional fees or subscriptions, was a long, hard struggle in the eastern colonies. As in most democratic countries, farmers and land owners did not take kindly to proposals for compulsory assessment to support schools. Progress toward the goal of education for all children was consequently retarded. In the 1850s probably no more than half the children in Nova Scotia, New Brunswick, and Prince Edward Island were attending school for even a minimal period of twelve to eighteen months.

In Nova Scotia it took a fifty-year struggle before a free school system based on compulsory assessment was finally inaugurated in 1865. The same principle had been accepted in Prince Edward Island in 1852 but it was not until 1871 that New Brunswick had a Free School Act.

Newfoundland's educational and political development had been retarded for many years by the British policy of trying to retain the island as a fishing preserve and forbidding permanent settlement. Not until 1833 did that colony have an elected assembly, and in 1836 this body passed the first legislation to assist elementary schools. Newfoundland had to wait until the second half of the nineteen century before literacy became common.

With the exception of Newfoundland, the Atlantic colonies rejected attempts to set up denominational school systems supported by public funds. The issue seriously threatened the passage of both the Nova Scotia Free School Act of 1864 and the New Brunswick Free School Act of 1871. Prince Edward Island adopted the principle of non-sectarianism in its Public School Act of 1877. In Newfoundland, however, the earliest schools were established through the missionary efforts of the churches. This resulted in the growth of several sectarian school systems which won government recognition and financial support.

UPPER CANADA (ONTARIO). The settlement of what was first called Upper Canada (to-day the Province of Ontario) began with the revolt of the Thirteen

Colonies when Americans of anti-revolutionary sympathies fled from their homes in the insurgent colonies and sought refuge in Canada. These displaced persons were honoured by the British with the name *United Empire Loyalists* and were given land around Lake Ontario and along the Upper St. Lawrence. They were in later years joined by large numbers of American and British immigrants.

The first schools in Upper Canada were established privately, but in 1807 the colonial government passed its first school legislation. This was the *District Public School Act* of 1807 which gave state aid in establishing grammar schools in each of several large districts of Upper Canada even before any provision had been made for a system of elementary or "common schools." These district grammar schools were intended to be fee-paying and residential, a Canadian backwoods variant of the great English "public" schools of the time. They were placed under the control of appointed boards and soon were considered the schools for the upper class. Even after a common school system was established, in order to prepare children for the upper school grades these district grammar schools duplicated the work of the elementary or "common" schools. In fact, it was not unusual to find the majority of their pupils registered in the elementary or preparatory grades.

It was not until 1816 that Upper Canada passed legislation to give state support to a common school system. This Common School Act placed the responsibility on local initiative to elect three trustees, build a school, and produce twenty scholars before the district could be eligible for a government grant. In the establishment of the elected three-man board is seen the influence of the American settlers, who by this time formed a very considerable element of the population.

Popular demands from the colonists, through their elected Assembly, for increased aid to provide free common schools clashed with the policy of the "Family Compact" or government heirarchy to support the district grammar schools. This was one of the factors leading to the Rebellion of 1837. Without legislative authority a General Board of Education had been set up in 1822 under the chairmanship of the Reverend John Strachan, the Anglican Bishop of Toronto. His attempts to bring the public schools and the first university under the control of the established church led to bitter controversy.

The man whose leadership brought order out of chaos was a Methodist minister, the Reverend Egerton Ryerson, who was appointed superintendent of the Upper Canada school system in 1844. Ryerson prepared himself for his new duties by extensive travels through Europe observing the developments in state public education in Germany, France, Switzerland, and Ireland. He also followed closely the work of the American educational leaders, Horace Mann, Henry Barnard, and others. On his return from Europe, he was allowed to draft new legislation, the Common School Acts of 1846 and 1850 which created the original framework of the Ontario School system of today. The Act of 1850, by permitting property taxation for schools in place of the prevailing custom of charging the parents, ushered in the principle of free schooling, and by 1871 all common schools were supported by property assessment and were free with compulsory attendance. In 1847 Ryerson established the first Normal School, setting a pattern for teacher training which strongly influenced western Canada.

Before he resigned office in 1875 Ryerson had established in Ontario a modern public school system similar in many respects to those of the eastern United States with central control of curriculum and certification of teachers and with provincial school inspectors. It was an eclectic system with ideas of school law and finance borrowed from the United States, teacher-training from Germany and France, textbooks from Ireland, and Pestalozzian pedagogy from Switzerland and Germany.

During his period of office, Ryerson saw the district grammar schools evolve into high schools, forming an integral part of the public education system. In the period 1807 to 1853 the grammar schools made an unsuccessful attempt to carry on the English public school tradition. During this time they constituted the weakest link in the chain of education from common school to university. In 1849, from the whole thirty-nine grammar schools in Ontario only eight students matriculated to university. Many parents preferred to send their sons and daughters to private academies.

The first step to place the grammar schools fully under democratic control came with the *School Act* of 1853. They now became part of the provincial system, although administered by county councils which were empowered to support them through local taxation.

Originally intended to be largely autonomous, to be restricted in admissions to boys, and to follow a classical curriculum, they had gradually come under public control and provincial inspection. Economy and other realistic factors had forced coeducation upon them and the demands of the Canadian environment had determined a broader curriculum.

Finally in 1871 the grammar schools became high schools similar to the American pattern, although the classical tradition was maintained by recognizing a category of academic high schools of superior qualifications as "Collegiate Institutes."

CONFEDERATION AND EDUCATION. Such were the main developments in public education in the British North American colonies which in 1867 confederated to form the small Dominion of Canada. The original union consisted of the former colonies (now provinces) of Nova Scotia, New Brunswick, Quebec, and Ontario. The legislation which incorporated the new country and which became its constitution was the

British North America Act (1867). Section 93 of this Act stated that each provincial legislature may "exclusively make laws in relation to education," subject however to certain provisions which protect "any right or privilege with respect to denominational schools which any class of persons have by law in the Province at the union."

SEPARATE SCHOOLS. This clause points to one of the distinguishing features of Canadian public education—the existence in some provinces of separate denominational schools protected by the constitution, forming part of the provincial school system and receiving public support. What are the origins of the separate school systems?

The first move to create separate schools originated in predominantly French-speaking, Roman Catholic Quebec. The rapid influx of British settlers into this colony when it came under British rule in 1763 soon created a cultural and religious minority problem. The predominantly Protestant, English-speaking settlers established a school system under the auspices of the Royal Institution for the Advancement of Learning, incorporated by an Act of 1801. The fact that this Institution was largely under English-speaking Protestant leadership accounted for the failure to attract French Canadians to its schools. Not until an Act of 1829 constituting parish school boards and permitting the use of parish revenues for school purposes did the French Canadians begin to show an interest in public schools of their own. From the beginning, therefore, *both* English- and French-speaking communities of Quebec chose to have their own distinct education *systems*.

In 1841 the two colonies of Upper and Lower Canada were united to form one country under one government—Canada. In this new country the numbers of English-speaking and French-speaking Canadians were about evenly divided. When the new government faced the task of devising school legislation which would apply to both groups it introduced in the *Common School Act* of 1842 a provision permitting persons of a minority religious faith in an area to set up their own school board and operate a *dissentient* school. This was the germ of the *separate* school systems of Canada.

The new government of Canada, recognizing the great cultural differences between Canada West (Ontario) which was predominantly Anglo-Saxon and Canada East (Quebec), almost entirely French and Roman Catholic, decided to set up separate and distinct systems in each province.

In Quebec two school systems developed, a Roman Catholic and a Protestant system. The latter in reality included any non-Roman Catholics, such as the Jewish population. A Council of Education was set up in 1859 and administered each system through a committee. Each system had its own organization, administration, curriculum, and Normal Schools.

In Ontario, however, *separate* schools were less separate. Here there was a large minority of Irish Roman Catholics. The aim of the government in this province was to retain as much unity as possible while conceding to the minority group the right to operate its own separate schools but within a public school system as public schools of a special category.

Legislation permitting separate schools had been enacted in Ontario when Ryerson was on his European tour. Although personally opposed to the divisive tendency of separate schools, he accepted them and tried to establish them on a fair and workable basis. He protected the freedom of the individual Catholic to support the ordinary public schools and to send his children there if he chose so to do. As late as 1865 the majority of Roman Catholics in Ontario were sending their children to those schools operated by the public rather than separate school boards. As Superintendent of Education, Ryerson insisted on a unified Departmental control of texts, curriculum, teacher-training, and school supervision, in return for which there would be equal grants to both public and separate schools.

In Ontario the term *separate school* was not exclusively applied to a Roman Catholic School. A minority Protestant group within a largely Roman Catholic area could petition to form its own separate school board. The "public school" board represented simply the dominant religious group in an area. People who gave notice to the municipal authorities that they wished to support the separate school had their local tax levy directed to the separate school board.

The small bi-cultural colony of Canada existed from 1841 to 1867 when it joined with two other British North American colonies, Nova Scotia and New Brunswick, to form the Dominion of Canada. During this period prior to 1867 the Protestant minority of Quebec could look for support to Ontario where Protestants were in the majority. Similarly the Roman Catholic minority in Ontario enjoyed the protection in the Canadian legislature of Catholic Quebec. When confederation with other colonies loomed as a possibility in the 1860s this balance of power was threatened in the new political union and supporters of minority school systems in both Quebec and Ontario sought assurance that their privileged position would be protected in the new Canadian confederacy. This was accordingly guaranteed in Section 93 of the *British North America Act* with the result that the separate school now had the sanction and protection of the Federal Government.

Consequently, when that Government later decided to organize the provinces of Alberta and Saskatchewan out of its own North West Territories, the Acts constituting these new provinces contained provisions for separate schools. Later still, when in 1949 Newfoundland finally decided to become the tenth Canadian province, the protection of Section 93 of the *British North America Act* was extended to the several denominational school systems that had been recognized previously by the Newfoundland Government. Such, in brief, is the background of a characteristic feature of Canadian education. Today separate schools, in one form or another, exist in Ontario, Quebec, Newfoundland, Alberta, and Saskatchewan as well as in the North West Territories. These areas are the homes of 77 percent of the Canadian people. Even in some provinces which do not have separate school legislation, certain concessions have been made to permit Roman Catholic schools to operate as recognized public schools and receive the regular school grants. This is so in the provinces of Prince Edward Island, New Brunswick, and Nova Scotia.

THE OPENING OF THE WEST. In 1867 at the time of Confederation the infant Dominion of Canada stretched from the Great Lakes eastward to the Atlantic but plans were already afoot to annex the vast wilderness of the West. It was significant that the official insignia of the new country carried the prophetic words A Mare Usque ad Mare—"from sea to sea."

West of the Great Lakes the forty-ninth parallel divided the territories of the United States from the British possessions. These latter consisted of the Crown Colony of British Columbia, extending from the Pacific to the Rockies. From thence to the Great Lakes and from the forty-ninth parallel to the Arctic spread the huge domain of the Hudson's Bay Company. This area was all that now remained of half a continent which had been granted by charter to this fur-trading company by the British crown in 1670.

Aside from roving Indian tribes these vast plains were almost uninhabited. There was no reason to prompt a fur-trading company to encourage settlement. Only in the Red River Valley where Scottish Lord Selkirk had secured land for a colonization venture for his fellow Scotsmen was there any considerable agricultural settlement. The Hudson's Bay Company had employed large numbers of French Canadians as *voyageurs* (packers or canoemen) and as servants of the Company. These and the Scottish employees of the Company had married Indian women and fathered a mixed race known throughout the west as *métis*.

The Company had encouraged the churches, both Roman Catholic and Protestant, to establish mission stations at the various forts and settlements and had granted subsidies to these missions to start schools. By 1867 there had grown up a small Roman Catholic education system of about seventeen schools. Protestant schools were fewer in number. The chief concentration of population and therefore of schools was in the Red River region where by 1870 there dwelt about 12,000 people, mostly French-speaking *métis*.

MANITOBA. In 1868 the infant Dominion of Canada managed to acquire from the British Government possession of all the Hudson's Bay Company lands. These were constituted as the *North West Territories*. An insurrection of *métis* in the Red River region against the new Canadian Government led to the granting of provincial status to that part of the North West Territories, when the Province of Manitoba was created in 1870 to become Canada's fifth province. The Canadian Act incorporating the new Province made it bi-lingual (French and English) and decreed that it have a dual school system, Roman Catholic and Protestant, similar to Quebec's, to be supported equally by Provincial grants.

Between 1871 and 1890 the influx of new settlers in great numbers changed the whole character of the population of Manitoba. Most of these new settlers were English-speaking Protestants from Ontario. By 1876 the school population showed approximately 1600 Protestant to 1100 Roman Catholic pupils but by 1890 the disproportion had grown to 11,000 Protestant and 2,000 Roman Catholic pupils. The result was a change of school policy by the Manitoba legislature in 1890 when it abolished the dual religious school system in favour of a united non-secetarian one. To seek restoration of their schools the Roman Catholic minority appealed to the Canadian Government under Section 93 of the British North America Act. When the Canadian Government tried to force the Provincial Government to rescind its legislation, a national election resulted in which the Federal Government fell. This "Manitoba School Dispute" has been the only major educational issue to enter federal politics.

Since 1890 Manitoba has maintained its unified education system although strong efforts were being made in the 1960s to force the Provincial Government to give financial assistance to Roman Catholic parochial schools. In 1897 the Canadian Prime Minister, Laurier, and the Manitoba Premier, Greenway, arrived at a compromise to alleviate somewhat the position of the French-speaking Roman Catholic Manitobians. The "Laurier-Greenway Compromise" permitted religious teaching by Protestants or Roman Catholic clerics in the last half-hour of the public school day. This instruction was to be given in segregated groups but no further separation of children by religion was permitted.

Another feature of the compromise was to permit bi-lingual teaching "when the pupils in any school speak the French language or any language other than English as their native language."

This clause was seized upon by ethnic groups other than the French to enable them to set up their own bi-lingual schools. The turn of the century was the period of the opening of the West to European immigration and large numbers of Polish and Ukrainians, attracted by cheap land, came swarming into the province. The bi-lingual agreement was soon found to be hampering the schools in their effort to assimilate and Canadianize the new immigrants, and efforts to train and supply suitably bi-lingual teachers were not successful. An investigation by the Manitoba Department of Education into the bi-lingual schools disclosed that these were poorly attended and failing to provide a sufficiently high standard of education in English. In consequence the bi-lingual clause in the Education Act was repealed in 1916 and henceforth English became the sole language of instruction in the public schools.

When in 1870 the Canadian Government had carved out Manitoba from the newly-created North West Territories, this had left a wide expanse of prairies still to be administered as the North West Territories. The first schools in this area had been mission schools operated by the churches at the little, isolated fur posts of the Hudson's Bay Company. In 1875 a dual system of schools for the Territories, similar to the original arrangement in Manitoba, was recognized by the Canadian Government. These were administered until 1905 by the Territorial Government through a Board of Education consisting of two sections, Catholic and Protestant, each responsible for the schools of its own faith. Difficulties between the two sections arose, particularly over areas where the population was of several religious groups. In 1892, therefore, the Territorial legislature abolished the Board of Education and placed all schools under the unified control of the Cabinet, although maintaining separate school districts where constituted. In 1901 control of the school system of the Territories was vested in a Ministry of Education with a Superintendent and Department.

By this time the once-empty prairies had become well populated by Eastern Canadian and European settlers. Completion of the first Canadian transcontinental railway in 1885 had accelerated the migration. Accordingly, in 1905 the Canadian Government created two new provinces from the North West Territories, Alberta and Saskatchewan.

ALBERTA AND SASKATCHEWAN. The constitution of each of the new provinces specifically recognized the right to establish separate schools on a Roman Catholic or Protestant basis. Alberta's separate school system maintains the separation through both elementary and high school grades. Saskatchewan, on the other hand, has followed the Ontario pattern, limiting separate schools to grades one to eight inclusive.

BRITISH COLUMBIA. The westernmost province of Canada, British Columbia, was admitted to the Canadian Union in the year 1871. It entered confederation with a school system already functioning and committed to the principle of non-denominational schools.

The first public schools were established in the separate Crown Colony of Vancouver Island in the 1850s with the Colonial Government paying grants of one hundred fifty pounds per teacher. To maintain the schools the grants were supplemented by fees. In 1865 a *Free School Act* was passed by the Vancouver Island Legislative Assembly which gave the little colony free and non-sectarian schools and a very highly centralized system with all authority vested in a General Board, its Superintendent and Department.

The mainland of British Columbia constituted another and separate crown colony following the gold rush to the Fraser River in 1857 and succeeding years. Its first schools were largely privately initiated but subsidized in part by grants from the Government. When the mining industry declined, the economy of both the Vancouver Island and mainland colonies was severely affected, with the result that the two colonies combined to form the Crown Colony of British Columbia in 1866.

In 1869 the new Colonial Government established a state-aided public school system for the whole of British Columbia. Financial difficulties had forced the Government to depart from the free school principle which Vancouver Island had endorsed in 1865 but immediately after confederation with Canada, the new Province passed a *Public School Act* of 1872 which restored free schools, and established a Superintendent and Department of Education. It maintained the non-sectarian principle.

TRENDS AND DEVELOPMENTS IN CANADIAN EDUCATION

Developments of the Local Authority

The American principle of local control of common or elementary schools by elected school boards had been established in most parts of Canada well before Confederation. The school districts were originally small. In Quebec and in parts of New Brunswick the unit was the parish. In other provinces it was the small school district, small enough to be within the walking distance of its pupils.

The first large administrative units appeared when cities and towns amalgamated the school districts within their boundaries. The small district governed by a three-man school board and supporting what was frequently no more than a one-room school survived in the thousands until the depression days of the 1930s when most provinces realized that the small school district was a very expensive anachronism. Its area was too small to provide a sufficient basis for the school. The cost per pupil in small districts was excessive because of the small pupil-teacher ratio. Educationally these small districts could provide little or no secondary education and their low salaries and poor promotional opportunities could not attract good teachers.

From the 1930s on, one of the most important movements in Canadian education was the development of larger units of local administration, usually through the consolidation of several small school districts. Three main factors combined to bring about this trend: the depression with its acute problems of educational finance; the improved roads and advances in transportation which made possible school bus routes bringing children in from an extensive area to a central "consolidated" school; and the growing popular demand for a better education for rural children.

In Eastern Canada, the development of larger units of administration proceeded slowly, particularly in Quebec where the parish in most areas continued to be the local unit. Ontario favoured as its larger unit, the township. By 1950 that province had 3465 small rural school sections with 536 township areas. By 1964 the Ontario Government was insisting that no local unit be smaller than the township. In Nova Scotia and New Brunswick somewhat of a compromise was reached between small and large districts. Royal commissions in both provinces had in the 1940s recommended the consolidation of rural districts into county or municipal areas each with a central board for taxation and school finance, but the actual administration of the schools was left in the hands of the smaller school district board. By 1950 this system had become standard throughout these provinces.

The most significant and most rapid development of large administrative units occurred in the western provinces beginning in Alberta. Here the first large rural unit was developed in the Turner Valley following oil discoveries there in 1928. The success of this venture led rapidly to the spread of the large school *division* throughout the province. By 1949, fifty-seven large divisions were in operation providing consolidated elementary and secondary school systems. A second type of large administrative structure developed in some parts of Alberta in the 1950s. This was the county unit organized like the English local authority on a county or municipal basis, with the county council assuming the powers of a school board and operating the schools through an education committee.

Saskatchewan, impressed by the success of the large units in Alberta, passed its *Large Units Act* in 1944 and within five years forty-six larger units had been formed. By 1960 both Alberta and Saskatchewan had brought almost all their schools under large units of local administration.

British Columbia, influenced also by the Alberta precedent, developed several experimental large units in the period 1936-1942. In 1945 the Maxwell Cameron Commission, investigating educational finance and administration in the province, urged the abolition of the hundreds of small local units except in isolated areas and recommended that the province be divided into seventy-four large districts. The British Columbia Government adopted the Cameron Report and carried out its recommendations in 1946.

Slowest of the western provinces to adopt the larger unit of administration was Manitoba where until 1958 it continued to support the small rural school district. The Macfarlane Royal Commission of 1958 recommended the larger units be organized for secondary education with permission for the inclusion of small elementary school districts within these. By 1960 all but four superintendencies had been organized into large secondary school units.

The educational advantages of the larger unit have become apparent throughout Canada, offering to rural children much improved elementary education and consolidated secondary schools where often no high schools had existed before. Economically the larger unit permits a more equitable distribution of the tax-load over a larger area. Administratively it provides a large enough organization to permit good supervisory services and for teachers greater opportunity and incentive for professional growth.

Financing of Education

Success of public education, in Canada as elsewhere, has depended very largely on the system of educational financing at the local and provincial levels. Dr. H. P. Moffatt in his book, *Educational Finance in Canada,* distinguishes four stages in the history of educational finance in Canada.

At first in the early colonial days the government looked to the church to provide some measure of schooling and to finance it. In French Canada, this was done through the parish schools and through the teaching orders of the Roman Catholic Church. In the English-speaking colonies, church-sponsored philanthropic organizations such as the Society for the Propagation of the Gospel in Foreign Parts established church schools. In some cases the government assisted these with regular or occasional grants.

The second stage, occurring mainly in the second half of the eighteenth century, saw the parents of school children taking the initiative. As in eastern Canada, after building a school house and hiring a teacher, they could then apply for state aid from the government. Evidence of local initiative and good faith was thus demanded before the state gave assistance.

The next step was the gradual acknowledgement by the provincial governments of their responsibility for public education. In line with this trend, grants were increased. There were wide differences between provinces, however, in the extent of such aid, ranging from a small part of the total costs of education (Ontario) to the assumption of the full costs of education as in British Columbia (up to 1889). By 1900 provincial contributions to the total cost of education amounted to about 10 percent.

In most provinces the government grant was supplemented by locally raised funds, at first by subscription lists and later, after considerable reluctance, by compulsory assessment.

The final and present stage in the development of educational finance was the attempt to achieve, through some kind of a finance formula, the aim of equality of opportunity. Beginning in the period following World War I, a number of causes contributed to this trend: the economic depression, the rapidly rising cost of education, and the increased holding power of secondary schools. With rising costs and expenditures, educational inequalities which had previously existed, but in less marked contrast, were now magnified, giving cause for democratic concern. The financial burden was felt most by the school boards of poorer districts. A Nova Scotian Commission in 1958 revealed, for example, that tax rates in that province varied from 3 to 150 mills. Provincial governments heretofore had in most cases given flat grants of so much per teacher employed. To assist certain depressed areas they had occasionally added special *ad hoc* grants. From 1905 onward the provinces adopted some equalization formula aimed at assisting districts according to local ability to pay. The formula and method varied from province to province. Alberta, for example, in 1925 offered a special equalization grant to those districts whose per-classroom assessment was less than $75,000. British Columbia after 1945 made its equalization factor a set mill rate with the Government paying all operational costs less what could be raised locally by the set mill rate. One effect of the trend toward equalization was generally to increase the proportion of the total cost borne by the provincial governments from about 11 percent in 1936 to 35 percent in 1950. The most radical proposal for achieving complete equalization within a province has come recently from the 1963 Royal Commission on Finance and Municipal Taxation in New Brunswick. This commission recommended that the province's educational system be placed under a *Public Schools Commission* which would pay most of the costs of education by levying a provincial property tax of 1 1/2 percent of the market value of property. Local authorities would in effect cease to function fiscally and would retain merely an administrative role.

The trend in Canada toward equalization, together with the growth of the large school district, has in general placed educational finance upon a much more secure and equitable basis and has gone far to ensure a higher quality of education within each province. It has not, of course, had any effect on reducing the wide discrepancies in per-pupil expenditure which have existed between the "have" and "have not" provinces. In 1952, for example, in comparison with $239 which British Columbia was spending per child, Newfoundland's figure was $86 and yet Newfoundland's spending was high in terms of average personal income. Such inequalities could only be corrected by federal aid to education.

In this respect, although by Section 93 of the *British North America Act* which is the Canadian constitution, education was placed under the jurisdiction of the provinces, yet the term "education" was nowhere defined in the Act. Consequently the Federal Government has been able to extend its authority over certain fields not specifically stated

to be provincial. Since the provincial field of taxation has not grown proportionately to the ever-increasing commitments of the provinces, particularly in education, the Federal Government has from time to time resorted to subsidies of one kind or another to help the situation. Since 1913 agricultural education has been federally assisted and since 1919 technical education has also. The *Vocational Training Coordination Act* of 1942 and subsequent legislation made available to the provinces large Federal grants for vocational training in secondary schools. The *Family Allowances Act* of 1944 authorized payments from the Canadian treasury to every family of a monthly allowance for each school-age child. Acting on the recommendation of the Massey Commission, the Federal Government has since 1951 given large annual grants to all recognized Canadian universities.

Developments in Elementary Education

The elementary school in Canada has followed a line of evolution similar to its growth in the United States.

The original ungraded schools of the pioneer era were gradually replaced by multi-roomed graded institutions. In Canada the earliest forms of grading or grouping were introduced by nineteenth-century monitorial schools which were very active in the Atlantic Provinces. Another form of early grouping was by subjects, the first "grade" being the "spelling class" from which the pupil progressed to the "reading class" and on successively to writing, arithmetic, geography, and grammar.

In Ontario, Ryerson's introduction of a graded series of readers (the Irish National Series) in the 1850s led to grading in the same way that it developed in the American elementary school. By the 1870s fully graded schools were well established in Canadian cities. New Brunswick was the first province to introduce the eight-grade system (in 1878). By 1923 this had become the common pattern throughout Canada.

Kindergartens were first recognized as a feature of the public education system when Ontario passed legislation in 1885 permitting their inclusion by school districts. Most provinces were reluctant to sanction them until the post-World War II period when the high birth rate, combined with the increased employment of young mothers, were no doubt factors of public pressure. By 1948 kindergartens could be included for provincial grants from Quebec westward.

F. H. Johnson (in *Elementary Education in Canada*, J. Katz, editor), cited eight major trends in the development of elementary education over the past century:

1. The curriculum has been broadened from its original 3 *R*'s to include the language arts, the social studies, music, art, physical education, nature study (later

science), manual training, home economics, and in some provinces, religious instruction and French.

2. Canadian teachers have, in common with their colleagues in other countries in the last half century, greatly increased their understanding of the learning process. In the latter half of the nineteenth century, the more professionally-minded teachers were following the educational theories of Pestalozzi and Herbart. The twentieth century ushered in the era of scientific child study. The writings of G. Stanley Hall, F. N. Parker, Earl Barnes, William T. Harris, and other American educators were followed with interest in Canada until the 1920s when the developments in educational psychology which were taking place in both Britain and the United States began to influence Canadian schools.

3. With the newer theories of education came newer techniques of teaching. The teacher-centered school of the Herbartians gave way to the more child-centered classroom advocated by John Dewey and the Progressives. Dewey's stress on the active nature of child learning and on the importance of socialized and cooperative endeavor was reflected in most school systems. Canadian teachers, however, tended to accept with some caution and moderation the ideas of the Progressive Movement. In Saskatchewan and Alberta the "enterprise method," a Canadian version of the activity methods of the Progressives, was popular in the period 1940-1960.

4. One of the noticeable improvements in the Canadian classroom over the past century has been in the relationship between teacher and pupils. The strict discipline of the old school has given way to a much more humane and understanding attitude toward child learning. Pupil-teacher relations have become friendly and relaxed and the elementary school has become a pleasant, enjoyable environment for learning.

5. Greater concern for the individual differences of children has characterized education in Canada, particularly since the 1940s. Most school systems now use some form of grouping within the grades, such as the reading group. Some have introduced continuous promotion plans permitting children to progress through school at varying rates of speed according to their ability. Saskatchewan instituted such a system for its schools in 1964.

6. Canadian teaching in recent years has increasingly been influenced by the vast body of published research into educational methods and curriculum, particularly in such fields as reading and the teaching of arithmetic.

7. Administrative developments, especially the widespread acceptance of the larger school district, have done much to improve elementary education by providing larger and better schools and better supervisory services. Teacher-consultants and subject supervisors can be employed by the larger systems to assist with the in-service education of their teachers.

8. Improvements in the education and training of elementary teachers have occurred but progress in this field has been much slower than in the United States. No province in Canada yet requires a degree for teaching in the elementary school. As little as one year of post-high school training is still sufficient for certification in some provinces. Since 1945, however, the three westernmost provinces together with Protestant Quebec and Newfoundland have abolished the nineteenth-century Normal Schools and have transferred all elementary as well as secondary teacher-education to the universities. In Eastern Canada non-degree-granting training colleges for elementary teachers are still maintained by the Provincial Departments of Education.

Developments in Secondary Education

Evolution of the secondary school in Canada reflects the bi-cultural character of the country and also the fact that Canada is a North American nation. Two quite different patterns of secondary schools have developed, one in French Canada and another, following closely the American pattern, in English-speaking Canada.

The recognized academic type of secondary school in French-speaking Quebec is the *Collège Classique*. This combination high school and college can trace its geneology in direct line from the original Jesuit College, the *Petit Séminaire*, founded in Quebec by Bishop Laval in 1668. Not until after the British conquest were other classical colleges established on this model. In 1963 the number of such colleges had increased to over a hundred, mostly in Quebec, enrolling some 37,000 boys and 11,500 girls. These schools are not public institutions but are, in almost all cases, operated and administered by teaching orders of the Roman Catholic Church. However, they are subsidized by the Provincial Government and those which are recognized by the National Conference of Canadian Universities and Colleges receive Federal aid.

Any student wishing to proceed to a French-speaking Canadian university must attend a *collège classique*. Here he enters at the end of elementary school (grade seven in Quebec) and follows an intensive eight-year course. Traditionally this has been strongly classical in content, although in recent years it has offered two programmes, the one stressing Latin and Modern Languages and the other Latin and the Sciences. Students may receive the high school graduation diploma at the end of the fourth year although 38 percent go on to complete the eight-year course culminating, as in the case of the French *lycée*, in the *baccalauréat*. This degree will admit the student to a French-speaking university either in Canada or in France. In 1964 the Classical College programme was the subject of much discussion in Quebec where many feel that these schools should be brought more closely under public control and that their curriculum should be modified and modernized. The defenders of the *collège classique* support the programme with the arguments for a liberal education, *i.e.* that these studies develop the mind and character. Most of the graduates of the *collèges* proceed to such professions as the clergy (25 percent), medicine (17 percent), science (17 percent), education and liberal arts (12 percent), law and diplomacy (9 percent), and commerce and finance (7 percent).

Due to the selective nature of the *collège classique* and to the fact that fees are charged, only a small proportion of the French-Canadian youth can attend them. In 1962 only 10 percent of the boys of the age group and 3 percent of the girls attended the *collèges*.

Other post-elementary schools of a vocational type are provided in French Canada, but 50 percent of the pupils in the Province of Quebec leave school at the age of fifteen.

In English-speaking Canada the evolution of the secondary school has been toward a type of institution quite American in character. It has been noted how the Province of Ontario developed its modern high schools from district grammar schools modelled on English prototypes. In other provinces high schools developed more democratically by extension of the elementary school grade by grade, but all the English-speaking provinces today have developed much the same characteristics of secondary education.

There are today three main types of high schools in Canada. (a) The small local high school with up to a hundred students offering only an academic programme. This is a type which is gradually disappearing. (b) The larger regional high school formed often by consolidating two or more local high schools. In most cases these schools would have from two hundred to four hundred students and would be able to offer, besides an academic matriculation course, certain non-academic electives such as technical, commercial, or industrial arts. (c) The third type of high school is the large composite secondary school with an enrollment of perhaps two thousand. Here the student could choose one of several complete programmes, *i.e.* academic, technical, commercial, or general.

In some parts of English-speaking Canada, particularly in the four western provinces, the Junior High School has developed. Winnipeg and Vancouver were the first Canadian cities to experiment with this type of school (in 1919 and 1922 respectively). The Province of British Columbia adopted the junior high school and a 6-3-3 system of public schools following the Report of the Putman-Weir Commission in 1926. In this province the 6-3-3 system was soon modified in response to geographical conditions to a 6-6 system. This happened where the six-year *Junior-Senior* High School was favoured on the basis of economy and other considerations. In Ontario the separate school system which operates up to the end of grade eight has made it difficult to introduce the usual grade seven to nine Junior High School although some centres have established junior highs limited to grades seven and eight.

Introduction of the junior high school has been but one of the contributing factors to a general trend which has been developing since the 1920s in secondary education, a process which might be described as the democratizing of the high school. Other elements which have contributed to this movement have been the abolition of fees (achieved in most provinces by the 1930s); the raising of the compulsory school age to fifteen and the abolition of the external examination for entrance to high school. In some provinces students may now enter high school on the recommendation of the elementary school.

As the high school became less selective in response to social pressure it had to modify its programme to accommodate the wider ranges of abilities and vocational interests of its students. The result has been an increased emphasis on technical and vocational training.

The first technical school to operate in the daytime was opened in Toronto in 1901. By 1916 such schools were operating in the principal large cities. When the *Technical Education Act* of the Dominion Government in 1919 gave matching grants to the provinces and when vocational training legislation of 1931 and 1942 carried on this precedent, the movement gained great impetus. Finally the *Technical and Vocational Training Assistance Act* of 1960 continued and expanded Federal Assistance which now amounts to 75 percent of provincial expenditures in retraining unemployed, and 50 percent of provincial capital expenditures for vocational training facilities.

Development of Higher Education

The beginnings of higher education in Canada and in the United States were roughly concurrent. Laval in Quebec was contemporary with Harvard and William and Mary as seventeenth-century foundations. King's University in Nova Scotia and the early colleges in the American colonies date from the eighteenth century. Most of the older eastern Canadian universities were founded in the first half of the nineteenth century—*i.e.* Dalhousie (1820), Acadia (1838), New Brunswick (1828), McGill (1829), Toronto (1822), and Queens (1841).

Of the western universities only Manitoba dates its origin to the nineteenth century. The others were all products of the twentieth century.

All the early Canadian universities, with the exception of Dalhousie, were founded by churches. In general, most of the eastern universities have been church-sponsored while the western ones have been established under provincial auspices as non-sectarian institutions.

No country in the Commonwealth today has more universities than Canada. The United Kingdom, with twice the Canadian population, has approximately half the number of universities that Canada has.

Canadian universities have their own unique characteristics, distinguishing them from both American and British institutions. There is perhaps less of a range in quality than one might find in American colleges. All Canadian universities are coeducational, Mount Allison (New Brunswick) having been the first in the country to admit women. Men, however, outnumber female students by three to one. Most Canadian students finance themselves through university or are assisted by their families. Compared with the United Kingdom, Canada does little to assist its own students by scholarships. Nevertheless in comparison with the 5 percent of British youth in universities, Canada has 10 per cent. This figure is small again by contrast with the 20 percent attending colleges in the United States.

University finance depends mainly upon provincial government grants. Fees cover only 28 percent of the cost of education. Federal assistance is on the basis of two dollars per head of the general population.

The great problem today in Canada is to keep pace with the increasing demand for university education. In the decade from 1953 to 1963 the university population doubled. Today new universities are springing up at a rapid rate. Ontario, since 1960, has chartered seven new universities. In the year 1963 British Columbia created three new universities. When the projected institutions are built there should be no city of more than thirty thousand population in Canada without its own college or university or without one in the near vicinity.

To provide the professorial staff for these new and expanding universities is a presently unsolved problem. Canada has been slow in developing graduate studies and only in the post-World War II era has this been an important area of growth. In 1961-2 there were only 7347 full time graduate students out of a national university enrollment of 125,000. The country at present needs an increase of two thousand university teachers annually while producing less than one hundred Ph.D.'s per year. Ontario has recently taken a step to encourage graduate work by offering $1500 fellowships to all students accepted by graduate schools.

One solution which is being advanced to help solve the demand for post-high school education is the junior college. At present the western provinces, particularly Alberta and British Columbia, have shown the most interest in this type of institution.

Teacher Education

Canada has been slower to effect improvements in its training of teachers than in perhaps any other field of education. Although it developed its first normal schools contemporary with the first in the United States, it has continued to retain the old normal school much longer than its southern neighbour. The first government-controlled normal school in North America was begun in Montreal in 1836 but closed in 1842. New Brunswick and Ontario both established permanent normal schools in 1847, and these were the precursors of similar establishments modelled after them in the other provinces. By 1908, from the Atlantic to the Pacific the normal school had become the accepted training institution for elementary school teachers.

The first normal schools began with the most humble entrance requirements (elementary schooling) and with the briefest of terms (ten weeks). They gradually raised their standards of admission and training until by the 1920s high school graduation was the generally accepted admission requirement and nine months was the usual training period.

While the Normal school in the United States was experiencing a metamorphosis from a one-year training school to a four-year teachers' college and on to a state college and in many cases to a state university, the Canadian normal school remained static, changing only its name to a *teachers' college* and continuing to offer a one-year programme. The first province to break with this tradition was Alberta which in 1945 abolished its normal schools and placed all teacher education under its provincial university carrying degree credit. Other provinces soon took similar action, Newfoundland in 1946, Protestant Quebec in 1955, British Columbia in 1956, and Saskatchewan in 1964. Nova Scotia and New Brunswick in the 1960s arranged to give credit in their universities for certain of the normal-school training courses.

Ontario, Manitoba, and Catholic Quebec systems still keep the training of elementary teachers separate from the universities in normal schools (now called Teachers' Colleges) operated by the Provincial Departments of Education.

Standards for secondary school teaching have generally been high in Canada. The traditional type of training has for many years been an Arts or Science degree plus a post-graduate year of teacher-training taken in a faculty of education at a university. The University of Alberta introduced the American pattern of an undergraduate Bachelor of Education degree for secondary as well as for elementary teachers, and at Alberta, British Columbia, McGill, and Memorial Universities, this programme integrating arts and science courses with professional courses is more commonly chosen by student teachers today.

Teachers' Associations

Provincial teachers' associations have become an important force in Canadian education. Originally teachers' associations developed from "teachers' institutes" organized largely as in-service training sessions by the provincial Departments of Education. Most of the present provincial teachers' associations were formed in the post-World War I period when more men with stronger feelings of professionalism were choosing teaching not merely as a stepping-stone to some better paid vocation but as a life work. In most provinces, particularly in the west, the teachers are represented by one provincial association although special interest organizations of teachers may exist in affiliation with the main body. In Ontario, legislation in 1944 united five organizations in affiliation under one provincial body known as the Ontario Teachers' Federation.

A national teachers' association was organized in Canada in 1919 as the Canadian Teachers' Federation. By 1927 it included all provincial associations with the exception of the Roman Catholic teachers of Quebec. It speaks on behalf of Canadian Teachers to the Federal Government and in international organizations.

The teachers' associations in Canada have made a great contribution to the improvement of teaching as a profession. They have played an active part in provincial curriculum revisions and in the in-service training of teachers through conventions and workshops. They have exerted pressure to raise the minimum requirements for the certification of teachers and have cooperated with Departments in recruiting young people for the profession. Largely through their efforts, Canadian teachers enjoy security of tenure, respectable salary schedules, pension schemes, and other fringe benefits. Between 1942 and 1962 the median salaries of all Canadian teachers had risen from $1057 to $4522, an increase of 328 percent. There remains, however, a very wide range in median salaries in 1962-3 from $2667 for the teacher in Newfoundland to $4522 for the British Columbia teacher. Between rural and urban centres there was also great variation in median salaries—in 1962-3 from $2983 for the teacher in a one-room rural school to $5306 for the teacher in a city of 100,000 population or more.

Royal Commissions

No study of Canadian education could be complete without mention of the important role in this country of the Royal Commissions. One of the traditional devices of a Canadian government, federal or provincial, when faced with a difficult issue, and especially one which may cut across political lines, is to appoint a Royal Commission to study and report on it to the government. Education has been a favourite field for such commissions. Between 1950 and 1963 every province, with the exception of Newfoundland, has had commissions of inquiry studying some aspect of education, and in addition, the national government in 1951 appointed its own Royal Commission on National Development of the Arts, Letters, and Sciences.

While governments are not bound to accept the advice of commissions, nevertheless in most cases the commission reports have been printed, have won public support and have, in large part, been implemented

by legislation or other action. In British Columbia, to take one province as an example, the Putman-Weir Commission Report of 1925 gave the province its 6-3-3 school system and shaped its curriculum until the Chant Royal Commission Report of 1960 advocated revisions which are now being implemented. This province's modern and efficient system of large school administrative districts owes its creation to yet another commission report of 1945.

Royal Commissions on education have since 1950 made recommendations concerning almost every conceivable aspect of education from its basic philosophy to details of curriculum, examination, religious education, length of instructional time, school organization, and even methods of teaching.

How competent are commissions to advise on these matters? In most cases in recent years, Royal Commissions on education have been composed largely of laymen with a sprinkling of experienced educators. To take the three recent commissions in British Columbia, Alberta, and Manitoba which studied education during the period 1958-1960, of the total of fourteen members, three were professional educators, three were Roman Catholic members, two were women, and the six others might be considered to represent the general public. The predominance of laymen does not preclude the members from receiving and acting on expert advice. Frequently education commissions employ professional educators as secretaries and as researchers. The fact that non-professional members predominate in numbers merely indicates that the Royal Commission is a genuine democratic device to enable the government and the people of a province to see for themselves what the schools have been doing.

The views of recent Royal Commissions on what should be the aims of education are interesting, offering as they do a good indication of Canada's educational objectives. The Alberta and British Columbia commissions of 1959 and 1960 emphasized intellectual self-development as the schools' principal, although not its exclusive, role. The Ontario commission of 1950 stated no less than nine aims of education, ranging from developing good health and family relations to training the child to think clearly. The Quebec Commission of 1963 considered that the school system should "prepare the individual for life in society" as well as to train him for "the working world." The Manitoba Report of 1959 stressed also the social aim of "developing in each child the desire and capacity to become an acceptable member of a society of free men."

These may suggest much the same divergence of views on the function of public education which has characterized the thought of educational philosophers since the days of Plato.

Developments since 1966-7 have included increased attention to inter-provincial cooperation in education, seeking more equitable ways of handling federal aid to education, more school consolidation moves, increases in special services to students, and more attention to underprivileged students.

BIBLIOGRAPHY

For General Reference

ALTHOUSE, J. G. *Structure and Aims of Canadian Education*. Toronto: W. J. Gage, 1949.

KATZ, J., ed. *Canadian Education To-day: A Symposium*. Toronto: McGraw-Hill Book Co., 1956.

PHILLIPS, C. E. *The Development of Education in Canada*. Toronto: W. J. Gage, 1957.

SWIFT, W. H. *Trends in Canadian Education*. Toronto: W. J. Gage, 1958.

For More Particular Reference

CAMPBELL, H. L. *Curriculum Trends in Canadian Education*. Toronto: W. J. Gage, 1952.

FLOWER, G. E., and STEWART, F. *Leadership in Action: The Superintendent of Schools in Canada*. Toronto: W. J. Gage, 1957.

FRECKER, G. A. *Education in the Atlantic Provinces*. Toronto: W. J. Gage, 1956.

JACKSON, R. W. B. *Educational Research in Canada To-day and To-morrow*. Toronto: W. J. Gage, 1961.

JOHNSON, F. H. *A History of Public Education in British Columbia*. Vancouver: University of British Columbia, 1964.

KATZ, J., ed. *Elementary Education in Canada*. Toronto: McGraw-Hill Book Co., 1961.

LAYCOCK, S. R. *Special Education in Canada*. Toronto: W. J. Gage, 1963.

LAZERTE, M. E. *Teacher Education in Canada*. Toronto: W. J. Gage, 1950.

LLOYD, W. S. *The Role of Government in Canadian Education*. Toronto: W. J. Gage, 1959.

LUSSIER, I. *Roman Catholic Education and French Canada*. Toronto: W. J. Gage, 1960.

MOFFATT, H. P. *Educational Finance in Canada*. Toronto: W. J. Gage, 1957.

PATON, J. M. *The Role of Teachers' Organizations in Canadian Education*. Toronto: W. J. Gage, 1962.

PHILLIPS, C. E. *Public Secondary Education in Canada*. Toronto: W. J. Gage, 1955.

PUTNAM, J. H. *Egerton Ryerson and Education in Upper Canada*. Toronto: Ryerson, 1912.

ROWE, F. W. *The History of Education in Newfoundland*. Toronto: Ryerson, 1952.

Royal Commission Reports on Canadian Education:
Report of the Royal Commission on Education in Alberta. Edmonton: Queen's Printer, 1959.
Report of the Royal Commission on National Development of the Arts, Letters, and Sciences. Ottawa: King's Printer, 1951.
Report of the Royal Commission on Education in British Columbia. Victoria: Queen's Printer, 1960.
Report of the Manitoba Royal Commission in Education. Winnipeg: Queen's Printer, 1959.
Report of the Royal Commission on Education in Ontario. Toronto: King's Printer, 1951.
Report of the Royal Commission on Education in the Province of Quebec. Quebec: Queen's Printer, 1963.

SISSONS, C. B. *Egerton Ryerson. His Life and Letters*. Toronto: Clarke, Irwin, 1947.

———. *Church and State in Canadian Education: An Historical Study*. Toronto: Ryerson, 1959.

WALKER, F. A. *Catholic Education and Politics in Upper Canada*. Toronto: J. M. Dent & Sons, 1955.

WEIR, G. M. *The Separate School Question in Canada*. Toronto: Ryerson, 1934.

WOODSIDE, W. *The University Question*. Toronto: Ryerson, 1958.

UNITED STATES OF AMERICA

Carlton E. Beck

Education in the United States, one of the most complex of all nations, has been discussed and dissected in literally thousands of books and long articles. The task in this essay is to delimit that history and to present developments of major interest to readers who wish a summary of such materials. Those wishing to pursue in depth any of the phases of topics mentioned will find such information in the books listed in the bibliography.

Education in the United States is usually described as (a) almost universal, (b) expensive to finance, (c) decentralized, (d) primarily locally controlled, (e) of public, private, and parochial types, (f) unevenly distributed in urban and rural areas, (g) having racial troubles, and (h) vital to the way of life found in the United States.

From the earliest days of the seventeenth century when the first permanent settlers came to the northeastern section of what is now the United States, education has been regarded as of great importance. The early settlers came from Europe, primarily from northern and western Europe, seeking religious freedom and economic opportunity. During the early years of that century, there was so much work to be done that education was not a systematized endeavor: forests were to be cleared, houses were to be built, negotiations or fighting with the natives had to be handled, and the ravages of disease had to be taken into account. To this confusion were added the strained relationships among all nations which laid claim to sections of the "New World"; the various colonies were torn between allegiance to their native lands and to their neighbors in the new land. The problem of what the colonies owed to their former homelands and what the homelands owed to the colonists had grave implications for education and for economic development as time passed.

EARLY LAWS AND DEVELOPMENTS

In the earliest days of the colonies, education was limited to that which a child received from his parents, or from attending a "Dame School," a term used to mean schooling received from any woman of the community who was willing to instruct children in her home for a small fee. Reading, writing, and religion were the major elements of such education, with some attention to domestic skills for the girls. The women were, in the main, untrained for teaching, passing along as best they could what they knew of these subjects. The quality of education was most uneven, since some of these women were only semiliterate themselves.

It soon became apparent that this type of "education" would not suffice, and a matter of major importance to the settlers was that it certainly would not provide students who would be qualified to man the pulpits of the Puritan church in the future. The deaths of a few key ministers and church elders brought about some changes relatively early in the life of the New England colonies. Between 1642 and 1693 laws were passed which made mandatory the establishment of a reading and writing school in every settlement of fifty families or more. Settlements of one hundred or more families were required to have a Latin grammar school, where, in addition, the Greek language was studied, also a prerequisite for entering Harvard College, which was founded in 1636 and was the first training place in America for ministers of the Puritan faith.

The early laws set important precedents for American education. The Selectmen's Act of 1654 provided that a number of citizens should be elected by the people to oversee the affairs of the school, including the hiring of teachers. Previously, school affairs had been left to the ministers of each individual community. Parents wanted to have a more direct voice in education, because often the schoolmaster chosen by the minister was a strong moral man, but not a person skilled in the art of teaching. This law is a major precedent for the "local control" style of education which is difficult for many visitors to the United States of America to understand.

Stated in its simplest terms, "local control" means that every city, town, and village in the United States of America selects members of its own community to serve on a "school board" or "board of education" for that locality. The board hires teachers, dismisses teachers, plans for needed improvements, and oversees all business and curricular affairs of the school district, whatever its size. The only limitations placed upon the local school board are those of state or national law. For example, each school district plans its own sequence of courses, but in some states three years of English is required by state law, as is a year of American History or U. S. Government in secondary schools. Beyond simple limits such as these, the local district is free to decide what shall be studied in its schools. The local school board has control over only the public schools of the district, that is, only those which are wholly supported by tax funds and are open to all students who wish to attend. Parochial (church-financed) schools and private schools (those established by any group other than churches or local government) likewise select their own "boards of education" (called locally by various names) which serve the same functions.

Two other early laws passed in the seventeenth century, together with the Selectmen's Act of 1654 mentioned above, shaped the American system of local control—the so-called "Old Deluder Satan Act" of 1647 and the Massachusetts Bay Law of 1693. The former, taking its name from the wording of the law which was intended to keep "that old deluder Satan" from the minds of the young by furthering education and stressing religion, stated that there must be schools available to all children for the basic elements of education, and that in larger communities there must be an opportunity for further schooling. The latter law established that once the "Selectmen" (school board) had proposed a budget for the coming school year, the matter must be put on a ballot for public vote. If the voters today decide via ballot that the expenditures or the purposes for which they were intended do not meet the wishes of the people, the board must then revise the budget, indicating changes, and resubmit it for another vote. The intent is that local people shall have a great degree of control over their schools, and that schools provided by public tax funds shall be available to all children.

States have the function of specifying the *minimum* limits of professional training which teachers must have and of issuing at the state level a teaching certificate. Of course, any school district within the state may decide that it desires more training and

may refuse to hire teachers who meet only minimum state requirements. The states also set the age for compulsory attendance at school for all children. The age typically is six. Again, local districts may provide preschool experiences for their own children (kindergarten and/or nursery school) if they wish. All states give a certain amount from state tax revenues to the local districts to aid them in financing their schools, the amount to be determined by the voters of each state. Much of the local money for supporting schools, however, comes from local real-estate taxes. It is not unusual for poorer communities to receive a great proportion of their total school budget from the state treasury, while wealthier districts are given less. This is only one of the ways in which the United States tries to approach the goal of equality of educational opportunity.

Returning to educational history, one might state that in the United States education has passed through six major stages.[1] These might be labeled as follows: (1) education for salvation, (2) education for livelihood, (3) education for productive citizenship, (4) education for moral inspiration, (5) education for patriotism, and (6) education for world society. It would be difficult to assign dates to these since the nation is so large and has distinct sectional histories, but in general, the first stage extended from the arrival of the first settlers in the first decade of the seventeenth century to approximately the middle of the eighteenth century. The second spanned the latter half of the eighteenth century; the third, the first half of the nineteenth century; the fourth, the second half of the nineteenth century; the fifth, from the beginning of the twentieth century until the end of World War II; and the sixth, from then until the present. The future will be determined not only by domestic developments but also by results of the United States involvements in foreign affairs.

These suggested dates are intended to stress the *emphasis* current in schools in the United States at the times indicated. They are not intended as definite and identifiable beginnings or ends of trends; rather, they represent overlap and merging of trends. For example, United States schools are still concerned with making a living, still stress productive citizenship, and still have ideals of patriotism discussed in classrooms. In a very real sense, no stage ever really ends; it simply merges with newer concerns and is less emphasized, as happens in many nations.

The major concern of seventeenth-century education was the perpetuation of the various religious groups. Since each religious group settled almost exclusively in communities of their own, the desirability of teaching religion in the schools was not ques-

1. For a more lengthy and detailed discussion of these stages, see Carlton E. Beck, *et al., Education for Relevance* (Boston: Houghton Mifflin Co., 1968), pp. 10-29.

tioned. Salvation of one's soul was thought to be the overriding consideration of education. As cities came into being, and as religious groups found themselves in proximity to other religious faiths, questions arose as to the role of the tax-funded public schools in the teaching of religion. Thomas Jefferson, third president of the United States, felt that there should be a "wall of separation between church and state" in order to safeguard the interests of each and to obviate the functions of each. The teaching of religion in government-supported public schools was deemed by Jefferson as undesirable at best, and extremely dangerous at worst. Jefferson felt that no man should be taxed to support a religion in which he does not believe. This principle is today the subject of extensive debate in the United States and is discussed under the heading of "Problems" later in this essay.

Education in the schools of the seventeenth century (chiefly in the northeastern section of what was to become the United States of America and termed "New England") centered about basic skills of reading, writing, arithmetic, and religion at the primary level; on the second level—not typically attended by any except those boys who were bound for the ministry of the Puritan Church—the emphasis was on Latin and Greek language and literature, which were prerequisites for entering college to prepare for the ministry. The wisdom of the past and the style of the ancients were the emphases of the schools, not critical thinking or originality. The so-called "classical" emphasis maintained a strong grip upon secondary education in the United States for almost two centuries, a condition which Alfred North Whitehead termed "the dead hand of the past." Even today there are those who feel that drill, repetition, and the "mental discipline" value of the classical type of education is a mark of distinction, but their number is decreasing. That outlook was typified in its extreme form by a statement from a parent who once said, "It doesn't make any difference what a child studies, just so long as he doesn't like it!" It was difficult to "like" the monotonous read-and-recite form of learning found in primary schools and Latin grammar schools of the seventeenth and eighteenth centuries.

The first real challenge to the dominance of classic education and the small number of students who chose to continue school past the reading and writing stage was issued by Benjamin Franklin, who founded an "academy" in Philadelphia in 1751. Franklin was one of the first to do something about the realization that the United States was changing in many ways which made the older, classic-centered form of education irrelevant to the needs and wishes of most of its young citizens. Franklin introduced an emphasis on *English* language and literature, *science,* and *modern* foreign languages. His justification was that in the rapidly urbanizing way of life in the United States with its manufacturing and trade, classical languages

were irrelevant to the vast majority of the people. Since he believed also that no nation, not even Greece and Rome, had a monopoly on truth and wisdom, the study of modern languages seemed necessary and desirable. Science was to become the wave of the future. Franklin saw this even in the 1750s and made it a mainstay of his academy. Science was later to produce a standard of living which was to become an example to much of the rest of the world.

Gradually the "academy" type of education spread, thrusting into American education a note of practicality instead of the classical emphasis. Franklin had also added to the curriculum the "practical" studies such as bookkeeping, surveying, and navigation, all a welcome addition to a nation engaged in commerce, world trade, and an increasingly urban way of life. Perhaps the best statement in concise form which typified the outlook of the academy came not from Franklin, its founder, but from Jefferson. In speaking of a proposed law for extending education, he stated that its goal was ". . . to provide an education adapted to the years, to the capacity, and to the condition of every one, and directed to their freedom and happiness."

If one truly emphasizes the latter part of the statement, the goal of modern education in the United States remains as Jefferson stated it, a goal worthy of consideration throughout the world. The form it takes in a given nation would be relatively unimportant if those ends were served for all mankind. All nations fall short of those ideals.

At the time of Jefferson and Franklin, the belief was growing that every citizen must attain literacy so that all could handle their own business affairs and partake of the duties of citizenship in some informed manner. Jefferson's phrase, "an aristocracy of talent," became the keynote of several generations of competitive Americans. "Equality of opportunity" was advocated to make life a fair race at the start, but one's own industry and native abilities—developed through relevant education—would determine one's place in the world. Men began to realize that all would benefit from the maximum development of talents in all men, especially as society became increasingly interdependent and as division of labor expanded. Many talents were needed, not just the verbal ability which marked the successful "classical" student.

As the United States expanded westward, it became increasingly apparent that formal education was indeed only that: education in *forms*—forms which had no real relationship to life as it was lived on the frontier, where men lived by courage, intelligence, strength, and improvisation. To the call for practicality issued by Franklin was added the voice of noted thinkers called the Transcendentalists, among them Henry David Thoreau and Ralph Waldo Emerson, in the early and mid-nineteenth-century. They issued a call for self-reliance, for a focus on living closer to nature, for finding one's own meanings in life and not merely accepting those of others, for aspiring, for "hitching your wagon to a star." They recognized the futility of much which passed under the name of education in their time. A new education somehow had to be born, one which made contact with the lives of men. They called for men to receive, either from themselves or from others, what has been termed "Education for Moral Inspiration." Both men lived during a time when European philosophers were examining intricate systems which were intended to explain the totality of the universe. Emerson, too, had faith in a Grand Design in nature, but this included man's coming to a personal relationship with the universe. No one else could give it to him; he had to discover it through living, learning, and contemplating. Education to Emerson was not the narrowing and specializing which produced only lawyers, accountants, and other jobholders, but rather it was a broadening, searching endeavor which would produce "great-hearted men."

To aid in the search for this sort of education, the number of institutions bearing the name of "state universities" was expanded. What Jefferson and Emerson dreamed of would not be possible without expanded equality of educational opportunity. The state university, conceived in the 1780s, became the vehicle for providing low-cost education beyond primary and secondary school for any talented and ambitious young person. The state university was to be one totally supported by tax funds (later, it drew part of its sustinence from tuition, but even today the cost of attending a state university is comparatively nominal), and one free from the dominance of religion. Jefferson envisioned it as a place where only secular subjects would be taught. It was to be an institution in which any bright young man might find a truly liberal education and perhaps a profession worthy of his deepest commitments.

The first few decades of the nineteenth century brought changes of far-sweeping importance to education in the United States. Among them were the following, each of which is a story in itself, and each has been the subject of many books and scholarly researches:

The common school movement
The founding of the first high schools (secondary schools)
The "lyceum movement"
Free elementary schools
The first coeducational colleges and universities
Quality colleges for women
Publicly supported normal schools to provide teachers
Legal decisions supporting the right of religious schools to exist unharmed
The strengthening of the movement to abolish slavery.

Horace Mann and others recognized the importance of providing a "common school" in which all the children, of all the people who wished, could attend a well-conceived, well-equipped, well-taught place for learning the common branches of study. This was deemed necessary in a land which was to be ruled by "an informed electorate," a land which was becoming increasingly complex, urbanized, and diverse. Mann studied Prussian schools and others and read widely in the writings of major educational theorists in order to bring to bear the best thinking and practice on the formation of American public schools. These schools were to become the unifying influence in a nation which prided itself on many ethnic stocks, religions, and diverse cultures. Common schools were to be eventually free of charge and staffed by the best teachers available.

Education was also to be compulsory. Of course, if a child's parents wanted to send him to a church-operated school, this was an acceptable means of educating him, as was his attendance at any private school. But the influence of the common school movement in the United States was that education was to be compulsory at the elementary school level. Every child was to have the opportunity to learn, despite parental objections to denying the family the small wages a child laborer might earn; despite customs which in the "old country" might have dictated that "education is not for people like us"; and despite the cost to the public as a whole. Pennsylvania was the first state to pass a law in 1834 making common-school education free of charge, although local communities elsewhere had done so by choice (under local control). Other states followed suit shortly after.

But a common-school education was not enough. In the 1820s, a new educational institution, the high school, began in Boston, Massachusetts. The first high schools were much like the academies and were maintained separately for boys and girls. Nevertheless, the whole idea of education for girls beyond the elementary stages was in keeping with the idea of equality of opportunity for all. By the 1850s high schools were coeducational in several parts of the nation and quickly replaced the separate schools for boys and girls. A high school grew to be the "common school extended." At first, no one *had* to attend it, but it was there for all who *wished* to attend, assuming one had the ability to achieve. It was furnished at no cost (sometimes a tuition was charged early in its development) to the student, in contradistinction to most of the academies, which were typically privately-owned and charged tuition as had the Latin grammar schools before them. Soon the curriculum of the high school broadened to accommodate the wide range of interests and abilities found in the increasing number of students who chose (or later, by state laws, were compelled) to attend to the ages of fifteen or sixteen. One fundamental principle of universal, free, and compulsory secondary education is that it makes no sense to increase the diversity of the student population without a corresponding broadening of the curriculum. True equality of educational opportunity implies this in a society which prides itself on diverse talents and ideas.

At about the same time that high schools were coming into acceptance, replacing academies, coeducation at the college level was beginning at Oberlin College in Ohio, and quality education in a college exclusively for women was beginning in Massachusetts at Mt. Holyoke College. It was only a short step from this expansion of educational opportunities for women to expanded professional choice for those women who chose a career outside the home. No nation can speak honestly about having equality of opportunity when any large minority is denied access to choice of occupation and education.

While women were winning equality of educational opportunity, the large majority of Negro slaves laboring on Southern plantations were being denied it, as they had been since the founding of the nation. The historical "reasons" for the justification of slavery are well known in the literature of many nations, but none of them fit well in a nation supposedly dedicated to individual freedom and worth. The movement to abolish slavery was gathering momentum in the 1830s and 1840s, culminating in the War Between the States (American Civil War) of the early 1860s. After the war, the freed slaves were faced with many problems, one of the chief of which was how to win one's way in a world which placed increasing emphasis on education, a commodity which the slave had not possessed. There had been some education given by benevolent masters and some at the hands of religious groups which maintained charity schools in the South (but these were often primarily evangelistic efforts rather than educational ones). The vast majority of Negroes had no education at all and hence no access into the larger society, even if the prejudice of skin color had not been against them. One of the first orders of business of the Freedman's Bureau, a government agency set up to aid the former slaves in adjusting to life as free men, was to provide schools. In addition to requiring the states to set up schools for Negroes at the elementary and high school levels, federal money was spent to aid in the establishment of colleges for Negroes. Integration of the races in schools, especially in the South, was far in the future.

The "lyceum movement," mentioned earlier, was another attempt at extending the scope of education. Originating in New England, the lyceum was somewhat like a town meeting in which entertainment, discussion of current topics of interest, educational lectures, or other requested activities were provided. This form of meeting, based on interest and sustained by its quality, was the true beginning of adult education in the United States. Men were beginning to realize that formal education could not be the end of learning; education had to have a lateral as well as a vertical dimension. Learning continues throughout life; what changes is simply the source and focus of it. Adult education in the United States today is ever-expanding. Skills are taught, upgraded, or refreshed; cultural activities are explored; recreation is provided. Virtually anything which one wishes to learn is available somewhere in adult education programs sponsored by public schools (at night and on weekends), by religious groups, by community centers, local government departments, or others. One example is called the "Opportunity School" sponsored by the Shorewood, Wisconsin, Public Schools. Any resident of that village, located near the city of Milwaukee, can enroll in any course free of charge (or in the case of some shop courses, and so forth, by payment of a small materials fee), while those from neighboring cities or villages can enroll there for fees of $5.00 per semester. Subjects taught include cooking and sewing, woodworking, modern languages (seven), swimming, card-playing, dancing, history and other recognized academic subjects, shorthand, typing, genealogy, and cryptography—all offered in the evenings during the school year. None of this would have been possible without an adequate supply of well-educated teachers and a commitment to a broad curriculum.

The first step toward supplying the type and number of teachers required for a system which was intended to become universal, free, and compulsory was the establishment of the first state-supported normal schools in the late 1830s and early 1840s. The content of the training centered at that time on practice teaching, methodology, and principles of education. The length varied from weeks to months in the beginning, and later was extended to two years. The present teacher education institutions in many cases evolved from normal schools to state colleges, and later to state universities. Every major university and nearly all colleges today have a program or department of teacher *education*. The older term "teacher *training*" has been discarded, since it connotes a bag of tricks or habit formation, an outmoded conception of the task of the teacher in the United States today. Teachers today are required by law to possess at least the bachelor's degree from a college or university, with some states (*e.g.*, California) insisting on a master's degree. It is not uncommon for teachers to hold master's degrees, especially in urban areas. Increasing numbers of teachers are working toward the doctorate either in education or in their academic specialty. Those who choose to do graduate work in education often have in mind a change from classroom teaching to supervision, counseling, administration, school psychology, school social work, or some other ancillary position.

RELIGION AND PUBLIC EDUCATION

In the second decade of the nineteenth century, a famous legal battle established once and for all the right of churches to operate and continue to maintain their own schools. The famous Dartmouth Decision involved the desire of the state of New Hampshire to take over a church-related college for use as a state university. In ruling against the state and for the church officials in this case, the court stated that to do so would mingle church and state unnecessarily. The wisdom of the decision is apparent. If one church-related college could be taken over "for the public good," no church-operated institution would be safe. Any minority could be put in the position of not having a place in which to provide for the training of its ministers, nor having the special brand of education for its young people which it might desire. Soon after this decision was rendered, a great number of church-related colleges and lower schools began springing up across the country.

While the courts have affirmed the right of the churches to operate schools, the relationship between church-affiliated schools and governmental units has not been clarified. Were the United States to follow the thinking of Jefferson concerning a necessary "wall of separation" between church and state, no money or other encouragement from the city, state, or federal government could be spent in any way to benefit churches or church schools. However, much to the dismay of those who wish to see complete separation maintained, states and local governments have exercised their local options in various ways to aid indirectly the church-supported schools. Operating under what is referred to as the "child benefit theory," local and state governments in some areas of the country (usually having a large Roman Catholic population among its voters) have "helped children, not churches" by providing tax-supported, free school-bus transportation to schools operated by churches, by providing free or inexpensive hot lunch programs at government expense, by buying textbooks for such schools from public funds, and by employing nuns or other religious to teach in public schools which have a large Catholic population. Of course, the counterargument to "child benefits" is that any such expenditures relieve the church of expenses, and money so released can be used to further the religious work of the church, thus indirectly aiding the church via public funds. The church schools remind the public often that were the parochial and private schools in the United States to close, the resulting influx of new students in the public schools would create an emergency situation and call for far more expenditures than the present unsettled state of affairs costs. Religiously-sponsored schools are, in fact, closing, one by one; the cost of education has risen greatly in the United States, and the people demand good schools. The religious schools have extreme difficulty competing with the publicly-financed schools for quality teachers and good facilities. While it is not expected that religious schools will cease operations completely, the number of such schools seems almost certain to decline greatly within the next decade. The historical reason for the existence of Catholic schools, namely, that "public" schools in the last two centuries in fact taught Protestant religion, seems no longer a good reason. Recent U. S. Supreme Court decisions have banned religion in almost every form from public school classrooms, even ruling out an opening prayer and a prayer before the noon meal. It is unlikely that the old reason will continue to convince Catholic parents. The other reason given for the existence of Catholic schools in the United States deals with giving religious sanction and interpretation to the various areas of study. This, too, has waned as an effective argument in times when ecumenism and social changes within the Catholic Church have all but removed "orthodoxy" as a cogent reason for the existence of the parochial schools. The only noticeable increase in parochial and private school enrollment has taken place in urban areas where some parents feel that public schools are not as good academically because of disruptive students, and some of these feelings have racial overtones. It is not a well-kept secret that many U. S. government officials in Washington, D. C., either have moved outside the District of Columbia in which the nation's capital stands because of the reasons mentioned above, or have placed their own children in private or parochial schools, often for the same reasons. Whether there is any basis in fact for these actions in Washington or elsewhere is not relevant here. The fact is that parental *feelings* along these lines have led to an increase of parochial and private schools in some urban areas.

POST-CIVIL WAR INFLUENCES ON EDUCATION

Several events of the period during and after the Civil War of the 1860s exerted great influence on the direction of education. The passage of the Morrill Act in 1862 established land-grant colleges and universities which assured lost-cost, flexible, and practical higher education across the newer parts of the nation. The creation of a federal Department of Education, charged with collecting and disseminating information about education, was another step toward professionalization of teaching. The establishment of Johns Hopkins University's first-rate graduate school was another. One of the early students at Hopkins was young John Dewey, later to become America's foremost philosopher and educator.

A legal decision at Kalamazoo, Michigan, in the 1870s set the legal precedent for the use of public tax money for secondary education. Although this *practice* had been followed in many places prior to the court test of its legality, the case removed any doubt as to the *legality* of supporting a level of education, in this case secondary education, of which the majority of the population had not yet availed itself. The court pointed out that there were many indirect benefits to all citizens arising from the existence of further educational opportunity. This decision led later to the establishment of what are called community colleges and junior colleges at the expense of state, regional, or local treasuries. The purposes of these types of higher education are many, but three stand out quite clearly as important: (1) Some types of technician training require post-secondary study and can be met without the usual two years of liberal arts education which comprise the first two years of American college and university education; (2) Some people desire only the first two years of college for "cultural broadening" instead of preparing for a profession; and (3) Some view the junior college or the community college as an inexpensive way to complete the first two years of college (by living at home) and saving money in order to go away for the final two years at a four-year college or university. In addition to these three major reasons, others find the junior college desirable as an adult education "cafeteria," a place to which any high school graduate (or in some case, those who have had less than that amount of schooling) can take one course or a few courses in whatever field he may at some time need to know about, or about which he is curious. The first publicly-supported junior college was established just after the twentieth century began.

Correspondence courses also came into existence in the 1880s, providing another way for adults to upgrade or attain job skills as well as to add to their general educational background.

THE VOCATIONAL EDUCATION MOVEMENT

Because of large waves of immigrants which had been inundating the cities, and the resultant demand for their making a living, the public schools took the position that education must be broadened to include job skills, or at least work habits and acumen, in order to serve well its now-diverse population. The first manual training high school in the United States was established in Baltimore, Maryland, in the mid-1880s, soon to be followed by similar institutions in many other large cities. Those which did not do so usually added another "stream" or "major" within existing high schools for those who wished to concentrate primarily upon trades, business, or industrially useful learnings. It was only a short step from this to work-study (cooperative programs with local industries and businesses) plans in which the student would study part of the day and then enter a work-study job in which he might put to use what he had learned under the supervision of local businessmen or industrial supervisors, earning money at the same time. This type of program reduced the drop-out rate for students who ordinarily might not have stayed in school had the school been traditionally academic.

The first law insisting upon *full-time* attendance for all students came in Connecticut in 1890 and was followed soon after by similar laws in other states. This was an attempt to assure at least more exposure to knowledge while serving the dual purpose of keeping youngsters off the labor market a bit longer. Again, schools which so expanded their clientele were faced with broadening and individualizing what it offered to its now-captive audience, or suffering the consequences in its classrooms.

At about the same time, an influential report called the Report of the Committee of Ten recommended changes in the entrance requirements for colleges, among them the dropping of a foreign language requirement for admission. The committee questioned the relevance of some time-honored traditional standards for admission which showed again the "dead hand of the past." Another influential group called the Committee of Fifteen published a list of changes deemed necessary in the education and training of teachers. The traditional type of teacher, the skillful taskmaster who knew what had to be done in order that a student might begin to achieve mastery in his field, was now being put on notice that there was more to his task than subject matter.

Together with these developments, the twentieth century produced an emphasis on scientific inquiry in the behavioral sciences. The beginning of the guidance and counseling movement, chiefly vocational counseling at first, came about through the work of Boston social worker Frank Parsons. Parsons' book, *Choosing a Vocation,* stated that in order to help people find rewarding jobs, the counselor must (a) know the man, (b) know the world of work, and (c) match the man with the job. Through psychological tests which were produced in great numbers over the next three decades, the counselor could "know" his client better and more empirically; through monographs about jobs and through the study of job requirements in counselor education programs, the counselor could know better the world of work. The "matching" process became a matter of skill in interviewing and in test interpretation.

The emphasis of John Dewey's philosophy of education fit well with these events. In his major works Dewey stressed that we live in a changing world, that man must "find himself" somehow within a social frame of reference, that education must play up the strengths and interests of an individual and de-emphasize weaknesses, that individuals must be treated as unique persons worthy of respect and possessing dignity, and that practicality or the "consequences of an act" are important in education as well as in life outside the classroom. Dewey further wanted schools to be miniature societies in which the student lived and learned concurrently.

The emphasis upon meeting individual needs, social as well as academic, required better educated teachers, and more of them. Teacher education underwent many changes during the first four decades of the twentieth century. "Progressive" education, a much-misused term, became the collective name for the combined effect of these emphases.

GOALS OF TWENTIETH-CENTURY EDUCATION IN THE UNITED STATES

Several statements of purpose or goal have been made during the twentieth century. Such objectives as self-realization, effective human relationships, economic efficiency, and civic responsibility have been advocated as the desired ends of education in the United States. Other stated objectives have been developing salable skills, physical fitness, democratic citizenship, satisfying family life, consumer skills, use of scientific method in problem-solving, appreciation of beauty, satisfying use of leisure time, cooperation with others, and self-expression. From the composite list above, it is clear that not only purely academic outcomes are sought in United States schools. The ideal of the "educated man" in the United States varies from social group to social group, but some of the elements mentioned seem important to all groups and individuals. A definition of education which has recently become popular in the United States is "Education is composed of all activities and learnings which enable a man to take charge of his own life." Coupled with the general tone of the previously mentioned goal statements, that definition would come close to being typical of thought concerning education in the United States today.

National pride in the many scientific, commercial, and industrial accomplishments of the young United States reached a peak during World War II. The United States of America was then truly a leader among nations, and its destiny was involved with that of the entire world in many ways. The sobering developments during and after that war led to the realization that no form of isolation from the rest of the world was either possible or desirable. Education for living in a world society became a major aim, added to the others.

TODAY'S EDUCATIONAL SYSTEM

In the United States today, state laws typically require children to enter school (public, parochial, or private) at age six. Many communities choose to maintain preschool classes or kindergartens to aid in social development of the children, but these are voluntary both for communities and for children. Depending upon the preference of local communities, children attend eight years of elementary school and four years of high school; or six years of elementary school, three years of junior high school, and three years of senior high school; or other local variations of these patterns. The local community determines the pattern to be used, but twelve years of schooling, consisting of literacy skills, mathematics, sciences, art, music, social studies, and various locally-chosen "elective" subjects are to be found nearly everywhere. Because of excellent roads in most parts of the country, school buses are used to transport the children from rural areas to centrally located or "consolidated" schools at no cost to the children. This grouping makes possible efficient operation and a broad curriculum which is in keeping with United States emphasis on individual choice in education.

As stated previously, those parents who choose to send their children to schools other than public schools must pay tuition and whatever other charges are deemed necessary by the school concerned.

The average number of years of schooling of United States citizens today is approximately 10.7, but there is wide variation in various sections of the country, ranging from about 12.3 years of schooling in states such as Utah and California to just over 8 years of schooling in parts of the South and the various parts of the Appalachian hill regions. Several factors in addition to the previously described historical ones combine to produce these variances. Among these are wide variations in teacher salaries being offered, rural versus urban ways of life, the existence of free, or nearly free, junior college education in some areas, views taken by various ethnic and religious groups concerning education, and a degree of racial discrimination against Negroes, American Indians, and others. Discrimination is officially outlawed but persists despite earnest attempts at eradicating it. Special governmental programs and local efforts are being made to remedy the situation.

Although each locality sets up its own curriculum, selects its own teachers, sets its own pay scales, and conducts its own educational affairs, certain rather common patterns may be observed. In virtually all sections of the nation the emphasis in elementary education is upon basic skills such as reading, writing, usage and grammar, science, arithmetic, and good study habits. Varying amounts of attention are given to music, art, hygiene, history, geography, and current events. Good citizenship is a continuing emphasis at all levels. The extent of time and emphasis given to each subject matter area depends in large measure upon the qualifications of the teachers, local attitudes, local conditions, and financial support available to the local district.

The quality of the various subjects taught in secondary schools and the emphasis on these subjects also depend upon the factors just mentioned, but certain identifiable patterns again emerge in nearly all sections of the country. Most of the high schools, especially medium-sized and larger ones, offer the student a choice of "major"—college preparatory, commercial, vocational, or general. Once the student has made his choice, he pursues a core of courses intended to aid him in preparing for his objectives. There is still some measure of electives within each program, and a student may at his own request change from one curriculum or "major" to one of the others at any time. Certain basic courses are rather standard fare at nearly all high schools—English usage and literature, foreign languages, mathematics (usually including algebra, geometry, trigonometry, and some higher forms in larger schools), biology, chemistry, physics, world history, American history, U. S. Government, social problems, and some forms of vocational or commercial training such as woodworking, metal shop, typing, shorthand, and similar courses. Not all students take all of these, of course, but some mathematics, science, English, and social studies are included in the curriculum of each child.

Problems and Directions

Education in the United States today is its life's blood. The great technological advances and the high standard of living found among most of the citizens have come about largely through the extension of opportunities for a good education to vast numbers of people, and at public expense. The major problems facing the nation's educational systems are entwined with the overall problems and commitments of the United States as a whole. International involvements, space exploration, and unrest among groups within the nation affect the amount of money available for education as well as the emphases, especially those of the type subsidized by federal funds. Currently, special programs are being pursued in extending equality of educational opportunity to more and more people, retraining adults whose jobs have been eliminated by automation, providing health care in larger measure to children from underprivileged homes, researching better ways of teaching, and helping emotionally disturbed, mentally handicapped, or physically handicapped children through special education programs. Among some of the most promising of such programs are such things as the "G. I. Bill of Rights," which is a system of supporting the higher education, at federal expense, of young men and women who have served in the armed forces; Project Head Start, a preschool program which is now being continued into elementary schools to help culturally different or disadvantaged children to compensate for lacks in their home environment which may be detrimental to at least the early stages of learning in school; and certain recent loans, scholarships, and experimental programs financed chiefly by federal funds especially to meet these needs.

While this chapter has presented few statistics on education, those interested in such data can find up-to-date information in such sources as UNESCO's *World Survey of Education,* its *International Yearbook of Education,* various U. S. Government publications, and by consulting the National Education Association or the U.S. Office of Education in Washington, D.C., U.S.A.

SELECTED BIBLIOGRAPHY

BECK, CARLTON *et al. Education for Relevance.* Boston: Houghton Mifflin Co., 1968.

BELL, HOWARD M. *Youths Tell Their Story: A Study of the Conditions and Attitudes of Young People in Maryland between the Ages of 16 and 24.* Washington, D. C.: American Youth Commission, 1938.

BUTTS, R. FREEMAN. *The American Tradition in Religion and Education.* Boston: Beacon Press, 1950.

BUTTS, R. FREEMAN, and CREMIN, LAWRENCE A. *A History of Education in American Culture.* New York: Henry Holt & Co., 1953.

CREMIN, LAWRENCE A. *The American Common School.* New York: Teachers College, Columbia University, 1951.

CUBBERLEY, ELWOOD P. *Readings in Public Education in the U. S.* Boston: Houghton Mifflin Co., 1934.

CURTI, MERLE. *The Social Ideas of American Educators.* New York: Charles Scribner's & Sons, 1935.

HARPER, CHARLES A. *A Century of Public Teacher Education.* Washington, D. C.: National Education Association, 1939.

JOHNSON, CLIFTON. *Old-Time Schools and School-books.* New York: Macmillan & Co., 1904.

KNIGHT, EDGAR W. *A Documentary History of Education in the South before 1860.* Chapel Hill, N. Carolina: University of North Carolina, 1949.

———. *Public Education in the South.* Boston: Ginn & Co., 1922.

KNIGHT, EDGAR W., and HALL, CLIFTON L. *Readings in American Educational History.* New York: Appleton-Century-Crofts, 1951.

KRAUS, CHARLES A. "The Evolution of the American Graduate School," *American Association of University Professors Bulletin,* vol. 37, no. 3, Autumn 1951.

LEE, GORDON C. *An Introduction to Education in Modern America.* New York: Henry Holt & Co., 1953.

MONROE, PAUL. *Founding of the American Public School System.* New York: Macmillan & Co., 1940.

POTTER, ROBERT E. *The Stream of American Education.* New York: American Book Co., 1967.

REISNER, EDWARD H. *The Evolution of the Common School.* New York: Macmillan & Co., 1930.

THWING, CHARLES F. *A History of Higher Education in America.* New York: Appleton-Century-Crofts, 1906.

Part Five

Education in Latin
America

AREA ESSAY: LATIN AMERICA

Murdo J. MacLeod

In a short article which purports to give a historical background for the whole of Latin America, one must generalize. And in Latin America, so little understood and so quickly dismissed in the past, such generalization can lead even further astray than elsewhere. It is well, therefore, before embarking on this synthesis, to repeat some warnings.

Latin America is not one. This seems a commonplace and is endlessly repeated by students of the area but is seldom heeded. Backward, French-speaking, Negro Haiti is not recognizable in Uruguay of the rolling plains and many Italian immigrants. Bolivia, heavily Indian, divided over questions of language, race, and caste, is startlingly different from its immediate neighbor Argentina.

Nor is Latin America one in attitudes and self-images. One may read in any textbook on Latin America that there is no statue to Cortes in the whole of Mexico, and one quickly discovers in Mexican literature that he is often considered to be a prototype of the imperialistic adventurer, destroying civilizations, enslaving races, lusting for gold, all without any understanding, so it is claimed, of what he was doing. How different is the attitude in Peru, the other great center of Spanish civilization during the colonial period. Here, if one must pass such a moral judgment, the *conquistadores* led by Pizarro were more cruel, more ignorant of their surroundings, more treacherous, and more avaricious than in Mexico. Yet today the statue of Pizarro the Conqueror dominates the Plaza de Armas in downtown Lima, and a mummy, widely held to be that of Pizarro, lies in state in the cathedral on the other side of the square.

In the case of Brazil one is continually impressed by a significant difference in its historical patterns when compared to those of Spanish America. Independence was accomplished with hardly any gore. Divisive issues have not produced the lengthy, racking civil wars which have troubled its neighbors, in spite of the fact that Brazil is larger and more divided than

they are. The political and economic questions of the nineteenth and twentieth centuries generally have been settled by compromise and accommodation; all very different from the revolutions and wars of Mexico, where even today many issues are immediately seen in terms of black and white.

Without going too far along the outmoded road of geographical determinism, the student of Latin America cannot help being impressed by the effects of geography and geology on the history of the area. Most of the inhabited parts of Latin America suffer from a chronic shortage of water, while mighty rivers such as the Amazon and the Orinoco flow through empty and hitherto useless regions. The Andes form a massive barrier dividing east from west and have made transportation and communications difficult. Many would blame the tininess and even the unruliness of some Latin American states on the particularism and regionalism which this difficult geography has fostered.

Geologically Latin America lacks coal, and many of its best mineral deposits are located at great distances from centers of population and convenient land or sea routes.

It is safe to say, in fact, that the major impression which Latin America leaves on the foreign traveller is one of diversity both in the cultural and physical realms.

Yet another warning which the student of Latin American history must continually heed is that the normal terminology of history and politics may be of very diminished usefulness in the Latin American setting. What is one to say of wars of independence which left so very few people even relatively independent? How many of the hundreds of "revolutions" can really qualify as social and economic upheavals at all? In the area of everyday party politics casual observers are constantly puzzled by the strange use of adjectives in party labels. Revolutionary parties which are quite content with the *status quo* are numerous, parties which proclaim themselves "socialist" may be far to the right in the political spectrum, and several "radical" and "radical liberal" parties in Latin America have disillusioned their followers by the mildness and cautiousness of all their legislation once in power. The government *Party of Revolutionary Institutions* of Mexico provides an excellent example of this confusion. Once the student of Mexican politics has overcome the contradiction implicit in the very name (for how can an institution be revolutionary?) he is left to consider the growing complaints that the party is bourgeois, complacent, and very much in a rut. An even greater contradiction is evident in the strange label taken by a prominent Bolivian party, the *Bolivian Socialist Phalange*.

Latin America, as we conceive of it, began with the Spanish-sponsored discovery of 1492 and the subsequent conquests and occupations. Before discussing the impact of Spain in America, however, it would be well to consider some of the more salient features of the civilizations of those whom the Spaniards found in America and some of the dominant characteristics of the Spaniards themselves at that historical period.

Whatever the quantitative or qualitative measurements, it is clear that several of the Indian civilizations found in Meso-America and South America by the Spaniards were far superior to anything found in North America by the English or the French. Peoples such as the Aztecs, Mayas, Chibchas, and Incas had developed far beyond the stage of hunting and gathering. In the areas dominated by these peoples the Spaniards found complex societies, urban centers, and population densities which did not exist to the north. These civilizations, it is significant to note, were very closely tied to the soil. Nearly all active individuals played some part in the seasonal cycle, and all depended on one, or at most two, basic crops. Maize and potatoes were the bases of all activity. Although the Indian civilizations had long and bloody military histories, the student of the conquest finds that in every case the Spaniards had relatively little difficulty in subjugating these sedentary peoples. They lacked the ability to disappear into the wilderness or even to sustain a long campaign in the field. After a month or two of fighting they had to surrender or starve. Often they simply laid down their arms and lost interest in the matter, such was their anxiety to get back to the neglected staple crops. It is worth noting that wherever the invading Spaniards found nomadic peoples, in the rain forests of southern Chile, in the Caribbean islands, or on the Pampas, they failed to pacify these wanderers, and, through one means or another, exterminated the vast majority of them just as was done in North America.

The Spaniard was just as much a creature of his historical past as was the conquered Indian. Ferdinand of Aragon supervised the taking of Granada in 1492, the same year as the discovery of America by Columbus, thus bringing to a close about 780 years of intermittent warfare against the invading Moors. This long war, especially in its final stages, was a war between two religions more than between two peoples. By the time of the fall of Granada it had assumed many of the characteristics of a crusade, and after so many centuries of struggle, it is clear why this crusading spirit was so military in character. Obviously then, after eight hundred years of war, it became evident to many Spaniards that there could be no more glorious work than fighting the infidel. It was a holy task and one's king and fellow-countrymen were grateful for the protection. Then again, part of the reason for the reconquest was booty, and this booty was considered honorably won when taken from pagan Moors. A war of this nature and duration severely discourages agriculture and commerce. There is little honor to be gained in such pursuits, and the rewards of soldiering tend to be more tangible and movable. In a war of ever-shifting frontiers, movable wealth, or booty, becomes far more valuable than a rich farm, be it ever so large.

Spaniards who arrived in America in the sixteenth century were often the results of such historical conditioning. They looked for conquests, not settlements, quick returns not steady development, and, of course, resident populations which would do the work for which long centuries of warfare had made them unsuited. It would not be accurate, however, to confuse a disinclination to engage in manual labor or commerce with a lack of energy or an inability to bear hardships. The energy and endurance of the sixteenth-century Spaniard was prodigious, and the exploits of the great conquerors through jungles and deserts are now legend.

One important trait which this long war with the Moors helped to stamp on the Spanish soul was individualism. In a disjointed war of that duration, with one group of Christians separated from another by Moors and mountains, regionalism flourished and remains as one of the dominant features of modern Spain and Latin America. This individualism was further fostered by the impossible nature of Latin American geography when the Spaniards finally settled in the New World.

When the Spaniards arrived in the Americas, therefore, they found several sedentary, agricultural peoples unprepared for long wars and used to steady and prolonged manual labor. The invaders were militaristic, energetic, and fanatically religious seekers after gold and glory. The outcome could not long be in doubt.

Two features of the colonial period are of great significance. The colonial period saw the gradual establishment of one of the most intricate and successful administrative systems which the world has seen and was the stage for the most intense struggle for justice between harsh realists and idealistic humanitarians which has taken place there until the present.

Two fears lay behind the type of colonial administrative system which developed. One, of course, arose out of logistics. The crown correctly felt that such large distances would tend to diminish its authority and would cause a disregard of the interests of the mother country or open rebellion. (This fear was confirmed early in the colonial period by the civil wars in Peru.) The other fear came from Spanish historical experience. The crown had emerged as a centralizing, cohesive force after centuries of struggle, not only against the alien Moors but also against the recalcitrant, individualistic nobility of feudal Spain. In this, if in little else, the crown can be said to have learned from bitter historical experience. It was determined from the beginning to prevent the creation of a powerful local nobility independent of its influence. The early *conquistadores* and *adelantados* were quickly replaced by administrators from the Peninsula, often in the most ungrateful and ungracious way, and throughout the colonial period powerful administrative positions were almost always filled by individuals from the mother country, and their appointments were always for a fixed term. Many scholars have commented on this exclusion of all Americans from the higher posts in colonial administration. It tended to inhibit local initiative and deprived the Creole population of administrative experience, with disastrous results, if one admits the validity of this theory, after the wars of independence.

The feelings of insecurity and distrust which obsessed the Spanish monarchs were reflected throughout the system. While two, and later four, viceroys acted as the king's supreme representatives in the New World, yet each viceroy was subject to the most intricate system of checks and balances. All his work was open to inspection and criticism from any of his minor officials, each one of whom could complain or inform directly to the crown over the viceroy's head, if he so wished. At the end of the viceroy's term, or even during it in some cases, he was hailed before sudden courts of inspection conducted by outsiders responsible to the crown. The safest line of conduct was to do nothing which could possibly bring a reprimand.

At the lower echelons there was constant overlapping of jurisdiction, a situation which delayed decisions and caused a veritable plague of lawsuits all through the colonial period. These delays and administrative squabbles seem to have been preferable, from the crown's point of view, to the uncertainty which would have arisen if administrators had been left on their own to initiate and carry out policy. This strange system of legalistic delay may have been deliberate. One Spanish ambassador in Paris hoped that death would come to him as slowly as the news and decisions from Madrid, for if that could be assured he would live forever. In the New World, thanks to the *Patronato Real* or royal patronage, the Church, which was the most important single entity in the colony, also felt the full weight of royal surveillance and sanctions.

Considering the problem from the viewpoint of the twentieth century, one is forced to admit that many of the crown's suspicions were fully justified. The monarchs simply knew their subjects rather well. The individualistic and separatist propensities of Spaniards have already been mentioned. Recent research has also proved that the historical tradition of the quiet colony and the "colonial siesta" is largely a myth. Not only was the region constantly troubled by Indian revolts, as was to be expected, but it was also the scene of frequent Creole conspiracies and even open rebellions. The revolt of the Contreras brothers in Nicaragua, which included the assassination of the local bishop, and the *comuneros* revolt in Paraguay in 1730 are only two of the more obvious examples. The acid test of the Spanish administrative system must be its duration. It persevered for over three hundred years, and half of this period was a time of great stress for the Spanish crown itself. To hold together a scattered empire of such dimensions, and at such a distance, during the period of Spain's deepest decadence was no mean administrative and political feat.

Throughout its period of domination in the Americas the Spanish monarchy was harassed by a difficult juxtaposition of the real and the ideal. According to the prevailing mercantilistic theories of the time, the colony existed primarily for the use and benefit of the mother country. Quite simply, it was supposed to show a profit. And as the Spanish crown's financial difficulties and obligations multiplied, the importance of this profit increased. In order to show a profit, the mines, pearl fisheries, and farms had to be worked. Negro slaves were imported in large numbers and partially resolved this problem in the hot coastal areas, but in the highland mines such as Potosí, Huancavelica, Guanajuato, and Zacatecas the only apparent solution was the Indian. The same was true in all the farming areas of temperate climate. The crown was caught in a dilemma between its humanistic concern for the welfare of the Indians and its urgent need for the gold and silver from the treasure fleets. The religious orders, and in particular the Franciscans, working hard to convert the Indians and seeing much of their work frustrated, played on the crown's humanistic concern; the Creole entrepreneurs and landowners, who needed the reluctant labor of the Indians, played on the crown's dire financial straits; the puzzled royal administrators, most of whom faithfully tried to follow the zigzags of regal decisions, often found themselves condemned by both sides of the argument.

This centuries-long debate is largely responsible for the creation of the so-called "black legend." Eager to win a hearing for their point of view, such early missionaries as Fray Bartolomé de Las Casas publicized their cause as widely as possible, talking of the destruction of the Indies, the monstrous massacres of the indigenous population, and the cruel exploitation to which the surviving Indians were subject. Nations and individuals hostile to Spain, of which there were many in the sixteenth and seventeenth centuries, capitalized on this issue for political and religious advantage; the result was that even today the average British schoolboy's first introduction to Spain in the New World is closely tied to the novels of Charles Kingsley and the glorious exploits of Sir Francis Drake (which, it is interesting to note, is a name still used to terrify naughty children in some parts of Latin America).

Evolution of colonial labor systems closely reflects the twists and turns of this prolonged argument. The crown, under strong religious promptings, quickly abolished widespread enslavement of the Indians, decreeing that they were to be considered as rational human beings. It comprised, however, by admitting that their innocence and lack of the Catholic religion made of them special cases, wards of the crown, who could not be trusted for the moment to know their own best interests. The result was the *encomienda* system whereby Indians were "entrusted" to supposedly responsible Spaniards for indoctrination and physical care. In return the *encomenderos* were permitted to exact work from them. Laws governing how much work and when and where it was to be done were quite stringent.

Although the system worked efficiently in some areas, it soon became obvious that many clerics and some administrators were far from satisfied that all exploitation of the Indians had ceased. Persistent complaints from these two sources eventually caused the crown to over-react. The famous "New Laws" of 1542 were the result. They called for a gradual but definite abolition of the *encomienda* system and the substitution of wage labor. These laws caused open rebellion in some cases and shocked pleas to the crown in others. Even loyal Guatemala City councilors sent a message to the king complaining that they felt as if their heads had been cut off and warning him that he should not listen too closely to the exaggerations of meddlesome friars such as Las Casas. The crown was forced to proceed more slowly in its program for the abolition of the *encomienda,* but gradually a new system emerged. Known variously as the *mita* or *repartimiento*, it provided for forced, paid, Indian labor on a selective service basis. In many cases a certain number of Indians from selected villages were gathered together in the public square of the principal town on a fixed day of the week or month, and there *repartidos* were divided among the local Spanish employers.

Complaints about this system from the usual sources were almost immediate, and it too was abolished before the end of the colonial period. Many Indians eventually found their way into a free market situation where their exploitation continued on a cultural rather than a formalized basis. Others, especially those in the isolated agricultural areas, soon fell under the labor system known as "debt peonage," whereby, through various devices, they and their descendants became so hopelessly indebted to the owners or administrators of the *hacienda* or workshop that their departure was impossible. Many also became sharecroppers, which, given their lack of education and their conditioning to a life of servility, effectively tied them to one employ. These two labor systems exist and coexist in many parts of Highland Latin America to this day.

When studying this long debate, the twentieth-century observer feels a reluctant sympathy for the Spanish monarchy. Its motives were often of the best as can be seen clearly when one considers the number of humanitarian laws, far in advance of their times, which were promulgated for the relief of the Indians. And yet massive and costly embroilments in Europe and the restiveness of the Creole population in the New World caused constant compromises. Economic necessity and fear of revolt stifled much of the best and most imaginative thinking of the Spanish crown.

One important aspect of Latin American colonial history which has been almost totally neglected is the impact of Spain's rapid seventeenth-century decline on the institutions and society across the Atlantic. The descendants of the great *conquistadores* were often made painfully aware that their once great country was hard put to defend their coasts against pirate raids; they saw the decline of Spanish trade and the disappearance of industries; the news from Spain, when it got through, was almost always bad, and the culture which came from there became increasingly escapist and rigid as Luis de Góngora and his school began to dominate all writing.

In the colony itself all was far from well by the middle of the seventeenth century. The Indian population continued to decline, which meant that formerly prosperous industries and agricultural areas were abandoned. The intellectuals of the period gave themselves over to the same escapist, intricate poetry as was current in the Peninsula, and much of the vigor went out of society. When one reads the town council records of the period, it becomes plain that the major preoccupations were ones of precedent and ceremony.

It is well to remember that this seventeenth century which saw the decline of Spain was the first truly formative era in the colony. The new society was settling down, a large *mestizo* class was coming into being, Spaniards were being born who had never seen Spain and who thought of themselves as Creoles and Americans, and in spite of the efforts of the

Church, which steadily pushed back the "rim of Christendom," the boundaries of the occupied and productive areas had been fairly definitively staked out.

So, to overstate a point, one may claim that Latin American society first coalesced in an atmosphere of decline and doubt. Pessimism was rife and some of the most obscurantist extremes of the European baroque made their permanent home in Latin America. The effects of such a childhood on a society are bound to be profound and are certainly worthy of much more research.

———

It has been customary when studying Latin American history to consider the wars of independence as the important watershed. The cultural historian, however, while not denying the significance of these struggles, feels more inclined to consider the coming of the European Enlightenment as the dividing line between what was medieval and what is modern. To put the matter simply, the present-day historian finds it easier to identify with the problems and decisions of the Latin Americans after the Enlightenment. They are talking about a world which he feels that he knows.

The intellectual movement known as the Enlightenment reached Latin America in the latter half of the seventeenth century but did not gain momentum until 1700 and after when the Bourbons, having replaced the pathetic Hapsburg line, sought to open Spain to the world, or at least to Europe. The Enlightenment, simplified, represented a skeptical revolt against traditional dogmas and an attempt to replace undisputed and traditional authority by a desire to verify by investigation and experiment. To many historians these thinkers were the first "modern" men.

The impact of this movement on Latin America was certainly not so profound as in Europe, but to the young, disgruntled, upperclass Creoles it represented a set of ideas which coincided with their economic and sociological frustrations with the Spanish crown and colonial system. In spite of belated attempts at reform by the Spanish monarchy, it was from such ideas and such frustrations that the dream of independence was born.

The modern world seeks accomplishments and progress when it studies history, but when faced with the need to justify the wars of independence in these terms, the student of Latin America is left with precious little. It is true that the Creoles threw off the restrictive government of Spain, but to the great majority the turmoil brought few changes. In some areas such as Central America there was little disturbance; in others, such as Venezuela, the wars brought widespread death and destruction. The Andean Indian certainly did not profit by the wars, and there is considerable evidence that his status and level of living actually deteriorated after independence. After all the Creole was his exploiter and traditional enemy.

What little protection he had ever obtained had been from the crown. After the wars the crown was gone and the exploiters controlled the new societies. Peru even witnessed a brief Indian revolt which proclaimed the desirability of the return of Ferdinand VII of Spain. Of even more significance is the fact that the new rulers of Peru and Bolivia quickly restored the Indian tribute payments which had been abolished by the Spaniards. Also worthy of consideration is the very short time in power which was given to Bolívar, Sucre, and San Martín, the idealistic leaders of the struggle for independence in South America. Without admitting to a conspiracy theory of history, one is forced to admit that these children of the Enlightenment were obliged to withdraw as soon as their usefulness to the Creole upper classes had diminished.

The wars of independence, to the chagrin of Simón Bolívar, did not transform Latin America society. They simply left a political vacuum. There was as yet no spirit of nationalism or solidarity in the infant nations, and the lack of administrative and political experience was to leave many of the new societies at the mercy of the most unscrupulous adventurers. In addition, the newly independent Latin America was sparsely populated (perhaps a total of sixteen million inhabitants), and the centers of population were separated from each other by empty areas of difficult geography. Obviously regionalism would flourish in such circumstances and would present yet another formidable obstacle to the formation of truly integrated national states. These very geographical and population factors, however, have spared Latin America from futile international wars of which there have been surprisingly few since independence. Much more in evidence have been civil wars, revolts, and regional strife within the boundaries of each individual nation.

Another vain hope of the revolutionaries was that the wars would free them from outside direction to such an extent that they would be able to play a larger role in world affairs and especially in world trade. And indeed, after the restrictive hand of Spain had been removed trade did flourish in many parts of Latin America. But to the dismay of the new leaders it was soon found that they were simple amateurs compared to the trading powers of the world, and many were presented with the paradox of seeing their trade increase while the economic situation of the nation deteriorated rapidly.

The often-expressed feeling that the history of Latin America since the wars of independence has been the history of attempts to reconcile individualism with authority has particular relevance to the early struggles to organize viable nations. Would the old Spanish craving for individual liberty lead to anarchy, or would the need to create a coherent state be such as to crush the individual through emphatic assertions of authority? The early history of many of the national states presents a distressing picture of anarchy alternating with dictatorship, of federalists who represented regional and occasionally individual liberties struggling against centralists who longed for discipline and a truly national state.

One of Latin America's most persistent problems is that it has remained for so long a cultural and political child of Europe. In literature, for example, the latest vogue in Paris or Madrid is soon copied slavishly in Latin America. Only in the last two or three decades has the purely indigenous in the area received intensive notice from the local intellectuals.

This tendency to adopt ideas and modes from Europe, whether or not they fit the New World environment, had a somewhat pernicious effect on the organizers of the new nations. It happened that the middle of the nineteenth century, when so many of the Latin American states were struggling to set their houses in order, was the era when Europe was swept by the twin waves of Liberalism and Romanticism. In many ways these were the wrong theories and emotions for the area at that time. Liberalism as it was then practiced placed great stress on written codes and constitutions, claiming that if the law of the land abolished tyrany and injustice, then surely some approximation to the earthly paradise would follow. This fallacy caused even greater havoc and disillusionment in Latin America than in Europe, and needlessly so. Latin Americans, with their long tradition of honoring the king but not obeying him, would have been the first to realize, one would suppose, that written codes are subject to wide interpretation, that they are easily replaced or amended at the whim of any dictator, and that if they do not reflect the real nature of a society, then they are at best only wistful hopes for the future. This urge to legislate progress rather than plan it is very much a part of today's Latin America. The biggest argument in both Ecuador and Honduras at this historical moment is what should go into the new constitutions and what should be left out of them. Both countries are close to setting records in the number of constitutions which they have had in about one hundred forty years of independence. Several Latin American nations have had about twenty, a new constitution every seven years, and that is leaving aside the number of times these inspiring charters have been radically amended!

These constitutions, with their constant proclamations of separation of powers and political equality for all citizens can only have added to the pessimism and cynicism of many thinking Latin Americans. What separation of powers can be said to exist when the *caudillo* of the moment controls the courts, "rigs" the elections, and fills the representative bodies of the nation with his sycophants? It is small wonder that so many Latin American intellectuals have become either hopelessly alienated, losing all faith in representative democracy, or have tried to work with the system already in existence, while professing open-

ly that things do not change in Latin America whatever one chooses to call the latest government and leaders.

Another tenet of nineteenth-century "classical" Liberalism which was completely out of place in many parts of Latin America was laissez faire economics and government. This theory claimed that every man should be considered enlightened enough, and free enough, to know his own best interests. The government and laws, therefore, should withdraw from the scene as much as possible and leave commerce in peace. But in Latin America all economic decisions had been made by an outside agency for over three hundred years, and the traders and businessmen were simply novices vis-à-vis their European and North American counterparts. Nevertheless, in many cases they were deprived of all protection from their national governments.

Within the boundaries of each nation the results of laissez faire were sometimes even worse. When a majority of the population is illiterate and lives in semi-slavery because of caste and language, it is ridiculous to speak of the enlightened self-interest of the individual. Yet in the Andean countries the Indian was declared a free individual, subject to the same laws as other citizens, with no special code for his protection for such a code would degrade him! (Other laws, of course, stated that only literates could vote or hold public office, thus excluding nearly all Indians.) With all laws for his protection swept away, the Indian was cast into the open market in matters of commerce and real estate. Conditioned to obey every whim of his white and *mestizo* fellow-countrymen, the Indian was exploited and cheated on every side, and all this, paradoxically, according to the letter of the new, enlightened law. In Bolivia and Peru the Indians lost much of their tribal and individual holdings not to the Spaniards of the sixteenth and seventeenth centuries, but rather to avaricious entrepreneurs of the ninteenth century operating under the laws of laissez faire.

All these various Liberal dogmas had the effect in Latin America of reinforcing the *status quo*. Eventually the Liberal leaders were indistinguishable from the conservatives whom they fought.

The wars of independence had also legitimized the use of force. The kings of Spain had ruled by divine right and had been supported by legend and long tradition. The leaders of the independence movement won their right to command through violence. A new tradition was soon established. The peoples of Latin America had been accustomed to domination from above. The democratic tradition was a local matter, when it existed at all, and is notoriously slow to develop. Pointing to the examples provided by the wars, profiting from the inexperience of the Latin American peoples in governing themselves, the *caudillos* stepped into the political vacuum left by the the departure of Spain.

The *caudillo*, or personalistic, charismatic leader, has been one of the most distinctive features of Latin American national life. He varies according to the country and the historical moment, proclaiming himself, at will, liberal or conservative, federalist or centralist, revolutionary or renovator; but basic to all his policies is self-perpetuation in power. The shock which occurs when a *caudillo* voluntarily resigns from office is considerable, and there have been few examples. Some *caudillos* have been freely elected and even reelected such has been their popularity, and occasionally, their ability, but most have come to power through *coups d'état* of one kind or another. Many claim as justification that their long-suffering nations are not ready for the blessings and responsibilities of representative democracy, that the common people have been the dupes of clever coteries of unscrupulous politicians, that much has to be done and there is no time for the wasteful processes of debate and vote, and that, in the final analysis, they represent the total voice and aspirations of the people better than any one political party or group. As the twentieth century has advanced, the typical *caudillo* has had to adopt the protective coloring of the age (especially if he wants quick diplomatic recognition from the United States and the accompanying funds), so that many of them are as at home mouthing the current shibboleths of land reform, economic imperialism, universal compulsory education, and the like, as their nineteenth-century predecessors were when they shouted "federalism or death."

What cannot be denied is the decisive role which some of these dictators have played in the creation of nationhood. Whatever the moralist may think of his methods it is an historical fact that Argentina did not exist as a cohesive entity until it was brutally welded together by Juan Manuel Rosas, who, incidentally, proclaimed himself a federalist. It is hardly an exaggeration to say that the outlying regions of Mexico first felt the full weight and dominance of Mexico City in the days of Porfirio Díaz. And without Diego Portales directing national affairs behind the scenes it might have taken Chile many long decades to resolve its internal quarrels and begin its national life.

The fragmentation of Latin America after independence weakened the area and its component parts vis-à-vis the powerful nations of the Western world. Latin America, throughout the nineteenth and twentieth centuries, has been subject to steady economic penetration from without and has suffered recurrent interference in its internal affairs. Its dominant military establishments have been powerless against foreign incursions. Because of the relative weakness of the area in the modern world it has developed a pathological fear of some of the powerful nations, particularly the United States, the "Colossus of the North." United States intervention has been frequent, particularly in Mexico and the Caribbean, and Latin Americans believe, with some justification given recent events in Guatemala and Cuba, that such interference has far from ended. Certainly economic penetration of the smaller countries is massive, and the nationalization of tin mines in Bolivia, the recent arrangements with oil companies in Venezuela, with fruit companies in Guatemala and Honduras, and with copper companies in Chile, all reflect the Latin Americans' suspicion and fear that they are not effective masters of their own house.

As the nineteenth century drew to a close, Latin America was swept by a new wave of ideology from Europe. While this new set of dogmas has sometimes been called "The New Liberalism" in an effort to distinguish it from the early classical Liberalism which proved so harmful, and finally so sterile, in Latin America, yet perhaps "Liberalism" is a complete misnomer for what was now happening. By implication at least the new ideas were authoritarian. The Positivists believed that scientific laws governed the functioning of society and that once such laws had been discovered it was the duty of governments to intervene, whether asked to or not, to enforce these laws on society for its own good. Implicit in this argument was a denial of representative democracy, although this was seldom admitted. Positivism implied that there would be an oligarchy of scientifically educated investigators who would determine what were the basic laws governing the satisfactory functioning of society and who would then persuade or force society to adopt appropriate legislation or mores, even if it were reluctant, simply because these scientists knew what was good for people better than the people themselves. It is obvious that the so-called "New Liberalism" was in many ways the exact opposite of the old classical Liberalism. It certainly did not believe in laissez faire either in economics or politics or in a neutral, non-participating government. Rather it called for heavy government intervention as the only means of guiding society toward its proper goals. This primitive Positivism had a profound impact on Brazil and Mexico. Even today the Brazilian flag bears the legend "Order and Progress" (not "Democracy and Progress" which would be much closer to the aspirations of most present-day Brazilians). In Mexico, directly contradicting the representative Liberalism advocated by Benito Juárez, Porfirio Díaz, who claimed to be his spiritual heir, became convinced by the new Positivism. Starting from the assumption that most Mexicans were little better than children who could not be trusted to know what was good for them, Díaz, one of Latin America's longest ruling *caudillos*, gathered around him a scientific elite of planners, the famous *científicos*, who set about planning society, using where necessary the most extreme forms of repression and inhumanity.

Fortunately perhaps for most Latin Americans the new scientific Positivism (or scientific materialism as some have called it) soon lost its more doctrinaire and exclusive aspects in the stresses of day-to-day political and social life. The idea of popular representation, even though so often frustrated, was too firmly established to allow much peace to any group of elite scientific planners. The humanization, if one may so call it, of the new Positivism came about because of widely different pressures from country to country.

In Argentina, Brazil, Uruguay, and to a lesser extent Chile, massive European immigration after 1870 proved to be the principal enemy of doctrinaire Positivism. These new immigrants were not conditioned to servility as were the Andean or Meso-American Indians, and they were certainly not prepared to allow all political and social decisions to be made for them. Nearly all were Western Europeans and as such their history had made them very political and social beings. Many were preoccupied with driving social ambitions which seemed new and startling to caste-bound, carefully stratified Latin America. A significant minority of them soon began to assume middle-class attributes and attitudes and began to have an important voice in national decision-making. These new citizens did, of course, believe in Mammon. They were as attracted to scientific progress, to the railways across the Pampas, to capital investment, and to new inventions in machinery as any Positivist. They emphatically did not believe, however, that one small elite held the keys to the future. Most of them wanted to decide their own futures and to play a part in deciding the future of their new homelands. Thus one can generalize by saying that the new urge for material progress was humanized by the old ideas of representative government and social justice.

In Argentina and Uruguay the immigrant inspired desire for material progress plus social justice led to the founding of urban and heavily immigrant political parties.

Largely because of the personality of some of its early leaders the *Radical Civic Union* of Argentina was the more cautious. Its ideals of that time appear narrow today and its social reform program seemed far from ambitious to many of its followers once it reached power. In Uruguay, where the reformers took over a traditional party called the *Colorados,* the movement was much more dynamic. Under the aegis of one man, José Batlle y Ordóñez, who dominated Uruguayan politics for the first twenty years of this century, the country was completely transformed. Batlle was very much a Positivist and believed in massive government participation in national life. Many basic industries were nationalized and welfare services such as old-age pensions, minimum wages, the eight-hour day, and free education were begun far ahead of their time. Yet Batlle realized that his program depended on popular acceptance and could not be foisted upon the nation by a distant elite. By a series of legislative measures and presidential de-

crees he turned Uruguay into an extremely democratic state, establishing complete freedom of the press, secret ballot, and separation of church and state. In his last term he even went so far as to curtail the powers of the presidency by the introduction of a collegiate or *colegiado* system of government. While it must be admitted that Batlle made intensive and skillful use of propaganda, nevertheless he was so convinced that people could be persuaded to vote to their own advantage that he continually jeopardized his own program by seeking popular approval for it. The early Positivists of Latin America would have considered such an attitude as rank stupidity, for how can the individual know what is to his own advantage? (There are many examples which support this argument in Latin American history!)

In Mexico the humanization of doctrinaire, scientific Positivism was a violent and destructive process in which frustrations and hatreds dating back to the early days of the colonial period found expression through a bloody social revolution.

Porfirio Díaz and his coterie of planners rationalized his long and ruthless rule by claiming that he was establishing a scientific basis for Mexico's future prosperity. To him and his clinical *científicos* the Indians and uneducated lower classes were a negative factor in the national picture, and as such were only fit to be used expendably for Mexico's progress. But these Indian and lower classes comprised 80 to 90 percent of the total population. Mexicans of all classes became increasingly disgruntled as they saw that all the repression and lack of representation, while it did bring heavy foreign investment and enriched a select few, was not even attempting to solve the centuries-old problems of the country. A generation may be persuaded or forced to sacrifice itself for the sake of its descendants or for the nation, but it is much harder to force it to sacrifice itself for the benefit of a handful of contemporaries.

The Mexican Revolution created its ideology as it progressed. Originally concerned with a more extensive suffrage and a ban on reelection to the presidency, it widened its credo during years of chaos to include an intense nationalism, a desire to keep foreign investment and interference under strict control, a humanitarian concern for the poor of the country, especially the rural peon, and a constitution in 1917 which embodied many of the principles of social justice which Batlle brought to Uruguay. In this manner violent social revolution softened materialistic national progress with some measure of social justice.

The impact of the Mexican Revolution on the rest of Latin America has been deep and long-lasting. It was, after all, a purely Mexican phenomenon, little concerned with foreign ideologies or European intellectual fashions. Inasmuch as it was indigenous it satisfied the Latin American craving for cultural and political independence, giving new inspiration to the many jaded intellectuals and politicians who had become convinced that Latin America was too divided and too impotent to bring about needed changes through its own efforts. Here, after so many barracks revolts and pseudo-reformers, was a movement which could be defined as a genuine revolution, and not only Mexicans but many other Latin Americans are quick to point out that "their" revolution antedates the one in Russia.

The Mexican Revolution was one of the principal causes of a new creativity in the Arts. The young, *engagé* artists and writers found to their surprise that their own homelands presented a variety of themes which they were better equipped to study than the themes of Paris and Madrid. In such novelists as Ciro Alegería and Jorge Icaza of Peru and Ecuador, and in such painters as Diego Rivera and José Clemente Orozco of Mexico the new concern for the Indian and the downtrodden found fresh and vital expression.

The awakened interest in things properly Latin American has not saved the region from involvement in the events and ideologies which trouble the modern world. The several nations discovered that they were not to be left alone to work out their destinies according to local needs and conditions. In an ever-shrinking world, ideologies and the polarization of ideologies have become international, and the wars between these different systems have involved all nations to varying degrees. Latin America, for so long an outpost in world affairs, was to discover that a desire to play a leading role in the wider world also brought a reciprocal intrusion by the troubles of the world on domestic problems and solutions.

The political life of the last forty years has produced an entirely new group of political parties. These parties claim to be purely national with few ties to the great international ideologies. A basic premise is the conviction that solutions to national problems must be found within the nation itself, for Latin America is too much a special case to be susceptible to correction by fixed international dogmas. The indigenous parties have had widely varying results in their attempts to win the support of the discontented masses, and some have shown signs of age.

The *National Revolutionary Movement* of Bolivia came to power by revolution in 1952, Latin America's second "true" revolution, and until 1964, and perhaps even today, seemed to enjoy the support of most of the peasants in the largely rural nation. Yet Bolivia's gigantic problems, the lack of trained personnel to carry out ambitious reform programs, and the entrenched tradition of corruption in government, all contributed to a series of blunders and an unleashing of civil strife which the national government had difficulty in controlling. It may well be true that the *National Revolutionary Movement* (*M.N.R.*) has at least laid the foundations for a new and better Bolivia, but the country's poverty and divisiveness is such that to the hungry Bolivian peasant the promised land and

its wealth, or even an approximation to it, seems far beyond his lifetime or that of his son.

In Peru the original national revolutionary party has never come to power, but the *Popular Revolutionary Alliance of America*, (*APRA*), while never becoming the international party which it had hoped to be, has had such an influence on Peruvian politics since 1924 that nearly all large political groups in the nation now find themselves at least professing similar aims. Many of *APRA*'s original programs are now law and became law while the party's most hated enemies were in power. *APRA* and its leaders now seem old and tired while Peru has hardly begun to solve its national problems, but its rivals may very well carry forward its program.

Democratic Action of Venezuela appears at this historical moment to be the most successful of these parties. Partly because of oil revenues and partly because of the astuteness and dynamism of its leaders, it has brought many profound changes to the country in recent years in spite of terrorism and a hypersensitive military establishment.

In several small nations such as Nicaragua and Haiti, attempts to form indigenous reformist parties have been abortive. Another group of countries does not seem to have awakened to the realities of modern life. In Ecuador and Colombia *Liberals* and *Conservatives* still squabble interminably about such questions as lay schools, laws permitting divorce, or separation of church and state, just as they did in the nineteenth century. Colombia, which still suffers the consequences of a decade and more of civil war and terrorism, may have realized at last the dangers of political chauvinism, but generals and demagogues may not permit much time to the traditional parties for the carrying out of constructive reforms.

The indigenous reform parties are under constant pressure from the outside world. Whether it be the United States with its conviction that a mixed economy is the best possible solution or tiny groups of Communists who promise the discontented that they can bring about the same reforms quicker and better, these parties are under heavy siege and are often self-consciously defensive.

The other problem facing the indigenous reform parties is the, to them, negative side of the dynamic Latin American political tradition. Mention has already been made of the old *caudillo* in modern dress, the Porfirio Díaz who has learned to speak convincingly of land reform and dialectical materialism. The Latin American masses are still instinctively drawn to the charismatic leader and the new forces have found few antidotes to his charms. In several countries, including the two largest in South America, skillful dictators won the allegiance of the masses to such an extent that they inhibited the development of the democratic parties and their programs. The popularity of exiled Juan Domingo Perón with city workers still troubles Argentina, and most of Brazil's ineffectual parties are the brainchildren of the late Getulio Vargas. In little Ecuador the great demagogue José María Velasco Ibarra has been president four times and has completed only one term. Yet he easily won the elections of 1960 against candidates of both traditional parties, and they all fear that if he came back from exile he would win again. Disillusioned Liberals and Conservatives now find themselves uttering the same beliefs as the typical *caudillo*. "The common people are like children. They are unable to understand what is to their own advantage."

The new parties themselves are reluctant slaves to the area's political heritage. Many of them owe their successes not to imaginative and appealing programs but rather to the popularity of their leader and the impression which he has conveyed of a dominant personality. *APRA*'s history is essentially the story of the struggles of Victor Raúl Haya de la Torre, and until his retirement all students of *Democratic Action* of Venezuela thought in terms of Rómulo Betancourt. The history of the *National Revolutionary Movement* of Bolivia is closely tied to the career of Victor Paz Estenssoro, and even in Cuba, where foreign ideology has made such an impression on the native reform movement, the present situation is hard to imagine without the dominant figure of Fidel Castro.

———

Latin America has entered the world scene only to find that it is "underdeveloped," or as the more positive and optimistic economists phrase it, "in the process of development." It is part of the revolution of rising expectations. Population is exploding while good agricultural land erodes and slums multiply. Land reform proposals are debated endlessly while Indians invade rich *haciendas*. Governments desperately provide "bread and circuses" by building handsome sports stadiums or by reviving old and forgotten boundary disputes. Efforts at hemispheric integration are hampered by petty jealousies. And the students of political situations of this kind warn that there is little time left. The illiterate peoples have been introduced to the marvels of radio and cinema and the contentment, which arises from ignorance, is gone. The Andean peasants, or at least a significant number of them, are now aware that others in the world and even in their own country live much more fully and comfortably than they do. Some tell them to wait, others ask them to work constructively for a glorious future, still other voices tell them that they can have it all now. To the illiterate Indians or slum dwellers who spend their lives in an agonizing pursuit of a few necessities, and who are slowly becoming aware of their numbers and their importance to the various nations, the third alternative looks attractive and more easily attained. They have heard centuries of promises but, before, they were simply promises. Now the miserable listeners believe, rightly or wrongly,

that it can all be won, and woe to those who frustrate their hopes.

What is the role to be played by the outside world in this drama? A dominant feature of today's Latin America is the presence of planners and technicians, many of whom are foreigners from agencies of the United Nations or from United States aid missions of various kinds. While these agencies play important roles in development, nevertheless their relationships with the people whom they serve are often poor. Many Latin Americans have an undefined but firm suspicion that technical aid is some new kind of foreign penetration or at best a variety of condescending paternalism. The Latin American needs help but he is at pains to point out that despite the confusion and unrest which has troubled much of visible Latin America his civilization is not exactly an infant one and that many Universities in Latin America were functioning long before Harvard. The Latin American is fond of suggesting that the developed nations, with their neuroses, their super-bombs, and their armaments races, may present an even greater threat to the world than his many problems. His conclusion that he may have just as much to give to the developed world in the way of advice and that aid to be effective should not all be in one direction has some validity and would certainly be an interesting experiment.

Another complaint which the Latin American nationalists often voice is that foreigners, and especially the government of the United States, are so preoccupied with trying to forecast the direction which turbulent Latin America will take that they have no time left to try to understand the people of the area. This sounds like a typical, vague complaint from people of small nations who are worried about the omnipresence of more powerful ones. Nevertheless, just as in the previous assertion, there is a grain of truth in the complaint which is worthy of investigation. Latin America remains one of the least known and least studied areas of the world. Before prescribing remedies for its multiple modern ills it would be well to engage in much deeper study of the historical, cultural, and psychological roots of Latin America's varied societies. The Latin American, even when ill-informed, is deeply conscious of his history and wonders how one may help him without knowing it.

If people do not attempt to know and understand Latin America and its heritage then it is surely presumptuous to encourage radical change among its peoples.

SELECTED BIBLIOGRAPHY

BERLE, ADOLF A. *Latin America: Diplomacy and Reality.* New York and Evanston: Harper & Row Publishers, Incorporated, Published for the Council on Foreign Relations, 1962.
BOURNE, EDWARD GAYLORD. *Spain in America, 1450-1580.* New York: Barnes & Noble, Inc., University

Paperbacks, 1962. The latest edition of an old classic.

Dozer, Donald Marquand. *Latin America: An Interpretive History*. New York: McGraw-Hill Book Company, Inc., 1962.

Hanke, Lewis. *The Spanish Struggle for Justice in the Conquest of America*. New York: Oxford University Press, 1949.

Morse, Richard M. "The Strange Career of 'Latin-American Studies.'" *The Annals of the American Academy of Political and Social Sciences*, Vol. 356, November, 1964.

Needler, Martin C. *Latin American Politics in Perspective*. Princeton, New Jersey: D. Van Nostrand Company, Inc., 1963.

Onis, Harriet de, ed. *The Golden Land: an Anthology of Latin American Folklore in Literature*. New York: Alfred A. Knopf, Inc., 1961.

Pike, Frederick B., ed. *Freedom and Reform in Latin America*. Notre Dame, Indiana: University of Notre Dame Press, International Studies, 1959.

Tannenbaum, Frank. *Ten Keys to Latin America*. New York: Alfred A. Knopf, Inc., 1963.

Torres-Rioseco, Arturo. *The Epic of Latin American Literature*. Berkeley and Los Angeles: University of California Press, 1961.

Whitaker, Arthur P., ed. *Latin America and the Enlightenment*. Ithaca, New York: Cornell University Press, Great Seal Books, 1961.

BRAZIL

Richard Cummings

Brazilian education may be conveniently divided into six historical periods, each of which has been a reflection of the culture and most commonly analyzed within macro-level economic, social, or political frames of reference. For nearly four centuries, and four of the six periods cited here, Brazilian education served as an instrument for the maintenance of the *status quo* in an agriculturally based senhorial society. However, beginning about 1930 the nation began an intensive effort to diversify its economy and to modify its social structure to serve an economy and society characterized by a growing awareness of the economic, political, and social potential inherent in the achievement of literacy for a significantly expanded segment of the nation's population.[1] The current basic issues are popular education versus education for a small, privileged group;[2] instrumental versus speculative academic curricular orientations; and, at the secondary level, public versus private control of the educational system.[3] These issues have engendered efforts to develop transformed and/or new institutional structures that may provide the nation's school-age population of approximately 35 million[4] with the education and training appropriate to living and working in an exponentially diversifying economy and an urbanizing society.

FOUR STAGES FROM 1500-1930

The estimated one million Indians of Brazil at the beginning of the sixteenth century lived in the most primitive cultures found in the Western Hemisphere. They consisted of four main stocks: the Tupi, Carib, and Arawak (classified together as Tropical Forest Indians), and Ge-speaking peoples classified as Marginal Cultures. Economies of the Tropical Forest tribes were based upon agriculture while the Marginal Culture people were nomadic hunters, fishermen, and gatherers. None of the groups had developed a written language, and the skills and traditions of their cultures were acquired by modeling the be-

havior of adults and by engaging in the ceremonial rites-of-passage appropriate to an individual's sex, age, and status position.

The first European educators to visit Brazil were six Jesuits who arrived in Salvador, Bahia, in 1549.[5] While limited numbers of Benedictines, Carmelites, and Franciscans also entered Brazil, the Society of Jesus dominated the educational effort for over two centuries during which time they laid the foundations of Brazilian educational philosophy. During the first century of the tenure of the Jesuits, literacy training was initiated as the basis for Christianizing the Indians, and a limited number of *Colégios* (secondary schools) were developed which offered more advanced training in writing, arithmetic, Latin, and sacred history along the lines outlined in the *Ratio Studiorum*.[6] The emphasis upon grammar, rhetoric, and humanities undergirds the educational legacy of 210 years of Jesuit preeminence.

A third period of Brazilian Educational history began with the banishment of the Jesuits from Brazil in 1759. The ouster left an educational vacuum; edu-

1. Ministerio de Educação e Cultura (MEC). "Educação e Desenvolvimento Economico." Brazilian position paper presented at the Latin-American Conference on Education and Social and Economic Development, Santiago, Chile, March 5-19, 1962 (mimeo).

2. MEC. "Pre-Investment for Perfecting Human Factor." Rio de Janeiro, Undated (1961?, mimeo).

3. Jaime Abreu. "Situação Atual e Tendências do Ensino Medio no Brasil," found in "Educação e Desenvolvimento Econômico," *op. cit.*, pp. 174-96.

4. According to the 1960 census, almost 42 percent of the total population was under 14 years of age and only 2.4 percent was over 65, leaving little over half between the ages of 15 and 65, most of whom were under 30. Applying these data to an estimated 1968 population of 85 million one identifies approximately 46 million persons age 21 or less of whom one-fourth are considered to be pre-school age. Overall, about one-third of the 5-to-21 age group is currently accommodated in schools (see Table 1).

5. Fernando de Azevedo, *A Cultura Brasileira*, São Paulo: Edições Melhoramentos, 1965 (4th Edition), p. 501.

6. *Ibid.*, p. 519.

cation entered into and remained in the doldrums until the arrival of the Portuguese Court in Brazil in 1808 at which time the ideas, concepts, and thought of the Encyclopedists and Positivists were introduced.

During the fourth period, the need to provide for the military defense of the colony of Brazil precipitated a call for the preparation of military and civil engineers. Hence, a Naval Academy and a Military Academy were established in 1808 and 1810. These institutions, of a directly instrumental nature, represented a break with the scholastic traditions of the earlier established educational enterprises in the colony. However, schools of this "technical" character were antithetical to the culture of the erudite elites and the results of various efforts to foster a broadly based system of education were abortive.

In 1823 concern for free popular education was espoused, but under a decentralized system of control the program had little effect. In 1834 the Ato Adicional called for Provincial Assemblies to be responsible for primary and secondary education while higher education would be centrally administered. By 1872 less than 2 percent of an estimated population of ten million was enrolled in elementary level schools. The structure of the social order with an elite of *Doutores* (frequently educated abroad and intellectually far removed from the lesser educated class) remained little changed during the Empire Period (1822-1889) although the seeds of social and educational change had been planted during this period.

At the time of the founding of the Republic (1889) approximately 250,000 children were enrolled in elementary education, some 10,400 students were in secondary schools, and 2,300 students were attending institutions of higher education out of an estimated total population of fourteen million. The system of secondary[7] and higher education was designed to continue to prepare the elite of the nation while the popular system consisted of primary schools, normal schools, and a limited technical education, all administered at the State level.

In the decade of the 1920s the so-called Washington Luis reforms affected primary education as the State of São Paulo *democratized* primary schools and established the pattern of three years of schooling in rural areas and four years in urban areas. The end result of this reform provided a tripartite system, one rudimentary and restricted portion with little probability of emancipating the rural peasantry from the burden of illiteracy, another portion not well providing for the urban middle class and its aspirations for upward social mobility via education; and one portion for the economic and social elite. A more universal system of education was espoused in the Federal District in 1928 but was aborted during the Vargas-led Revolution of 1930.

TWO STAGES FROM 1930 TO PRESENT

Centralization of education increased during the fifth period as the Ministry of Education and Public Health was established in 1931 and the Federal Constitution of 1934 called for the Federal Government to establish a national education plan to cover all "levels and branches" of education in the nation. Criteria were established for the development of a University system, secondary education was extended to a two-cycle, seven-year system, former legislation was revised to facilitate the expansion of private secondary schools while primary schools and normal schools generally remained in the doldrums. Following World War II the Congress passed legislation calling for the equivalence of secondary "tracks" in order to permit the transfer of students from one curriculum to another and to make it legally possible for graduates of all secondary-level courses to enter university.

The sixth period may be defined as beginning with the advocacy of the "Law of Guidelines and Bases of National Education" in 1948. The "Law," as promulgated in 1961, is a compromise document calling for a moderate degree of decentralization and provides the potential for increased Federal, State, and County cooperation. By the 1960s the concept of explicitly planning for the development of human resources via programs including education had taken root. The Federal Council of Education made the following statement in 1961:

If some culture or civilization enters on a phase of transformation in consequence of a change of the structure and working conditions of society, as is the case of Brazil, the contingency of transforming schools and increasing their number *so as to attend to the new needs of a society in transformation* becomes a real condition of its survival.[8]

And in 1962, spokesmen such as Anísio Teixeira were being more specific in calling for reform measures:[9]

For many years we have been in the condition of our Xavante Indians, who, having learned to use steel axes, could no longer do without them and saw themselves tied to those who supplied the axes. Now that we already produce steel, telephones, and penicillin, thereby increasing our autonomy, we risk to subordinate ourselves to foreign standards and skills. We will really be autonomous only when the renovation of our factories can be performed by our own engineers and technicians, according to procedures resulting from our own special conditions.

---

7. Secondary education was transferred to federal jurisdiction in 1911 but retained the predominant encyclopedic, literary traditions of the Empire period.

8. MEC, "Pre-Investment for Perfecting Human Factor," Rio de Janeiro, Undated (1961?) p. 8 (mimeo).

9. Anísio S. Teixeira and Darcy Ribeiro, "The University of Brasília." United Nations Conference on the Application of Science and Technology for the Benefit of the Less Developed Areas, E/Conf., 39/K/19, October, 1962, p. 1.

This is the road we must follow if we are to step up the rate of our production and reduce the distance between Brazil and the technically advanced nations. They will be ahead of us unless and until we develop a new kind of *higher education* to produce scientists and technicians of our own; in other words: unless and until we have education for development.

Since 1930 the pace and pattern of Brazil's economic life and social structure have been structurally modified. Educational leaders continue to contribute to the transformation of the schools so as to attend to the new needs of a transforming society.

CURRENT PATTERNS

Perhaps the most significant of the quantitative measures of education is that of students enrolled. In 1964 the primary, secondary, and higher education enrollments were calculated in round numbers as follows:

TABLE 1

School Enrollment, 1964

Level	Number	Percentage of Total
Primary	10 million	82
Secondary	2 million	17
Higher	150 thousand	1

Primary Education

In 1964 Brazil's primary school population age groups (7-11) totaled 9.4 million of which 6.2 million were enrolled. There were some ten million children aged seven to fourteen enrolled in the first four years of schooling as demonstrated in Table 2.

Over half (5.2 million) of the total primary enrollment of ten million is in the first grade and about

TABLE 2

Percentual Distribution of Ages
in Grades 1–4, 1964*

Grade	Age							
	7	8	9	10	11	12	13	14
1	19.0	23.2	17.2	14.6	9.5	7.9	5.1	3.5
2	2.1	12.5	19.7	20.9	16.0	3.8	8.9	5.8
3	–	1.7	11.1	21.8	20.8	20.1	14.5	9.9
4	–	–	1.6	13.5	22.8	25.7	20.7	15.5

*Escritório de Pesquisa Econômica Aplicada (EPEA), *Plano Decenal de Desenvolvimento Economico e Social,* Educacão I e II Dianóstico Preliminar, 1966, p.26. An additional estimated 5 million children age 7-14 were not enrolled.

three-quarters (7.5 million) of the total enrollment is in grades one and two.

Completion figures demonstrate that about 15 percent of those beginning first grade graduate from the fourth grade. Thus, Brazil is faced with the need to deal with the high financial and psychological costs of massive numbers of dropouts and repeaters clogging the educational pipeline at a time when the nation is undergoing a net annual infant increase of over 40 per thousand of total population.

Secondary Education

Secondary level schools are divided into two "cycles"; the lower cycle (*ginásio*) consists of four years and the upper cycle (*colégio*) of three years.[10] In 1960, for example, of the more than 3,000 counties (*municipios*) in Brazil, about 1,400 had no secondary schools, 800 had only lower-cycle schools, about 800 had both lower- and upper-cycle schools. Overall, 69 percent of the secondary schools were private, tuition-charging institutions.

There are five tracks in the established secondary sequence only one of which, the academic, is intended to prepare its graduates for post-secondary studies. The distribution of students within the two cycles and five tracks in 1960 is presented in Table 3.

The academic curricula, divided in the second cycle into a classic or a science-oriented sequence, is designed to provide a general, intellectual training. The nationally prescribed content in effect in the early 1960s is presented in Table 4.

The 1960 data demonstrate that approximately 74 percent of secondary students were enrolled in academic courses generally considered university preparatory, 16 percent were in commercial courses, 8 percent were in Normal courses and only about 2 percent were in industrial- and agriculturally-oriented programs.

Two National Apprenticeship Systems (Serviço Nacional de Aprendizagem Industrial, SENAI, and Serviço Nacional de Aprendizagem Comercial, SENAC) were initiated in 1942 to provide better for the expanded need for technicians, foremen, artisans and other middle-level personnel in the nation's expanding secondary sector. SENAI and SENAC are administered by the National Confederations of Industries and Commerce which support on-the-job training programs through applying contributions of 1 percent of member firms' payroll costs to these programs. In 1964 SENAI enrolled nearly 50,000 pupils in 114 apprenticeship schools.

Higher Education

In early 1965 Brazil had twenty federal, thirteen private, and two state universities, 93 schools of Phi-

10. The schools that offer the traditional college-entrance academic curricula are most frequently called *ginasios* and *colegios* while the Commercial, Agricultural, Normal, and Industrial schools are less frequently identified by these terms.

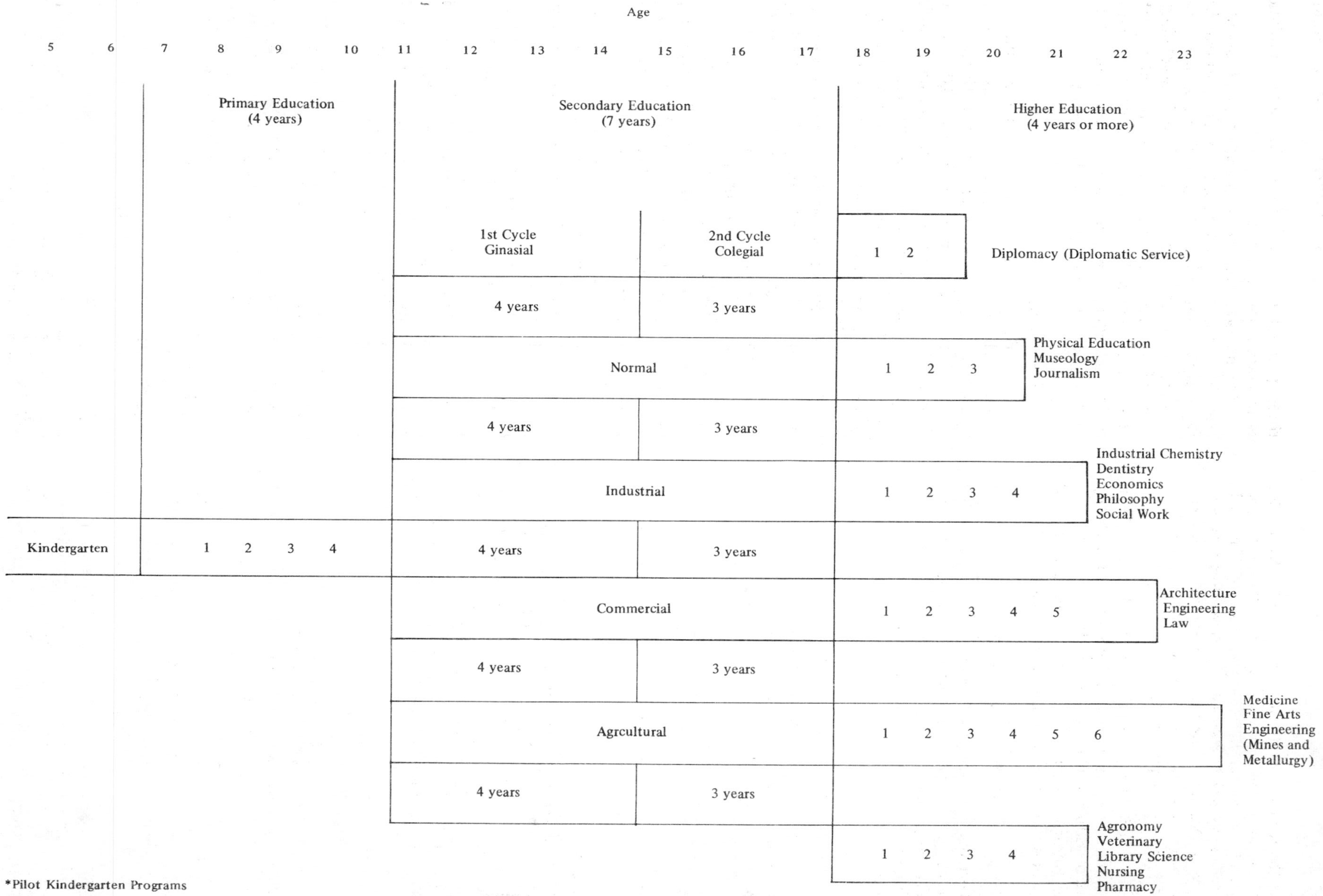

Figure 1. Brazilian education—a general overview.

TABLE 3

Distribution of Students

	Enrollments 1960	Graduates 1960
LOWER CYCLE SCHOOLS		
Ginásios	754,608	98,344
Commercial Schools	104,676	11,839
Agricultural Schools	5,062	1,461
Normal Schools	25,964	3,791
Industrial Schools	19,973	2,610
Sub-Total	910,283	118,045
UPPER CYCLE SCHOOLS		
Colégios	113,570	23,025
Commercial Technical	81,258	17,667
Agricultural Technical	1,601	439
Pedagogical Normal	64,763	18,948
Industrial Technical	5,952	1,022
Sub-Total	267,144	61,101
Total	1,177,427	179,146

*"Educacao e Desenvolvimento Economico," Brazilian report to the Conference on Education and Economic and Social Development in Latin America, Santiago, Chile, 5 to 19 March, 1962, p. 49.

TABLE 4

Time-Table in General Secondary Schools*
(in hours per week)

Subject	First Cycle				Second Cycle Classical Course			Science Course		
	1	2	3	4	5	6	7	5	6	7
Portuguese	3	3	3	3	3	3	3	3	3	3
Latin	2	2	2	2	3	2	3			
Greek (optional)					3	2	-			
French	3	2	2	2	3	2	-	2	2	-
English	-	3	2	2	3	2	-	3	2	-
Spanish	-	3	2	2	2	-	-	2	-	-
Mathematics	3	3	3	3	3	3	3	3	3	3
Natural Science	-	-	3	3						
Physics					-	2	3	3	3	3
Chemistry					-	2	3	3	3	3
Natural History					-	-	3	-	3	3
History of Brazil	2	-	-	2	-	2	2	-	2	2
World History	-	2	2	2	2	2	2	2	2	2
Geography of Brazil	-	-	2	2	-	-	2	-	-	2
World Geography	2	2	-	-	2	2	-			
Philosophy					-	3	3	-	-	3
Manual Training	2	2	-	-						
Drawing	3	2	2	1				2	2	2
Choral Singing	1	1	1	1						
Physical Training	2	2	2	1	2	2	1	2	2	2
Totals per week	23	24	24	24	23	28	28	25	27	28

*UNESCO. *World Survey of Education III* (Secondary Education), New York: Columbia University Press, 1961, p. 271.

TABLE 5

Higher Education Enrollments*

	Registrations at the Beginning of the year	
	Number	Percentages
Law	26,140	24.4
Phil., Sciences, & Letters	24,170	22.5
Engineering	13,129	12.2
Medicine	10,838	10.1
Econ. & Accounting	10,275	9.6
Dentistry	5,552	5.2
Agronomy	2,546	2.4
Art	2,360	2.2
Pharmacy	2,021	1.9
Architecture	1,903	1.8
Social Work	1,800	1.7
Nursing	1,358	1.2
Pub./Private Admin.	1,077	1.0
Veterinary Science	902	0.8
Others	3,228	3.0
Total	107,229	100.0

*Sinopse Estatistica do Ensino Superior. Rio de Janeiro, MEC, 1962.

losophy, Sciences and Letters not incorporated within a university, and over 410 other institutions offering a total of 31 certificate-granting curricula recognized by the Ministry of Education and Culture. Curricular patterns are prescribed by law and, consequently, diplomas from institutions not accredited by federal inspectors have no legal value.

The higher education system presently provides facilities for only 2 percent of the 20-to-25-years-old age group. Rigorous competitive entrance examinations are required for admission to the most prestigious schools of Law, Medicine, and Engineering; *e.g.* in 1962 there were 17,092 candidates for 2,008 places in first-year medical courses, 16,519 candidates for 4,020 places in engineering schools, and 13,635 candidates for 6,812 law-school openings. In the same year, however, there were fewer than two candidates for every three openings in Schools of Philosophy, Science, and Letters. A total of some 20,000 undergraduate degrees were granted in 1962 while graduate programs and research activities were the exception.

The expectation on the part of the nation's leaders to extend the total system of education focuses first upon the university level because of both the recognized currently increasing high-level manpower needs of the society and its modern institutions and the ubiquitous political influence of the very articulate and active lobby conducted in urban areas by the university-age population and their families.

Brazil is in the midst of a clearly visible revolution of rising educational expectations and is vigorously engaged in determining the overall goals and priorities of operational objectives to be implemented in order to meet this challenge.

SELECTED BIBLIOGRAPHY

AZEVEDO, FERNANDO DE. *A Cultura Brasileira*. São Paulo: Edições Melhoramentos, 1964 (4a. Edição).

BENJAMIN, HAROLD. *Higher Education in the American Republics*. New York: McGraw-Hill Book Co., 1965.

CAPES. *Sinopse Retrospectiva do Ensino no Brasil, 1933/1958*. Rio de Janeiro: CAPES, 1959.

Conselho Federal de Educacao. "Plano Nacional de Educacao." Rio de Janeiro: Ministerio da Educacao e Cultura, Revisao de 1965.

CRUZ, GEORGE F. *A History of Ideas in Brazil*. Berkeley: University of California Press, 1964.

"Educacao de Desenvolvimento Economico": Relatorio Brasileiro para a Conferencia sôbre Educacao e Desenvolvimento Econômico e Social na America Latina. INEP, 1962. (mimeo).

Escritorio de Pesquisa Econômica Aplicada (EPEA). *Plano Decenal de Desenvolvimento Econômico e Social, Educacao I e II Diagnostico Preliminar*, 1966.

Estados Unidos do Brasil. "Diretrizes e Bases da Educacao Nacional," Rio de Janeiro: Departamento de Imprensa Nacional, 1963.

FAUST, AUGUSTUS. *Brazil: Education in an Expanding Economy*. Washington, D. C.: U. S. Government Printing Office, 1959.

GARCIA WEREBE, MARIA JOSE. *Grandezas e Miserias do Ensino Brasileiro*. Sao Paulo: Difusao Europeia do Livro, 1963.

HAVIGHURST, ROBERT J., and MOREIRA, J. ROBERTO. *Society and Education in Brazil*. Pittsburgh: University of Pittsburgh Press, 1965.

MEC. "Pre-investment for Perfecting the Human Factor." National Education Plan, 1961 (mimeo).

SMITH, T. LYNN. *Brazil: People and Institutions*. Baton Rouge: Louisiana State University Press, 1963.

TEIXEIRA, ANISIO. *A Educacao e a Crise Brasileira*. Sao Paulo: Cia. Editora Nacional, 1956.

UNESCO. "Education in Brazil." Education Abstracts (Paris: UNESCO) Vol. X, No. 9, November, 1958.

———. *World Survey of Education: Handbook*. Paris: 1952.

———. *World Survey of Education, II: Primary Education* (1958).

———. *World Survey of Education III: Secondary Education* (1961).

CARIBBEAN ISLANDS (SELECTED)

Earl and Elizabeth Anttila

European-affiliated areas of the Caribbean are islands of the archipelago forming the eastern boundary of the Caribbean Sea, islands off the coast of Venezuela, parts of the South American mainland, a section of Central America, and islands in the Central Caribbean. The largest area is that of the British with the islands of Barbados, the Windward and Leeward Islands, Jamaica, Trinidad-Tobago, and British Guiana bordering Venezuela on the northern coast of South America, and British Honduras on the eastern coast of Central America. The Bahamas are also British, but they are farther north in the Atlantic and do not consider themselves Caribbean.

The Netherlands-affiliated areas are the two political units of Surinam (Dutch Guiana) and the Netherlands Antilles. The latter consists of the Netherlands Leeward Islands off the coast of Venezuela (Aruba, Bonaire, and Curacao), and the Netherlands Windward Islands in the northeast Caribbean (Saba, St. Eustatius, and the Dutch part of St. Martin).

The French areas consist of French Guiana, bordering Surinam on the northern coast of South America, and Martinique, Guadeloupe, St. Barthelmy, and the French part of St. Martin.

Only the European-affiliated islands of the Lesser Antilles are discussed here. The British areas in Central and South America are omitted as well as Jamaica in the Caribbean. The French and Dutch parts of South America are also eliminated. Since World War II, the Caribbean islands formerly held as colonies by European powers have assumed a great measure of self-rule, and with political changes have come new concepts of their political, social, economic, cultural, and educational development.

The great majority of island inhabitants are descended from African slaves brought to the Caribbean primarily as laborers on sugar plantations, the chief resource in the early days of settlement. In Trinidad there are significant numbers of East Indians, Indonesians, and Chinese. Everywhere there are people of European origins, although they form a small minority, and many racially mixed people.

The most important British-affiliated islands are Trinidad and Jamaica. The latter is discussed elsewhere. Although the British islands differ socially, culturally, politically, racially, and even linguistically, they have enough in common that educational developments are similar.

Before the emancipation of the slaves in 1833, the British colonies had a large measure of self-rule with locally elected legislatures. When the Negroes were freed, however, the area became Crown colonies directly ruled by officials appointed from England. The slaves far outnumbered the Europeans, and their freedom presented a staggering educational problem. Plantation owners had endeavored to keep their slaves in ignorance and even refused, for the most part, to permit them to become Christianized. The families who held slaves felt that educating them would bring trouble, and they balked at the thought of a fellow Christian in bondage. There were missionaries who worked among the Negroes, and on some plantations they were permitted to conduct schools. For most Negro children, however, there was no instruction except that given by the old people in whose care they were left while their parents worked. The British government vainly urged religious instruction for all slaves as early as 1823. The Protestant missionaries were the first to teach the slaves. The Moravians came in 1756 and were well established in St. Kitts and Antigua by 1800. There are few records regarding education prior to 1833, but it is clear that whatever education the masses received was rudimentary and haphazard at best. The white population looked to England as "home"; and whoever could afford to do so sent his sons there to be educated. The Codrington estate left funds for a school to educate ministers on Barbados in 1745, but it became a gentleman's school with a classical course of study. Barbados alone had a superior grammar school before 1833. Both Catholic and Protestant private schools undoubtedly existed, but records are available only for Trinidad. In 1823, that island reported in an educational census one English Female Boarding School and three French day schools in Port-of-Spain with a total of 175 scholars, and one small day school teaching only Spanish in an Indian village. After Emancipation Day, there were an estimated 53,565 pupils receiving religious school instruction, but very few were actually in day school. The number of children between the ages of three and twelve in the British colonies was believed to have been about 112,000 at that time. During the period of slavery, education was for the white elite, it was classical in nature with a great deal of memoriter work, young boys prepared for a university education in England by laboring at Latin and Greek, less attention was paid to the education of girls, and criticisms were made that education in the colonies did not follow the changes taking place in England.[1]

The report of the Reverend J. Sterling to the British Government, May 11, 1835, noted that some 770,000 people had been freed from slavery, and there was an immediate need for education and development. The prospects for the Negroes' future were not optimistic. The newly-freed slave was usually trained only in agricultural labor, and when England discontinued preferential treatment for West Indian sugar in 1846, the colonies suffered. Many plantation owners left, the sugar lands went back to jungle, and great estate houses fell into ruins. The British Government had recognized that the colonies could not at once assume the financial burden of establishing an education system, so in the Act of Emancipation there was included the Negro Education Grant. It provided £30,000 a year for five years, then gradually decreased the amount until 1845 when it ceased altogether. Religious schools were given aid, and thus the character of education maintained up to the present was set. Education, historically, had a religious association. After Emancipation, the problem of education was widely discussed. The people were divided as to the kind of education to be offered. Latrobe, reporting on the Windwards and Leewards in 1838, observed that the Negroes were violently opposed to "practical" education, that is, anything that had to do with working with one's hands. It was an attitude that grew out of their background of slavery that caused them to regard manual work as demeaning. They also had an exaggerated regard for education. Their belief that schooling" should be "bookish" and should prepare them for white-collar jobs was opposed by the planters. Not until after World War II did the islanders begin to have any appreciation for vocational or technological education. During the period of the Negro Education Act, schools were built, some native teachers were trained, religious groups contributed both money and teachers, but development varied greatly among the colonies. The more urban areas showed the greatest development. There were numerous mission schools on Antigua and Barbados, for example, as early as 1838. On St. Lucia and Dominica, there were many obstacles to education, such as language and the diversity of religious faiths among the Negroes. The Mico Charity opened promising schools in Trinidad during the decade following Emancipation. The great enthusiasm with which education was reviewed by the free Negroes became clouded by disappointments as early as 1837 because the funds were insufficient even for the mission schools. In 1845, the Grant ended and the duty to support education fell to the local areas. One lasting value of the Grant was that it implanted the idea of popular education for the first time. Local problems, such as race, religion, and language, particularly in Trinidad and the Windwards, the severe lack of funds, and the lack of trained teachers plagued the colonies. In the 1850s, there was a series of epidemics of cholera, yellow fever, and smallpox that so drastically depleted colonial coffers that sometimes no grants were made for education at all. In Trinidad, because of religious differences and the foreign elements, the government established secular schools in 1851. Secular schools were tried on Dominica, but failed in 1867. It was deemed impossible to exclude priests from the schools in Catholic Dominica. For social reasons, Barbados clung to religious schools. The Codrington Estate school on Barbados used the monitor system in 1848, and the headmaster reported it was very efficiently run. An Infant School Experiment was tried there the following year. In 1859, Trinidad reported that children went to ward schools at an early age speaking only a French *patois*.

During the emancipation period, governments began to participate in education, usually through grants and the establishment of boards and school committees. Departments of Education were organized in several British territories, as were Boards to advise the Department of Education heads. A dual control of education by church and state was affected. Measures were adopted to make education free and compulsory, although the lack of facilities made universal education impossible. Industrial education was little understood or practiced. Education consisted largely of the 3 *R's*, because of poorly trained teachers. During the Colonial Administration, 1865-1885, systems of "payment by results" were inaugurated to increase the efficiency of elementary schools. Under these systems, grants were made to schools on the basis of the pupils' performances in the 3 *R's*. Criticism of the method was remarkably small, and during its operation many children were attracted to the schools.[2]

During the colonial period, only a few teacher training schools were opened. Teachers were qualified everywhere by examination, and the pupil-teacher system was used. Secondary education was rare, but

1. Shirley C. Gordon, *A Century of West Indian Education.*
2. *Ibid.*

Barbados managed to maintain a scheme of first and second grade schools open to all. Religious groups also conducted some secondary schools. By the end of the nineteenth century, beet sugar competition in Europe further depressed West Indian sugar, and delinquent young people, especially in the towns, became a serious problem. The Royal Commission of 1882, which studied the financial depressions, criticized education as inefficient and the teachers as very poor. However, funds were not available to remedy the deficiencies which continued to recent times. Although few students attended secondary schools, there was an increase in such schools during the latter part of the nineteenth century, and their graduates could compete for a small number of scholarships offered by English universities. Secondary education was classical and bore little relationship to elementary work. It was not considered a continuing process. The secondary school became largely training for the competitive examinations. In one or two places, commercial subjects and agriculture were introduced into the secondary schools. Cambridge Examinations were adopted almost everywhere as the yardstick for education for both boys and girls, although few students took them and the failure rate was high.

During the twentieth century, secondary schools continued to increase, and religious schools, most of which received government grants, spread. Still the secondary school population was less than 1 percent of the age group. The secondary school curriculum continued largely on the pattern of the nineteenth century in spite of administrators who pled for a more realistic curriculum including science, commercial subjects, art, and domestic science. A few of these subjects were introduced, but the secondary school was still dominated by the scholarship examinations. Secondary education was largely controlled by religious or other voluntary agencies. The government provided subsidies for secondary education early in the twentieth century but did not have the right to inspect and supervise it.

During the last ten years, educational growth has reflected the greater political autonomy of the islands. Attention has been given to adapting education to the needs of the people rather than imposing upon them an alien, imported system. The area is still economically underdeveloped, and an elementary schooling of eight years has been the maximum most children could hope for, and certainly not all have obtained it. Lack of family ties among people of African origin has impeded the development of stable homes favorable to the education of children. Further, the language of instruction may be different from that used at home by the child. Economic changes have brought some industrialization and diversification of the economy, especially in Curaçao and Aruba where oil refining is the chief business and in Trinidad which has both oil refining and bauxite. A need for technological education has arisen. Most of the territories recognize that educational development is an essential part of economic growth. The old attitude toward working with one's hands persists and has impeded the development of vocational education, so sorely needed in an area that is still basically agricultural. Since World War II, however, some change is evident since the pecuniary rewards have become greater, but most islanders still regard vocational education as inferior. At the present time, educational trends are indicative of a more realistic approach. The schools' functions have generally expanded, and attention is being directed more toward vocational and commercial subjects, home economics, and adult education. Work is progressing in guidance services, agricultural training, trade and industrial training, apprenticeship and on-the-job training, and teacher training for vocational education. Conferences, seminars, and workshops have been held in connection with members of the now defunct Caribbean Organization which was organized in 1946 as an intergovernmental consultative and advisory body. Puerto Rico has been training personnel from the British areas in trade and industrial education, teaching of vocational education in agriculture, community education, home economics, cooperatives, social work, and public health among other fields. Measures have been taken to secure UNESCO help.

In the modern period, from 1940 on, the state has recognized its responsibility for education, and government education departments have been set up under the British Crown Colony System. Each area has acquired a large degree of home rule, and, as there is no central government, each area has been developing education in its own way. Everywhere, however, the government supports education through government schools and by subsidies to denominational and private schools. Generally, the governments have operated a higher percentage of elementary than secondary schools. The latter are still largely denominational or private. In Trinidad there are Hindu, Moslem, Catholic, and various Protestant schools. The government has assumed more and more of the responsibility for school costs and operation, has set the pattern of policies and regulations, and has provided for inspection and overall administration, whereas the religious bodies often have supplied school buildings and have administered the day-to-day operation of the schools. Therefore, religious schools can be considered as a part of the regular school system.

Charles C. Hauch points out the modern educational trends in the British-affiliated Caribbean. He found that the fundamental problems are the necessity of remedying deficiencies in buildings, staff, books, and equipment; the rapidly increasing school population; and the poverty of the region. Most local governments have evolved educational development plans covering five- to ten-year periods to cope with the difficulties. Each area feels that with greater self-government there is a greater need for an enlightened populace. Most schools, in recent years, have been organized into departments known as infant (ages five to six), junior or primary (ages seven to eleven) and senior or post-primary (ages twelve to fourteen or fifteen). There is a tendency for the latter to be in separate schools and to be regarded as the equivalent of the modern English secondary school which combines academic and "practical" subjects. Percentages of children of elementary school age not in school in 1957 give an idea of the work yet to be done—2 percent in Barbados, Antigua, and Montserrat, 12 percent in Trinidad, and 30 percent in Dominica. Actual attendance is frequently far below enrollment, whereas chronic tardiness also is a special problem. Hauch saw progress in building programs, a recognition of need for materials and books adapted to the local areas, the beginnings of a movement to articulate elementary and secondary education, a curriculum better adjusted to the demands of the area, developments both in traditional secondary schools and new schools of shorter duration devoted to commercial subjects, a re-evaluation of traditional examinations and certificates, and an increasing interest in teacher preparation. No longer is the elementary school graduate who has studied in his free time and qualified on certain examinations everywhere regarded as a teacher. College-trained teachers in no area made up 50 percent of the teaching staff as late as 1957, but thinking is directed toward making it possible for all teachers to be professionally prepared on a college level. Colleges exist in Antigua, Barbados, and Trinidad for the purpose. The programs of technical education on the post-primary level have assumed greater significance. Both day and evening classes are being opened. Advanced technical education is available in Trinidad, which also offers work in practical agriculture at the Eastern Caribbean Farm Institute. Various parts of the British Caribbean are working toward the establishment and growth of adult and community education programs.[3]

The problems of the Netherlands-affiliated Caribbean islands are frequently similar to those of the British areas. The Netherlands Antilles are co-partners with the Kingdom of the Netherlands and are responsible for financing their own educational programs with no regular aid from the Netherlands. The Netherlands Antilles enjoy a rather high economic level for the Caribbean, particularly in the Leewards where most of the population is urban-oriented and is connected in some way with the petroleum refineries. Large segments of the population, however, do not speak Dutch. The problem has been met by offering Dutch in the elementary grades as a foreign language and increasing its use to the medium of instruction on the upper elementary level, as in the Windward Islands. English is the language of instruction in the lower grades in the Windwards, but it is Dutch in the Netherlands Antilles Leeward Islands, where

Papiamento is the vernacular. The education system has been organized into two parallel branches. One set of schools is for children from Dutch-speaking homes and the other is for children from non-Dutch-speaking homes. Generally, education is based on Netherlands models except for a few local variations. As in the British islands, both governmental and private organizations share education, and the government aids private as well as public schools in cost, provides programs of study, and government inspection. In the Antilles, most of the schools are church-affiliated, largely Catholic. The Dutch areas aim to provide six years of elementary education for all children ages six to twelve. In the Antilles, nearly all that age group was in school by 1955.[4]

In the Netherlands Caribbean education is not compulsory in the Antilles. Children are obliged to pay in some measure for schooling. Only the *B* grade and rural elementary schools offer free school supplies. There is an overall lack of teachers and facilities for training them. As in the British islands, training colleges help with examinations for students under the departments of education.

Students desiring further education usually must win a scholarship to a Netherlands university. The insular governments are generally regarded as the ones responsible for governmental contributions, although the central government may take up the problem, as it has done in Bonaire and the Windwards, meeting nearly all the costs. At present, teachers are mostly recruited from Holland or, if locally recruited, are Holland-trained in the secondary schools. The largest part of all public expenditure on education is for primary and elementary education, largely in the form of grants to assisted schools. Secondary education has generally been limited to one school, or perhaps two where the sexes were divided, in larger urban areas, but some extension has been made because of the government grants to private schools. Fees of varying amounts are charged secondary school students. Although audiovisual education has progressed very little, if at all, nearly all areas now have adult education programs which are being broadened. In addition to other fields, Curaçao has offered extension courses in Latin, Greek, and instrumental music, and Aruba has had special courses in musical theory.[5] The people of the Netherlands Antilles are beginning to develop concepts of the place and function of education in their lives, and keen interest has been evinced in deciding upon the type of education which will best suit their needs. They are more politically autonomous than at any time in the past, the economy of the Caribbean is changing, and through greater contacts with other Caribbean areas, common problems and

---

3. Charles C. Hauch, *Educational Trends in the Caribbean*, pp. 32-70.
4. *Ibid.*, pp. 107-109.
5. *Foreign Education Digest*, Vol. 24, 1959, pp. 108-117.

interests have been studied. As a result, most areas are expanding school activities and are thinking in terms of universal education.

The French Caribbean islands of Martinique, Guadaloupe, St. Barthelmy, and the French part of St. Martin (St. Maarten) became, in 1946, the Departments of Martinque and Guadaloupe. For administrative purposes, the two small areas of St. Barthelmy and French St. Martin were included in the Guadaloupe Department. The two Caribbean Departments thus formed are integral parts of the French nation and are coequal with the Departments of European France. Education, although offered to a people primarily of African origin living in heavy-populated tropical islands almost totally dependent on agriculture, was made to conform in practically every particular with education in France. The organization, methods, principles, programs of study, examinations, and all other aspects were those of France. Complete assimilation was the aim with a few local variations permitted. Each Caribbean Department is attached to the *académie* (educational region) of Bordeaux and through it to the Ministry of National Education. Vice-Rectors or regional inspectors in Martinique and in Guadaloupe represent the Rector of the *académie* of Bordeaux. The education laws and regulations of France apply to the Caribbean Departments. As in France, financial responsibility is divided among the National government, Department, and "communes" (local governments). Most educational costs in the French Caribbean are met by the national budget, in actual practice. Education in the French Caribbean is predominently public government schools, with a few Catholic institutions. Since graduates from both private and public schools take the same examinations at levels of schooling, the curricula tend to be similar. Enrollment is predominantly in the elementary schools. The system, broadly, is made up of an eight-year elementary program and a four-year complementary course. After five years of elementary, some pupils may be selected for the complementary course, some for the *lycées* (secondary schools) or the *Collége Technique* (vocational secondary schools). Pupils completing the eight-year elementary receive the primary school certificate. The complementary course is one year longer and has become, as a rule, the highest education to which pupils may progress. From this group of graduates come most of the future elementary teachers. Instruction in elementary and complementary courses is basically the same as in France, with some attention to Caribbean history and geography. French is the language of instruction in all Departments, causing difficulties for some of the non-French-speaking islanders. Secondary education is highly selective and follows French designs. Vocational education is quite new and is called technical. The chief needs in the French Caribbean are greater facilities in education to accommodate the increasing school population, adult education to combat illiter-

acy, and institutions that provide teacher-training facilities and programs. Only one institute of higher learning exists—the Law School (Ecole de Droit) in Martinique. Generally, the education pattern is the same as European France with "a 3-year course at a *lycée* in preparation for the *brevet supérieur*, a fourth year of intensive actual teacher training, including practice teaching. Secondary school teachers are either recruited from France, or from local men and women who have been trained in France."[6]

In all the Lesser Antilles, education for the masses is still largely elementary. The chief problems yet to be solved are the development of educational programs within a philosophy that will be adapted to the needs of the localities, greater financial resources for instituting broader educational programs, and overcoming attitudes against vocational and technical training. Buildings, equipment, books, and other physical facilities need to be modernized and expanded. Efforts must be made to bring greater numbers of children and adults into the schools. The people of the Lesser Antilles have an increasing awareness of the role of education in their development and are taking steps toward building broader and more efficient programs for the future.

EDUCATION IN PUERTO RICO

When the United States occupied Puerto Rico, in 1898, it had a population of about one million. Most of these were country people, 800,000 of them. In 1900 there were very few schools and only 45,000 children were in attendance, or fifteen out of every hundred. Most children left school by the third grade. An American-type school system had been introduced by the occupation authorities, but with a completely centralized control in San Juan and with local Puerto Rican financial support.

The three basic policies of the school system were (1) to provide a common school education for as many children as possible, (2) to Americanize and assimilate the Puerto Ricans as soon as possible, and (3) to teach English.

President McKinley appointed Dr. Martin G. Brumbaugh the first American commissioner of education for Puerto Rico under the Foraker Act. He was given almost unlimited powers to reorganize the schools left by the United States Army.

The second commissioner of education, Dr. Samuel McCune Lindsay, expanded the schools and increased the number of American teachers. The expenses of school operations were borne by the people of Puerto Rico, but the commissioner of education derived his authority from Washington.

The third commissioner of education was Roland F. Falkner. His administration of the schools faced rising anti-Americanism.

6. *Foreign Education Digest,* Vol. 24, 1959, p. 113.

In 1909, Edward G. Dexter became commissioner of education. In 1910, he found 121,453 children in school; by 1912, enrollment had increased to 160,657. When Dexter left the island, he was replaced by Edward W. Bainter.

Commissioner Bainter faced the opposition of the Puerto Rican faculty and politicians to American policy. Puerto Ricans were becoming restive under "Americanization." School enrollment, however, increased. In 1914; 207,101 children were in attendance.

When Commissioner Paul G. Miller (1915-1921) became the head of the department of education, he was faced with three problems: (1) the world-wide depression of 1914 reduced funds, (2) the outbreak of World War I made civilian administration difficult, and (3) the government of Puerto Rico was democratized by the Jones Act of 1917, which curtailed some of the power of the commissioner of education. By 1921, school enrollment had dropped to 193,369. Dr. Miller was the last continental American head of the Puerto Rican school system.

In 1921, the first Puerto Rican was appointed commissioner of education, Juan B. Huyke. He expanded the schools and stimulated Americanization. He is remembered as having stifled all opposition to his policies. American attitude, however, was becoming more liberal. Policy was directed toward giving Puerto Ricans a greater share in their own government. When Huyke's term of office ended in 1930, he was replaced by Dr. Padín.

Dr. Padín was well liked by the Puerto Rican faculty. He stimulated the faith of the teachers in the future of education. He was thought to be anti-American by the opposition. His educational reforms, particularly those dealing with language, were unpopular with the Republican Party.

The last commissioner of education to be appointed by an American president was Dr. José M. Gallardo. He was practically unknown when he arrived in Puerto Rico, although he had at one time been employed by the Department of Education. He set aside Dr. Padín's reforms and followed highly confused policies, particularly in language matters. By 1942, however, he had returned to Dr. Padín's ideas. At the end of his second term of office, in 1945, no new commissioner was approved by the American government. In 1947, Puerto Ricans were given complete control of their own educational system.

By 1954 practically all six-year-olds were able to enter school for the first time. By 1964 more schools had been built and the enrollment reached 606,000. Illiteracy had been reduced to 17 percent. There still remained the problem of double enrollment.

Puerto Rican education in this decade faces problems similar to those in the United States. A rapid industrialization fills the cities with former country people. Rural education must be developed along new lines, technical education becomes more and more a need for the growing economy, and expenses mount. New educational approaches are being attempted through model schools, thirty at present. These schools work closely with the community in which they are located. Since 1945 to the present it is estimated that 900,000 persons have received vocational training of some sort. In nine high schools 1,623 children who are planning to go on to the University are given special programs. Results had been very good under the stimulus of Dr. Angel Quintero, the Assistant Secretary of Education who was recently appointed Secretary of Education.

In attempts to decentralize the education system, more local supervision is emphasized. Six regional nuclei of supervision have been set up over the island. Each has its own director.

By 1964 Puerto Rico had reached a population of 2,554,000. Over 84 percent of the children between six and twelve were in school and over 54 percent from thirteen to fifteen. Costs have gone up. In 1947, 30 million dollars was spent. This had risen to 100 million dollars by 1960. Salaries for teachers are still low, but a new bill supported by the powerful Teachers Association will provide a salary of $460.00 a month for teachers with a bachelor degree. Per student expenditures are around $185.00 per annum.

The University of Puerto Rico has grown to an enrollment of over 21,000 students. It is an American land-grant type school but includes various campuses, Río Piedras, San Juan (Medical and Dental Schools), Mayaguez (Agriculture and Engineering), the Humacao Regional College (Junior College), and various agricultural extension installations. Plans are being made to extend the junior colleges to include additional campuses. The University is accredited by, the Mid-Atlantic Accrediting Association. Professors salaries are comparatively low, but the University gives special consideration for teachers who wish to do research. There is a liberal sabbatical leave (with full pay) policy, grants to study off the island, and a fair retirement system.

Other aspects of the education of Puerto Rican children are found in the private schools. Close to 130,000 children are in private institutions, mostly Catholic parochial schools. It is doubted that so large a number of parents desire religious education as such. Puerto Rico is not a fanatically Catholic land. More likely, the large private school enrollment indicates a dissatisfaction with the overcrowded and often poorly staffed public schools. In addition to the elementary and secondary schools, there are three private colleges and a private junior college as well as a multitude of business schools, language schools, and others, as found in most areas of the United States.

The historical problem of Puerto Rican education that has not been discussed in detail is that of language. Since this question has been revived by the former Secretary of Education, Cándido Oliveras, in an attack on the use of English as the medium of instruction in private schools, a consideration of the developments regarding English in the public schools would be valuable.

When the United States Army established schools in Puerto Rico, most of them were conducted in Spanish. English was emphasized, but there were few American teachers available and few Puerto Ricans who knew English. Under civilian government, the use of English as the language of instruction was gradually increased through the administrations of American commissioners of education from Dr. Brumbaugh (1900-02) to Dr. Miller (1915-21).

When the first Puerto Rican, Juan B. Huyke, was appointed commissioner, he continued the policy of using English as the medium of instruction as much as possible. It was not until Dr. Padín was made head of the department of education that a study was made of the problem. He recommended that all elementary education be conducted in the vernacular, Spanish, and that English be taught as a foreign language. On the high school level, English was to be the language of instruction, and Spanish was to be taught as a subject. This policy was put into effect but was revised in 1937 by Dr. José M. Gallardo, who became commissioner of education in that year.

Dr. Gallardo set up a complicated program of teaching partly in English and partly in Spanish on the elementary grade level. By 1942, however, he returned substantially to the Padín policy.

In 1947, Puerto Rico was granted educational autonomy, Spanish was made the language of instruction, and English was to be taught as a foreign language.

EDUCATION IN THE VIRGIN ISLANDS

Colonial history of the Virgin Islands is similar to that of the rest of the Caribbean. Various powers, Spain, England, France, the Dutch, and the Danes laid claim to the islands. The Danes, the final power before American purchase, imported slaves from Africa. Hence, almost the entire population is Negro. There are groups of Puerto Rican and French settlers as well as tourists and seasonal residents. Thousands of Virgin Islanders live in New York. The typical Virgin Islander is not an illiterate peasant as are so many other Caribbean islanders. They are independent-minded. Even though ex-President Hoover referred to the Islands as the American poorhouse, rum taxes have contributed more to the Federal treasury than the United States paid for them in 1917. The fact that the Danes were masters and not the English or Spaniards did not ameliorate the condition of slavery. Slave revolts occurred as early as 1773, and, by revolt, the Danish West-Indian slaves secured their own freedom in 1848.

The three islands, St. Thomas, St. John, and St. Croix, have a combined population of over 31,000. The largest urban center is Charlotte Amalie on St. Thomas which is also the administrative center. St.

Croix is rural with two small towns, Fredriksted and Christiansted. St. John has a very small population and a great part of the Island is a national forest.

American interest in the islands dates back to 1865, when the United States Navy began pressing the government for a base in the Lesser Antilles. As fear of German overseas power developed, the American government negotiated the purchase of the islands for $25,000,000 in 1917.

The administration under the United States Navy retained most of the Danish school system. The language of instruction was English, and so no language problem existed. Other problems, however, had to be solved. Teacher training, school construction, increased enrollments, vocational and agricultural training, and a new school law were needed.

Expansion of the school system brought greater enrollment figures. In 1921, a new school law, based on that of New Mexico, was enacted. In 1927, 3,083 pupils were in school.

In 1931, the Virgin Islands were transferred by the Navy to the Department of Interior. The first civilian governor, Paul M. Pearson, tried to stimulate interest in education. By 1934, enrollment stood at 3,485 out of a total population of about 23,000.

Federal aid was extended to the Virgin Islands schools from the very beginning of American control. This was extended after the election of President F. D. Roosevelt to include a school lunch program and special education.

In 1939, a new school law replaced that of 1921. In 1941, it was revised. School boards with certain duties, authorities, and responsibilities were set up on St. Thomas and St. Croix. A schedule of salaries providing for raises was approved. As a result of better salaries, all teachers were required to have at least high school certificates. One additional year beyond high school was required for a permanent certificate.

In 1946, President Harry Truman named William H. Hastie the first Negro governor of the Islands. Under his administration school expenditures rose to $250,000 for St. Thomas and St. John and $77,000 for St. Croix. In St. Thomas, 2,494 students were enrolled. School lunches were served without charge to 1,700 children in thirteen schools in St. Thomas alone. In 1947, 171,628 lunches were served in all the Virgin Islands to a total school population of 6,111. In 1948-49, 400,583 lunches were served. The municipality of St. Thomas and St. John appropriated $66,441.18 and the United States Department of Agriculture contributed $12,000 in food for this program.

In 1950, President Truman appointed Morris F. de Castro the first native-born governor. In the same year the House of Representatives Education and Labor Committee visited the islands. It recommended the extension of the Vocational Act of 1946 to the Virgin Islands.

By the school year 1950-51, it may be said that the Virgin Islands school system was a replica of the usual American school system, from elementary, to junior, to senior high school.

Under Chapter XI of the Charter of the United Nations entitled "Declaration Regarding Non-Self-Governing Territories" the United States accepted the right of United Nations survey of its development of the Virgin Islands and the people of the area. Under Article 73 the United States agreed to give "due respect for the culture of the people concerned and to promote their educational advancement." The people of the Virgin Islands were not consulted as to their reactions regarding such reporting and in 1964 when a majority of the members of the Committee for Non-Self-Governing Territories expressed concern over the balance of free elections they felt themselves betrayed.

In 1954, a revised organic act set up a unicameral legislature of eleven senators. At present, the Virgin Islands are an "unincorporated territory" but have financial autonomy and can issue bonds. This should promote educational development.

By the school year 1962-63, the Virgin Islands were spending $389 per pupil, or were thirty-first as compared to the fifty states, ahead of such giants as Texas (thirty-fourth) which has never been called a poorhouse. The average salary of teachers is low at $4,200.646 (forty-sixth among the states).

In 1962-63 the operating budget reached $3,499,-326.13 and the capital budget was $1,376,000, no small achievement for a population of slightly over 31,000 people. Scholarships given college students amounted to $72,000.

A new development of education in the Virgin Islands is the Virgin Islands College, opened in 1963. The governor of the Islands has warmly supported this project.

SELECTED BIBLIOGRAPHY

Bulletins and Periodicals

Annual Reports of the Department of Education of:

Antigua	Barbados
Bahamas	Dominica
Grenada	St. Lucia
Leward Islands	St. Vincent
Montserrat	Trinidad
St. Kitts	Virgin Islands

Bulletin Administratif et pedagogique. Annee Scolaire 1964-65, No. 1, Feb. 1964.

Bureau of Insular Affairs. Report of the Commissioner of Education of Puerto Rico, 1900-1917, *passim*.

Great Britain Colonial Office. *Education in the Windward and Leeward Islands: Report of the Educational Commissioners.* London: 1938, 1939.

Institute of Field Studies, Teachers' College, Columbia University. *Public Education and the Future of Puerto Rico.* New York: Teachers' College, 1950.

International Institute, Teachers' College, Columbia University. *A Survey of the Public System of Puerto Rico.* New York: Bureau of Publications, Teachers' College, Columbia University, 1926.

Puerto Rico Department of Education. *Reports of the Commissioner of Education.* San Juan: Bureau of Supplies, Printing, and Transportation, 1929-1951, *passim*.

Republica Dominica. *Revista de Educacion,* Volume III. Santo Domingo: Garcia, 1920.

United States, Department of the Interior. *Annual Report of the Governor of the Virgin Islands.* Washington: 1931-1950, *passim*.

U.S.O.E. *Educational Trends in the Caribbean: European Affiliated Areas,* edited by C. C. Hanch, Washington: 1950.

Books

GORDON, SHIRLEY. *A Century of West Indian Education.* London: 1963.

HOWES, H. M. *Survey Recommendations on Adult and Youth Education in Dominica.* UNESCO Adult Situation Mission in Dominica, 1962.

JARVIS, J. A. *The Virgin Islands and Their People.* New York: Dorance & Co., 1945.

KNOX, JOHN P. *Original History of the Danish West Indian Islands.* New York: Charles Scribner, 1852.

OSUNA, JUAN J. *A History of Education in Puerto Rico.* Rio Piedras: Editorial de la Universidad de Puerto Rico, 1949.

TUGWELL, REXFORD. *The Stricken Land, Story of Puerto Rico.* New York: Doubleday, 1947.

ZABRISKIE, LUTHER K. *The Virgin Islands of the United States of America.* New York: Putnam, 1918.

CUBA

Joseph S. Roucek

Only ninety days after it took power, the Kennedy administration suffered quite an international setback by not giving a full support to the "Bay of Pigs" invasion of Cuba which had hoped to eliminate the Communist regime of Fidel Castro. Furthermore, the failure to overthrow Castro eventually culminated in a crisis which nearly led to World War III. It began on October 15, 1962, when the analysis of aerial photographs revealed the presence in Cuba of medium and intermediate range missiles capable of the nuclear bombing of a large part of the Western Hemisphere. The crisis seemingly ended on October 28, 1962, when Chairman Khrushchev notified President Kennedy that he had ordered the dismantling of the sites and the shipment of the equipment back to the Soviet Union.

Why such an international flare-up over such a small island?

Cuba lies only 1,260 miles from New York, and about 90 miles from the tip of Florida.

The location of Caribbean America between the North and South American continents gives this region importance both politically and economically; first, it forms an important part of the larger political region of Latin America; and, second, it has extensive communication with the United States directly to the north. The importance of the area is certified to by the vital interests of the United States in the building and protection of the Panama Canal, the acquisition of Puerto Rico, and the sending, during the early part of the twentieth century, of U. S. military forces to the Middle American Republics for the purpose of maintaining law and order, a step repeated again in 1965.

More specifically, today the continued presence of the Communist regime so close to the shores of the United States is a source of a profound embarrassment to the United States. Although the United States and Cuba have no diplomatic relations, the former continues to maintain its naval base at Guantanamo Bay at the southeastern end of the island.

Cuba, the largest and most populous of the islands of the West Indies, covers 44,218 square miles and is about 759 miles in length with a width at the widest part of about 195 miles and at the narrowest 36 miles. Its coast line is about 2,000 miles. Unlike Puerto Rico, Cuba is not densely populated, and its agricultural potential is high. Much of the land is level or gently rolling, and more than one-third of the island is in cultivation.

The island was discovered by Christopher Columbus on October 27, 1492, during his first voyage; he landed at what is called the Bay of Nuevitas and took possession of the country in the name of the King of Spain. Named successively Juana, Santiago, and Ave Maria, the island finally regained its original Indian name of Cuba. In 1511 Diego Velazquez was appointed Governor and to him fell the task of subduing the aborigines, the warlike Caribs and Nabacs. From that date, except for a brief period of British occupancy from August 12, 1762, to June 6, 1763, the island remained a Spanish possession until December 10, 1898, when sovereignty was relinquished under the terms of the Treaty of Paris, which ended the armed intervention of the United States in the struggle of the Cubans against Spanish rule. Cuba became free and independent, although the U. S. maintained a governor there for some time.

On February 24, 1902, Tomas Estrada Palma was elected President; upon his inauguration on May 20, 1902, the United States representative was withdrawn.

Accompanying the proclamation of Cuba's Independence was the Platt Amendment, granting the United States the right to maintain coaling and naval bases on Cuban soil and to intervene in internal affairs "for the preservation of Cuban independence . . . for the protection of life, property, and individual liberty." This right was exercised in 1906, 1912, and from 1917 to 1922.

As a result of the Platt Amendment and of Cuba's economic position relative to the United States, the island existed in a protectorate type of status from 1901 until the development of the United States "Good Neighbor" policy in the mid-1930s. But even after the abrogation of the Platt Amendment, Cuba continued in a position of economic dependence upon the U. S. For example, the U. S. took over half of Cuba's sugar crop and provided three-quarters of Cuba's export earnings; American investments in Cuba were extensive before the Castro take-over.

THE RISE OF PRO-COMMUNIST CASTRO

Much has been written, after the fact, stating that the United States government should have realized from the very beginning that Castro was a Communist and should have taken steps to prevent his ever coming to power. Many of his closest associates, even those who had fought with him in the mountains, were equally mistaken in their evaluation of the man. (Of the nineteen members of his first Cabinet for the revolutionary government, over two-thirds are now dead, in prison, or in exile.) When Castro fled to the mountains in December, 1956, to carry on the fight against the Batista government, he did not have the support of the Cuban Communist Party, which dismissed him as "bourgeois." Only when the party saw he had a chance of winning did it lend him support.

On January 1, 1959, the rebel forces of Fidel Castro, after more than two years of guerrilla fighting, ousted the corrupt and repressive regime of Cuba's dictator Fulgencio Batista. The victory of the "twenty-sixth of July Movement"—named after Castro's first abortive rising against Batista on July 26, 1953— ushered in a revolution aimed at bringing social justice and economic betterment to the island's 6.5 million people. The leaders were all young men in their early thirties, headed by Castro, a dynamic leader; his program called for agrarian reform, industrialization, and a far-reaching public-works program. It had strong socialistic overtones and to observers smacked of communism. But Castro asserted that the revolution was "humanist and not Communist."

Reaction of Washington was at first quite friendly. In April, 1959, Prime Minister Castro paid an unofficial visit to the United States and was given a warm reception. But the good feeling did not last long; there had been disillusionment over the many summary executions. Hopes for a democratic government were squelched when Castro postponed elections indefinitely. By mid-1960s Cuba's entire agricultural economy and much of her industry had been nationalized, usually without compensaton. And there was growing concern over the influence which men of known Communist leanings were gaining in Cuban affairs.

Once in power, Castro appeared throughout the Latin American Hemisphere as the symbol of the independence of the Latin American nations—and the Communists started to move in. Although he had defeated an ill-conceived invasion by an ill-supplied group of exiles, he presented himself as the David who had defeated Goliath. More significantly, Soviet Russia was henceforth clearly committed to the defense of Cuban independence, and Castro posed as the hero of a Pan-American revolution against American imperialism.

Since 1959, relations between Cuba and the United States have deteriorated rapidly.

To meet the imaginary threat of an American invasion, a large popular militia has been trained to supplement the regular army. As Castro started to confiscate more and more American property, Washington began to realize the pro-Communist forces in Havana. In February, 1960, Ernesto Guevara signed a commercial treaty with the U.S.S.R. under which the Soviets agreed to buy Cuba's sugar and give Cuba a hundred-million-dollar credit to buy Russian oil and machinery; the agreement was followed by trade pacts with several Soviet satellites and with Communist China. Upon authorization from Congress, President Eisenhower halted, in July, 1960, American imports of Cuba's sugar, causing Cuba to lose an estimated 150 million dollars per year. This strengthened Castro's defiance, especially when Premier Khrushchev threatened to launch intercontinental missiles against the U. S. if it intervened in Cuba. The threat of a Soviet satellite on America's doorsteps had suddenly become terribly real. The Cuban crisis in October, 1962, induced Premier Khrushchev to promise to dismantle the sites of missiles in Cuba.

Thus Castro's government has in a sense become a "pawn" in the Cold-War struggle between the U. S. and the U.S.S.R. as well as Communist China.

PRE-CASTRO EDUCATION

Castro's revolutionary changes in Cuba's education have been made easier because Cuba was also probably the most literate nation in the Caribbean area prior to his assumption of power.

Formally, before 1959, Cuba's educational system had an end-to-end organization, the elementary school leading directly to the secondary which in turn (except for secular and technical schools) led directly to the University. The elementary school had an eight-year program, and the secondary (*Instituto*) consisted of a four-year course. (A new type, the Higher Primary School, paralleling three years of secondary education, was not an integral part of a primary-secondary-universities structure.) Elementary school was compulsory and free for children from six to fourteen years of age; but school attendance was extremely low and upwards of two-thirds of Cuba's one million children of primary school age, during 1942-1943, for instance, were not attending schools. There was shortage of buildings, teachers, and facilities. According to the 1953 census, only 61.49 percent of Cuba's population could read. There were some church schools but not enough of them. There was also the eternal problem of troublesome University students; most were working while attending the University, and the idea of full-time faculties serving full-time students had yet to be developed. Many students joined Castro's movement, although Castro's strength depended originally on Cuba's middle classes, attracted to him by resenting the discredited old political parties.

Of the many changes that have influenced the basic form of Cuba's life, two big ones are most profound and irrevocable. One is the land reform which has broken up big holdings and made communal farms where many peasants work, although the state owns them. The other is the explosion of schools and education, under the direction of the Minister of Education.

Castro's "indoctrinated" generation is a product and staunch supporter of the "new Socialist Cuba."

Castro has reorganized completely the pre-Revolution system of education. Scores of brand-new schools have been built all over the island. The government provides thousands of scholarships and students wear special uniforms which set them apart as "becados" (scholarship holders). The schools have also the task of regimentation; students march in military steps to and from classrooms, and even sports take place under strict discipline. Boarding schools, even in mountainous areas, were opened in 1967.

EDUCATION UNDER CASTRO

On the assumption of power in January, 1959, the new Minister of Education proclaimed immediately its intention to reorganize schools at all levels so that they would mirror the political, economic, and social changes of the revolution. The following objectives were proclaimed: (1) quantitative and qualitative development of educational services; (2) decentralization of administrative and technical functions; (3) establishment of a modern system of educational planning to synchronize all plans and services; (4) technical improvement of all branches of education; and (5) general educational reform.

Decree No. 2099, published on October 13, 1959, provided for the regulatory powers of the Ministry of Education over all education. Since then, private schools have been either nationalized or closed.

In the same year, education departments were set up de facto in each province and municipality to handle the problems of elementary, secondary, and vocational education. The Central Planning Board (Junta Central de Planificacion, JUCEPLAN) created twenty-four regional zones for overall government purposes, including regional departments of education. A Commission of Educational Planning operates directly under the Minister and has authority over all educational operations.

The structure of elementary and secondary education has been converted to six-year elementary, three-year basic secondary, and three-year upper secondary. Elementary education was declared compulsory.

After completion of elementary grades, students take examinations given by the Ministry of Education in order to enter a national basic secondary school. The three-year basic secondary program is a pre-vocational period when the student's abilities are observed and then channeled into one of several upper secondary programs, including university preparatory, commercial, technical, art, home economics, and teacher-training programs. Each municipality is to have at least one school offering basic secondary education. In addition, there are technological, agricultural, and industrial schools (escuelas tecnologicas, agricolas e industriales) of three years. Upper secondary schools (escuelas secundarias superiores) comprise pre-university schools (institutos preuniversitarios); schools of surveying (escuelas de comercio); schools of fine arts (escuelas de bellas artes); agricultural and industrial, technical schools (institutos tecnologicos, agricolas, e industriales); and elementary teacher-training schools (escuelas de maestros primarios). The upper secondary programs are, in general, three years in length, while the teacher-training programs take four years.

Several steps were taken to reorganize teacher training. After the new regime took over, numerous teachers (especially those employed since 1952, when the previous government had come to power) were dismissed; some 600 secondary school teachers were released, and some immediately re-employed for the rest of the academic year. But both groups were permitted to take competitive examinations in September, 1959, leading to possible tenure-bearing positions, and new laws provided a pension for secondary and elementary school teachers with more than twenty years of experience. Special schools, such as the Home Economics School and the Normal School for Kindergarten Teachers, were abolished; specialized elementary school teachers (such as teachers of home economics and physical education) were to teach all subjects and, eventually, plans were announced that all new elementary school teachers were to be graduates of the new Escuela de Maestros Primarios. At the same time, the government ran training and orientation courses to prepare them as "integral" teachers (teachers of all subjects).

In 1960, the Higher Institute of Education (Instituto Superior de Educacion) was founded to determine teaching qualifications, qualify teachers for specific teaching assignments, act as the government liaison office in matters of international educational exchange, and to organize educational conferences, seminars, and other professional activities.

A Volunteer Teacher Corps (Cuerpo de Maestros Voluntarios) was created of upper secondary school students prepared through emergency teacher-training courses; university students were trained through similar emergency training; and for vocational and technical schools, workers without previous training as teachers were placed as instructors in such schools. In 1961, a group of 1,000 applicants with basic secondary school background was selected and granted scholarships to attend a first-year course at the Vocational Initiation Center for Elementary School Teachers (*Centro de Iniciacion Vocacional del Magisterio Primario*), in the Sierra Maestra Mountains; the members were to have three years of pedagogical-cultural education in schools located in rural communities and one year of practice teaching. In addition, three to six months' special training courses were initiated in April, 1961, in order to qualify immediately as teachers those students who were nearing completion of their normal school education.

Schools for Secondary School Teacher Preparation (*Escuelas del Profesorado Secundario*) were founded in 1959 in the universities, with programs from four to five years in length. Formerly, regular university graduates could be appointed to teaching positions; these new schools required teachers to be trained in an integrated program, including general culture, special subjects, and methodological principles. Schools for Fine Arts Inspectors were also created, and graduates of an emergency provision one- or two-year programs were assigned to People's Farms and Agrarian Cooperatives to foster artistic recreation in rural communities. Plans were also made for Farms for Youths (*Granjas Juveniles*) for students from rural communities who would pursue general secondary and technical schools, and included free room, board, and medical facilities.

Politically involved in the struggle for power during 1956-1958, the Universities of Havana and the University de las Villas at Santa Clara and the University of Oriente were closed; the private University of Villanueva was shut down briefly but was reopened in early 1958.

Under Castro, the University de las Villas was the first to reopen, in February, 1959, with 1,000 students; the University of Oriente reopened in March, 1959, but both campuses had been purged of alleged collaborators. The University of Havana, occupied by the military between January first and May, 1959, was the last to reopen. But there were troubles between the University and the students in regard to procedures for purging professors; the FEU (Federation of University Students) took control. Elaborate reforms were initiated, including reorganization of the curriculum, rewriting of university statutes, clarification of the obligations of professors, and greater voice for students in the administration and operation of the university.

Law 11 of January 14, 1959, invalidated courses taken and degrees given by the University of Villanueva and other private universities between November, 1956, and January, 1959; but the resentment and arguments over this step led to the modification of the decree in May. Students of private institutions who had received degrees between November, 1956, and January, 1959, were not allowed to practice their professions for one year. Eventually, however, all universities—with the exception of the three public institutions—were closed, and credits and degrees earned by students were subject to review by government boards.

The remaining three institutions (*Universidad de la Havana, Universidad Central "Marta Abreu" de las Villas,* and *Universidad de Oriente*) had their faculties and fields of studies reorganized, and radical changes were introduced in content of courses and textbooks.

In January, 1960, the Mixed Commission (students and professors) of the University of Havana approved an article for university statutes requiring university students to give a year of service to the government, after the completion of their courses, to qualify for their degree.

The glaring shortage of professors and doctors induced the government search for importing such specialists from communist countries, especially for the Faculty of Medicine of the University of Havana. More than 1,500 of Cuba's physicians had fled the country, although as a group they had been some of the early supporters of the Castro government. Their principal complaint is that most doctors were unwilling to tolerate the restrictions on free professional practice. The government dissolved the Cuban Medical Association and tried to make all physicians join the *Sindicato Unico de Trabajadores de le Medicinia* (Single Union of Medical Workers); the regime also exerted pressure on physicians to volunteer for service with the militia and harassed physicians who refused to sign up were deprived of gasoline rations. The earnings of physicians remaining in Cuba are believed to average about $500 a month; most of them work fixed hours under the direction of the Ministry of Health.[1]

A reorganized Ministry of Health took control of all but a few of the nation's hospitals, and medical care was offered to all without direct charge. Most physicians are now connected either with the Ministry of Health or are employed by mutual aid societies; those who wish to continue private practice may do so. Medical education is being accelerated at Havana University School of Medicine and a second medical school has been established at Santiago.

In January, 1962, the President of the Cuban Communist Party had been named Rector of the University of Havana, and the goal of training 25,000 engineers and technicians in their specialties and in Marxist-Leninist principles was set for the next eight

---

1. "Cuba: Physicians and Patients," *Medical Magazine,* VII, 2, February, 1963, 75-76.

years. The new programs for university degrees in all fields include a required subject entitled "Historic and Dialectical Materialism" throughout the first year and a half of study.

OPERATION OF THE EDUCATIONAL SYSTEM

While pupils and students learn to read and write and master modern technology in contemporary Cuba, they also get a steady diet of Marxist theories and slogans.

Within the Marxist-Leninist framework, an important element in the indoctrination is the concept of "revolution." The word "revolution" is regarded differently in Latin America than in the U. S., where "revolution" has come to be a bad word. In Latin America, "revolution" is a magic word which carries very favorable connotations. It symbolizes the hope that things are going to be better. Latin America saw old-style revolutions played by generals as a game of musical chairs for power in a series of social revolutions.

In many Latin American countries, unless reforms are soon made, revolution is definitely on the horizon. In fact, in one sense, the only question in Latin America might be: "What kind of revolution will there be?" "A Sovietized social revolution, such as the Communists were able to accomplish in Cuba or a gradual, peaceful social revolution, into a better world for Latin America's people?"

There is no question that Cuba is a Communist country, or "Socialist country," as Castro prefers to call it. Yet it is far from being a duplicate of the U.S.S.R. or Communist China.

On ideological issues, Premier Castro strives to be neutral between the U.S.S.R. and China; at the same time, he declares that Cuba is firmly "Marxist-Leninist" and the Cuban Communist Party—the United Party of the Socialist Revolution in Cuba—appears to be considerably advanced in its organization. The party permeates most of the public and private activities of the island.

Castro also claims that each country must work out its own Marxist-Leninist system to suit local conditions. Certainly Cuba has done that; the flavor and atmosphere of Cuban Communism must be unique in the Communist World.

The government subsidizes all sports and encourages youngsters to join political organizations, such as the Young Pioneers of the Union of Communist Youth. Complementing these are the schools of revolutionary instruction, where the student is thoroughly coached in the intricacies of Marxism-Leninism.

Castro's regime is especially proud of its experiment in raising a new crop of "elite" youngsters by providing it with special scholarships (an experiment resembling Khruschev's "boarding schools"). Thus, today, some 70,000 becados (scholarship students)

are living in Havana's suburbs in expropriated hotels or in the former homes of the self-exiled rich middle class. Fresh farm boys are housed there, on a nine-months schedule, learning, from 8 A.M. to 5 P.M. daily, classical ballet, music, Marxism, general subjects, and French (taught by a Swiss). The girl students study languages, the arts, or a few home economics courses seven hours a day, and then receive also two hours of Leninism-Marxism after supper (while boys' courses lean to engineering and related fields).[2] All becados live away from home and are shielded from parental influence, but they can visit their families on vacations; non-Marxist education is not available.

THE DRIVE ON ILLITERACY

In 1961-2, most becados "volunteered" for the patriotic task of the government's plan to conquer illiteracy.

The year 1961 was declared the Year for Illiteracy Eradication (Ano de la Alfabetizacion), as well as the Year of Education (Ano de la Educacion). Illiteracy had been estimated in 1958 at 900,000, or approximately 22 percent of the population age fifteen and above, one of the lowest rates among the Latin American Republics.

The National Commission for Literacy, established by the new government to organize the campaign, is composed of technical officials of the Ministry of Education, delegates from university schools of education, and lectures in teacher-training schools. It was reported that since April, 1959, 817 literacy centers have been operating with 2,751 teachers and more than 16,000 students.

An "Army of Education" of 100,000 students over twelve years of age was organized in 1961 to go into the interior and teach illiterates. The regular schools were closed on April 15 for this purpose, several months earlier than usual, and were not reopened for the 1961-62 school year until February, 1962 (several months later than usual). The students selected from the "Army of Education" were organized into uniformed brigades and were given special courses of indoctrination which were to be passed on to the peasants in the course of the literacy campaign. Two manuals were issued by the Ministry of Education: Venceremos (We Shall Conquer), a primer for students; and Alfabeticemos (Let's Teach Reading and Writing), a guide of instructions for teachers on how to overcome illiteracy and at the same time to indoctrinate students in the "ideological objectives of the revolution." Cuban teen-agers (brigafistas) clad in Cuban blue jeans and equipped with lamps made-in-China, were let out of school for eight months. The government claims that as a result of this campaign practically everyone in Cuba has learned to read and write, and that "the peasants at least felt that some-

2. "Cubans Show School Setup," Christian Science Monitor, January 31, 1963.

body in the city cared about them, and the youngsters came back burning with a zeal to do something about the countryside. Everywhere, you see *seguimiento*, or follow-up classes, which take the newly literate up to the third grade."[3]

On the other hand, today, by the thousands, young and old Cubans are trekking to Prague, Moscow, and Leningrad to learn fishing, technology, Russian, and, of course, Marxism-Leninism. Most, if not all, return convinced that Communism is the only way of life.

THE WEB OF CONTROL

The educational structure, as in all Communist countries, is inseparably related to the whole "way of life" of the Cuban people.

Most Cubans live according to the orders and directives of the Committee for the Defense of the Revolution—really thousands of small committees organized down to the block level, whose most active members belong to ORI, an organization made up of both Castro's supporters and other Communists. They know everything in the life of everyone and can give or take away favors.

The Committee does social work, distributes clothing, gives vaccinations, and fights juvenile delinquency. Above all, however, its task is to defend each block against counter-revolution. Its job was originally vigilance. Now, these defenders, mostly middle-aged housewives, shoulder fourteen duties in all for the regime. Issuing ration books is just a start; they also see that children on the block are vaccinated; that everyone learns to read and write; that the local butchers dole out meat fairly; that "culture" is encouraged; and that neighbors are indoctrinated with good revolutionary principles. It runs "indoctrination" sessions in kitchens, garages, and on porches.[4] "Criticism and self-criticism" sessions are frequent and big occasions at these "reunions."

The cultural orientation is directed by the powerful Council of Culture, which promotes art all the way down to folk dancing on state farms. Castro is also trying to attract the intellectuals; painters, for example, glory in their freedom to paint abstract art, something which is not tolerated in other Communist countries, and, in fact, a tourist exhibit of Cuban modern art was banned in East Germany.

This type of organized and directed system of life is strengthened by all available social control means. On the communal farms, for instance, all Cubans work together, eating in mess halls. The press is always full of propaganda; messages are crude and in stereotyped Marxist lingo. Numberless posters plaster the billboards and walls and feature social and political ideas or boast of production figures. One of the most popular ones shouts: "A country that studies is a country that wins!"

Adult education is also promoted by Soviet technicians who are especially engaged in the instruction in the workings of imported machinery (mainly the tractors, jeeps, and trucks) to the farm boys.

THE CATHOLIC CHURCH, CASTRO, AND RELIGION

Cuba, colonized and Christianized by Spain, has belonged, since its origins, both in culture and religion to the Catholic Church, which has played a leading part in the struggle against other Latin American dictatorships (Argentina, Venezuela) thanks to its authority.

Before Castro's seizure of power, Cuba had more than 700 parish priests and numerous religious orders. Today, only about 125 remain to minister to the entire population; according to Vatican sources, 598 priests had been expelled or forced to leave the country.[5]

In pre-Castro Cuba there had been Catholic primary and secondary schools and a Catholic University; all of these institutions have been nationalized.

But this process of separating the Catholic Church from the people has had other than religious roots. The majority of practicing Cuban Catholics belong to the middle class. But, as a consequence, there were few native Cuban priests and the church administration in Cuba had to depend on large numbers of Spanish priests. As immigrants and Spaniards they occupied the positions of social inferiority and were labeled by liberal extremists as *Falangists* and *bodegueros* (grocers—the popular term for Spanish immigrants in Cuba). This tendency to undermine the social position of the clergy was used by Castro, who finally ordered the expulsion of the Spanish priests and members of religious orders.

Although the Cuban Catholics have tried to resist the new government openly, and especially its Communist policies, their reaction came too late.

There is also evidence that Catholic and Protestant churches are still operating in Cuba, in spite of their difficulties. In fact, "in no other Communist country . . . does one see high government officials attending church regularly. Cuba is the only Communist country that exchanges diplomatic representatives with the Vatican."[6]

CUBAN REFUGEES IN UNITED STATES

Establishment of the Castro dictatorship brought about a refugee problem that, almost overnight, made the United States a country of first asylum for 1,000 Cubans each week. By the middle of 1968, there were

---

3. Berquist, Laura, "My 28 Days in Communist Cuba," *Look,* XXVII, 7, April, 1963, pp. 15-27, 20.
4. Berquist, *op. cit.*, 20.
5. *L'Observatore Romano,* January 24, 1962.
6. Donald Grant, "Cuba is Evolving Her Own Ideology," *New York Times,* August 2, 1963.

over 200,000 Cuban refugees in the United States, located mostly in the Miami area, with smaller numbers in the New York and Tampa areas.

The first refugees were largely educated, middle- or upper-class Cubans. Almost all had to accept jobs for which they were not fitted.

Today, many Cuban teachers are training in the University of Florida (Tallahassee) in the hope of securing certificates to teach in United States schools.

SELECTED BIBLIOGRAPHY

BATISTA Y ZALDIVAR, FULGENCIO. *Cuba Betrayed.* New York: Vantage Press, 1962.

BELSON, LOWREY. *Rural Cuba.* Minneapolis: University of Minnesota Press, 1950.

BERQUIST, LAURA. "My 28 Days in Communist Cuba." *Look,* XXVII, No. 7, April, 1963, 15-27.

BRENNAN, RAY. *Castro, Cuba and Justice.* New York: Doubleday & Co., Inc., 1959.

CASUSO, TERESA. *Cuba and Castro.* New York: Random House, Inc., 1961.

DRAPER, THEODORE. *Castro's Cuba: Myths and Revolution.* New York: Frederick A. Praeger, Inc., 1962.

DUBOIS, JULES. *Fidel Castro: Rebel-Liberator or Dictator?* Indianapolis: The Bobbs Merrill Co., Inc., 1959.

JAMES, DANIEL. *Cuba: The First Soviet Satellite in the Americas.* New York: Avon Book Division—The Hearst Corp., 1961.

KEIMWIEDE, GRACE I., FREEBERGER, ADELA R., and HAUCH, CHARLES. *Educational Data: Cuba.* Washington: USOE GPO, November, 1962.

UNESCO. *World Survey of Education,* 1955 ff.

(Booklets in Spanish are also available from Ministerio de Educacion, Havana, Cuba.)

DOMINICAN REPUBLIC

Roger W. Axford

The Island of Hispaniola was discovered by Christopher Columbus in 1492. Hispaniola, the second largest of the Greater Antilles, is between Cuba and Puerto Rico. The climate of the Island of Hispaniola is subtropical throughout the year. The Dominican Republic occupies the eastern two-thirds of the Island, and the Republic of Haiti occupies the one-third to the west. A long conflict has existed for over one hundred years between the two countries, and the fears and animosities have come to the fore periodically through the century.

Founded in 1496, the ancient city of Santo Domingo is claimed by some to be the oldest settlement on the western hemisphere. The remains of Columbus are supposed to be in the old cathedral in Santo Domingo.

GEOGRAPHY OF DOMINICAN REPUBLIC

The Dominican Republic is bounded on the North by the Atlantic Ocean, on the South by the Caribbean Sea, to the East by the Mona Channel, and to the West by the Republic of Haiti. There are three major mountain ranges that cross the island: Central, Northern, and Southern. The highest mountain is in the Central Range, called Pico Duarte, 3,175 meters high. The best fruits, sugar cane, and vegetables are found in the grassy plains known as "The Garden of the West Indies" (El Jardin de las Antillas). Both Christopher Columbus in his diary of his voyage and Father Bartolome de las Casas in his History of the Indians related that the grassy plains made superior pasturage for cattle.

The international river between the republics (Dominican and Haiti) is Higuamo and Artibonito. Other important rivers are: Ozama, Yuna, Yaque del Northe, and Yaque del Sur. The largest lake is Lake Qnriquillo.

Santo Domingo de Guzman is the Capital, called Ciudad Trujillo during the Dictatorship of the cruel tyrant Trujillo. The Republic occupies 19,333 square miles.

The Dominican Republic is much less densely populated than Haiti. As one travels from Santo Domingo to Santiago there are long stretches of hilly lands with only a hut here and there. Small towns dot the now modern highway connecting the two cities, built by the "benevolent Dictator Trujillo." Ethnologically, the Dominicans are a contrast with the Haitians. Dominicans are a Spanish-speaking people, predominately of mixed Negro and European descent, while the Haitians are mostly Negro and speak French.

GOVERNMENT AND HISTORY

Both the French and the Americans have played important roles in Dominican Republic history, as have the powerful Spanish. Santo Domingo was ceded to France by Spain in 1795. Then in 1801 Toussaint L'Ouverture, the leader from Haiti captured the country. During the period 1803-1821 Spain recaptured control and a number of native governments were established and deposed. Haiti governed the entire Island from 1822 to 1844. But the Dominican Republic dates its beginning from 1844. Spain again occupied the republic from 1861-63.

The United States became involved directly when the American Marines occupied the country from 1916 through 1924. It was in 1924 when a constitutionally elected government was established. The republic is divided into twenty-five provinces and a national district whose governors and councilmen are named by direct popular vote every two years. The President is elected by direct vote every five years during normal times. All persons over eighteen have the right to vote.

ERA OF CRUELTY AND TYRANNY—TRUJILLO

Rafael Leonidas Trujillo Molina (1891-1961) played such an important role in the Dominican Republic that to understand the contemporary scene one must understand the happenings during his rule, a cruel and tyrannical epoch. Seizing power in 1930 by means of elections held under a terror Trujillo imposed as Army Commander, he ruled for thirty-one years. He maintained power by means of an army of one hundred thousand men. Mainly they protected Trujillo, his family, and family enterprises. According to Alejandro E. Grullon, President of the Banco Popular Dominicano, the Trujillo family owned and managed all the major enterprises in the country. The national treasury was drained for the military, 38 percent of the national budget was used to maintain the army, while *only 7 percent* was allocated to the Ministry of Education. Trujillo set up a strict vigilance over the entire country subdividing the country into seventy-two communes, and then into Sections and Districts. In this way military and civilian authorities had charge of only a small area. They could prevent or extinguish the outbreak of protesters or uprisings. The period was a rule of terror. Important authorities were shifted often. Officers were transferred from one city to another as often as every two or three months. No accurate estimate of the number of Dominicans killed under Trujillo has been established, but some estimate as high as 10 percent of the total population was eliminated. When Trujillo slaughtered some 20,000 Haitians in October, 1937, he had an indemnity of $750,000 and the omission of his name as a candidate for President in 1938-42. He picked Jacinto B. Peynado as President for that term, a man whom he owned and controlled. Trujillo built canals and good roads but took 10 percent profit for himself on all Public Works and from the public employees' salaries. Luis Augusto Caminero says that Trujillo was probably the most powerful and wealthiest man in America. Through a fabulous fortune Trujillo learned what price each man had who visited him. His wealth was estimated over one thousand million dollars. This does not count the wealth of his children and relatives. On August 16, 1959, the Organization of American States at its Sixth Meeting of Foreign Ministers held in San Jose, Costa Rico, found Trujillo guilty of attempted assassination of the Social Democratic President of Venezuela Romulo Betancourt. Economic and commercial sanctions were placed against the Dominican Republic. Then Trujillo wanted the Church to bestow the title "Benefactor of the Church." This was to have offset this guilt for heinous crimes. Failing this, he started anti-religious campaigns and this led to his undoing. Rafael Leonidas Trujillo "The Benefactor" was murdered on May 30, 1961 (some sources say May 27th). Only two persons in the original plot survived while more than ten were killed in the uprising.[1] Antoni Imbert and Luis Amiama Tio became a part of the Council of State which tried to lead the country to a democratic state. Dr. Joaquin Balaguer became President, a man who made himself out to be a victim of Trujillo's

tyranny. He made some democratic concessions, but the people did not accept him. Freedom was finally won on January 19, 1962, following months of internal revolution.

Rafael F. Bonnelly was named President January 18, 1962, by a seven-member Council of State. But on December 20, 1962, Juan Bosch, poet and author, was elected president in the first free elections in thirty-eight years. The United States expanded financial aid after having broken diplomatic relations for seventeen months, and projects such as the Agency for International Development began as joint efforts with the United States. Peace Corps had more than 200 workers in the Dominican Republic country in 1964. Three civilians took over from Juan Bosch in September, 1963, after a military coup.

ECONOMY AND INDUSTRY

Agriculture and raising of stock are the principal sources of income. The land is very fertile in most of the country, with an estimated 15,000 square miles tillable. The leading manufactures are sugar, alcohol, lumber, cement, chocolate, molasses, rum, peanut oil, tobacco products, furniture, cordage, and wearing apparel. An estimated 50 percent of the exports go to the United States, and about half of the imports come from the United States.

In agriculture, rice, sugar, cacao, coffee, corn, and tobacco are the leading crops. Much of the manufacturing is related to processing the agricultural products from the farms.

POPULATION AND RELIGION

The United Nations estimated the population of the Dominican Republic as 3,600,000[2] in 1965. The population is composed of approximately 19 percent Negroes, mulattoes, and whites. The religion of the country is predominately Roman Catholic, although there is the claim of religious tolerance. There is said to be no state religion. From the date of the discovery of the Island until the period of the French Revolution, the ecclesiastical and civil history of the Dominican Republic are inseparably intertwined. It is recorded that the first Bishop of San Domingo sent an idol of aboriginal workmanship as a present to Leo X (Moroni, Dizionario, XX, s. v. Domingo). In the Gothic Chapel in the Cathedral, San Domingo, are claimed to be the relics of Columbus.

EDUCATIONAL SYSTEM

On April 5, 1918, the Constitution of the Republic vested direction and control of the system of educa-

1. For a detailed account of the terror of Trujillo see Chapter 28, pp. 441-445, "The Dominican Republic," Hubert Herring, *A History of Latin America,* (2nd edition). New York: A. A. Knopf, 1962, also *New York Times,* April 4, 5, 6, 1960, Edward C. Burks.
2. *United Nations Yearbook,* 1966.

tion in the National Council of Education known as Consejo Nacional de Educacion. This body consists of the Secretary of Public Education and Fine Arts, who is also a member of the President's cabinet, in addition to four members appointed by the Chief Executive. Members serve for a four-year term. The Secretary of Public Education and Fine Arts is ex-officio Chairman of the Council.

The National Council of Education has broad powers. It is the regulatory agency for the organization and maintenance of the public-school system in the country. This includes all levels of education and every type of school. The Council determines the following: number and location of schools; diplomas to be issued; plans for study and curricula; teacher qualifications, salaries, examinations to be taken; and all the basic instructional controls for the system.

Three types of schools are to be found in the Dominican Republic: official public schools, semi-official public schools, and private schools. The State entirely maintains the official public schools, while the semi-official public schools receive only partial support. Any individual or group may found a private school, but it receives no Governmental help. Only in the lower elementary schools can the state intervene, for these schools must conform to the official programs, the textbook requirements, and the program prescribed by the government.

Teaching of political propaganda is forbidden as is the teaching of religious creeds or dogma. A more humane treatment of students is encouraged, for the employment of any cruel or degrading forms of punishment is forbidden by law.

It is reported that resulting from the change in the political situation a major reorganization of the national education service has resulted. In 1962 the Secretariat of State for Education, Fine Arts, and Religion reestablished the former National Board of Education. A national commission for broad educational planning will be responsible for preparing short- and long-range plans for education. The two bodies, the National Council for Education and the National Commission for the National Education Project, are responsible for the preparation of projects and plans for educational reform which will ensure a firm and systematic organization of national education looking to the future.

FINANCE

A marked advance in financing education was observed between 1962 and 1964. The budget for the education department at the beginning of 1962 was 9,844,851 pesos. This rose to 13,344,851 pesos (40 percent); 5,000,000 pesos was added by the Alliance for Progress, a total of 18,344,851.[3] Improved financing brought improvement in teachers' salaries. By June 1962, 3,500,000 pesos had been allocated to increase teachers salaries. In the case of teachers of literacy,

some increased 150 percent. Illiteracy, as late as 1967, was still over 60 percent. Secondary school teachers, inspectors, and departmental directors received salary increases up to 40 percent. An extensive program was undertaken by the government of up-grading teacher training, and services of institutions of higher education abroad were utilized. Teachers were sent to summer institutes. During the summer of 1963, more than 322 teachers participated in workshops of eight-weeks duration at the University of Puerto Rico. More extensive training programs included sending teachers to the Pennsylvania State University, University of Wisconsin-Milwaukee, and other institutions of higher learning for a study of such topics as the comprehensive high school. In 1963 it was determined to send more than 300 teachers and personnel from the technical staff abroad to take part in intensive studies.

An effort has been made at reform in the structure and organization of education in the Dominican Republic. In 1963 a commission was set up to study the reform of primary and secondary education in order to create a six-year baccalaureate course to be divided into two states (four and two years).

In March 1962, the Ministry of Education, Fine Arts, and Religion of the Dominican Republic reported the following quantitative development:

	SCHOOLS	TEACHERS	PUPILS
Three-year rural schools	2,357	2,360	102,657
Five-year rural schools	1,880	3,490	238,932
Urban schools	274	3,027	132,472
School homes	232	237	11,674
Schools for adults	7	23	622
Intermediate schools	235	729	20,417
Lower Secondary Schools	80	711	14,171
Teacher Training Schools	4	36	288
Art education	99	272	13,933
Technical education	88	399	11,195
	5,260	11,374	551,094

The training course for teaching in the rural schools has been extended from a two-year program to three years. Modern languages were removed in the secondary school curriculum but were replaced in 1961. A five-year course is supposed to be provided in English and a two-year program in French.

STRUCTURE OF THE SCHOOL SYSTEM

The Organic Law on Education recognizes in Article 3 (1951) the types of education within the Dominican Republic: nursery; primary; intermediate; secondary; rural primary and secondary teacher training; further vocational, technical and artistic education; special; and university.

The constitution provides for compulsory education for children. Freedom of education is recognized as an inherent right of the human personality in

3. *International Yearbook of Education,* 1963, p. 124.

Article 6 of the Dominican Republic Constitution. It states, "Primary instruction shall be under the supervision of the State, and shall be compulsory for children of school age, in the form established by law. In official institutions, this instruction, as well as that provided by schools of agriculture, manual arts, and domestic economy, shall be free."

TEACHER TRAINING

Teachers prepare to teach in either urban or rural schools. Teachers may receive their schooling at rural teacher-training schools. Primary teacher-training schools and teacher-training colleges train the urban primary teachers. Regular summer courses are offered to broaden teachers' knowledge about educational methods and new materials for teaching. Special courses are organized for supervising teachers and inspectors of education. Teachers who are candidates for teaching posts in rural and urban primary and intermediate schools must satisfy certain requirements: must have reached the age of eighteen; have no communicable disease or physical defect which would incapacitate them for teaching; obtain a primary teacher's diploma for urban primary and intermediate education, or a rural teacher's diploma for rural education. Because there is often a shortage of teachers qualified for positions, the Executive may upon the recommendation of the Secretariat of State for Education and Fine Arts appoint persons as teachers who possess the ability and experience for teaching. Some protection is afforded the teacher, at least on paper, for no qualified teacher may be suspended or dismissed except on evidence of serious reasons affecting his competence or his moral character.

SECONDARY EDUCATION

Education in the state general secondary school (liceo de educación) is free. But a student must be at least twelve years old and have completed a higher-primary or intermediate school-leaving certificate. He must have an official certificate granting admission to secondary studies. The purpose of the secondary schools is twofold: to give the youth a broad cultural education to prepare him to take part in the life of the community and to prepare young people for higher education by developing a specialty. The first three years of the four-year course provide a general education, and the program is the same for all students. During the fourth year specialization may be in natural sciences, philosophy and letters, or physics and mathematics. The specialty depends upon the university field of study chosen by the student.

Examinations determining the *bachillerato* diplomas to be given students is defined and determined by the National Board of Education. Examinations are also taken along the way to determine progress. Women can take a special *bachillerato en artes y*

letras if they do not wish to go to the University. This program provides general culture and some domestic skills. The subjects included in the three-year program provide languages, gardening, sports, dressmaking, history of art, music, painting, and general culture.

TECHNICAL AND VOCATIONAL SCHOOLS

The San Ignacio de Loyola Institute of Technology has a curriculum which includes subjects for special preparation such as mechanics, electricians, plumbers, cabinet-makers, agricultural specialists. The teaching is divided into different stages.

The National School of Arts and Crafts (Escuela National de Artes y Oficios) trains skilled workers and craftsmen in carpentry, engineering, electricity, automobile mechanics, and radio engineering.

One of the exciting new institutions developing is the new Agricultural Institute at Santiago in the middle of the island. Here members of the Peace Corps are working and teaching English. The Institute was opened in 1963 and is headed by Professors from Texas Agricultural and Mechanical College. The director's salary is being paid by the Ford Foundation, U.S.A. This school is preparing teachers and agricultural agents. The school has programs in poultry, dairy, and animal husbandry with an experimental farm. Best methods of agriculture are demonstrated. The founder of this school was Luis B. Crouch, a Dominican businessman from a prominent family. Crouch is a plastics manufacturer who has interested other businessmen, the Ford Foundation, Agency for International Development, and the Ministry of Education in quality agricultural training. Crouch is himself a graduate of Georgia Tech in the United States.

Vocational training for women is provided by special schools. These include a school of industrial training for girls, school of nursing, the school of hairdressing and beauty culture, and the school of home economics.

A three-stage program prepares students in business training. The State subsidizes semi-official schools for elementary commercial courses. A three-year curriculum is included in the secondary commercial course in state business-training schools, leading to the secondary school-leaving certificate. A diploma in accountancy is obtained by attending a four-year program in the College of Accountancy.

Special teachers in the fine arts are trained in the National School of Fine Arts. Teachers are taught painting, sculpture, drawing. Such schools are the National Conservatory of Music and Elocution, and the Liceo Musical Pablo Claudio at San Cristobal which is a college of music.

HIGHER EDUCATION

The University of Santo Domingo at the capital of the country claims to be the oldest university on the western hemisphere. The University of Santo Domingo was established in 1538 by Dominican fathers. Professional training is provided by the University through faculties of law, dentistry, medicine, pharmacy, chemistry, science and engineering, philosophy, agronomy, and veterinary science. The University is planning an expansion program, and in the summer of 1964 the Agency for International Development through the U. S. State Department sent seven professors from the University representing the various professional schools to study the planning and architecture of institutions of higher learning in the United States. The University of Santo Domingo has over 5,000 students and is a prime source of intellectual leadership for the country.

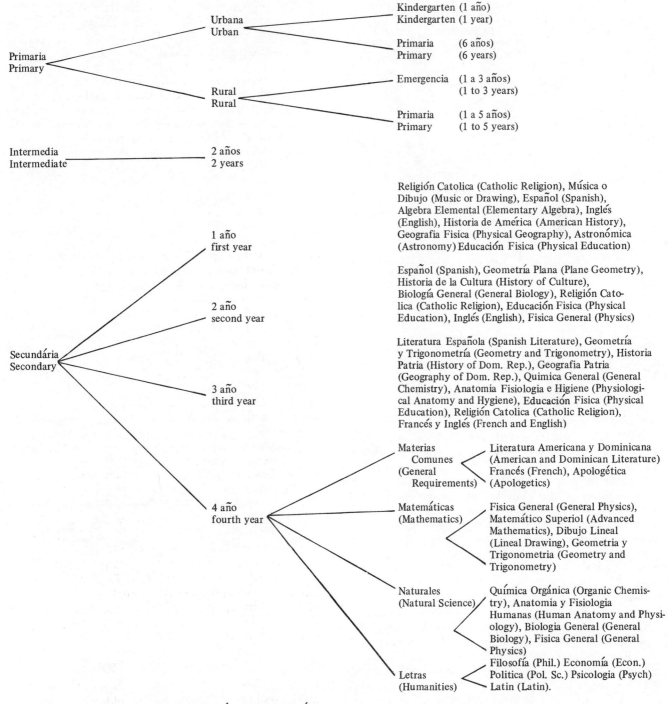

Figure 1. Sistema de la educación en la República Dominicana (the educational system in the Dominican Republic).

A new university has been started at Santiago, the University Madre y Maestra de Santiago. This is a Catholic university which served 160 students in 1964, according to Luis B. Crouch, Trustee.

LOOK TO THE FUTURE

There are some bright spots to be observed on the horizon of a dark thirty-one years of oppression by a cruel dictator. In 1962 it was reported that over one hundred inspectors, school principals, and teachers in various capacities took training in the United States and other countries to improve their professional training. According to a leading banker, who is also a member of Fomento, the national planning board, astounding things are happening in the economy. Bank deposits doubled during the three years following the overthrow of Trujillo. Rice consumption has doubled, and rice is a staple food. More than 80 percent more peanut oil is being consumed. In 1964, cement production had increased 120 percent since the Trujillo ouster. Lumber production, which was twenty million board feet per year under Trujillo, is now thirty-five million board feet per year.

It is reported that the nutrition of the children is being improved through auxiliary services in the schools. Through help from international organizations such as CARE and Caritas, between 150,000 and 200,000 school children have received meals since 1963.

A special program has been inaugurated for the education of adults. According to Mr. Buenaventura Sanchez Feliz, Delegate of the Government of the Dominican Republic to the XXIVth International Conference on Public Education, a particular effort has been made in campaigns to promote literacy education, basic education, and adult education. A program of civic education has been organized to accomplish these ends.

With the new-found freedom and promise of elections and a new democratic constitution, the schools in the Dominican Republic may fare better than in the past. There is a need to build a middle class; this is recognized by the leaders. Some of the young educators are active in the political life of the country and may play an important role in cultivating democratic institutions. One of the major objections of the teachers in the projects on the study of comprehensive high schools was the amount of involvement of students in politics, even at the secondary level of education. Now that the chains of dictatorship have been broken, perhaps new leadership will provide for better education, and more education at all levels.

BIBLIOGRAPHY

AXFORD, ROGER W. "New Freedom in Dominican Republic," *The Milwaukee Journal*, July 12, 1964, part 5, p. 3.

———. 1962-3 Annual Report, Latin American Project, AID (University of Wisconsin-Milwaukee).

HEATH, KATHRYN G., *Ministries of Education, Their Functions and Organization*. U. S. Department of Health, Education, and Welfare, Bulletin 1961, No. 21 OE-14064.

HERRING, HUBERT. *A History of Latin America*, 2nd ed. New York: Alfred A. Knopf, Inc., 1962.

International Yearbook of Education, 1963-1967.

LOWENTHAL, ABRAHAM F. "Limits of American Power: Lesson of Dominican Republic," *Harper's*, June, 1964, pp. 87-95.

———. "Neighbors at Odds in Hispaniola," *London Times*, July 4, 1964.

POTTER, GLADYS L., and EBAUGH, CAMERON D. *Education in the Dominican Republic*, Federal Security Agency, U. S. Office of Education Bulletin, 1947, No. 10.

Revista de Educacion. Secretaria de Estado de Educacion. Bellas Artes & Cultos Santo Domingo, Republica Dominicana, 1964.

RUIZ COEN, PROSPER, and LITTLE MARY A. *Algunas Ideas Sobre Ensenañza*. Cuidad Trujillo Servicio Cooperativo Interamericano de Eucacion (SCIDE) 1956, 58 pp. (Series of letters written to a young teacher in the Dominican Republic, gives suggestions for teaching in rural normal schools.)

United Nations Yearbook, 1962-63.

World Survey of Education. Paris UNESCO,
Vol. I, 1955 Handbook of Educational Organization, and Statistics. Dominican Republic, pp. 202-207.
Volume II, 1958 Primary Education, Dominican Republic, pp. 315-324.
Volume III, 1961 Secondary Education, Dominican Republic, pp. 427-433.

(Special Thanks to Miss Irene Zimmerman, Librarian, The University of Florida, and to the Reference Library staff, Robert Manning Strozier Library, Florida State University, Tallahassee, Florida.)

ECUADOR

Hazel J. Tucker

HISTORY OF EDUCATION

The history of education in Ecuador begins with the arrival of the Spaniards in 1534. The Spanish priests assumed responsibility for the organization of educational institutions and established a control which persisted for many decades.

Fray Jodoco Ricke founded a school which was known as "Colegio de San Andrés." When this school was taken over by the Augustinian Fathers, the name was changed to the "Colegio de San Nicolás de Tolerino." The Dominican Fathers established a charity school. The first university in Quito, the "Universidad de San Fulgencio" was founded in 1586 by the Augustinian Fathers. In addition to these, and always under clerical supervision, many other educational institutions were established throughout the country, such as the "Real Colegio de San Fernando," the "Universidad de Santo Tomás de Aquine," and the "Universidad de San Gregorio Magno" where the most brilliant men of the period were educated.[1]

Julio Tobar characterizes the first twenty years of education after Ecuadorian independence from Spain in 1822 as a continuance of the colonial policy of cruelty and abuse, of virtual slavery of the Negroes and the Indians, and of abandonment of the lower classes, a situation which was democratic in name only.[2]

In 1830 Ecuador withdrew from the Federation "Gran Colombia" to initiate its own government. During the early years, in conformance with the pattern in most South American countries, education continued to be reserved for the select few, for those of potential leadership, and chiefly for those from the upper classes.[3]

In 1835 President Vicente Rocafuerte outlined education as a public function, secular in nature, and national in scope. For the first time, he attempted to subject the clergy to state control, but his efforts were mitigated by the continuing power of a negative environment.[4]

Dictator García Moreno, in power three decades later, was vitally concerned with education, yet his interest in the preservation of the landowner class, and his religiously-oriented politics permitted the clergy to regain their former control.[5]

The liberals came to power under President Eloy Alfaro in 1895, and the concept of a nation, of Ecuador for the Ecuadorians, was re-established. The constitution of 1897 mentioned elementary education as a public function to be supported by state funds. President Alfaro began the process of secularization of education which continues to the present. In order to provide lay teachers for state schools, Alfaro founded the normal schools, "Juan Montalvo" for men, and "Manuela Cañizares" for women. Other educational institutions founded during his presidency were the Military School, the National Conservatory of Music, the School of Fine Arts, and the Mejia High School, all in existence up to the present time.

General Leonidas Plaza, twice president of Ecuador, from 1901 to 1905 and from 1912 to 1916, defined liberal doctrines, implanting and legalizing them with a concreteness not previously seen. Staunchly opposed to clerical influence in all matters of government, he appointed a Minister of Education as a member of the President's Cabinet, thus truly effecting federal control of education, a characteristic feature persisting over the years with few digressions. With vigor and with enthusiasm, General Plaza selected excellent ministers to head the Ministry of Education, increased the national budget to support the foundation of schools, brought specialists from Germany to aid in the technical transformation of national educational

1. Jorge Enrique Adoum, "Cultural Facets," in *Ecuador, Andean Mosaic*, Rolf Blomberg, ed., pp. 286-287.
2. Julio Tobar, *Apuntes para la historia de la educacion laica en el Ecuador*, pp. 7, 8.
3. John J. Johnson, *Political Change in Latin America*.
4. Julio Tobar, *op. cit.*, p. 8.
5. *Ibid.*

laws and programs of study, and extended aid to elementary education and the masses.[6]

Although 1906 had marked the inclusion of secular education as a part of the Constitution, numerous political changes hindered the effectiveness of its application. Table 1 is a record of changes of government from 1900 to 1948:

An analysis of Table 1 reveals that few Presidents completed their terms of office, and within some periods there were many changes of ministers. Many excellent programs initiated by men with vision were dropped by their successors, motivated by personal political aspirations.

TABLE 1

Changes in Government, 1900 to 1948

Heads of State	Term of Office	Number of Ministers of Education
1. General Eloy Alfaro	1895-1901	1
2. General Leonidas Plaza	1901-1905	3
3. Don Lizardo García	1905-1906	1
4. General Eloy Alfaro	1906-1911	5
5. Don Emilio Estrada	September-December 1911	1
6. Don Carlos Freile Zaldumbide	December 1911-March 1912	1
7. Dr. Francisco Andrade Marín	March-August 1912	1
8. Dr. Alfredo Baquerizo Moreno	August 1912	1
9. General Leonidas Plaza	1912-1916	3
10. Dr. Alfredo Baquerizo	1916-1920	3
11. Dr. José Luis Tamayo	1920-1924	1
12. Dr. Gonzalo S. Córdova	1924-1925	3
13. Military Dictatorship	1925-1926	4
14. Dr. Isidro Ayora	1926-1931	3
15. Col. Luis Larrea Alba	August-October 1931	1
16. Dr. Luis Baquerizo Moreno	1931-1932	2
17. Dr. Alberto Guerrero Martínez	September-December 1932	2
18. Don Juan de Dios Martínez Mera	December 1932-December 1933	4
19. Dr. Abelardo Montalvo	1933-1934	2
20. Dr. José Velasco Ibarra	1934-1935	6
21. Dr. Antonio Pons	August-September 1935	1
22. Engineer Federico Paéz	1935-1937	3
23. General Alberto Enríquez	1937-1938	3
24. Dr. Manuel M. Borrero	August-December 1938	1
25. Dr. Aurelio Mosquera Narvaéz	1938-1939	1
26. Dr. Andrés F. Córdova	December 1939-August 1940	*
27. Dr. Carlos Arroyo del Río	1940-1944	2
28. Dr. José N. Velasco Ibarra	May 1944-August 1947	5
29. Col. Carlos Mancheno	August 1947-10 days	1
30. Dr. Mariano Súorez Veintimilla	September 1947-11 days	1
31. Don Carlos Julio Arosemena	1947-1948	*
32. Don Galo Plaza Lasso	1948-1952	2
33. Dr. José M. Velasco Ibarra	1952-1956	
34. Dr. Camilo Ponce	1956-1960	2
35. Dr. José Velasco Ibarra	September 1960-November 1961	1
36. Dr. Carlos Julio Arosemena Jr.	November 1961-July 1963	
37. Military Dictatorship	July 1963-March 1966	1
38. Dr. Otto Arosemena Gomez	October 1966-Present	

NOTE: The asterisk indicates that the suceeding Chief of State did not change the incumbant Minister of Education.

Many times the office of Minister of Education has been held by men of distinction who have, however, been educated in professions other than education. Without special training, they sometimes approached the problem of educational reforms by contracting special missions from other countries, such as the United States and Chile in 1901, Spain in 1906, Germany in 1913, Colombia in 1924, Germany in 1922, and Spain in 1942. The success of these missions was closely linked to that of the political party in power, and often there were few lasting results.

The struggle for power between the two major political parties, the Church-related Conservatives and the nationalistic Liberals is reflected in the struggle for control of education. The members of the clergy, strongly entrenched in the lives of the people by tradition and by religion, continued to exert great control under various administrations. The Liberals were equally determined to strengthen lay education directed toward building a strong national unity.

With frequent changes of political direction, progress was slow and uneven, and indeed, often nonexistent. However, some milestones should be noted: the First National Educational Conference in 1916, the first retirement laws in 1923, vacation institutes in 1926, publication of textbooks by the government in 1926, labor laws for women and children in 1928, the first Educational Congress in 1930, the first national program of studies in 1932, the first national salary schedule in 1932, and attention to rural schools on a national scale in 1934. Normal schools had also been established in the outlying provinces before 1911. Other important schools founded by various administrations were the Espejo School in 1915 in Quito, the Rita Lucumberry Normal School in 1917 in Guayaquil, the Manuel J. Calle Normal School in 1927 in Cuenca, the 24th of May High School (girls) in 1934 in Quito, and the Polytechnic Institute in 1935 in Quito.[7]

In summary, it can be said that fundamental characteristics of the history of education in Ecuador are the subservience of education to the political scene, lack of consistent programs based on long-range goals, dissension between Church and State over the control of education, and financial support at frequently changing levels. Although education was many times served by sincere and dedicated men, their work was often discarded by those who followed them. Progress has been slow and has not kept pace with the challenges of the twentieth century.

MAJOR PROBLEMS

Ecuador is a country whose past cannot be separated from its present. The prehistoric and the historic are two contrasting streams which exist side by side and effect a set of traditions and mores unique to Ecuador. The Indian tills the soil on the mountain slopes or weaves at his loom using methods inherited from the Incas. The Ecuadorian feels a close tie with Spain, conquerors and destroyers of the Incan Empire in 1533. Ecuador's language is Spanish, the religion is predominately Catholic, and the traditions and customs are inherited, in large part, from the mother country. Yet all Ecuadorians glow with pride over the achievement of their independence in 1822, and they are intensely nationalistic since they withdrew from the Federation "Gran Colombia" in 1830 to initiate their own government.

Ecuador is a country of magnificent potential and startling contrasts. Astride the equator, the source

6. Emilio Uzcategui, *Paginas de cultura y educación*, p. 139.
7. *Ibid.*, pp. 7-80.

of its name, its geographical position and its varying levels of altitude make it possible to raise almost every agricultural product known to man. Yet its economy, although extremely sound in late 1969, is virtually limited to exportation of bananas, coffee, and cacao. On the other hand, the government must sometimes be concerned over the possible shortage of rice, a basic foodstuff for most of the people.

Since the time of the Spanish conquest, the white Creole has assumed the role of ownership and leadership formerly held by the Spanish grandees. Ownership of lands has been concentrated in the hands of a few. There have been the rich and the poor; the latter, subservient in the role of *huasipungueros* (tenant farmers) have generally been ignored in programs of education and social betterment.

There are also problems of sectionalism and of race. The port city of Guayaquil, a thriving, bustling, modern metropolis, represents the low-lying coastal areas which produce bananas. Guayaquil wants more prominence in the affairs of state because it is supporting the country's rapidly improving economy. Quito, a charming city of colonial flavor and Spanish formality, holds the reins of government. Sectionalism was fomented in the early days by lack of transportation and inadequate communication. Though the Air Age was an immediate solution on the physical side, it served to make more apparent the inequalities in the various sections of the country; indeed, little attention had been given over the years to outlying provinces. The racial makeup of the masses in the coastal area is ethnically white, Indian, and Negro; in the sierras, there are few Negroes. In temperament the coastal people are more volatile than those in the high country; and their lesser importance in the political scene often makes Guayaquil the focal point of uprisings.

Ecuador is still an agricultural country where only recently small industries have been initiated under the sponsorship of the United States Agency for International Development. Great masses of Indians are still content to live in mud huts and till small plots of land under the protection of the landowner. They resist, to some degree, efforts to move them into better living quarters; such housing projects have been initiated in several rural areas, and Peace Corps workers report little initial enthusiasm on the part of the prospective owners. Mechanization on a large scale is rare; there is no local production of farm and industrial equipment. Isolation of Ecuador together with isolation of provinces within the country itself delayed the transitional changes needed to face the challenges of a modern industrialized world.

A very high illiteracy rate among the masses of Indians has been an important factor in resistance to change. In addition, the Indians are divided into several important groups, Otovalans, Salasacans, Colorados, and others, which have contact with civilization although they continue to live in closely-knit units. Other Indian groups, the Jivaros and the Aucas, are uncivilized. Of the Indian languages, Quechua is the most important, and for all, Spanish is a foreign language. Long years of subjection to the domination of the Creole ruling class has made the Indian humble, unsure, suspicious of the motives of the government, and highly resistant to change.[8]

The mestizo, a member of the lower economic level, is a laborer, a mason, brick-layer, gardener, servant, janitor, a person who works with his hands. As a class the mestizos do not enjoy social prestige. Some have risen to a slightly higher social by becoming small tradesmen, seamstresses and tailors, mechanics, electricians, and members of other trades where some degree of skill must be obtained through training. This second group, although financially better off than the first, still ranks low in a social sense. Teachers, office workers, lesser government employees, members of the Armed Forces, owners of small businesses and small industries represent the middle class which is presently struggling to establish itself in leadership. The prestige professions are medicine, law, engineering, architecture, and government.

Economic pressure at the lower social levels makes these groups an easy prey to promises of aspiring politicians. With little to lose, they are ready and willing to foment any change which promises some relief from their impoverished state. They do not understand political systems, but they do understand and want some of the benefits of education, material possessions, and freedom from want. These are the people who loved Franklin D. Roosevelt and who worshipped John Kennedy, placing small paper flags on their homes to show their grief after his death. But just as easily they are misled by the leaders of Communism, and they represent a genuine hazard for political stability.

GOALS OF EDUCATION

In July, 1963, just when it seemed that the attainment of most goals had receded into the realm of improbability, the respective heads of the Armed Forces assumed control of the government. Immediately, the Military issued a decree outlawing Communism. With internal political stability once reestablished, appointments to cabinet posts were made. Under the present system, the Military Junta holds the executive power and the legislative power, and the judicial power remains in control of the Supreme Court. The Military Junta has, with broad vision and sound goals, sought to solve many pressing problems. The economy of the country has been strengthened, and the value of the sucre, the local monetary unit, has increased its buying power by 20 percent. Loans and technical assistance have been secured from the United States to build roads, improve agricultural

8. Segundo B. Maiguashea, *El indio, corebro y corazon de America*, pp. 84-90.

methods, promote low-cost housing, provide basic utilities for the masses, organize small industries, assist in educational reform at all levels, improve communication within the country, and other needed reforms. Of all the special decrees issued by the Military Junta, none is more important than the Agrarian Reform Act of early October, 1964, a decree which firmly outlines the Junta's concern for the masses at the lower economic levels. A most significant statement which incorporates the basic philosophy was made by the Military Junta on October 10, 1964:

It is necessary to transform the institutions of the country, and it is necessary to effect a (social) revolution which will make a complete turn away from the past. The State must become an instrument of service for the majority, not groups or special social circles. . . . Let us make reality that which we have been longing for during several generations of this century, a new country where there is for all a little more justice and equality.[9]

In a system of planned economy motivated by humanitarian impulses and practical approaches, education plays an important part in the present and the future. Licenciado Humberto Vacas Gómez, in 1964 Minister of Education, supported by the Military Junta and with the assistance of administrators, teachers, representatives of the press, business, agriculture, artisans, and other national organizations, formulated a ten-year plan for the development of national progress based on needs in all areas. Licenciado Vacas believed that the school must render to society an accounting for the preparation of youth in the following areas:

1. The field of employment, with its socio-economic consequences for the individual and the country.
2. The area of life at the sociological level which extends from the individual to that of participation in government.
3. The area concerning the individual in all of its physical, moral, and cultural aspects.[10]

Educators must use the following criteria in their planning and subsequent evaluation:

1. A maximum use of human resources.
2. Parallel development and integration of education and economic development.
3. Harmonization of the cultural and practical facets of education.[11]

A practical application of Ecuador's philosophy can be seen in the following goals:

1. To re-organize elementary education as follows: provide six years, not four, for all children, improve teacher preparation and in-service training, improve supervision, re-orient the programs of study toward the fulfillment of environmental needs, improve special services (lunches, health, clothing, and scholarships), and provide textbooks, supplies, and teaching aids.

2. To re-organize secondary education as follows: aid in the formation of a middle class composed of potential employers as well as employees, broaden the programs so that there may be greater mobility among various types of employment, give opportunity for selection between careers of either short or long-term preparation, provide for more guidance in career selection, emphasize active participation and experimentation, and reduce the number of failures and drop-outs.[12]

3. To re-organize higher education as follows: structure a plan, educational, scientific, technical, and cultural, which will better meet the needs of Ecuadorian youth, coordinate the program with that of the secondary level, re-define the duties and responsibilities of all personnel, and limit the rights of students to participation in university affairs, not interference in affairs of state.[13]

4. To re-organize adult education programs as follows: provide literacy programs, first, second, and third levels within the framework of a structured program designed to help the adult complete his elementary education, organize rural curricula, health, agriculture, home management, recreation, and citizenship for Indian communities, provide professional and technical training for workers, artisans, and other types of workers at the low economic level, provide cultural programs through correspondence, night school, radio and institutes for young and old, and give special attention to maladjusted young people.[14]

The budget for the academic year 1963-1964, $21,718,445 (390.932.000 sucres) was the highest in national history and represented almost 15 percent over the previous year's appropriation. By its own effort, the Ministry constructed seventy-nine elementary and secondary schools during that year. Other buildings were constructed under the terms of a tripartite agreement whose participants were the National Government, the local Municipality, and the United States Agency for International Development. By their own efforts, provinces (states), municipalities, local communities, and private schools have also built new units. Construction, in addition to elementary and secondary levels, has been extended to include other levels, such as five technical institutes, the new Agronomy Center at the Central University, the University of Loja, the Quito Polytechnic, and a number of normal schools.[15]

The Ministry has made notable progress in initiating and extending services in other areas: (1) in

9. *El Comercio*, Quito, Ecuador, October 10, 1964, pp. 1, 5.
10. Humberto Vacas Gómez, *Informes de labores del Ministerio de Educación Pública*, Quito, Ecuador, p. 55.
11. *Ibid.*, p. 56.
12. *Ibid.*, pp. 81-83.
13. *Ibid.*, pp. 104-106.
14. *Ibid.*, pp. 106-108.
15. *Ibid.*, pp. 5-8.

cooperation with CARE the school lunch program has been augmented, (2) health units have been added, (3) 1,653 additional teachers have been hired, (4) special institutes have been held for teachers with sub-standard credentials as well as in-service training for other personnel, (5) two pilot night schools have been created in Quito and Guayaquil with both elementary and secondary programs, (6) pilot schools have been selected to demonstrate the new programs of study, (7) equipment for technical schools amounting to $1,142,670 has been purchased; USAID contributed an additional sum, $122,594, (8) courses for supervisors have been organized, (9) support of physical education and music programs, competitive sports, and folk festivals has been enthusiastic, and (10) 1500 centers for adult literacy programs have been initiated; and instructional materials and student supplies have been provided in each case.[16]

In addition to the technical and economic support of the United States Agency for International Development, UNESCO has maintained a special mission in Ecuador since 1963 to aid in the literacy campaign, formation of the national program of education with special emphasis on technical curricula, teacher-training programs, and special studies in marine, biology, astronomy, the dramatic arts, and library organization. The Fulbright Program and the Andean Mission also have cooperated with the Ministry.

Local organizations which cooperate closely with the Ministry of Education are the Ministry of Social Welfare, National Council for the Promotion of Literacy, National Council for Economic Planning and Coordination, and state and city governments.

Long-range planning is not concerned alone with the correction of problems of the present but also with the problems, caused by a population explosion, which will bring a big burden of the absorption of youth into areas of employment. Table 2 shows projected numbers of students to be educated.[17]

TABLE 2

Projected Number of Students
To Be Educated

Year	Elementary	Secondary
1965-1966	865,000	113,814
1966-1967	892,000	124,583
1967-1968	920,000	136,026
1968-1969	948,000	148,141
1969-1970	973,000	160,930
1970-1971	1,000,000	174,392
1971-1972	1,037,000	188,528
1972-1973	1,076,000	203,336
1973-1974	1,103,000	218,817

It is believed that (beginning with approximately 87 percent in 1963-1964) increasing numbers of the possible elementary school population will actually register in school; by 1972 the percentage is projected to be 100 percent. Projected percentages are not available for the secondary school population. At both levels, the burden of education is to be borne by the government, municipalities, and private schools.[18]

Projected costs (in sucres) are indicated in Table 3.

TABLE 3

Projected Costs

Year	Elem. Personnel	Elem. Bldg. and Equipment	Sec. Personnel	Sec. Bldg. and Equipment
1965-1966	$ 15,370,000	$ 29,840,000	$ 6,651,840	$ 5,895,000
1966-1967	24,750,000	32,216,000	7,098,000	6,300,000
1967-1968	34,763,000	33,977,000	7,544,160	6,705,000
1968-1969	45,196,000	35,396,000	7,990,320	7,110,000
1969-1970	402,868,000	188,142,000	36,362,040	32,265,000
TOTAL	$530,075,000	$344,700,000	$71,852,040	$63,765,000

*Humberto Vacas Gómez, *Informes de labores del Ministerio de Educación Publica,* Quito, Ecuador, pp. 75, 77, 78, 105.

The literacy campaign, also scheduled for a ten-year period, proposes to reduce illiteracy from 44 percent in 1963 to approximately 34 percent in 1973 at a cost of 190,394,753 sucres for the entire program.[19]

The very serious problem of student failure at the various levels, repetition of the year, and drop-outs is one of preoccupation. Figures show that out of a determined number of students who enter the first grade of elementary, only 17 percent will be able to enter the first year of secondary; drop-out occurs every year. Also it has been shown that approximately 18 percent repeat the year; these students occupy space needed by other students. Figures for the secondary level show that 16.63 percent fail the year, 9.89 percent are drop-outs, and 11.36 percent repeat the year. Losses to the government and parents are thus severe, and the student is faced with the stigma of failure. The new curricula has been designed to solve some of these problems.[20]

In summary, it is evident that Ecuador's present plan of education is comprehensive in nature. Long-term goals have been determined, and there is evi-

16. *Ibid.,* pp. 57-61.
17. *Ibid.,* p. 72, p. 101.
18. *Ibid.,* p. 72.
19. *Ibid.,* p. 111.
20. *Ibid.,* p. 58, 60.

dence of practicality in making them a reality. The success of the program is linked to internal political stability and the level of economic development able to support the proposed budget planned for the next ten years. Sincere, dedicated men must labor at all levels to assure continuity of the program.

DESCRIPTION OF THE EDUCATIONAL SYSTEM

All education in Ecuador is controlled by the Ministry of Education. The Minister of Education, the Undersecretary of Education, and the Director General of Education are in command in that order. The Minister works directly with UNESCO, Point IV, and the National Scholarship Commission. The Undersecretary works with the National Council of Education and the Department of Educational Planning, public relations, printing, statistics, and other related areas. The Director General of Education has charge of the various sections, elementary, secondary, higher education, adult education, technical education, extension programs, and such special entities as the National Theater "Sucre," the Symphony Orchestra, the Ecuadorian Cultural Center (Casa de la Cultura), the National Library, the Astronomical Observatory, the Folklore Institute, the museums, and a radio station "Radio Nacional." There are also directors for each of the provinces, a position similar to that of State Superintendent of Public Instruction.

Educational facilities are provided at the kindergarten, elementary (six years), secondary (six years), and higher education levels. Kindergartens are limited to cities, and the minimum age is five years. Elementary education is provided in both urban and rural areas and differs in curriculum according to the need. Secondary education, almost always divided by sexes, is of three types: The first program, in classic or modern humanities, leads to the *bachillerato,* a term not easily translated since the curriculum includes philosophy, psychology, and economics before graduation. The second program is one of technical specialization. The third program is devoted to teacher preparation in normal schools, again of two types. University education is devoted to career preparation, medicine, nursing, law, engineering, architecture, economics, education, and humanities. The polytechnic institutes are limited to fundamental preparation in the sciences and mathematics. In addition, specialized study is provided in the Bi-national Center, the Alliance Française, the American Junior College, and numerous other small institutions.

One degree awarded at the university level is the *licenciatura,* approximately equivalent to a Master's Degree, and is awarded after five or six years of study, depending on the major field. The doctorate may be secured after six to eight years of study, depending on the field. Institutions giving specialized study at the higher levels give a variety of titles; the American Junior College awards the Associate of Science Degree.

Final examinations at all levels, kindergarten, elementary, and secondary, are given each year by delegates named by the Ministry of Education. In addition, sixth graders must take a secondary entrance examination, and twelfth-grade students must present oral examinations in the presence of Ministry delegates. Students also must take university entrance examinations. If a student fails one subject during any level, he must repeat all subjects listed on the official program. He must secure forty-five points out of a maximum eighty in order to pass; he does, however, have a chance to repeat the final examination just previous to the opening of the following new school year. Beginning at the secondary level, all promotions and records must be recorded on tax-bearing official paper.

The academic year is arranged on a trimestral basis. The school year in the high country is from October through July; in the coastal areas inclement weather makes it necessary to schedule school from April through January. Some unsuccessful attempts have been made to coordinate the school year, but climatic factors have made it impossible.

Schools are government-supported, municipality-supported, and privately supported. Among the private schools are those organized and supported by religious groups, mostly Catholic orders, and others bi-national in nature, such as the American School of Quito, the German School, and the French School. Since private schools do not enjoy state support, parents must pay registration fees, monthly tuition, and must purchase all texts and school supplies. Despite the fundamental interest in national problems of education manifested by Ecuadorian leaders in all areas, they still prefer to educate their children in private schools.

Ecuadorian education has been strongly influenced by Europe with respect to its curriculum content. Typical curricula and distribution of classtime are shown in Table 4.

The official Ministry-approved secondary curriculum now includes a three-year program of basic studies.[21] (See p. 353.)

After the third year, majors to be selected are Mathematics-Physics, Biology, Social Science, Classic Humanities, Literature, Music, or Fine Arts.

In 1964 the universities organized a cycle of basic studies for first-year students, thus delaying the selection of the major; previously, there was no possibility of transferring credits from one college to another. Under the new system, students will not be forced to repeat subjects already completed, and they will have more time to reach a decision concerning a major. Three United States universities, Pittsburgh, St. Louis, and Houston, financially sponsored by United States

---

21. *Ibid.,* p. 95.

TABLE 4

Elementary Schedule*

Subject	1st	2nd	3rd	4th	5th	6th
Reading	10	10	6	6	4	4
Penmanship	5	3	2	2	1	1
Grammar, spelling	-	2	4	4	6	6
Composition	-	2	4	4	4	4
Arithmetic	10	10	10	10	10	10
Study of immediate surroundings	10	10	-	-	-	-
Civics (city, state, nation)	-	-	10	10	-	-
Geography	-	-	-	-	3	3
History	-	-	-	-	3	3
Science	-	-	-	-	5	5
Health education	2	2	1	1	1	1
Music, dancing	5	5	2	2	2	2
Dramatic play	5	5	2	2	2	2
Drawing	5	5	2	2	2	2
Practical arts	5	5	10	10	10	10
Social adjustment, school activities	5	5	5	5	5	5
Free activity	3	1	1	1	1	1
Physical education	-	-	3	3	3	3

NOTE: Numbers are number of periods per week; each period is 25 minutes in length.

*Humberto Vacas Gómez, *Informes de labores del Ministerio de Educación Publica*, Quito, Ecuador, p. 80.

Classification	Subject	Periods Weekly		
		7th	8th	9th
Basic	Spanish	5	5	5
	Mathematics	5	5	5
	Foreign language	3	3	3
General culture	Natural sciences	2	-	-
	Physics, chemistry and natural sciences	-	3	-
	Physics, chemistry	-	-	3
	History of Ecuador, America, World	2	2	2
	Geography of Ecuador, America, World	2	2	2
	Health, physical education	2	2	2
Social activities	Clubs, music, art, archeology, hobbies	1	1	1
Electives	Agriculture, industrial arts, secretarial subjects, arts and crafts, homemaking, music, Latin	10	10	10
Extra hours to be used at the discretion of each school to augment hours of the above.		4	3	3

organizations, are providing technical advice concerning reorganization of higher education.

The Ministry of Social Welfare has control of several types of institutions for minors which incorporate educational programs. There are day nurseries, one group for infants of one day of age to three years, and another group for children from three to six years. Orphanages, one for each of the two sexes, accept children from six to twelve years of age. A sanitarioum accepts children between the same age levels who are ill or undernourished; a staff of doctors and nurses is in charge. A deaf-mute school in Quito accepts children of both sexes on a boarding-school basis from eight to eighteen years of age. There are three schools of correction, also with boarding facilities; two are for girls and one is for boys. Students from twelve to eighteen years of age are taught home-making skills and agriculture together with a program of education. Three work camps for boys from twelve to eighteen years of age have programs of rehabilitation; boys in these camps are wards of the Juvenile Court. The state also supports two special homes through which all cases must pass for observation, psychological studies, and health examinations.[22]

The Ministry of National Defense has charge of the Military School and the Engineering Institute, the latter for special training in Communications, Artillery, Cavalry, Infantry, and other related areas and with special emphasis on officer training. The Armed Forces also have other schools, one for training pilots, another for aviation mechanics, and another for training navy personnel.[23]

The Ministry of Agriculture controls a School of Agriculture, of secondary level, in Ambato. The course of study has both general studies and technical subjects; in addition, the students are given practical experience in crop selection, rotation, care, and harvesting. Students who successfully complete this program have an opportunity to continue their education in the College of Agronomy at the Central University. There are also several rural schools with agricultural programs, one with the express purpose of promoting the production of coffee, another to emphasize tropical crops, and a third to train hacienda overseers.[24]

Illiteracy is a major problem in Ecuador. In 1962, out of the total population of 2,478,133 persons fifteen years of age and above, 32.69 percent were unable to read the newspaper or to sign their names. It is well known that great masses of rural citizens have had no schooling. Only in isolated instances are efforts made by landowners to provide schooling for the children of the workers; one of the outstanding examples of such effort is the Zuleta School located on the hacienda of Mr. Gale Plaza, ex-President of Ecuador, and in part financed by him personally. Even in urban areas many children never enter school; every year the newspaper publishes pictures of children looking wistfully through the gate of an over-crowded school. Others who do enter may finish one or two grades

22. Leonidas García: *Panorama y orientaciones de la educación ecuatoriana*, pp. 54-56.
23. *Ibid.*, pp. 57-61.
24. *Ibid.*, pp. 62-67.

and then drop, either because the family cannot afford a book, notebook, and pencil, or because the child must help at home.

A survey made by the National Planning Commission in 1956 showed that 2,851,038 inhabitants had a monthly income of 142 sucres (approximately seven dollars); during recent years this figure has increased, but at the same time, it has been offset by increases in the cost of living. Under such circumstances, education is a luxury these families, always large in number, must forego to provide the barest necessities. It is estimated that approximately 20 percent of the children of school age do not enroll. Of the number enrolling there are many losses from grade to grade: 50 percent to second, 49 percent go to third, 37 percent to fourth, 25 percent to fifth, and 21 percent to sixth. Only 17 percent of the original first-grade enrollment finish sixth grade.[25]

Secondary education is a luxury and a special privilege. For example, in 1961-1962, 608,814 children were enrolled in the elementary schools. At the secondary level the same year, there were 78,550 students enrolled in the academic high schools. Given the need for special materials, in themselves costly, together with the loss of earning power of a member of a large family, it is understandable that the registration rate is low.

If a student succeeds in finishing secondary education, he finds it easier to continue at the university level. Classes are held in the early morning and late evening hours, and a student can thus seek employment during the ordinary workday. Compared with university fees in the United States, yearly costs are very low and range between 65 and 100 dollars, not including books.

Teachers at the elementary level are generally products of the normal schools, special six-year secondary schools. Secondary teachers generally have university training in the School of Education or are specialists who have graduated from other sections of the university. Teachers may apply directly for employment in private schools. There is a national salary schedule, and by a special decree in August 20, 1963, the schedule was made effective. Placement on the salary schedule depends on preparation and years of experience. Steps on the salary schedule are on a four-year basis. A beginning teacher will earn twice as much salary as a domestic, approximately the same as a lower-level office worker, less than a chauffeur, and one-third as much as a bi-lingual secretary. After fifteen years of experience, a teacher will earn as much as a bi-lingual secretary, or a governmental employee in a minor administrative capacity. Physicians, dentists, self-employed engineers, skilled tradesmen, and businessmen may make five or six times the salary of a teacher; higher earning ability also comes much more rapidly to these groups. Despite these unfavorable comparisons, young people still feel that teaching is an attractive profession be-cause of the limited time on duty; also, for some it has a very valuable prestige factor, and the time spent in preparation, especially at the elementary level, is relatively short. A teacher, if immediately employed following graduation from the normal school, may continue with a program of higher education while employed. Also, the local Social Security program has many worthwhile features, medical care, hospitalization, loan privileges for homes, burial expenses, excellent pension systems, and financial support of widows and orphans. It must be noted that members of the top professions are generally engaged in teaching, usually at the secondary and university levels, for a few hours per week. Some are motivated by a desire to have special privileges with respect to tuition, but the vast majority are greatly concerned with the improvement of education in the country and want to help in the general effort. Generally speaking, teachers do not leave the profession for more lucrative positions; rather, they look for extra employment to increase their income. Also, husbands and wives both work, a very important change in a culture where wives formerly remained at home. Teachers, by combining two incomes, are purchasing modest homes, automobiles, radios, televisions, refrigerators, generally on credit; they educate their children in prestige schools and enjoy modest vacation excursions within the country. Teachers constitute a vigorous, hard-working, public-spirited group at the middle-class level, a dynamic potential in the future development of Ecuador.

Past efforts to form a Teachers' Union have been unsuccessful. Rather, teachers meet on local, provincial, and national levels under the Ministry of Education control. If teachers on any level feel that a problem must be solved, an elected commission visits the Minister to explain the problem. Often individual prominent schools act as leaders in such action. In addition, each secondary school has an elected commission, composed of three members, which can act in an official capacity in presenting petitions. The national press is interested in education and gives excellent coverage to such requests. Thus teachers in general are always informed and can support seemingly isolated efforts.

PERTINENT DATA

According to the 1962 census figures, the population of Ecuador numbered 4,539,650 persons. Of this total, 50 percent reside in the highlands (Sierra), 44.5 percent live in the lowlands (Costa), and 6.5 percent live in the inland lowlands on the eastern side of the Andes Mountains. The total population of the Galapagos Islands, a sector usually treated alone, is approximately 2,000 persons. A study of the

25. Humberto Vacas Gómez, op. cit., p. 59.

various areas shows that, generally speaking, much of Ecuador is rural in nature:[26]

Section	Urban	Rural
Highlands	31%	69%
Coastal lowlands	40%	60%
Inland lowlands	11%	89%
Galapagos Islands	——	100%

Since a large percentage of the population is concentrated in rural areas, the emphasis on agricultural pursuits is great:

Section	Agriculture	Cattle
Highlands	69.3%	30.7%
Coastal lowlands	91.2%	8.8%
Inland lowlands	14.8%	25.2%

Figures also show that only 15.62 percent of the land suitable for cultivation is presently in use; 84.38 percent of the land remains untilled. Distribution of uncultivated land according to sections is as follows:

Section	Land suitable for cultivation
Highlands	14.75%
Coastal lowlands	16.04%
Inland lowlands	69.18%

Despite the heavy emphasis on agriculture, some industries have acquired important status in Ecuador. Life Laboratories, a pharmaceutical house established in 1940, now exports 60 percent of its medicinal products to Central and South American countries. A plywood manufacturing company exports the same percentage to other countries. The fishing industry, particularly shrimp and tuna, has made steady growth in production for national consumption and for export. A number of factories produce excellent woolen and cotton materials, still largely for national use. The production of rope and sacking has recently made great strides. Sally Victor's visit in 1964 provided great impetus in the production of straw hats, commonly attributed to Panama. One of the industries which has long been in operation is the production of beer, largely for national consumption, of excellent quality, and a source of important income for the national government.

Industries established since 1963 and 1964 are cement, tires, ceramics, glass, new sugar refining processes, chemicals, refrigerators, gas stoves, minor agricultural implements, and assembly of radios and automobiles. These new industries still produce for national consumption, and, for the most part, in insufficient quantity to supply the needs of the country.

Electrification of Ecuador has proceeded slowly; there is still insufficient production in most of the country.

Roads and highways total 18,000 kilometers; only 12 percent is paved with asphalt, and only 40 percent is considered to be first class, that is, paved with asphalt or cobblestones. There are two principal highways from north to south, the Pan-American Highway, which crosses the highland area from Colombia to Peru, and the coast highway, still unfinished, which unites the lowland provinces. These two highways are linked by a series of cross-country highways, some still in the process of construction:[27]

1. Quito-Santo Domingo-Esmeraldas
2. Quito-Santo Domingo-Quevedo-Guayaquil
3. Latacunga-Quevedo-Manta
4. Cuenca-Guayaquil
5. Cuenca-Machala
6. Ambato-Puyo-Tena
7. Cuenca-Limón
8. Quito-Baeza

Railways total 1,100 kilometers the principal line is from Quito to Guayaquil, a route of great scenic beauty and engineering achievement.[28]

Ecuador has the following commercial airports: two international, ten classified as second rate, and fifteen as third rate. Several international lines provide jet service to Quito and Guayaquil. Ecuador has one company which provides international service and several companies for local service.

Communication within the country is via telephone and telegraph. Cable service and telephone communication via International Radio connect Ecuador with other countries. The government as well as private organizations maintain both types of services.

Automobiles are, for the most part, strictly limited by importation regulations. Trucks, pick-ups, and closed panel delivery units are the vehicles considered to be necessary to the general economy.

Mining is limited to the following: lignite, coal, ochre, sulphur, clay for pottery, and gypsum. Gold, formerly produced in quantity by two United States companies, is now reduced to 4,000 ounces, troy weight. The production of silver is also greatly reduced.

Ecuador exports primarily the following food products to the United States: bananas, cacao, coffee, shrimp, and sugar.

Studies of illegitimacy show high rates in the tropical coastal areas and elsewhere. However, these figures do not reveal the number of illegitimate children who died at birth or the number of abortions. It is also necessary to remember that according to Ecuadorian law, recognition by the father removes

26. Jaime Arturo Chiriboga, unpublished studies made by senior students of the American School under the direction of Dr. Jaime Arturo Chiriboga, professor of economic history and geography of Ecuador in the American School and Central University of Quito.

27. *Ibid.*

28. *Ibid.*

illegitimacy; it is not necessary for the two parents to marry.

One of the gravest problems confronting Ecuador over the years has been the loss of territory:

Event and Date	Size of Ecuador	Territory Lost
Royal Charter of 1563	1,200,000 sq. km.	
Royal Charter of 1740	1,107,290 sq. km.	130,000 sq. km.
Act of 1777	967,290 sq. km.	140,000 sq. km.
Gran Colombia, 1824	886,000 sq. km.	81,290 sq. km.
Pedemonte-Mosquera Treaty of 1830	705,000 sq. km.	181,000 sq. km.
Tobar-Riobranco Treaty of 1904	645,000 sq. km.	60,000 sq. km.
Muñez Vernaza-Suarez Treaty of 1922	470,000 sq. km.	175,000 sq. km.
Río de Janeiro Protocolo of 1942	270,000 sq. km.	200,000 sq. km.

The present size of Ecuador is 270,000 square kilometers; this figure, when compared with that of the size allowed by Royal Charter in 1563, shows a decrease of 77.5 percent. The effect of loss of territory is serious, both with respect to the economy of the country and to the morale of its citizens. The last decision, formulated in Río de Janeiro in 1942, has never been accepted as just; rather, there is still great bitterness and disheartenment on the part of all nationals at all levels.[29]

In summary, Ecuador is a small country whose agricultural economy places it in a position of great disadvantage in any program of competition with other highly industrialized nations. With the economic and technical assistance of the United States, Ecuador is making a great effort to foment industries, provide public utilities in all sections, and improve transportation to all areas. At the same time, exports to other countries are increasing each year, thus providing a balance in the general economic structure.

QUALITIES OF AN EDUCATED MAN

Leonidas García enumerates some desired end products of education, "love of liberty, respect for others, devotion to truth, love of work, respect for and appreciation of law, care of one's health, and love for one's country." He also states that education must prepare one to meet the needs of his time, and that in future years action will be more valuable than erudition, deeds of more value than beautiful words.[30]

Julio Larrea speaks of the essential qualities of an educated man, the education of his esthetic tastes, of his moral standards, of his intellectual initiative, and of his manual skills. "He is a solid personality with purposes and the will to achieve them with sincerity and courage." In order to be classified as an educated man "it is necessary to develop esthetic tastes, the spirit of observation, intellectual penetration and initiative, moral sensibility, and the comprehension of others."[31]

Emilio Uzcátegui writes, "An educated man must be versed in philosophy, science, art, literature, and technology, for these occupy the position of greatest importance; they are subjects both useful and creative, and they develop moral values which are, after all, our most precious possession.[32]

BIBLIOGRAPHY

ADOUM, JORGE ENRIQUE. "Cultural Facets," *Ecuador, Andean Mosaic*, Rolf Blomberg, ed. Stockholm, Sweden: Huge Gebers Förlag, 1952.

ALEXANDER, ROBERT J. *Today's Latin America*. New York: Doubleday and Co., 1962.

CHIRIBOGA, JAIME ARTURO. Unpublished studies made by senior students of the American School of Quito, Ecuador, 1964.

————. "El Comercio," a daily newspaper, Carlos Mantilla, ed.

GARCÍA, Leonidas. *Panorama y orientaciones de la educación ecuatoriana*. Quito: Casa de la Cultura, 1951.

JOHNSON, JOHN J. *Political Change in Latin America; The Emergence of the Middle Sector*. Stanford, California: Stanford University Press, 1958.

LARREA, JULIO. *La educación nueva*. Quito: Imprenta Ministerio de Educación, 1951.

MAIGUASHCA, SEGUNDO B. *El indio, cerebro y corazón de América* Quito: Editorial Fray Jodoco Ricke, 1949.

MURGUEYTIE, REINALDO, *Cerro arriba y río abajo*. Quito: Casa de la Cultura, 1959.

————. *Tierra, cultura y libertad*. Quito: Talleres Gráfices Minerva, 1961.

TOBAR, JULIO. *Apuntes para la historia de la educación laica en el Ecuador*. Imprenta del Ministerio del Tesoro, 1948.

UZCÁTEGUI, EMILIO. *Páginas de cultura y educacion*. Quito: Imprenta de la Universidad Central, 1953.

VACAS GÓMEZ, HUMBERTO. *Informe de labores, Ministerio de Educación Publica, Julio 11 del '63 a Julio del '64*. Quito: Talleres Gráficas de Educación, 1964.

29. *Ibid.*
30. Leonidas García, *op. cit.*, p. 152.
31. Julio Larrea, *La educación nueva*, pp. 218-224.
32. Emilio Uzcátegui, *op. cit.*, p. 23.

GUATEMALA

Robert V. MacVean

INTRODUCTION

The Republic of Guatemala is located in the northern part of Central America with Mexico on the north and El Salvador and Honduras on the south. With altitudes from sea level to about 15,000 feet, Guatemala has a varied climate ranging from tropical to cool. Temperatures range from forty to eighty degrees in the highlands and from seventy-seven to eighty-six degrees in the lowlands. There are two seasons, rainy and dry. From November through April little or no rain falls in most of Guatemala. In the rainy season, May to October, the rainfall is heavy in most parts with annual precipitation ranging from fifty to one hundred sixty-five inches.

About 60 percent of the population is indigenous (Maya Indian). According to recent estimates, about 70 percent of the total population is illiterate. In some rural areas, as many as 90 percent are illiterate. According to the 1964 census there were 4,278,241 inhabitants in Guatemala. The area of Guatemala is 50,647 square miles.

Agriculture is Guatemala's principal source of wealth, with coffee, bananas, cotton, and essential oils the chief products. Export of these agricultural products is the main source of dollar exchange to Guatemala. Most manufactured products and all heavy industrial items are imported, and importation represents the main dollar outflow from Guatemala. There is an increasing development of small and medium industry, encouraged in part by the Central American Common Market, within which goods manufactured in the area are distributed without customs duties. Automobile tires, paint products, plastics, paper, chemicals, textiles, pharmaceuticals, and other light industrial products are now produced in Guatemala and distributed throughout the Central American area.

There are two petroleum refineries to supply part of the Guatemalan market. Guatemala does not have any oil or coal resources, so far as is known. Lead is exported from Guatemala in small amounts and a nickel mine is in development.

HISTORY OF EDUCATION IN GUATEMALA

Education Before the Spanish Conquest

Information concerning education among the Maya Indian group, the original population found in Guatemala by the Spanish explorers in the early sixteenth century, is scarce. The highly developed culture of the Mayas, the most significant pre-Colombian culture in this hemisphere, clearly indicates that there was transmission of knowledge and accumulation of experience. It is not certain, however, to what extent formal education was a part of this process.

Most of the reference works on the civilization of the Maya, including Morley's well-known work *The Ancient Maya*, make only incidental references to education; none has a complete chapter on the subject.

It is probable that education was incidental, personal, and non-systematized. Probably it was related to agriculture, astronomy, mathematics, and crafts and was intended to perpetuate knowledge for an elite of religious and political leaders, to prepare craftsmen, and to maintain customs. Certainly, knowledge of the written language of the Maya was restricted to the very few. The high priest had specific responsibility for teaching language, genealogy, ceremonial rites, astronomy, and astronomical calculations for their accurate calendar to the religious elite. All education, in the home and outside it, was ruled by moral and religious considerations.

Several structures found at the Maya sites may have had something to do with education. Archeologists have given such designations as "nunnery quadrangle" to certain structures; just what the activities and objectives of these structures were, however, is not clear.

It is certain that there was no carry-over of the Maya education into the colonial period following the arrival of the Spaniards.

Education During the Colonial Period

Guatemala's educational system has its origin in the Spanish conquest of Central America in the early sixteenth century. Education during the colonial period was the responsibility of the Catholic Church, and the first school was established in 1534, mainly for educating the children of Spanish settlers; gradually, Indian children were taken into the school and more schools were created to prepare children for secondary and higher education. By 1575 the San Francisco Convent had established a school for religious studies.

In 1620 the first secondary school was established in Guatemala. The Jesuits established a school which had the right to confer degrees and professional licenses. Religious schools continued to grant degrees and to serve the purposes of a university until 1676 when the University of San Carlos was established. Education in Guatemala received great impetus during the seventeenth century from the founding of the University of San Carlos and the introduction of printing in Guatemala.

Education in the original University of San Carlos was aimed at supplying trained people for the professions of theology, medicine, and law. The University of Salamanca in Spain provided most of the professors, and instruction was in Latin with the exception of certain classes which were taught in Spanish.

By 1796 specialized guild schools were established for training in mathematics and drafting. A society was established for the instruction of workers and the improvement of arts, sciences, letters, agriculture, commerce, industry, and education. The society attempted to reorganize the guilds and to provide specific education for craftsmen. Instruction in mathematics and in arts was intended to improve the skills of the workers in the various handicrafts. Girls were taught to work in textiles.

Education in Guatemala From 1821 to 1871

After achieving independence from Spain in 1821, the Republic of Guatemala attempted to increase the emphasis on education. The first Government agency with responsibilities for education was the Academy of Studies, which had jurisdiction over elementary, secondary, and higher education. In 1835, the first statute of primary education was issued. Provision was made for the organization of public and private schools and for the instruction of the indigenous population. For the first time the principles of obligatory free education were announced.

In the same year, the first normal school was established but was of short duration due to political changes. During most of the nineteenth century, the University of San Carlos continued to function as it had during the colonial period.

The objectives of obligatory and free education were not achieved during the nineteenth century. Most of the population was illiterate and only a small fraction of school-age children attended regularly; women particularly did not attend school and most of them did not know how to read and write. The women who dedicate themselves to activities requiring reading and writing were rarities. From 1821 to 1871, there were a few public and private elementary schools and a somewhat unsystematized secondary education, a university based on its colonial organization, and a small or non-existent budget for public education.

Education From 1871 to 1944

With the triumph of the liberal revolution of General Justo Rufino Barrios in 1871, again great emphasis was put on education. Normal schools were established in the capital and in five departments; the colonial university was converted into separate professional schools. Renewed emphasis was placed on the principles of obligatory free education. The schools were made the responsibility of the state, and separation of church and state was established. Academic freedom was accepted as a principle.

In 1875 the first organic law of public elementary instruction was issued. Education was made obligatory to fourteen years of age. Differentiations among students on the basis of social class, nationality, and color were to be eradicated.

Educational policy changed radically from government to government during the latter part of the nineteenth century and the early part of the twentieth. Each succeeding government developed its own educational policy. During some governments the educational system was militarized. From 1871 on, education in Guatemala was the responsibility of the central government through a Ministry of Education. The general characteristics of education have been those typical of the centralized system, in which all authority over schools is vested in one department of the executive branch of the government.

Elementary schools have usually been for boys and girls separately, and the secondary schools have been of two kinds: (1) the normal schools for the training of teachers and (2) the public institutes to provide the academic secondary curriculum required for admission to the University of San Carlos.

The University of San Carlos was also the responsibility of the central government and was administered by the Ministry of Education. Until 1945 the rector of the University was appointed by the chief executive.

A military school was established in 1872. A national agricultural school and a commercial school were established in 1880. Gradually other schools were established at the secondary level for special training.

A popular university (Universidad Popular) was established as a private institution in 1923 and has been dedicated to night-school teaching of workers. It provides elementary and secondary instruction for adolescents and adults who otherwise would not be able to attend school.

Education From 1944 to 1965

The Guatemalan educational system began to take its present form in 1944. General Jorge Ubico was president of Guatemala from 1930 to 1944 at which time his government fell through popular revolution. The new government proceeded immediately to establish social security, to permit the organization of labor unions, to develop a labor code, and to introduce social legislation which, although revolutionary in Guatemala, had existed in some Latin American countries for a decade or more.

Fundamental changes in education also took place. The newly elected president in 1945, Dr. Juan José Arévalo, held a Ph.D. degree in education. New programs of study were put into effect in 1946-47. Many new school buildings were built, some of which were of the circular type called "Federation Schools," a design intended to promote progressive methods of teaching and school organization.

The academic program of the secondary school, *bachillerato,* was increased from four to five years in 1946. (Traditionally the secondary program had been five years, but was reduced to four a few years previously.) A two-six-five type of education was established and is still in effect: two years of pre-school for five- and six-year-old children (attendance not compulsory); first through sixth grades of the elementary school with compulsory attendance; five years of secondary education leading to the *bachillerato* diploma. The normal school provided teacher training during the last two secondary years as before, but there was an emphasis on progressive teaching methods in the elementary school. More attention was given to democratic procedure, and student government was encouraged at the secondary level. All secondary schools were de-militarized, for under the previous administration military training had been a part of secondary education for boys.

Half-day sessions were organized because of the scarcity of classrooms, and some of the schools even had three sessions per day, one in the morning, one in the afternoon, and one in the evening.

The first national salary schedule was put into effect in 1947, providing elementary school salaries ranging from $900 to $1,800. A full-time salary was earned by working the morning, afternoon, or evening session in an elementary school.

Great emphasis was immediately given by the Arévalo government to rural education. Literacy pro-

grams and ambulatory missions for the remote areas were organized.

Although there were great increases in the number of children attending school in the decade from 1944 to 1954, the rapidly increasing population caused the percent of attendance to remain more or less stable.

In 1955-56, new programs of study were issued for the elementary and secondary schools and a gradual reorganization of the secondary schools began, to be completed in 1961. Through this gradual reorganization plan, the first cycle of three years was made prerequisite to all terminal education programs, thus raising the level of general education from the sixth grade of the elementary school to the third year of the secondary school. Previously, students had gone from elementary school directly into special programs of commerce, bookkeeping, industrial arts, military training, and the like. Vocational and educational guidance services were established for the pre-vocational program. The last two years of the secondary school completed the college preparatory curriculum and permitted some selection of courses in accordance with the student's future plans.

In 1945, the University of San Carlos was granted autonomous status by the new constitution. A superior council made up of representatives of the ten faculties, the professional colleges of alumni, and the students became the governing board of the University. Thus, the faculties, the alumni, and the students had about equal representation in the superior council. The rector, the highest official of the university, and the deans of the faculties were elected every four years. Again the professional organizations, the faculties, and the students had about equal representation in elections.

Enrollments in the University have increased rapidly since 1946. Some diversification of professional training has been introduced.

In 1945 the Faculty of Humanities was established, within which the Department of Education for the preparation of secondary teachers was organized. Only a few degrees have been granted in education, but many teachers have achieved several years of professional and liberal arts training through part-time attendance at the university. About one-half of the secondary teachers of Guatemala have some university training.

THE GUATEMALAN EDUCATIONAL SYSTEM

The educational system in Guatemala consists of two years of pre-school, six years of elementary school, and five years of secondary school. Table 1 shows how the grades in Guatemala compare with those in the United States.

In both Guatemala and the United States the total number of years of education is thirteen. The two pre-school years in Guatemala are not compul-

TABLE 1

Grades in the Elementary and Secondary Schools of
Guatemala and the United States
By Ages

Age	Guatemala	United States
5	Párvulos	Kindergarten
6	Preparatoria	1st grade
7	1st grade	2nd grade
8	2nd grade	3rd grade
9	3rd grade	4th grade
10	4th grade	5th grade
11	5th grade	6th grade
12	6th grade	7th grade
13	1st bachillerato	8th grade
14	2nd bachillerato	9th grade
15	3rd bachillerato	10th grade
16	4th bachillerato	11th grade
17	5th bachillerato	12th grade

sory, but attendance is required in grades one through six. Children who have finished the elementary school in Guatemala have done work more or less the equivalent of the seventh grade in the United States.

The school year in Guatemala is from January through October and children are in attendance from 150 to 190 days per year. The school year is not dictated by the seasons, for it comprises five months of dry weather and five of rainy, but the vacation months of November and December, which are dry, do coincide with the coffee-picking season in certain areas of the country.

Elementary Education

As shown above, elementary education in Guatemala is divided into two phases totaling eight years, for children from five to twelve years of age.

Elementary Teachers

Elementary teachers are graduates of the normal school and some of them have advanced work at the Faculty of Humanities of the University of San Carlos. Normal school training is given at the secondary level. Secondary education for teachers was of five years' duration previous to 1961. In 1961, a sixth year was added, making the normal school program one year longer than the academic curriculum. A permanent certificate for teaching in the elementary schools is issued on completion of the program, at which point the teacher is about eighteen or nineteen years of age.

In the city schools all of the teachers are licensed. In the rural schools, many teachers do not have the teaching certificate granted by the normal school.

Salaries

The beginning teacher receives a salary of $1,200 per year. Increases of 20 percent are made every five years in accordance with the salary schedule which takes into account length of service and additional training. Each teacher's performance is evaluated by his principal each year and the Ministry of Education also considers this appraisal in granting increases.

In the public schools the teacher may work in the morning or in the afternoon and receive the full salary for either shift. The morning schedule is from 7:00 A.M. to 1:00 P.M.; the afternoon schedule is from 1:00 P.M. to 7:00 P.M. There are some evening elementary schools but they operate on a modified program and are mostly for adults.

Curriculum

The curriculum of the elementary school has undergone three revisions since 1944. New courses of study were put into effect in 1946 and were substantially revised in 1957 and 1964. Through this series of revisions, the courses of study have progressed from lists of rather isolated points of content to comprehensive statements of the educational experiences the students are to have. The traditional course of study outlining content only has now been combined with the guidance the teachers need in a prescribed, centrally-controlled program.

The courses of study cover in detail the usual content of mathematics, sciences, social studies, and language as the basic academic program in addition to courses in music, art, physical education, and manual arts.

The teaching varies from traditional to progressive. Although the course content is prescribed, no attempt is made to dictate methods or to specify materials.

Teaching materials are not usually furnished by the Ministry of Education. The teachers select the best they can find from commercial sources and students pay for the materials a little at a time through sales activities and assessments made by the teachers.

Some teachers provide a list of the required materials at the beginning of the year and the student is to purchase them as best he can.

Teaching methods, particularly in relation to beginning reading, vary greatly in accordance with the teacher's experience, preparation, the enrollment, the size of the classroom, the materials available, and the attendance of the pupils. Attendance in the public schools varies from school to school but is often irregular because of sickness and family problems. The dropout rate is high after the third grade, for many children begin to help their families through work or by taking care of younger children. Transfers from one school to another are frequent in some areas.

Results of the final examinations, which are prepared or approved by the Ministry of Education, count one-third in determining promotion. If a child in the first grade fails reading, he is not promoted; if a child in second grade or above fails reading and mathematics, he is not promoted. Often over-aged children are found in the lower grades.

Personnel for the Elementary Schools

The average school has a director, who does little or no teaching, and a secretary in addition to the required number of teachers. The large elementary schools have additional administrative personnel.

Secondary Education

About 80 percent of the children who finish the elementary school enter secondary education. Of this 80 percent, 24 percent finish the secondary school. Attendance in the secondary school is more or less regular, for if a student has more than 25 percent absences he is not eligible to take the final examinations. The number of days in the school year varies from about 150 to 190 days in session.

Teacher Preparation

Generally the secondary school teacher is an elementary teacher with some advanced or special training. Some have completed the training for secondary teachers provided by the Faculty of Humanities, which leads to a University degree and a teacher's certificate after four years of study. Most secondary teachers, however, have completed only part of this university training and do not yet have the degree.

Salaries

Secondary teachers are paid on a salary schedule which provides a minimum wage of $360 per year per class meeting five periods per week. A teacher is limited to six such classes. As a teacher moves up in the salary schedule, he receives a 20 percent increase for every five years of experience or sooner if he has taken additional preparation and receives a favorable rating by his superiors. The maximum salary for a secondary teacher in the public schools is $4,320 per year if he teaches six classes meeting five days per week.

Curriculum

The secondary school curriculum is divided into two cycles, the pre-vocational cycle of three years and the diversified cycle of two or three years. In the first three years all students study the courses shown at top of next column, Pre-Vocational Program.

The pre-vocational program is prerequisite to all of the programs in the diversified cycle: agriculture, commerce, military, teacher training, and the college preparatory course. The curriculum of the college preparatory program is shown in next column, College Preparatory Program.

PRE-VOCATIONAL PROGRAM

First Year	Second Year	Third Year
Mathematics	Mathematics	Mathematics
Spanish	Spanish	Spanish
Social Studies	Social Studies	Social Studies
General Sciences	General Sciences	General Sciences
Foreign Language	Foreign Language	Foreign Language
Music	Music	Music
Art	Art	Art
Physical Education	Physical Education	Physical Education
	Industrial Arts	Industrial Arts
		Typing

COLLEGE PREPARATORY PROGRAM

First Year	Second Year
World Literature	Spanish-American Literature
Mathematics	Mathematics
Social Studies	Social Studies
Physics	Chemistry
Foreign Language	Foreign Language
Biology	Psycho-Biology
Applied Statistics	Introduction to Philosophy
Art or Music	History of Art of Guatemala
Physical Education	Art or Music
	Physical Education

Teaching methods range from the purely traditional to the most modern. Since many of the teachers are part-time, teaching one or two classes in a school, they tend to use lecture or discussion-type procedures. There are secondary teachers, however, who make use of the community resources and do imaginative teaching. Teaching materials are prescribed by the teachers and it is up to the students to secure the books and other materials. Textbooks of some description are available for nearly all courses.

Laboratories and shops are increasingly common, although in some schools the teaching of science and manual arts is theoretical.

Guidance

Guidance services are available in the public secondary schools. Interest, aptitude, and general ability tests are given and students are provided with group and a limited amount of individual guidance.

Promotion

Promotion is by subject and the final examination counts two-thirds of the final mark. If a student fails a course, he has two opportunities to take a make-up examination the following year. If he fails more than two courses and does not make them up at the beginning of the following year, he has to repeat the grade.

Non-academic Secondary Programs

In addition to the academic curriculum described above, there are a number of other secondary courses. Industrial schools exist in the capital city and in several departmental capitals. After completing the pre-vocational program, a student is eligible to seek admission into a commercial school, the military school, the agricultural school, the conservatory of music, forestry school, school of social work, and other terminal educational programs offered at the secondary level. These programs are two or three years in length and provide a special diploma.

Teacher Training

The normal schools operate under the Ministry of Education. Teacher education is now three years in length following the pre-vocational cycle, one year more than the academic curriculum. In addition to courses in language, science, social studies, and mathematics similar to those of the academic curriculum, the student in the teacher-training program studies several education courses and does practice teaching.

HIGHER EDUCATION

Higher education in Guatemala is provided by the University of San Carlos, one private university (Roman Catholic), the National School of Nursing, and other post-secondary educational programs.

The University of San Carlos

The University of San Carlos was founded in 1676, more than a hundred years after the first Spanish settlers came to Guatemala. It was granted autonomous status in 1945 and is guaranteed 2 percent of the national income of Guatemala by the Constitution. Other income is from tuition and fees. Each student pays about $60 a year for tuition, unless a reduced fee is granted on the basis of need. Table 2 shows the enrollment by schools for 1965.

TABLE 2

Enrollment by Faculties
University of San Carlos
1965

Department of Basic Studies	2,330
Faculties:	
Agriculture	103
Architecture	196
Chemistry and Pharmacy	152
Dentistry	148
Economics	1,062
Engineering	739
Humanities	472
Law	1,296
Medicine	542
Veterinary Science and Zoology	85
Quezaltenango branch	350
	7,475

The Superior Council

The Superior Council of the University of San Carlos is made up of forty-two members: the rector (the highest administrative official of the university), the secretary, the treasurer, the deans of the ten faculties, one professor from each faculty, one student from each faculty, and one representative from each professional organization of alumni. The Superior Council meets an average of once every two weeks and makes many administrative decisions in addition to acting as the legislative body of the University.

Administration of the University

The central administration of the university is made up of a rector, elected for a four-year term, a secretary, a treasurer, a registrar, and several minor officials. Each faculty has a dean and a secretary in addition to teaching personnel. Each faculty also has a board of directors with responsibility for certain administrative decisions. The members of the boards are the dean, the secretary, two professors, one representative of the professional organization, and two students.

The Faculties

The University of San Carlos comprises ten faculties: Agriculture, Architecture, Economics, Engineering, Humanities, Law, Dentistry, Pharmacy, Medicine, and Veterinary Science. Traditionally the separate faculties have been autonomous and only a small degree of coordination has existed. The administration of the University has been strengthened in the past few years, however, and the services of registration, admission, and finances are now centralized. All faculties are located in different buildings and most of them in different parts of the city. The Faculties of Agriculture, Architecture, Engineering, and Veterinary Sciences are located at University City, the new campus of the University on the outskirts of the city.

The Department of Basic Studies

In 1964 a new department of basic studies was established to provide a two-year program to all students entering the university. The curriculum is made up of survey courses in mathematics, science, social studies, language, and philosophy. All the students take the same courses and must finish the two-year program before being admitted to a faculty for professional training of two to five years more to receive a degree.

Some of the new services of the university, such as admissions and guidance, are being established in the department of basic studies even though they will serve the whole university. At the present time about 2,000 of the 7,000 students are enrolled in basic studies.

University Professors

Most of the professors of the University of San Carlos are graduates of the same university; many of them are part-time, devoting one, two, or three hours to university work. An increasing number of professors, however, are full-time and all of the professors of basic studies are full-time employees of the university.

Salaries

A full-time university professor receives over $7,200 per year, almost double the maximum paid to secondary school teachers. Part-time professors are usually hired by class; if a professor is hired to teach one class he is paid $720 yearly. Most full-time teachers have a combination of teaching and research activities, whereas part-time professors usually are hired for teaching only.

Department heads and deans receive additions to their regular salaries as teachers.

Campus

A new university campus of 156 acres is being developed on the southwest side of the capital city of Guatemala. The central administration building (Rectoría), the faculties of Agriculture, Architecture, Engineering, Veterinary Science, and Department of Basic Studies are located there. About half of the university students now take their classes at the main campus.

University Buildings

All of the buildings at the University City are new. The other buildings occupied by the University of San Carlos in the City of Guatemala are of various ages and types of architecture.

Elections

The Rector of the University and the Deans of the Faculties are elected for four-year terms. The professional organizations, the faculties, and the students have about the same number of votes. The representatives to the Superior Council from the professional associations and the student groups are also elected by their respective groups.

Other Institutions of Higher Education

Rafael Landívar University

The only independent university in Guatemala is the Rafael Landívar University, Roman Catholic in denomination. It was established in 1961 and operates three faculties (Law, Economics, and Humanities) and a Department of Basic Studies. At the present time, it has an enrollment of 777.

The National School of Nursing

The National School of Nursing is operated as a post-secondary program under the Ministry of Public Health. It admits about thirty-five students each year from Guatemala and other Central American countries. In 1964, twenty-two nurses were graduated.

THE MINISTRY OF EDUCATION

The Minister of Education is appointed by the chief executive and is a member of his cabinet. The Vice-Minister is the second highest official and acts in place of the minister during his absence. The next highest officials are the Director General of Education, the Director General of Culture and Fine Arts, and the Director General of Basic Services who coordinate the activities of the departments of secondary education, elementary education, commercial education, technical education, adult education, rural education, art and musical education, and personnel. Each department has a head and a number of supervisors and clerks. The supervisors visit the various schools and are designated to interpret ministry policy to the individual school directors.

Outside the capital city of Guatemala there are twenty-one departmental offices of the Ministry. As is natural in a centralized system of education, the Ministry of Education is responsible for all educational activities throughout the country. All teachers are employed and paid by the Ministry of Education. The Ministry is also responsible for the curriculum and the testing program. All promotion and graduation certificates are signed by representatives of the Ministry of Education.

GOALS OF EDUCATION IN GUATEMALA

Goals of education in Guatemala as revealed in the Constitution and the Organic Law of Education are those consistent with a democratic form of government. Education is designed to promote a literate and intelligent electorate, a greater participation in the cultural activities of the country, reasonable competence in economic affairs, and respect for human rights and the basic freedoms. The goals of education in Guatemala are not greatly different from those of democratic governments set up to protect human rights, freedom, and individual well-being.

Considering the more immediate purposes of education in Guatemala, emphasis is placed on literacy programs. The illiterates in the Guatemalan population on the basis of the census of 1950 were about 72 percent.

Another important aim of education in Guatemala is to extend the privileges of the elementary school to all children, particularly to those in rural areas who now attend school little or not at all.

Still another objective is to improve the diet of the children in Guatemala. The Institute of Nutrition of Central America and Panama has provided abundant evidence that poor diet is the cause of much human suffering and death. Improved understanding and practices in nutrition are important in Guatemalan education.

Guatemala is also trying to improve the preparation of teachers, particularly at the secondary level, and there is a desire to reduce the number of teachers in the rural schools who do not have the requisite training.

Lack of adequate preparation for admission to the university is a wide-spread concern. Secondary education in Guatemala receives the same criticism it receives the world around for not providing better-trained people for higher education.

BIBLIOGRAPHY

ARÉVALO BERMEJO, J. J. "Educational Developments." *International Yearbook of Education.* Geneva, 1952.

Catálogo de Estudios. Guatemala: Imprenta Universitaria, 1963.

EBAUGH, CAMERON D. *Education in Guatemala.* Washington, D. C.: Federal Security Agency, Office of Education, Bulletin 1947, No. 7.

——. "University of San Carlos de Guatemala," *Higher Education,* III, November 1, 1946.

ESPENDEZ NAVARRO, JUAN, and SMITH, HENRY LESTER. "Education in Guatemala." *Bulletin of the School of Education,* Indiana University, Vol. XVIII, No. 2, March, 1942.

GILLIN, JOHN P. "Parallel Cultures and the Inhibitions to Acculturation in a Guatemalan Community," *Social Forces,* Vol. 24, No. 1, October, 1945.

HOLLERAN, MARY P. *Church and State in Guatemala,* doctoral thesis, Columbia University, 1949.

KANDEL, I. L., ed. *Education in the Latin American Countries.* New York: Teachers' College, Columbia University, 1942.

LA FARGE, OLIVER. *Santa Eulalia: the Religion of a Cuchumatan Indian Town.* Chicago: University of Chicago Press, 1947.

LANNING, JOHN T. *The University in the Kingdom of Guatemala.* New York: Cornell University Press, 1955.

Leyes, Estatutos y Reglamentos Generales de la Universidad de San Carlos de Guatemala. Guatemala: Imprenta Universitaria, lo. de diciembre de 1961.

MATA GAVIDIA, JOSÉ. *Anotaciones de Historia Patria Centroamericana.* Guatemala: Cultural Centroamericana, S. A., 1953.

Memoria de Labores 1948-1949. Guatemala: Imprenta Universitaria, 1950.

MORLEY, SYLVANUS GRISWOLD. *The Ancient Maya.* 3rd ed., revised by George W. Brainerd. California: Stanford University Press, October, 1956.

Union Panamericana. *La Educacion,* 33. Washington, D. C.: Secretaria General, Organizacion de los Estados Americanos, Union Panamericana, enero-marzo 1964, ano IX.

VAILLANT, GEORGE C. *The Aztecs of Mexico.* Origin, Rise and Fall of the Aztec Nation. Maryland: Penguin Book.

WILLEMIN, ALBERT DUPONT. "Guatemala," *International Yearbook of Education,* Geneva, 1953.

MEXICO

James J. Van Patten

Mexico's educational system has evolved throughout a long period of metamorphosis which is continuing in the twentieth century. Across the pages of Mexican history, many and diverse cultures met and joined to form an indigenous populace. Forces of geography, economics, ethnic groups, space, and time have left an indelible imprint on the face of her peoples. It is a face of tremendous complexity, combined with a certain naiveté which make the study of Mexico one of perplexity, paradox, and contrast.

From this indigenous populace a great new nation has been molded. A key factor in this molding has been the Revolution of 1910 which became and continues to be a dynamic, living, moving force in building a twentieth-century Mexico. This force has been propelled toward social reconstruction through education which seeks to enable the people of Mexico to govern themselves and improve their standard of living.

In an attempt to understand Mexico's educational system, one must first note its cultural perspective. This perspective is made clear in the words of one of Mexico's great educational leaders, Rafael Ramirez:

We are more interested that our population should be cultured than that it should be learned, and we will continue to sustain and support this school which we have created and which cultivates culture.[1]

In the cultural heritage and the continuing emphasis upon cultural identity and values lies the essence of the historical and philosophical base for Mexico's educational system. In order to understand Mexican education, one must examine the history of Mexico.

HISTORY

"Mexico's cultural heritage began fifteen to twenty-five thousand years ago when men of Mongoloid stock, in search of food, made their way across the frozen Bering Strait from Asia to the North American continent."[2]

These people moved slowly south, settling in what is now Mexico and building giant civilizations such as the Mayan, Toltec, and Olmec. The Aztec civilization was most highly developed at the time of the Spanish Conquest. Aztec education was traditionalist with prime emphasis on preserving the cultural heritage of the past and guiding youth into a highly structured society. Education began in the home with the father teaching his son his craft or trade and the mother teaching her daughter to cook, perform wifely duties, and keep house. Education in the home stressed a high degree of moral structure and obligation.

Once Aztec family education was complete, state education began for the boys. There were two types of schools, one for the wealthy or nobility and one for a type of low middle class. Most of the population were slaves (captured from other tribes) and were not eligible for state education. Training for the nobility centered around religious instruction. Curriculum for the lower middle class was oriented to practical military training with some basic religious education.

With the Spanish Conquest of Mexico completed about 1521, the educational system of Spain was superimposed on that of the great Aztec civilization. Since the Aztecs had a strong religious cast to their educational aim, so the Spanish as representatives of the Crown and the Catholic Church strove to establish religious indoctrination in education.

One of the first schools (of European origin) established in the new world was founded by Fray Pedro do Gante in 1523 at Texcoco. This school was

---

1. George I. Sanchez, "Education," *Annals of the American Academy of Political and Social Science,* CCVIII (March, 1940), pp. 144-152.
2. Alfonso Caso, *The Aztecs, People of The Sun,* Norman: University of Oklahoma Press, 1958, p. viii.

oriented to the indigenous culture and was devoted to religious instruction, elementary instruction in political institutions, and some trade training. This school, and a few others like it, were the exception, not the rule. Education, in general, was non-existent throughout all but populous areas.

In 1551 the Royal or Pontifical University of Mexico was established (now National Autonomous University) and opened its doors in 1533. The majority of the pupils enrolled in higher education were sons of Spanish nobility in the new world. Jesuits contributed much to Mexican higher education, but their philosophy of education was deeply committed to medieval scholasticism which in time fell into useless, if not meaningless, linguistic acrobatics.

In 1821, Mexico gained her independence from Spain; from then to 1910, education continued for the most part in the hands of the church. There were several attempts to wrest education from church control and put it in the hands of the state, but they were notably unsuccessful. These attempts were confined generally, with the exception of the reform laws of the Constitution of 1857, to written decrees, laws, and constitutional changes. They were seldom carried out in practice.

Gabino Barreda and Justo Sierra, in the late nineteenth century, were leading educational theorists who moved the educational effort toward the sciences and away from traditional argumentation or medieval scholasticism. Many Mexican humanists, however, felt these reformers moved too far in the direction of positivism as a reaction against religious control of education. Their efforts proved to be too little too late, however, because Mexico's peasant population as well as many intellectual elite were ready for nothing less than social and economic justice, calling for reform of the whole social structure. Their cry for social and economic justice was based on the facts that estimates of illiteracy ran as high as 90 percent and that only 2 percent of the population owned 70 percent of all the land.[3]

REVOLUTION OF 1910 TO DATE

The cry for "land and liberty" was becoming increasingly loud, and in 1910 one of the bloodiest conflicts of Mexican history broke out—the Revolution of 1910. Through this revolution the demand for social justice found an outlet in a new Constitution of 1917. The Constitution and the Revolution on which it was based demanded continual reconstruction of individual and social life through improvement of culture based on the philosophical position *educar es redimir*, "to educate is to redeem."

Antonio Caso and José Vasconcelos were educational leaders born of the Revolution. Both men set goals for education which have been carried with enthusiasm into modern Mexico. They sought to revitalize Mexican education and redefine its goals in terms of cultural identity and perspective. The rebirth of national purpose and cultural awareness, however, did not ignore Mexico's place in the world community. Antonio Caso spoke of Mexican education in proper perspective when he wrote:

All education has a double purpose, human and national; because every man is bound by tradition to his people at the same time that he is part of humanity. It is false to educate solely for the nation . . . but to educate solely with a view toward humanity, excluding sacred patriotic traditions, constitutes on the face of it a grave and serious error.[4]

Caso set the stage for present-day emphasis on United Nations Day and other school events designed to create an awareness of the concept of the brotherhood of man and nations. Thus appears a deep strain of humanism in Mexican educational thought. Caso also set in motion Mexican education's continuing and deep concern for the individual development of each pupil. He rejected, however, both the extremes of individualism and socialism which ignored the type of well-balanced individual with which he desired Mexican education to be intimately concerned.

José Vasconcelos joined Caso in rejuvenating Mexican education. Vasconcelos could be called the John Dewey of Mexican education. He was appointed Mexico's first Secretary of Public Education by President Alvaro Obregon in 1921. Vasconcelos reorganized the administration of education and broadened its scope and goals. He stressed cultural identity and advocated that all Mexican youth be exposed to art as a creative experience. He saw the importance of art as not only developing a cultural consciousness, but more importantly as developing a deep love and respect for the greatness of Mexico's artistic heritage. Under Vasconcelos' direction, a system of rural education on a nationwide basis was developed for the first time in Mexico. He developed rural teacher-training institutions and sought to disseminate the basic elements of culture and civilization throughout the isolated rural areas.

Under the direction of education leaders such as Vasconcelos, the school became a propaganda arm of the Federal government. It was designed to teach everyone the what and why of governmental policy. The school became the Federal Government's expression of a desire and drive to educate all the people to govern themselves. In the years following Vasconcelos and Caso, every attempt was made to replace superstition, dogma, and prejudice with a rational concept of man and the universe. This was an attempt to fulfill Article 3 of the Constitution of 1917 as amended in 1934.

---

3. Victor Gallo Martinez and Donaciano Gutierrez Garduno, *organization y administracion escolares* (Mexico, Secretaria de Educacion Publica, Institute de Capacitacion del Magisterio, 1957), pp. 9-10.

4. George F. Kneller, *The Education of the Mexican Nation*, New York: The Columbia University Press, 1951, p. 59.

OVERVIEW OF MEXICAN EDUCATION

Through the years, particularly since the Revolution, the Federal Government has played an increasingly larger role in Mexican education. The post of Secretariat of Public Education, created in 1921, is a full-fledged member of the governmental cabinet. The Secretary of Public Education is appointed by the President and generally serves six years. In many instances, however, the President reappoints the Secretary particularly if he is an outstanding educational leader. This was the case with Jaime Torres Bodet who has been an extraordinary figure in Mexican education. Since the Secretary is a Presidential appointee and a member of the executive cabinet he generally reflects the philosophy of the prevailing leadership in Mexico.

In recent years, the Federal Government has devoted a large percentage of its total budget to education. In 1964 the government allotted over 22 percent of its funds to education. This reveals clearly the exceptional value Mexico's leaders have placed in education.

The Secretariat of Public Education determines the distribution of its share of the national budget among the various education levels and schools according to a national comprehensive educational plan. This plan has long been concerned with providing universal free public education for all. However, the enormity of the task to be accomplished has made it mandatory in the eyes of Mexico's educational leaders to place the bulk of its funds and efforts at the elementary school level. It is felt that as elementary education is provided for all, a firm base for Democracy will thereby be provided. Once this is accomplished more funds will be allotted to secondary and higher education.

Since its inception in 1921, the Secretariat has grown from six departments to over fifty-four offices, departments, and institutions. New political administrations (a President may serve only six years and is not eligible for reelection) often create additional departments within the Secretariat. UNESCO in its *World Survey of Education* has perhaps the most complete account of the organization of the Secretariat.[5] A brief glance at the organizational chart of the Secretariat reveals the comprehensiveness of the Federal Government effort in education. Among the many divisions, besides administrative offices such as finance and accounting, are those devoted to every educational level as well as a bureau devoted to relations with parents' associations, the National Institute of Fine Arts, and the Director General of Social Welfare. The national system of education, directed by the Secretariat, includes the following levels:

Pre-school
Elementary
Secondary
Normal Schools (Teacher Training Secondary and Higher)
Vocational
Advanced technical or professional (National Polytechnical Institute)
Institutes of Scientific Investigation
Extracurricular (Cultural Missions and Literacy Training)
Special (handicapped and delinquent children)[6]

The present size of the program of the Secretariat is a recognition that only the Federal government has the finances to carry out the major educational effort required in Mexico. However, it is now obvious that even the Federal Government, devoting a large percentage of its budget to education, cannot meet the demand for classrooms and plants. Therefore efforts are being made to gain more state, municipal, and private support.

Although the greatest share of the educational effort is carried by the Federal Government, the Constitution of 1917, as revised in 1933, and the Organic Law of 1941 all recognize the rights of states to engage in public education. All the states have availed themselves of this right. States may enter into agreement with the Federal Government and many have done so. These agreements are called "federalization" or "coordination" of education. When the agreement authorizes the Secretariat of Public Education to handle only the technical direction of the school it is one of coordination. In this case the state provides full financial support for the school. If, however, the State authorizes the Federal Government to handle both the technical and administrative direction of the educational system, the agreement is one of "federalization." In this case local governments turn over to the general treasury of the national government those amounts that their own state budgets set aside for education. The Federal Government has a representative of the Secretariat in all twenty-nine states, the Federal District, and two Territories. They supervise all Federal schools and other schools which have entered into agreements of the type noted above. The state maintains its own Director of Education who supervises state schools. Education in the Federal District and the two territories of Mexico is under the direction of the Secretariat of Public Education.

Private schools (including religious schools) may exist only if they meet requirements of the Secretariat of Public Education. Not only must they meet requirements stipulated by law but they are under supervision of the Secretariat. The supervision of all schools under the direction of the Secretariat is carried out by an elaborate system of inspection. Chiefs of school inspection zones (*Jefes de Zona de Inspeccion Escolar*) coordinate and control all levels

---

5. *World Survey of Education,* Zurich, Switzerland: UNESCO, 1958, II, pp. 706-707.

6. Further information pertaining to the organization of the Secretariat can be obtained from a doctoral dissertation: James Van Patten, "Education in the United Mexican States," unpublished doctoral dissertation, Austin: University of Texas, 1962.

and types of Federal Education in a specific region. There are additional inspectors for each education level. These inspectors attempt to see that uniformity is carried out in plans, programs, and methods of instruction for all education dependent on the Federal Government. An important point to be noted is that provision is made to allow sufficient flexibility for the instructor to adapt his teaching to regional needs such as differences in climate.[7]

The Federal budget for education has moved steadily upward until it is now over twenty-two percent of the total governmental expenditure. This year a record of 380 million dollars is being spent on public education. As will be seen these expenditures are inadequate due to rapidly increasing population figures.

SPECIFICS OF MEXICAN EDUCATION

Preschool

The philosophy of preschool education is that "the plant that would grow tall must sink its roots deep." The government is making every effort to extend education at this level. Private initiative to support these schools is solicited and encouraged by the government. At this time preschool education is not compulsory nor requisite for entrance into primary schools. Children age three to six are eligible, when facilities exist, to enter pre-primary school. The school contains three cycles or grades each of which deals with primary elements of language and physical education seeking to expand the child's understanding in these areas. Teachers for this level are selected when possible from those who have had special teacher training in normal schools. One of the most comprehensive, interpretative, statistical reports done in Mexico in recent years may be found in Victor Gallo Martinez' *Estructura economica de la educacion mexicana.*[8]

At this point it would be appropriate to caution the reader to note that statistics in Mexico have often been highly unreliable. Part of the problem has been due to pockets of isolation and language differences throughout the country. Much progress has been made in recent years, however, and it is felt that the data used in this report are substantially correct and will aid the reader in interpreting Mexico's educational problems and her educational effort. Statistical information used in this essay will be based on several charts and on the work of the various statistical surveys made by the government in addition to Martinez' report.

In 1957 there were approximately 1,964,131 children of pre-primary age. The pre-primary school enrollment was 199,951. These kindergartens were operated principally in Mexico City and other populous centers. In 1964 there were approximately 2,500,-000 children of pre-primary age. The kindergarten was 317,154.

Primary School

As noted previously, the primary educational effort in Mexico has received the most attention. The Revolution and the Constitution of 1917 were seen as a mandate to provide literacy for all Mexicans. Primary education in rural Mexico where the majority of the people live had to be built from the ground up. This building process is still taking place under a new eleven-year program adopted in 1959. This program seeks to provide educational facilities for all primary-age children by 1970. This plan seeks to increase opportunities for enrollment in first grade for pupils who haven't attended school and secondly, to establish higher grades which are needed in rural areas of the country.[9] Under this plan at least ten portable schools are being built every day in Mexico. These schools are designed to serve not only the needs of the pupils in rural areas but also to stimulate teachers to serve in these areas. The buildings are attractive in design and provide living facilities for teachers. Local communities build the foundation and provide the labor. The Secretariat provides all other building and educational material needed. Such schools become the focal point for the communities' activities and are used for civic events. "House of the people" may be an appropriate title for these new schools.

Primary education is divided into six grades. They are grouped into three cycles of two years each. Primary education is compulsory for all children from age six to twelve where facilities are available. The Organic Law of 1941 levies fines on parents or guardians who do not see that their children attend school. This law is not yet rigidly enforced due to the lack of personnel and facilities.

In 1957 there were about 6,742,495 children of primary school age. Four million five hundred thousand attended primary school. In 1964 over six million pupils were attending primary school of a school population for this level of over eight million. Many of Mexico's primary schools are running two shifts (morning and afternoon) just to keep up with the population growth. It is the primary educational effort that has cut illiteracy to 28.91 percent.[10]

Secondary Education

Secondary education in Mexico has not received the bulk of the Secretariat's attention since primary

---

7. An excellent review of laws, regulations, programs and plans for teachers is to be found in Julio Rubio Villagran's, *Agenda Del Maestro*, Mexico: Impresora Galve, 1964.

8. Victor Gallo Martinez, *Estructura economica de la educacion mexicana*, tomos I y II, Mexico: Academia Mexicana de la Educacion, 1959.

9. For a comprehensive report see *A Panorama of Mexico Education Today*, Mexico: Secretariat of Public Education, 1961.

10. Literacy in some instances refers to about a second grade education. A Literacy Law in 1944 indicated literacy to be ability to read and write and understand basic elements of culture.

education is considered more essential at this point. Increasing attention is being given to secondary education, however, due in no small measure to Mexico's need for technical training for her growing industry.

Mexico follows the European two-ladder system of secondary education more closely than that of the United States. Secondary education is divided into two main stages. The first stage is three years and is provided in lower general secondary, lower vocational secondary, agricultural, industrial, and arts and crafts schools. Pupils enroll at age thirteen and complete the program at about sixteen. Permission may be obtained, however, to enroll at ages far above this since educational officials are aware that many pupils have to work full or part time at an early age.

Two exceptions are to be noted in this general secondary level of education. The secondary schools for nurses and midwives run a full six years as does the vocational training schools for music, dancing, and the fine arts.

A major expansion program is taking place in the secondary technical education program. A number of new educational plants were former prisons remodeled to handle growing numbers of boys and girls interested in technical education. One school, opened in September, 1964, had facilities for over 2,000 pupils. Rooms for arts and crafts, laboratories, and home economics facilities were provided with the latest equipment. It is inspiring to note the enthusiasm of administrators and pupils for their new schools.

The second stage of secondary education varies from two to three years. Pupils enroll at age sixteen or seventeen and generally complete their program at age twenty. Two-year courses are provided in secondary vocational schools and in preparatory schools. The preparatory schools grant degrees in science (*bachillerato de ciencias*) and art (*bachillerato de humanidades*). These degrees provide entrance to the University of Mexico and to other universities throughout the country. Three-year secondary programs are provided for teacher training, Army, and Navy education.

In the curricula or syllabi requirements, the first stage of secondary education is regulated by the Secretariat of Public Education. In the second stage, the Secretariat governs matters of curricula and syllabi with regard to vocational schools while the universities govern the establishment of these matters for *baccalaureate* or preparatory schools.[11] Local governments in the States may modify requirements to meet regional needs as long as they adhere to general Secretariat policy. The governors of the several states can, at regional levels, issue syllabi as long as they do not differ in content or aim from those of the Secretariat.

It is important to note at this point that private schools are important in secondary education. In 1958, private schools enrolled about 48,834 pupils compared to a school population of about 125,170, in schools run by or with cooperation of the Federal Government. The enrollment in secondary schools was far short of the number of youngsters in the eligible age group, over 2.25 million. In 1964 there were about 796,621 students enrolled in both cycles of the secondary school.

Before leaving the secondary level it should be noted that there is increasing interest and attention to the National Polytechnic Institute which is an important source of the governments technical skills. This Institute administers, as an arm of the Secretariat, all public institutions concerned with technical education outside of the universities. The National Polytechnic Institute in Mexico city enrolls some 30,000 students in both secondary and professional (higher education) schools and divisions.

A goal of humanism runs throughout secondary education as it does with all other levels. The goals of the National Polytechnic Institute reveal this thread of concern for the dignity and worth of man. These goals are devoted to developing good technicians while creating the type of man who is capable of being a good citizen and individual. Technical education is not considered an end in itself but a means of developing a skill to further elevate the standard of living of all Mexicans.

Teacher Training

As a bridge to exploring higher education, one might begin by viewing teacher training in Mexico. Teacher-training institutions are in both the secondary level and higher or professional level. Teacher training (escuela normales) for secondary teaching is a six-year program of two cycles the last of which is a three-year program of professionalization. Variations are made in the second three-year cycle to meet the needs of those preferring to teach in specific areas such as physical education. Primary and pre-primary teachers are prepared in the six-year secondary program, while secondary teachers are selected where possible from those who have four years of successful elementary teaching experience and who graduate from a four-year higher normal school.

The person who desires to teach in the secondary school may elect to study in specific subject matter areas at the university level. After three years of study, a degree of *maestro* is awarded. A master of science degree in education may be granted after an additional year of study. Thus secondary school teachers may go to a four-year higher normal school or four years to a university to complete the requirements for teaching.

All workers in Mexico belong to a union, the Federation of Union State Employees. Teachers are

---

11. The Secretariat has moved toward encompassing secondary schools that are presently part of universities within the plan of studies that it formulates.

no exception this rule. All must become members of the Sindicato Nacional de Trabajadores de Educacion, a branch of the National Workers Union. Membership in this union gives the teachers an opportunity to explore with other workers ways and means of raising the level of working standards, health and retirement programs, as well as increasing salaries.

In 1964 there were over 200 normal schools at both secondary and higher level enrolling over 50,000 pupils, as opposed to some 120 schools with 27,000 pupils in 1957. In the period 1952-1957 the graduates of normal schools averaged 2,184, whereas in 1964 approximately 5,000 pupils were graduated from these schools. As will be noted later, this effort falls short of meeting the demand for qualified teachers. The eleven-year plan previously noted provides for the building of new normal schools and the enlargement of existing schools. This plan also devotes funds to the Federal Institute for Teacher Training (Instituto Federal de Capacitacion del Magisterio) in order to train teachers in the field who have not met certification requirements. The Institute reaches presently inadequately-trained teachers through extension and correspondence courses as well as through radio programs. Summer teaching institutes are conducted to enable teachers to gain certification and to keep up with advances in the teaching field. The Federal Institute for Teacher Training is reaching over 26,000 teachers in the field through eleven regional branch offices and thirty-one state coordinating agencies.

Teachers' salaries vary greatly according to efficiency reports made by school principals and inspectors, merits and demerits for work performed, professional preparation and experience. It would be inappropriate and misleading to list scale of teacher salaries because of the wide differences between country and city, large populous area and smaller community, public and private schools, but it can be stated without qualification that great progress has been made in improving teacher salaries throughout the nation. In the larger communities, especially in Mexico City, teachers are paid as well as those in other learned professions. In certain of the isolated areas, however, teachers are paid at an abysmally low rate. This accounts for the fact that a large number of teachers in the field are inadequately trained. Those who graduate yearly tend to congregate in the larger communities where salaries are higher and opportunity for promotion is greater. The Secretariat, however, is doing everything possible to correct deficiencies in teacher salaries.

Throughout Mexico there are a number of very young people on teaching staffs. Many of these individuals have had only two or three cycles of primary school and in some instances are serving on secondary school staffs. These teachers are encouraged to continue their education through correspondence and extension courses. One is impressed with the enthusiasm with which these young teachers perform their duties. On the whole, students in Mexico are diligent and attentive learners, respecting their teachers and the teaching profession.

In concluding this picture of teacher training in Mexico, it would seem appropriate to note the thread of humanism continuing in this area of the nation's educational effort. This may be noted in the six-year report (1952-1958) of the Secretariat of Public Education picturing the teacher Mexico seeks. The report states a teacher should have the following characteristics:[12]

1. An integral, whole man of solid moral character with a clear sense of professional responsibility.
2. A revolutionary and a patriot with a basic commitment to liberty and social justice and to the principles and practices of democracy.
3. A professional individual with the drive to develop the creative potentiality of the Mexican people. (Influence of Vasconcelos and others).
4. A tireless worker who does not give up in the face of adversity and who remains a militant worker in the cause of Mexican progress.

Higher Education

Higher education has a long history in Mexico beginning with church colleges for the Indians as early as 1536. The National Autonomous University of Mexico opened its doors in 1553. The highest technical training school in the country is the National Polytechnical Institution which was discussed briefly with the secondary school system. This school was founded in 1937 from a previous technical school and has grown until it now includes several pre-vocational schools, six vocational schools (in engineering, mathematics, medical biological science, and social science), two intermediate technical training schools, and nine higher schools (engineering, chemistry, veterinary medicine, and business). This school with its divisions is under the direction and is an integral part of the Secretariat of Public Education.

Educational leaders in 1960 founded a Center of Advanced Studies for the purpose of research for those who wish to study for the degrees of Master and Doctor in Sciences.

Other technical-training institutions exist in Mexico under the direction of the Federal Government or supported by the Federal Government. State and private initiative often supports these institutes as is the case for the Technological Institute of Monterrey which is a private institution supported and operated by the community. An interesting sidelight is the founding of this school by funds obtained from a lottery. This school has a high quality program and staff and is attended by many American students during the summer months. Other regional institutes

---

12. Secretaria de Educacion Publica, *Direccion General de Ensenanza Normal, 1952-1958, Seis anos de labor*, Mexico, 1958, pp. 7-49.

exist for the study of specific industrial and engineering problems.

Over thirty institutions of higher education exist in the States and every State is participating in the higher education effort. The Federal Government is providing funds for the operation of most of these institutions and doing so without influencing the direction of the school program. The most noteworthy instance of Federal aid without Federal control is the operation of the National Autonomous University of Mexico which is subsidized by the Federal Government but not controlled in any way. This University is the largest school and offers the most comprehensive program of studies in the nation. The National University encompasses seventeen teaching faculties and schools and sixteen research institutes, including the National Preparatory school. The University enrollment was well over 30,000 in 1964.[13]

There are also private schools of higher education devoted to research and study in the humanities. Noteworthy among these are the Colegio de Mexico and Mexico City College. The Secretariat is most interested in coordinating the higher educational effort throughout the nation to eliminate expensive duplication of effort. Since many universities in the States are autonomous, the decisions with regard to coordinating the educational effort must be made by the institutions themselves. That universities recognize this is noted by the fact that the National Association of Universities and Institutes of Higher education in Mexico is devoting more time and attention each year in its regional conferences to finding ways and means of coordinating the educational effort throughout the nation. This augurs well for the nation especially since the Secretariat and other educational leaders recognize the advantage of improving many of the State Universities through restricting their activities somewhat and concentrating on strengthening a few facilities and departments.

Cultural Missions

Cultural missions provide a unique program for elevating the standard of living in Mexico. They are an operation bootstrap by which Mexicans are lifting the cultural level of the populace through a grassroots effort. Visiting many cultural missions in Mexico provides an opportunity to see how a nation is seeking to bring civilization to isolated areas.

The first cultural mission was established in 1923 primarily to improve the training of rural school teachers. Its first teachers were called *misioners*. They were sent out to promote a cultural revolution. These teachers were reformers. They were enthusiastic about the possibilities for improving the working and living conditions of Mexico.

Throughout the years, with the exception of a brief period of disbandment, the cultural mission movement has expanded until in 1961 there were over 1,000 teachers working throughout the country in some ninety cultural missions, seventy-eight of which were in rural areas.

Each mission team generally comprises a supervisor, social workers, nurse or midwife, a recreational director, teachers of music, agriculture, industry, and trades such as carpentry, plastic arts, masonry, also ten specialists in literacy programs. The mobile mission staff consists of a supervisor who is a professional educator, a physician, three literacy workers, three recreational directors, three agricultural teachers, three shop teachers (arts, crafts, industrial), and three social workers. Attached to each mobile unit are three individuals who drive and repair the vehicles as well as run the audiovisual equipment. In 1961, some ten motorized missions operated in ten states reaching some 250,000 people.

The mobile or motorized mission generally has three vehicles with audiovisual equipment; arts and crafts shops; library and medical material designed to enable the unit to operate as a traveling school with a full complement of teachers.

Cultural mission teachers live and work in isolated rural areas with the residents of the community. They teach peasants the cultural heritage of Mexico through folk songs and dances as well as arts and crafts. They also teach the importance of the family as a social unity and basic elements of sanitation. Some missions teach basic elements of hygiene through instruction in vaccination of animals and water purification. Cultural mission teachers become close to the people and thus are able to teach them how to use their own energies to build a better community. After three months, the mobile mission workers move on to another community, returning only to see how much progress has been made. The missions work to develop libraries in the communities where literacy programs may be carried out and where individuals can continue to expand their reading as their ability improves. The mission program is a gigantic attempt to bring social justice to all Mexicans and help thousands of isolated residents become part of the mainstream of twentieth-century life and society.

GOALS AND OBSTACLES TO THEIR ATTAINMENT

First consideration will be given to the broad general goals of Mexican education based on publications by the Secretariat synthesizing this with the author's observation and experience of the system. In doing this one must note that the literature of the Secretariat must be viewed with some degree of caution since in some instances it may be the basis for a request for funds from the general treasurer. In

---

13. A good view of the National Autonomous University and its scope may be found in the *Anuario General* (Mexico: Direccion General De Publicaciones, 1963), Universidad Nacional Autonoma de Mexico.

other cases, the Secretariat may be overglorifying the work accomplished to show how well the general funds have been spent. It is important, therefore, in dealing with official reports to examine them circumspectively. There seems to be in Mexican official educational writings a tendency to deal with an ideal picture that should exist rather than a situation as it exists.

With this word of caution, the broad goals of Mexican education may be viewed as intimately concerned with dissemination of democratic thought and practice. A prime goal is to teach Mexicans how to govern themselves to eliminate the age-old cancers of *mordida,* or bribery, and *empleomania,* or eagerness, to hold public office and to add relatives to the public payroll. That much progress has been made is evident. It requires a major effort to eliminate abuses because of age-old customs. The *caudillo,* or leader, is as old as time itself in Mexico, and rural residents still regard governmnt leaders with some degree of awe. The answer to the problem seems to lie in the philosophical position noted previously— *educar es redimir,* "to educate is to redeem."

Mexican education having the goal of democratic thought and practice is in reality universal. It opens its schools to everyone regardless of race, color, or creed. There is little racial discrimination in Mexico outside of a Spanish carry-over of paternalism toward the Indian. All schools are thoroughly integrated. Furthermore, Mexican law seeks to protect and aid citizens who are in isolated cultural pockets. Programs such as the *ejido,* or communal land projects, are designed to provide a degree of security to rural peasants.

Throughout Mexican education one finds an expression of cultural identity. At all levels pupils are taught the rich history of Mexico. They gain a sense of unity of purpose and of the meaning of social justice not only for Mexico but also for the greater community of nations. Vasconcelos in an earlier period sought to pull divergent streams of Mexico's varying ethnic groups into a sense of national purpose. His efforts are being rewarded today as more and more isolated groups are being brought into the mainstream of Mexican twentieth century. Sometimes they peer out only to withdraw into their own cultural island. Still the nation's educational effort seeks to draw them out just a little further until finally they become part of a greater Mexico.

Mexican education seeks to bring theory and practice into a working unity through emphasis on practical agrarian reform and expansion of her industrial arm along with an awareness of the need for more education for more people. This emphasis on the practical never overlooks the humanism which seeks always to "cultivate culture," to develop a well-balanced individual, a builder of a finer tomorrow.

The emphasis in education is on a scientific approach to man and his universe. This is the goal of all education and has been so since the promulgation of the constitution of 1917.

Thus the educational goals concern themselves with building a sound democracy based on universal, free public education, motivating Mexicans to improve their standard of living and to correct age-old abuses. The prime concern is with the present improvement of culture but not to the detriment of deep and abiding concern with the dignity and worth of the individual in future generations.

Obstacles to these goals are many and serious. Perhaps the foremost obstacle is the population explosion in Mexico. Her population moved from 16,552,722 in 1930 to 32.3 million in 1958 and in 1964 stood at a record 38 million with over 40 percent under the age of fifteen. Mexico has to run just to keep up with the population growth.[14] The annual rate of population growth is over 3 percent. Projecting this rate into the future, the population would double every twenty to twenty-five years. The rate of growth is due mostly to a natural increase but is coupled with a decrease in death rate due to better health control. These figures reveal in sharp outline the difficulty faced by Mexico in providing universal education. Today with an expenditure of well over $300 million amounting to in excess of 22 percent of the national budget, Mexico is unable to provide educational facilities for all of its children. The Secretariat of Public Education has long concerned itself primarily with elementary education hoping to provide educational facilities for all eligible children at this level before devoting necessary funds to higher levels of education. With the rate of population growth, however, the Secretariat has opened a national campaign to gain financial and other support for education. Private schools are being asked to take some of the student load and industry is called upon to give money, land, and buildings to meet the educational need. States and local governments are being asked to increase and coordinate their educational effort. The Federal Government does not have the finances to provide for universal education. The response to the government's request for aid in its educational program has been excellent. Parents' organizations donate time, labor, money, and buildings for education. The National Advertising Council is sponsoring radio programs and carrying out an educational campaign at its own expense. With a gigantic national effort, what seems to many educational experts in Mexico to be insurmountable obstacles may well be overcome.

Another obstacle to fulfilling educational goals lies in the poverty of many of the people. Although the gross national product has increased annually for

---

14. For an excellent analysis see Louis J. Ducoff, "La poblacion y la fuerza del trabajo futuras de Mexico, Centro America y Panama: Algunas inferencias para el desarrollo economico." Reprinted from Estadistica, *Journal of the InterAmerican Statistical Institute,* September, 1950.

some years by over 3.2 percent, the population growth places an increasingly heavy burden on the nation's financial structure. A study of population movement reveals gravitation to major population centers at an alarming rate. This adds to the poverty problem although the government is moving as rapidly as possible to provide food and clothing at minimal prices for the indigent. In Mexico City a large distribution center maintains a fleet of trucks which each day distributes low-cost food and supplies. In rural areas industrial enterprises are called upon by law to provide educational facilities and pay teacher salaries.[15] Every effort is made to teach crafts and arts to citizens so they will be self-supporting. To eliminate some rural pockets of poverty the government is seeking to teach the value and worth of moving to undeveloped areas of fertile land such as may be found in the states of Veracruz and Yucatan. This attempt finds much resistance due to age-old traditions which encourage people to cling to the land of their forefathers.

Space does not permit an extensive exploration of obstacles to fulfilling educational goals, but lack of adequate sanitation in some areas leads to health problems and thus reduces class attendance. Health programs carried on throughout the educational system are resolving this difficulty.

Many Mexican students who live along the American frontier attend schools outside of Mexico. In order to prevent this flow of talent outside the country, Mexico has developed a National Frontier Program which is seeking to strengthen educational programs along the border and beautify frontier communities to keep the students in Mexico and to attract tourists to the country so as to gain additional, much-needed income.

Finally, there is a problem of school failure. Part of the cause of this problem is a tendency toward authoritarian teaching and rote memorization of material difficult for pupils to comprehend. The Secretariat is seeking to eliminate this problem through encouraging an ever larger number of teachers to enroll in teacher-training courses. Lack of school books, long a serious problem in the nation, is being met by a program inaugurated by President Lopez Mateos in 1959 to supply free textbooks from the first to fourth grade. Many parents need further instruction as to the value of education. They often keep their child out of school to help with farm work, and in some instances children are kept out of school a number of days to observe religious holidays. The Secretariat is conducting a campaign through the cultural mission and literacy programs to teach parents the goals and rewards of education. It also has moved toward permitting greater flexibility in the school schedule so that pupils who have to work part of the day can still attend school. It is to be noted that not enough has been done in this direction. Further work in this area would be of real benefit to the educational effort. As far as religious holidays are concerned, the Secretariat attempts to build a curriculum that will use these holidays as a device to bring parents to schools to participate in a fiesta where teaching is carried on by enabling the parent to feel he is part of the school's effort and enrolling the pupil to show the parent his work.

Regardless of the problems, the confidence of educational leaders in Mexico that they will be solved is unshaken.

THE FUTURE

This essay has pointed to many serious problems facing Mexico's continuing attempt to provide free and universal education. Progressive educational leaders, however, such as Secretary of Public Education, Jaime Torres Bodet, have demonstrated energy, capacity, and innovation in attempting to solve these problems. They are carrying on the spirit of the Revolution which has come of age with a stable economy and a rising middle class which demands more and more of the educational effort. This new class is willing to give more to make the educational effort a success.

Mexico's leadership in the past twenty-six years has been middle-of-the-road and, with her new President Gustavo Diaz Ordaz, this trend will continue with perhaps a tilt in the direction of conservatism. Regardless of the president in office, however, a major part of the budget in the last twenty-six years has gone into education. This trend will continue since it is the route to the continuation of democracy based on social justice.

All the statistical evaluation possible cannot adequately appraise the ability of the Mexican people to surmount obstacles to fulfill the mandates of the Constitution of 1917 for free and universal education. Mexico remains a nation of culture and humanism which seeks to build a finer tomorrow through education. It is hoped this essay will stimulate the reader's further investigation of the educational plant to south of the United States which for all its dimensions of complexity is a study in the efforts of a people to build and maintain a working democracy.

BIBLIOGRAPHY

ALEGRIA, PAULA. *La educacion en Mexico antes y despues de la Conquista.* Mexico: Editorial Cultura, 1936.

CASO, ANTONIO. *Discursos a la nacion mexicana.* Mexico: Libreria de Porrua, 1922.

COWART, BILLY F. *The Educational Philosophy of Jaime Torres Bodet and Its Implications for Mexican and World Education,* unpublished doctoral dissertation, Austin: University of Texas, 1963.

FABILA, ALFONSO. *La mision cultural de Amanalco, escuela sin muros.* Mexico: Editorial Bolivar, 1948.

---

15. Article 123 of the Constitution of 1917.

GALLO MARTINEZ, VICTOR. *Estructura economica de la educacion Mexicana*. Tomo I y II. Mexico: Academia Mexicana de la Educacion, 1959.

GIL, EMILIO PORTES. *The Mexican Schools and the Peasantry*. Mexico City: Press of the Ministry of Foreign Relations, 1936.

GILL, CLARK CYRUS. *The Role of the Federal Government in Public Education in Mexico*, unpublished doctoral dissertation, University of Minnesota, May, 1948.

GUZMAN, MARTIN LUIS. *Escuelas laicas, textos y documentos*. Mexico: Empresas Editoriales, 1948.

HUGHES, LLOYD H. *The Mexican Cultural Mission Programme*. Paris: UNESCO, 1950.

JOHNSTON, MARJORIE C. *Education in Mexico*. Washington: U. S. Government Printing Office, 1956.

KNELLER, GEORGE F. *The Education of the Mexican Nation*. New York: The Columbia University Press, 1951.

LARROYO, FRANCISCO. *Historia comparada de la educacion en Mexico*. Mexico: Editorial Porrua, 1947.

MINANO GARCIA, MAX H. *La educacion rural en Mexico*. Mexico: Ediciones de la Secretaria de Educacion Publica, 1943.

PARKES, HENRY BAMFORD. *A History of Mexico*. Boston: Houghton Mifflin Co., 1960.

SANCHEZ, GEORGE I. *The Development of Higher Education in Mexico*. New York: King's Crown Press, 1944.

——. *Mexico: A Revolution by Education*. New York: The Viking Press, 1936.

Secretaria de Educacion Publica:
A Panorama of Mexican Education Today, Mexico, 1961.
Direction general de ensenanza normal, 1952-1958. Seis anos de Labor., Mexico, 1959.
Importancia de la Lectura-Escritura y sus Metodos de Ensenanza, Mexico, 1956.
Ley Organica de La Educacion Publica, Mexico, 1942.
Misiones Culturales, Mexico, 1961.
Presupuesto y Administracion, 1952-1958, Mexico, 1959.
Programas de educacion primaria aprobados por el Consejo Nacional Tecnico de la Educacion, Mexico, 1958.
Realizaciones de la Direccion General de Segunda Ensenanza en el sexenio, 1952-1958, Mexico, 1958.

VAN PATTEN, JAMES J. *Education in the United Mexican States*, unpublished doctoral dissertation, University of Texas, 1962.

VILLAGRAN, JULIO RUBIO. *Agenda Del Maestro*. Impresora Galve, Mexico, D. F., 1964.

WILSON, IRMA. *Mexico: A Century of Educational Thought*. New York: Lancaster Press, Inc., 1941.

World Survey of Education. Vol. II. Zurich, Switzerland: UNESCO, 1958.

"Preparation of General Secondary School Curricula," International Conference on Public Education, Publication No. 216. Paris: International Bureau of Education, 1960.

PERU

Raúl Acosta Rengifo

The evolution of Peruvian education is presented for the three major periods in Peruvian history: Inca, Viceroyal, and Republic. Each of these periods was marked by political, economic, and social factors which had a bearing on the prevailing educational system. The three principal influences on Peruvian education throughout the three periods are those stemming from Spain, France, and the United States. José Carlos Mariátegui in *Siete Ensayos* (Seven Essays) comments that the precise limits of these influences are unclear.

Inca education has had very little influence on later developments of Peruvian education because the Spanish conquest virtually wiped out this as well as other institutions of importance in Inca civilization. Nevertheless, from an historical point of view, the inclusion of a brief resumé of education during the Inca period is necessary in order to point out its most important aspects.

INCA EDUCATION

Education during the period of the Inca empire faithfully reflected the vastly different social levels characteristic of the society and was characterized by aristocratic and class-conscious concepts. It had a twofold purpose: (1) to prepare the nobility, religious leaders, and military class to govern and (2) to guarantee submissiveness on the part of the general population. The repressing of individual personalities and the molding of the individual to the needs of the group were indeed prime goals of Incan education. By fulfilling the educational precepts of the society, the daily necessities of both the individual and of the society were met. To be sure, during this remote period neither schools nor professional teachers existed; nevertheless the educational process was an intimate and essential part of Inca life.

The first step in Inca education coincided in its major characteristics, although not in its chronology,

with the Homeric period of Greek pedagogy and with the so-called primitive period of the Ancient Rome. Garcilaso de la Vega attributes to the founders of the Inca Empire the functions of teachers and educators. In the eyes of their subjects the founders of the Inca Imperium represented over the generations the prestige of their divine origin. Their educational precepts therefore were seen as coming directly from the gods, and those who ignored them were deserving of divine wrath.

The system was essentially a practical one, revolving around the preparation of individuals to correctly carry out their assigned duties, which were essential to the Inca system. Cieza de León says: "Many were not skilled in the cultivation of the land, not as teachable as they might have been. Therefore every nobleman on certain days went to the field and took the plough in his hands and tilled the soil. And even the Incas themselves did this in order to show a good example."

The family-centered nature of Inca education during early childhood was consistent with teaching practices throughout the whole society. The Peruvian sociologist, Roberto MacLean y Estenós, writes: "The family, together with the priesthood, have been the only educational influences throughout human history which extended from the origin of man until the appearance of the earliest civilizations."

Referring to the obligation of parents to educate their children, the chronicler Guamán Poma wrote:

Children from birth until the age of two were under the control of the mother. From 2 to 5 girls were taken care of by their parents and boys by the older brother. From five to nine they helped their parents to the extent that they were able, and played mainly with their younger brothers and sisters. Parents taught children the occupations appropriate to their sex. From nine to twelve the educational system for boys consisted of hunting birds with slingshots, and drying the meat for human consumption and saving the feathers for clothing for the military officers—and for the Inca himself. During the same period girls picked flowers and dyed wool and newly made clothing. Children and youth were required to be obedient to their parents, to their elders and indeed to all persons older than themselves. The first incidence of disobedience was punished by whipping and if repeated the child was required to work in the gold or silver mines. Equally severe was the punishment of the lazy and the unproductive, because only the industrious could support themselves and their dependents.

One can distinguish three aspects of Inca education: moral, physical, and intellectual. Moral education was for all social classes; everyone was required to be reared according to the strict moral rules of the classical Inca maxim: "Do not rob, do not lie, don't be lazy, don't kill, don't injure anyone, don't be an adulterer." (In Quechua: "Ama sua, ama llulla, ama ccella, ama aipex, ama mappa, ama huachicanqui.")

Physical education was common for all boys and youth of the nation and included fasting, athletic contests, and personal combat, but the purposes for the two major social classes were regarded as different. For children of the ruling classes physical education was "to prepare for the rigors of government." For the common man it was to serve as *chasquis,* runners famous for their endurance, carriers of the mail from Tahuantinsuyo who participated in a marathon relay, jogging over the highways of the vast rugged Inca territory. So dependable and swift were the *chasquis* that, according to oral tradition, the Inca rulers in Cuzco were able to eat fresh fish from the sea, 300 miles distant.

Celebration of the Inca version of commencement or school graduation for the nobility traditionally took place on a special day (*Huarachico*) in November. The ceremony was similar in purpose to the practises in Mediaeval Europe when young noblemen qualified for knighthood.

Education in an intellectual sense was confined to the tiny upper-class groups and was regarded as a class privilege. The use of *quipus* (kee-poo-s) a kind of counting process using knotted cords, and the teaching of geography, astronomy, and history made up the curriculum of the young Inca nobility. According to Porras Barrenechea, a famous Peruvian historian, "The *quipu* served as a numerical record system, as well as aid to memory, and the process functioned as an important supplement to oral tradition." It cannot be properly called writing because it is not a phonetic reproduction of words. It was not the invention of the Incas nor was it for private use, inasmuch as it was also used by many others.

Scientific education achieved a relatively high level of development although there were a number of mutual inconsistencies between Inca religion and medicine. Scholars have identified two schools of surgery in Peru during the Inca period in which bone surgery at an advanced level, the trephination of skulls, was taught. It is estimated that 60 percent of the patients who underwent this type of surgery survived and perhaps enjoyed improved health. Dr. Pedro Weiss notes the possibility that in ancient Peru there were schools of both surgery and anatomy.

Two types of educational institutions for the Inca elite, one for men and one for women, are known to have existed (*Yacha-huasi* and *Aclla-huasi*). The Inca Roca is credited with establishing *Yacha-huasi* (house of teaching). Sons of the nobles lived there, together with their teachers who are described as "philosophers and poets." The *Aclla-huasi* were centers of domestic education for young women. They were known as Houses of the Virgins of the Sun. In order to qualify for admission the applicant must "be a virgin and not have bastard blood." They were cared for by a particular type of woman teacher.

The Incas recognized the importance of language and were far ahead of their times in the care they exercised to assure linguistic unity throughout the empire as a major factor in maintaining national unity.

Manual dexterity and mechanical ability characterized the education content designed for the common people, with the double objectives of producing good farmers and able artisans. Occupations and positions were to a large extent hereditary. Among the laws handed down by the Inca Roca concerning popular education which were preserved in oral tradition and recorded by the Spanish chroniclers, was one which stated:

It was appropriate that the sons of the common man were not to learn sciences which were the exclusive province of the nobility, in order that the common man might not become self-important and threaten the established order. It was sufficient that the ordinary man be taught the occupation of his father. Children should serve their parents until the age of twenty-five and thereafter place themselves in the service of the nation.

The education of the Incas, according to Mac-Lean y Estenós,

was a faithful reflection of social stratification, but guaranteed individual and collective morality, physical vigour of the entire population, and assured continued dominance of the ruling classes. The intellectual preparation of the elite nobility also resulted from the prevailing educational practices. The unification of the Empire, also resulted from attempts to harmonize by means of a pedagogical system the differing characteristics of the various ethnic groups which fell before the Inca conquests and made up the population of the Empire.

SCHOOLS UNDER THE VICEROYS

When the vice-royalty was established in Peru on November 20, 1542, an absolutist political regime came into being as well as an intellectual and individualist type of religion which influenced instruction and classical feudalism in economic affairs. Spanish culture brought a new outlook on life with its language, religion, arts and crafts, as well as a new idea of personal dignity and honor. Viceroyal education was the right of the nobility. The church, however, carried on educational activities among the Indians. With the establishment of the universities, San Marcos in Lima (1551), San Antonio de Abad in Cuzco (1568), San Cristobal de Huamanga in Ayacucho (1677), and the Convictorio of San Carlos in Lima (1770) a new period of restructuring education was initiated. Toribio Rodriguez de Mendoza, who helped to prepare Peru for later independence, was joined by other teachers in establishing a printing press in 1581 and newspapers in 1791 which helped to spread new ideas and European culture.

Schools of the level now known as "primary" (elementary) education were in the hands of teachers whose competency and methods "varied from satisfactory to deplorable." Secondary education, which followed directly upon primary education, was the responsibility of the religious orders which established *colegios* where theology, philosophy, and letters were taught according to the dogmatic requirements of scholastic methods. The sciences were not merely untaught, they were explicitly excluded from secondary schools of the period.

The principal high schools (*colegios máximos*) of the new country included Colegio Mayor de San Felipe (1592), San Pablo (1568), and San Martín (1582)—all in Lima. San Martín was established by the Jesuits. In Cuzco the Colegio de San Bernardo opened its doors. San Felipe and San Bernardo admitted only the sons and the descendants of the Spanish conquerors.

The Viceroy Prince Esquilache established secondary schools in Lima (*El Principe*—the Prince) and in Cuzco (*San Borja*) for the children of the Indian nobility who had become wards of the new government, when they were taught "the Christian religion and Latin."

Almost two centuries afterwards, upon the exclusion from Peru of the Jesuits, a boarding school of university level (Convictorio San Carlos, 1770) was established in Lima. The new institution was made up of the *Colegios* of San Martín and San Felipe. In 1791 an academy for pilots was established in Callao, the port of Lima, to teach navigation. An "Amphitheater of Anatomy" was established in 1796 for medical studies. It was followed in 1811 by a school of medicine, the work of Hipólito Unanue, who afterward reorganized Cayetano Heredia. Since the beginning of the sixteenth century, higher education has been the responsibility of the universities. San Carlos was perhaps the most important cultural influence of this period because a generation known as "the Próceres," the leaders for the struggle for independence, was educated there.

During the administration of Toribio Rodríguez the teaching of mathematics, physics, and natural sciences got under way. With the aid of Father Cisneros, Rodríguez de Mendoza brought about a complete reorganization in the course of study which resulted in his being dismissed from his post. However, he was able to continue his work of reforming Peruvian education as a professor in San Marcos University and as a leader of the society "Amantes del País" (Those Who Love Peru).

The University of San Marcos was established by the Viceroy Amat under Royal decree (Real Cédula) of May 11, 1551, on the request of the Provincial of the Order of Santo Domingo, Father Tomás de San Martín. Only courses in General Studies were offered until 1577, when Viceroy Toledo undertook its reorganization using the University of Salamanca in Spain as a model. By the end of the eighteenth century the University of San Marcos was known throughout the world.

The University of San Antonio Abad del Cuzco was first established under Royal decree dated December 25, 1568, as a seminary and courses were inaugurated by Viceroy Toledo in 1571. In the same year the Jesuits founded the Colegio of the Compañia de Jesús (a secondary school) which by order of Gregory XV dated August 8, 1621, was raised to university level and commended to the protection of Saint Ignacio of Loyola. After the Jesuits were expelled from the country, the Seminary of San Antonio de Abad was transformed by order of Innocent III into a university.

The University of San Cristobal of Huamanga in Ayacucho was established in August 3, 1677, and Pope Innocent XI approved its establishment by Papal Bull of May 11, 1648. The University of San Ildefonso was established by the Augustinians in 1608, and the University of San Pedro de Nolasco was established by the Mercedarians in 1626. The University of San Martin in Cuzco was established on January 29, 1648, by order of the Viceroy, the Marquis of Mancera.

Peruvian historian José Valega, in his book "*El Virreynato del Peru*" (The Viceroyalty of Peru), notes that the concerns of the students were bounded by Mass which opened the day, sacred reading by a student during the hour of the mid-day meal, and psalms sung in chorus at the beginning of the afternoon work period. Then came meditation, during "the period for digestion" in the silent cloisters. Any manifestation of mirth or happiness was considered sinful. Mystical contemplation on the completion of the work of the day and prayers for the Pope and for the King, "religious conversation" around the tables in the afternoons, litanies in the Chapel before going to their cells at nine and instruction in morality, logic, theology, philosophy, and the arts—always within the confines of religiosity—made up the students' day.

The concept of "probability" which was introduced into the University of San Marcos from Spain in the eighteenth century was summarized in the Jesuit maxim: "The opinion least probable in relation to the most probable, may be accepted as true." The Jesuit concept of probability provided an outlet for youth of that day which served as an escape valve for their tremendous vitality. The most serious problems could be discussed on the basis of this tentative initiation of the right to think, unprecedented in their school experience up to that time. For this reason Alexander VII in 1665 and Innocent XI in 1680 prohibited this method of examining what ideas one should follow. Viceroy Amat in 1768 ordered the elimination of the doctrine from San Marcos University, going to the extreme of imposing upon students and pupils an oath or pledge that they would not listen to nor discuss it.

EDUCATION DURING THE REPUBLIC

When Peru achieved independence in 1821 the thinking of its people was not prepared for the new freedom. Dr. Roberto MacLean y Estenós in his admirable work *San Martín y Bolívar en la Historia de la Pedagogía Peruana (San Martín and Bolívar in the History of Peruvian Education)* ably describes the educational situation of that day.

Far from being flourishing, it was not even satisfactory except in a few instances. For the state of education in Peru essential for its development was unsatisfactory, now that the country has ceased being a Spanish colony and has begun its life as a free and sovereign country.

Spain, like the other great colonizing powers of the past centuries, projected its social values to its overseas colonies and possessions. And in Spain of the eighteen hundreds, according to the observation of the erudite Feijóo, education was in a deplorable state. The philosophers of that century had discovered the art of opposing the fruits of judgment and of discounting whatever was reasonable. A lock-step attachment to traditional routine obstructed, especially in the metropolitan centers, any important intellectual progress. The achievements in the physical and natural sciences of other countries were ignored by Spain. Physics was studied from a metaphysical point of view and was reduced to mere scholastic polemics. Arguments were frequently passionate concerning "the essence of matter, or *la union* material, and movement." Medicine was reduced to theories or mere speculation, and natural sciences suffered from unbelievable underdevelopment. When the intelligent ruler, Carlos III, attempted to come to grips with tradition and routine by reestablishing scientific studies in the universities of Salamanca and the Alcalá de Henares, the monarch was told that their systems could not be changed, that the doctrines of Newton and Galileo were not in accord with revealed truth, and that legal studies should not depart from the limits set by the wisdom of Roman law—which were "eternal as the city in which it was produced."

Bernardo Monteagudo, one of San Martín's ministers, writing of the need to reform teaching, held that

It is necessary to leave the Temple of Jano and enter that of Minerva, because so long as we continue to think about war-like things, and are deaf to the clamorous cries of humanity for justice, there cannot be a solid basis for our planning.

In observance of Independence Day, the 28th of July, 1821, General San Martin established the national library in Lima and sometime later established the "Society of Patriots."

Another indication of concern for education of the children of the common people was the establishment of the Normal School in Lima July 6, 1822, which under the administration of Diego Thompson propounded the Lancastrian system, using facilities furnished by the Dominicans. General San Martín himself decreed in 1821 that all owners of slaves were required to feed *and to educate* the children of slave mothers.

It is important to note that the Constitution of 1823 required as a condition for citizenship that all "know how to read and write," but illiteracy was so widespread that the legislation was not put into effect until 1840. However, it was a clear declaration that education was an individual and social necessity for Peruvian citizenship.

Arrival of Bolívar in Peru on September 1, 1823, provided another impulse for the development of education. An Administrative Decree (May 10, 1824) established the University of Trujillo with professorships of Philosophy and Humanities, Religious Sciences, Exact and Natural Sciences, Public and Civil Law. The University of the Convent of the Jesuits began to operate October 12, 1831, and was called "Freedom University" according to an official resolution of the Jesuit body dated November 4, 1831, and was entrusted to the protection of Saint Thomas and of Saint Rose of Lima.

The University of Arequipa was established by an administrative decree of August 6, 1825. A few weeks later, September 20, 1825, Hipólito Unanue was able to see the opening of the Convictorio de San Carlos. In Ayacucho, the University of San Cristobal was combined with the seminary of the same name and was known as "Colegio, Seminary, and University of San Cristobal."

Bolívar, having assured the independence of Peru by the battles of Junin and Ayacucho, took upon himself the task of stimulating elementary and secondary education throughout the country. Speaking on the first day of the year of 1825 he declared, "The Lancastrian System gives the best results known, and ought to be established in every province throughout the whole territory of the Republic." He recommended the establishment of a normal school in every capital of every province in order "to prepare teachers in order to bring about the education of all the people." He also recommended to the "Society of Patriots" the establishment of a normal school for girls. The objectives and programs of primary schools in the convents were specified in an official statement published August 6, 1825, in which the programs of "Schools of First Letters" and "Higher Elementary Studies" were differentiated.

The Colegio operated by the missionaries of the Convent of Santa Rosa of Ocopa of Jauja, was turned into a public high school by an administrative decree dated November 1, 1824. The Colegio San Luis Gonzaga of Ica was established by administrative decree June 1, 1821, and the program of its first years included the teaching of jurisprudence, philosophy, and mathematics.

An Institution in the south of Peru which has had a distinguished tradition, the National Colegio of Sciences of Cuzco, was begun in 1825 (Administrative Decree of July 8). During the same period a secondary institution for girls was also established in Cuzco, and in August of the same year the Colegio of Arts and Sciences came into being in Puno, on the shores of Lake Titicaca. Bolivar also established the Colegio San Simón in Moquegua on the southern Peruvian coast in April of 1826, which offered instruction in rhetoric, latin, natural law, and citizenship. Some years later its name was changed to Colegio de La Libertad for women and received a good deal of attention during this period. A "Gymnasium" offering elementary and secondary studies deemed appropriate for the education of girls was operated in the Convent of the Conception, for which its great carved doors were opened October 6, 1825. It was later known as the Central Lancastrian School for Women.

A general high school of sciences and arts (*Colegio General de Ciencias y Artes de la Independencia Americana*) was established in Arequipa February 4, 1827. The curriculum later served as the basis of the University of San Agustin, which opened and was formally recognized November 11, 1828.

PUBLIC EDUCATION

Bolivar struck another decisive blow for education by decreeing in 1825 that secondary schools should function in the buildings which had been used by convents but later closed, and stipulated further that the income received by the convents should be used for the operation of the schools. In Bolivar's Constitution the three bodies which formed the legislative arm of the state were required to "prepare courses of study and teaching methods for the public schools."

During the period of the Peruvian-Bolivian Confederation, Santa Cruz specified the functions of the office of director general of instruction (Dirección General de Estudios). Even in those days both English and French were taught at the National Library, and in Independence High School (Colegio de la Independencia) the teaching of science attracted much attention.

The General College of Science and Art of American Independence (*Colegio General de Ciencias y Artes de la Independencia Americana*) was established in Arequipa February 4, 1827. This was a secondary school patterned after the Lauretana Academy and later served as the model for the University of San Agustin. Classes in the university began November 11, 1828, but it was not officially recognized by the government of General Luis José de Orbegozo until May 6, 1825.

During the administration of Santa Cruz a number of other high schools were established including the Colegio Nacional de San Ramon in Cajamarca (September 8, 1831), the Colegio Nacional de San José in Chiclayo (December 22, 1832), Colegio San Carlos in Puno (April 16, 1830), Colegio San Miguel in Piura (May 1827), a Colegio for Teachers in Ica (May 24, 1828), the Colegio of the Holy Spirit (July 19, 1830), and many others.

It was during the Peruvian-Bolivian Confederation that the Ministry of Public Instruction was established (February 4, 1837). This Ministry was also responsible for public welfare and ecclesiastical matters. Up to this time all of these activities had been the responsibility of the Ministry of Government.

A guarantee of "primary education for all citizens and respect for the 'intellectual integrity' of educational institutions which teach the sciences, literature, and arts" was contained in the Constitution of Huancayo (Article 164), the sixth Peruvian Constitution, which went into effect November 5, 1839.

During the government of Ramón Castilla, one of the most illustrious of Peruvian Presidents, the Ninth Constitution (Article 25) guaranteed that "All those who qualify by competency and morality as prescribed by law may freely exercise the teaching function and may direct educational establishments under the inspection of the qualified authorities."

The Constitution of 1867 again guaranteed free primary education and the development of public institutions to teach science and the arts. Article 24 stated: "Primary, secondary, and higher education are completely free and new universities may be established."

Compulsory education for both boys and girls from the age of six was guaranteed in the Constitution of 1920. This document assured that

The Nation guarantees free education, and there shall be at least one primary school for boys and another for girls in every capital city of each district. There shall also be a higher school for each sex in the capitals of the several provinces. Public school teaching is recognized and its practitioners are entitled to all of the benefits established by the law.

The cornerstone of public education in Peru consists of the General Regulation for Public Instruction dated April 7, 1855, drafted by Sebastián Lorente, one of the distinguished directors of the Colegio Nacional de Guadalupe. Teaching conditions, administrative organization, as well as how to carry on the education of women, were specified in considerable detail in the Regulation.

But in spite of repeated efforts during the early period of the Republic to promote public education there was a conspicuous absence of programs of study which were well constructed and organized. The constant disturbances which characterized the early years of the Republic, interspersed by periods of anarchy and barracks revolutions, prevented the organization of education on solid bases. During the government of Castilla the first serious attempt to systematize education programs was made, and the first regulations for general instruction (issued June 14, 1850, by the Ministry of Government under Juan Manuel del Mar) formally identified three levels of teaching: elementary, secondary, and higher.

Castilla was also the initiator of university reform establishing a new set of regulations in August, 1861, for the University of San Marcos in Lima. Only three months before, the university professorship had been formally recognized as a government position (from *Proceso Historico de la Educación en el Perú*, Jorge Castro Harrison).

The "Plan of Studies" handed down to the universities and to the high schools in 1863 classified universities as "major" (mayores) or "minor" (menores) determined by whether they had more, or fewer, than "five faculties or departments of instruction which had been established by the law dated April 7, 1855." Secondary education consisted of two cycles, the first four years of general study and the second of two years which included and required elective courses grouped under either "sciences" or "letters."

The period of secondary education, however, was lengthened by the "Law of Teaching" of 1901 which set six years as the period for secondary education to be taught in *liceos* and high schools (*colegios*). It was shortened, however, in 1941 when the secondary school was established as a basic cycle of three years plus a second of two years. The same numbers of years were again approved in 1950, following a study carried on in the Colegio Nacional Alfonso Ugarte in Lima. The basic period of three years is followed by a differentiated cycle of two years during which students select one from (1) sciences, (2) letters, (3) arts and techniques, and (4) general culture.

In 1952, directors of the major secondary schools of the country (*Grandes Unidades Escolares and Colegios Nacionales*) under the leadership of Dr. Walter Peñaloza, with the advisory assistance of Chester Wood, a U. S. educator, reorganized the programs of secondary education within the already established framework of two cycles, one for three years plus a differentiated cycle of two years. The latest major curriculum reorganization of Peruvian public secondary schools took place in 1954 by a committee directed by Dr. Mario Alzamora Valdéz. This group recommended changes in the second differen-

tiated cycle of two years in order that it consist of (1) letters, (2) sciences, and (3) technical education, a plan which is presently in effect (see Jorge Castro Harrison cited above).

Peru now has 391 major secondary schools. A pre-school period of one year, followed by one year of "transition" (kindergarten), and five years of elementary school precede a five-year high school program. In addition, there are elementary schools which prepare only for vocational training; these offer the same number of years as the regular elementary school program. All elementary school education is compulsory and free in schools which are supported by the Peruvian government.

Technical education is growing noticeably at the present time. Technical secondary schools specialize in either agriculture or industrial and trades activities. The latter prepare for carpentry and for mechanical and electrical vocations.

The Government is increasingly supporting adult education. The percentage of illiteracy is being steadily reduced due to coordination of public and private educational efforts. During 1964 a general campaign of literacy mobilized the participation of teachers and students at all levels. Religious schools and industrial organizations as well as international organizations such as UNESCO are participating. Schools for adults have been established. In general these function in school plants used during the day for younger students and are operated in the late afternoon and evenings to permit attendance of office workers and laborers.

Private schools both for primary and secondary as well as normal school education are increasing in number and help reduce the gap between the limited numbers which can be enrolled in public schools and a rapidly expanding child and youth population. Not only the general operation of private schools but their programs of studies and fees and other charges made are under the control of the Government. In general the salaries of private school teachers is less than those paid for services in the public educational institutions. By law, however, no private school may pay less than half of the salary which would be paid for the same level and type of work in a government institution. It should be noted that 80 percent of the private schools in Peru are administered by Catholic religious orders, whose educational programs have benefited not only urban centers but the most isolated sections of the Andes and Amazonian areas.

Preparation of teachers is a responsibility of the Government as well as of the universities and private teacher-training institutions. Normal schools serve as sources of teachers for public schools and are operated by the Government. There are four normal schools of university level, one the higher normal school Enrique Guzman y Valle of la Cantuta, Chosica (near Lima) for young men, and the Women's Normal School of Monterrico in Lima. Also the *In-*

stituto Pedagógico Nacional in Lima and *Escuela Normal Superior* in Urubamba near Cuzco. In these institutions teachers for elementary, secondary, and technical schools are prepared. There are presently in operation in Peru sixty public and twenty private normal schools which train elementary school teachers. The Schools of Education of the universities prepare secondary teachers.

University education in Peru has undergone marked development in recent years. There are presently in Peru twenty-one universities, the majority of which have been established in the last five years and there are approximately 50,000 students including 37,000 men and 13,000 women. Seven of these universities are private, including one dedicated exclusively to medical sciences (*Universidad Peruana de Ciencias Medicas y Biologicas*) and another is for women (Universidad Femenina del Sagrado Corazón).

Sixty-five thousand Peruvian teachers at all levels enjoy benefits of social security which include medical care, disability, maternity, and pension; upon retirement or after thirty years (for men) or twenty-five (for women) service, survivor's pension and death benefits. Teachers salaries are also adjusted according to years of service, according to the elevation and location of place assigned, number of children, and other factors.

In 1964 a law regarding salary schedule and related legislation was passed in an attempt to improve the economic positions of Peruvian teachers. Major concerns since 1966 have been increasing the number of schools available and trying to encourage better teaching techniques.

BIBLIOGRAPHY

Astete Abril, M. Antonio. *Significado de la Educación en la Vida del Pueblo Peruano.* Cuzco (Ed. H. G. Rojas, S. A.), 1956.

Barreda y Laos, Felipe—1888. *Historia de la Instrucción Pública en el Perú Independiente,* Bibliografía Principal Congreso Internacional de Historia de América, 2do., Buenos Aires, 1937, 1938.

Bazán, Reyna M.—1957. *Contribución a la Historia de la Educación en el Perú,* Lima 1942. Tesis (Dr.) Pontif. Univ. Cat. del Peru 1939. Bibliografía pg. 112-114.

Castro Harrison, Jorge—1915. *Proceso Histórico de la Educación en el Perú.* (Pueblo Libre, Dpto. impresiones G. U. E. Bartolomé Herrera), 1959.

Cornejo Foronda, David. *Don Manuel Pardo y la Educación Nacional.* Lima, Pontif. Univ. Cat. 1953.

Encinas José Antonio—1888-1958. *Un Ensayo de Escuela Nueva en el Perú.* Lima: Librería e Imprenta Minerva, 1959.

Infante, Luis C.—1887. *Education in Perú,* 2nd ed. Lima: 1941.

MacLean Estenós, Roberto—1904. *La Educación en el Imperio de los Incas.* Lima: Ed. San Marcos, 1952 (Ediciones del Instituto Peruano de Sociología).

————1904. *San Martín y Bolívar en la Historia de la Educación Peruana.* Córdova (R. A.): Imp. de la Universidad, 1943, (Antes del título: *Sociología educacional del Perú*).

Mori Revoredo, Angel. *Compendio histórico-crítico de la educación en el Perú.* Huancayo: Andrés A. Salazar, 1921.

Varetto, Juan C. *Diego Thomson, apóstol de la instrucción pública e iniciador de la obra evangélica en América Latina.* Buenos Aires: Imp. Evangélico, 1918.

Villar Córdova, Aníbal S. *Educación Incaica.* Huancayo, Imp. "El Heraldo," 1929.

Valcárcel, Carlos Daniel, 1911. *La Educación en el Perú autóctono y virreynal.* Sevilla (Escuela de Estudios Hispanoamericanos, Consejo Superior de Inv. Científicas, 1956).

———, 1911. *Historia de la Educación incaica.* Lima, Imp. de la Univ. Nac. de San Marcos, 1961.

Part Six

Education in Africa

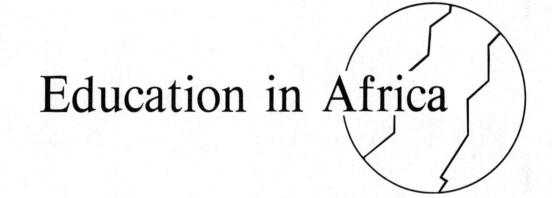

AREA ESSAY: AFRICA

Bruce Fetter

Much of African history cannot be documented by written evidence, and for this reason, many historians have concluded that Africa has no history at all. This is not the case, for a great deal is known about the last two thousand years in Africa, but the knowledge is of necessity based on kinds of evidence which are not often used by other historians. Linguistics, geography, anthropology, and the oral traditions of non-literate states are only a few of the disciplines which have contributed to the picture.

Geography has been an extremely important factor in determining the course of Africa's history. The western nine-tenths of the continent is divided into four nearly symmetrical zones. The best known of these zones is the rain forest, a kind of jungle, which covers a surprisingly small area restricted to the Congo basin and at the southern edge of West Africa. To the north and south of the rain forest is savanna, a grassland, which supports game, livestock, and some farming. Beyond the savanna are the Sahara and Kalahari deserts, which give way to a Mediterranean climate on the northern and southern fringes of the continent.

Except for the Mediterranean zones and some regions of volcanic soil in the Center, Africa is a very poor continent. Neither rain forest nor the deserts support more than the sparsest population, and the savannas are infertile except in the river valleys. The poverty of the soil has prevented the concentration of population normally associated with higher civilizations in other parts of the world, and a further barrier to the development of the area has been the difficulty of communications. Sea travel on the Atlantic was impossible until the Portuguese maritime innovations of the fifteenth century, and although the Indian Ocean has long been a world highway, communications between the coast and the hinterland were not established until the 1790s. Land travel was hampered by the barriers of the Sahara and the rain forest, which, although passable, did not allow any large-scale transportation. In the savanna, animal parasites killed draft animals, leaving human portage the only means of transportation. These natural barriers insulated most Africans from the rest of the world and from each other. Inhabitants of isolated regions developed languages which were totally unrelated to those spoken in other parts of the Continent. Although one cannot entirely reconstruct the history of the African languages, approximate distribution of the four great language families as of 2000 years ago is known. Speakers of Afro-Asiatic languages lived in the Sahara and Mediterranean belt. Macro-Sudanic languages were spoken by people living between the Nile and the Great Lakes of Central Africa and by a few people living near the Niger River. The remainder of Africans north of the rain forest spoke languages of the Niger-Congo family, while Africans south of the rain forest seem to have spoken Khoisan (Click) languages.

Changes of language often indicate population movement, and African history, as we now know it, begins with the migration of people who spoke Bantu languages (of the Niger-Congo family) across the rain forest and into the southern savanna. These Bantu-speakers spread over the southern third of the continent, overwhelming the previous inhabitants by their advanced technology and by the new diseases which they brought. Their material culture, which included settled agriculture, domesticated animals, and the use of iron made possible greater densities of population than the earlier inhabitants had been able to produce, and states eventually emerged in the more fertile regions of central and southern Africa.

Until quite recently most historians believed that the states of Africa owed their existence to conquest by outsiders of European or "Hamitic" blood, who established themselves as kings and aristocrats over the local inhabitants. It is true that some states, notably those of the Central African Lakes region, were founded by outsiders from the North, but most of the other states of sub-Saharan Africa seem to have arisen as a response to two purely local factors, relative fertility of the soil and trade.

The more fertile river valleys developed denser populations than the territories which surrounded them. Within these agglomerations, communication was easy, and the inhabitants soon devised common customs—peculiarities of speech, family patterns, and religious practices—although they lacked any central political institutions. An additional stimulus was provided when these centers were on the border between different geographical zones, such as desert and savanna or savanna and forest, because local products of the two regions could be exchanged through the population center.

Government developed when some villages in the fertile region became stronger than their neighbors and conquered them. Victorious units increased in size until a few kingdoms dominated relatively large areas. This was the case of Ghana, Mali, and Songhay in the Niger Valley; Ashanti and Dahomey in the Guinea Forest; the Kongo and Luba-Lunda kingdoms in the southern savanna; and the Zulu empire in northern Natal.

These kingdoms endured for considerable periods of time, but their territories were limited by the absence of efficient communications. Lacking writing, government officials had great difficulties in transmitting and preserving their orders and laws. Outlying areas were many days removed from the capitals, so the kings could not act quickly in the case of emergency. If a king appointed a lieutenant to govern an outer province, his appointee might rebel in the safety of distance.

Before the penetration of Europeans, the strongest African states were the Muslim kingdoms of North Africa, which had a number of advantages over kingdoms farther to the south. Touching the Mediterranean, their peoples had long been in contact with other parts of the world. Draft animals made the exchange of goods possible on a relatively large scale. Most important, Islam encouraged the loyalty of the people to their kings and provided the kings with writing and other necessary tools of administration.

Islam quickly crossed the Sahara, although initially it took forms that were different from those of North Africa. Rulers in the northern savanna, who had previously lacked written languages in their administration, encouraged Muslims to settle their countries as traders, scribes, and royal advisors. Some kings became Muslims, but their states were not as deeply Islamized as those of North Africa, so that the religion, and the literacy which accompanied it, was often limited to urban centers and the king's immediate entourage. Before the eighteenth century, the masses of the population were little affected, adding a few Islamic practices to their local rites.

Large-scale conversion to Islam was not the work of kings, but of holy men and their religious brotherhood, the Qadiríyya, which reached the northern savanna from Morocco in the sixteenth century. The holy men, who were called marabouts, concentrated at first on conversion, but as the membership in the Qadiríyya grew, they began calling for the establishment of theocratic states, which, unlike the earlier states in the northern savanna, would be legitimated by Islam rather than by animistic practices. The first state having Islam legitimation was Bondu, which was founded in the 1680s, and the process of conversion and state-building continued until the European conquest some two hundred years later. Thwarted politically, Islam continued to grow during the colonial period, perhaps as a means of resisting European rule, and most of the inhabitants of the northern savanna today are Muslims.

Islam spread into the Guinea forest of West Africa in much the same way as in the northern savanna, by means of traders and technical advisors to the kings, but the states of the forest had outside influences other than Islam. Beginning in the fifteenth century, European ships sailed to the coast of West Africa to purchase gum, ivory, gold and slaves. Africans on the coast responded to these demands and as elsewhere on the continent, political units coalesced into increasingly large states. In the early years of contact, the interests of the European traders were more or less identical to those of the Africans—both wanted a maximum flow of goods. In the seventeenth and eighteenth centuries, however, fundamental differences arose. Europeans wanted enormous quantities of slaves to stock their sugar plantations in the western hemisphere, while the larger kingdoms, although profiting from the slave trade, wanted to limit slave shipments in order to prevent the enslavement of their own people and the excessive effort that would be necessitated by continual wars against their neighbors. Europeans continued to trade with large kingdoms, where the available slaves could be quickly loaded onto slave ships, but more slaves could be generated in areas where many small kingdoms were at war with one another. The Portuguese, in fact, encouraged various provinces of the Kongo kingdom to revolt against the king so that more men would be enslaved in civil war.

Europeans brought still greater problems to the states on the western coast of Africa during the nineteenth century. Led by England, which was guided by humanitarian sentiment and a decreased dependence on the products of slave labor, the European powers abruptly reversed their attitude toward slavery and attempted to abolish the slave trade entirely. African rulers were unwilling to accept this abolition because slaves could still profitably be sent to the United States, Cuba, and Brazil, and because European anti-slave patrols were not strong enough to prevent the Africans from trading. Throughout the nineteenth century, European navies patrolled the coast of Africa with the aim of suppressing both the slave trade and the independent states that were participating in it.

European activity was not, however, limited to the negative goal of destroying the slave trade and the states which participated in it. As an alternative, European governments encouraged trade in other items such as gum, ivory, and palm oil. Improvements in tropical medicine enabled governments and private groups to send explorers into the interior to evaluate the resources of Africa. Missionaries, too, penetrated the interior, but unlike the traders, their task was an ambivalent one. They saw themselves as servants of God, while Africans often saw Christianity as a means of acquiring Western technology. Due to the efforts of traders, explorers, and missionaries, then, African societies began adapting to European culture before the European conquest.

In eastern Africa during the nineteenth century, the most influential foreigners were Muslims who were attracted to the interior by slave trade in countries bordering the Indian Ocean. These Muslims, who were more often than not Negroes, entered East and Central from the Nile Valley and the coast of Kenya and Tanzania. Their slave trade brought the same kind of changes to eastern Africa that the European slave trade had brought to western Africa at an earlier period. Strong states, often founded by outsiders, prospered and the inhabitants of weaker political units were enslaved. The new states, however, did not have as much time to develop as their predecessors in West Africa because Europeans were soon in the area, trying to suppress the slave trade.

In the period between 1880 and 1914, Europeans conquered most of the African continent. Most often, they attributed humanitarian motives to their action: to end the slave trade, to spread Christianity, to open the area to trade—to impart to Africa that spirit of progress which nineteenth-century Europe alone of all the nations of world history had engendered. In reality, the conquest of "benighted" Africa was undertaken because of nationalism in Europe. Territorial claims in Africa had become tokens for measuring the power and prestige of western European governments. At first they limited their activities to coastal regions but the rules of the game came to include boundaries in the interior, so representatives of the various European governments raced each other to the center, establishing borders; when at last they met their competitors, European weapons in particular and technology in general made concerted African resistance impossible. The larger states fell first because they were easier to locate. Smaller states fell when the Europeans got around to subduing them. Only European opposition could halt the expansion of a European power.

Once boundaries had been established, the Europeans organized their colonial government. Their aims, in general, were twofold: to establish the cheapest practical administration of their new territories and to find economic assets which would justify the expenses incurred in the conquest. Although Europeans insisted on their mission to civilize Africans, they insisted that Africans should bear the entire expense. The most common method for keeping down costs was the liberal system, through which colonial administrations assigned activities which in Europe would have been performed by the government to private groups. Thus, missionaries monopolized the educational facilities in most of tropical Africa, and industrial concessionaires gained unlimited powers over their employees.

Running parallel to the minimization of expenditures on Africans was the assumption that African interests should be strictly subordinated to those of Europeans. This endemic racism was applied most harshly in areas which were considered most suitable for European settlement: South Africa and Southern Rhodesia, Algeria, and Kenya. In these territories, Africans were removed from their land and forced into the service of settlers. Elsewhere the resident Europeans were either government officials, entrepreneurs, or missionaries, who demanded obedience from all Africans. In all but a few British territories, Africans who had been politically important before the conquest were systematically denied offices in the colonial administration. In the handful of exceptions to the foregoing rule (which included Uganda, Northern Nigeria, and Northwestern Rhodesia), British officials governed through the chiefs to create what was called "indirect rule." Even in areas of "indirect rule," however, European officials made a continuous effort to limit rather than to extend the power of the chiefs.

Given the imposition of an alien ruling caste and the subversion of local political authorities, Africa inevitably underwent a social revolution. The elite which emerged at the end of the colonial period was comprised of those Africans who had attached themselves most firmly to the Europeans. Thus, former slaves had the least objection to joining the colonial armies, and formerly oppressed groups such as the Ibos of eastern Nigeria and the Luba-Kasai of central Congo applied themselves most vigorously to mission schools. These were the men who rose to the highest positions available to Africans in the colonial administrations—the non-commissioned officers, the foremen, the chief clerks. These were the first high school graduates, the first doctors, the first graduates of metropolitan military academies, who, though adopting the servile attitude which was necessary for survival in a colonial society, raised their childern to be the leaders of contemporary Africa.

Members of this new elite made enormous personal advances in the first forty years of the twentieth century but their power was in no way sufficient to gain independence without outside help. The European hold on Africa was undermined by the death struggle between European nations which took place during the Second World War. In Asia, moreover, colonies of the same metropoles were pushed to the point of independence by the Japanese invasion and occupation. When the war was over, some Asian colonies gained their independence immediately, while others had to fight protracted guerilla wars in order to win it. The lesson to European powers, however, was clear; due to advances in the design of small arms and the perfection of guerilla techniques, Europeans could not put down popular uprisings without great cost. An African colony would have to be of enormous value to justify the expense of subduing a rebellion.

In most cases the metropoles decided to grant African colonies their independence rather than to provoke their resistance. The first countries to gain their independence were the Muslim countries north of the Sahara: Libya, the Sudan, Tunisia, and Morocco. Then came those areas below the Sahara which had no European settlers. Europeans tried to hold the line in three areas: Kenya, Algeria, and southern Africa. In the first two cases, Africans mounted bloody revolutions which, although defeated militarily, proved so costly that the colonial powers were forced to abandon their white settlers. In southern Africa, local settlers and the Portuguese have thus far been able to withstand African demands, but at the terrible cost of the creation of police states in which white as well as black people must live.

Africa today is thus divided between the independent states and the remaining settler areas, both groups having unique problems. The independent states, having gained their independence either through revolution or through events in Asia, have not yet produced elites capable of bringing their countries to European standards of wealth and technology. Lacking many natural resources, they may never be able to do so without foreign aid. The settler areas must maintain large military machines in order to protect themselves from internal insurrection and invasion from the free countries of Africa. Both groups will have to make considerable adjustments before they reach the living standard of the developed world.

SELECTED BIBLIOGRAPHY

General Texts

OLIVER, R., and FAGE, J. *A Short History of Africa*. Baltimore, Md.: Penguin Books, 1965.

OLIVER R., and ATMORE, A. *Africa Since 1800*. London: Cambridge University Press, 1967.

ROTBERG, R. *A Political History of Africa*. New York: Harcourt, Brace & World, Inc., 1965.

Specialized Works (arranged by region)

GIBB, H. *Mohammedanism*. New York: Oxford University Press, 1962.

GALLAGHER, C. *The United States and North Africa*. Cambridge: Harvard University Press, 1963.

DAVIDSON, B. *A History of West Africa*. Garden City, N. Y.: Anchor Books, 1966.

CROWDER, M. *A Short History of Nigeria*. London: Faber and Faber, Ltd., 1966.

———. *Senegal*. New York: Oxford University Press, 1962.

HARGREAVES, J. *West Africa: The Former French States*. Englewood Cliffs, N. J.: Prentice-Hall, Inc., 1967.

HOLT, P. M. *A Modern History of the Sudan*. New York: Grove Press, Inc., 1961.

GREENFIELD, R. *Ethiopia*. London: Pall Mall Press, 1965.

OLIVER, R., and MATHEW, G. *A History of East Africa I*. Oxford, Eng.: Clarendon Press, 1963.

HARLOW, V., and CHILVER, M. *A History of East Africa II*. Oxford, Eng.: Clarendon Press, 1966.

VANSINA, J. *Kingdoms of the Savanna*. Madison: University of Wisconsin Press, 1966.

DUFFY, J. *Portugal in Africa*. Cambridge: Harvard University Press, 1962.

HALL, R. *Zambia*. New York: Frederick A. Praeger, Inc., 1966.

MASON, P. *Birth of a Dilemma*. New York: Oxford University Press, 1958.

OMER-COOPER, J. *The Zulu Aftermath*. Evanston: Northwestern University Press, 1966.

DE KIEWET, C. *A History of South Africa*. Oxford, Eng.: Clarendon Press, 1941.

ROUX, E. *Time Longer than Rope*. Madison: University of Wisconsin Press, 1964.

SLADE, R. *King Leopold's Congo*. New York: Oxford University Press, 1962.

Specialized Works (arranged by topic)

The Oxford Regional Geography of Africa. Oxford, Eng.: Clarendon Press, 1965.

CURTIN, P. *The Image of Africa*. Madison: University of Wisconsin Press, 1964.

ROBINSON, R., and GALLAGHER. *Africa and the Victorious*. New York: St. Martin's Press, Inc., 1961.

SCANLON, D. *Traditions of African Education*. New York: Columbia University Press, 1964.

HODGKIN, T. *Nationalism in Colonial Africa*. New York: New York University Press, 1957.

CENTRAL AFRICAN REPUBLIC

Joseph S. Roucek

Known until 1958 as Ubangi-Chari, the Central African Republic was the birthplace of a short-lived dream of unity for the peoples of Afro-Latin culture; the dream died with its originator, Barthélemy Boganda, when he was killed in a plane crash in 1959.

It was one of the territories of Africa which voted "Yes" in the referendum of September 28, 1958; the people, under the leadership of Boganda, returned a 98 percent vote in favor of the French Constitution which gave each territory a free choice as to its future ties with the French Republic. On December 1, 1958, the Legislative Assembly of the Central African Republic voted for membership in the new Community of Self-Governing States. On July 12, 1960, agreements of cooperation and transfer of jurisdiction were signed with the French Republic; independence was proclaimed on August 13, 1960.

The Constitution, adopted on February 9, 1959, by the Constituent Legislative Assembly, proclaimed the nation's "attachment to the Rights of Man, to the principles of democracy and to the self-determination of peoples." The Republic is "indivisible, secular, democratic, and social." Its motto is "Unity, Dignity, Work," and its official language is French. Suffrage is universal, equal, and secret, and all citizens of both sexes who have reached majority may vote.

A large landlocked country, 238,000 square miles, the Republic lies almost in the middle of the African Continent, bordered on the east by the Sudan, on the south by both Republics of the Congo, on the west by Cameroon, and on the north by Chad. It is more than 300 miles from the sea, and consists of a vast rolling plateau with an average altitude of around 2,000 feet, most of the land draining toward the Congo basin. There are many rivers, but navigation is often difficult.

The history of the nation, like that of other regions of tropical Africa, has been marked by successive waves of migration of which little is known and which explain the complex ethnic and linguistic pattern of the area. It has been a major crossroad and trading center of Africa's heartland since its early history.

In fact, all that is known is that successive waves of people from the northeast were pushed into the western coastal regions of Africa by more aggressive peoples who came after them.

French explorers from Gabon and the Middle Congo, as the Congo (Brazzaville) was known, reached the area in 1887, and the first French outpost was established in Bangui in 1889. The area became a territory in 1894, and in 1906 it united with Chad, forming the Ubangi-Shari-Chad colony. In 1910 Ubangi-Shari became one of the four territories of the Federation of French Equatorial Africa (which also included Gabon, the Middle Congo, and Chad). This administrative structure lasted through World War II, during which the area gave active support to the Free French and their allies.

The country is a showcase of the flora and fauna of tropical Africa; nearly every species of African animals can be found here. Elephants were once very common; but, by now, ivory hunters have depopulated the herds. The great equatorial rain forest, the largest of the fabled rain forests in Africa and the least influenced by civilization, stretches across most of the southern half of the Republic.

The people are of great interest to anthropologists. They are primarily subsistence farmers with some Hamite-Negro herdsmen in the northern part of the country. There are four main ethnic groups: the Mandjia-Baya, the M'Baka, the Banda, and the Zandé; they speak many Bantu and Sudanic dialects. Sangho is the widely used *lingua franca* of the market place, and French, the official language, is widely spoken. Most of the people are animists, but there are small Christian and Moslem minorities.

Substantial Moslem immigration to the Republic has taken place in recent years. The Moslems, comparatively well educated and better off financially, are good traders and administrators and often hold government posts. European residents, mostly French, number about 6,000 and live principally in Bangui, the capital city on the Ubangi. Laws require employers to give job preference to Central Africans, and many Nigerians and others have been expelled from the country.

Abroad, the Republic is known primarily for its folkways and mores among certain tribes which use huge discs to extend the lips of their women. It has been believed that originally this disfigurement was effected so that Arab slave traders would become disenchanted by those grotesque faces and would not carry off the women. But among the tribes neighboring the Ubangi River, the custom became widespread and fashionable; huge, plattered lips are now considered a mark of great beauty.

POLITICS

President David Dacko's Movement d'Evolution Sociale on Afrique Noire (MESAN—Social Evolution Movement of Black Africa) controls all of the fifty seats of the National Assembly. President Dacko, who started his career as a teacher, succeeded his uncle, Barthelemy Boganda, the founder of the MESAN and one of the best known political figures in Equatorial Africa, as Head of Government in April, 1959, following the latter's death in an airplane accident.

The principal opposition party, The Movement d'Evolution Démocratique en Afrique Centrale (MEDAC), was dissolved in December, 1960, after an existence of only seven months; in November, 1962, all opposition parties were banned. The President pledged, however, that no important decision would be made without consulting labor, women's and youth organizations, and other representative groups.

During 1963, the Government undertook through MESAN an intensive campaign in the provinces to instill a sense of national unity and purpose in the isolated and diversified citizenry. At the end of the year, the President started a campaign for a three-year austerity program to permit investment in the country's development and in the economic and social needs of the people. On January 5, 1964, President Dacko was reelected for a seven-year term by a majority of 99.4 percent.

THE ECONOMY

Essentially an agricultural country, The Republic exports cotton, coffee, and lumber. Food crops are raised mostly for consumption. Cotton continues to be the chief export crop and is cultivated throughout the country with the exception of the forest regions and along the northeast border. Coffee-growing first became important in 1925; after 1956 it spread widely among the farmers, and its production has been increasingly successful. The herds are too small to sup-

ply all the meat the country needs, and additional animals must be imported from Chad. Stock-raising has been carried on only in those few regions where the tsetse fly is not prevalent. The extensive forests represent the greatest potential for export earnings if the transportation problems could be solved. (The other two export crops, cotton and coffee, are both surplus in the world market). Equatorial wood, on the contrary, enjoys such strong demand that sales are assured for all wood which can be placed at boatside in Atlantic ports. Diamonds are the only mineral mined in the Republic.

TRANSPORTATION

A great effort is being made to improve existing facilities in transportation as a first step in the Republic's economic development. The Government has been considering using the country's position in the heart of Africa to turn it into a transportation center for that continent.

There are more than 370 miles of navigable waterways in the Republic, which, however, are not always usable as trade routes. The flow of water varies from season to season, and the unevenness of the river beds makes it difficult for boats to pass. The flow of the chief river, the Ubangi, is quite irregular, and work now underway to improve this watercourse will take years to complete. The tributaries, the Ouka and Kotto, are overgrown with thick vegetation. New installations at the river port of Bangui have already begun. The present road system seems to satisfy the country's economic needs and can, without large-scale improvements, keep pace with the anticipated economic development. There are 10,900 miles of roads, 3,600 of which are passable all year. The most important task at present is to maintain them in good condition for traffic, and various schemes are aimed at improving main roads and bridges and the trails leading to remote villages.

The Republic has three major airports and several secondary ones. The Bangui airport may be turned into a major stopping point on the trans-African air routes. There are no railroads.

Foreign assistance is of major importance to the Republic's development efforts. While the major burden is borne by France (approximately $20 million annually), assistance also has been received from the EEC, the UN, Israel, and the United States. The United States has granted assistance in control of endemic diseases, road maintenance, agricultural extension services, and the National Pioneer Youth Program, which combines civic education with training in modern agricultural methods.

FOREIGN RELATIONS

The Republic has retained close ties with France. The Republic is a member of the fourteen-nation African and Malagasy Union and the Organization of

African Unity. Relations with the United States have been friendly. In November, 1964, the Chinese Communists established diplomatic relations with the Republic; 25 Chinese technicians formed the first detachment to Bangui "to study the site for a Chinese Embassy."

EDUCATION

History of the country has offered it a very poor educational background. French explorers reached the country somewhat later than its southern neighbors, and military forces had to subdue dissidence directed initially at the exploitative policies of the concessionary companies. The French established a permanent administration only after 1910, and the country's inland insulated position postponed the arrival of missionaries and limited their numbers.

The situation became even more difficult when the Ubangui territorial assembly was reluctant to subsidize mission schools; in fact, the territorial education service and the territorial assembly were periodically at sword's points, with the result that at least on two occasions numerous French teachers left their posts.

One of the primary aims of the new Republic has been the extension of educational facilities. A considerable effort has been made by the Ministry of Education and Labor to increase the rate of school enrollment, not only in state schools but also in private ones, allowed to function under state control. Realizing that elementary education is the basic need, particularly in the rural areas, efforts have been made to increase the number of children attending schools in the villages. These schools have been expanding, and buses are used to transport children from outlying districts. In 1951, 9.5 percent of children of school age were enrolled in schools; by 1960, the proportion had reached 27.3 percent.

Of the 61,428 primary-school students in 1960, 37.8 percent attended mission schools; over 90 percent of these were Catholic. The pupil-teacher ratio in the mission schools was 57 to 1; in the public schools, it was 65 to 1.

When Boganda, a former priest, became the country's leading political personality in the early 1950s, the allocations to mission institutions were greatly increased, and their attendance also rose. But, in spite of these subsidies, the Catholic missions were in such financial straits by 1958 that their staff had to decide whether to resign or accept big salary cuts. The Africans struck, insisting on the government help. The Minister of Education tried to hold out, but public opinion forced him to raise the mission subsidy by more than a third, to almost $350,000 in 1959; and by the end of that year, the government was paying 80 percent of the cost of operating these missionary establishments.

The difficulties between the territorial education service and the territorial Assembly can be traced to the period after the end of World War II, when a new head of the education service was sent from Paris to replace an acting territorial inspector. In spite of the territorial assembly's approval of the dismissal of the acting inspector, he was upheld by the local French administration, and three newly-arrived professors from France left abruptly in the resulting skirmish. Then, in 1956, Boganda asked for a "profound reform" of the inspectorate—with the result that another exodus of about fifty European teachers took place; this represented a substantial proportion of the country's secondary and administrative staffs.

A persistent problem that has been plaguing the educational efforts is the absenteeism of students in the rural areas because of rain during the rainy season and the need to pick cotton, hunt, or fish when it is dry.

The whole system of secondary education, financed entirely by FAC (Fund for Aid and Cooperation, a French government agency for economic and technical assistance to the new states in Africa), has been closely modelled on the French system. Many new buildings have been constructed, and the distribution of educational institutions has been improved. In 1960, 1,560 students attended the seven public and eight private secondary schools (an increase of about 500 students since 1958). One-third of secondary-level students attend private schools, a slightly higher proportion than in 1958. Almost all the students in mission secondary schools in 1958 were Catholic. Of those in secondary schools in 1958, 13 percent were girls, of which only a minority of 16 percent atttended Catholic schools. Of the seventeen students taking the baccalauréat examination in 1957, six passed. In the same year, 55 out of 100 succeeded in achieving their BE or BEPC diplomas.

Since there are only limited facilities for secondary education, the stress is placed on technical centers and on teacher-training schools which will make it possible to train the teachers and technicians that the young Republic needs. In 1960, there were 1,412 students in the twenty-two technical (vocational) schools, of which only one (with twenty students) is private. This is a marked increase over the 1958 figure of 436.

In November, 1959, a school for girls, constructed with FIDES funds, opened. Three sections were offered: lingerie embroidery, sewing, and social work; there were ninety students in five classes, about equally divided between Europeans and Africans.

As in all other central African territories, preventive medicine is the most important aspect of public health in the Republic. The health service is organized into two separate administrative units: the African Medical Assistance, in charge of hospitals and dispensaries, and the Mobile Health and Prophylaxis Units. A new hospital with 350 beds has recently been opened in Bangui, and dispensaries and clinics have been set up. The ratio of doctors to the total population is still inadequate (one doctor for each 44,000 inhabitants); even this, however, is a drain on the national budget, as public health expenditure accounts for 14 percent of the total.

The Republic has been unable to set up any institutions of higher learning; so its students continue to go to the University of Dakar in Senegal, or to French institutions. The Republic is a signatory to the accord establishing a new university at Brazzaville as the center of higher learning for Chad, Congo, and the Central African Republic.

Compared with the requirements of the country and size of its population, these achievements may seem insignificant; but if the short space of time in which they have been accomplished is taken into account, they are by no means neglible. In spite of its limited resources, the Republic has been able to organize a sound educational system, with schools staffed primarily by French teachers until enough Central Africans can be trained to take their place.

Developments since 1966-67 have included the placing of radio and television under plans for "national education," a substantially higher expenditure (17 percent of State monies) for education (e.g., an increase of 15 percent from 1966 to 1967), and greatly expanded enrollments at all levels (primary, about 149,000 pupils; secondary, 5,000 pupils; technical-vocational, 800; teacher training, 230; higher education, 100). The European Development Fund built 150 new primary school classrooms in 1967 alone. More stress is being placed on African history and culture than previously.

BIBLIOGRAPHY

The Central African Republic, Hour of Independence. New York: Embassade de France, Service de Presse et d'information, December, 1960.

COLEMAN, JAMES S., and ROSBERG C. G., JR. *Political Parties and National Integration in Tropical Africa.* Berkeley: University of California Press, 1964.

Department of State. *Central African Republic.* Department of State Publication 7285, African Series. Washington, D. C.: Government Printing Office, April, 1962.

DOXEY, G. V., and M. P. *Problems of Transition in East and Central Africa.* Toronto: Canadian Institute of International Affairs, 1963.

FRANKLIN, HARRY. *Unholy Wedlock.* London: Allen & Unwin, 1964.

GUSSMAN, BORIS. *Out in the Mid-day Sun.* New York: Oxford University Press, Inc., 1963.

JARRETT, H. R. *Africa.* Chapter XI, "Central Africa," pp. 250-277. New York: London House, 1962.

KITCHEN, HELEN, ed. *A Handbook of African Affairs.* New York: Frederick A. Praeger, Inc., 1964, pp. 23-25, 192-3.

LEGUM, COLIN, ed. *Africa: A Handbook to the Continent.* New York: Frederick A. Praeger, Inc., 1962.

MELADY, THOMAS PATRICK. *Faces of Africa.* New York: The Macmillan Co., 1964, pp. 107-110.

SEGAL, RONALD. *African Profiles.* "The Equatorial Quarter." Baltimore: Penguin Books, Inc., 1962. chap. 11, pp. 173-185.

WATTENBERG, BEN, and SMITH, RALPH LEE. *The New Nations of Africa.* New York: Hart, 1963, pp. 68-77.

WILLS, A. J. *An Introduction to the History of Central Africa.* New York: Oxford University Press, Inc., 1964.

EGYPT-U.A.R.

G. B. Ghobrial

The fundamental fact that emerges from any study of the Egyptian educational system is that Egypt, during her long history, has been an educational battleground where many cultural, economic, and political forces met and mingled and left on the present educational system their indelible marks. The present Egyptian educational system has inherited four major handicaps: (1) An emphasis upon memorization of factual information, rote learning and slavish adherence to textbooks, discouraging creative thinking and scientific investigation. As a result, instead of tending to produce citizens endowed with intelligence and vision, it tends to produce "automatons" who can only "act" in a monotonous and routine manner. (2) An inadequate opportunity to develop individual potential and personality. The leaders imbued with enthusiasm, culture, and above all, conscientiousness, who should emerge from an educational institution become "wooden" products manufactured in an atmosphere in which these qualities are stifled or frozen. (3) An authoritarian environment largely excluding the beneficial attitudes of love, understanding, cooperation, and freedom. The soldierly atmosphere and freedom-denying measures employed by the school inhibit the pupil's awareness of individual rights and future responsibilities and breed men and women amenable to exploitation. (4) An almost exclusive orientation toward qualification for the school certificate, virtual employment insurance, the certificate leading to government employment. Youth are not educated to meet political issues or the social problems of their community. As a result, the secondary school graduate joins the ranks of the unemployed if he fails to secure a government post.

This essay will present the educational systems which have existed in Egypt since the earliest known times in order to determine the prevalence of these several maladies: where they came from, when they were instituted, and how they were perpetuated. After a consideration of education in Ancient Egypt, the respective cultural and/or political impacts of the Arabs, the French, Mohammed Ali and his successors, and the British will be treated.

THE EDUCATIONAL SYSTEM IN ANCIENT EGYPT

Among the ancient Egyptians, learning was valued for at least three reasons. Apparently learned men enjoyed privileges unavailable to the unlearned; learning divided the ruling class from the classes of the ruled. By following learned studies and becoming a "scribe," one was able to enter into the hierarchy of official life, and all the offices of the state seemed to be open to him. "As for the scribe," wrote Duauf (2000 B.C.), "any position at court may be his, he needs not to be a beggar therein."[1] A second reason was that the scribe was exempt from labor. "Put writing in thine heart that thou mayest protect thyself from hard labor of any kind and be a magistrate of high repute" enjoined an anonymous sage.[2] Third, learning was "the way to renown. The ignorant man, whose name is unknown, is like a heavily-laden donkey; he is driven by the scribe, while the fortunate man who has set his heart upon learning is above hard work and becomes a wise prince."[3]

It was not without reason that the high officials were so fond of having themselves represented in the act of writing. It was to writing, to being a scribe, that they owed their status. Most probably it was for the same reason that ancient Egyptian literature is woven with such enthusiastic reverence for learning as is evident in the remark of Ptah-Hotep who lived *circa* 3550 B.C.:

1. Sir Wallis Budge, *The Teaching of Amenemapt,* London: Martin Hopkins and Co., 1924, p. 68.
2. Adolf Erman, *The Literature of the Ancient Egyptians,* London: Macmillan and Co., 1927, p. 193.
3. A. Erman, *Life in Ancient Egypt,* London: Macmillan and Co., 1894, p. 328.

Train thy son to be a teachable man whose wisdom is agreeable to the great. . . . A son who attends [schools] is like a follower of Horus; he is happy after having attended. He becomes great, he arrives at dignity, he gives the same lesson to his children. . . . As for the man without experience who listens not, he affects nothing whatsoever. He seeks knowledge in ignorance, profit in loss, he commits all kinds of errors, always accordingly choosing the contrary of what is praiseworthy.[4]

One of the Egyptologists by whom King Amenemapt's writings were examined, Professor J. P. Mahaffy, took pains to remark the avidity of the ancient Egyptians for learning:

There have been only two earlier nations and one later which could compete with the Greeks in their treatment of this perpetual problem in human progress. We have first the Egyptian nation, which by its thorough and widely diffused culture, attained a duration of national prosperity and happiness perhaps never since equalled.[5]

A note of Professor M. Howell's parallels the reflection of Professor Mahaffy:

It was in Egypt that the first University of which we have any knowledge was located, and of which Abraham, Isaac, and Jacob may have served as members of the Board of Trustees. I have sometimes thought, indeed I think it most probable, that it was, as I have therefore stated, at the Heliopolis University that Joseph, the son of Jacob, was educated as was Moses.[6]

THE PRIMARY COURSE OF INSTRUCTION

At the outset, it is necessary to distinguish between the attendance at the palace schools and at the public schools.

For the highest class, *viz.* the heir to the throne, the king's other sons, and the resident foreign princes, the training was in the nursery of the palace. Dating from the nineteenth Dynasty (1300 B.C.) there was a tradition that all the children born on the same day as the royal heir were to be brought up with him. Perhaps this was connected with their sharing the same horoscope and therefore the same fortune. A large staff of nurses and attendants managed the younger scholars, while the elder ones had tutors called "father nurses" who educated them and who were represented on their tombs holding a prince on their knees.

The public schools existed for the education of boys of the lower classes. Even children from the poorest classes attended such schools, and from them came high priests, governors of provinces, architects, engineers, physicians, poets, and astronomers. School life began at the age of four and the school day evidently lasted until noon.

The primary course of instruction, both in the palace schools and the public schools, lasted twelve years and included instruction in writing, arithmetic, and ethics.

Writing was important for three reasons: First, because of the veneration the Egyptians had for the character of their scripts, which they called the "divine words" and which they believe to have been an invention of the God Thoth, who had taught them to the inhabitants of Egypt; Second, coincident with the creation and organization of the State, writing became indispensable for conducting governmental affairs, business, and commerce. Furthermore, the man of culture was distinguished from the less educated by acquiring this art to the greatest proficiency. Hence, writing was in a peculiar fashion the real foundation of Egyptian education and became uniquely the process by which the Egyptians acquired their learning, whereas in the schools of other peoples the main effort has always been to master the lesson by verbal repetition.

The method of teaching writing consisted chiefly in giving the pupils passages to copy in order that while practicing their calligraphy and orthography, they might at the same time form their style. These passages were sometimes model letters and literary compositions, but more frequently the teachers chose specimens which contained rules for wise conduct and good manners.

The second subject which the school boy learned was mathematics. Egyptian mathematics was developed to solve daily problems encountered in the transactions of business and government. Inasmuch as this science attempted to solve the problems of daily life, its instruction in Ancient Egypt centered around exactly such problems. At the elementary level Plato was particularly struck by one teaching method which he described as follows:

In Egypt, systems of calculation have been actually invented for the use of children, which they learn as a pleasure and as amusement.[7]

Continually emphasizing the practical tendency of Egyptian mathematics, Professor Steindorff remarks, "It must be admitted in this connection, that the Egyptian handbooks on the subject [mathematics] were devoted exclusively to the treatment of practical problems."[8]

Morality constituted the third subject of the ancient Egyptian curriculum. The textbooks used were written by sages who maintained in their morality a wholesome regard for the highest practical

4. Ptah-hotep, *The Teaching of Ptah-hotep*, Quoted from A. H. Sayce (ed.) *Records of the Past*. London: Samuel Bagster and Sons, 1890, Vol. III, pp. 32-33.

5. J. P. Mahaffy, *Old Greek Education*, London: Harper and Bros., 1905, p. 4.

6. M. Howell, *Egypt's Past, Present, and Future*, Dayton, O.: Service Publishing Co., 1929, p. 323.

7. Plato, *The Laws of Plato*, Jowett's translation, Vol. IV, p. 336. Quoted from *The Catholic Quarterly Review*, Philadelphia: Hardy and Mahoney, 1893, Vol. XVIII, p. 180.

8. G. Steindorff and K. Seele, *When Egypt Ruled the East*, Chicago: The University of Chicago Press, 1942, p. 128.

ideals, touching always on everyday moral situations.[9] All their writings were a series of moral aphorisms and incidents, the distilled experience and wisdom of the fathers to guide their sons in their coming life. In all these writings there was nothing of speculation, no theoretical questioning, only the practical reflections on life as it had been experienced by themselves. By adopting these ethical works, the schools indicated that they aimed to instruct their young in a wholly practical way in the art of virtuous living.

Such is the picture of the primary course of instruction in Ancient Egypt. From what has been shown, further education was designed on equally practical lines with respect to equipping the scholar with the necessary tools to earn his living. Nevertheless, if he wanted to complete his education, he would enter one of the department schools or one of the temple schools, the universities of the day.

HIGHER COURSE OF INSTRUCTION

The "department schools" were so called because they were connected with various government departments in order to train candidates for the respective official positions. Examples of these were the schools attached to the Royal Treasury, the Royal Workshop, and the Royal Library. In these institutions the individual training of the young scribes was carried on by one of the higher officials of the department to whom they were assigned as pupils and subordinates. Here the scholar was trained in form and good style, spending entire months in copying letters, circulars, legal documents, and admonitions. At his disposal were books full of extracts taken from well-known authors which he studied perpetually. When the apprentice could write all the formulas from memory, the master then entrusted him with composing original efforts to suit occasions such as Journeys of the Pharaohs and higher officials, the building of temples or cities, repairing of ships or chariots, and petitions of lower officials to their superiors and the replies of the latter, requests for furlough, complaints, and many other official situations.

During this period the masters constantly endeavored to instill in the minds of the pupils several important principles. The official scribe should be impartial, protecting the weak against the powerful; capable, knowing the way out in the midst of the greatest difficulties; and humble, never thrusting himself forward, and yet one whose opinion is heard with respect in the council. His every writing and utterance, too, must be distinct from the vulgar, reflecting his adherence to the ideal of learning.

Besides training in literary style, the master used to accompany his student to the workyards to observe and help him in keeping documents of the material delivered and used there and to assist him in gathering material for his reports.

Apparently this course of training lasted throughout four years and having acquired the knowledge and skill needed for everyday use, the education of the trainee was considered complete; he became a scribe, and a job was sought for him in some office at the bottom of the ladder.

Training for professional careers was undertaken in the Temple Schools which were located at Heliopolis, Thebes, Memphis, Heracliopolis, and Tel-El-Amarna. It was at Heliopolis, the most flourishing city of all, that many of the master minds of antiquity, Egyptians and others, spent time in study; among these were Moses, Thales, Selon, and Plato. Each of these universities had a large library on which was inscribed "Remedy of the Soul." These institutions were open to every Egyptian youth, even though one must not imagine that the children of the lower classes formed a large proportion of the students; these were boarding schools which made heavy demands on the father's purse. A passage in the Harris papyrus informs one that if the fathers had five slaves, he must give up three of the five to pay for the boy's education.

Among the studies pursued at these schools were medicine, astronomy, engineering, sculpture, and drawing. And practice, not theory, underlay the method of education.

As for medicine, Professor Hebermann has pointed out that whereas in Babylonia and Greece the resort of the sick man was to have himself carried to the market place and treated according to the suggestions of the good-natured passerby, medicine in Egypt was systematically taught and performed.[10] In recent years many writers have equally revered the Egyptians for their medical knowledge and skill. Breasted, for example, has written:

Medicine was already in possession of much empirical wisdom, displaying close and accurate observation; the calling of a physician already existed and the court physician of the Pharaoh was a man of rank and influence. . . . Some of his recipes crossed with the Greeks to Europe where they are still in use among the peasantry of the present day.[11]

It is a noteworthy fact that medical knowledge in ancient Egypt was developed to meet an extremely important problem, namely, the embalming of the bodies of the dead, since the Egyptians believed in physical life after death and they wanted to keep the body in exemplary condition for this after-life.

The way in which the young man was trained in medicine was comparable to the training of the

---

9. For more information on these texts see: G. Ghobrial, *The Maladies of the Egyptian Secondary Education in Historical Perspective.* Ph.D. Thesis, University of Minnesota 1960, pp. 31-42.
10. American Catholic Quarterly Review, "Education in Ancient Egypt," Vol. 18, 1893: p. 194.
11. J. H. Breasted, *The History of Egypt from the Earliest Times to the Persian Conquest,* p. 201.

scribe; he studied the textbooks to master the medical knowledge contained in them, then practiced extensively under the supervision of his master.[12]

Sculpture served practical purposes; the statues were not erected in the market place but were masoned within the tomb where they might be of advantage to the deceased in the hereafter. The sculptor's training proceeded in the same practical fashion as the training of the scribe and the physician. Professor G. Haspero has given a vivid description of the training of the Egyptian sculptor:

As soon as the learner knew how to manage the point and the mallet, his master set him to copy a series of graduated models representing an animal in various stages of completion, or a part of a human body, or the whole human body, from the first rough sketch to the finished design.[13]

When the student mastered this step, he proceeded to the next; here the master would ask him to put the separate parts together to compose a complete figure of a man or a woman in various postures, kneeling, seated, squatting, the arm extended or falling passively to the sides. Executed by the master, these models were copied over and over again by his students till they could produce them with exact fidelity. This practical method produced works which have been described by M. C. Perrat as not to be surpassed in their way by the greatest portraits of modern Europe.[14]

Such, in outline, is the picture of education in ancient Egypt. Two generalizations have bearing here. The first is that there was no gap separating scientific and moral education; the moral precepts were given to the students throughout his education, whether he was trained to become a scribe, a physician, an engineer, or a priest. The second is that Ancient Egyptian education centered around daily-life problems, problems which, once observed, they sought information about, then analyzed; and reaching practical solution, they proceeded to effectuate these solutions in action. And, not least important, they perpetuated their methods through their education.

It has been seen that Ancient Egyptian education, on each level, in all its aspects, was dominated by a wholly practical interest. The following will be concerned with the breakdown of that educational position, its supplanting by others, and an evaluation of the consequences.

EDUCATION FROM THE ARABS

Of the influences which may be discerned in present-day Egyptian education, the earliest is that of the Arabs who included Egypt within their empire during the seventh century A.D., a generation after the death of the Prophet Mohammad. The Arab conquest proved to be the most persuasive influence: it brought with it a new religion, Islam, a new language,

Arabic, and a new educational system the remnant of which is still operating in the country.

Into Egypt the Arabs carried an educational system which consisted of the *Kuttab* where the young underwent their elementary training and the *Madaris* where they received advanced instruction. As in schools elsewhere in the Arab world, the attendance here was throughout centuries limited to those of the male sex and those whose parents were eager and able to provide for their education.

The Egyptian *Kuttab*, which survived until after 1949, occupied one schoolroom where the students began by learning the individual Arabic letters; from them they proceeded to words and phrases, mostly taken from the Koran. When the child knew how to read, he then began to memorize parts of the Koran. As there was rarely more than one copy of the Holy Book in the school, the teacher wrote on the child's slate verse after verse to be memorized. This study of the Koran, however, was entirely mechanical, no explanation or commentary whatever being given.

When the child had gone through half of the Koran in this manner, his education was judged to be complete. No arithmetic was taught in these schools; if the child was obliged to have some knowledge of that science, he studied it with the public weigher or was apprenticed to a merchant. Hence, the course provided no real intellectual education or training in reflective thinking. And as the knowledge of reading and writing was closely related to knowledge of the Koran, even this gradually vanished from want of exercise, when the adolescent left the *Kuttab*.

The *Kuttab fiky* (or instructor) was not generally a man of any great attainment. Indeed, his standard of learning seems to have been so low that cases of actual illiteracy have been reported. Unsalaried, the *fiky* lived mainly on gifts from his students' parents. With the *falaka*, a thick stick with a loop of cord in it, to which the pupils' feet are strapped down while they are being whipped, the *fiky* guaranteed the education of the most backward and mentally defective as well as the most talented children.

It has been remarked that the main emphasis in the Kuttab was the learning by heart of parts of the Koran rather than necessarily the understanding of it. The parents were often illiterate and therefore could not be expected to judge about the standard of their children's education; as long as their sons could recite the Koran in loud, clear voices, they were considered well educated. The fiky was thus the sole authority to the student, and whether the student

12. For information on these texts see: G. Ghobrial, *op. cit.*, pp. 50-51.
13. G. Maspero, *Egyptian Archeology*, London: H. Grevel and Co., 1889, p. 192.
14. Perrat and Chipiez, *History of Art*, Vol. II, p. 194. Quoted from J. Breasted, *The History of Egypt from the Ancient Times to the Persian Conquest*, p. 106.

understood what he was reciting or not depended upon the fiky's own understanding of the Koran, a matter which was in many cases doubtful. Moreover, students were not encouraged to ask questions since the idea that, in general, questioning the Koran was a sin was deeply enrouted in the student at an early stage.

Having completed his Kuttab studies, the youth was ready to launch his career. In most cases, the son followed his father's trade or profession; he very often underwent his period of apprenticeship with his father. If, however, he wanted to continue his education he might go to any of the higher schools; if he wanted to enter some trade other than his father's, he could become an apprentice to a member of the particular corporation; otherwise he could make a living by reciting the Koran and carrying on his social obligations.

This Kuttab education fulfilled a social function once needed. This institution gave the young child all he was expected to know, namely, the recitation of the Koran by heart, as well as the recitation of various prayers and the correct performance of the movements that accompanied them. The kuttab discipline thus brought the pupil into line with the rest of the Moslem community life; the main ideal was moral and religious, preparing him for social acceptability in accordance with Moslem ethics, and making him part of the religious system which controlled almost every art of life.

Secondary and higher education in Egypt since the Arabs has traditionally been offered at the *Madaris* of which the earliest and most important in this country is al *Azhar*. Al *Azhar* had admitted students at almost any age and with little regard to preparation. Traditionally, students have previously learned the Koran by heart in a Kuttab and also have known the rudiments of reading, writing, and arithmetic. Often, however, these were learned at al *Azhar* itself. Once a student has inscribed his name on the register, he can remain at al *Azhar* as long as he wishes. Each chooses the subject and teachers he desires and advances at his own pace. No tuition is charged and students are distributed according to their place of origin, each province or country having its own hostel where the students are lodged, fed, and taught. The students scarcely ever leave the campus; al *Azhar* becomes to them an adopted home to which they always remain faithful.

The curriculum of al *Azhar* is divided into two sections, the most important of which is constituted by *al ulum al nakliah* (transmitted or traditional sciences) which includes dogmatic theology, interpretation of the Koran, traditions and jurisprudence. These are all based upon divine revelation, and consequently their sources are not subject to investigation or criticism. Next came *al ulum al akliah* (the rational sciences) which include the grammar and syntax of the Arabic language, prosody, and rhetoric. Other fields such as history, geography, and mathematics have, since the Middle Ages, fallen into neglect, or if taught at all, have been taught in a very inadequate way.

In al *Azhar* teaching has always taken exclusively the form of lectures. These were based upon the text of some author of bygone centuries who is regarded as an authority on the subject at hand; but rarely is the text in the hands of the students themselves. Rather, the student sets himself to memorize by rote the commentary of some later writer upon the original text, or the glosses of a still later writer upon the commentary, or still further superglosses and notes upon this.

There is no graduation as such; no diplomas or degrees are granted. Students may leave at any point. If not far advanced, they are likely to be absorbed in various walks of life, including teaching in the Kuttabs. The more advanced are likely to become "preachers" of mosques. Many, however, continue their studies until they feel competent to become teachers at al *Azhar* itself. Then they start lecturing, and if they attract increasing numbers of students, they will be licensed by the rector of al *Azhar* and so eventually come to be counted among the official faculty of the institution.

The spirit which has dominated instruction in al *Azhar* for centuries has been severely traditional. The chief object of the education which it imparted was not research and investigation for the purpose of improving the state of the sciences taught, but rather the transmission of these sciences exactly as they had been handed down by the early fathers of the faith, without deviation. The doors of independent investigation of the sources of the faith and the formulation of independent opinion concerning them were closed in Islam by the middle of the eleventh century, and consequently the authoritative interpreters of religion were those of the dim and distant past.

To show that the *Azhar* lives in the past, hedged in by a narrow formalism, and its main interest is the dogmas, the theology, and the traditions of Islam, rather than modern science, modern literature, modern history, and modern philosophy, no better evidence could be given than a few anecdotes. The first concerns a conversation which took place in 1914 between Lord Cromer, British High Commissioner to Egypt, and the president of al *Azhar*. Lord Cromer asked the president whether he believed that the sun went around the earth or the earth went around the sun. To this question the learned person replied that he was not sure; that one nation taught one way, and another a different way; that his own general impression was that the sun went around the earth, but he had never paid much attention to the subject which, in any case, was too unimportant to merit serious discussion. The other anecdote, which sheds further light on the whole spirit of this institution, concerns a conversation that took place in 1930 between the distinguished Orientalist M. P. Grabites and one of the *Azhar* professors.

"Our Azharites," said the professor, "do not have to attempt to demonstrate the correctness of the thesis expounded by them. They simply set forth what our great scholars of bygone days have proven hundreds of years ago to be the truth. Any controversy that might have existed as to the orthodoxy of such doctrines has been settled ages ago. Today the matter is removed from the domain of doubt. You Occidentals," he continued, "with your modernism imagine that new matters of inquiry are arising everyday. You are wrong. We stay put. Our scholars have long since molded into authoritative form all that an educated man is required to know, or should be allowed to know."

Existence of this authoritarian type of medieval education, which exalted memory and which employed memorization as its chief pedagogical method, has exerted a specific and penetrating influence on education in modern Egypt.

First, it has impregnated all Egyptian education with its own dominant characteristic: cramming the memory instead of developing the powers of thought. While it may be said that this is not an evil peculiar to Egypt, it has certainly been carried to extraordinary lengths there. For at least a thousand years the idea of securing knowledge by memorizing the authorized and revered texts has been the normal Egyptian method.

A second defect came as a result of the fact the Islam has always been impervious to change and consequently al Azhar has been the arsenal manufacturing once and for all a set of values and thereafter resisting change and resenting criticism, thus stifling in its students any initiative. While change is not in itself necessarily progress, yet without change progress obviously is impossible. Where there is no freedom to engage in new ideas, where the beaten path must forever be adhered to, where the eyes are constantly turned backward in the complacent glorification of a distant past, all hope for advancement is paralyzed. In view of the conservatism of al Azhar's influence on one hand and the valuable social changes which only educational experimentation could bring on the other, the damage done to the nation by the killing of this vital social function of the schools is beyond calculation; this is particularly true since Egypt has possessed no other agency capable of bringing such necessary change.

Third, this system of education has a great influence on the social outlook of Egypt. It has been a great agent of conservatism, fanaticism, and hostility toward modern civilization. It has created an atmosphere of its own and has imbued its youth with a peculiar mentality which has affected the masses considerably, not only in Egypt, but also in the whole Arabic-speaking world.

It is hard to predict the future of al Azhar. Today the country is patterned on western standards; the modern lawyer has replaced the Azhar-trained juris-

consultant. As a result, with each succeeding year, the position of the Azhar graduate is becoming more and more precarious. Having devoted long years to acquire knowledge, he cannot merely sit idle and nurse his grievance. Something must be done. The modern world has to invade the citadel of al Azhar; to invade it not with electric lights and modern desks (which the institution now has), but with a new philosophy to replace its traditional medievalism. Once this has been done, the Azhar graduate will become a force of enlightening the general public in Egypt and the rest of the Moslem world.

THE FRENCH AND THEIR IMPACT

In 1798 Napoleon's forces landed in Egypt, the first western invasion since the Crusaders left the country in the thirteenth century. And it was not until the arrival of Napoleon that any decisive change was effected in Egyptian education, the Arab educational system remaining essentially unaltered throughout the dynasties of the Fatimides, the Aiyubites, and the Mamelukes. While otherwise Egypt underwent many vicissitudes, education there remained the same. The French occupation which lasted from 1798 to 1801 opened up to outside influences a country that for nearly four centuries had been isolated from the growing civilization of the western world. The object of the following pages, therefore, is to discuss what Napoleon brought from France, the impact of his innovations on the Egyptians; to analyze what the French leader established in the country and the French influence on the people; and to study the implications of the French invasion for the educational outlook of the country.

To consider the first matter, Napoleon brought with him 165 *savants* who composed a living encyclopedia, representing a summary of everything useful or decorative that an advanced civilization could produce. Among these were mathematicians, astronomers, naturalists, and mining engineers, one sculptor, engineering draftsmen, gunpowder experts, men of letters and secretaries, consuls and interpreters, health officers, quarantine officers, painters, and musicians.

Second, the occupation brought with it 500 volumes which included the famous *L'Encyclopedie;* the collection of transactions of the *Academie de Sciences;* technical works on medicine and surgery; and works on architecture, and civil engineering. Also included were works of more humanistic interest, such as those of Voltaire; volumes of history and geography, travellers' records, notably those of Savary and Valney; seven copies of the series of maps by the geographer D'Auville, relating not only to Egypt, but also to other parts of the Eastern and African world. These volumes constituted the library which was open to visitors from ten in the morning until dusk.

Third, Napoleon brought with him two printing presses. One was official, supplied by the State Printing Department, and the other was private, belonging to a citizen who followed Napoleon as an independent printer. The official press owned French, Arabic, and Greek types and was divided into two sections, one oriental and the other French. This plant printed official memorandums and proclamations. The private printing plant published two periodicals, one of which was *Le Courier de L'Egypt* which appeared every fifth day, gave local news and news from Europe. All articles that were of interest to the natives were translated into Arabic and issued as a tract. The other periodical was *La Decade Egyptienne* which applied itself to the domains of science, art, commerce, civil and criminal legislation, moral and religious institutions, and had room for articles on climate and diseases. Different issues included lessons on the grammar of spoken Arabic for the use of the French and Egyptians, a description of ophthalmia in Italian and Arabic, and essays on smallpox in French and Arabic.

Fourth, many French artisans accompanied the expedition; musicographers, actors, dancers, and gardeners. The activities of this "artistic baggage" gave a French air to the capital of Egypt. Boulevards were constructed, restaurants in French style were opened, cafes and casinos with salons came into being, shops of all sorts sprouted in the capital, and articles of European furniture, such as beds, tables, and chairs started to be in demand in a country where a room was supposed to be completely furnished when it had some cushions and a carpet.

Fifth, Napoleon established two institutions in the country. The first, established in Cairo in August, 1798, was an academy of science and fine arts which was given the name *Institute d'Egypt*. This establishment had for its principal objectives the research into and publication of the natural, industrial, and historical data of Egypt and the giving of advice on the ordinary problems of government. Related to the institute there were the engineering workshops which supplied all that was asked from them; surgical instruments, telescopes, compasses, and pencils, lenses and microscopes, and machinery for the printing works. On October 5, 1798, another institution emerged. The Egyptian notables from all parts of the country were invited by Napoleon to come to Cairo to form an assembly known as the "General Divan," the objective of which was, in Napoleon's words, "to accustom the notables of Egypt to the ideas of assembly and government." This institution consisted of a General Divan at Cairo, and Provincial Divans in the capitals of the provinces. This divan system was an integral organization which invited the Egyptians for the first time in their history to deliberate in common on their country's affairs. It was, in effect, the first "school" where the notables of Egypt received their beginning lessons in self-government. This "course of political education" which lasted throughout the period of the French rule, bore its fruits in 1805 when these notables became the political power which made Mohammad Ali the Pasha of Egypt.

The French invasion marked an epoch in the history of education in Egypt. The old education of the *madaris* remained unchallenged until the beginning of the nineteenth century when it was subjected to a severe test that shook it to its very roots. Napoleon instructed the Egyptians to appreciate French culture, and when Mohammad Ali came to power and took tentative steps toward introducing European civilization into Egypt, his love for this civilization showed itself in two ways: The first was that the Pasha turned to France for assistance. From it he "imported" his educational exports, and to it he sent his educational missions. As a result, in 1837, when the *Divan al Madaris* or ministry of schools was established, it was composed of six Egyptians and five Frenchmen. Second, the first missionary educators that Mohammad Ali encouraged to come to Egypt were the French who started to open their schools in 1840. The *Bon Pasteur*, Lazarists and Jesuit Fathers, and the *Mere De Dieu* and *Sacre Coeur* Sisters launched the first parochial schools the country had ever seen. The successful spreading of these parochial schools led to the endowment of several private and secular schools. Four French Colleges were opened by the French state in Egypt: the *Lycée Francais* in Alexandria, the *Lycée Francais, Ecole de Droit*, and *L'institut Francais d'Archiologie* in Cairo. The French rightly boasted that Egypt was one of their cultural provinces. Despite the British Occupation which lasted for more than sixty years, French educational and cultural influences were solidly established in the country.

Into the medieval orthodoxy of the Arabic system the French influence came like a breeze. It was the first refreshing and creative force, bringing those scientific and dynamic ideas present in the physical and natural sciences and the social sciences of the West. All this wealth of man's progress, which had been excluded from the traditional Arabic education, was thoroughly embodied in the Europeanized schools which had their origin under Mohammad Ali.

At the same time that this tribute is paid, it must also be recorded that the French influence has not been an unmixed blessing. French culture carried with it the French system of bureaucratic centralization. Into Egyptian education this centralization reinforced formal learning, discipline by punishment, reverence for traditions, and the acceptance of authority. The result was a wide gap between what was laboriously memorized and crammed in the schools and what was individually and socially useful and significant for life.

Moreover, this centralization brought with it its inevitable accompanying bureaucracy, which dominated the country. This bureaucracy became so large that whatever its intentions, it blocked reform, became a petty aristocracy and an end in itself rather than a servant to the people. The aloofness of the government official became a characteristic in Egypt and the schools were no exception. As government officials, teachers removed themselves to realms far above their pupils, and lack of sympathy for their students became a characteristic of too many Egyptian teachers.

These two maladies, centralization and bureaucracy, found in Mohammad Ali's authoritarian outlook a congenial soil to grow steadily and as will be seen in the next pages, they are still existing in the Egyptian ministry of education.

MOHAMMAD ALI AND HIS EDUCATIONAL SYSTEM

Mohammad Ali, an Albanian mercenary, landed in Egypt as a commander of a force of cavalry dispatched by the Sultan of Turkey to assist the British in expelling the French from Egypt. Once the Turko-British mission had achieved its purpose and had withdrawn from the country, Mohammad Ali was left behind as one of the two leaders of the Albanian troops. Mohammad Ali who had the horse-sense of the born diplomat saw that the Ottoman Empire was gradually disintegrating and that the power of the Sultan over Egypt was consequently in decline. He realized that in this state of affairs Egypt offered an arena of tremendous potentiality, and he decided to go into business for himself. In 1805 and at the age of 36 he was installed as the Pasha of Egypt.

This new Pasha of Egypt was completely uneducated but despite his illiteracy he placed a high value on "European" knowledge and founded in Egypt a system of Western education which by 1830 had an imposing apparatus of primary, secondary, and technical schools. These pages, accordingly, propose to study the circumstances that urged the Pasha to introduce a European educational system into the country; to investigate the nature of this system and to see whether the Pasha wanted to raise the masses from the ignorance in which they were steeped or merely to achieve personal ambition; and to discuss the maladies that the present educational system inherited from the Pasha's rule.

Helpful for an understanding of why Mohammad Ali introduced Western education in Egypt, it may be useful to first discuss the circumstances in which Mohammad Ali worked after his accession to power. On the first hand, Mohammad Ali wanted to obtain independence from the Ottoman Empire and secure hereditary authority over Egypt. The most promising manner in which to get what he wanted from Constantinople was to make himself invincible as well as necessary to the Sultan who, having troubles in Saudi Arabia and Greece, was wont to call on the Pasha of Egypt for help. On the other hand, Napoleon's invasion of Egypt revealed the importance of its geographical situation to the West, especially to Britain, which realized that the key to the East lay in the hands of any country that occupied Egypt. Of that

Mohammad Ali was aware. "England," he confided to Bruckhart, the emissary of the British Africa Society, "will take Egypt as her share of the Ottoman Empire."[15] Having no intention of hastening that day, he decided to excel in the same weapons and tactics which made the British so powerful.

To satisfy the needs of his master, the Sultan, to rule eventually, not on behalf of another but as an independent sovereign, and to resist any Western attack, Mohammad Ali required a strong army and navy. In achieving this objective, he made up his mind to adapt entirely different methods than those of the East. During his early career he saw enough to convince himself of the superiority of European tactics over Eastern. He was himself engaged against the French army in Egypt, saw the strength of this army which destroyed the Mameluke soldiery, and realized that it was due to this same power of arms that the French were in turn expelled from the country. One may conjecture that such reflections as these led Mohammad Ali to announce, in 1815, that the new Egyptian army was not going to be *a la Tourque*, a turbulent militia, but an army subjected to rigorous discipline that would adopt Western military tactics and thus insure success in the field. It was this decision which gave birth to Mohammad Ali's military schools.

The first obstacle which Mohammad Ali encountered in reconstructing the military force was the lack of experts and competent personnel. As early as 1809 Mohammad Ali sent missions to France. Between 1809 and 1818, the Pasha sent forty-four future officers to French military schools. In 1844, Mohammad Ali dispatched yet another large mission, which was placed under the directorship of the French Minister of War and was housed in a special building in Paris which was given the name of the *Ecole Militarie Egyptienne*.

The Pasha was not idle while awaiting the return of his missions. He looked to Paris for immediate assistance, employing French experts to train the Egyptian army. It was with the help of those experts that the military schools were launched. Four military schools were established in the country, and these schools produced an army that fought in Saudi Arabia and crushed the Wahhabi rebellion against the Sultan between 1811 and 1819, conquered the Sudan between 1820 and 1821, and gained victory over the Greeks in their struggle for independence from Turkey between 1822 and 1828. These victories which astonished the Western world, encouraged the Pasha to set up more organized military schools in Cairo and Alexandria. The latter military institutions included diverse units; a cavalry school, an infantry school, a school of signaling, a school of artillery, a school of war munition, a naval school, and a school of music. Mohammad Ali's new military organization expanded at an enormous rate, and to meet its needs

---

15. George Young, *Egypt,* London: Ernest Beuu, 1927, p. 50.

the entire Egyptian economy was dedicated; foundries, arsenals, workshops, and dockyards were established. Nor was Egyptian education unaffected because when the army and its auxiliaries had sufficiently expanded, the Pasha realized that these require technicians, engineers, administrators, doctors, veterinarians, and the like. It was in the response to these demands that the technical schools, for which he felt the most immediate need, came into being.

When the Pasha started to establish his technical schools, he realized that the old Islamic institutions of the *Madaris* were totally out of harmony with modern life, which left him with the alternatives: either to introduce new scientific subjects into the old system or to create a new one which could provide the modern sciences he needed for his military expansion. In making his decision, Mohammad Ali refrained from attempting to introduce any reform in the *Madaris*, deciding instead to start a new system modeled on the French.

The first of these "technical" schools was the school of medicine. The objective of this school was not to prepare physicians for the people but solely to prepare officers for the medical department of the army. Consequently, its enrollment expanded and decreased according to army needs. In 1840, when the army numbered 300,000, the enrollment went up to 300; while in 1841, when the army numbered only 18,000, the enrollment went down to 130. The second school was the Veterinary School which provided the army with the needed veterinary surgeons and to take care of the thousand horses of the Pasha's private guard. The polytechnical school was the third to appear and its objective was the provision of officers for the military engineering services and to train engineers for the military industrial establishments. All these schools until 1837 were part of the Department of War. Their organization and administration was military.

Students for these schools were at first recruited from al *Azhar* and other *Madaris*. When, later, it became clear that some kind of preparation in the languages and sciences was necessary before medical and scientific studies could be approached, preparatory schools were opened. These preparatory schools were military establishments in every sense of the word, the staff having military rank, pay, and ration, the students wearing uniforms and being subject to the same code of punishment as the army. It was further discovered that the traditional *Kuttab* was inadequate to equip young men for the preparatory school course. Hence, new primary schools were established. Students for these schools were between the ages of seven and twelve and were recruited from the towns and villages exactly as the soldiers were recruited.

EDUCATIONAL MALADIES INHERITED

The notion of having schools only to satisfy the needs of the army had its obvious shortcomings. Schools, as has been seen, were military establishments, and this military atmosphere has lived with the secondary school ever since; even today it is undisguised. This military atmosphere is not the only malady bequeathed to the Egyptian schools by Mohammad Ali. Because the army was the *raison d'etre* for the Pasha's innovations and because he wanted to arrive at the greatest degree of military efficiency in the shortest order, his educational system started inversely: higher schools first, then preparatory schools, and only finally primary schools. This narrowed the scope of each level, limiting it only to the preparation of student to the higher level. This concept of education, which was introduced by Mohammad Ali in the last century, has continued. The third educational malady came as a result of the authoritarian outlook of the Pasha which produced deep effects in the field of education. Until 1821, all matters concerning education were settled by the Pasha himself. In 1821, the Ministry of War was established, and education was placed in its care until 1837. In 1837 the Ministry of Schools was ordained and was composed of six Egyptians and five Frenchmen. The Pasha, the Minister, and the French advisors set up among them a great bureaucracy which made the ministry the final authority on all matters connected with education. This bureaucratic spirit, which entered with the French and so appealed to Mohammad Ali, persists to the time of this writing. The fourth malady came as a result of Mohammad Ali's policy toward the ancient *Azhar* which he maintained while continuing to establish the modern Western institutions. This procedure created a dual system which gave rise to many serious problems. The first arose through overlooking the creation of a training school for teachers and employing *Azhar* graduates to teach in the modern schools. Thus teachers brought with them their traditional teaching techniques, and beginning with Mohammad Ali's rule, the modern schools thus inherited the bad tradition of the old which stamped them with the *Azhar* way of teaching. Moreover, since the *Azhar* graduates were the only literate group in the country, students for the modern schools were recruited from among them. Naturally enough, they brought with them their ancient method of memorization and treated Western science in the same way they treated Eastern theology. Consequently, it is found that the students put the greatest emphasis on committing scientific information to memory without understanding it experimentally. This peculiar characteristic of al *Azhar*—memorization instead of the assimilation of subject matter—permeated all Egyptian education. A further problem occurred as a result of having two different educational systems in the country. In the one, the main emphasis was on religion, while in the other, secular education predominated. This duality in the system of education created two different streams of thought. One was a product of the twelfth and thirteenth centuries, medieval, conservative, and hostile to modern civilization, while the other was a product of the nineteenth century, modern, progressive, and in harmony with Western science. Here, one finds that the influence of the method of learning described above had a broad influence on the whole intellectual life of the country. It had created a type of mentality that isolates what is called "the *Azhar* type" from the rest of the people, a mentality consonant with the primitiveness and antequarianism of this institution.

THE BRITISH AND THEIR EDUCATIONAL SYSTEM

Mohammad Ali died in 1845 and the last half of the nineteenth century witnessed the steady and increasing encroachment of the British Empire on Egyptian affairs, an encroachment which began with the signing of the Suez Canal concession in 1858 and ended in 1922 when the British occupied the country. From 1882 to 1922, the British High Commissioner in Cairo, assisted by a number of his fellow countrymen attached to the various departments, had complete control of the Egyptian administration and full responsibility for shaping its policy.

The educational program centered around two men, Lord Cromer, High Commissioner from 1883 to 1907, and G. Dunlop, the Educational advisor whom Lord Cromer appointed in 1906. In expressing his educational intentions toward the Egyptians, Lord Cromer said in an interview with the Frenchman, De Guerville, "I have considered always, and before everything else, the interests of Egypt, and the welfare of her people."[16]

In ascertaining the sincerity of Lord Cromer's intentions, the pages that follow will state his educational objectives, which promulgated for the country, and investigate the extent to which these were achieved.

Main objectives of Lord Cromer's educational program, as stated by the High Commissioner himself, were "the raising of the educational level of the illiterate masses through the agency of the existing *Kuttabs*, the creation of an efficient civil service by encouraging young Egyptians to work for the secondary certificate, the development of female education, and the promotion of technical education.[17]

Emphasizing the importance of raising the educational level of the illiterate masses, Lord Cromer's language was most forthright: "It is on every ground of the highest importance that a sustained effort should be made to place elementary education in Egypt on a sound footing."[18] However, the number of the *Kuttabs* connected with the education department in 1899, seven years after the occupation, was only fifty-five compared with 1,223 in 1878. The curriculum was strictly limited to the four *R*'s, religion being the fourth. As for the standard of teaching in these *Kuttabs*, Harris scathingly reported:

The Kuttabs at which the majority of the Egyptians learn their *ABC* impart a schooling which would have been considered barbarous in the middle ages. Recitation from the Koran in archaic Arabic, which most of the pupils do not even understand, the thousand rules of grammar, and calligraphy are to all intents and purposes the sole subject of the curriculum.[19]

It is noteworthy that until 1905 there were no institutions for training teachers for these *Kuttabs* which the British considered the basis of national education. It is equally noteworthy that in 1891, the teachers of these *Kuttabs* were subjected to an examination of but the simplest character on the subjects of writing and arithmetic. The result of this examination was significant. Out of fifty-seven teachers, eighteen failed to appear. Of the thirty-nine who took the examination, only fifteen satisfied the examiners in arithmetic, while no single teacher passed in writing. Of the twenty-four who failed, moreover, seventeen received no credit at all in arithmetic. Yet again, when 301 Kuttabs asked for financial assistance from the Government in 1897 to improve their situation, only 110 were given any.

Now the second objective which Lord Cromer alleged for his educational program was to encourage young Egyptians to work for the secondary certificate in order to become efficient civil servants. But what measures did the British adopt for teaching them? With a keen desire on the part of the governed and good intentions on the part of the governor, many Egyptians were led to believe that the expenditure on a modern course of education would be generous and adequate. Relevant statistics, however, do not sustain optimism. In 1884 the figure allowed for education was 91,000 Egyptian pounds[20] and decreased to 70,000 in 1885, which amounted only to 1 percent of the annual budget. Moreover, after forty-seven years of British domination the expenditure on education went up to no more than 2 percent of the annual budget. The slim budget allowed for Egyptian education led to the logical step, the abolition of free education. Not only that, but in 1901 the British raised the school fees. These measures had a tremendous effect on the enrollment both in primary and secondary schools. G. Stievens, an English observer, was struck by the low enrollment in the primary schools:

First we went into the primary school. There were not many pupils, because the fees in this school are high—

16. A. B. De Guerville, *New Egypt*, London: William Heinnman, 1905, p. 48.
17. The Earl of Cromer, *Modern Egypt*, New York: The Macmillan Company, 1928, Vol. 11, p. 534.
18. W. B. Worsfold, *The Redemption of Egypt*, New York: Longman, Green & Co., 1899, p. 146.
19. Murray Harris, *Egypt Under the Egyptians*, London: Chapman and Hall, 1925, p. 15.
20. The Egyptian pound is $2.8.

as much as twelve and fifteen pounds a year for day boys.[21]

In the secondary schools, the situation was even worse. Arthur White, another Englishman, who visited Egypt in 1899, noted, "Few boys survive the secondary course. They enter at the age of 14, or under, and drop off steadily year by year because parents get weary of paying fees."[22]

The second measure which was taken by the British toward stimulating the young Egyptians to work for the secondary certificate was the rigid and formal examinations which became the Alpha and the Omega of the Egyptian educational system. Under the British, Egypt saw for the first time "The Board of Examiners" which was charged with imposing predetermined questions on the whole country. The examinations were of two kinds; the Primary Certificate Examination and the Secondary Certificate Examination. The proportion of the successful pupils in the primary examination was hardly one in three in 1893. In 1898 the proportion was equally low. The results of the secondary examinations were also discouraging. In 1891 only 28 out of 128 passed and in 1920 the result was considered a catastrophe. With results as low as this, one wonders whether the fault lay with the students or with the tests. Concerning the student's ability, De Leon gave this opinion:

For the Arab [meaning Egyptian] child is remarkably bright and intelligent, and loves learning, when there is any possible chance for his acquiring it. At some of the schools I visited, I was struck by the quickness of the boys, and their memories seemed surprising.[23]

Stievens commented on the same phenomenon:

He [the student] is astonishingly industrious; the difficulty is not to make him work, but to prevent him from working. . . . Some of his work in English literature I saw, compares quite well with that of University extension students at home.[24]

If this is true, the fault certainly lay in the examinations themselves and in the purposes they sought to achieve. In 1921, Sir Valentine Chirol, the Foreign Editor of the London Times acknowledged this:

Our failure as far as the higher purposes of education are concerned was not so conspicuous during the first period of the Occupation as it has now become, and the extent of our failure, even judged by the narrow test of the examinations which dominated the whole system, has only been recently disclosed.[25]

Ostensibly, with respect to female education, Lord Cromer's third desideratum, the British believed that "the hand that rocks the cradle rules the world." Lord Cromer, in his High Commissioner's report of 1899, mentioned that the Government "was endeavouring to educate the girls, whose subsequent influence on the family life and morals should be beneficial to the state."[26] However, in 1912 A. Cunningham, an English journalist, remarked on the high percentage

of illiteracy among girls, saying that the state of female ignorance "was indeed appalling."[27] In 1915, Egypt had only forty-five *Kuttabs* for instructing girls, and it might be interesting to note that the Government admitted in the same year that, "a good many of the women teachers in these *Kuttabs* were themselves unable to read and write."[28]

The last of Lord Cromer's objectives was the promotion of technical education. Emphasizing the importance of this kind of education, the High Commissioner declared that what Egypt most required was a supply of agriculturalists, up-to-date horticulturalists, mechanics, electricians, carpenters, and skilled workmen.[29] Nevertheless, even by 1909, after twenty-seven years of British Occupation, there were only seven vocational schools in the country. Four of these, with 586 students, were trade schools which were suffering, according to an official report, from a severe shortage of trained staff. This left Egypt with only three technical schools which started after a sum of 51,000 pounds was collected locally and an income of 3,600 pounds was endowed yearly for their maintenance.

The record of higher education was no better. The School of Medicine was wanting. Studies in this school were reduced to bare theory, and the enrollment was extremely low: two in 1892; none in 1893; four in 1894; five in 1895; six in 1896; fourteen in 1899; twenty-one in 1898, which was increased to fifty in 1910. Similarly the school of agriculture was not flourishing. In 1909 it enrolled thirty-three students and in 1912 it registered eighty. The enrollment of the school of engineering was small and it graduated only twenty-eight students in 1900. The training of teachers was no more adequate. In 1909 the teachers' Training College graduated nine secondary school teachers, four primary school teachers, forty-seven *Kuttab* teachers, and fourteen women teachers altogether.

Did the British then really endeavor to educate the Egyptians, or did they only consider this country a large market for their goods, a magnificent training ground for their officers, civil servants, and young

21. G. Stievens, *Egypt in 1898*, London, William Blackwood & Sons, 1898, p. 107.

22. Arthur White, *The Expansion of Egypt*, London, Methuen and Co., 1899, p. 229.

23. Edwin De Leon, *Egypt Under Its Khedives*, London, 1882, p. 159.

24. G. Stievens, *op. cit.*, p. 118.

25. Sir Valentine Chirol, *The Egyptian Problem*, London: Macmillan and Co., 1921, p. 77.

26. Lord Cromer's report for 1899. Quoted from A. S. White, *The Expansion of Egypt*, London: Methuen and Co., 1899, p. 218.

27. Alfred Cunningham, *Today in Egypt*, London: Hurst and Blackelt, 1912, p. 60.

28. U. S. Bureau of Education, *Education in Parts of the British Empire*, Washington, D. C.: Government Press, 1919, Bulletin No. 19, p. 94.

29. A. B. De Guerville, *op. cit.*, p. 170.

officials? Three statistics are enough to imply the whole story; the percentage of illiteracy in 1882 was 96.7, in 1907 it was 97, and in 1917 it was 91.3. This record of achievement, however, cannot be called an unqualified success.

EDUCATIONAL PROBLEMS INHERITED FROM BRITISH

When the British came to Egypt, one might have imagined that they would bring with them their system of decentralized education founded on the principle of freedom and dedicated to the development of individual personality and character. The paradox of the British administered education was that England, the champion of decentralized education at home, perpetuated in Egypt a centralized system which outdid the French in its inflexibility. Dunlop, the British educational adviser, kept the machinery of education and the records of its results to himself and under him the Anglo-Egyptian bureaucracy became more rigid in its complete centralization. Of Dunlop's policy Lord Lloyd wrote:

Mr. Dunlop was a Scot, with all the tenacity of his race. His administration of the educational department could hardly have been described as alight with either insight or imagination, but he certainly succeeded in keeping the direction of Egyptian education tightly in his own grasp, and he maintained throughout a dour bureaucratic efficiency which was proof against all attacks.[30]

So despite the fact that the French sowed the seed for centralization, it was under the British that the crop matured, and with the educational policy in their hands, Egyptian education became more rigid, more bureaucratic, and more centralized than it had ever been before.

The second defeat was present in the final product the British wanted to have from the "modern" schools which they maintained. Lord Cromer, in his annual report for 1898, indicated that the primary object of these schools was to turn out a number of young men who would be able to take a useful part in the administration of their country. Did these schools, therefore, train the Egyptian youth in modern conceptions of progress and freedom in order to produce intelligent citizens who would occupy, with advantage to their country, the administrative jobs held by the British? To answer this question one should first ascertain the educational practices the British offered in these schools. What initially attracts attention is the course of study in the secondary schools which was reduced from five to three years. The second fact is that the method of teaching encouraged rote learning and memorization instead of creative thinking and scientific investigation. The third fact is that Arabic was replaced by English as the medium of instruction, and the periods assigned to the teaching of Arabic were reduced to a minimum. The fourth is that the soldierly atmosphere still prevailed. The

effect of this kind of discipline on the young students was recognized by Lord Lloyd:

The standard of discipline maintained in the State Schools was a crying scandal, and not only became eventually a cause of constant political trouble but had further a disastrous effect upon the characters of the younger generation.[31]

Obviously this type of education did not offer adequate opportunity for creating leaders imbued with enthusiasm, culture, and above all, conscientiousness. Instead it turned Egypt into a submissive minion to serve Britain on its highway to India. As Professor Young has acknowledged:

Education was neglected not only scholastically, but in the large field of schooling in affairs. Education in self-government by development of democratic institutions, had been suspended.[32]

At this point it is safe to say that the main goal of these schools was to produce young men fitted for nothing else than to be lower-capacity government employees. And the most tragic part about this is that the majority of Egyptians have not yet passed beyond the stage of looking upon education as the avenue that leads to government employment. Where other nations sought, through education, to create national culture, national solidarity, equality of opportunity, an intellectual elite, personality, moral character, or new economic and political ideals, the schools of Egypt have had as their outstanding goal merely the preparation of candidates for government service.

THE PRESENT EDUCATIONAL SYSTEM

Egypt obtained her independence in 1922 and consequently took over the control of education from the British. The shortcomings of the situation were glaringly obvious; three, however, were of major importance: (1) Illiteracy was almost 90 percent, and elementary education facilities in the *Kuttabs* were limited to only 10 percent of the population. (2) Primary and secondary education was the privilege of the very few. There was a small number of primary and secondary schools, all requiring tuition, with no room for the able but needy. The whole machine was devised to provide the administration with the necessary number of employees and mediocre practitioners who would preserve the *status quo* in subservience to authority. (3) Although there existed a number of higher schools for different branches of learning, there was no state university.

The elementary and the primary school systems existed until 1949 when Egypt realized that the cultural unity of the society, a requisite for social progress, requires that the children of the country share

30. Lord George Lloyd, *Egypt Since Cromer,* London: Macmillan and Co., 1933, Vol. 1, p. 161.

31. Lord George Lloyd, *op. cit.,* p. 265.

32. George Young, *Egypt,* London: Ernest Beun, 1927, p. 166.

a minimum of common understandings in their lives by means of a universal education at least during the early years of the educational system. To this end the Ministry of Education welded in 1949 the elementary and primary schools into one school for all children. This does not mean that there is one educational system in the country, actually there are two. These are described in the following paragraphs.

1. THE TRADITIONAL RELIGIOUS SYSTEM: In al *Azhar* which is now considered the Oxford of Islam and the oldest continuously operating school in the world, education starts with four years in the primary section, then five years in the secondary section, after which the student is given four years of study in its colleges. Following this there are also two years of specialization making a total of fifteen years. Students at al *Azhar* are provided free lodging and are partly supplied with food and sometimes money. Funds for the support of the students and for the salaries of the faculty come from endowments which were settled by rulers or wealthy families. This institution enrolls about thirty-three thousand students most of whom would become clergymen with an average salary of ten pounds a month.

2. THE MODERN SYSTEM OF EDUCATION: This system is styled on Western lines and leads to studies in modern universities of Egypt. It is also free for students of both sexes at all stages. At the bottom of this system is the primary school. The period of study is four years, from age six to ten. After the fourth year, the students are required to take a general examination for the "Primary School Certificate." Holders of this certificate are then admitted to the preparatory school (equivalent to the junior high school in the United States) where they stay for another four years until the age of fourteen, after which the children are required to take another general examination for the "Preparatory School Certificate." There are more than eight thousand primary schools in the country which could absorb 85 percent of all school-age children. The curriculum of the primary and preparatory schools is meant to produce a good citizen with a special stress on the national culture. At the preparatory school the pupil begins to learn his first foreign language, English or French.

Pupils with the preparatory school certificate are then admitted to the secondary school. There are three categories of secondary schools:

a. The academic secondary school is chiefly for studies that lead to the university. It is a three-year course, the first year of which is given to general studies to serve as a continuation of the preceding stage in the preparatory school. In the remaining two years, students are subdivided into two main lines of specialization: (1) literary and (2) scientific. It is left to the student to choose whichever branch of specialization he likes since on his choice here depends that section of the university he intends to join. However, the students are advised to pursue studies which are more suitable to their aptitudes as shown in their grades in the Preparatory School Certificate.

Since education at this stage is free and since the state budget cannot accommodate all possible candidates, the selection of those eligible to such course is based on ability alone. Students who fail to prove capable to the academic study in these schools have to leave to make room for others. Nevertheless, the chance of education is not lost forever for these failures. They may still try their luck in private schools, which charge tuition.

b. The technical secondary school may either be an end in itself, or, if the student prefers, may lead to the vocational schools: agricultural, commercial, or industrial. The aim of this kind of school is to create a class of technicians who stand halfway between the ordinary workers and the highly qualified university graduates. These vocational schools of industry, agriculture, and commerce are primarily meant to meet the vast economic needs of a country which is rapidly expanding in these areas. The average salary of the graduate of the vocational schools is ten pounds.

c. While girls share with boys the same schools at every stage, there are certain schools particularly divided for girls alone. These schools, secondary schools for girls, are geared to produce enlightened housewives.

There are four state universities in the country: University of Cairo (founded in 1908) enrolls thirty thousand, Alexandria University (founded in 1942) enrolls fifteen thousand, Ayin Shams University (Cairo 1950) with a population of twenty thousand, and Asyut University (1950) with a student body of about three thousand. The average salary of the university graduate is fifteen pounds a month.

ADMINISTRATION OF EGYPTIAN EDUCATION

The most outstanding feature of the administration of education in Egypt is its excessive centralization in a Ministry of Education at Cairo. The Ministry of Education is organized on the French plan. At the head of the Ministry is the Minister of Education with great powers. Going down the ladder there is a bureaucracy of officials with descending and diminishing powers. Next to the Minister come the Under-Secretaries, on the next lower rung come the controllers and sub-controllers of various grand-divisions of the Ministry such as Primary Education, Secondary Education, Girl's Education, Vocational Education,

Higher Education. Next in order come the inspectors, the connecting links between the central office and the schools scattered throughout the country. Next come the principals of schools, and finally the teachers.

In these pages an attempt has been made to present the salient maladies of contemporary Egyptian education along with their historical sources. In addition to the historical diagnosis of the maladies themselves, the example of the educational system of Ancient Egypt has been provided for its normative significance; whatever its limitation, that system encouraged in the student a problem-solving attitude toward the world around him, a respect in which all later systems in Egypt have failed. It is hoped that, recognizing the sources of the maladies and recalling the nature of the education which once existed in the country, the modern Egyptian educator may work more effectively toward reshaping his country's education. And only through schools can Egypt undo what the schools have done.

BIBLIOGRAPHY

Official Documents

The Association of the Graduates of the Institute of Education. *Conference for Applying Progressive Methods in Education.* Cairo: The Association, 1945 (in Arabic).

CLAPAREDE, ED. *Report General Presente au Ministere de L'instruction Publique.* Cairo: Ministry of Instruction, 1929.

EL HILALI, AHMAD. *Report on Educational Reform in Egypt.* Cairo: Ministry of Education, 1943.

————. *Secondary Education, Its Defects and Means of Reform.* Cairo: Ministry of Education, 1935.

MANN, F. O. *Report on Certain Aspects of Egyptian Education.* Cairo: Ministry of Education, 1932.

The Ministry of Education, Bureau of Educational Research. *Memorandum on Secondary Education.* Cairo, 1945.

National Income of Egypt for 1953. Ministry of Finance and Economy. Cairo: Government Press, 1954.

Permanent Council for the Development of National Production. Cairo: Government Press, 1955 (in Arabic).

Books

ADAMS, CHARLES. *Islam and Modernism in Egypt.* London: Oxford University Press, 1933.

AKRAWI, METTA, and MATHEWS, RODERIC. *Education in Arab Countries of the Near East.* Washington, D. C.: American Council on Education, 1949.

ARTIN, YAKOUB. *Consideration Sur L'instruction Publique en Egypte,* Le Caire: Impremerie Nationale, 1894.

BONWICK, JAMES. *Egyptian Belief and Modern Thought.* Indian Halls, Colorado: Falcon's Wing Press, 1956.

BREASTED, J. H. *A History of Egypt from the Earliest Times to the Persian Conquest,* New York: Charles Scribner's Sons, 1926.

BUDGE, SIR ERNEST ALFRED. *A Short History of Egyptian People.* London: M. Dent and Sons, 1923.

CHIRAL, SIR VALENTINE. *The Egyptian Problem.* London: Macmillan and Co., 1921.

CLOT, ANTONIE, B. *Apercu Generale sur L'Egypte.* Paris: Fortin, Masson, 1840.

CROMER, THE EARL OF. *Modern Egypt.* New York: The Macmillan Co., 1908.

CUNNINGHAM, ALFRED. *Today in Egypt.* London: Hurst and Blackett, 1912.

DEGUERVILLE, A. B. *New Egypt,* London: William Hienemann, 1905.

DELEON, EDWIN. *Egypt Under Its Khedives.* London: Sampson Law, Martson, Searle, and Rivington, 1892.

ERMAN, ADOLF. *Life In Ancient Egypt.* London: Macmillan and Co., 1894.

————. *The Literature of the Ancient Egyptians.* London: Methuen and Co., 1927.

GHOBRIAL, GIRGIS BAKHOUM. *The Maladies of the Egyptian Secondary Education in Historical Perspective.* Ph.D. thesis, University of Minnesota, 1960.

HARRIS, MURRAY. *Egypt Under the Egyptians.* London: Chapman and Hall, 1925.

HOWELL, J. M. *Egypt's Past, Present and Future.* Dayton, Ohio: Service Publishing Co., 1929.

KARIM, AHMAD. *History of Education in Egypt Under Mohammad Ali.* Cairo: El Nahda Bookshop, 1938 (in Arabic).

LORD LLOYD, GEORGE. *Egypt Since Cromer.* London: Macmillan and Co., 1933.

MAHAFFY, J. P. *Old Greek Education.* London: Harper and Brothers, 1905.

MASPERO, G. *Egyptian Archeology.* London: H. Grevel and Co., 1889.

PLATO. *The Works of Plato.* Jowett translation. New York: Tudor Publishing Co., 1949.

SAYCE, A. H., ed. *Records of the Past.* New Series, London: Samuel and Bagster, 1890. Vol. III.

STIEVENS, G. W. *Egypt In 1898.* London: William Blackwood and Sons, 1898.

STEINDORFF, G., and SEELE, K. *When Egypt Ruled the East.* Chicago: The University of Chicago Press, 1942.

The Story of Education In Egypt. Washington, D. C.: Embassy of Egypt, 1955.

U. S. Bureau of Education. *Education in Parts of the British Empire.* Washington, D. C.: Government Print, 1919.

WHITE, ARTHUR. *The Expansion of Egypt.* London: Methuen and Co., 1899.

WORSFOLD, W. BASIL. *The Redemption of Egypt.* New York: Longmans, Green and Co., 1899.

YOUNG, GEORGE. *Egypt.* London: Ernest Beun, 1927.

Periodicals

AL AHRAM. "Causes and Weakness of the Secondary Course of Study," August 17, 1932. In Arabic.

American Catholic Quarterly Review. "Education in Ancient Egypt," Vol. 18, 1893: 176-201.

Bureau of Education. *U. S. A. Circulars of Information.* "Public Instruction in Egypt," Vol. 3, 1875. Washington, D. C., Government Printing Press, 1875.

Bureau of Education. *U. S. A. Circulars of Information.* Vol. 3, 1875: 101-108. Washington, D. C., Government Printing Press, 1875.

Journal Asiatique. "Lettre sur les ecoles et l'impremiere du Pasha d'Egypte," 1843: 5-61.

Revue Des Deux Mondes. "Lettre sur L'Egypte," 1834: 671-685.

Revue Palitique et Parlementaire. "Le Domaine intellectule de la France en Egypte," Vol. 139, 251, 1929.

IVORY COAST

R. Clignet

The Ivory Coast is roughly shaped like a square whose sides are approximately 400 miles long, comprising various climatic zones. It is covered by a tropical rain forest in its southern parts, which progressively gives way to a park savannah in the northern part of the country. This implies a variety of natural regions which do not enjoy similar opportunities for economic development.

The country has a little more than three and a half million inhabitants with a yearly rate of increase of about 3 percent. This population comprises seven major ethnic clusters of varying size whose traditional social, political, and religious organizations differ to a considerable extent. Thus, some Ivory Coast societies are matrilineal while others are patrilineal. Some present a complex political organization whereas others are politically segmented and acephalous in character. Originally animists, the peoples of the South have been exposed for more than a half century to the influence of Christian missions while the north West tribes are predominantly Moslem. These distinct cultures have responded differently to forces making for modernization.[1]

The first contact between France and the Ivory Coast was made at the end of the seventeenth century. A religious mission was begun on the Eastern part of the coast but survived only a decade. Contacts were reestablished during the middle of the nineteenth century but were only sporadic.[2] These pioneers did not receive warm support, since the metropolitan government was less committed to the idea of an active colonization of the area than it was to prevent further expansion of British activities in this part of Africa. Ultimately, a merchant already settled in the then small village of Grand Bassam on the eastern part of the coast was appointed in 1878 as French Resident. His functions were to strengthen French influence around Grand Bassam and to explore the hinterland. However, it was only during the last two decades of the century, when the French colonial army had gained control of the territories situated north of the Ivory Coast and when the desire of creating a new colonial empire grew stronger among French metropolitan circles, that real attempts to gain control over the hinterland were really undertaken. Expeditions were launched northward from the coast, and at the same time military outposts established in the then French Sudan and Upper Volta extended their influence southward. The core of the Ivory Coast became a French colony at the turn of the century but complete military pacification was not effected until the end of the first world war.[3]

The character of the French colonization in the Ivory Coast has had two implications for the spread of formal schooling. First, since it was undertaken rather late and met a pervasive local resistance, French overrule was not accompanied by educational efforts commensurate with those displayed in other parts of French-speaking West Africa. For example, until the period following World War II, enrollments in the Ivory Coast lagged far behind those in Dahomey and Senegal. Second, the economic development of the various areas of the Ivory Coast has been largely a function of the duration of the French presence. The higher the level of economic development of a subregion, the higher its school enrollments.

HISTORY OF EDUCATION

The pattern of development of educational facilities in the Ivory Coast can be divided into five

1. A. R. Zolberg in *The One Party Government of the Ivory Coast* (Princeton, 1964) gives a very clear and accurate account of the geographical and historical background of this country. One will observe that, in a same region, the level of participation to crashcrop economy varies significantly with ethnicity. One will also note that ethnicity determines the volume and the form of urbanization in this country. Some ethnic groups are underrepresented in the population of the capital, others are overrepresented. Similarly some are heavily concentrated in low status occupations.

2. See P. Atger, *La France en Cote d'Ivoire de 1843 a 1893* (Dakar universite de Dakar, 1962).

3. See G. Mary, *Precis historique de la colonisation francaise en Afrique Occidentale depuis les premiers siecles jusqu en 1910* (Paris Larose, 1937).

periods. First, the earliest French policy was influenced by a desire to counter the attractiveness exerted by British social, commercial, and military enterprises on the coastal populations. Schools were opened by Missions and then by the Government on the border between the Gold Coast and the Ivory Coast in the avowed hope of weaning the Nzima people from the British influence.[4] At this time and until the end of the first decade of the twentieth century, the French Government allowed local Governors considerable latitude in adapting educational institutions to local needs. The latter had the final word as to how many schools should be opened, where they should operate, and what should be the nature of their curricula.[5] Thus, the idea of a French Government attempting to "assimilate" African populations on the basis of a preestablished and centralized program does not hold true during this period.[6]

During this first period, the development of schools followed a very clear pattern. Educational institutions were founded on the coast westward from Grand Bassam in each of the commercial outposts created by the French (Dabou, Jacqueville, Grand Lahou, Tabou) and northward from the coast (Bondoukou Dabakala). The teaching force comprised some Europeans, both laymen and missionaries, and a number of Senegalese soldiers who served as teaching assistants and were progressively replaced by Senegalese graduates of the Teachers' College of Senegal (*Ecole Normale d'Instituteurs*). A female European teacher was appointed for the first time in the early part of the twentieth century and the school system was incorporated in a superintendency (*Inspection primaire*) in 1910.[7]

The second period began after the first World War and lasted until the end of the second. It was characterized by the fact that educational structures were increasingly centralized and subject to a tight control by the General Governor of West Africa in Dakar and by Metropolitan authorities. Although it implies the development of uniform curricula and uniform types of educational institutions, the tightening of this control should not be equated with the emergence of a consistently assimilationist policy. First, the financial efforts undertaken by the Metropole in order to expend schooling varied markedly from territory to territory. In 1935, the part of the Ivory Coast budget devoted to educational purposes was only 4 percent of the whole, whereas for Senegal which had a much smaller population and a budget of a similar size, the corresponding figure exceeded 6 percent. Similarly, as time passed, the percentage differences of budget devoted to educational enterprises in the Ivory Coast and in Dahomey increased consistently. This increased trend was associated with growing inequalities in the importance of the respective school enrollments of the two countries. Since the population of Dahomey was smaller than that of the Ivory Coast and enjoyed a higher level of economic development, the educational policies followed by colonial authorities were not only determined by economic considerations but also by political principles. Within the West African Federation, Dahomey was supposed to act as a reservoir of semi-skilled manual and clerical manpower, whereas the economic development of the Ivory Coast was to be implemented by French settlers with the help of an absolutely unskilled agricultural labor force.

Second, there were continual controversies during this period between educational administrators.[8] Some were eager to replicate Metropolitan schools in the Ivory Coast. Others urged the adjustment of these educational institutions to local needs, although the problem remained to ascertain the nature of such needs. In the latter group some administrators emphasized the agricultural nature of traditional societies and attempted to multiply the number of schools where agricultural components of the curriculum would be stressed. Others were concerned chiefly with the growth of private and public bureaucracies and wanted schools primarily to train an industrial and clerical semi-skilled labor force. Between 1903 and 1945, every student began his studies in the rural areas of the Ivory Coast with a *cycle* of two years in *ecoles rurales* whose curriculum centered around agricultural topics (each school had a garden whose size was defined by regulations).[9] For the best of these students this period was followed by an additional *cycle* of four years in *ecoles regionales*. In urban centers, these two *cycles* were combined in one single period of six years called *ecoles urbaines*. Again, a highly selective examination occurred at that point to determine who should be allowed to the *ecole primaire superieure*. In fact, in the late thirties, access to this school was reserved to the most able students of a new type of institution intermediate between

---

4. See *Archives de l'ancien Ministere de la France d'Outre mer* (Cote d'Ivoire, XX, 2 encl. 1).

5. See *Bulletin du Comite de l'Afrique Francaise* (1920-1939). See also G. Hardy, *Une Conquete morale l'enseignement en AOF* (Paris Armand Colin, 1917) and in English Jerry Bolibaugh *Education as an instrument of national policy in selected newly developing nations* (Stanford, Comparative Education Center, mimeo, 1964).

6. On this point, see R. Clignet et P. Foster, "French and British colonial education in Africa" (*Comparative Education Review*, VIII, 2, 1964), pp. 191-198.

7. These details are drawn from *Annuaire du Ministere des Colonies* (1898-1914).

8. Concerning the details and the changes of the educational system at that time see J. Bolibaugh, *op. cit.* In French, see Ray Antra, "Historique de l' Enseignement "Misere de l'enseignement en AOF" (*Presence Africaine*, December, 1956, January, 1957), pp. 57-70.

9. At the end of the pre-war period in the Ivory Coast, schools with three classes were obliged to plant 2.5 acres under coffee. The gardens attached to these schools were sometimes a source of profits for the school teachers. Bitterly criticized by many African leaders, these gardens were suppressed by the regulations following the Brazzaville Conference. The bad reputation attached to rural schools has persisted so long that, even today, the sole concept of "school-gardens" is associated with negative emotional reactions on the part of many Africans.

ecoles regionales and ecoles primaires superieures, called *cours de selection*. Thus, steps were taken to limit the number of individuals gaining access to a post-primary education. The students of the ecoles primaires superieures were trained to become primary school teachers, nurses, veterinary assistants, or skilled clerical workers destined to serve in the railroad system, in the general administration, or in government services. Parallel to this school, there were vocational training schools specializing in mechanics, which absorbed one-third of the output of the ecoles regionales.[10]

By the early 1930s, there were twenty-seven rural schools with 4500 pupils, of which 4200 were male; twelve *ecoles regionales* with 400 students of which 370 were boys; one urban school with 100 girls; one ecole primaire superieure with 138 male students; and one ecole professionnelle with 90 students. In addition there were eleven Catholic mission schools training 700 individuals.[11] Until the middle thirties, the best students of the country were obliged to go to Senegal for their post-primary education. There, only a limited number of seats were made available annually for each colony of the federation. It was only in the late thirties that a Teachers' College, originally specializing in the training of rural school teachers, was opened in the Ivory Coast at Dabou.

Theoretically, however, African students were not eligible for secondary studies of a metropolitan type. Yet, a Lycée identical with those in France had been functioning in Saint Louis since 1928 to serve the needs of the local European population. In a very small number of cases, it seems that some Africans (among whom was at least one Ivory Coaster) were allowed to undergo regular secondary schooling.

In summary the main features of this period were the diversity of the educational efforts undertaken in the various components of French West Africa and the ambiguity of the educational aims of the French colonial administration. This ambiguity explains why local circumstances played such an important role in the determination and the attainment of educational goals. In the Ivory Coast itself, primary school enrollments remained limited because of pressures exerted on local administrators by European settlers who owned large-scale plantations and were hostile to educational development, and feared losing the unskilled labor force they needed in their farms.

The third period began with the end of the second World War and with the implementations made at the Conference of Brazzaville in 1944. Two basic aims undergirded plans for educational developments in colonial areas: first was to increase school enrollments to a considerable extent and second was to provide African children with an education equivalent to that available in France itself. The small-sized African elite was already in a position to exert increased pressure upon metropolitan authorities, and they received active support from many of the leaders

of the French resistance movements.[12] However, there were variations in the degree to which these recommendations were carried out. The proportion of the Ivory Coast budget devoted to educational investments remained lower than the corresponding figure for other colonies.[13] Enrollments were still limited because of the reluctance of the French Government to provide the Ivory Coast with increased assistance, in view of the radical political orientation of this latter territory.

In 1950, this orientation changed because of an agreement concluded between the Minister of Overseas Affairs and the local political leaders.[14] As a result, the number of schools, the number of seats available per school, and the number of scholarships granted to Ivory Coast gradually increased.[15] Only the technical schools were not involved in this process of general expansion of the post-primary system. The European *planteurs* still had enough power to prevent the development of a skilled labor force which would have raised the general wage level to an extent which they thought undesirable. Since such expenditures would have been handled by the General Government of the federation, these *planteurs* were, strangely enough, supported in their opposition by some African politicians who were afraid that such measures would maintain or even increase the influence of federal authorities over local problems.[16] In 1955 on the eve of the *loi cadre* when it became obvious that African territories were to acquire their independence (either within or outside of the French

---

10. See J. Bolibaugh, *op. cit.*, pp. 36 and ff.

11. See *Bulletin du Comite de L'Afrique francaise* (5, 1932), p. 82. See also Bryant Mumford, *Africans learn to be French* (London Evans Brothers), p. 170; for instance between 1921 and 1936, 22 graduates from the Nurses School only were from the Ivory Coast as compared with 34 from Dahomey, 34 from Senegal, and 36 from French Sudan.

12. These leaders did not belong to the conservative parties who had been engaged in close collaboration with German authorities during the Vichy regime and were therefore in no position to criticize the promises made to African leaders by the more liberal parties.

13. See *Enseignement d'Outre Mer* (December, 1955, 7), p. 22. Only 15 percent of the Ivory Coast budget was devoted to educational enterprises as against 19 percent of the budget of Guinea, 18 percent of that of Senegal and 24 percent of that of Dahomey which had less resources and a smaller population.

14. See A. R. Zolberg, *op. cit.*, and F. Mitterand, *Presence francaise et Abandon* (Paris, 1957).

15. See *Encyclopedie Mensuelle d'Outre Mer* (June, 1956, 70), p. 250. No less than 2541 scholarships for secondary students were granted at that time to the Ivory Coast as opposed to 2349 to Senegal and only 110 to Guinea. Out of 469 scholarships enabling pupils to be enrolled in secondary institutions in the Metropole itself, no less than 269 were granted to the Ivory Coast.

16. For instance, the representative of Ivory Coast to the West Africa *Grand Conseil* consistently opposed the appropriations necessary to the functioning of the *Centres de Formation Professionnelles Rapide*, schools which attempted to adapt TWI programs to an African context. In 1958, the Ivory Coast representatives took initiative to have these institutions closed in spite of the great success of these operations.

community), educational efforts were sharply intensified. The demands of Africanization of the civil service led to a drastic expansion of the school system particularly on the secondary school level.

With the *loi cadre* itself, the last period began in 1957. The rate of expansion was even further increased as the new African government was installed and was therefore in a position to fulfill part of its promises to make schooling available for everyone. A multi-track system analogous to that prevailing in France was progressively put into operation. Ironically, it is the acquisition of statehood which has fostered the most extreme form of assimilation in the Ivory Coast.

The Present Profile of the System

The present primary school system comprised almost two thousand schools in 1963 with no less than 300,000 pupils.[17] This system represents six years of studies taught entirely in French and divided into three periods of two years each: *Cours preparatoire* where the children acquire the basic elements of the three R's, *cours complementaire* where these basic elements are progressively integrated into a more complex program, and *Cours Moyen* where the pupils prepare the final examination of the primary studies the *Certificat de fin d'etudes primaires* (CEP).

Primary enrollments average 40 percent of the corresponding age group, reflecting the determined efforts of the Government to provide each child with a primary education. However, there are considerable inequalities in the size of enrollments between the various parts of the Ivory Coast. Thus 90 percent of children resident in the immediate vicinity of Abidjan, the main city, attend primary schools while the corresponding percentages for the northern sections of the country are only 13 percent (Korhogo) and 11 percent (Seguela). In fact, rates of enrollment decline consistently when one moves westward and northward from Abidjan. As suggested, this decline is associated with contrasts in the level of economic development of the subparts of the Ivory Coast. The more backward the economy, the fewer chances there are that parents will want their children to receive any form of formal schooling. If there are disparities between the enrollments of the various regions of the country, there are similar contrasts between the enrollments of the sexes. For the entire nation, girls constitute only one-third of the total number of students, and female enrollments vary sharply between regions. They are much lower in the northern sections of the country than in the south.

The second characteristic of the system is that wastage and attrition are very high. Of a sample numbering of 10,000 pupils, only 2,065 reach the stage of the final examination, and half of these take eight years instead of six to do it, since it is possible, within such a system, to repeat one or several classes.[18] Drop-out rates are higher for girls than for boys. As in other parts of Africa, research is needed to ascertain the factors which account for such high rates of waste. A *priori*, it is possible to suggest that the following factors might be involved. First, it should be observed that there is a certain amount of temporary migration among the peoples of the Ivory Coast, which prevents pupils from regular attendance. More generally, although the system is tuition-free, it may be that beyond a certain level of education, families view the unemployment of their offspring as an undesirable cost. Second, it is noteworthy that curricula are not necessarily adapted to the needs, the motivations, and the abilities of rural children so that their academic experience is hardly rewarding. Third, because of the decline in prestige of teaching as an occupation, the teaching force is increasingly composed of individuals who have only had between three and four years of post-primary education themselves. In this situation, any increase in the size of enrollments obliges the Government to lower the level of the academic prerequisites demanded of teachers.

At the same time, educational costs at this level are very high and exceed those prevailing in other parts of Africa. They amount to $40 per year and student.[19]

The secondary system (Figure 1) is highly differentiated and can be divided into three main streams: the academic, the technical, and the agricultural.

The first of these streams is itself divided into three segments: the long academic *Lycées and Colléges*, the short academic *Cours Complementaires*, and the short academic *Cours Normaux*.

Originally it was intended that there should be a marked difference between the *Lycées* and the *Cours Complementaires* in curriculum and academic prerequisites. The second of these institutions was supposed to train semi-skilled administrative personnel in order to meet the needs of the unevenly economically-developed sections of the country. Their curricula were supposed to be regionalized. The candidates to *Cours Complementaires* sat for the same kind of examination as that required for the individual attempting to gain access to the *Lycées* but were supposed to be less talented. In fact, the *Cours Complementaires* have acted as substitutes for the overcrowded lycées. In both cases, a period of four years of studies is terminated by an examination, the *Brevet d'Etudes de fin du Premier cycle* (BEPC). In the Lycées, these studies are either classical or modern, in which case stress is placed on mathematics, physics,

17. See Republique de la Cote d'Ivoire Ministere des Affaires Economiques et du Plan, *Supplement trimestriel au Bulletin Mensuel de Statistiques* (3eme annee 2eme trimestre, 1961), See also UNESCO, *Premiere Mission du Groupe de Planification* (Paris, 1963), pp. 37-52.

18. UNESCO, *op. cit.*, p. 44.

19. UNESCO, *op. cit.*, p. 46.

natural sciences, or modern languages. The second cycle of post-primary studies, access to which is theoretically reserved to the pupils of the long *Lycées* and *Collèges*, comprises three years of study terminated by the examination *Baccalaureat*, which leads to university studies.

In 1963 there were 26 *Cours Complementaires* scattered throughout the country and ten *Lycées and Collèges*, the majority of which were heavily concentrated in the environs of Abidjan. All these schools had in 1963 an enrollment of about 13,000 students. Catholic and protestant missions have been eager to help the Government in the attainment of its educational goals, and no less than 2,500 pupils are enrolled in five private *Lycées and Collèges* and in nine private *Cours Complementaires* operated either by the Catholic church or protestant missions or former teachers from the public system.

Ethnic and socio-economic groups are unevenly represented in the post-primary systems. However, as in other parts of Africa, the desire for receiving a post-primary education is becoming more widespread among the various segments of the population. The recent character of the post-primary schools probably accounts for the lack of differentiation in the representation of the distinctive ethnic minorities or socioeconomic groups in the different components of the post-primary educational system. For the time being, the critical issue involves access to the post-primary system as a *whole* rather than to any *part* of it. There are signs that a change is taking place. Thus, there are contrasts in the social profile of the population of technical schools, which are derived chiefly from urban centers, and in that of agricultural schools, which are derived from the rural areas of the country. Similarly such contrasts seem to be developing between the populations of classical and modern sections of the long academic Lycées.[20]

In a similar fashion, the underrepresentation of girls in the post-primary system is even more marked than in the primary schools. They do not constitute more than 15 percent of the entire pupil population and tend to be concentrated either in private schools or in technical institutions.

There is an even higher level of student wastage in the secondary stream. Out of a sample of 10,000 individuals beginning their education in the secondary stream, only 850 will finish their two "cycles" of study, and one-third of these will do so only after ten years instead of the prescribed seven. As in the primary schools, this delay is accounted for by the large incidence of doubling.[21]

At present, the secondary school teaching force is almost entirely European. This leads to a relatively high amount of turnover among teaching personnel and represents a source of considerable difficulties for the Ivory Coast.

Access to the *Cours Normaux* depends on the success in a special examination taken by pupils finishing their primary school studies and who are at least fourteen years of age. They contract with the Government to teach for a period of ten years following their graduation from the *Cours Normaux*. There are ten such institutions (seven public and three private) with more than 2,000 pupils out of which only 350 are females. These pupils undertake a cycle of four years of study terminated by an examination called *Brevet elementaire* which is usually followed by one year of teacher training, for improving the quality of teaching is a permanent concern of the Government.

The most able students of these institutions are allowed to take an entrance examination to a second cycle of study in the only *Ecole Normale* of the country. This school has about 160 students who prepare for the Baccalaureat under the same conditions as the students of the Lycée but who also receive more advanced training in teaching.

At the secondary level, educational costs are comparatively very high, amounting to $500 per student per year.

The technical stream of the post-primary system also is divided into two cycles. The Vocational Training Centers (*Centres d'Apprentissage*) offer four years of study in mechanics, woodwork, construction, and other industrial skills or in accounting, typing, and other clerical duties.[22] In 1962, there were about 600 students in these institutions recruited by examination among the graduates of primary schools. In fact, a substantial minority of these pupils are drawn from academic secondary schools where they fail to pass their examinations. As in other parts of Africa, the value of these "short-cycle" technical institutions is questionable insofar as they are not flexible enough to adjust in time to the variations of the labor market. There is much evidence that the graduates of the *Centres d'Apprentissage* are unable to find work in the occupation for which they have been trained. Furthermore, many firms prefer to hire individuals with a more general background who can be trained on the job. There is also some evidence that present rates of unemployment among the graduates of such institutions are exceptionally high.[23]

---

20. As far as the recruitment processes into secondary schools are concerned see R. Clignet and P. Foster, Potential elites in Ghana and the Ivory Coast in *American Journal of Sociology*, (LXX, 3 November, 1964), pp. 349-362. See also R. Clignet et P. Foster, "Un exemple d'Assimilation: la preeminence de l'enseignement classique en Cote d'Ivoire," *Revue Francaise de Sociologie* (June, 1965).

21. UNESCO, *op. cit.*, pp. 66 and ff.

22. To these sections should be added the section of Home Economics, training 100 girls in dressmaking and child care.

23. The Office de main d'Oeuvre de la Cote d'Ivoire was able to conduct a survey among the graduates of the Centres d'Apprentissage which showed that 45 percent of the output of this school between 1955 and 1960 were engaged in occupations different from those for which they had been trained and that 12 percent of them were unemployed at the time of the survey. In a survey conducted in 1963, Clignet and Foster obtained similar results.

Abidjan's *Lycée Technique,* access to which is reserved for pupils who have completed at least two years of general secondary school, offers a cycle of six years of study and prepares individuals for an advanced but terminal degree in industrial or clerical work (*Brevet d'Etudes industrielles, brevet d'etudes commerciales*). Also, a full cycle of seven years exists, which is terminated by the technical *Baccalaureat.* In 1963, almost one thousand pupils were enrolled in the various programs offered by this school.

The last stream of post-primary study comprises an agricultural training center (*Centre de Formation Rurale*) which enables individuals who have already completed one or two years of secondary study to take three years of instructions in agricultural subjects. This "cycle" leads to a final examination which guarantees access to middle positions in the Department of Agriculture. A second cycle of three years (*College Technique d'Agriculture*) leads to a sort of *Agricultural Baccalaureat* examination which guarantees access to higher positions within the Agricultural bureaucracy. There were 200 students in both of these cycles in 1963.

Increased output of all these schools entails serious problems of employment. Until now, many students have been absorbed by the various government agencies which have set up specialized training programs whose academic prerequisites and duration differ but whose function is to facilitate the adjustment of these educated individuals to the positions available in the public bureaucracy. The Ministry of Public Works alone sponsors a dozen such programs. Thus by 1963, a course for construction foremen was

open to the graduate of the Centres d'Apprentissage, (seven individuals recruited every year) and for bulldozer crewmen (twenty yearly recruits) or foremen (twelve yearly recruits). Above the post-primary system, there is now a university preparing students for the *Licence* in law, science, and literature, with schools of engineering, medicine, and secondary school teaching.[24] In recent years, just over 400 students prepared for all post-secondary examinations. The difficulties evident at the post-primary level also characterize the functioning of the university. For a long time the teaching force will be predominantly European, which in itself makes the functioning of this higher institution rather expensive. Further, since for a long time studies in France were unquestionable sources not only of prestige but of high income, the government is at great pains to require students to remain in the Ivory Coast.[25]

SUMMARY AND CONCLUSIONS

As in France itself, the educational system of the Ivory Coast is characterized by the multiplicity of its tracks. The differentiation of various types of post-primary education is meaningful, insofar as these do not enjoy parity of prestige and do not provide equal access to the most financially rewarding and prestigious types of occupation. If, as suggested, there

24. The level of the license is roughly equivalent to that of the U. S. master's degree.
25. For the significance of the studies undertaken in France see J. P. N. diaye *Enquete sur les etudiants Noirs en France* (Paris, Realites Africaines, 1962).

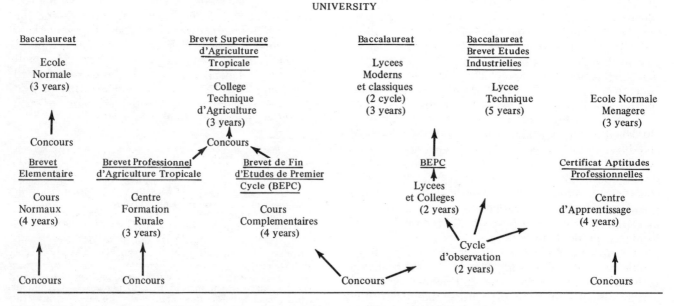

Primary System: Cours Moyens (2 years); Cours Elementaires (2 years); Cours Preparatoires (2 years).

Figure 1. The structure of the educational system in the Ivory Coast in 1963.

is presently no inequality of access into the distinctive components of the post-primary school system, such inequalities do exist with regard to entrance to the system. Thus southeastern tribes are overrepresented in the schools, boys are more numerous than girls, and the level of paternal and maternal education are in fact good predictors of the chances that an individual has to reach the highest rungs of the educational ladder.

In the long run, there is no doubt that the educational endeavors of the government will pay off. In the short run, they may lead to serious problems. First, the increased demand for education is associated with a decline of the efficiency with which the system is run, insofar as it is impossible to exert an adequate control on the age of students. As a result, the progress of a group may be retarded by the presence of overaged individuals who do not have the intellectual abilities to proceed further.

Second, the initial advantages in education gained by some ethnic groups are maintained if not increased. They lead to disparities in levels of participation in political and occupational structures, which may reinforce ethnic particularism. In effect, similar academic experiences do not necessarily give birth to similar sets of attitudes. Ethnic and socio-economic inequalities in access to schooling reinforce ethnic and socio-economic tensions. These tensions are likely to increase since the government seems ready to reduce the generous allowance it was granting uniformly to students in the various parts of the school system.[26]

Third, the increase in the output of the schools is not associated with increases of a similar magnitude in the labor market. As a consequence, educated individuals are obliged to accept occupations which do not correspond with their expectations. Unemployment is likely to increase among the educated segments of the population, creating a potential source of political discontent.

In the complex educational structure of the Ivory Coast, difficulties in employment are aggravated by the lack of adequate information given to pupils about educational and occupational opportunities.[27]

Fourth, there has never been any serious attempt to Africanize the curricula, and the original nationalist platform of the government in this respect has not been enforced.

Fifth, a one-party system presents tendencies to overcentralization which are analogous to those of the former colonial bureaucratic structure.[28] The growing influence of a centralized bureaucracy leads many talents to be diverted from entrepreneurial activities into employment in the central branches of the various public agencies. As a result, the concentration of educated *cadres* in the major city of the Ivory Coast may widen the gap already existing between the rural and urban segments of the population. Additionally, the increase of positions in the power structure of the country may account for the

teaching profession's loss of prestige. Formerly considered to be occupying a position near the top of the occupational structure, teachers are increasingly looked upon with disdain; their power as a pressure group has consistently declined.[29] Further, teaching often entails the obligation to reside in small villages where amenities are rare and where the cost of living for an educated individual is actually higher than in an urban center.

Finally, access to key power positions becomes more and more difficult, since these were filled by senior cadres at the time of independence. Hence the growing conflict between present office holders whose educational level is necessarily lower because of the limitations imposed upon them during the colonial period, and younger groups are graduating now from more advanced institutions. In this case, educational progress has tended to accentuate generational conflicts.[30]

This enumeration of the bottlenecks and tensions which characterize the functioning of the contemporary Ivory Coast educational system must not be overemphasized. They are, after all, not an evil specific to this African country. Further, there are some signs that the various "actors" are beginning to adjust to the new situation. For example, although the majority of present secondary school pupils overwhelmingly desire employment in the public sector of the economy, those in the higher educational classes are increasingly interested in participating in the private sector of the economy. In this free-enterprise African country, they seem to realize that large European concerns, which are under pressure to "Africanize" their personnel, offer increasingly rewarding careers.

Many of the tensions described here reflect the crucial role played by education in the placement of individuals in the occupational structure. Most of the segments of the Ivory Coast population are aware of this role, and this fosters gaps between the demand for education and the supply of schooling that the government can provide. When enrollments will exceed a certain level, one can predict that education will cease to be looked upon as the only instrument

26. Up to now, most students receive books, dresses, and clothes free of charge. They receive additionally free room and board.

27. See R. Clignet, Education et Aspirations Professionnelles *Tiers Monde* (V, 17, 1964), pp. 61-82.

28. For the characteristics of the French educational bureaucracy see M. Crozier, *The bureaucratic phenomenon*, (Chicago: University of Chicago Press, 1964), pp. 307 and ff. See also M. Crozier "Administration et bureaucratie: les problemes organisationnels du developpement (*Sociologie du Travail*, 4, 1962), pp. 367-378 and S. N. Eisenstadt, Problems of emerging bureaucracies in developing areas and new states in B. Hoselitz and W. Moore (ed.), *Industrialisation and Society* (The Hague Mouton, 1963), pp. 167-68.

29. The teachers' union has played a determinant role in the political development of the country until 1960.

30. See A. R. Zolberg, *op. cit.*, pp. 279-280.

of economic development and of social differentiation. Education will lose its irresistible appeal, and the entrepreneurial qualities displayed by individuals will be as important determinants of their occupational roles as their level of formal schooling.

SELECTED BIBLIOGRAPHY

Articles

ANTRA, RAY. "Historique de l'Enseignement en AOF." *Presence Africaine.* February-March, 1956, 68-86.

CLIGNET, REMI. "Education et Aspirations Professionnelles." *Tiers-Monde*, V, 17, 1964, 61-82.

CLIGNET, REMI, and FOSTER, PHILIP. "French and British Colonial Education in Africa." *Comparative Education Review*, VII, 2, 1964, 191-198.

————. "Potential Elites in Ghana and the Ivory Coast." *American Journal of Sociology*, LXX, 3, 1964, 349-362.

————. "Une Exemple d'Assimilation la Preeminence de l'Enseignement Classique en Cote d'Ivoire." *Revue Francaise de Sociologie*, June 1965.

Books

BOLIBAUGH, JERRY. "Education as an Instrument of National Policy," in *Selected Newly Developing Nations.* Stanford: Comparative Education Center, 1964, mimeo.

CROZIER, MICHEL. *The Bureaucratic Phenomenon.* Chicago: University of Chicago Press, 1964.

HARDY, GEORGES. *Une Conquete Morale*: *L'Enseignement en A. O. F.* Paris: Armand Colin, 1917.

MUMFORD, BRYANT. *Africans Learn to Be French.* London: Evans Brothers, *n.d.*

N'DIAYE, JEAN PIERRE. *Enquete sur les Etudiants Noirs en France.* Paris: Realites Africaines, 1962.

ZOLBERG, ARISTID. *The One-Party Government of the Ivory Coast.* Princeton: Princeton University Press, 1964.

LIBERIA

A. Doris Banks Henries

From the beginning of the Liberian nation, education has been stressed as a basis for development. The early colonists taxed themselves to provide public schools, while missionaries and religious institutions executed a program of a private nature. People who were skilled in trades took apprentices from among the settlers and tribal groups and taught them a vocation. The first elementary school opened at Caldwell in Montserrado County in 1824; but its existence was short-lived because of lack of funds. In government, mission and private school elementary education was stressed throughout the Colonial Period of Liberia 1822-1838. There was no standard curriculum except for the teaching of reading, writing, and arithmetic. Textbooks and other instructional materials were quite unsuitable, for most of them were discarded books from America and Europe.

As might be expected, religious instruction was greatly emphasized in schools, the majority of which were supported by churches and other religious groups. The Baptists who led the way in home missionary work also pioneered in translating the Bible and other instructional materials into tribal dialects and languages. In 1838 Mr. W. G. Crocker started this important work by writing for the Bassa school children.

Very little supervision by government was given to schools until the Commonwealth Period (1839-1847). It may be noted that an attempt had been made in the early years of the colony when The Reverend Calvin Holton of Boston, Massachusetts, had been invited to organize a school system in Liberia in 1826, but he died soon after his arrival in Liberia. John Brown Russwurm came to Liberia in 1835 to be superintendent of schools. But the cornerstone of supervision was laid in September, 1839, when an act was passed by the Legislative Council establishing a School Committee in every township and settlement. The duty of each committee was to supervise and control activities of public schools and to see that all

laws pertaining to education were carried out. Among the laws was one on compulsory education, requiring school attendance for all children between the ages of five and twelve years. A fine of three dollars was imposed on the parent or guardian who violated this law.

The Commonwealth Period was characterized by expansion of elementary education and the advent of secondary education. The pattern adopted was that of American Schools of the same type. The Protestant Episcopal Mission High School at Cavalla in Maryland County was probably the first secondary school to be established in Liberia. Subsequently high schools were opened in other parts of the country, chiefly along the coast until the Republican Period, which began in 1847. High schools were not established in interior areas until after World War I and they developed very slowly until the period following the second World War. The reason for the lack of secondary schools in the hinterland is probably that the elementary schools in the region did not graduate many students, and missions bore most of the responsibility for rural schools which provided evangelistic workers for their organizations. Education has been boosted recently by a Rural Area Development Program.

Higher education was initiated in Liberia during the Republican Period. With the assistance of the Board of Trustees of Donations for Education in Liberia, located in Boston, Massachusetts, U. S. A., Liberia College was opened in 1862. It was a liberal arts college designed to provide statesmen for the country. For many years this institution adequately fulfilled its objective. The second institution of higher education was founded by the Protestant Episcopal Church. Cuttington College and Divinity School began as a high school in 1889. It was not incorporated to confer degrees until 1922, although it offered college courses before that date and awarded certificates to graduates. Because of an administrative controversy, Cuttington closed in 1928 and did not open again until 1949. Meanwhile, engulfed in financial difficulties and other problems, Liberia College continued its struggle for existence. In 1953 Catholics ventured into higher education with the opening of the College of our Lady of Fatima to train teachers in Harper, Cape Palmas. Thus Liberia became the home of three institutions of college level. In 1951 Liberia College had been absorbed as the College of Liberal Arts and Science in the formation of the University of Liberia which was chartered by the Liberian Legislature. Other degree-granting schools incorporated in the University are the Wm. V. S. Tubman Teachers' College, The Louis Arthur Grimes School of Law, The College of Forestry, and the College of Agriculture.

With the opening of the first University in Liberia, Technical Assistance came to Liberia. First the UNESCO Science team arrived in 1951 to strengthen the university science program. This mission remained in Liberia for ten years during which time the turnover in personnel was so frequent that students were continually beginning because of a lack of continuity in the program. It had been planned that, at the end of ten years, Liberian counterparts would be qualified to take over full responsibility for the university science program. However, this objective was not realized and Liberia subsequently has continued to employ expatriates as its own citizens continued their preparation to replace foreign personnel. Other technical assistance has come to the University of Liberia through FAO and the United States Agency for International Development.

As the country moved forward in its rapid development following World War II, the lack of skilled workers became increasingly acute and more and more labor had to be imported from abroad. Booker Washington Institute which had been founded in 1928 could not meet the demands in vocational education. The government of West Germany and Sweden agreed to assist in this area by building two additional vocational schools and training teachers to staff them. A vocational school was opened in 1964 as a cooperative undertaking of the Swedish and Liberian Governments. It is located at Nimba near the iron ore mines. Schools of Home Arts and Beauty Culture have made it possible for women and girls to pursue attractive careers.

The shortage of teachers has caused grave concern among Liberian educators and other government officials. It has made the compulsory education law of little effect, since the number of children of school age should be limited to the number of teachers and physical accommodations available for educational use. For this reason a number of emergency programs for teacher training have been launched. Two- and three-year certificate courses for the training of high school students and graduates have been given in Rural Teacher Training Institutes, the first of which

was opened at Zorzor in 1960. Extension Schools and Vacation Schools have been other sources for preparing and upgrading teachers. The latter programs have replaced the annual two-week vacation institutes which lasted from 1938-1952. These short training courses have supplemented the degree courses offered by the William V. S. Tubman Teachers' College which began in 1947, the Education courses at Cuttington College and Divinity School which reopened in 1949, and the program of the College of Our Lady of Fatima which started in 1953. As a result of the combined efforts of these institutions the number of teachers has increased and more pupils have been enrolled in elementary schools, thus expanding the reservoir for secondary education.

Adult education has received a considerable amount of attention since the Literacy Campaign was begun in 1951. Besides classes in various communities, there was established, with the aid of UNESCO, Klay Fundamental Education Center where teachers were trained in Community Development. Literature in tribal languages and in English has been produced for this program. At the University of Liberia the People's College for Mass Education has made it possible for adults to begin and complete secondary school. Public and private high schools are attended by large numbers of adults. Also, at the University, degree courses are given in the afternoon where working people may earn credits toward graduation.

Educational administration has expanded and has grown stronger over a long period. New divisions in the Department of Education have been organized to give more attention to various phases of the system. Assistant and Undersecretaries as well as Directors have been employed to strengthen the educational system. Supervisors and principals have benefitted from foreign scholarships resulting in a corps of professional administrators distributed over the entire country. The latest experiment in educational administration is the consolidation of schools in Monrovia under the direction of a Superintendent. A special contract team from San Francisco State College in 1962 was engaged to initiate this administrative unit. The success of this undertaking in decentralization will influence other parts of the country. Within the Monrovia district will be a number of new elementary schools along with modern junior and senior comprehensive high schools.

Another major development of education since 1950 is in the area of instructional materials. For many years educators have realized the handicap Liberian children suffered as a result of importation of school books written for children in America and Europe, but foreign to the experience and background of people in Liberia. In 1956 there was created a Division of Higher Education and Textbook Research. One responsibility of this division is to see that essential research is carried on for the purpose of producing suitable textbooks for Liberian schools. The lack of writers has retarded progress in this area. However, a few textbooks and other instructional materials have been completed and distributed to schools. In addition, the services of a professional writer of children's books have been made available through USAID to train Liberian writers. This project began in April, 1964, and continued for eighteen months. Writers' workshops have been conducted and individual assistance has been given as progress has been made on manuscripts. Also, some scholarships to train writers have been obtained through the same agency. By these means, Liberia expects to develop some writers of school textbooks.

Since 1944 the Liberian government has invested heavily in local and foreign scholarships in an effort to encourage more young people to complete their education and meet the professional and vocational needs of the country. Although some students have disappointed the authorities and taxpayers, the majority have measured up to expectations, and large numbers have returned home to join those qualified students who did not go abroad, to make a worthy contribution to their country. Supplementing Liberian government scholarships, other countries have financed education of Liberians who study in foreign institutions.

Through participation in international educational organizations and conferences, Liberia has been greatly enriched. The benefits derived in this manner cannot be measured in terms of money. The government has put forth much effort to make it possible for citizens to attend important conferences on education.

In 1938 the first professional organization in Liberia was formed. The National Teachers' Association brought together teachers and other educators for mutual and national benefits and improvement. It became a foundation member of the World Confederation of Organizations of the Teaching Profession at the organizational meeting in Denmark in 1952. It has been influential in bringing about increments in salary and better conditions of work. The NTA compiled the first history of education in Liberia. Annual observances of Education Week make the public aware of the importance of education in social development.

In harmony with the United Nations Development Decade, Liberia has obtained assistance through UNESCO in the preparation of a five-year development plan. Liberia is confident that with determination and cooperation of all citizens, education in this country will meet the social, technical, professional, and moral demands of Liberia's development program.

GOALS OF EDUCATION IN LIBERIA

The Republic of Liberia is aware of the increasing complexity of life in the modern world and the great responsibility of the government to prepare its citizenry to make suitable adjustments and worthy contributions to national development and progress. It recognizes the importance of technological and social advancement in national and international relations. It realizes that the danger of complete annihilation of mankind may be averted by educating individuals so that they will be responsible members of society motivated to work for peace and goodwill among men. By imbuing citizens with solid principles of democracy through education, the government of Liberia hopes to lay the foundation for wise choices and use of freedom.

The Department of Education in Liberia is charged with these tasks:

1. Raise the quality of educational performance.
2. Broaden the scope of education to serve educable citizens, adult as well as youth.
3. Make better use of the human resources available in the nation and, where necessary, bring in technical know-how from abroad.
4. Train education leaders and trainers of teachers in every way possible in Liberia and in foreign countries.
5. Improve the organization, administration, cooperation, and supervision of the educational system at the local as well as at the national level.
6. Assume adequate long-term financing and full support by the government to perform this task.

In the Five-Year Plan for Education in Liberia, goals and means for achieving goals are outlined under the following headings:

> Organization and Administration
> Elementary Education
> Secondary Education
> Higher Education
> Teacher Education
> Adult Education
> Vocational Education
> Scholarships
> Materials

Organization and Administration Goals

Goals for organization and administration in Liberia are as follows:

1. To develop and implement a modern organization for administering and supervising the nation's school system.
2. To upgrade Department of Education headquarters and field office employees through in-service and participant (scholarship) training.
3. To improve the administration of the departmental and field offices so that they will better supply essential instructional materials, equipment, and services to the schools on time and at the least possible expense to the Government.
4. To develop the type of supervision for the school system that will demand from all the employees

the self-discipline required in a professional school program.

5. To make full use of staff through well defined assignments and follow-up instruction where assistance is needed.

6. To develop personnel health, time, and attendance record cards as well as a proper reporting and evaluation system for Department of Education headquarters and field office personnel and the members of the supervisory and instructional staff of schools in Liberia.

7. To consolidate the Monrovia schools into a single district and to form similar districts in the counties on a step by step basis.

Goals for Elementary Education

Goals for elementary education in Liberia over the coming years are the following:

1. INCREASE SCHOOL BUILDINGS. The culture and progress of a people or nation may be determined by the extent to which education is supported and financed including facilities made available for its schools in the form of building and equipment, libraries, and instructional materials. One of the first goals established in one Five-Year Plan was the building of approximately 180 new elementary schools over the five-year period, at a total cost of approximately 3.8 million dollars. In the years 1964-1965 there was an annual construction of thirty elementary schools in the rural areas, and thereafter, for the next three years (1966-1968), forty schools a year were built to accommodate increasing enrollments.

2. INCREASE SCHOOL EQUIPMENT, MATERIALS, AND SUPPLIES. One of the greatest handicaps is the lack of adequate instructional materials. Teachers need a substantial supply of instructional materials, teaching aids, and other media of teaching, which by virtue of their nature will induce students to take an interest in learning because the heart and core of any adequate education system is reflected by the standards of its library program. Any education program which lacks a sufficient supply of printed matter (textbooks, library books) for its reading public is unrealistic. Therefore an initial step hopefully will be to attach to each elementary school a well-equipped library and reading facilities. It is estimated that over the five-year period more than 3 1/2 million dollars will be required for the purchase of school equipment, supplies, and materials (out of which $306,700 will be for instructional supplies alone and $504,850 for maintenance and repairs) little of which has hitherto been available for proper instruction. In addition, free textbooks will be provided by the Department of Education for all elementary grades. This equipment, supplies, and materials are essential to curriculum change designed to offer opportunity

to both academic and non-academic students. It is estimated that in 1968 there was a total of 648 elementary schools throughout the republic. Only through such adequately supported schools and curriculums can it be expected that students will remain in school and the economic progress of the nation be promoted.

3. INCREASE STUDENT AND TEACHER ENROLLMENT. Based upon 1964 statistics, there were 53,998 pupils (39,253 boys and 14,745 girls), and 1,602 teachers in the 519 public elementary schools outside Monrovia. It is estimated that within the five-year period (1964-1968) there were 79,700 pupils and 2,214 teachers in the public schools. Teachers' salaries for this period amounted to $4,681,300. In addition to the Liberian teaching staff, the nation depends on large numbers of foreign teachers in the elementary schools. The teachers are acquired under the following international exchange programs: the U. S. Peace Corps, the U. N. multilateral program, and special French teachers from adjacent French-speaking African countries. The number decreases yearly as qualified Liberians replace them.

4. RETAIN AND EXPAND LOCAL SCHOLARSHIPS. The objective of the scholarship program is to discover and develop talents of youths who possess intelligence but whose families lack the means to enable them to take advantage of the educational facilities provided and maintained by the state. By this means efforts will be made to improve the quality of citizenship and promote progress.

Toward these ends, the Department of Education gives both local and foreign scholarships to deserving students. Despite this incentive offered by the Government and the fact that education is free in terms of tuition, fees, and textbooks on the elementary level, many rural girls do not attend school for long. This is due in part to the socioeconomic status of parents and tribal marriage customs. In order to encourage girls to continue in school and their parents to permit them to do so, elementary scholarships consisting of maintenance in a dormitory, subsistence and books will be given to more pupils. Presently, only a very small number of elementary school girls are receiving this type of local grant-in-aid. These scholarships need to be continued on an increasing scale in the future. It is estimated that 170 students were recipients of such local scholarships amounting to a total of $20,500 for the years 1964-1968.

Goals for Secondary Education

Recognizing that secondary education can be improved, Liberia has as its goals for this area:

1. To implement the secondary school curriculum in order to

a. Better prepare an increasingly large number of students qualified to enter university;

b. Prepare a proportionate number of students qualified to enter directly upon graduation into the agricultural, business, and industrial programs of the nation or into advanced vocational schools.

2. To upgrade the standards of the secondary school through
   a. Improvement of the instructional program,
   b. Improvement of facilities.

Goals for Higher Education

With the great demands made on a developing nation in a complex world society, leaders are seeking a clear definition of national goals. Goals in higher education are inextricably bound to national goals. The following are the goals for higher education:

1. To encourage superior students to have a higher education to meet the demands of the nation for professional and technical personnel. In order to achieve the above broad national goals it is imperative that strong leadership and material support be provided.

2. To provide a faculty to staff institutions of higher education.

3. To develop to the fullest extent the individual's intellectual, ethical, moral, and spiritual capacities, thus insuring responsible leadership as well as the protection and perpetuation of the Liberian democracy.
   a. This indicates that the primary purpose of higher education is to disseminate knowledge and cultivate the intellect.
   b. This also indicates that broad cultural development is as important as technical advancement insofar as national strength is concerned.

4. To provide adequate facilities to educate required personnel.

5. To meet the nation's need for administrators in government and private endeavors as well as in all professions.

6. To stimulate and develop research in essential fields.

7. To stimulate and encourage literary efforts in social science, literature, music, and art as well as in the field of technology and science.

Goals for Teacher Education

The overall goal of the program is preparation of professionally competent teachers with good personal, social, and emotional qualities who will contribute significantly to society as active and informed citizens and leaders in their communities. At present, teacher education in Liberia must face two challenges:

1. The training of an adequate number of qualified teaching personnel to staff existing and anticipated elementary schools.

2. The development of more and adequate teacher education programs that will provide the quality of teaching demanded by the nation's rapidly developing economy and meet the social and political needs of the country.

Goals for Adult Education

More specifically, major goals of adult education in Liberia to have been attained by 1968 were as follows:

1. Teach 18,000 adults and youths the basic skills in speaking, writing, and reading English. With this knowledge they will be taught fundamental understanding of how to improve home and community and will gain valuable information on agriculture.

2. Provide continuing education for 1,200 persons.

3. Offer to approximately 10,000 persons courses designed for cultural advancement and citizenship training through seminars, lectures, regular classes, and radio programs.

4. Accelerate present programs, to include approximately 10,000 people, particularly women, through classes, demonstrations, and other means in areas of home and family living.

5. Promote vocational interests and assist with vocational training in providing courses in occupational fields for 6,000 persons.

6. Develop programs, organizations, and activities for the youths of Liberia. Provide opportunities for approximately 20,000 young people and children to participate in creative activities (crafts, arts, sports) which will contribute to their development through use of leisure time.

7. Construct buildings for a National Museum and a National Library and develop programs in keeping with this expansion.

Goals for Vocational Education

Goals for greater adequacy in meeting vocational needs include the following:

1. Booker Washington Institute: This Institute needs further development as a vocational school. The enrollment will be increased in order to serve the urgent needs of Liberia and to reduce the per student cost. It has planned to have increased the enrollment to 650 students by 1966 and to have produced annually, by 1966, 125 vocational high school graduates, 200 graduates of special short-term courses for sub-high school students and 15 graduates for practical arts instruction for junior high schools.

2. Vocational Training Center, Monrovia (Federal Republic of Germany): This adult education vo-

cational training center is being established to train Liberian skilled and semi-skilled workers by means of practical and theoretical instruction and to provide advanced training for employed Liberians.

Full-time day courses will cover two years and will be continued for a third year in industrial workshops (on-the-job). Advanced training will be conducted during evenings. About 100 students will be admitted annually to the day courses. The courses given will be consistent with the needs of Liberian industry.

3. Vocational Training Center, LAMCO, NIMBA (Royal Swedish Government): This Vocational training center has been established to train skilled workers, foremen, supervisors, and instructors in the following trade areas: carpentry, joinery, cabinet making, welding and forging, electrical installation, and motor mechanic. The Royal Swedish Government and the GOL will share equally in the cost of operating the center on the basis of special arrangements. A three-year training program is planned and the center will serve about 100 students annually in this adult education project.

One of the goals of the division is the introduction of practical arts instruction (Agriculture, Business, Home, and Industrial) in selected public junior and senior high schools.

Goals for Scholarships

Since scholarships are important on all levels of education, this phase, too, has goals:

1. Foreign scholarships
   a. To carefully select graduate students to qualify for essential work in Liberia and send them to accredited universities abroad.
   b. To check on students' programs so that they will complete the required work within the limited period.
   c. To provide scholarships in accord with national needs.
2. Local scholarships
   a. To provide local scholarships on all levels in order to make elementary and secondary education available and vocational and professional education possible for those who qualify and desire it.
   b. To select students for scholarships on the basis of need, ability, and area of the country so that every section may participate in the scholarship program.
   c. To check on students' programs to see that only deserving students receive government assistance.
   d. To give special attention to scholarships for girls to encourage more of them to seek advanced education.

Goals for Materials

Materials are important to an educational program; therefore goals for materials are as follows:

1. To revise and produce curriculum guides in various subject areas to help teachers in the elementary and secondary schools to improve instruction.
2. To provide scholarships for Liberians to complete required work and return to work in the Department of Education:
   a. One librarian for the Educational Materials and Research Center
   b. Four writers to produce textbooks and other educational materials
   c. One specialist in Curriculum Development
   d. One artist
3. To conduct annual writers' workshops.
4. To develop an Educational Materials and Research Center.
5. To produce textbooks and other instructional materials.
6. To provide training in developing and using instructional materials.

Obstacles to the Attainment of Goals

The chief handicap to attainment of goals in education is chiefly a lack of adequate financing. Money is required to construct and equip suitable buildings, to provide transportation for teachers and students, to educate administrators and teachers to instruct students, and to prepare all professional and non-professional workers to develop the economy and perform all the tasks required in national and international activities. Money is essential in producing and purchasing textbooks and other instructional materials. The country is tapping all sources of income available to overcome the problems resulting from shortage of capital. Through a program of Operation Production the country as a whole is working to expand and improve agricultural yields as well as to develop local industries. An Emergency Education Relief Fund has been established requiring every adult citizen to annually contribute ten dollars for education. Emphasis is placed on a minimum of elementary education for all citizens and on each adult's being taught a profession or vocation in order to make his maximum contribution to national progress and stability.

Major Problems

Major problems in Liberia which might change education in the future include the following:

1. There is a lack of skilled manpower to deal with technological developments. Foreign industrialists are investing in local businesses. Because few skilled Liberian workers are available, large numbers of laborers are imported from other countries. As a result, students are sent abroad to learn required skills while facilities within the country are

being provided to train a larger number at home.

2. An increase in modern inventions reduces necessity for numerous servants; hence workers must learn other skills to earn a living. Concomitantly, workers must be trained to maintain machines which replace men.

3. The problem of polygamy among some tribes is gradually disappearing as urbanization eliminates the extended family and as plurality of wives becomes burdensome and uneconomical.

4. The problem of the fear of spinsterhood will disappear as women enter careers of various types. More girls will seek education so that the school population will no longer be excessively male.

5. The tribal schools or "societies" have caused many rural Liberians to remain out of school for long periods of time, thus retarding students.

THE SCHOOL SYSTEM IN LIBERIA

The school system of Liberia is highly centralized, following the form of the national government. The Secretary of Education is a cabinet minister placed in charge of all education within the Republic of Liberia —public, private, and philanthropic. He is assisted in his duties by three Undersecretaries and a group of Directors who head divisions in the central office. Each of the nine counties of the country has a Supervisor who is responsible for education in the area. All of these officials are commissioned by the President of Liberia. Besides them there are many lesser officials. In the field away from the central office, School Committees assist Supervisors with problems arising in connection with principals, teachers, students, and school facilities and equipment.

Before World War I there were more church mission schools than public schools. These were subsidized by the government in recognition of the republic's responsibility to educate its children. But since World War II public schools and enrollment far outnumber similar private institutions. Besides government and church mission schools there are private schools and those which are a joint venture of two governments (*e.g.*, the Vocational School at Nimba was built by the Swedish government while the Liberian government invests a considerable sum to operate the institution). Likewise, a joint Liberian-West German project is underway.

Organization of the school system is largely patterned after that in the United States of America. For many years it consisted of eight years of elementary education, four years of secondary education, and above the secondary school was the four-year college degree program. Because many students entered school late and left early, the government decided to guide students into suitable studies for terminal education, with skills, on a less-than-college level. Therefore, the system was changed in 1962 to six years of elementary school, three years of junior high school, and three years of senior high school. During the junior high school course, guidance is given so that early school leavers may be directed into vocational training by which they can earn a livelihood; those who plan to go on to college are given a more academic program of studies. Because of the large numbers of over-age students in school an attempt has been made to separate children for instruction so that proper age groups are together.

For a long time the poor salaries of teachers did not attract many people to educational work. Those who could not find other work turned to teaching. In this way many poorly trained and untrained individuals entered the teaching profession. In the early years of the nation the government of Liberia sought to remedy this situation by requiring teachers to study at Teachers' Institutes during the long vacation period. Two-week institutes were extended to four-week Vacation Schools in 1952 and later to six-week Vacation Schools. Besides this, the first Teacher Training School was opened in Monrovia in 1947. Four years later the first graduates were awarded Bachelor of Science degrees. Since that time, education degrees have been awarded at the University of Liberia annually. Other teacher-training programs have been outlined in the historical section at the beginning of this essay. In addition to local graduates, hundreds of students are sent abroad on scholarships to prepare for work in education.

All licensed teachers are eligible for membership in the National Teachers' Association. Other members consist of educators in general, regardless of the specialized field. The National Teachers' Association is composed of nine county Teachers' Associations which, in turn, consist of several local Teachers' Associations. All of these aim to raise the standard of education and to solve problems of educators.

At present, Liberia has no accurate statistics on literacy. Some say that illiteracy is as high as 85 percent. Since the launching of the National Literacy Campaign in 1951, thousands of adults, chiefly in rural areas, have learned to read and write. To help them keep their reading skill alive, a monthly periodical is published together with a number of booklets on various subjects of current events, health, and citizenship. The work in literacy and adult education proceeds at an encouraging pace.

Regular public schools are completely supported by the government. In addition, subsidies continue to be granted to certain acceptable private institutions. As government appropriations for education increase, the need for private schools will decrease and subsidies will be correspondingly reduced.

An educational survey made in 1963 revealed that about 30 percent of school-age children were then actually in school. Of this number 31 percent were pre-school, 48 percent were in grades one to three and 21 percent were in grades four to six. The reason for this small percentage, despite a compulsory

1963 STATISTICS ON 1429 GOVERNMENT ELEMENTARY SCHOOL TEACHERS
(HIGHEST GRADE COMPLETED)[1]

	GRADE							COLLEGE TRAINING			
	6	7	8	9	10	11	12	1 Year	2 Years	3 Years	4 Years
No. of Teachers	7	92	371	209	188	142	209	27	45	27	110

education law, lies in the impossibility of enforcement of the law because of (1) lack of adequate school buildings to meet the growing enrollment and improved curriculums being offered, (2) limited number of qualified school teachers, and (3) shortage of textbooks and other instructional materials and equipment. These weaknesses and limitations have proved a great hindrance to the country's educational progress.[2]

In 1963 the 1429 teachers in 471 public elementary schools (grades K-6) instructed 45,487 students.

As in many countries, the salaries of teachers are generally low. But during the past twenty years they have risen at least by 300 percent. Doctors and lawyers who are employed by the government usually can triple their salaries by returns received from their private practice. Some secretaries with lower qualifications than teachers receive higher salaries. Because of more attractive salaries in industry and other services, young people tend to avoid the teaching profession. Teachers have deserted the classroom to engage in other types of work which bring more money. Furthermore, more prestige is attached to many government positions than to the teaching profession.

Although education is free in elementary school and can be pursued at a very low cost on the secondary and college level, many young people find it impossible to remain in school for many years. The cost of living is high and part-time employment is at a premium. Some scholarships are given to deserving students by the government and more are made available each year. The foreign scholarship program of Liberia has resulted in providing the country with a large number of college graduates and skilled workers who have filled strategic posts in the economy.

The Department of Education now recommends a gradual reduction in foreign scholarships and an increase in local scholarships. This is because colleges in the country are raising their standards and can meet the needs of students on the undergraduate level leading to a bachelor's degree in the humanities, science, agriculture, forestry; and on the graduate level in law. If this proposal is followed, education will be made available on all levels to a larger number of worthy young people.

Liberia believes that the educated person should be able and willing to participate intelligently and constructively in the economic and social life of the nation and of the world. He should be industrious, tolerant, and congenial. He should be willing to function beyond the limits of duty without a desire for financial compensation or personal gain. His chief objective should be to serve his fellowman and to help in building a society in which all may live happily.

SELECTED BIBLIOGRAPHY

The African Repository

Annual Reports of the Secretary of Education, R. L.

Convocation Journals, Protestant Episcopal Church, 1836-1953.

GARDNER ALLEN. *The Trustees of Donation for Education in Liberia,* 1923.

HUBERICH, CHARLES. *Political and Legislative History of Liberia.* New York: Central Book Company, 1947.

JOHNSTON, HARRY. *Liberia.* Volume 1, 1906.

National Teachers' Association of Liberia. *Education in Liberia.* Mimeographed history, 1954.

---

1. See "A Five Year Plan For Education in Liberia," 1963. Department of Education, R. L., pp. 25 and 26.
2. *Ibid.*

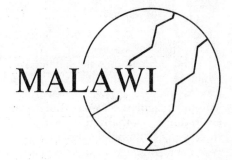

MALAWI

James E. Blackwell

The new nation of Malawi came into existence on July 6, 1964, but the history of the country is deeply rooted in antiquity. Much of its history is unrecorded, but oral traditions, folklore, and deductions from linguistic and racial attributes provide a vivid source of information about the development of Malawi to modern times. The early inhabitants of what was, between 1891-1963, the British Protectorate of Nyasaland were probably related to the Bushmen and Hottentots of South Africa and Bechuanaland and of the great Zulu people. It is also claimed that the ancient Maravians, a Bantu word which refers to "reflected light" (denoting both geographic features near Lake Malawi as well as the people who lived near the lake), developed a well-organized social and political system and their Kingdom is believed to have once encompassed all of the territory presently occupied by Portuguese East Africa, present-day Tanzania and much of what is now the Republic of Kenya.

While it is true that during the fifteenth century the Portuguese were the first Europeans to enter the territory, it is generally agreed that David Livingstone did more than any other individual to open up the territory for European settlement and the Christianization of Malawi. Observing the brutalities inflicted upon the indigenous Africans by the Arab slave traders, Livingstone was convinced that Malawi "ought to be Christianized" and between 1858-1864 led the Zambezi Expedition into Central Africa for the dual purposes of ridding the area of the Arabs and for an imminent introduction of Christianity into Central Africa. By 1891 the British were so firmly entrenched that Nyasaland was declared a British Protectorate and for the next seventy-three years the British ruled Nyasaland by what may best be termed "benevolent paternalism." (Note: the names Nyasaland and Malawi are used interchangeably in this discussion.)

In 1953, the British Parliament enacted legislation which created the Central African Federation; an artificial union which comprised Nyasaland, Southern Rhodesia, and Northern Rhodesia. The Federation was to become Britain's Waterloo in Central Africa. The probabilities that it would succeed were minimal even at its inception, primarily because the African population was not consulted before it was imposed upon them and because it was inconsistent with the rising tide of nationalism that had already begun in other parts of Africa.

The unpopularity of the Federation in Malawi was so pronounced, the nationalism movement so stringent, and the demands for independence so forceful that in 1958 Dr. Hastings Kamuzu Banda returned to his country after an absence of forty years to lead it to independence and self-government. A state of emergency was declared in 1959 and Dr. Banda with many of his followers were imprisoned in Gwelo, Southern Rhodesia. Disruptions followed throughout the country, and by 1961 Britain began to work with the African population to plan for the dissolution of the loosely-joined Federation and for the establishment of an independent Malawi. The Federation was dissolved at midnight on December 31, 1963, and Nyasaland became independent Malawi on July 6, 1964. It became a Republic on July 6, 1966, with Ngwazi Dr. Hastings Kamuzu Banda as President.

Today, Malawi is a small land-locked nation comprising some 45,000 square miles, approximately one-third of which is taken up by Lake Malawi. About the size of New York, the country is 520 miles long and varies in width from fifty to one hundred miles. It is bordered on its north by Tanzania, its south and southwest and east by Mozambique (Portuguese East Africa), and on its northwest by Zambia (formerly Northern Rhodesia). Its 1966 population was estimated to be slightly less than 3,900,000 and its population density of 82 persons per square mile made it one of the most densely populated nations of Africa. The population consists of approximately 3,800,000

Africans, 16,000 Asians and "Coloureds," and 12,000 "Europeans" or Caucasians.

The African people belong to the Bantu stock which in Malawi divides itself into seven major tribal groups; namely, Nyanji, Chewa, Yao, Nguru, Ngoni, Tumbuku, and the Cena. Although tribal differences are minimal, perhaps the three dominant groups are the Nyanji, Tumbuku, and the Yao. Tumbuku is the dominant language of the Northern Region; Nyanji is principally spoken in the Central and Southern regions. English is the official language of the government and is taught in most schools of the country as early as the first grade.

Malawi is economically impoverished, and most of its people live on subsistence agriculture. One-eighth of the Africans are wage-earners and it is estimated that more than 150,000 Malawians are employed outside Malawi, principally in the mines of South Africa, Zambia, and Southern Rhodesia. The per capita income in Malawi was estimated at $64 per annum in 1964 but that of its "working force" at approximately $200 per year. Tea is the most important export; other cash crops include tobacco, ground nuts, tung oil, and cotton.

Politically, Malawi is divided into three regions and twenty-five districts. The Government consists of a President, eleven appointed cabinet members, and fifty-three elected members of the National Assembly. The Malawi Congress Party is the only political party functioning in Malawi.

It is estimated that there are 1,000,000 Moslems, 1,000,000 Animists (comprising traditional religious groups), 750,000 Protestants, and 557,953 Roman Catholics in Malawi. The largest Protestant group is the Church of Central Africa, Presbyterian, with 150,000 members. Other Protestant groups are the United Bible Societies, Assemblies of God, Seventh-Day Adventists, the National Baptist Convention, and the African Evangelical Fellowship, formerly called the South Africa General Mission.

EDUCATIONAL DEVELOPMENT AND HISTORY

Role of Missions and Voluntary Agencies

Malawi owes much of its educational development to the dedication and tenacity of various missionary bodies and voluntary agencies. Missionaries established the first schools in the country, most of which were basic or primary schools that emphasized the rudiments of "reading, writing, and numbers." As early as 1880, the Anglican Church had established missions along the east shore of the lake in Yao country but were unable to establish an effective mission until 1903 at Likoma Island. The Anglican Church was concerned with the fundamental problem of how to advance the education of the indigenous people of the country. Early after their arrival the missionaries established numerous primary schools and train-

ing institutes for nurses as well as for hospital attendants and midwives.

The Church of Central Africa, Presbyterian (CCAP), now includes three groups: the United Free Church of Scotland, the Dutch Reformed Church of South Africa, and the Church of Scotland (Presbyterian). Through their respective leaders in Malawi, Dr. Robert Laws who spent fifty years at Livingstonia, Dr. Andrew Murray, and the Reverend Clement Scott, these churches established hundreds of schools, introduced printing presses throughout the country, constructed hospitals, inaugurated teacher-training programs, developed institutes for agricultural training as well as custodial care and training for the blind.

The first impact of the Catholic Church on education in Malawi came with the White Fathers who made their way to the Country in 1889 and established their first permanent mission in 1902. Throughout the nation's history, the Catholic Church has experienced conspicuous success toward advancing education. Today, more than 1000 African schools, six recognized teacher-training colleges, several hospitals, and two leper clinics are operated by the Roman Catholic Church in Malawi.

Although religious organizations provided the first systematic opportunities for educational achievement by Africans, the major defects of the primary school system and most teacher-training institutions today are the legacy of their early inadequacies. Without an organized and governmentally controlled school system and with the missions supplying most of the financial support for education in the country, church-related schools were left to set their own standards for both the schools and all of their functionaries. The school systems that were constructed without assistance from public funds became unbalanced; many were commenced without either an adequate staff or financial support to develop a full course. This situation accounted for much of the excessive attrition or "wastage" which characterized the primary school system and the teacher-training colleges for several decades. Uncontrolled proselyting engendered discrimination in the school system because of the tendency to admit to schools only those persons who were members of one's own religious denomination.

In spite of the basic problems which characterized church-related schools, the Malawians' insatiable appetite for education today remains as perhaps the most important contribution of the churches. It is said that at the age of twelve, Dr. Banda walked over a thousand miles from his home in Malawi to Johannesburg, South Africa, to work in the mines and to further his education. There is considerable evidence that walking hundreds of miles to school was at one time a common practice, and as late as 1963 this situation still existed because of the inaccessibility of various schools, particularly secondary schools, in the country.

The Phelps-Stokes Fund made an intensive investigation in Malawi in 1924 and published its report under the title, *Memorandums On Native Education In The Tropical Dependencies.* The response to this report and the insistence of the various denominations for educational reforms were instrumental in the appointment of the first Director of Education for Nyasaland in 1925 and for the establishment of the Nyasaland Department of Education in 1926. A Native Education Conference, convened by the Governor in 1927, was attended by representatives of all missionary societies and addressed itself to the problem of African education. The conference appointed committees to consider "Education Rules" to be established under the Education Ordinance which had been prepared to consider teacher training, female education, and the expansion of primary education.

By the end of 1927, there were 2,788 village schools with 4,481 teachers; the majority of whom were untrained and unqualified. All of the instruction was in the vernacular and, with notable exceptions, did not proceed beyond the rudiments of reading, writing, and arithmetic. The decade of the twenties marked the beginning of a genuinely organized plan for African education in Malawi.

Educational Ordinances and Policy

Legislation in the area of education in Malawi reflects the attempt of both the British and the Africans to deal with critical needs in the general field of education. The first education ordinance was enacted in May, 1927. The important aspects of this ordinance were its provisions for (1) a Board of Education to act as the advisory body on all educational matters and (2) for district school committees, which were organized during the next year but short-lived and unable to function properly. In 1930, a new education ordinance was enacted to control expenditures on education and to establish an Advisory Committee which replaced the Board of Education. This ordinance was revised in 1938 in order to permit the Governor of the Protectorate to decide the precise composition of the Advisory Committee and in 1939 to provide a legitimate vehicle through which the members of the District Committees could object to the opening of new schools. The latter revision reflected a local concern for the indiscriminate opening of schools devoid of a trained staff and without appropriations of government expenditures for the maintenance and support of the schools.

In 1945, a new ordinance was enacted which attempted to (1) define the relative positions of voluntary agencies and the Department of Education, (2) establish a measure of control over education, and (3) set rules for teaching service. This ordinance was followed by the appointment of a Committee a year later by the Governor to "investigate and review the whole question of African education" which accomplished little more than a rubber-stamp report justifying the *status quo.*

In 1951 the East and Central Africa Study Group, commonly known as the Binns Commission and sponsored jointly by the Nuffield Foundation and the Colonial Office, visited Malawi. This commission recommended far-reaching changes in the organization and financing of education for the Country, influenced the approach to education in Malawi, and became the basis for a more detailed study of the problem of education for Africans which was commenced in 1961.

A revision of the Ordinance of 1952 provided for the establishment of District Education Committees to replace the District School Committees which had previously served as the advisory body on educational development at the district level. These District Education Committees were empowered to "establish, build, equip, maintain, and manage schools and other educational institutions." Legislation in 1953 and 1958 attempted to clarify and systematize the Unified African Teaching Service Rules.

The Phillips Commission spent several months in 1961 in Nyasaland investigating all aspects of African education. The report of the Commission was published in 1962 under the title, *Report By The Committee Of Inquiry Into African Education.* Its major findings underscored the urgent need for expansion of secondary education as the most important dimension of a development program. It also urged improvements in the training of teachers, increase of facilities for technical education, an expansion of the Inspectorate in the Ministry of Education, the development of a comprehensive district system of educational administration, and admonished the Government to devolve this responsibility to elected local government bodies. Aside from the importance justifiably attached to the expansion of secondary education, the most important recommendation was for assuring greater public control of the development and organization of the primary school system with a concomitant restriction of the activities of voluntary agencies involved in education which would eventuate into their withdrawal from the more significant aspects of the administration of primary schools. The findings and recommendations of the Phillips Commission were the foundation for the Education Ordinance of 1962.

By 1962 the political realities evidenced by the 1959-60 state of emergency had resulted in an almost universally accepted fact that political independence for Nyasaland was almost a *fait accompli.*

The major purposes of the 1962 law were to strengthen the powers of public control over education and to enable the development of education on the lines of national planning required by the people as a whole. Its specific provisions were designed to (1) establish a greater degree of autonomy for local Education Authorities, (2) establish Advisory Councils, (3) centralize and standardize the registration of teachers, (4) provide for registration and control of schools, (5) regulate the prescription of fees and syllabi, and (6) establish overall powers and responsibilities for the Minister of Education.

The 1962 Ordinance had the direct effect of abolishing all ineffective district committees and promulgating a major breakthrough for the participation of the community in the task of developing education by devolving the responsibility for primary education to the Local Government level. It clearly delineated the functions of Local Authorities and differentiated these functions from those of the Minister of Education.

Intention of the Ministry to devolve these responsibilities for primary education to the local levels was reinforced in both persuasive and precise terms in a policy statement issued in 1963. It stated that this responsibility was in fact that of the popularly elected Local Education Authorities, which outside the urban areas of Blantyre-Limbe, Zomba, and Lilongwe is the District Council. The Local Government Authority has jurisdiction over the Local Education Authority and its subordinate Education Committee. The Education Committee of the Local Education Authority presently consists of up to twelve members, of whom one is the Ex-Officio Chairman of the Local Education Authority. As many as six members of the Education Committee are appointed from the membership of the Local Education Authority and no more than five can be nominated by the Minister of Education to represent national interest in educational activities at the local level.

Primary duties and powers of the Local Education Authorities are to (1) receive subventions and grants-in-aid, (2) receive tuition and other educational fees, (3) provide and allocate funds for primary education and ancillary services as well as for scholarships and bursaries at secondary schools, (4) advise the Minister on matters pertaining to primary education, (5) exercise control over the proprietors of schools and to provide equipment services, and (6) be responsible for the control and management of schools. The Executive Officer of the Education Committee is the District Education Officer who is appointed by the Minister of Education and has the responsibility for advising the Committee on Ministry Policy and for the implementation of the decisions of the Committee.

A new three-year National Development Plan, underwritten largely by Great Britain, was announced in 1962. This Plan placed special emphasis on both secondary and higher education. It allocated $2,520,-000 of the total proposed budget of $5,459,600 for education on secondary education and $1,876,000 to higher education both inside and external to Malawi. It also proposed some $1,246,000 for the construction of a Polytechnic Institute, $1,036,000 of that sum to be contributed by the United States Agency for Inter-

national Development. The Plan provided for the following expenditures over the three-year period, 1962-65: primary education, $196,000; secondary education $2,520,000; teacher training, $336,000; technical training, $196,000; University College, $1,400,000; Polytechnic College, $1,246,000; scholarships for higher education, $476,000; Blind Training Center, $28,000; and Localization or Africanization, $61,600.

The School System

Until 1948, the pattern of education was a 4-3 (or 4) -3 scheme divided into village or vernacular schools, central or lower middle schools and station or upper middle schools. The age ranges in these schools were five to fourteen, ten to eighteen, and twelve to twenty years, respectively. It was more or less expected that a child would take approximately ten years to reach the highest class in the upper middle or station school, and it was not uncommon for many students to require a much longer period of time than that mainly because of the constraints placed upon them by lack of funds, responsibilities at home, and lack of propinquity to the school.

In 1949, several voluntary agencies, primarily unassisted missions, began to open Junior Secondary Schools which provided a two-year post-primary course. Provisions for these schools were incorporated into the 1954-59 national education system and were designated as a basic course for potential civil service employees. These schools were to be considered as a complete course, separate and distinct from the first two years of a regular secondary school. In practice, this system was dysfunctional because the students in the Junior Secondary Schools sat for the same examinations at the completion of Standard VIII as did the students in the regular systems, a practice which obviated distinctions between the two categories of students.

By 1960, the system was transformed into a 5-3-4-2 pattern. The corresponding nomenclature was as follows: primary, senior primary, a four-year secondary course which led to the Cambridge School Certificate, and a two-year sixth form (comparable to the American Junior college). The pattern of education was again changed in 1963 to a seven-year primary course, each grade called a Standard, and a five-year secondary course with each grade referred to as a Form.

With the dissolution of the Central African Federation in 1963, the Government decided that responsibility for the schools previously administered by the Federal Ministry of Education must be transferred to the Government of Nyasaland. The transfer of these schools occurred in December, 1963, and the Nyasaland Government received control of two secondary schools and twenty-six primary schools. The Government also decided that the European schools should remain exclusively for Europeans but that all other schools would become fully integrated with the existing system of the Ministry. Therefore, in European schools, the education fee would cover the cost of education provided, less the present grant or contribution made at other schools. From that point, the actual fees became $126 per year for primary education, $144.20 for secondary education plus $268 per annum for boarding. This action sanctioned the existence of three separate school systems in Malawi; one each for Europeans, Africans, and Asians and Coloureds. Since 1964, there has been a movement toward racial integration in a single system of education in Malawi. Presently, the principle of integrated education is accepted and most of the schools that were once segregated schools are now integrated.

Upon the recommendation of the Advisory Council, several changes were made in the system of education in 1965. Among these were a reversion to the previous pattern of an eight-year primary course, followed by four years of secondary education, mandatory internal examinations for all pupils at the conclusion of each school term and at the conclusion of a school year, a reintroduction of the Primary School Leaving Examination which became mandatory for all students in Standard VIII. Others included a requirement that satisfactory completion of the Junior Certificate Examination was a *sine qua non* for admission to the second half of the secondary school course, a substantial increase in the number of in-service courses for teachers combined with regular guidance visits to schools by members of the Inspectorate, and renewed emphasis on the T.3 courses (two years of teacher-training college training plus a Junior Certificate of Education) for increasing the number of qualified teachers in the primary schools. Provisions for retaining or deferring promotion of students in grade and firm guidelines for the expulsion of students from school were established for the first time. These changes became effective at the beginning of the 1966 school year.

In addition to the various internal examinations now required of all students, other examinations include (1) the Primary School Leaving Examination taken at the completion of Standard VIII and used as a basis for selection for entry into Form I of the secondary school, (2) the Cambridge Overseas School Certificate taken at the completion of Form II or twelve years of schooling, (3) the Cambridge Overseas Higher School Certificate, taken after the completion of Form IV or fourteen years of formal education.

Students now enter the first grade or Standard I between the ages of six and eight but age limits are not rigidly enforced and there is no compulsory education in Malawi. The present national objective is free primary education for everyone by 1980. Students are taught in the vernacular, either Nyanji in the Central and Southern Regions or Tumbuka in the Northern Region, until the third year at which time

instruction in English commences. All students are required to pay school fees which vary from $3.00 for Standards I-V, $5.00 for Standards VI-VIII and $21.00 for secondary schools per annum plus boarding expenses. Students at Teacher Training Colleges are paid a stipend of $5.60 per month for each month of study.

Historical Perspective of the School Systems

PRIMARY EDUCATION: For more than a half-century Christian Missions provided the foundation for the educational system, but their schools are now becoming the casualties of time, more effective planning, and organization. In 1960, for the first time, the number of children in "assisted" or financially-aided schools exceeded the number of students in Mission "unassisted" schools. Even as late as 1960, however, the majority of the primary schools were owned and managed by Christian missions and churches. Others were owned and operated by agencies who provided education for the children of their employees. Notably, few schools were owned by Muslims and private individuals. The owners of the schools were responsible for their management and supervision and were persuaded to establish liaison with the Department of Education which has led to distinctive improvements in the curricular offerings and general development of the unassisted mission schools.

The number of students in the primary schools has shown dramatic increases in recent years, but the number of educable students in the general population is not always reflected in the number of pupils who actually enter schools. For example, the estimated child population in 1963 was 658,315, but the number of school places that were filled in all primary schools was 367,348; 144,099 of those were in "unassisted schools" where enrollment figures are not always accurate. It is apparent that less than 50 percent of the children of primary school age are in fact enrolled in primary schools today.

There are twice as many boys in school as girls mainly because the attrition rate for girls during the primary school years is about 60 percent while that for boys is only about 8 percent. As a result, three times as many boys complete their primary education than girls. About 42 percent of the entrants into Standard I are girls, but they tend to drop out of school before completing Standard VI for work at home, marriage, and because it is still not a fully accepted norm that the education of girls is as important as that of a boy. The 1964 Report of the Survey Team on Education in Malawi, *Education For Development*, stressed, *inter alia*, the value of reducing the wastage or attrition rate among female students at all levels of education for meeting the national objectives of the Country. The education of girls is improving as evidenced by the fact that the

1965 literacy rate among females over the age of seven in Malawi stood at 40 percent while that for men was 60 percent.

The primary system of education currently receives its financial assistance from three principal sources; Central funds, Local Authority funds, and Agency funds. The latter are derived primarily from contributions from overseas and local churches, school fees, and costs of services rendered. Expenditures by Local Education Authorities on primary education in 1965 were $1,318,444.40.

Critical but remediable problems confront the primary education system. One of the more acute problems is that of raising the level of trained teachers in the school system. Although there were 5,000 professionally qualified teachers at the end of 1965 holding positions in the primary schools, most of these teachers were in the T.4 category (*i.e.,* holding a Primary School Leaving Certificate plus two years of teacher training). Over 3,000 teachers were "without professional qualifications;" two-thirds of whom held only the Primary school Leaving Certificate and 600 were "without any qualifications."

It is the lack of adequately trained teachers that exacerbates and magnifies other insidious conditions which affect the primary school system. It accounts in part for such a rigid adherence to the syllabus and the exaggerated emphasis on examinations that the student is neither encouraged to be imaginative nor to participate in problem-solving activity. Nor is he encouraged to develop his capacity to think systematically and logically. The Education Survey Team Report pointed out the disturbing consequence of this approach in that it produces a student whose "learning is repetitive, mechanistic, and regurgitative." These conditions parallel the problems of poor equipment, lack of furniture, inadequate supply of books and library materials, and lack of educational reinforcement in the home.

These difficulties do not belie the fact that Malawi is determined to make education a powerful instrument for national development. Nor do these criticisms deny the fact that the new nation is coming to grips with some of its more urgent problems. It is committed to educational expansion commensurate with the available financial resources and established priorities. The Ministry of Education has decreed that there must be a significant reduction in the wastage or attrition rate at all levels and that the school system must retain a much larger proportion of all pupils who enter each Standard or Form. It has embarked on a bold plan to improve instructions qualitatively by improving the curriculum, the course content, upgrading the teaching profession, acquiring better equipment, and expanding facilities, and by devising techniques for identifying the talented students and encouraging such students to develop their educational potential maximally.

SECONDARY EDUCATION: There was no recognized secondary course in Malawi until 1940 when the Blantyre Secondary School was opened by the Church of Central Africa, Presbyterian. The school was built with the aid of an initial government grant of $12,486. Other secondary schools were constructed by the Roman Catholic Church at Zomba in 1942 and by the Nyasaland Protectorate in Dedza in 1951 and Mzuzu in 1959. As late as 1960, there were only four secondary schools and 1,478 pupils in all of the country. Only 3 percent of the primary school leavers could proceed to the School Certificate level. However, 10.1 percent of the boys and 17.8 percent of the girls who left primary schools entered these four secondary schools. Because of a desire to exact in 1960 high entrance standards and the limited space available for positions, *inter alia,* admission to secondary schools has traditionally been by competitive examinations.

A "Sixth Form" opened at Dedza Government School in 1958 which offered a two-year course preparatory for admission to the Cambridge Higher School Certificate. Previously, a number of Malawians were accepted for this course in the Rhodesias.

By 1962, Malawi had committed itself to devote maximum attention to secondary education in order to meet the anticipated needs consequent to independence and to develop the Country's national potential. Ten new streams opened which enabled an intake of 996 pupils as compared to an intake of 446 during 1961. Seventy-five students were accepted for post-school certificate studies and all students who entered the secondary school course were expected to complete it, an expectation which marked what was then believed to be an end to the Junior Certificate Examination. There were ninety-six professionally qualified teachers and thirty-two in the "without professional qualifications" category. The Government made arrangements for the recruitment of forty-two Peace Corps Volunteers and additional recruits from the British-Government-sponsored Volunteer Service Overseas for teaching duties in the secondary schools. All but 4 percent of the qualified teachers were employed in the Government Secondary School.

By 1965, the secondary school enrollment stood at 7,578 with 185 "professionally qualified teachers," including 74 trained graduates and 32 trained teachers, and 196 teachers "without professional qualifications," including 182 degree holders and 14 teachers who held higher school certificates. There were twice as many male students as females, the number of girls diminishing significantly in the higher forms. As of July 5, 1966, even with the reversion to the four-year secondary school pattern, there were 7,958 pupils in the secondary schools and 381 teachers. The United States Peace Corps accounted for more than 50 percent of all the teachers at the secondary school level in Malawi.

Since 1961, Malawi has embarked on an ambitious program for the expansion of secondary school facilities. In the six-year period between 1959 and 1965, the number of secondary schools rose dramatically from four to thirty-nine, an increase of 925 percent. The number of classes in the secondary schools stood at 246 and there were more than 70 streams in these 39 schools.

The secondary school curriculum is dictated primarily by the requirements of the Cambridge Overseas School Certificate. The basic subjects taught at the secondary school level are English, mathematics, French, Nyanji, Latin (to a small extent), general science, physics, chemistry, biology, history, geography, and domestic science. Other subjects may also be taught, but the actual range varies greatly between schools according to local circumstances and availability of staff.

Stress on the development of secondary education is reflected in the overall increase in the national budget for education as well as the specific increase in the allocations for secondary education. The 1966 Central or National Government expenditure on education was 14.8 percent of the national budget, an increase of 3.3 percent over the rate spent in 1963. The percentage of expenditure on education as compared with the country's gross national product is 29.5 percent. The actual amount expended for secondary education in 1965 was $1,420,538.80.

The problems developed consequent to the increasing emphasis on secondary education have challenged the imagination of education officials and strained the resources available at local levels. One of the more urgent problems is the need for hostels and living accommodations near the twenty recently-constructed day secondary schools. Inadequate accommodations restrict the opportunities for organized and productive study and affect the general morale of the students. Outside study away from boarding schools presents numerous difficulties for the pupil, especially those living at homes devoid of reading lights, books, resource materials, and a suitable place for studying.

Most schools face the complex problems associated with inadequate library facilities, inadequate supply of texts, outdated texts, insufficient equipment, including writing paper, furniture, electricity for both reading and laboratory experiments, and gas. The attention given to the syllabus and the concomitant emphasis on studying for the examination are special problems at the secondary level. Success on the Cambridge Examinations not only has a social importance but is of inestimable economic significance. The fears associated with the danger of failure on the Cambridge engender a penchant for rigid adherence to the syllabus and renders deviations from the syllabus unlikely. This situation is likely to be perpetuated, consciously or unconsciously, until such time that Malawi develops an educational system that is distinctively Malawian.

TECHNICAL AND VOCATIONAL EDUCATION: The Report of the Survey Team in 1964 stressed the need for the development of technical and vocational education as a necessary instrument for national development. The team viewed this type of education as not only one solution for the unemployment problem of the country but as an informal means for continuing education for school dropouts. A technical education officer had been appointed in 1962 to advise the Ministry on the development of technical education and to establish standards for training programs. However, the recommendations of the Survey team led to the establishment of a Further Education Center in Blantyre to provide training in industrial and vocational education. This center became the forerunner of a million dollar Polytechnic College which opened in September, 1965. It also gave impetus for the construction of the Nyasaland College of Commerce in Blantyre which provides instruction in a variety of commercial and general subjects. A Government Technical School opened at Lilongwe in 1963; a total of six technical and trade schools for men existed by that year. Several facilities existed for the training of women in domestic science and housecrafts. The basic technical courses are now designed to lead to the City and Guilds Ordinary Levels. The fact that it is extremely difficult to arrange for satisfactory apprenticeship duties in this non-industrialized Country agitates the opportunities for experience in on-the-job training and encourages theoretical instruction with little practical application. As the nation builds its own industries and attracts investments in local industries by external business enterprises, these opportunities for apprenticeship training will increase. More, than 300 students are presently enrolled in apprenticeship courses at the Polytechnic College and over a thousand are enrolled in other technical and vocational courses elsewhere.

TEACHER-TRAINING COLLEGES: Teacher training began with the establishment of the first mission schools and operated on an apprenticeship or pupil-teacher basis. Up to 1929, when a Jeanes Training Center was opened, there was no coordination of standards of entry to training programs or of the training itself. The Jeanes Center provided a modicum of standards, established a training format and curriculum for the elementary vernacular schools and for the lower and upper middle schools. It was not until 1955 that the first post-school certificate was accepted as a requisite for entry into teacher training and currently most of the 1,319 students in the teacher-training colleges are persons who have completed primary school education and no secondary school training.

There are twelve teacher-training colleges, of which only two are managed and owned by the Ministry of Education. Six of the remaining ten are operated by the Roman Catholic Church and four are owned in association with the Christian Council. A "Further College" is operated by the Seventh-Day Adventists, but receives no financial help from the Central Government In general, these colleges are too small and have more than 3:1 male-female ratio.

Soche Hill Teacher-Training College, opened near Blantyre in 1962 primarily for training teachers for secondary school positions, offers a Diploma in Education course. This three-year course has as its major objective the production of teachers who will have a sufficient knowledge of two teaching subjects for effective teaching in the lower levels of the secondary school.

Development of the Inspectorate has encouraged improvements in methods of teacher training in the colleges. The selection committee is the same committee that serves the secondary schools. Presently, the 500 selectees, obtained on an annual basis, are required to serve one year as a pupil-teacher before they can enter a college. They teach in a local school and are observed for potentiality as a student and as a teacher. There is a continued emphasis on refresher courses, workshops for improving teaching effectiveness and competency, opportunities for professional development, and cooperative projects with external teacher associations. The Malawi Teachers' Association has taken a special interest in such projects.

As of 1965, there were ninety-seven "professionally qualified" teachers in all of the training colleges, including nineteen trained graduates and twenty-nine trained teachers and five diploma teachers. Of the thirty-seven staff members listed in the "without professional qualifications" category, thirty-six held the bacculaureate degree and only one person was teaching with a Higher School Certificate. A lack of women teachers continues to be noted but the number seems to be increasing slightly.

Funds allocated for teacher training in 1965 were slightly more than a half million dollars ($542,553.20).

Several classes of teachers exist in Malawi today which can be summarized as follows: A "trained graduate" is a person who holds a university degree or its equivalent and who also has professional training as a teacher. A "trained teacher" is a person who holds a Ministry of Education provisional teaching certificate. The T.2 teachers have completed Form IV plus two years of teacher training; a T.3 teacher has completed Form II plus two years of training; a T.4 teacher has completed primary education plus two years of teacher training, and a T.5 teacher, practically non-existent today, has two years of training and no academic qualifications.

It is still somewhat difficult to attract the better students into the teaching profession primarily because of the low salary in comparison to salaries paid civil servants and persons in other professional services, plus the tendency of the better students to continue their education. In recent years, the teaching field has lost a number of highly competent teachers to various government posts, including ambassadorial and diplomatic services. The basic annual salary for a qualified single teacher in the secondary school is $1,960 while that for a married teacher is $2,200.80. Primary school teachers average about 40 percent of the average salary of secondary school teachers.

HIGHER EDUCATION: With the achievement of self-government in 1963, the American Council on Education was invited to sponsor a survey of education in Malawi. Their report recommended the establishment of a University and outlined a suggested form for it. The British Government added its support to the proposal and the University was created by an Act of the Malawi Parliament on October 30, 1964. Dr. Hastings Banda accepted the invitation of the Provisional Council to serve as the University's first president and Dr. Ian Michael was appointed by the council to serve as the vice-chancellor. The main campus is presently located at Blantyre but will eventually be relocated at Lilongwe.

The core of the new University is the new Liberal Arts College whose curriculum now includes chemistry, physics, mathematics, biology, geography, English, history, and French. In September, 1966, courses were started in agriculture, economics, and in psychology, philosophy, and sociology.

Other previously existing institutions which have been integrated as constituents of the University structure and which form the remaining components of the University are Soche Hill Teacher-Training College which serves as the School of Education; the Malawi Polytechnic College; the Institute for Public Administration at Mpemba, which provides training for civil service positions and fundamentals of law, and an Agricultural College at Bunda. The four of these institutions award diplomas after three years but the Liberal Arts College awards an ordinary degree after four years and an honors degree after five years. Students normally enter the University after twelve years of schooling. Presently 490 students, including 180 in the Liberal Arts College, are enrolled in the University.

Establishment of the University does not mean that higher education for Malawians external to the Country will cease but it is likely to be curtailed. Between 1960 and 1965, the number of Malawians pursuing degree or postgraduate studies outside the Country increased from 91 to 282 and by 1965 about 293 Malawians were engaged in non-degree or diploma courses in foreign countries. Most of the degree-oriented students were studying in the United States, Great Britain, and India while the non-degree and diploma students were located in Great Britain, West Germany, and Kenya.

The Government and the people of Malawi are cognizant of their opportunities to use education as an instrument for national development and solidarity. They are mindful of the disjunctive forces that can be unleashed on the country by rapid technological changes and ineffective preparation to cope with these changes and by the concomitants of uncontrolled population increases and unsatisfied social appetites of the masses. The manner in which Malawi approaches these problems will materially affect her ability to capitalize upon her present moment of opportunity to make education the dominant influence on its entire social, economic, and political system. If major social problems are to be eschewed in this developing nation, the entire fabric of education must be continually strengthened, and if the national welfare of the people is to be protected, the educational system must be expanded so that the life chances of the population as a whole will be substantially augmented. The overall quality of education in Malawi will be assured as long as the type of education espoused is appropriate for the requirements of national development and national unity.

SELECTED BIBLIOGRAPHY

"African Education in Nyasaland." *The Times Educational Supplement No. 1356*. London: April 24, 1941, p. 192.

American Council on Education. *Education For Development*. Washington, D. C.: U. S. Agency For International Development, 1964.

Annual Report of the Education Department, 1960. Zomba, Nyasaland: The Government Printer, 1961.

Annual Report of the Ministry of Education and Social Development, 1962. Zomba, Nyasaland: The Government Printer, 1963.

Annual Report of the Ministry of Education, 1963. Zomba, Malawi: The Government Printer, 1965.

Annual Report of the Ministry of Education, 1964. Zomba, Malawi: The Government Printer, 1965.

Annual Report of the Ministry of Education, 1965. Zomba, Malawi: The Government Printer, 1966.

Bowman, E. D., "Jeanes Training in Nyasaland," *Overseas Education*, Vol. 16. London: April 1945, pp. 97-103.

Bray, F. *Report of Survey of Facilities for Technical Education in the Federation*. Salisbury: Government Printer, 1958.

Brown, Edward E., et al. *A Bibliography of Malawi*. Syracuse, New York: Syracuse University Press, 1965.

Coupland, Sir Reginald. *East Africa and Its Invaders*. Oxford: Clarendon, 1938.

Debenham, Frank. *Nyasaland, The Land of the Lake*. London: Her Majesty's Stationary Office, 1955.

Education Project—International Development Association. Zomba, Malawi: Ministry of Education.

Fletcher, Basil A. *The Background of Educational Development in the Federation*. Salisbury: University College of Rhodesia and Nyasaland, 1959.

———. "Research Projects in Education: University College of Rhodesia and Nyasaland." *Teacher Education* (London) Vol. 1, May 1960, pp. 31-9.

George, Archdeacon. "Village Schools, Lake Nyasa." *Overseas Education* (London), Vol. 2, October 1930, p. 44.

Hazelwood, Arthur and Henderson, P. D., *Nyasaland, The Economics of Federation*. Oxford: Blackwell, 1960.

Hunter, Guy. "Emerging Africans." *Adult Education* (London), Vol. 32, Autumn 1959, pp. 101-7.

Irvine, S. H. "Education for Africans in an Industrial Society." *Teachers Education* (London), Vol. 1, November 1960, pp. 39-44.

———. "Education for Africans in an Industrial Society. The Aspects of Wastage in Formal Education." *Teachers Education* (London) Vol. 1, February 1961, pp. 43-57.

Jones, Thomas Jesse. *Education in East Africa: A Study of East, Central and South Africa, by the Second African Education Commission Under the Auspices of the Phelps-Stokes Fund*. New York: Phelps-Stokes Fund, 1925.

Kitchen, Helen, ed. *The Educated African*. New York: Frederick A. Praeger, Inc., 1962, pp. 215-231.

Livingstone, David. *Narrative of an Expedition to the Zambesi*. New York: Harpers, 1866.

Oliver, Roland. *The Missionary Factor in East Africa*. London: Longmans, 1952.

Parker, Franklin. "Education in the Federation of Rhodesia and Nyasaland." *Journal of Negro Education*, Vol. 30, Summer 1961, pp. 286-93.

Report on Education Development 1965-66. Zomba, Malawi. Presented at the XXIX Session of the International Conference on Public Education, Geneva, July 1966.

Thomson, Frances T. *Africa Fact Sheet No. 7*. New York: National Council of the Churches of Christ, 1965.

University of Malawi Provisional Council Act, 1964. Zomba, Malawi. The Government Printer, 1964.

Ward, W. E. R. "Education in British Africa Existing Patterns: Suggestions for the Future in View of Changing Political Status," *British Affairs*, Vol. 4, September 1960, pp. 128-35.

Wrong, Margaret. "Education in British Central and South Africa," *Journal of Negro Education*, Vol. 15, July 1946, pp. 370-81.

UPPER VOLTA

Joseph S. Roucek

Being landlocked, the Republic of Upper Volta is in a delicate geopolitical position. Its export trade depends on Ghana; it depends on France, for its import trade. Its attitude toward Communism is negative, and yet the government must also remain friendly with Ghana which tends to be rather receptive to overtures from Soviet Russia and Communist China.

Thus it was a pleasant trick of destiny that the first foreign chief of state received (in April, 1965) by President Johnson since his inauguration came from one of the poorest, weakest, and most remote countries in the world; he was President Maurice Yaméogo of Upper Volta, this landlocked country that once was part of French West Africa.

Yet history, which chastens pride, indicates that President Yaméogo comes from a region and a tribe that had a brilliant kingdom—the Mossi Empire—as far back as the twelfth century. The capital from which he came to the United States, Ouagadougou, was an imperial capital ages before Washington was built.

Upper Volta has always remained closely linked to France, which has been extending technical and cultural assistance at the rate of about $50 million a year. The economy is almost entirely agricultural.

Despite these links, Upper Volta is as jealous of its independence as are all the new African states.

The young, outspoken President Yaméogo has been more and more pro-Western. He has sided with the United States against Soviet and Communist Chinese inroads in Africa; he has backed the Tshombe government in the Congo and has supported a resolution condemning Ghana for letting its territory be used as a training ground for subversive elements.

As a spokesman for fourteen nations of the Inter-African and Malagasy Organization, Yaméogo brought to Washington the message that the future of Africa lies with the Africans and not with the Chinese or other communists.

He also brought to Washington the sense of the African transition from tribal culture to the modern age. A Mossi tribesman whose face bears the tribe's ritual scars, Yaméogo is a modern-minded and experienced administrator and an adroit politician in an area that has known continuous unrest since independence came to the West African nations.

A Roman Catholic in a country where 75 percent of the population still practices animism, President Yaméogo was the first African chief of state to be received by the Pope. (He was educated in Catholic mission schools and at a Catholic seminary.) He is a farmer and was interested in agricultural and irrigation projects during his visit of the United States. (Upper Volta is almost entirely an agricultural country, with cattle as its main wealth.)

Yaméogo became the first President of Upper Volta at the age of thirty-nine, in August, 1960. Although the average income in his country is $50 a year, he represents the country so well that he is one of the most influential men in West Africa. In 1961, he was chosen President of the Entente Council, a regional organization composed of Upper Volta, Togo, Niger, and the Ivory Coast. Subsequently, he became the moving power behind the inter-African-Malagasy group.

HISTORY

Exact roots of the Mossi people are somewhat of a mystery, although it is known that they reached this area from somewhere in the East. As empire builders they founded two settlements in what is now Ghana and they spread northward, setting up a series of feudal empires on their way. The tribal folklore claims that the Mossi continued conquering the surrounding regions and founded the ancient empire of Moro Naba under the leadership of Quedraogo (stallion); after his passing, the Empire was divided among his heirs, and a new Kingdom, the Yatemga, was founded. Centered at Ouagadouga (now the Capital), its people opposed the aggressive proponents of Islam and have been able to save their own folkways and mores down to modern times; they won against the nearby Mandingo and Songhai Empires and sacked the city of Timbuktu in 1333; two centuries later they defeated the invading Moroccans.

In 1900 the French reached Upper Volta, and the region was part of the administration of Upper Senegal and Niger. It was reconstituted as a distinct territory in 1919, part of French West Africa. Following World War II, the political scene started to change very rapidly. The *loi cadre* of 1956 gave the country direct universal suffrage. It had become a self-governing republic by 1958 and was granted independence on August 5, 1960. (Just prior to independence, President Yaméogo joined the Council of the Entente with the Ivory Coast, Niger, and Dahomey; the council is mainly a customs union, although some disagreements have been troubling the relations between Ivory Coast and Upper Volta in regard to duties; as a result, Upper Volta formed a separate customs arrangement with Ghana, and today three-fourths of Upper Volta's export trade is with Ghana.)

POLITICS

The Constitution of 1959 provides that the Republic adheres to the principles of democracy and human rights. The President of the Council is elected and responsible to the legislative assembly, composed of seventy-five members, elected for a five-year term. The judicial branch is independent of both the executive and the legislative. The High Court of Justice is empowered to judge the President of the council and other officials impeached by the Assembly. (It is similar to the Supreme Court of the United States, as it determines the constitutionality of laws by the legislature or any of the thirty-seven local *cercles*.

SOCIO-ECONOMIC CONDITIONS

Covering 105,811 square miles, Upper Volta has a population of a little more than 3,500,000 people. More than 1.7 million strong, the Mossi live in the central region of the country and, for the most part, make their living by farming. Their society is family-centered; parents and their adult offsprings make up the larger family unit and occupy a group of huts surrounding a small court.

The Republic, which is the geographic center of French-speaking western Black Africa (bounded on the north and west by the Republic of Mali, on the east by the Republic of Niger, on the South by the Republics of Ghana, Togo, Dahomey, and the Ivory Coast), is a vast plateau, varying in altitude from 7 to 1,100 feet. None of the rivers is navigable for any appreciable length, and the country's transportation system is limited on the Ouagadougou-Abidjan railroad, the only one in the country.

Consumer goods are so scarce that Ouagadougou is one of the world's most expensive cities. To make some goods available to the natives, the government has experimented with a nonprofit cooperative which sells consumer goods at considerably lower prices. Erosion, primitive agricultural methods, and poor strains of livestock have kept the country in a depressed condition. The government has been using the funds available from FIDES (FAC) to promote agricultural development. Cattle represents more than half of the total value of exports, most going to the neighboring countries of the customs union. A program of forestation has been undertaken that is to prevent further dessication of the soil. There are about 1,300 telephones, and all but fifty are in Ouagadougou and Bobo Dioulasso; there are two radio stations but no daily newspapers.

EDUCATION

Like all other newly-formed African countries, Upper Volta has been feverishly experimenting with promoting education, especially on the elementary level.

Education in Upper Volta in any modern sense is a product of the twentieth century. Almost no information is available concerning education before colonial times.

Since 1951, school enrollments have increased threefold, and the number of public and private schools more than doubled between 1959 and 1965.

Education is based on the French model as is that of most of West Africa. The importance of education in the overall plan for the development of Upper Volta was set forth in the Constitution: "The State and the local communities shall have the right and the duty of creating the preliminary conditions and the public institutions which shall guarantee the education of the children."

Nevertheless, education is not a state monopoly. "Private Schools may be opened with the authorization of the State," and are placed under its control.

The government has been trying desperately to increase the ratio of school attendance, one of the lowest in French-speaking Africa; the figure had been raised, by 1965, to 9 percent.

Thanks to the aid of the FIDES and FAC, the number of children receiving elementary education quintupled during the 1947-1963 period.

In order to recruit more teaching personnel and to meet the growing educational needs of the nation, the government has been intensifying the teacher-training program. Simultaneously, numerous new buildings are being constructed to house educational facilities. In Ouagadougou, a high school, a technical training college, a teacher-training school for girls, and a domestic science college are being built. In Bobo-Dioulasso, the Quezzin Coulibaly High School is preparing students for the "Baccalauréat." A high school with an accelerated program was also opened there in October, 1962, and is preparing its students for the B.E.P.C. Since 1952, two teacher-training schools for boys were opened, one in Dougougou and the other in Ouahigouya. High Schools, offering complete programs of studies were opened in Banfora, Fada N'Gourma, Kaya, and Ouahigouya.

A program of accelerated education is now being studied and it is expected that within fifteen years all children of school-going age will be absorbed into the educational system. For a population of nearly 5,000,000, Upper Volta has a great number of children of school-going age; it has been estimated that this figure increased to about 900,000 by 1969.

The enrollment for 1961-1962 was only 64,000, about 9.8 percent of the total number of children of school-going age. Even then, this modest figure has been achieved through a strong and concerted financial effort by the government; education takes 23 percent of the national budget.

Authorities acknowledge frankly that "the total expenditure desirable for education is rather impractical as of the moment. This is the reason why a rational method has to be sought, which will permit the greatest amount of education for the children for the least expenditure of money."

The Government has been employing comparative education experts to improve the country's educational program. Among them were Messrs. Christol and Medard. Mr. Christol, working for SEDES, carried out economic, demographic, and financial research; Mr. Medard, who was attached to the Office of Training Research, Paris, delved into technical questions regarding education. The work of these two experts resulted in a subsequent reorganization of the educational system under the "Christol Plan," permitting a maximum school attendance for the minimum of expenditure. Under the system, there is shorter school attendance with curricula adapted for the purpose of securing the most education for the given period of school attendance. This intensive type of education allows the enrollment of children between the ages of twelve and fourteen years who, under the former system, could not attend school when they were between the ages of six and twelve.

The Christol Plan was approved by the Legislative Assembly on November 26, 1959, and put into operation during 1961. At the beginning of 1962, about 183 centers to carry out the program were in operation.

A new technical boarding school was opened in 1962 in Ouagadougou. Here the students specialized in such subjects as building trades (bricklaying, carpentry, ironwork, locksmith, mechanics, and maintenance). There are also three private Catholic technical centers in Bobo-Dioulasso, Fada, N'Gourma, and Nonna. In 1962, there was a total of 141 private schools with 24,890 pupils (of which 16,505 were boys and 8,385 girls).

Upper Volta's financial situation in education is grave, a story often repeated in Africa today. Recent developments (1966-1969) include plans for a university in the capital, more stress on vocational-technical education, expanded teacher education, attacks on illiteracy among adults, improved agricultural techniques, and better education on sanitation in rural areas.

SELECTED BIBLIOGRAPHY

CHURCH, R. J. H. *West Africa: A Study of the Environment and of Man's Use of It*. New York: Longmans, Green & Co., Inc., 1957.

DUGUE, GIL. *Vers Les Etats-Unis D'Afrique*, Dakar, 1960.

DUMONT, RENE. *Afrique Noire: Developpement Agricole*. Presses Universitaires, 1961.

FAGE, J. D. *An Introduction to the History of West Africa*. New York: Cambridge University Press, 1955.

KITCHEN, HELEN, ed. *The Educated African*. New York: Frederick A. Praeger, Inc., 1962, Chapter 27.

———. *A Handbook of African Affairs*. New York: Frederick A. Praeger, Inc., 1964.

MELADY, THOMAS P. *Faces of Africa*. New York: The Macmillan Company, 1964, Chapter 11.

NERES, PHILIP. *French-Speaking West Africa: From Colonial Status to Independence*. New York: Oxford University Press, 1962.

PEDLER, F. J. *Economic Geography of West Africa*. New York: Longmans, Green & Co., Inc., 1955.

POQUIN, J. J. *Les Relations Economiques Exterieures Des Pay D' Afrique Noire de L'Union Francaise*. Paris: Colin, 1957.

RICHARD-MOOLARD, JACQUES. *Problems Humains en Afrique Occidentale*. Paris, 1958.

ROUCEK, JOSEPH S. "Focus on Upper Volta." *New Africa*, April, 1963, 14-16.

SKINNER, E. P. *The Mossi of Upper Volta*. California: Stanford University Press, 1964.

THOMPSON, V. M., and ADLOFF, R. *French West Africa*. California: Stanford University Press, 1958.

WATTENBERG, BEN, and SMITH, RALPH L. *The New Nations of Africa*. New York: Hart Publishing Co., Inc., 1963, 442-452.

West Africa Annual. London: Clarke, 1962, ff.